1999

SOUTHWI

The Lav

Healthc

Administr

Third Ed

SOUTHWICK'S

The Law of Healthcare Administration

Third Edition

J. Stuart Showalter

HEALTH ADMINISTRATION PRESS
CHICAGO, ILLINOIS

03 02 01 00 99   5 4 3 2 1

Library of Congress Cataloging-in-Publication Data

Showalter, J. Stuart.
     Southwick's the law of healthcare administration / J. Stuart
Showalter.—3rd ed.
        p. cm.
     Rev. ed. of: The law of hospital and health care administration /
Arthur F. Southwick. 2nd ed. 1988.
      ISBN 1-56793-101-4 (alk. paper)
      1. Medical care—Law and legislation—United States.
2. Hospitals—Law and legislation—United States.   3. Medical laws
and legislation—United States.   I. Southwick, Arthur F. Law of
hospital and health care administration.   II. Title.
III. Title: Southwick's the law of health care administration.
      KF3825.S65   1998
      344.73'0321—dc21   98-53747
                                                                      CIP

The paper used in this publication meets the minimum requirements of American National Standards for Information Sciences—Permanence of Paper for Printed Library Materials, ANSI Z39.48–1984. ⊚ ™

Health Administration Press
A division of the Foundation
   of the American College of
   Healthcare Executives
One North Franklin Street
Chicago, IL 60606
(312) 424-2800

CONTENTS

v

PREFACE

Since its original publication in 1978, *The Law of Hospital and Health Care Administration* by Arthur F. Southwick has been a guiding light in the field of health administration. This book was the first to capture the scope and intricacies of health law from the perspective of management. This perspective is, of course, crucial given the range of complex legal issues—many of which carry onerous consequences if not handled effectively—that healthcare executives face each day. Through his own teaching and through *The Law of Hospital and Health Care Administration,* Professor Southwick guided and influenced a generation of students.

The all-time best-selling book published by Health Administration Press, *The Law of Hospital and Health Care Administration* has had only two editions. The second, published in 1987, continues to enjoy wide classroom use. This continued popularity in a rapidly changing field is a powerful testament to the book's clear presentation, thorough examination, and insightful vision of health law. Inevitably, however, an update was necessary. The death of Professor Southwick on March 3, 1997, not only took from us a great teacher and scholar, but also the chance for him to share his thoughts on the current state of health administration law in a new edition of this book.

I was delighted when representatives of Health Administration Press approached me about developing a new edition of Professor Southwick's book. I had used the book for years in my classes at Washington University and St. Louis University. In addition, I had edited—with Bernard Reams, now of St. John's University in New York—a companion casebook and had developed a self-study course for the American College of Healthcare Executives based on the book. I had always found Professor Southwick's book to be the best among the competition and was eager to update the book for today's students.

My strategy in creating this new edition was to retain the book's basic format but to make the following important changes:

1. Each chapter has been updated by presenting significant developments that have occurred since the previous edition was published. These additions include discussions of and citations to recent case precedents and statutory and regulatory materials. For example:

- Included in Chapter 6, "Taxation of Healthcare Institutions," is an explanation of "excess benefits" and associated penalties, an issue that has arisen under the 1996 Taxpayer Bill of Rights 2.
- Included in Chapter 7, "Antitrust Law," is a discussion of current application of antitrust related to health planning, provider reimbursement, mergers and consolidations, and other activities.
- Included in Chapter 10, "Emergency Care," are the text of and cases interpreting the Emergency Medical Treatment and Active Labor Act (the "anti-dumping" statute).
- Included in Chapter 12, "Family Planning," are up-to-date cases on how the courts have ruled on abortion-related cases.

2. Case references and other illustrations and explanations have been judiciously trimmed with the goal of making the book even more accessible to health administration students (as opposed to law students). The chapter on peer review from the previous edition has been eliminated, with information on legal aspects of peer review and quality assurance monitoring of clinical care folded into Chapter 15, "Medical Staff Appointments and Privileges."

3. Chapter 8, "Healthcare Fraud and Abuse," has been added to cover prohibitions against false claims, kickbacks, and self-referral, as well as corporate compliance programs to prevent such violations.

4. Legal aspects of managed care are discussed in Chapter 5, "Liability of the Healthcare Institution"; Chapter 7, "Antitrust"; and Chapter 9, "Admission and Discharge."

Although subsequent editions of this book will undoubtedly introduce more substantive changes, this edition remains very much grounded in the scholarship, ideas, and writing of Arthur Southwick, updated for a more contemporary audience. The resulting work has been retitled *Southwick's The Law of Healthcare Administration* to acknowledge Professor Southwick's strong presence in this work and leadership in this field. I hope this book fills a need for a pragmatic health law text among health administration, executive education, nursing, and allied health faculty and students.

I wish to thank my friend and former student, Tadd M. Pullin, MHA, MA, for his encouragement and his astute management perspective in reviewing much of the new material in this edition. Thanks are also due to Eileen Wagner and Timothy Bullard, M.D., for their comments on the chapter on emergency care. Finally, I wish to thank the staff of Health Administration Press for their patience and professional support during the long process of bringing this third edition to press.

J. Stuart Showalter
Orlando, FL

INTRODUCTION TO THE ANGLO-AMERICAN LEGAL SYSTEM

I n recent years, law has assumed vast, some would say exaggerated, importance in the daily affairs of both individuals and business organizations. Nowhere have changes been greater and the legal issues more challenging than in healthcare. Because healthcare professionals cannot have an attorney constantly at hand, they must have a fundamental understanding of the law so that they can at least recognize serious legal problems that require professional legal counsel.

In this chapter some general concepts essential to any study of law will be examined, with special emphasis on three areas:

1. the sources of the law;
2. the court system; and
3. legal procedure.

First, however, a working definition of law will be useful. Defined in its simplest and broadest sense, *law* is a system of principles and rules devised by organized society for the purpose of controlling human conduct. Society must have certain specific standards of behavior and the means to enforce the standards. In the final analysis, the purpose of law is to avoid conflict between individuals and between government and subject. Inevitably conflicts do occur, however, and then legal institutions and doctrines supply means of resolving the disputes.

Because law is concerned with human behavior, it falls short of being an exact science. Many persons, in healthcare especially, find law frustrating because much of it is uncertain. Its rules often fail to guarantee particular results in individual controversies, and lawyers are many times unable to predict with authority the outcome of a given conflict or the proper course of action. But in a sense uncertainty about the law is a virtue and is the law's greatest strength. Its opposite, legal rigidity, produces decay by inhibiting initiative with respect to economic growth and the development of social institutions. Viewed in the proper light, the law is a beautiful and constantly (albeit slowly) changing tapestry that responds to economic and social developments and generally reflects the beliefs of society at any given location or point in time.

Sources of Law

Law can be classified as either public law or private law, depending on its subject matter. Law concerning the government or its relations with individuals and business organizations is classified as *public law*. In contrast, the term *private law* refers to the rules and principles that define and regulate rights and duties between or among persons and private business. Without doubt these two broad classifications of law overlap, but the classifications are useful in understanding Anglo-American legal doctrine.

The concept of private law embraces the law of contracts, property, and tort. *Contract law* is concerned with such matters as the sale of goods, the furnishing of services, the employment relationship, and the loan of money. In its broadest sense the *law of property* regulates the ownership, employment, and disposition of property, including the creation and operation of trusts. *Tort law* defines and enforces the duties and rights that exist among persons and business organizations but that are independent of contractual agreement between the parties. These three areas of private law significantly influence the conduct of all human enterprise and activity.

In contrast to private law, the purpose of public law is to define, regulate, and enforce rights where government is a party to the subject matter (e.g., labor relations, taxation, antitrust, environmental regulation). The principal sources of public law are written constitutions, statutory enactments by a legislative body, and administrative rules and regulations. This fact alone distinguishes public law from private law, because the primary source of private rights and duties is judicial decisions (subject to statutory modification and codification). The following paragraphs examine more closely these four primary sources of public and private law: constitutions, statutes, administrative law, and judicial decisions.

Constitutions

The U.S. Constitution is aptly called the "supreme law of the land" because the Constitution provides standards against which all statutory laws and administrative rules and regulations are judged. In the most basic terms the Constitution is a grant of power from the states to the federal government. All powers not granted to the federal government by the Constitution are reserved by the individual states. The grant of power to the federal government is both express and implied. The Constitution, for example, expressly authorizes Congress to lay and collect taxes, borrow and coin money, declare war, raise and support armies, and regulate interstate commerce. But Congress may also enact laws that are "necessary and proper" for exercising these express powers. For example, the express power of Congress to regulate interstate commerce carries with it the implied power to pass antidiscrimination legislation such as the Civil Rights Act of 1964, a statute that will be discussed in greater detail in later chapters.

The main body of the Constitution establishes, defines, and limits the power of the three branches of the federal government: (1) that of the legislature to make statutory laws; (2) that of the executive branch to enforce the laws; and (3) that of the judiciary to interpret the laws. Following the main body of the Constitution are 26 amendments. The first ten, the Bill of Rights, were ratified shortly after the adoption of the Constitution to, according to James Madison, calm the apprehensions of persons who felt that without the specific declarations the federal government might be held to possess an excessive degree of power. The provisions of the Bill of Rights include the well-known rights to freedom of speech and the free exercise of religion, to be secure from unreasonable searches and seizures, to bear arms, to demand a jury trial (whenever the right to a jury existed at common law), to be protected against self-incrimination, and to be accorded substantive and procedural due process of law.

Despite the breadth of the first ten amendments, in and of themselves they only apply to the federal government. However, the Fourteenth Amendment (ratified in 1870) provides " . . . nor shall any State deprive any person of life, liberty, or property, without due process of laws." The Fourteenth Amendment is especially important for two reasons. First, the Supreme Court has generally defined the process as specifically including most of the rights set forth in the Bill of Rights. Consequently neither the states nor the federal government may infringe on these rights. Second, and quite relevant to healthcare law, what constitutes the "state" or "state action" has been defined rather broadly. Even the activities of a private healthcare institution, for example, might fall under "state action" depending on the interplay of several factors, including the influence of government regulations on institutional policies, the availability of other facilities in a particular area, the receipt of federal or state funding, and the use of tax exemptions. Whether the activities of a private hospital constitute "state action" is especially important in regard to admission of patients to the hospital and granting hospital staff privileges to physicians and other professional persons. The numerous decisions on these issues will be discussed in later chapters.

In addition to the U.S. Constitution, each state has its own constitution, which is the supreme law of that state but is subordinate to the federal Constitution. The state and federal constitutions are often similar, although state constitutions are more detailed and cover such matters as the financing of public works and the organization of local governments.

Statutes

The second source of law, *statutory law*, is the law enacted by a legislative body, normally the U.S. Congress, a state legislature, or a local governmental unit such as a city council. Statutes enacted by each of these bodies will apply to healthcare organizations. In regard to discrimination in admitting patients, for example, hospitals must comply with federal statutes such as the Civil Rights

Act of 1964 and the Hill-Burton Act, as well as the relevant statutes enacted by states with respect to discrimination, taxation, and licensure, and with local laws. Most states and a number of large cities have enacted antidiscrimination statutes, although such laws may differ in breadth of coverage.

Although, as noted below, statutes have priority as a source of law over conflicting judicial decisions, judges are faced with the task of interpreting statutes; this is especially difficult if the wording is vague or ambiguous, as it often is. In interpreting statutes the courts have developed several rules of construction, and in some states these rules are themselves the subject of a separate statute. Whatever the source of the rules, it is generally agreed that they are designed to help one ascertain the intention of the legislature.

The following section from the Pennsylvania Statutory Construction Act illustrates the guidelines a court looks to in determining legislative intent.

a. The object of all interpretation and construction of statutes is to ascertain and effectuate the intention of the General Assembly. Every statute shall be construed, if possible, to give effect to all its provisions.
b. When the words of a statute are clear and free from all ambiguity, the letter of it is not to be disregarded under the pretext of pursuing its spirit.
c. When the words of the statute are not explicit, the intention of the General Assembly may be ascertained by considering, among other matters: (1) The occasion and necessity for the statute. (2) The circumstances under which it was enacted. (3) The mischief to be remedied. (4) The object to be attained. (5) The former law, if any, including other statutes upon the same or similar subjects. (6) The consequences of a particular interpretation. (7) The contemporaneous legislative history. (8) Legislative and administrative interpretations of such statute.[1]

Administrative Law

Administrative law is that division of public law relating to the administration of government. According to Sir Ivor Jennings, an English scholar, "Administrative law is the law relating to the administration. It determines the organization, powers and duties of administrative authorities."[2] Administrative law has greater scope and significance than is generally realized and is concerned with more than procedural matters. In fact, this division of public law is the source of much of the substantive law that directly affects the rights and duties of individuals and business organizations and their relation to governmental authority.

The executive branch of government is usually described as the branch charged with carrying out the law as enacted by the legislature and interpreted by the courts. This definition is an oversimplification, however, because administrative government often makes law and exercises a considerable amount of judicial or quasi-judicial power. In Anglo-American government, the phrase "administrative government" should be understood as embracing all departments of the executive branch and all governmental agencies created by legislation for specific public purposes.

Examples of administrative agencies or tribunals abound. In the United States they exist at all levels of government: local, state, and federal. Well-known federal agencies are the National Labor Relations Board, the Federal Trade Commission, the Health Care Financing Administration, and the Food and Drug Administration. At the state level there are worker's compensation commissions, labor relations boards, boards of medical registration, and numerous other agencies.

The law-making and judicial powers of administrative government are delegated by a legislative body. The U.S. Congress delegates to various administrative bodies the right to promulgate rules and regulations that have the force of law. The U.S. Food and Drug Administration, for example, although an administrative agency, has the power to promulgate rules controlling the manufacture, marketing, and advertising of foods, drugs, cosmetics, and medical devices. The Internal Revenue Service regulates tax administration. Many other examples could be given.

The amount of delegated legislation has increased tremendously in this century, particularly since World War II. The reasons are clear: economic and social conditions inevitably change as societies become more complicated, and (because of a lack of time and expertise in the details of policies' implementation) legislatures cannot directly provide the mass of rules necessary to govern the society. Delegating legislative authority makes it possible to put this responsibility in the hands of experts; however, a legislature may not abdicate its responsibility by delegating complete authority, even with respect to a specialized subject matter. Primary legislation must generally stipulate the standards to be followed by an administrative agency when promulgating regulations, and the quasi-judicial power of the administrative body must be limited because federal and state constitutions vest "judicial power" in the court systems.

Judicial Decisions

The last major source of law is the *judicial decision*. All legislation, whether federal or state in origin and application, must be consistent with the U.S. Constitution. The power to legislate is therefore limited by doctrines of the fundamental law, and the Supreme Court of the United States has the power to declare that an act of Congress or a state legislature is unconstitutional.[3] Judicial decisions are subordinate, of course, to the Constitution and also to statutes so long as the statute is consistent with the Constitution. Despite this subordinate role, however, judicial decisions are the primary source of private law. Private law, especially the law of contracts and tort, has traditionally had the most influence on healthcare law and is hence of particular interest here. Historically, the judicial decisions came either from the courts at common law or from equity.

Common law   The common law—that is, the law that is common to England—developed after the Norman invasion in 1066 and produced two important concepts that persist today: the writ and *stare decisis*. The *writ*, an order purchased by the plaintiff, directed the defendant to appear before the court or to perform or cease performing a certain act. Each writ, or form of action, differed from the others and carried with it the development of a separate body of substantive law, prompting Maitland to note that, although the old forms of action are buried and no longer used, "they still rule us from their graves."[4]

The doctrine of *stare decisis*, literally to abide by decided cases, required that courts look to past disputes involving similar facts and determine the outcome of the current case on the basis of the earlier decision. The use of earlier cases as precedent has made for stability in the Anglo-American legal system because persons embarking on a new enterprise can surmise the legal consequences of the endeavor from judicial decisions already rendered in similar circumstances. The use of earlier decisions to determine the substance of the law distinguishes the common law from the civil or Roman law system, which traditionally relied principally on a comprehensive code of laws to decide cases. Civil law is the basis for the law in Europe, Central and South America, Japan, Quebec, and (because of its French heritage) the state of Louisiana.

In the United States, *stare decisis* is a concept that is applied vertically, but not horizontally, to lower courts in the same system or to courts from other systems. An Ohio trial court, for example, is bound by the decisions of the higher Ohio courts (the state's intermediate appellate courts and supreme court) but is not bound by decisions of other Ohio trial courts or by the decisions of out-of-state courts. Likewise, the federal trial court—the district court—is bound by decisions of other Ohio courts (as to matters of Ohio law) and is bound by appellate court decisions for its own circuit but not by the federal appellate decisions of other circuits or by decisions of other district courts. The one exception applies where a federal court, in hearing a diversity of citizenship action (a case in which the plaintiff and defendant are from different states), must determine the law by following the decisions of the highest state court. While not bound to do so, courts in one system may examine judicial solutions in other systems to decide a case of "first impression."

Although *stare decisis* provides stability to the Anglo-American judicial system, the doctrine would lead to stagnation if courts were forced to adhere to precedents blindly. Consequently courts are given some flexibility in modifying the legal rule when the facts vary from the precedent, and they may even completely overturn their own earlier decisions. For instance, the Supreme Court of Pennsylvania overruled its own decisions and held in 1965 that charitable hospitals in Pennsylvania were no longer immune from tort liability when their employees are negligent.[5] Justice Musmanno noted:

> *Stare decisis* channels the law. It erects lighthouses and flys [*sic*] the signals of safety. The ships of jurisprudence must follow the

well-defined channel which, over the years, has been proved to be secure and trustworthy. But it would not comport with wisdom to insist that, should shoals rise in a heretofore safe course and rocks emerge to encumber the passage, the ship should nonetheless pursue the original course, merely because it presented no hazard in the past. The principle of *stare decisis* does not demand that we follow precedents which shipwreck justice.[6]

The doctrine of *stare decisis* should not be confused with another important common law doctrine also referred to in its Latin form, *res judicata*. *Res judicata* literally means "a thing or matter settled by judgment." In practical terms this means that, once a legal dispute has been decided by a court and all appeals exhausted, the same parties may not later bring suit regarding the same matters. *Res judicata*, as a general rule, will not be a defense, however, if the plaintiff has a different cause of action in the second suit, even if the same defendant is named in both cases.

The second source of judicial decisions, the *equity courts*, developed as a source of law because of deficiencies in the common law. By the Middle Ages common law procedures had become rigid, and courts could provide no relief to many parties who had just claims because the common law generally acted only after the fact. Thus, the common law court could grant damages to an injured party after an injury but would not order a wrongdoer to cease tortious behavior or threatened breach of contract before the injury occurred.

Equity courts

Parties began to seek relief from the king when the common law could provide no satisfaction. The king, through his chancellor, often aided the parties and eventually established a separate court, the Court of Chancery, to hear the cases. These courts, which attempted to "do equity" and to act in good conscience where the common law courts could not provide relief, developed the law of equity, which differed from the common law in two major respects. First, the courts in equity developed their own remedies—for example, the injunction, which enabled the court to provide relief before a wrong occurred. And, second, the procedure in the chancery court differed from that in the law courts. Most notably, the parties in the Court of Chancery had no right to a jury trial, and certain rules or maxims were frequently applied, for example, "he who comes into equity must have clean hands."

Gradually, with the development of these rules, equity became almost as inflexible as the common law, prompting Dickens to write in *Bleak House:* "Never can there come fog too thick, never can there come mud and mire too deep, to assort with the groping and floundering condition which [the] High Court of Chancery, most pestilent of hoary sinners, holds . . . in the sight of heaven and earth."

Although the dual system of law and equity was adopted in the United States, both here and in England law and equity eventually came to be administered by the same court. The relevant Michigan statute, for example, provides that the "[c]ircuit courts have the power and jurisdiction . . . possessed by courts of record at the common law . . . [and] possessed by courts and judges in Chancery in England."[7] Despite the merger of law and equity into one court, however, procedural and remedial distinctions remain. For example, the parties in an equitable action are still not entitled to a jury trial, and the equitable maxims are still applied by the courts.

The law derived from judicial decisions is sometimes referred to as the unwritten law because it is not a part of a formal statute or constitution. This term is misleading, however, because court decisions are in fact written, and many are published in bound volumes.[8] This law is also described, sometimes pejoratively, as "judge-made" law. It is important to note that judicially fashioned law is as old as the Anglo-American legal system, which has its roots in the eleventh century.

The Court System

The primary method of resolving disputes in the United States is through the court system. There are actually 52 different court systems in the United States, because each state and the District of Columbia has its own separate system in addition to the federal courts. The large number of court systems makes study of the law in the United States extremely complex, but the complexity adds strength and vitality because various resolutions to a particular problem can be tested in individual states before a consensus is reached regarding the most desirable solution.

State Courts

The federal court system and court systems of the more populous states use a three-tier structure comprising the trial courts, the intermediate courts of appeal, and a supreme court (see Figure 1.1). In a state court system, the lowest tier—the *trial courts*—is often divided into courts of limited jurisdiction and courts of general jurisdiction. Typically the courts of limited jurisdiction hear criminal trials involving lesser crimes (i.e., misdemeanors) and civil cases where the amount in dispute is limited (e.g., less than $10,000). The courts of limited jurisdiction often include a small claims court, where lawyers are not allowed to practice and the usual legal procedures are not followed. (Those who have watched "The Peoples' Court" or "Judge Judy" on television have viewed a small claims court in action.)

The state courts of general jurisdiction hear the more serious criminal cases involving felonies and civil cases where larger monetary amounts are in dispute. In some states only the courts of general jurisdiction may grant equitable relief, such as the issuance of an injunction. Because of the tremendous volume of cases, the courts of general jurisdiction are often divided into special courts: a family or domestic relations court, a juvenile court, and a probate court. The probate court is especially important to healthcare executives because, in addition to probating wills and administering estates, this court is

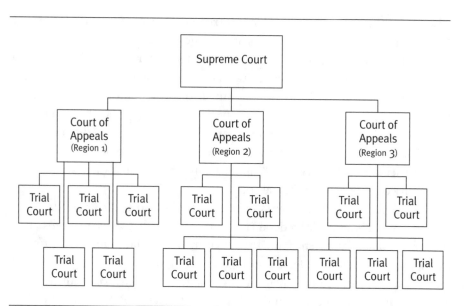

FIGURE 1.1
Model of
Typical
Three-Tier
Court Structure

often given jurisdiction to hear cases involving such matters as surgery for an incompetent person or the involuntary commitment of a mentally ill person.

At the next tier in the majority of state court systems are the *intermediate appellate courts*. These courts have appellate jurisdiction, that is, the power to hear appeals from final judgments of the trial courts. In exercising their appellate jurisdiction, appellate courts usually are limited to the record from the trial court and to questions of law, not of fact. In the appropriate circumstances, however, an appellate court may rule that a verdict of the jury was against the weight of the evidence.

The highest tier in the state court system is the *state supreme court*. This court hears appeals from the intermediate appellate courts (or from trial courts if the state does not have intermediate courts) and possesses limited original jurisdiction (jurisdiction to hear certain cases as if it were a trial court). The supreme court is often charged with other duties—for example, adopting rules of procedure and supervising the practice of law in the state.

The various states are not uniform in naming the tiers of courts. Trial courts of general jurisdiction, for example, may be named circuit, superior, common pleas, or county courts. New York is unique in the sense that its trial court is known as the supreme court. In most states the highest court is named the supreme court, but in Massachusetts the high court is called the Supreme Judicial Court, and in New York the highest court is the Court of Appeals. The intermediate appellate court in New York is the Supreme Court Appellate Division.

Federal Courts

At the bottom tier in the federal court system, the *district court* (the federal trial court) hears criminal cases involving both felonies and misdemeanors that arise under the federal statutes. The district court hears civil cases involving actions arising either under federal statutes, such as federal civil rights actions, or under the U.S. Constitution. The district court may also hear suits in which a citizen of one state sues a citizen of another state (i.e., where there is "diversity of citizenship") if the amount in dispute is more than $10,000. In such a case the court will apply the law of one of the states, because there generally is no federal common law.[9] There are 91 U.S. district courts established geographically in the 50 states. In addition, each of the following—the District of Columbia, the Virgin Islands, the Canal Zone, Guam, and Puerto Rico—has its own federal trial court.

The federal district courts have exclusive jurisdiction with respect to certain cases arising under federal law. This is to say that the state courts lack the power to hear and determine the outcome of such litigation. The primary examples of exclusive federal court jurisdiction relevant to the healthcare industry are cases alleging violation of the federal antitrust or securities laws and the Employee Retirement Income Security Act (ERISA). Additionally, bankruptcy is governed exclusively by federal legislation, and such cases are heard by the U.S. Bankruptcy Court. Each federal judicial district has a bankruptcy court where the judges hear only bankruptcy matters.

In contrast, federal and state courts have concurrent jurisdiction in cases arising under the federal Constitution or any of the federal statutes that do not confer exclusive jurisdiction to the federal court system. Further, there is concurrent jurisdiction whenever the litigation involves citizens of different states or foreign nations and the amount in controversy exceeds $10,000. Accordingly, plaintiffs who raise a federal question in their complaint or who meet the requirements of diversity of citizenship may choose to file their suit in either the state or the federal court having personal jurisdiction over the defendant. If suit is filed in a state court other than the defendant's home state, the defendant has the right to have the case removed to the federal court with jurisdiction.

Appeals from the district courts go to the U.S. *courts of appeals.* The United States, along with its territories named above, has 12 circuits, including a separate circuit for the District of Columbia, each of which has a court of appeals functioning in the same manner as the state appellate courts. In addition, there is a 13th Court of Appeals for the Federal Circuit hearing cases involving certain matters that are exclusively the province of federal law, including patents, trademarks, claims against the government, and appeals from the U.S. Claims Court.

At the highest rung in the federal court system is the U.S. Supreme Court. The *Supreme Court* hears appeals from the U.S. courts of appeals and from the highest state courts in cases involving federal statutes, treaties, or the U.S. Constitution. Generally a party has no absolute right to appeal to the Supreme Court. (One exception is a case in which a federal statute has been declared unconstitutional by the lower courts.) Instead, in most cases the Court's decision whether to hear a case is entirely discretionary. Parties must petition the Court for a *writ of certiorari*—an order to the lower court requiring that the case be sent up for the high court's review—and persuade at least four of the nine justices that the issue merits their attention. The Supreme Court normally decides only very a small percentage of the thousands of cases it is asked to consider each year.

Because the Supreme Court exercises considerable discretion in con-trolling its docket, many important legal issues are in effect decided by the lower federal or state courts. Typically the Court grants *certiorari* only in those cases that present current questions of extraordinary economic or social significance, or when the federal courts of appeals have differed in deciding cases involving the same legal issue.

Aside from the Supreme Court, which is created by Article III of the U.S. Constitution, the establishment and organization of the federal court system is the responsibility of Congress. Accordingly, Congress can create additional courts from time to time and define the jurisdiction of each. Complementing the district courts and the courts of appeals are several federal courts with specialized, limited jurisdictional functions. Congress has created, for example, the U.S. Claims Court, which hears certain claims brought against the government, the U.S. Court of International Trade, and the U.S. Tax Court.

Alternative Methods of Resolving Disputes

In addition to the court system, two alternative methods of resolving disputes are popular in the United States. First, *adjudication* of legal rights under administrative law is most often accomplished by an administrative agency or tribunal created by statute or constitution; hence, many private disputes controlled by administrative law are not resolved by judicial courts at all. (Workers' compensation cases are a familiar example.) Undoubtedly far more disputes are settled today by administrative adjudicative bodies than by the ordinary courts. Moreover, an administrative agency often has the statutory responsibility and power to initiate enforcement of statutory pronouncements. It may frequently happen that the same agency brings the initial proceeding, hears the case, and decides the dispute. The Federal Trade Commission, for example, is empowered to compel an alleged offender to cease and desist from practicing unfair methods of competition.

Thus, an ordinary court, following established and traditional methods of adjudication, might not be involved in administrative justice. Statutes, of course, prescribe the powers of administrative bodies. The role of ordinary courts generally will be limited to preventing administrative authorities from exceeding their powers and to granting remedies to individuals who have been injured by wrongful administrative action. Sometimes the statutes will give the right of appeal to a court from a judicial or quasi-judicial decision of administrative government. Generally the goals of administrative law are the same as those of common law in deciding matters of private law: to provide a day in "court," an independent "judge" or body to decide the dispute, and a rationally justified decision. A corollary aim is to provide for the traditional procedural protections (such as "due process") so far as it is consistent with notions of public welfare to do so.

The other alternative method for resolving disputes is *arbitration*, a method that is often quicker, less complicated, more confidential, and less costly than commencing an action in court. Arbitration in connection with the professional liability of physicians and other healthcare providers will be discussed in Chapter 2. Arbitration, generally defined, is the submission of a dispute for decision by a third person or a panel of experts outside the judicial trial process. When the parties to a dispute voluntarily agree to have their differences resolved by an arbitrator or by a panel of arbitrators and that the settlement will be binding, arbitration becomes a workable, viable alternative to the court system. Statutory law in most states favors voluntary, binding arbitration and frequently provides that an agreement to arbitrate is enforceable by the courts.[10]

In some circumstances arbitration may be required by law. Such statutes raise serious constitutional legal issues because they may deprive the parties of access to the court system and the right to a jury trial. Discussion of these significant issues is beyond the scope of this introductory chapter. The matter is reviewed in Chapter 2 in the context of statutory reform of the tort system.

A middle ground between voluntary, binding arbitration and compulsory, mandated arbitration is *"court-annexed" arbitration*. This occurs when state law or local rules of judicial procedure, including the rules of some of the federal district courts, permits a trial court to require the parties to submit the case to arbitration before trial. Various factors determine whether a particular case is referred to arbitration, including the nature of the case and the dollar amount in controversy. In any event, the purpose of the mandated referral is to encourage settlement of claims and thus avoid the costs of a lengthy trial. The decision of the arbitrator is not, however, binding in court-annexed arbitration. Either party may appeal the decision in a timely fashion and proceed to a trial *de novo* in court.

Arbitration must be distinguished from mediation, in which a third party, the mediator, simply attempts to persuade adverse parties to agree to settle their differences. The mediator has no power to require a settlement.

Legal Procedure

The law, either public or private, that creates and defines rights and duties is called *substantive law*, and most of this book is devoted to the substantive law as it relates to providers of healthcare. *Procedural law*, on the other hand, provides the means of enforcing and protecting rights granted by the substantive law. The branch of procedural law to be discussed below is the law relating to the litigation of a case.

The litigation process may be divided into six stages. It should be mentioned at the outset, however, that many cases involving a healthcare institution or professional practitioner are settled by negotiation before commencement of the litigation process.

Commencement of Legal Action

When claims do go to court, the first stage is commencement of legal action. A claimant who begins a lawsuit (an "action") becomes the plaintiff, and the other party to the action is the defendant. The plaintiff commences the action by filing a "complaint" that states the nature of the claim and the amount of damages or other remedy sought. The complaint and all papers subsequently filed in court are the "pleadings." A copy of the complaint, along with a summons, is then served on the defendant. The summons advises the defendant that the complaint must be answered or other action taken within a limited time—for example, 20 days—and that if the defendant fails to act the plaintiff will be granted judgment by default.

A problem sometimes arises when an action is commenced against a party out of state. As a general rule courts have decided that it is not consistent with procedural due process of law to force a defendant to defend a lawsuit in a state with which there has been no contact.[11]

The Defendant's Response

In the second stage of the litigation process, the defendant files an "answer" to the complaint admitting, denying, or pleading ignorance to each allegation in the complaint. The defendant may also file a complaint against the plaintiff (a "countersuit") or against a third party (a "third-party action"), thus bringing into the litigation a "third-party defendant" whom the original defendant believes is wholly or partially responsible for the plaintiff's alleged injuries.

A countersuit against the plaintiff may be filed in the original court proceeding (as when, for example, an institution that is being sued for negligence files a countersuit against the patient for unpaid bills) or, in some instances, after the conclusion of the original lawsuit. Such a counterattack is becoming especially popular with physicians who have defended and won malpractice cases and who then sue the patient and the attorney for malicious prosecution, abuse of process, defamation, or even barratry (illegally encouraging litigation). These claims are, however, often difficult to prove. Malicious prosecution, for example, requires proof that the plaintiff instituted suit without probable cause and with malicious motive, that the defendant won the lawsuit, and that damages were suffered as a result of the suit.[12]

The defendant has one other option at this stage in the proceeding: to ask that the court dismiss the plaintiff's complaint. The defendant may base the motion on a variety of grounds: the court's lack of jurisdiction, a prior judgment on the same matter, or the failure of the opposing party to state a legal claim. Although the terminology differs from state to state, the motion to dismiss is usually called either a motion for "summary judgment" or a "demurrer." When the motion to dismiss is granted by the court, the judgment is final and the losing party can appeal the decision immediately.

Methods of Discovery

In a few cases there is very little delay between the initial two stages and the decision by the court. In one instance a wife and mother of young children had lost two-thirds of her blood supply because of a ruptured ulcer, but her husband refused to approve blood transfusions because they were Jehovah's Witnesses. Within a matter of hours the hospital petitioned the district court for permission to administer blood, the district court denied permission, and the case was taken to a court of appeals where an order was signed allowing the transfusion.[13]

More frequently, however, especially in urban areas, there is a delay of several years between commencement of the action and trial. During this time, each party engages in the third stage of the litigation process, "discovery," which is an attempt to determine the strength of the other party's case. Discovery is a valuable device that can be used, for example, to ascertain the amount of malpractice insurance coverage or the identity of prospective defendants or witnesses. In *Cidilko v. Palestine*, for instance, a patient had fallen on the way to the washroom and fractured a hip.[14] The hospital was required to disclose the identity of the nurse who had directed the patient to the washroom instead of giving bedside attention.

Five methods may be used by parties to discover the strength of the other party's case. All are generally limited to matters that are relevant to the subject matter and that are not privileged or confidential.

The deposition The most common and effective discovery device is the *deposition*, whereby a party subpoenas a witness who, at a given time and place, will testify under oath before a reporter who transcribes the testimony. The opposing attorney will also be present during the deposition to make appropriate objections and, whenever appropriate, to cross-examine the witness. In addition to being useful as a discovery device, the deposition serves at least two other major purposes. First, it may be read into evidence at the trial itself when the witness is unable to testify in person (so long as the testimony is consistent with the rules of evidence). Second, it can be used to impeach the testimony of a witness. For these reasons, especially the latter, persons being deposed should answer the questions exactly as if they were testifying in court.

Interrogatories A second method of discovery, written *interrogatories*, is similar to the taking of depositions except that the questions are written. The procedure for using written interrogatories sometimes varies, depending on whether they are directed toward an adverse party or other witnesses. Interrogatories are some-times less effective than oral depositions because there is little opportunity to ask follow-up questions.

A party using the third method of discovery—a method especially relevant to healthcare law—may inspect and copy documents, inspect tangible items in the possession of the opposing party, enter and inspect land under the control of the other party, and inspect and copy things produced by a witness served with a subpoena duces tecum, that is, a subpoena requiring the witness to bring along certain books and documents. Some states have separate rules of court governing subpoenas for the production of hospital records. The special rules recognize that medical records contain sensitive information that is privileged or otherwise inadmissible at trial. Accordingly, the rules may provide that certain extraordinary security measures be employed. By way of example, the clerk of the court could be required to keep the record sealed pending a court order directing that the record be opened.

Discovery of documents

A physical or mental examination, the fourth discovery device, may be used when the physical or mental condition of a person is in dispute and good cause is shown for the examination. If the party being examined demands to see a report of the examination, that party waives any privilege that may be available regarding the testimony of other persons who have conducted similar examinations. In some states the privilege may be waived by simply bringing the lawsuit. Privilege and confidentiality of medical information are discussed in depth in Chapter 13.

Physical or mental examination of a party

The final discovery method is to request the opposing party to admit certain facts. By using these requests for admission, the parties may save the time and expense involved in unnecessary proof and may substantially limit the factual issues to be decided by the court.

Admission of facts

    In addition to the above methods of discovery, a pretrial conference will be held a few months before trial so that the judge and the parties may determine what issues are in dispute, discuss settlement, and set a date for trial if settlement is not possible. The pretrial conference also aids discovery because the court will require that parties specify all damage claims in detail, produce all exhibits to be used in the trial, and in some jurisdictions exchange lists of witnesses to be called at trial. With all these discovery devices available, the calling of an unexpected witness or presentation of other evidence that truly surprises opposing counsel should normally be extremely rare.

The Trial

A trial begins with the selection of a jury, if either party has requested a jury trial and if the case is one at law, not equity. After jury selection, each attorney makes an opening statement in which an explanation is given of matters to be proven during the trial. The plaintiff then calls witnesses and presents other evidence, and the defense attorney is given the opportunity to cross-examine each of the witnesses. After the plaintiff has rested the case, the defendant's attorney frequently asks the court to direct a verdict for the defense. Courts will grant the directed verdict if the jury, viewing the facts most favorably to plaintiff, could not reasonably return a verdict in the claimant's favor that would be in accord with the law. If the motion for directed verdict is denied, the defendant proceeds with evidence and witnesses in support of his or her case, subject to cross-examination by the plaintiff.

When all the evidence has been presented, either party may move for a directed verdict. If the judge denies the motion, "instructions" will be given to the jury regarding relevant law, and the jury will deliberate until reaching a verdict. Many times, after the jury has reached its decision, the losing party asks the court for a "judgment notwithstanding the verdict" and a new trial. The motion will be granted if the judge decides that the verdict is against the weight of the evidence.

The judge and the jury, of course, play key roles in the trial. The judge has the dominant role, deciding whether evidence is admissible and instructing the jury on the law before deliberation begins. As noted above, the judge also has the power to take the case away from the jury by means of a directed verdict or a judgment notwithstanding the verdict. The role of the jury is thus limited to deciding the facts and determining whether the plaintiff has proved the allegations by a preponderance of the evidence.

Because the jury's role is to decide the facts, it is of utmost importance that the members of the jury be impartial. If there is evidence that a jury member might have been biased, many courts will overturn the verdict. In cases tried without a jury, the judge assumes the jury's fact-finding role. (This function, because it can be performed by judge or jury, is often referred to as that of the "trier of fact" for ease of expression.)

Concluding Stages

The next stage in litigation is the appeal. In the appellate court the party who appeals the case (the losing party in the trial court) will usually be referred to as the "appellant" and the other party will be the "appellee." In reading appellate court decisions one must not assume that the first name in the case is the plaintiff because many appellate courts reverse the order of the names when the case is appealed. The case of *Smith v. Jones*, for example, where Smith sued Jones in the trial court, might become *Jones v. Smith* on appeal. The appellate court, as noted above, limits itself to a review of the law applied in the case; it normally will not review the facts as determined by the trier of fact. In reviewing the case the appellate court may affirm the trial court decision, modify or reverse the decision, or reverse it and remand the case for a new trial.

The final stage of the litigation process is collecting the judgment. The most common methods of collection are "execution" and "garnishment." A writ of execution entitles the plaintiff to have a local official seize the defendant's property and to have the property sold to satisfy the judgment. A garnishment is an order to a third person who is indebted to the defendant to pay the debt directly to the plaintiff to satisfy the judgment. Often the third party is the defendant's employer who, depending on local laws, may be ordered to pay a certain percentage of the defendant's wages directly to the plaintiff.

Conclusion

This chapter examined the sources of law, the court system, and legal procedure. The discussion of procedure focused primarily on civil lawsuits. It should be noted, however, that the procedure used in a criminal trial differs in several respects. A detailed discussion of criminal procedure is beyond the scope of this book, because it is the premise, and hope, of the author that healthcare professionals will minimize their contact with the criminal justice system.

Notes

1. PA. STAT. ANN. Tit. 1 § 1921 (Purdon Supp. 1987).
2. *See generally* W. JENNINGS, THE LAW AND THE CONSTITUTION (1959).
3. Marbury v. Madison, 5 U.S. (1 Cranch) 137 (1803) (established the court's power to declare federal legislation unconstitutional).
4. F. MAITLAND, THE FORMS OF ACTION AT COMMON LAW 2 (1965).
5. Flagiello v. Pennsylvania Hosp., 417 Pa. 486, 208 A.2d 193 (1965).
6. *Id.*, 208 A.2d at 205.
7. MICH. COMP. LAWS § 600.601 (1979).
8. In this book citations are given when cases are mentioned, not only to show where the complete court opinion can be found but also to indicate when and where the case was decided. The citation "374 Mich. 524, 132 N.W.2d 634 (1965)," for example, shows that the case was a 1965 Michigan case and that the complete opinion may be found in volume 374, page 524, of the Michigan reports and in volume 132, page 634, of a regional collection of cases, NORTH WESTERN REPORTER, second series. "309 F. Supp. 548 (D.C. Utah 1970)" indicates that the case was decided in 1970 by the U.S. District Court in Utah and may be found in the FEDERAL SUPPLEMENT. "504 F.2d 325 (5th Cir. 1974)" means the case was decided in 1974 by the U.S. Court of Appeals for the 5th Circuit and may be found in the FEDERAL REPORTER, second series; and "118 U.S. 356 (1886)" means the case was decided by the U.S. Supreme Court in 1886 and may be found in the UNITED STATES SUPREME COURT REPORTS. Supreme Court decisions are also reported in the SUPREME COURT REPORTER (S. Ct.) and LAWYERS' EDITION (L. Ed.).

9. Erie R.R. v. Tompkins, 304 U.S. 64 (1938).

10. *E.g.,* OHIO REV. COD ANN. § 2711.03 (Baldwin 1986).

11. World-Wide Volkswagen Corp. v. Woodson, 444 U.S. 286 (1980). *See also* Gelineau v. New York Univ. Hosp., 375 F. Supp. 661 (D.C. N.J. 1974), in which a New Jersey resident contracted hepatitis while being treated in a New York hospital. When the patient brought suit in New Jersey against the hospital the court dismissed the suit because the hospital had no facilities or agents in New Jersey and had done no business or committed a tort in that state. The court concluded that when patients travel to another state for treatment, they should expect to travel to the state again to bring suit against the hospital.

12. Adler, *Malicious Prosecution As Counterbalance to Medical Malpractice Suits,* 21 CLEV. ST. L.R. 51 (1972).

13. Application of President and Directors of Georgetown College, Inc., 331 F.2d 1000 (D.C. Dir. 1964), *cert. Denied, 377 U.S. 398 (1964).*

14. 24 Misc. 2d 19, 207 N.Y.S.2d 727 (1961).

2

BREACH OF CONTRACT AND
INTENTIONAL TORT[1]

Professional liability of healthcare providers is generally referred to as "medical malpractice," that is, a breach of the duty that arises out of the physician-patient relationship. The term covers such causes of action as breach of contract, intentional torts (for example, fraud and defamation), and negligence. In fact, many malpractice suits allege more than one cause of action, the reasons for which will be discussed below.[2]

The legal concept of professional liability is in part an attempt by society to compensate a patient for injury resulting from an adverse outcome. There is always a cost to such injuries, and society must determine when the cost will remain with the injured person and when it will shift to another. Such a shift may be through insurance, or by imposing civil liability, or in other ways to be noted in this chapter. Another major purpose of imposing legal liability is deterrence, the argument being that the threat of malpractice suits will deter healthcare providers from negligent actions. The system is thus seen as a means of ensuring that healthcare is acceptable in quality, although there has been considerable debate over the deterrent effect of the system in accomplishing this goal. A third reason is that patients may wish to exact retribution for what they feel has been mistreatment.[3]

In most instances civil liability is based on some fault or wrongdoing, intentional or unintentional, by the person to be held liable. Legal fault is not by any means the equivalent of moral fault, as will become clear. In fact, the law has not always required fault. Prior to the nineteenth century an individual acted at his or her peril and was responsible for any harm caused to another by his or her actions, even those that were entirely accidental and unavoidable. This standard changed in the United States by the mid-nineteenth century. For example, in *Brown v. Kendall* the defendant raised a stick to break up a dog fight and accidentally struck the plaintiff, who was standing behind him.[4] The plaintiff lost his suit for damages. The court held that the plaintiff must show either that the defendant's intention was unlawful or that he failed to use "that kind and degree of care which prudent and cautious men would use."[5]

The Nature of Legal Liability

Study of the law soon makes clear that not every wrong is a basis of legal liability; not every legitimate human interest is protected by the law. (For example, the law traditionally does not require a person to rescue another, no matter how easily the rescue might be accomplished.[6]) For a "cause of action" to be established, the plaintiff must have an interest that is protected by law. (Protected interests include life or health, property—including the right to earn a living—and the rights guaranteed by the federal and state constitutions.)

The burden of proof is initially on the plaintiff, meaning that the plaintiff must establish each element at least by a preponderance of the evidence. If the plaintiff succeeds in this task, the defendant may still offer a legal defense. Once the plaintiff establishes a case, however, the burden shifts to the defendant to prove the defense. If a legal defense is successfully shown, the plaintiff will lose the lawsuit. Sometimes the court decides that there are no issues of material fact and that the required elements do or do not exist (or that a legal defense does exist) as a matter of law. In such a case the court grants summary judgment in favor of the prevailing party and no trial occurs. If issues of material fact exist, the case must go to trial.

If liability is established, the plaintiff must then prove damages to recover money. Damages in a legal sense represent some harm which the plaintiff suffers that is compensable. Harm that is not compensable does not constitute damages; for example, pay for time lost from work to appear in court and in most cases attorneys' fees and costs are not recoverable as damages. Sometimes nominal or punitive damages are allowed, as will be seen later. In special cases a plaintiff may be permitted other kinds of legal relief, such as an injunction requiring the defendant to do or refrain from doing something.

The existence of a *legal duty* is essential to any legal liability, and the concept of duty tends to change as our society and values change to encompass different situations. The legal duty may be imposed by constitution, legislation, an existing contract, or a relationship concerning which common law imposes a duty. Legal duties arise from employer-employee relationships, fiduciary relationships, and so forth. In healthcare, a special legal duty arises from the physician-patient relationship.[7]

The Physician-Patient Relationship

The physician-patient relationship is founded on a contract in which the physician agrees to provide treatment in return for payment. Professional liability of the physician is usually founded on the breach of a duty arising from this contract. In the absence of a contract between physician and patient, the law usually imposes no duty on the physician to treat the patient, although it may impose other duties on the physician. For example, like other passersby, physicians have no legal obligation to help accident victims. The law in most states will not require them to be "Good Samaritans."[8]

This principle is illustrated in *Childs v. Weis.*[9] A Dallas woman seven months pregnant was visiting another town when she began to suffer labor pains and bleeding. At a local hospital's emergency room she was examined by a nurse who called the defendant physician and then advised the woman to go to her doctor in Dallas. The mother left the hospital and about an hour later the baby was born in a car. Twelve hours later the infant died. The court held that the physician had no duty to the woman because no physician-patient relationship had been established.[10] However, as noted in Chapter 10, "Emergency Care," federal law now requires emergency room personnel to stabilize emergency conditions irrespective of whether a provider-patient relationship exists.

Creation of the Relationship

A contract is necessary before the physician-patient relationship can exist. Contracts are generally created by mutual assent of the parties. A party purchasing an automobile, for example, makes an offer. If it is accepted by the other party, such details as price, terms of payment, date of delivery, and identity of the car are expressly agreed on, thus creating an *express contract*. On the other hand, a person may enter a bookstore, pick up the latest best-seller, pay a clerk, and leave the store without saying a word. This would be an *implied contract* because the terms of the contract were not expressly stated or written by the parties but were manifest by their actions.

The physician-patient relationship may be established by an express or an implied contract. A patient who has stepped on a rusty nail might go to a doctor's office. By doing so the patient is making an offer to enter into a contract. A physician who sends the patient away, as in *Weis*, has rejected the offer and owes no duty to the patient.[11] But if the physician begins to examine the injured foot the offer has been accepted, and an implied contract is created. An express contract would be created if the physician and patient manifestly agreed on the terms of the contract before the examination, including what the patient was to pay and what the physician was to do for the payment.

Sometimes the patient is unconscious or otherwise unable to express consent for treatment. Even in such circumstances the law may recognize a physician-patient contract. Despite the lack of mutuality of assent, a court might find that the contract was actually made with another party, such as a close relative or legal guardian acting for the benefit of the unconscious or incompetent person.[12] Under such an arrangement the patient, as the beneficiary of the contract between the physician and the third party, acquired the same rights as would a primary party to the contract. Second, even when no contract was made with another person, the law will treat the rendering of services to an unconscious person as a contract implied in law. Such a contract prevents "unjust enrichment" by requiring the patient to pay for services and imposes the same duties on the physician that would arise under an express or implied-in-fact contract.[13]

Although clear enough in the abstract, the principles of contract law discussed above are difficult to apply in the widely varying circumstances that arise in medical practice. For example, physicians commonly consult one another regarding diagnosis and treatment of patients. This often occurs informally, without fees, and the consulted physician often does not see the patient in question and may not even know his or her name. Do these informal consultations create a physician-patient relationship? Generally the answer is "no." In one instance a professor of medicine at the University of California at Los Angeles was speaking to a group of physicians at a medical meeting.[14] During the session a physician described a patient's medical history to the professor, who advised surgery. Later the patient sued the professor, claiming that the surgery had not been necessary. The court concluded that the professor had no duty to the plaintiff because there was no physician-patient relationship.

On the other hand, a physician need not come into direct contact with a patient for the doctor-patient contract to exist. In addition to providing advice over the telephone, a physician may provide services indirectly. A radiologist or pathologist, for example, has a contractual relationship with the patient.[15]

An important issue involves the duty of a physician providing services to someone who is not the other party to the contract. Such circumstances arise, for example, when a physician is conducting a pre-employment examination on behalf of the individual's potential employer, when a life insurance company employs a physician to examine an applicant for life insurance, and when a physician is asked by a court to examine a plaintiff in action for personal injuries. The general rule is that in these situations a physician-patient relationship is not established between the physician and the applicant or the plaintiff in the action and, therefore, the physician owes no duty to the individual being examined.

Some courts, however, have found at least a limited duty toward the plaintiff even in the absence of a contractual relationship. In *James v. United States* the plaintiff applied for a position at a shipyard and as a condition of employment was required to take a physical examination. A chest x-ray revealed an abnormality, but through a clerical error neither the x-ray nor the radiologist's report was seen by the examining physician. Almost two years later an inoperable cancer was diagnosed. The government defended the plaintiff's malpractice suit on the grounds that the absence of a physician-patient relationship precluded any duty of care. The court awarded damages to the plaintiff, however, finding that

> [h]aving made a chest X-ray an essential part of the preemployment examination to determine an applicant's physical fitness, however, defendant failed to use due care when . . . the report on the X-ray was not brought to the attention of the examining physician.[16]

A similar situation may arise for those already employed. In *Armstrong v. Morgan* the plaintiff was being promoted to company vice president and was requested by the company to have a physical examination. The defendant physician examined him and reported him to be in very bad physical condition. As a result of this report he lost his job and benefits. In suing the physician he contended that the report was false and that the physician was negligent in his diagnosis. The defendant argued that he had no duty to treat because there was no doctor-patient relationship. Although the court agreed that no such relationship existed, it nevertheless found that the defendant owed the plaintiff a duty not to injure him physically or otherwise. Furthermore, if he had injured the plaintiff as a result of a negligent examination and inaccurate report, actionable negligence would be shown.[17] The court quoted from Prosser's *Law of Torts*:

> [T]he problem of duty is as broad as the whole law of negligence, and . . . no universal test for it ever has been formulated. . . . It is embedded far too firmly in our law to be discarded, and no satisfactory substitute for it, by which the defendant's responsibility may be limited, has been devised. But it should be recognized that "duty" . . . is not sacrosanct in itself, but only an expression of the sum total of those considerations of policy which lead the law to say that the particular plaintiff is entitled to protection. . . . No better general statement can be made, than that the courts will find a duty where, in general, reasonable men would recognize it and agree that it exists.[18]

Employees' Remedies and Worker's Compensation Laws

When an employee suffers an injury or illness arising out of his or her employment, the worker's compensation laws generally provide the exclusive remedy for the employee. This means that workers are precluded from recovering from their employer or co-employees for negligence or other claims, apart from the worker's compensation claim. If an employee is injured on the job and negligently treated by the company physician or the physician in the course of examination or treatment fails to diagnose an illness, can the employee recover from either the employer or the physician on malpractice or other grounds?

Again, the general rule is that worker's compensation is the employee's exclusive remedy and that an employee's action for medical malpractice is barred.[19] However, some courts have found that when an employer operates in two capacities, as both an employer and a hospital, for example, the second capacity imposes obligations unrelated to and independent of the hospital's obligations as an employer. This is known as the "dual capacity doctrine." In *Guy v. Arthur H. Thomas Co.* the plaintiff worked as a laboratory technician at the defendant hospital and in the performance of her duties operated a magnetic blood gas apparatus that used mercury.[20] In her complaint against the hospital she alleged that she contracted mercury poisoning from the apparatus and that the hospital's employees negligently failed to diagnose her condition as mercury poisoning, thereby aggravating her injuries. The court held that as an employer the hospital was liable for worker's compensation benefits; as a hospital it was liable in tort. As another court put it, a physician-patient relationship is created between the employer and employee, and the employer takes on a different persona.[21]

Other exceptions to the exclusive remedy provision may exist when the employer commits an intentional tort against an employee because the intentional conduct does not arise out of the course of employment, and when there are two injuries: the work-related injury and the aggravation of the injury as a result of the employer's conduct. This last exception applies when the injury is concealed from the employee or the employer fails to disclose to the employee a noncompensable disease or injury detected during an examination by the employer. The exception for intentional torts is generally reserved for cases in which the employer actually intended to inflict injury on the employee. It does not cover accidental injuries caused by the employer's gross or willful negligence or tolerance of a dangerous condition.[22]

In addition to the issue of exclusive remedy, the other issue concerning worker's compensation laws is whether they protect a physician employed by a company from liability for negligent treatment of fellow employees. These laws generally provide immunity from suit for co-employees, and some courts have dismissed suits against physician-employees on this basis.[23] Others have found however, that a company physician is an independent contractor for purposes of the worker's compensation exclusion and have permitted actions against physician-employees.[24] The dual capacity doctrine has also been invoked to find physicians liable for negligent treatment of workers.[25]

Scope of the Duty Arising from the Relationship

When the physician and patient have entered into a contractual relationship, what have the parties agreed to do? Generally the physician has agreed to diagnose and treat the patient in accordance with the standards of acceptable medical practice and to continue to do so until the natural termination of the relationship.[26] The patient has agreed to pay the physician for the services rendered.[27] Ordinarily the doctor has not promised to cure the patient. In some cases, however, such a warranty or guarantee may be found from express promises made by the physician, and if no cure results he or she will be liable for breach of warranty.

The physician may limit the scope of the contract to a designated geographical area or medical specialty.[28] In *McNamara v. Emmons* a woman sustained a bad cut, which was treated by an associate of the defendant physician.[29] The next morning the patient left for a vacation in a town 20 miles away. While there she felt she needed further treatment and asked the physician to come to the town. He refused but gave her instructions and named a local physician whom she might call. The court held that in these circumstances the physician was justified in limiting his practice to his own town. In other cases the courts have decided that, at least when no emergency exists, the physician has no obligation to make house calls but instead may require the patient to come to the office for treatment.

Although traditionally the physician's duty has been only to the patient, the doctor's duties to persons other than the patient are increasingly at issue. One example is *Sylvia v. Gobeille*, a case in which a baby was born with serious defects because the physician failed to prescribe gamma globulin for the mother, even though he knew that she had been exposed to German measles.[30] The court held that these facts stated a cause of action for recovery of damages by the third party—the baby.

Duties to persons other than the patient

In some states the contractual relation between the patient and the physician not only allows the physician to warn certain persons when a patient has an infectious disease, but obligates the physician to do so. Similarly, a physician might be subject to liability when a patient injures a third party. In *Freese v. Lemmon* a pedestrian was injured by an automobile when the driver suffered a seizure.[31] Both the driver and his physician were sued by the injured person, the physician on the theory that he was negligent in diagnosing an earlier seizure and in advising the driver that he could operate an automobile. The trial court dismissed the complaint against the physician on the grounds, among others, that the pedestrian did not rely on the diagnosis and was not known to the physician. The Supreme Court of Iowa reversed and remanded the case for trial, however, on the theory that a physician is subject to liability to third persons for negligently treating or giving false information to a patient when an unreasonable risk of harm to a third party or class of persons was foreseeable.

In the well-publicized case *Tarasoff v. Regents of the University of California*, the California Supreme Court ruled that despite a confidential relationship to patients, a doctor has a duty to use reasonable care to warn persons threatened by a patient's condition.[32] The patient in *Tarasoff* had indicated to his psychotherapist that he intended to kill a certain person and later carried out his threat. On these facts the court determined that the victim's parents had a cause of action against the psychotherapist. An important consideration in such cases is whether the injury to the third parties was foreseeable. In *Brady v. Hopper* it was held that the psychiatrist who treated John Hinckley, Jr., the man who attempted to assassinate President Reagan, owed no duty to the plaintiffs because it was not alleged that Hinckley had conveyed to the defendant specific threats against the plaintiffs that would make his act foreseeable.[33]

Termination of the Relationship

Like all contracts, those between the physician and patient are at some point terminated: when the patient is cured (or dies), when the physician and the patient mutually consent to termination, when the patient dismisses the physician, or when the physician withdraws from the contract.[34] The first three methods of termination are usually legally uneventful; the fourth has frequently been the subject of litigation.

Withdrawals by a physician before the patient is cured often result in a claim of abandonment by the patient. Whether abandonment is a breach of contract, an intentional tort, or negligence has been a matter of considerable confusion. In many cases grounds for all three causes of action might exist, especially when the physician thought the patient had been cured and prematurely discharged him or her from the hospital.[35] The confusion has been compounded by the absence of a clear line between abandonment and lack of diligence in treating a patient—which, as will be seen later, is negligence. The distinction between negligence and breach of contract or intentional tort as grounds for a claim of abandonment is especially critical in regard to matters of proof, because plaintiffs relying on the latter two theories are often not required to present expert testimony.[36]

Abandonment may be either express or implied. *Express abandonment* occurs if a physician expressly notifies a patient of withdrawal from the case but fails to allow the patient enough time to locate another physician. In *Norton v. Hamilton* the plaintiff reported being in labor several weeks before her baby was due.[37] According to her allegations the physician examined her and concluded that she was not in labor. When the pains continued, the patient's husband called the physician twice to say that his wife was still in pain. At that point the physician said he was withdrawing from the case. While the husband was looking for a substitute physician, the patient delivered her child alone and consequently endured unnecessary pain and suffering. The court held that the physician's acts, if proven, constituted abandonment.

Implied abandonment occurs when the physician's conduct makes abandonment of the patient obvious. In *Johnson v. Vaughn* the plaintiff gave the following account. Dr. Vaughn initially admitted the patient to the hospital, treated him, and then went home, leaving word that he was to be called if the patient's condition grew worse. Because at the time the patient seemed dangerously ill, his son called a Dr. Kissinger who "gave such attention as appeared to be most urgent" but felt that he could not proceed further without a release from Dr. Vaughn. He called Dr. Vaughn on the telephone and told him that the patient was dying and needed immediate attention. At this, Dr. Vaughn became irate and abusive, called Dr. Kissinger a louse for trying to steal his patient, and hung up. A call from the patient's son produced more abuse. Finally Dr. Vaughn said he would release the patient if he was paid $50 by nine o'clock the next morning. Meanwhile 30 or 40 minutes had passed before Dr. Kissinger could operate, and the patient later died. The court held that these facts were sufficient to state a claim of negligent abandonment against Dr. Vaughn.[38]

Most physicians can raise a number of legal defenses to claims of abandonment. If the physician gives notice of withdrawal early enough for the patient to find another physician of equal ability, the claim will fail. As previously noted, physicians may also assert the right to limit their practice to a certain specialty or geographical area. A physician who is too ill to treat a patient or to find a substitute also has a valid defense to an abandonment claim. If physicians obtain a substitute physician, they have a valid defense so long as the substitute is qualified and the patient has enough time to find another if the substitute is unacceptable.[39]

Some defenses to abandonment claims have been found insufficient. A physician cannot rely on a claim that he stopped treating the patient because the patient was remiss in paying bills.[40] Nor was a physician successful in claiming that he was attending another patient, when it was shown that he had already given the plaintiff medicine to induce labor.[41]

Furthermore, a physician may not in every instance abandon a patient simply because another physician is reportedly handling the case. *Maltempo v. Cuthbert* is an example.[42] The plaintiff's diabetic son was in a county jail awaiting transportation to a state prison to serve a sentence for a drug violation. In jail the son's health deteriorated, and his mother called her family physician for assistance but could only reach the defendant physician, who was taking his calls. This man told the mother that he would investigate the matter and call back if there were any problems. He then called the jail, learned that the son was being treated by the jail physician, and did nothing further. The young man died while being transported to the state prison. The appellate court affirmed an award of $45,000 for the plaintiff, holding that even if it would have been unethical, for the physician to treat the young man without the jail physician's consent, the jury could find negligence from the doctor's failure to ask the other doctor about the man's condition or at least to inform the parents that he was proceeding no further. The physician's actions "lulled the Maltempos into believing that their son was being cared for, and effectively prevented them from seeking other emergency help."[43]

Two California cases have raised questions regarding the freedom of a healthcare provider to refuse initial or continued treatment of a patient whom the provider does not wish to treat. In *Payton v. Weaver* a physician informed his patient, a 35-year-old indigent woman with end-stage renal disease, that he would no longer continue as her physician because of her intensely uncooperative behavior, antisocial conduct, and refusal to follow instructions.[44] The patient tried without success to find alternative treatment and petitioned the court to compel the physician to continue treating her. The parties stipulated to an order providing that the physician would continue to treat her if she met reasonable conditions of cooperation. When she did not keep her part of the bargain, the doctor again notified her that he was withdrawing, and she again sought a court order. This time the trial court found that she had violated the previous conditions and in the process adversely affected other dialysis patients. The court also found that there was no emergency requiring treatment under a California statute,[45] that the physician's notice was sufficient to end the relationship, and that the doctor was not responsible for the fact that no other dialysis unit would accept the patient. The appellate court sustained the trial court.

A different situation resulted in the judgment that a medical group and hospital could not refuse nonemergency care to a husband and wife. In *Leach v. Drummond Medical Group, Inc.*, the plaintiffs, who were patients of the group, had written to a state agency commenting adversely on the performance of the group's physicians.[46] They were then informed by the group that because of the allegations made to the medical licensing board, "a proper physician-patient relationship" could not be maintained and the patients would receive only 30 days of care and that only in an emergency. The couple then brought suit to compel continued treatment of their many health problems, but the trial court denied relief. This judgment was reversed by the appellate court, however, which permitted the suit to continue. The court held that although one physician may not be required to treat a patient he or she does not like, a medical center or group may be ordered to. The court also held that the plaintiffs had stated a cause of action under the state civil rights act, which covered medical practices and physician services.[47] Because the patients had not publicly criticized the doctor but only discreetly contacted the appropriate state agency, the court held there was no justification for denying services to them. Thus the defendants' refusal constituted arbitrary discrimination in violation of the statute. It is significant in this case that the defendants provided the only medical care available within a hundred miles.

Duties following termination of the relationship

Recent cases have extended the physician's duty to the patient even after the doctor-patient relationship has clearly been terminated; in a sense, the relationship is continued as a matter of law. In *Tresemer v. Barke* the plaintiff's physician had implanted an intrauterine device (IUD) in 1972.[48] The physician had seen the patient only on that one occasion. The plaintiff later suffered injury from the device (a Dalkon shield) and filed suit against the physician. She alleged that he later learned the hazards from the IUD but failed to warn her. The court held that the defendant had a duty to warn the plaintiff, noting that a physician is in the best position to alert a patient and that death or great bodily harm might be avoided with much less inconvenience than the reasonable care required in the circumstances. The court held that breach of that duty gives rise to a malpractice action "from the imposed continuing status of physician-patient where the danger arose from that relationship. It is also a cause of action for common negligence."[49]

Liability for Breach of Contract

In the typical physician-patient contract, as has been pointed out, the physician expressly agrees or implies agreement to perform a service. Failure to perform the service with reasonable skill and care may give the patient a cause of action not only for negligence, the usual allegation, but also for breach of contract. Several breach of contract actions based on abandonment have already been discussed in connection with the scope and termination of the physician's contractual duty. *Alexandridis v. Jewett* offers one more example.[50] Two obstetricians implied that they would be available when the plaintiff went into labor. On learning that the woman was in labor, one of the obstetricians notified his partner, who was on call. The partner did not arrive on time, however, and an episiotomy performed by a first-year resident in obstetrics resulted in injury to the patient. In the suit that followed, the appellate court found enough evidence to go to a jury on the issue of negligence; furthermore, the court held that the partners would be liable for breach of contract if their superior skill would have protected the patient from injury. In a similar case the court noted that a cause of action could be stated for breach of contract against a urologist because he allegedly agreed to perform an operation on the plaintiff but was not present during the surgery; rather, two colleagues from his medical group performed the operation.[51]

A physician who uses a different procedure from that promised in the contract will also be liable for breach of contract. In *Stewart v. Rudner and Bunyan* the physician promised to arrange for an obstetrician to deliver a child by cesarean section.[52] The patient was a 37-year-old woman who had had two previous stillbirths and was extremely eager to have a "sound, healthy baby." While the patient was in labor the physician told an obstetrician to "take care of this case" but did not tell him about the promise to perform a cesarean section. At the end of a lengthy labor the baby was stillborn. The appellate court upheld a jury verdict for the patient on the grounds that the physician breached his promise that a cesarean operation would be used to deliver the baby.

Breach of Warranty

Physicians are especially susceptible to liability if they not only promise to perform a service, or to perform it in a certain manner as in *Stewart*, but also guarantee a specified result. Such a warranty does not exist unless expressly stated by the physician; consequently, the physician who guarantees a result gives the patient a separate cause of action if the treatment is not successful. In *Sullivan v. O'Conner* a professional entertainer contracted with a physician to have cosmetic surgery on her nose, which she felt was too long.[53] The physician promised that the surgery would "enhance her beauty and improve her appearance." In fact the surgery was unsuccessful, and after two more operations the nose looked worse than before. Although recognizing that physicians do not guarantee results simply by agreeing to perform an operation and that it is often difficult to draw the line between opinion and warranty, the appellate court nevertheless upheld a jury verdict for the plaintiff.

Another much-publicized case is *Guilmet v. Campbell*. The plaintiff in that case had a bleeding ulcer. He talked with one of the defendant surgeons regarding a possible operation and alleged that he was told (as summarized by the court):

> Once you have an operation it takes care of all your troubles. You can eat as you want to, you can drink as you want to, you can go as you please. Dr. Arena and I are specialists, there is nothing to it at all—it's a very simple operation. You'll be out of work three to four weeks at the most. There is no danger at all in this operation. After the operation you can throw away your pill box. In twenty years if you figure out what you spent for Maalox pills and doctor calls, you could buy an awful lot. Weigh it against an operation.[54]

With this alleged assurance the plaintiff underwent the operation. Diagnosis after the surgery showed that the patient had a ruptured esophagus; his weight dropped from 170 to 88 pounds, and he developed hepatitis. He then sued the physician on both a negligence theory and a warranty theory. The jury decided that the physicians were not negligent but had breached their promise to cure. This was affirmed by the state supreme court, which decided that the question was properly one for the jury. In an emotional dissent one justice observed:

> In these early weeks of 1971 an exuberant new majority of a once great appellate Court prepared to launch an unwarned, unprecedented, wholly gratuitous and destructive witless war of "contract liability" upon a brother profession which, by the multifold harassment of malpractice actions, has been forced already to undertake what is professionally known as "defensive medicine."[55]

Apparently the Michigan legislature agreed with the dissenting opinion. In an action that underscores the fact that hospital and professional liability law is derived from statutes as well as common law, the legislature in effect overruled *Guilmet* by passing the following statute in 1974:

> In the following cases an agreement, contract, or promise shall be void, unless that agreement, contract, or promise, or a note or memorandum thereof is in writing and signed by the party to be charged therewith, or by a person authorized by him:
>
>   (g) An agreement, promise, contract, or warranty of cure relating to medical care or treatment. Nothing in this paragraph shall affect the right to sue for malpractice or negligence.[56]

The *Guilmet* decision touched on another issue that is especially relevant in breach of contract cases: the necessity for *consideration*. If a person is to be held to a contractual promise, that person must receive something in exchange for the promise. In the physician-patient contract the physician will not be held to a promise to perform a medical or surgical procedure unless the patient gives something in return, usually a promise to pay the physician. In *Guilmet* the court decided that there was sufficient consideration because the physician promised to perform the surgery and to cure the patient in return for payment from the patient. If, however, the physician first promises to perform surgery, for which the patient promises to pay, and later adds an additional promise to cure or a guarantee of a particular result, the courts will not allow the patient recovery for failure to perform the additional promise or warranty unless there is additional consideration to support the promise.[57]

Liability for Intentional Tort

Another basis for professional liability of physicians is intentional tort. A *tort* is a civil wrong not based on contract that results in injury to another person or another person's property or reputation. Traditionally torts have been divided into three categories, each of which involves a different standard of proof for the plaintiff. An *intentional tort*, as the name implies, results when a person intends to do the wrongful act. *Negligence* occurs when a person intends no harm but fails to do what a reasonably prudent person would do in the same circumstances. *Strict liability* results when an act is wrongful, not because the actor intended the wrong or was negligent, but because the act involved a high risk of harm to others. As noted earlier, most malpractice actions are based on negligence.

Actions based on intentional tort are less common than negligence actions, but they are important because they allow a plaintiff procedural flexibility not otherwise available. There may also be multiple consequences for the physician who commits an intentional tort. Because intent is usually an essential element in proving both the intentional tort and a crime, many intentional torts such as assault and battery entail criminal as well as civil liability. The commission of a criminal act could lead to a third consequence for a physician: revocation of the license to practice medicine. The following discussion considers cases of intentional torts committed by physicians rendering healthcare. They are presented in alphabetical order.

Assault and Battery

Assault and battery is a combination of two intentional torts. An *assault* is conduct that places a person in reasonable apprehension of being touched in a manner that is insulting, provoking, or physically injurious. A *battery* is the actual touching. Both assault and battery denote acts done without lawful authority or permission. A threat to kiss someone without implied or express consent is an assault, and the act of kissing in such circumstances is an assault and battery. If the person were asleep when kissed there would be a battery without the assault. But kissing someone with express or implied permission is not an assault or a battery.

The question of permission or consent to medical or surgical treatment is complex and is treated more completely in Chapter 11. For present purposes assault and battery cases involving physicians may be grouped into three categories. First are the intentional acts committed by the physician with no consent whatever. In *Burton v. Leftwich*, for example, a physician who was removing sutures from the toe of a four-year-old child and having trouble controlling his patient hit the child's thigh several times with his open hand, leaving bruises that were visible for three weeks.[58] An appellate court upheld a jury verdict that the physician had committed an assault and battery, although it reduced the jury's damage award. This case should be compared with *Mattocks v. Bell*, where a 23-month-old girl, whom a medical student was treating for a lacerated tongue, clamped her teeth on the student's finger.[59] After trying unsuccessfully to free his finger by forcing a tongue depressor into the child's mouth, the student slapped her on the cheek. A suit by the parents for assault and battery failed, the court holding that the force used was proper under the circumstances.

In these situations a physician's liability for striking a person is similar to the liability of a lay person. The case is no different when a physician performs an operation without consent. In the oft-cited *Schloendorff v. Society of New York Hospital*, a doctor was held liable for intentional tort after he operated on a patient who, according to the jury's finding, had consented only to an examination under ether and had given no consent for an operation.[60] In a more recent case a patient signed a consent form naming a specific urologist to remove his kidney stones. After surgery, the patient discovered that the operation had been performed not by the urologist but by two other members of the urologist's medical group. He then sued all three physicians for malpractice and failure to obtain informed consent. On the plaintiff's appeal from a jury verdict in favor of the defendants, the appellate court affirmed, ruling that an operation performed by a surgeon other than the one named in the consent form is not malpractice but battery. The Supreme Court of New Jersey reversed, however, finding that the plaintiff had a cause of action for battery or malpractice and that even if no compensable injury resulted, damages for mental anguish and perhaps even punitive damages could be assessed.[61] The court stated:

> Even more private than the decision who may touch one's body is the decision who may cut it open and invade it with hands and instruments. Absent an emergency, patients have the right to determine not only whether surgery is to be performed on them, but who shall perform it.[62]

A second category of assault and battery comprises instances where the duty to obtain permission has been met but the physician goes beyond the scope of the permission. In a third category the physician acts within the scope of the consent, but because the doctor does not exercise ordinary care in advising the patient of the risks of the treatment, the patient's consent is not an informed one and the permission is invalid. As will be seen in Chapter 3, suit can be brought in both the second or third categories on either a negligence or an assault and battery theory. In recent years negligence has been charged in most cases, but liability has also been based on assault and battery.[63] *Mohr v. Williams*, although not recent, illustrates these latter cases.[64] In *Mohr* the plaintiff consented to an operation to remove a polyp from her right ear. After she was anesthetized, the defendant surgeon discovered that her left ear needed surgery more than the right ear and operated on the left one instead. On the grounds, among others, that his conduct amounted to a technical assault and battery, the appellate court upheld a trial court's decision to deny the surgeon's motion for judgment.

Although the surgeon in *Mohr* should have consulted the patient before operating on the other ear, a surgeon will sometimes be justified in operating beyond the scope of the consent, for instance when an emergency precludes obtaining the patient's consent. In *Barnett v. Bachrach* a surgeon operating on a patient who had been diagnosed as having an ectopic pregnancy discovered that the pregnancy was normal but that the woman had acute appendicitis.[65] He removed the appendix and later sued the patient for his fee. The patient defended the suit by alleging that the appendix was removed without her consent. In holding for the surgeon the court noted that if he had not taken out the appendix the patient and child might have been endangered.

Defamation

Defamation is wrongful injury to another person's reputation. Written defamation is *libel*, and oral defamation is *slander*. To be actionable, the defamatory statement must be "published"—that is, it must be made by the defendant to a third party and not just to the plaintiff. This point was made in *Shoemaker v. Friedberg*, in which a physician wrote to the patient that she had a venereal disease. The woman showed the letter to two or three other women and later, in the presence of a friend, discussed the diagnosis with the physician. In bringing the suit against him she alleged a breach of confidentiality, but the court held that no recovery should be allowed because the patient had "published" the diagnosis herself.[66]

Numerous defenses are available to a physician in an action for defamation. The truth of a defamatory statement is an absolute defense, although the defendant has the burden of proving the statement true.[67] Certain statements, such as those made during a judicial proceeding or by one physician to another in discussing a patient's treatment, are said to be absolutely privileged, thereby providing an absolute defense. In *Thornburg v. Long*, for example, a specialist incorrectly reported to a family physician that a patient had syphilis.[68] When a patient sued the specialist for libel, the court held that the statement was privileged because the specialist had a duty to communicate the information to the family physician.

Certain statements, although not absolutely privileged, are entitled to a qualified privilege if they were made to protect a private interest of the physician, the patient, or a third party. A qualified privilege requires good faith on the part of the physician making the statement. In *Simonsen v. Swenson* a physician believed that a patient had syphilis.[69] While he was awaiting additional tests, he advised the patient's hotel proprietor that the patient might have a contagious disease, and the proprietor forced the patient to move. It was later discovered that the patient did not have syphilis, but the court held that the physician was not liable for defamation because he had a duty to disclose information of this nature.

False Imprisonment

The intentional tort of false imprisonment arises from unlawful restriction of a person's freedom. Many false imprisonment actions involve patients who have been involuntarily committed to a mental hospital. In *Stowers v. Wolodzko* a psychiatrist was held liable for damages of $40,000 for his treatment of a woman who had suffered such involuntary commitment. Although her committal was allowed by a state statute, the court held that because the psychiatrist kept the woman from calling an attorney or a relative, his actions constituted false imprisonment because her freedom was unlawfully restrained.[70]

Closely related to false imprisonment is an action for abuse of process, which can be brought against a physician who wrongfully uses a commitment statute to commit a patient without justification. In *Maniaci v. Marquette University* a 16-year-old college freshman obtained her parents' permission to leave school.[71] College officials learned that she was leaving and, without asking whether she had her parents' permission to leave, stopped her by having her committed to a hospital. Hospital attendants removed the girl's clothes, bathed her, and gave her a housecoat to wear. Later she was locked in a room with several other female patients who engaged in sexual activities that shocked the girl. Eventually she established contact with her family through a social worker and was released. On these facts the trial court awarded the plaintiffs $20,001 on a false imprisonment theory. The Wisconsin Supreme Court reversed the decision on the ground that there was no "unlawful" restraint of freedom, the statutory procedures having been complied with. The court also determined, however, that the evidence showed a cause of action for abuse of process and remanded the case for trial on that theory.

Invasion of Privacy and Wrongful Disclosure of Confidential Information

Although truth is an absolute defense in defamation actions, two other bases for possible liability exist even when a physician's statement about the plaintiff is true: invasion of privacy and wrongful disclosure of confidential information. In actions for malpractice, *invasion of privacy* occurs when a patient is subjected to unwanted publicity. For example, in *Vassiliades v. Garfinckel's, Brooks Bros.* the plaintiff's evidence that the defendant physician and department store used "before" and "after" photographs of her cosmetic surgery without her permission was sufficient to support a jury verdict against the physician for invasion of privacy and breach of fiduciary duty.[72] Similarly, a Michigan physician was held liable for invasion of privacy when he allowed a lay friend to observe the delivery of a baby in the patient's home. Clearly, a patient's expectation of privacy should be respected.

An action for *wrongful disclosure* of confidential information was brought on behalf of a man who had been a patient at the Holyoke Geriatric and Convalescent Center.[73] His family had filed a petition seeking permission to remove him from the kidney dialysis treatments that were sustaining his life. When a court granted the petition, several nurses and aides from the center, with the approval of the center's administrator, wrote a letter to a local newspaper protesting the court order. The letter appeared on the front page of the paper. A jury awarded the plaintiff's wife and his estate $2.5 million for violation of a statute that prohibits release of personal data and gives a cause of action to an individual whose rights have been violated. A new trial was ordered, and the second jury granted an award of $1 million. Althouth this award was reversed on appeal because the center was owned by a governmental entity to which the statute did not apply, the case illustrates the danger of disclosing confidential patient information without proper authority.[74]

On occasion, disclosure of confidential information is required by state or federal law. For example, confidential information from a patient's medical record may be disclosed for the purpose of quality assurance and peer review activities and to state authorities in cases of suspected child abuse. Other reporting requirements include those relating to communicable disease, abortions, birth defects, injury or death resulting from use of a medical device, environmental illness and injury, injuries (such as knife or gunshot wounds) resulting from suspected criminal activities, and conditions (such as epilepsy) affecting one's ability to drive safely.

Obviously, disclosures made in conformity with law are not "wrongful," and no liability will attach in such circumstances. Similarly, there is no liability for disclosing otherwise confidential information in accordance with a valid authorization from the patient (or the patient's guardian) or pursuant to a search warrant or other legal process. Healthcare facilities must be aware of the federal and state requirements regarding confidentiality of medical records and must have policies and procedures in place to protect the information contained therein.

Misrepresentation

Misrepresentation is another tort for which physicians have been held liable. Misrepresentation is classified as either intentional—that is, fraudulent or deceitful—or negligent. In either case it must be shown that a present or past fact was falsely represented and was relied on by the person claiming injury. Both intentional and negligent cases of misrepresentation involving physicians fall generally into two other distinct categories: representations to induce a patient to undergo treatment and later representations concerning the treatment or its results.

Physicians who misrepresent the nature or results of treatment they render are liable for fraud even though they were not negligent in rendering the treatment. In *Johnson v. McMurray* a cause of action for fraud was stated by an allegation that the defendant physicians intentionally concealed the fact that Dr. McMurray operated on the plaintiff despite the plaintiff's specific refusal to have Dr. McMurray participate in the surgery.[75]

The presence of fraud sometimes enables a patient to bring suit after the statutory time limit for negligence. In *Hundley v. Martinez* a physician repeatedly assured his patient, an attorney, that his eye would be all right after a cataract operation.[76] In fact the attorney became virtually blind in that eye. Although the statute of limitations had run, the court held that the limitation was suspended if the jury found that the physician had obstructed the plaintiff's right of action by fraud or in other indirect ways.

Outrage

The intentional tort of *outrage* (sometimes called intentional infliction of *emotional distress*) arises from extreme and outrageous conduct by the defendant. The tort requires willful or reckless behavior rather than mere negligence. In *Rockhill v. Pollard* the plaintiff, her mother-in-law, and her ten-month-old daughter were injured in an automobile accident and the baby was rendered unconscious.[77] The defendant physician agreed to meet the family in his office, but when he arrived he was extremely rude and refused to examine them. Finally, after the plaintiff asked him several times, he made a cursory examination of the baby, who was still unconscious, and declared that there was nothing wrong with her. Even after the baby had vomited a considerable amount, the physician told the plaintiff that the cause was overfeeding. He gave the women no advice about further treatment and asked them to leave. They had to wait outside in freezing weather until the plaintiff's husband arrived to drive them to a hospital, where the baby underwent surgery for a depressed skull fracture.

According to the court, under these circumstances a jury could find that the defendant's conduct was outrageous in the extreme, even though the plaintiff did not allege negligence in the doctor's failure to diagnose the injuries properly. The court noted that an important factor was the particular relationship between the parties: the doctor had come to his office for the express purpose of rendering professional aid and had a special duty toward the plaintiff. The court also stated that the cause of action for outrage is "to compensate for real suffering intentionally or recklessly caused by socially intolerable behavior which invades plaintiff's interest in peace of mind."[78] The plaintiff had to show not only that the conduct was outrageous but also that she in fact suffered emotional distress as a result and that the distress was severe.[79]

Violation of Civil Rights

Recently, courts have recognized causes of action for violations of patients' civil rights. For example, in California a physician who failed to fulfill his agreement to treat a patient for reason of race was held liable under the state civil rights statute.[80] In *Eidgeion v. Eastern Shore Hospital Center*, the plaintiff had been involuntarily committed to a Maryland hospital after an *ex parte* hearing in which his wife testified that he had exhibited abnormal and violent behavior. He was examined by two physicians upon his arrival at the hospital, and although he showed no outward signs of mental illness the doctors ordered that he be held at the hospital. The plaintiff maintained that his wife lied about his behavior because she wanted to be free to join her male friend in Florida and that as soon as the two were together the hospital released him. The plaintiff sued his wife, the physicians, and the hospital for violation of federal and state civil rights statutes, negligence, false imprisonment, false arrest, defamation, intentional infliction of emotional distress, and conspiracy to commit these wrongs. The court held that the complaint stated a valid cause of action.[81]

Notes

1. Debora A. Slee, J.D., wrote this chapter for the second edition of this book.
2. Because negligence is by far the most common theory for recovery used by plaintiffs, most commentators use the term "malpractice" to refer only to negligence. Unfortunately this narrow definition has led many physicians and hospitals to believe thay have complete professional liability coverage under their malpractice insurance policies, when in fact they are covered only for negligent acts. For example, in Security Ins. Group v. Wilkinson, 297 So. 2d 113 (Fla. App. 1974), the court held that a hospital's professional liability policy did not cover a breach of contract to treat the plaintiff's wife. To obviate such confusion the discussion here will avoid using malpractice as a synonym for negligence.
3. For a thorough discussion of the history, purposes, and effectiveness of the tort system of professional liability, see Williams, *Abandoning Medical Malpractice*, 5 J. LEGAL MED. 549 (1984).
4. 60 Mass. (6 Cush.) 292 (1850).
5. *Id.* at 269.
6. Vermont and Minnesota have statutes, termed Good Samaritan laws, that go against this tradition by requiring a bystander to render reasonable assistance in an emergency. VT. STAT. ANN. Tit. 12 § 519 (1973); MINN. STAT. ANN. § 604.05 (Supp. 1985). Calling these laws Good Samaritan statutes is somewhat confusing. Most states already have Good Samaritan statutes that protect a person who voluntarily renders aid from liability; the Vermont and Minnesota laws go beyond this by requiring the aid. The implications for medical practitioners are unknown; for example, is a physician-bystander held to the standards for a lay person, or do the standards of medical practice apply?
7. Note that courts can and do apply legal principles to find legal duties where none had existed previously. In Tarasoff v. Regents of the Univ. of Cal., 118 Ca. Rptr. 129, 529 P.2d 553 (1974), aff'd, 131 Cal. Rptr. 14, 551 P.2d 334 (1976), the court found that a psychiatrist had a duty to warn the person whom the patient had threatened to kill, even though there was no relationship between the doctor and the threatened person and in spite of the fact that doctor-patient

communications are normally confidential. The court considered the following factors in determining whether liability should be imposed: (1) the foreseeability of harm to the plaintiff; (2) the degree of certainty that the plaintiff suffered injury; (3) the closeness of the connection between the defendant's conduct and the injury suffered; (4) the moral blame attached to the defendant's conduct; (5) the policy of preventing future harm; (6) the burden to the defendant and the consequences to the community; and (7) the availability, cost, and prevalence of insurance for the risk involved. Of these factors, foreseeability of harm is often most important to the court in determining whether a duty should be found. (This case is discussed in detail in Chapter 13, "Medical Records.")

8. For example, in Hurley v. Eddingfield, 156 Ind. 416, 59 N.E. 1058 (1901) the only physician available to aid a critically ill person refused, for no reason, to assist. The court stated that unless some special contract or other commitment exists physicians have no legal responsibility to treat people.

   Two states, Vermont and Minnesota, have statutes that require a bystander to render aid in an emergency. VT. STAT. ANN. TIT. 12, § 519 (1973); MINN. STAT. ANN. § 604.05 (Supp. 1985). See note 6, *supra*.

9. 440 S. W.2d 104 (Tex. Civ. App. 1969). This case is discussed in greater detail later in conjunction with hospital emergency care.

10. There was a dispute about what the doctor actually told the nurse. The physician said that he had instructed the nurse to have the woman call her own doctor and see what he wanted her to do.

11. This is so absent some other obligation, such as in an emergency room (as noted above) or in certain managed care situations.

12. Consent for a legally incompetent person is discussed in greater detail in Chapter 11, "Consent for Treatment and the Withholding of Consent."

13. J. WALTZ AND F. INBAU, MEDICAL JURISPRUDENCE 170 (1971).

14. Ranier v. Grossman, 31 Cal. App. 3d539, 107 Cal. Rptr. 469 (1973).

15. A. HOLDER, MEDICAL MALPRACTICE LAW 6 (2d ed. 1978).

16. 483 F. Supp. 581 (1980). *See also* Dornak v. Lafayette Federal Hosp., 399 So. 2d 168 (La. 1981) (defendants were negligent in failing to inform plaintiff-employee of tubercular condition disclosed during pre-employment physical examination).

17. Armstrong v. Morgan, 545 S.W.2d 45 (tex. Civ. Ct. App. 1977). *See also* Chiasera v. Employers Mut. & Bertola, 101 Misc. 2d 877, 422 N.Y.S.2d 341 (1979) (insurance company's physician had a duty not to injure plaintiff during course of examination).

18. 545 S.W.2d at 46, 47; W. PROSSER, LAW OF TORTS, § 53 (3d ed. 1964).

19. *See, e.g.* Young v. St. Elizabeth Hosp., 131 Ill. App. 3d 193, 475 N.E.2d 603 (1985) (plaintiff alleged negligent treatment of injuries sustained on the job; suit dismissed); McAlister v. Methodist Hosp. of Memphis, 550 S.W.2d 240 (Tenn. Sup. Ct. 1977) (hospital employee alleged negligent treatment of work-related back injury).

20. 55 Ohio S. 2d 183, 378 N.E.2d 488 (1978).

21. McCormick v. Caterpillar Tractor Co., 82 Ill. App. 3d 77, 402 N.E.2d 412 (1980), *aff'd in part and rev'd in part*, 423 N.E.2d 876 (1981).

22. Varnes v. Willis Day Moving and Storage Co., 6 Ohio B. 506 (6th Dist. Ct. App. 1983) (court also held that plaintiffs were estopped from bringing this

action because they had applied for and received worker's compensation benefits and had no right to dual compensation). *See also* A. LARSON, WORKMEN'S COMPENSATION LAW, §§ 68.11–.35 (1984).

23. *See e.g.*, Garcia v. Iserson, 42 A.D.2d 776, 346 N.Y.S.2d 572 (1973), *aff'd*, 33 N.Y.2d 421, 353 N.Y.S.2d 955, 309 N.E.2d 420 (1974).

24. *See e.g.*, Stevens v. Kimmel, 182 Ind. App. 187, 394 N.E.2d 232 (1979); Ross v. Schubert, 180 Ind. App. 402, 388 N.E.2d 623 (1979).

25. *See, e.g.*, Hoffman v. Rogers, 22 Cal. App. 3d 655, 99 Cal. Rptr. 455 (1972); Duprey v. Shane, 39 Cal. 2d 781, 249 P2d 8 (1952).

26. The standards of practice and termination of the relationship are discussed later in this chapter.

27. The patient has not agreed to follow the doctor's orders; failure to do so, however, may excuse the physician from liability for untoward results.

28. WALTZ AND INBAU, *supra* note 13, at 149.

29. 36 Cal. App. 2d 199, 97 P.2d 503 (1939).

30. 101 R.I. 78, 220 A.2d 222 (1966).

31. 210 N.W.2d 576 (Iowa 1973). *See also* Kaiser v. Suburban Transp. Sys., 65 Wash. 2d 461, 398 P.2d 14 (1965), *amended by* 65 Wash. 2d 461, 401 P.2d 350 (1965) (passengers in patient's bus were allowed to recover damages from defendant physician); Duvall v. Goldin, 139 Mich. App. 342, 362 N.W.2d 275 (1984) (physician owed a duty to third persons injured in auto accident after physician failed to warn his patient not to operate motor vehicle).

32. 118 Cal. Rptr. 129, 529 P.2d 553 (1974) *aff'd*, 131 Cal. Rptr. 14, 551 P.2d 334 (1976). *See also* Davis v. Lhim, 124 Mich. App. 291, 335 N.W.2d 481 (1983) (psychiatrist held liable for discharging patient who subsequently killed his mother and for failing to warn the patient's mother). *But see* Soto v. Frankford Hosp., 478 F. Supp. 1134 (E.D. Pa. 1979) (physician and hospital not liable for failure to warn patient's husband, after the patient's poisoning was incorrectly diagnosed, of the danger of carbon monoxide poisoning; the court, noting that the "physicians were not under a duty to control the conduct of Mrs. Soto," found that her husband's death was "one step removed" from cases where the patient's conduct injures a third party).

33. 751 F.2d 329 (10th Cir. 1984).

34. As a general rule the primary physician is relieved of duty when calling in a consultant to take over treatment of the patient. The primary physician would be liable, however, if negligent in the selection of a consultant or if working with the specialist in treating the patient. The consultant normally does not undertake continuing treatment after the consultation but has only the duty to treat the patient for the specific purposes relating to the referral. *See* A. HOLDER, MEDICAL MALPRACTICE LAW 34 (2d ed. 1978).

35. D. LOUISELL AND H. WILLIAMS, MEDICAL MALPRACTICE § 8.08, at 219 (1973); A. HOLDER, *id.*, at 374.

36. Holder, *Abandonment: Part I*, 225 J.A.M.A. 1157 (1973). Proof of negligence is discussed in the next chapter.

37. 92 Ga. App. 727, 89 S.E.2d 809 (1955).

38. 370 S.W.2d 591 (Ky. 1963).

39. WASMUTH, LAW FOR THE PHYSICIAN 26-29 (1966); SIEGAL, FORENSIC MEDICINE

5 (1963). *See, e.g.*, Stohlman v. Davis, 117 Neb. 178, 220 N.W. 247, 250 (1928) (child with osteomyelitis was being treated by a physician who was an expert on the subject. This physician went to Arizona to recuperate from an illness, however, and in his place substituted his son, who had practiced medicine for four years. The illness did not constitute an emergency. Because the patient and his father did not learn of the physician's departure until two weeks later, the court held the primary physician liable for abandonment because he had not given the plaintiff time to locate another physician. In the words of the court: "The clear duty, under the circumstances, was imposed upon him either to secure the patient's acceptance of the substitution of his son, Doctor Herbert Davis, or to give him notice so as to secure another physician or surgeon of his own choice").

40. Holder, *Abandonment: Part I*, 225 J.A.M.A. 1157, 1158 (1973).
41. Young v. Jordan, 106 W. Va. 139, 145 S.E. 41 (1928).
42. 504 F.2d 325 (5th Cir. 1974).
43. *Id.* at 327.
44. 131 Cal. App. 3d 38, 182 Cal Rptr. 225 (1982).
45. CAL. HEALTH & SAFETY CODE § 1317 (West 1979).
46. 144 Cal. App. 3d 362, 192 Cal. Rptr. 650 (1983).
47. CAL. CIV. CODE § 51.
48. 86 Cal. App. 3d 656, 150 Cal. Rptr. 384 (1978).
49. *Id.* at 672, 150 Cal. Rptr. at 394. *See also* Tuchman v. Cutter Laboratories (no. 976,275, Cuyahoga Cty., Ohio, Ct. of Common Pleas; unpublished) (failure to warn patient of allegedly defective prosthetic heart valve).
50. 388 F.2d 829 (1st Cir. 1968).
51. Perna v. Pirozzi, 92 N.J. 446, 457 A.2d 431 (1983). This case is discussed in more detail below in relation to assault and battery.
52. 349 Mich. 459, 84 N.W.2d 816 (1957).
53. 363 Mass. 579, 296 N.E.2d 183 (1973).
54. 385 Mich. 57, 68, 188 N.W.2d 601, 606 (1971).
55. *Id.* at 76, 188 N.W.2d at 610.
56. MICH. COMP. LAWS ANN. § 566.132 (Supp. 1985), *amending*, MICH. COMP. LAWS ANN. § 566.132 (1967).
57. 61 Am. Jur. 2d *Physicians, Surgeons* § 161 (1981).
58. 123 So. 2d 766 (La. Ct. App. 1960).
59. 194 A.2d 307 (D.C. Ct. App. 1963).
60. 211 N.Y. 125, 105 N.E. 92 (1914).
61. Perna v. Pirozzi, 92 N.J. 446, 438, 457, A.2d 431, 461 (1983) (as against the urologist, plaintiff had a cause of action for breach of contract and breach of fiduciary duty, as well as malpractice).
62. *Id.* at 461, 457 A.2d at 439.
63. W. PROSSER, LAW OF TORTS 189 (5th ed. 1984).
64. 95 Minn. 261, 104 N.W. 12 (1905).
65. 34 A.2d 626 (D.C. Mun. Ct. App. 1943).
66. 80 Cal. App. 2d 911, 916, 183 P.2d 318, 322 (1947).
67. Even a true disclosure, however, may give rise to liability for invasion of privacy or wrongful disclosure of confidential information (discussed below). *See also* the discussion on confidentiality of medical records in a later chapter.

68. 178 N.C. 589, 101 S.E. 99 (1919). *See* WALTZ AND INBAU, *supra* note 13, at 263-67.
69. 104 Neb. 224, 177 N.W. 831 (1920).
70. 386 Mich. 119, 191 N.W.2d 355 (1971) (court also held psychiatrist liable for assault and battery for giving patient involuntary medication beyond what was permitted by statute).
71. 50 Wis. 2d 287, 184 N.W.2d 168 (1971).
72. 492 A.2d 580 (D.C. App. 1985) (the department store was not liable because it had obtained assurances from the physician that the plaintiff had given her consent).
73. A disclosure of confidential information will not result in liability if it is privileged. Physicians have a duty to disclose suspected child abuse, for example. *See, e.g.,* ALA. CODE § 25-14-3 (1977); WASH. REV. CODE § 26.44.030 (Supp. 1984). This matter is discussed further in Chapter 13, "Medical Records."
74. Spring v. Geriatric Authority of Holyoke, 394 Mass. 274, 475 N.E.2d 727 (1985). The statute involved was MASS. GEN. LAWS ANN. ch. 66A.
75. 461 So. 2d 775 (Ala. 1984).
76. 151 W. Va. 977, 158 S.E.2d 159 (1967).
77. 259 Or. 54, 485 P.2d 28 (1971).
78. *Id.* at 63, 485 P.2d at 32.
79. Restatement (Second) of Torts § 46, comment j. *See also* Grimsby v. Samson, 85 Wash. 2d 52, 530 P.2d 291 (1975) (husband sued physician and hospital for abandoning his wife, claiming that as a result he was forced to witness the pain and agony of his dying wife. The court allowed the claim for the tort of "outrage" and listed four requirements for recovery by a third party on an outrage theory: (1) the act must be intentional or reckless; (2) the conduct must be outrageous and extreme; (3) the conduct must result in "severe emotional distress"; and (4) the plaintiff must be an immediate member of the family and present at the time of such conduct); Savage v. Boies, 77 Ariz. 355, 272 P.2d 349 (1954) (law enforcement officers, in order to get plaintiff to a hospital and confined as a mental patient, told her that her husband and child had been badly injured).
80. Washington v. Blampin, 226 Cal. App. 2d 604, 38 Cal. Rptr. 235 (1964).
81. 479 A.2d 921 (Md. 1984). *See also* Johnson v. Silvers, 742 F.2d 823 (4th Cir. 1984) (plaintiff's complaint, which stated that while voluntarily committed he had been forced to take antipsychotic medication against his will, alleged a deprivation of liberty within the contemplation of 42 U.S.C. § 1983); Leach v. Drummond Medical Group, Inc., 144 Cal. App. 3d 362, 192 Cal. Rptr. 650 (1983) (California's UNRUH Civil Rights Act prohibits healthcare providers from refusing services without justification; this case was discussed earlier in connection with termination of the physician-patient relationship).

NEGLIGENCE[1]

N egligence, the most common cause of action in medical malpractice cases, arises where injury results from the failure of the wrongdoer (also called the tort-feasor) to exercise due care. Normally four elements are essential to prove negligence: a duty of due care, breach of the duty, causation, and damages.

The Standard of Care

The *duty of due care* requires all persons to conduct themselves as any average, reasonable person would do in similar circumstances. One who fails to meet this standard has committed a breach of duty, and if the breach causes injury to another person or to property, the tort-feasor will be liable for resulting damages. The most common negligent tort is one in which the operator of a motor vehicle fails to do what the average, reasonable driver would do and causes an accident, thus becoming liable for resulting injuries.

The standard of care—the actions of an average reasonable person—although adequate in most cases, is unsuitable where the defendant is a physician. In cases of negligent driving, most members of the jury have driven cars themselves and can rely on their own experience, training, and common sense to determine whether the defendant was acting reasonably. In contrast, members of the jury usually do not have the requisite knowledge, skill, or experience to judge whether a physician has acted reasonably in a medical malpractice case. As a result, courts have adopted a special standard in such cases: physicians are measured against other physicians, not against the average person.

The standard of care used in malpractice cases has been stated in these words: "A physician is bound to bestow such reasonable and ordinary care, skill, and diligence as physicians and surgeons in good standing in the same neighborhood, in the same general line of practice, ordinarily have and exercise in like cases."[2] Courts generally agree with this concept, but like most such legal standards, it has been subject to various interpretations. The differences have to do with three aspects of the definition:

1. Against what other physicians is the physician in question to be measured? That is, who is "the reasonable physician"?
2. Where do these other physicians practice? That is, is a local, state, or national standard to be applied?
3. What school of medicine do these other physicians follow?

The Reasonable Physician

Because the standard requires such "reasonable and ordinary care, skill, and diligence as physicians and surgeons in good standing . . . ordinarily . . . exercise in like cases," physicians are not measured against their most knowledgeable, most highly skilled colleagues. Rather, the test is whether a physician has exercised the skill and care of other physicians in the same line of practice.[3]

If a physician chooses between alternative methods of treatment or uses experimental techniques, he or she will not be guilty of malpractice if the selection is one that in the physician's opinion best meets the patient's needs. It is sometimes stated that if the course of treatment is followed by a "respectable minority" of the medical profession, there will be no liability.[4] In one case a physician performing a thyroidectomy severed the patient's laryngeal nerves.[5] The patient did not claim that the physician was not careful but that two methods were in use and he should have chosen the other. The court rejected this argument because both methods were acceptable.

A more difficult problem arises when the physician treats the patient by a method that even a respectable minority would deem unacceptable because it verges on experimentation. Physicians are sometimes clearly justified in using innovative techniques when standard methods have failed and the condition is serious. In one case a surgeon performed an unorthodox operation on an ankle after trying standard techniques and when other physicians had advised amputation.[6] The court held that the operation was justified as a last resort. But a doctor who follows an experimental procedure before attempting standard methods is likely to be considered negligent. In one instance a physician treating an infant for a curvature of the spine used a surgical procedure he had developed but no one else had used. The child suffered a severe hemorrhage and died. In the case that followed, the court found both the doctor and the hospital liable for not disclosing to the child's parents that the procedure was novel and unorthodox.[7]

Local, State, or National Standard

The second aspect of the standard of care compares the treatment in question to that used by physicians and surgeons "in the same neighborhood." Generally the neighborhood may be limited to the community in which the physician practices or similar ones in the vicinity, the state, or the nation. This has been called the "locality rule" because it measures the standard of care in a given instance solely by the practices of other physicians in the same locality.[8]

> Such rule developed in early years upon the theory that doctors in a rural area should not be held to the same standards of medical expertise as doctors in urban areas because of difficulties of communication and travel, with restricted opportunities to be kept abreast of medical advances, and the necessity of practicing in often inadequate hospital facilities."[9]

The locality rule formerly referred to the same district in which the physician practiced, but it has been broadened in most jurisdictions.[10] Some courts consider medical practices not only in the same locality but also in similar places.[11] Expansion of the rule is especially appropriate when there are few if any physicians in the same locality whose practices offer a basis for comparison. The traditional locality rule has given way in most states to a broader standard because the original reasons for the rule have all but disappeared.[12] As one court stated:

> Locality rules have always had the practical difficulties of: (1) a scarcity of professional people in a locality or community qualified to testify; and (2) treating as acceptable a negligent standard of care created by a small and closed community of physicians in a narrow geographical region. Distinctions in the degree of care and skill to be exercised by physicians in the treatment of patients based upon geography can no longer be justified in light of the presently existing state of transportation, communications, and medical education and training which results in a standardization of care within the medical profession. There is no tenable policy reason why a physician should not be required to keep abreast of the advancements in his profession.[13]

For these reasons, the same court held that the "language 'same neighborhood' . . . refer[s] to the national *medical neighborhood* or *national medical community*, of reasonably competent physicians acting in the same or similar circumstances."[14] Thus, a "national standard" has been created.[15] In some cases the national standard appears to be limited to specialists. For example, in *Buck v. St. Clair* the Supreme Court of Idaho ruled that "for board-certified specialists, the local standard of care is equivalent to the national standard of care."[16]

For physicians practicing under less than ideal conditions the burden of meeting a national standard has been lightened by permitting "justifiable circumstances" as a defense.[17] The Mississippi Supreme Court stated the rule as follows:

> . . . [a] physician's non-delegable duty of care is this: given the circumstances of each patient, each physician has a duty to use his or her knowledge and therewith treat through maximum reasonable medical recovery, each patient, with such reasonable diligence, skill, competence, and prudence as are practiced by minimally competent physicians in the same specialty or general field of practice throughout the United States, who have available to them the same general facilities, services, equipment and options.[18]

Thus, presumably, a physician would not be responsible for providing certain care if, for example, the necessary facilities or resources were not available. The test is what is reasonable under the circumstances. All surrounding circumstances, including the "state of the art," are to be considered in determining whether there was a breach of the standard of care.[19]

The "School Rule"

The third consideration in determining the standard of care is whether the care is comparable to that of physicians and surgeons "in the same general line of practice." This rule, sometimes called the *school rule*, is a throwback to the days of different recognized schools of treatment. For example, the allopathic school treated diseases by using agents whose effects differed from the agent causing the disease. Its opposite was the homeopathic school. Many of these schools merged into what is known in some states as the regular practice of medicine, and in those states osteopaths for a time were not allowed to prescribe drugs or perform surgery; they were judged by the standards prevailing in their own school of medicine.[20] Today, most states allow osteopaths to perform surgery and prescribe drugs, and they are held to the standards established in the regular practice of medicine.

Despite the disappearance of several schools, the school rule is still important because a few such branches of medicine remain and the trend in medicine is toward specialization. The standard for judging practitioners in specialties or schools is established by the practices of others in the same school or specialty.

In applying the school rule, courts have first had to determine whether the school was legitimate. Legitimacy depends generally on whether rules and principles of practice have been set up to guide the members in treating patients. The existence of licensing requirements will usually suffice for recognition of a separate school when standard of care is in question.[21] In an early case the court did not recognize a spiritualist's practice as following a school of treatment because the practitioner's only principle was to diagnose and treat the disease by means of a trance. Because there was no legitimate school, the practitioner was held to the standards of medical practice.[22] In the case of a Christian Science practitioner, however, the court held the defendant to the standard of care, skill, and knowledge of ordinary Christian Science healers because he belonged to a recognized school.[23]

Within these school-rule standards, however, nonphysician practitioners will be held responsible for knowing which diagnoses are within their area of practice and which cases should be referred for medical treatment. For example, in *Mostrom v. Pettibon* a chiropractor was held liable for not identifying medical problems for which chiropractic treatment was not appropriate.[24] Physicians can also be held responsible for failing to refer a case to a specialist if the problem is beyond their training and experience. For example, a general practitioner was held liable for negligence when a patient died of a hemorrhage after coughing up blood for two days. The court found that the physician should have grasped the seriousness of the patient's condition and called in a thoracic surgeon who might have saved the patient's life.[25] On the other hand, a court found that a laminectomy and spinal fusion were within the scope of general surgeons and that the defendant, who was a general surgeon, had not been negligent in failing to call in an orthopedic or neurosurgeon.[26] (This decision might be questioned in today's era of greater specialization.)

Assuming that a general practitioner remains within his or her area of training and expertise and does not negligently fail to refer a patient to a specialist (if one is available), most courts hold the physician to the standards of general practitioners and not the standards of specialists.[27] Physicians who present themselves as specialists, however, will be held to a higher standard of care than that of general practitioners.[28]

Practitioners who are licensed, trained, or credentialed only in certain fields of medicine are held to higher standards of care if they go beyond what they are licensed, trained, or credentialed to do. This situation has arisen with licensed practitioners, such as chiropractors and podiatrists, and with nurses, medical students, and others among the growing number of allied health professionals. In *Thompson v. Brent* a medical assistant working in an orthopedist's office was held to the standard of care required of physicians in using a Stryker saw to remove a cast.[29]

Standard of Reasonable Prudence

Although the traditional standard of care in malpractice cases is derived from the practices of other physicians, and thus is set by the profession itself, courts have occasionally bypassed traditional standards. They have at times found the profession's standard inadequate, have permitted juries to judge for themselves whether a physician was negligent rather than rely on expert witnesses, and have found negligence "as a matter of law" from the facts of the case. Such approaches, illustrated below, tend to treat malpractice cases like ordinary negligence cases.

In *Favolora v. Aetna Casualty and Surety Company* a 71-year-old patient fell to the floor while being x-rayed and suffered a number of injuries, including a fractured femur.[30] The consequent prolonged hospitalization brought on pulmonary embolism and a kidney infection. In bringing suit the patient claimed that the fall would not have occurred if her radiologist had examined her medical records, which cited her history of sudden fainting spells. A lower court decision for defendants was reversed on the grounds that the professional standards, which did not require a radiologist to take into account the patient's history, were themselves negligent. In making this determination the court looked to teaching institutions, which required radiologists to examine the history of their patients.

In *Helling v. Carey* the plaintiff had been treated by two ophthalmologists from 1959 until 1968 while experiencing difficulty with her contact lenses.[31] In 1968, one of the ophthalmologists told her that tests of her eye pressure and field of vision showed she had glaucoma. She then sued the ophthalmologists because she alleged that permanent damage to her eyes had resulted from the defendants' negligence in not carrying out these tests nine years earlier. The trial and appellate court decisions were for the ophthalmologists. The Supreme Court of Washington reversed these decisions. According to medical experts for both plaintiff and defendants, the court noted, professional standards did not require routine testing for glaucoma for patients under age 40, a group in which the disease afflicts only one out of 25,000 persons. Although the plaintiff was only 32 when she learned she had glaucoma, the court concluded that because the test was simple, inexpensive, and painless, the standard adopted by the profession was itself negligent.[32]

The Washington legislature later passed a statute, apparently in response to the outcry that followed the *Helling* decision, that contained this provision:

> In any civil action for damages based on professional negligence against a hospital . . . or against a member of the healing arts . . . the plaintiff in order to prevail shall be required to prove by a preponderance of the evidence that the defendant or defendants failed to exercise that degree of skill, care, and learning possessed at that time by other persons in the same profession, and that as a proximate result of such failure the plaintiff suffered damages, but in no event shall the provisions of this section apply to an action based on the failure to obtain the informed consent of a patient.[33]

Even after the enactment of the statute, however, a later case, *Gates v. Jensen,* held that the rule of *Helling* that "reasonable prudence may require a standard of care higher than that exercised by the relevant professional group" was still effective.[34] The court noted that the original bill had used the word "practiced" rather than "possessed." According to the court the change by the legislature showed that the standard was not limited to what members of the profession actually did, but could be extended to what they ought to do.

A Michigan court allowed a jury to find negligence without requiring the plaintiff to prove the standard of care by expert testimony. In *Clapham v. Yanga* a 14-year-old girl and her mother had consulted the defendant physician because the girl complained of dizziness, nausea, and missed menstrual periods.[35] In fact the girl was pregnant. Although the defendant admitted he suspected pregnancy, he allegedly told the girl and her mother that the symptoms were caused by obesity and low blood pressure. He never tested for pregnancy, even though he saw the girl six times over a four-month period.[36] In noting that expert testimony is usually essential to establish whether the physician has violated the requisite standard of care, the court stated,

> if the physician's conduct is such that a layperson could ascertain that the medical practitioner's acts were negligent, such testimony is not needed. . . . We conclude that a jury could find, without specific testimony on the standard of care, that it is negligent not to give a patient who complains of the symptoms experienced by Loriann a

pregnancy test. *This is particularly true in light of defendant's admission that he suspected from the initial visit that Loriann was pregnant.*[37]

In another case the Supreme Court of Washington held that the trial court should have found negligence as a matter of law in the death of a patient.[38] Although the defendant physician suspected angina pectoris (chest pain caused by coronary artery disease), he neither informed the patient of his suspicion nor performed any of the three tests then readily available. The court held that the emergency room physician was also negligent as a matter of law in failing to take an electrocardiogram (EKG) of the patient, although uncontroverted testimony was heard that an EKG is medically indicated when any middle-aged man with mid-chest pain is rushed by ambulance to the hospital in the middle of the night, as this patient was. There was also testimony that in 95 percent of the cases the EKG would have shown the type of myocardial infarction that actually killed the patient.

Proving the Standard of Care and Breach of the Standard

To succeed in a medical negligence suit a plaintiff must first prove the standard of care and then show that it was breached by the physician. This proof usually demands expert testimony, which normally comes from the defendant's fellow practitioners because they alone know the standard. Moreover, unlike lay witnesses, physicians and other experts are not limited to testifying to facts they have observed but may give their opinion on the nature and cause of a patient's illness or injury. Because of the requirement for expert testimony, proving malpractice can be very difficult even if a valid case exists, because the plaintiff cannot always find a qualified expert witness. Some believe that a "conspiracy of silence" among physicians makes them reluctant to testify against fellow members of the profession,[39] and if a physician is not a party to the lawsuit, he or she cannot be forced to testify.[40] Evidence other than expert opinion is admissible in some instances to prove negligence, however, and occasionally even the defendant physician may provide the needed expert testimony. The various methods of proof are discussed below.

Expert Testimony

As mentioned, the normal method of providing professional negligence is to establish by expert testimony the appropriate standard of care and prove its breach. The expert witness who provides this testimony must be someone experienced and knowledgeable about the standard of care. Such a witness must meet certain conditions. First, the witness must be familiar with the standard of care required in the case. If the court follows the rule that specifies the standard in the same locality, the witness must practice in the same locality as the defendant physician. In some cases this rule is relaxed if the plaintiff can show that the witness is familiar with the local practice, even though practicing elsewhere.[41] If a national standard applies, any witness in the country is acceptable if otherwise qualified. A national standard of care therefore eases the burden of proof for the plaintiff because the search for a willing expert need not be limited to a particular locality. (This is another reason the "locality rule" has been relaxed: finding physicians in a particular town to testify against their colleagues and friends was often a daunting task.)

In addition to being familiar with the practices of the appropriate locality, the expert witness must also be professionally qualified. The basic requirement is knowledge of the standard of care to be applied. The witness need not practice the same specialty or even follow the same school of medicine, as long as familiarity with the standard of care can be established. For example, a specialist may testify about the standards for general practitioners, if knowledgeable about them.[42] Similarly, if the issue concerns the standards for doctors of osteopathy,[43] doctors of medicine can testify, although the school rule generally prohibits the imposition of their standards on the practice of others.[44]

The plaintiff must lay a foundation for expert testimony by persuading the judge that the witness has the appropriate training and experience to qualify as an expert. If the judge decides that the witness meets the qualifications, the testimony is allowed and the jury decides what weight to give it. Otherwise the witness is not permitted to testify. Qualification is a matter within the judge's discretion. For example, in *Gilmore v. O'Sullivan*, a 1981 case in which an obstetrician-gynecologist's negligence was alleged in the prenatal care and delivery of the plaintiffs' son, the court refused to permit the plaintiffs' expert to testify. Although the witness claimed to be familiar with the standard of care for a specialist in obstetrics and gynecology, the court found he was not qualified because he was not certified by the board of examiners in obstetrics and gynecology; there was no evidence of the number or types of maternity cases he had handled; he had not delivered a baby since 1959 or performed surgery since 1967; and he had pursued no research in or study of obstetrics and gynecology.[45]

Sometimes the defendant physician will be called as an expert witness. Unlike criminal defendants, who can invoke the privilege against self-incrimination, defendant physicians, like any other defendants in a civil case, must testify as to facts within their knowledge. Most courts have felt it is unfair to require the physician not only to testify regarding such facts but also to provide the expert testimony (opinion) needed by the plaintiff to establish the standard of care. A contrary trend, however, is illustrated by the New York decision in *McDermott v. Manhattan Eye, Ear and Throat Hospital*.[46] The defendant physicians, one of whom was one of the world's leading ophthalmologists, advised the plaintiff to undergo a series of operations to correct a corneal condition in her left eye. The operations resulted in blindness, and plaintiff claimed that the surgery was not approved by accepted medical practice, given the original diagnosis. At the trial the plaintiff presented no expert witness of her own but instead called on the defendant to testify to the standard of care required and the deviation from the standard in her case. The appellate court stated that the plaintiff had the right to require the defendant to testify both as to his actual knowledge of the case and, if he was so qualified, as an expert to establish the generally accepted medical practice.

In some cases the physician's out-of-court statements may be used as evidence of negligence, although statements made out of court are hearsay and normally excluded from evidence.[47] An admission (that is, a statement that a party to the suit makes against his or her own interest) is an exception to the hearsay rule. This is true even if the statement is made during negotiations for settlement and would not normally be allowed into evidence.[48] Courts face a difficult task in determining whether a given statement was really an admission of negligence or merely an expression of sympathy. After the death of one patient, for instance, the physician said, "I don't know, it never happened to me before, I must have gone too deep or severed a vein." This, the court held, was too vague and indefinite to establish negligence.[49] In another case a physician doing a sigmoidoscopic examination tore the patient's large intestine.[50] On the way from the operating room the patient's husband heard him say to another physician, "Boy, I sure made a mess of things." To the husband himself, he said, "In inserting the sigmoidoscope into the rectum, I busted the intestine." The court held that this admission could take the place of expert testimony because a jury could infer that the physician had not exercised the requisite degree of care.

In some instances a plaintiff is permitted to introduce medical treatises into evidence. Because medical publications are hearsay, most states limit their use to attacking the credibility of an expert witness[51] or reinforcing the opinion given in evidence by the expert.[52] A few states, however, by statute or court decision, permit medical books to be used as direct evidence to prove the standard of care. In a Wisconsin case the court took "judicial notice" of the standard of care set forth in a looseleaf reference service, "Lewis' Practice of Surgery," to determine whether an orthopedic surgeon was negligent in performing a laminectomy and diskectomy.[53] Even in states using the Wisconsin approach, however, the author of the treatise must be proved to be a recognized expert or the publication to be a reliable authority.

Written rules or procedures of the hospital, regulations of governmental agencies, standards of private agencies, and similar published material may be admissible to show the requisite standard of care. The landmark decision of *Darling v. Charleston Community Memorial Hospital* held, among other things, that the standards promulgated by the Joint Commission on the Accreditation of Hospitals (now the Joint Commission on Accreditation of Healthcare Organizations), standards of a governmental licensing authority, and provisions of the hospital's medical staff bylaws were admissible as evidence of negligence.[54]

Negligence Per Se

In some cases a statute or other law may be used to establish the standard of care.[55] Negligence that is established by showing a violation of law is called *negligence per se* or *statutory liability*. This doctrine requires several elements to be proved: that violation of the statute occurred and an injury resulted from the violation; the injured person was one whom the statute was meant to protect; and the harm was the type that the statute was enacted to prevent.[56] In *Landeros v. Flood* an 11-month-old child was examined by the defendant physician. She was suffering from a comminuted spiral fracture of the right tibia and fibula, which appeared to have been caused by a twisting force. Her mother gave no explanation for the injury, but in fact the child had been beaten repeatedly by both her mother and her mother's common-law husband. The physician failed to diagnose the battered child syndrome, and he did not take x-rays that would have revealed a skull fracture and other injuries. The child returned home where she was again severely injured. Because the doctor did not report the matter to the authorities, a civil damage action was allowed on the theory that the physician breached his statutory duty to report child abuse.[57]

Common-Knowledge Doctrine

Occasionally no expert testimony is required to establish professional negligence, such as when the negligence is so obvious that it is within common knowledge.[58] One clear example of such negligence would be amputation of the wrong leg. Similarly in *Hammer v. Rosen* three witnesses, not experts, testified that the defendant had been beating an incompetent patient.[59] Although the defendant physician claimed that without expert testimony it could not be shown that the beatings deviated from standard psychotherapy treatments, the court held otherwise because "the very nature of the acts complained of bespeaks improper treatment and malpractice."

Res Ipsa Loquitur

Perhaps the most complex exception to the expert-testimony rule is the doctrine of *res ipsa loquitur*, which means "the thing speaks for itself." The doctrine goes back to an English case decided in 1863, *Byrne v. Boadle*.[60] The plaintiff Byrne was walking down the street and was hit on the head by a barrel of flour that had rolled out of a warehouse owned by Boadle. Although the precise negligent act or omission could not be proved, the court found that Boadle was negligent because barrels of flour do not fall out of windows unless someone has been negligent.

Three conditions are essential to the use of *res ipsa loquitur*:

1. the accident must be of a type that normally would not occur without someone's negligence;

2. the defendant must have had control of the apparent cause of the accident; and

3. the plaintiff could not have contributed to the accident.

Whether the doctrine should be applied in a particular case is determined by the judge. Once a judge decides that *res ipsa loquitur* is applicable, most states have ruled that a permissible inference of negligence has been created; this in turn means that the case must go to the jury, who can then decide for plaintiff or defendant.[61] Some courts use the phrase *"prima facie* case" instead of *res ipsa loquitur* to describe essentially the same procedural effect.

In cases of medical treatment and resulting injury it may be impossible for patients to know the cause of the injury, particularly if they were unconscious during the treatment. If a plaintiff is permitted to invoke the doctrine of *res ipsa loquitur*, however, he or she may succeed in a malpractice claim even without proving any specific negligent acts of the defendant. The primary difficulty for malpractice plaintiffs has been the threshold requirement: the need to show an injury that ordinarily would not occur in the absence of negligence. The general test is whether in the light of ordinary experience and as a matter of common knowledge one could infer that the defendant was negligent.[62] In one example a patient underwent surgery for resection of the sigmoid colon.[63] The incision was closed with sutures, but eight days later it opened and a second operation was required to close it. The court held that *res ipsa loquitur* did not apply because a lay person would not know whether the incision failed to close because of the physician's negligence. Thus, the doctrine cannot be based simply on bad treatment results.

Leaving foreign objects in a patient after surgery is negligence within the common knowledge of lay people, however, and in such cases *res ipsa loquitur* is frequently used. In *Jefferson v. United States* the plaintiff was a soldier who had undergone a gall bladder operation in 1945.[64] Eight months later, after he had been suffering spells of nausea and vomiting, another operation disclosed that a towel had eroded into the duodenum. It was 30 inches long and 18 inches wide and was marked "Medical Department U.S. Army." These facts, the court held, showed negligence on the part of the defendants.

Some courts permit the common knowledge among physicians to satisfy the threshold test; that is, expert testimony is permitted to establish that the injury would ordinarily not occur without negligence. In *Hale v. Venuto* the plaintiff suffered from combined peroneal and tibial palsy of her left foot following surgery to correct a dislocation of her kneecap.[65] A neurologist and an orthopedic surgeon testified on her behalf at trial; they said that the injury was more likely than not to be a result of negligence. The appellate court ruled this sufficient to permit use of *res ipsa loquitur*, adding that California courts have relied on both common knowledge and expert testimony in determining probable negligence.

In addition to showing that the accident or injury would normally not occur without someone's negligence, the plaintiff must meet the second requirement for the use of *res ipsa loquitur* by showing that the defendant had exclusive control of the apparent cause of the accident. This requirement is often a problem for malpractice plaintiffs. Traditionally the doctrine cannot be applied in an action against several defendants, any one of whom could have caused the plaintiff's injury;[66] and this is very often the case for patients who have undergone surgery.

A major departure from the rule, however, was the California case of *Ybarra v. Spangard.*[67] After an appendectomy, the plaintiff felt sharp pains in his right shoulder and later suffered paralysis and atrophy of the shoulder muscles. The subsequent suit went to the California appellate court, which allowed the use of *res ipsa loquitur* against all of the defendants who had any control over the patient while he was anesthetized. These included the surgeon, the consulting physician, the anesthesiologist, the owner of the hospital, and several hospital employees, even though some of the defendants had probably not been negligent. The court held that the test had become one of "right of control rather than actual control."[68] The rationale for imposing on the defendants the burden of explaining the cause of the injury was that a special trust and responsibility arises from the physician-patient relationship.

The third requirement for use of *res ipsa loquitur* is a showing that the plaintiff could not have contributed to the accident. In many cases this is not difficult to prove: for instance, if the plaintiff was unconscious. If it is not clear, however, that the accident was not caused by the defendant's negligence, rather than the plaintiff's, the issue will not get to the jury. In *Rice v. California Lutheran Hospital* a hospital employee left a cup, saucer, tea bag, and hot water on a table beside a patient who was recovering from surgery and under the influence of pain-killing drugs.[69] The scalding hot water was spilled on the patient, who claimed that *res ipsa loquitur* should apply because the injury occurred while she was under sedation and did not understand what was going on. The court held that the doctrine did not apply in this case because witnesses testified that the plaintiff confessed to spilling the water on herself and that she was awake and alert at the time.

Strict Liability

By definition, strict liability does not naturally fall into a discussion of negligence because strict liability imposes liability without fault, that is, without any showing of negligence. A brief discussion is nevertheless relevant here because the concept is very closely tied to the doctrine of *res ipsa loquitur* and the standard of reasonable prudence discussed earlier.

A showing of fault was not required to impose liability until the mid-nineteenth century, at which time society decided that some wrongdoing must be shown to hold persons responsible for injury caused by their actions. Thus, at least negligence is required in most cases. Strict liability has been imposed, however, on those whose activities, such as using dynamite or keeping dangerous animals, entail a high degree of risk to others. The rationale behind strict liability is to place the burden of inevitable losses on those best able to bear them.[70]

Relatively recent developments in product liability law have imposed strict liability on manufacturers and sellers of products. The doctrine imposes liability on those responsible for defective goods that pose an unreasonable risk of injury and do in fact result in injury, regardless of how much care was taken to prevent the dangerous defect.[71] An important distinction has been made between products and services, and the doctrine does not normally apply to the latter. For example, in attempts to hold hospitals strictly liable for injuries caused by blood transfusions, courts generally have held that hospitals are providing a service and are not in the business of selling blood; therefore, strict liability does not apply.[72]

Courts generally reject attempts to hold physicians liable for adverse results without a showing of substandard care.[73] For example, in *Hoven v. Kelble* the plaintiff suffered injuries while undergoing a lung biopsy; in his action for malpractice he argued that strict liability for defective medical services should apply because a hypothetical, well-informed physician, working in a perfectly equipped hospital, could have avoided the injury.[74] Rejecting this argument, the court noted that the adoption of strict liability for medical services "would set the standard of performance for the entire medical profession at the zenith of that profession's achievement, a level at which by definition virtually no one could perform all the time."[75]

Causation and Damages

In addition to proving that a physician failed to meet the standard of care and that the patient was injured, a malpractice plaintiff must also prove that the injury resulted from the negligence. Although this element of proof is called "causation," the term has a different sense from that used in medical circles. The law considers an injury to be caused by a negligent act if the injury would not have occurred *but for* the defendant's act or was a foreseeable result of the negligent conduct. The legal cause of an injury is often termed the "proximate cause." Note that the plaintiff need not prove that the negligence in fact caused the result but only the strong likelihood that it did. Also, the negligence need not be the sole cause but only a significant factor in the injury. It must be remembered that the purpose of a malpractice trial is not to *convict* the defendants of malpractice but to decide whether the loss caused by the injury should be allocated to the defendants. The standards of proof are thus lower than for a criminal trial, for example.

If a physician has failed to meet the standard of care, the injuries resulting from that lapse, if any, may be difficult to determine. This is especially true in medical care because the patient presumably already had some illness or injury resulting from other causes. A number of physicians have been completely absolved from liability, despite their negligence, because of inadequate proof of causation. In one such case a 16-year-old boy was treated at an emergency room after being hit by a truck.[76] A physician there examined the boy and sent him home, where he died early the next morning from a basal skull fracture. The appellate court found sufficient evidence that the physician was negligent in not taking vital signs or ascertaining whether anyone else had taken them. According to the court, however, there was inadequate proof that the alleged negligence was the cause of death. One expert witness testified, "There is no possible way for a physician or anyone else to ascertain with any degree of certainty whether with medical intervention, the individual would have survived or died." Another expert noted, "There certainly is a chance and I can't say exactly what—maybe some place around 50 percent—that he would survive the surgery."[77] The court held that these statements did not show the defendant's negligence to have been the "proximate" cause of death. A similar result was reached in *Henderson v. Mason*, where the defendant physician failed to discover a piece of steel embedded in the patient's eye. The steel was eventually discovered and removed by another physician.[78] The court denied recovery because testimony showed that the patient would have suffered infection and loss of vision even if the defendant's diagnosis had been correct.

A court may determine that only some of a patient's injuries resulted from negligence. In one case a woman and her obstetrician lived near each other. In the sixth month of pregnancy she experienced labor pains, and her husband summoned the doctor. He did not arrive for several hours, however, and the patient miscarried. In the suit charging him with negligence in failing to treat her, the court decided that the obstetrician's negligence did not cause the miscarriage because his presence in the house would not have prevented it. He was nevertheless held liable for the patient's pain and suffering that he might have eased or prevented by his attendance.[79]

"Loss of a Chance"

Situations arise where, because of the nature of the disease, patients have virtually no chance of long-term survival but an early diagnosis may prolong life or permit a chance of survival, however slim. Should a practitioner who negligently fails to make that early diagnosis be liable even though the chances are that he or she could not prevent or forestall the patient's death? The courts have been divided on this question. Some jurisdictions have held that the defendant should not be liable if it was more likely than not that the patient would have died anyway.[80] Other courts have concluded that if the defendant increased the risk of death by lessening the chance of survival, such conduct was enough to permit the jury to decide the proximate cause issue, at least where the chance of survival was significant.[81] "The underlying reason is that it is not for the wrongdoer, who put the possibility of recovery beyond realization, to say afterward that the result was inevitable."[82]

In a Washington case the defendant allegedly failed to make an early diagnosis of the patient's lung cancer and the patient eventually died.[83] The defendants offered evidence that, given that type of lung cancer, death within several years was virtually certain, regardless of how early the diagnosis was made. The defendants moved for summary judgment. Because the plaintiff could not produce expert testimony that the delay in diagnosis "more likely than not" caused her husband's death, the trial court dismissed the suit. For purposes of appeal, both parties stipulated to these assumptions: the defendants were negligent; the patient had never had more than a 50 percent chance of survival; if the cancer had been diagnosed when the patient first saw the defendants, his chances of surviving five years would have been 39 percent; and at the time the cancer was actually diagnosed his chances were 25 percent. The delay in diagnosis may thus have reduced the chance of a five-year survival by 14 percent. The appellate court held that such reduction was sufficient evidence of causation to allow the proximate cause issue to go to the jury, who would then decide whether the negligence was a "substantial factor" in producing the injury. "To decide otherwise would be a blanket release from liability for doctors and hospitals any time there was less than a 50 percent chance of survival, regardless of how flagrant the negligence."[84] The court also noted, however, that should the jury find the defendants liable, they would not necessarily be liable for all damages caused by the patient's death but only those resulting from the premature death.

The question of damages is closely related to the element of causation. In addition to proving that the injury was caused by negligence the plaintiff must demonstrate the amount of damages he or she is entitled to recover; that is, which injuries resulted from the negligent conduct and what these injuries are worth. The most common damages are called "actual" or "compensatory" damages. These compensate the plaintiff for economic loss, such as the cost of medical and rehabilitation treatments and lost earnings, and for noneconomic loss, such as pain and suffering.[85] Punitive damages are seldom awarded in negligence cases.

Defenses to Negligence and Other Malpractice Actions

A physician involved in a malpractice suit may have legal defenses that can avoid or reduce liability even if a plaintiff can establish all the necessary elements of a cause of action. A statute of limitations can keep the case from ever going to trial; other defenses, such as comparative negligence, require a decision by the trier of fact. Defenses especially relevant in malpractice actions are discussed below. Other legal defenses, such as the *res judicata* theory discussed in Chapter 1, are of course available but have no unique significance in malpractice cases.

Assumption of Risk

A defendant in a tort action can occasionally raise *assumption of risk* as a defense. In many jurisdictions people who perceive the risk and still voluntarily expose themselves to it will be precluded from recovering damages if injury results. In medical malpractice cases the risk is often in a new method of treatment, and an important issue is whether the possible effects of such treatment were made known to the patient. This issue is closely related to informed consent, for a physician who informs the patient of the risk will not be liable if the danger materializes. He or she will also be able to assert that the patient knowingly assumed the risk. In *Karp v. Cooley,* for example, the surgeon was not held liable for the patient's death after a heart transplant because he had fully informed the patient and obtained consent to perform the operation.[86] The risks that the patient has assumed do not usually include the physician's negligence in treating the patient. In *Karp,* if death had resulted from the surgeon's failure to exercise the standard of care required in heart transplants, the surgeon would probably have been liable.

Contributory and Comparative Negligence

Even if a physician has been negligent, contributory negligence is a complete defense in many states. Under this theory, if the patient failed to act as a reasonably prudent person would have, and if the plaintiff's negligence contributed in any way to the injury, he or she cannot recover damages for the physician's negligence. In one case a physician who was grossly intoxicated treated a patient negligently.[87] The court refused to hold the doctor liable on the grounds that the patient was negligent in accepting treatment from a physician who was obviously drunk.

There are cases, however, where the patient's contributory negligence merely aggravated an injury caused by the physician's negligence. If the injury would have occurred despite due care by the patient, the plaintiff will be allowed at least a partial recovery. In a Wisconsin case, *Schultz v. Tasche,* an 18-year-old woman was negligently treated for a fracture of the right femur.[88] As a result the right leg was one and one-half inches shorter than the left and was deformed and painful. The appellate court decided that the patient could recover for the doctor's negligence despite her own negligence in leaving the hospital early, driving 15 miles to her home, and failing to return for additional treatment. The plaintiff's negligence, the court decided, merely aggravated the existing injury, and its only relevance was to reduce the damage award.

The *Schultz* case was based on a contributory negligence theory that has since been replaced in Wisconsin and most other states by a "comparative negligence" approach. Different theories of comparative negligence exist, but all attempt to compensate the injured parties in some way despite their own negligence. A later Wisconsin case illustrated one variation.[89] A hospital patient slipped while taking a shower and was injured. The jury decided that the hospital was 20 percent negligent, possibly for failing to install safety devices in the shower, but the patient was found 80 percent negligent and was awarded only $4,500.

Exculpatory Contract

Occasionally a defendant physician will raise as a defense a contract clause in which the patient agrees to forfeit the right to sue the physician for negligence. Such contracts are usually executed prior to treatment. The general rule that exculpatory contracts are invalid has been applied to physician-patient contracts, and the same rule applies to hospitals. In *Tunkle v. Regents of the University of California* the court held that a contract between a hospital and a patient that attempted to release the hospital from all liability was against public policy.[90]

Release

In contrast to an exculpatory contract, a *release* executed by a patient following treatment may operate as a defense for a physician. If a physician and patient reach a settlement on a malpractice claim, a release given by the patient will bar a later suit for injuries arising from the same negligent act. A more complicated situation results when one person wrongfully injures a patient and a physician aggravates the injury by negligence. If the patient settles with the original tort-feasor and gives that person a release, does the release also cover the physician? In *Whitt v. Hutchison* the plaintiff, who was injured at a ski resort, claimed that his injuries were aggravated by the negligence of the physicians treating him. Three and a half years after the original injury, the plaintiff settled with the ski resort for $6,000 and signed a form releasing the resort

> from any and all liability . . . and any and all other loss and damages of every kind and nature sustained by or hereafter resulting to the undersigned . . . from an accident which occurred on or about the first day of March, 1969, at Clear Fork Ski Resort, Butler, Richland County, Ohio, and of and from all liability, claims, demands, controversies, damages, actions, and causes of action whatsoever, either in law or equity, which the undersigned, individually or in any other capacity, their heirs, executors, administrators, successors and assigns, can, shall or may have by reason of or in any wise incident [to] or resulting from the accident hereinbefore mentioned.[91]

The court held that this release was broad enough to include malpractice claims and upheld a dismissal of the suit against the defendant physicians and hospital. The reasoning was that aggravation of the injury because of malpractice is considered a "proximate result of the negligence of the original tort-feasor," and the original tort-feasor, or one tort-feasor, releases all wrongdoers, whether concurrent or subsequent. In some cases courts have held the release effective for all tort-feasors even when there was an express provision to the contrary.[92] In most instances, however, a release will not be effective for those explicitly excluded. In *Whitt* the physicians and hospital were not excluded from the release, and hence the release was considered unconditional. "Such a release is presumed in law to be a release for the benefit of all the wrongdoers who might also be liable, and to be a satisfaction of the injury."[93]

"Good Samaritan" Statutes

"Good Samaritan" statutes, discussed more completely in Chapter 10, on "Emergency Care," offer a defense if the physician has rendered aid at the scene of an accident. These statutes, which most states have in some form, commonly provide that a physician rendering emergency care will not be held liable for negligence unless he or she is grossly negligent or acts in a reckless manner.[94] Most of these statutes do not *require* doctors to assist in emergencies but only protect those who volunteer their aid. Some states, however, have gone further and created a duty to assist along with immunity from civil suit for persons complying with the law.[95] References to a Good Samaritan statute may thus indicate either immunity or a duty to assist, or both.[96]

Worker's Compensation Laws

Worker's compensation statutes may provide a defense to physicians who are employed by companies and are sued by employees whom they treat in the course of their employment. In some instances the worker's compensation laws provide the exclusive remedy for such a patient, and a malpractice suit against the physician will not be permitted, but some courts have allowed such suits.[97]

Governmental Immunity

For government-employed physicians there are statues providing governmental immunity (also called "sovereign immunity") from civil liability for treatment rendered in the course of such employment. A unit of government cannot be sued unless a statute exists waiving sovereign immunity as to such cases. Generally, immunity applies to acts of discretion by public officials and governmental agents but not to "ministerial" acts. A ministerial act is one performed without exercise of judgment in accordance with a mandate of legal authority. For example, in *Tobias v. Phelps* a woman, committed to a state psychiatric hospital, died after physicians at the hospital cut down her medication for asthma in preparation for surgery, although she soon experienced difficulties.[98] Her personal representative sued the physicians alleging, among other things, that they failed to monitor the patient's condition properly and did not instruct the hospital staff adequately about her care. The physicians raised governmental immunity as a defense to the suit. The court ruled that the decision to wean the patient from the medication was a discretionary act and therefore the physicians could not be sued. However, the court found that the execution of the decision was ministerial; if the physicians decided that close monitoring was necessary but failed to ensure such monitoring, they would not be protected by governmental immunity but would be liable for negligence in executing the decision. The court therefore permitted the suit to proceed on the issue of negligence in the performance of ministerial acts.[99]

Governmental immunity is usually applicable only to negligent acts and will not protect intentional or grossly negligent conduct.[100] A government physician will also not be immune from suit under civil rights acts for deprivation of medical treatment if the alleged acts or omissions are "sufficiently harmful to evidence deliberate indifference to serious medical needs."[101] As discussed earlier, a physician may also be sued under these kinds of statutes for violation of other civil rights.[102]

Statutes of Limitations

Statutes of limitations specify a period during which lawsuits must be filed. The time allowed for malpractice actions (often two years) is generally shorter than for other actions, although the statutory provisions vary greatly from state to state.[103] California's statute of limitations for medical malpractice applies to "any action for damages arising out of the professional negligence" of a physician.[104] This leaves in doubt whether the statute applies only to suits that specifically plead negligence or to all causes of action—such as breach of contract, intentional tort, or negligence—resulting from a negligent act. Florida's statute, on the other hand, seems clearly intended to apply to any cause of action commonly referred to as malpractice, not only those based on a theory of negligence:

> An "action for medical malpractice" is defined as a claim in tort or in contract for damages because of the death, injury, or monetary loss to any person arising out of any medical, dental, or surgical diagnosis, treatment, or care by any provider of health care.[105]

Statutes of limitation generally specify that the period begins when the cause of action "accrues." A cause of action in an assault and battery case, for example, accrues the moment the defendant threatens or touches the plaintiff. In malpractice cases, however, it is often difficult to determine when the statutory period begins, particularly if the adverse result appears much later. There are three specific times when the statute might begin, depending on the state's law and the particular circumstances.

First, many states interpret the statute literally and have decided that the limitations period begins when the alleged negligence treatment is performed.[106] Second, a number of other states use the "discovery rule," under which the period begins when the patient discovers or should have discovered the alleged malpractice. In Michigan an appellate court decided that the two-year statute of limitations began when the plaintiff discovered that a surgical needle had been left in her abdomen, even though the needle had been there since 1949, 25 years before the court's decision.[107] Some courts, however, make such exceptions only if a foreign object is found in the patient. The third possibility is the "termination rule," under which the period begins when the treatment ends or, in a few states, when the physician-patient relationship ends.[108]

In many states particular circumstances create other possibilities. If a physician fraudulently conceals the malpractice, the statutory period will begin only with discovery of the negligence.[109] The beginning is often delayed also for patients who are minors. In *Chaffin v. Nicosia* a physician's negligent use of forceps during a birth caused almost complete loss of sight in the child's right eye.[110] Suit was allowed 22 years later because it was brought within two years after the injured person reached the age of majority. Moreover, some courts have decided, despite the discovery rule, that an action for wrongful death accrues at the date of the death.[111]

Liability for Acts of Others: Vicarious Liability

A physician who has not been personally negligent may be held liable for the negligence of others. This is called *vicarious liability* and is usually based on the principle of *respondeat superior:* that is, let the superior be responsible for the negligence of agents or employees. In the hospital there is sometimes a question as to whether the physician or the hospital must answer for the negligence of hospital employees, an issue thoroughly discussed elsewhere. Physicians whose offices are outside the hospital are responsible for the negligent acts of nurses, paramedics, x-ray technicians, and other physicians in their employ.[112]

Liability under the theory of *respondeat superior* does not depend on the negligent person's being on the payroll of the superior (although this might be a consideration) but on whether the person was under the direction and control of the superior. In *Baird v. Sickler* a surgeon was held liable for the acts of a nurse-anesthetist employed by the hospital. The court judged that the close relationship between the surgeon and the anesthetist resembled that of an employer and employee in that the former had the right of control over the latter. Perhaps a more important fact in this case was that the surgeon had instructed the anesthetist in some of the procedures and participated in positioning the patient and administering the anesthetic. These facts created a "master-servant" relationship, and the physician "had to answer for the servant's failures." By contrast, when a nurse had negligently administered an injection ordered by a physician, the physician was found not vicariously liable for the negligent act because he did not control the administering of the medicine.[113]

In addition to being liable for acts of employees, physicians who refer cases to physicians not in their employ may also be held liable. In general physicians are not liable when a substitute physician or a specialist takes over a case, but if they are careless in selecting the substitute or the specialist, they will be liable for their own negligence. And one who continues to participate in the treatment of the patient becomes by law a joint venturer and will be liable for the negligence of the other physician.[114]

A physician in partnership with other physicians is liable for the torts of the partners, as long as they acted within the scope of the partnership, because each partner is legally an agent of each other partner. If judgment is against a partnership with insufficient assets, the physician's personal assets may be used to satisfy the judgment. In one extreme case a man sued a medical partnership for alienation of affections, claiming that his wife had an affair with one of the partners.[115] Normally there is no vicarious liability for intentional torts; in this case, however, the court decided that the partnership was liable if the other partners did not use reasonable means to prevent their associate from wrongfully injuring the plaintiff's family relations. (Liability of this type could be limited by incorporating the partnership. The corporation would then have to respond in damages, although physicians who personally committed such torts would of course still be individually liable for their own wrongful acts.)

Distinctions Among Causes of Action

Although a single set of facts may constitute more than one cause of action, there may be tactical or legal advantages and disadvantages to each cause of action in a particular case. These depend on the time the action commenced, the legal defenses available, the need for expert witnesses, insurance coverage, and the money that the plaintiff is permitted to recover in damages.

Statutes of limitation, discussed above, vary according to the cause of action. For example, actions claiming malpractice, defamation, assault and battery, or false imprisonment in Ohio must be brought within one year, other personal injury actions within two years, wrongful death actions within two years of the date of death, actions based on an oral contract within six years, and written contract actions within fifteen years.[116] If an Ohio patient visited an attorney one year and one week after learning of complications resulting from an incident that took place in Ohio, it would be too late to sue for malpractice, though malpractice might not encompass all possible causes of action against the physician in this instance.[117] If only professional negligence were covered by the one-year limitation, the patient might base a suit on an intentional tort theory within two years or on breach of contract within 6 or 15 years.[118]

Other legal defenses, also discussed earlier, are not available in every cause of action. Assumption of risk, contributory and comparative negligence, Good Samaritan statutes, worker's compensation law, and governmental immunity usually apply only to suits for negligence, and intentional torts are almost always excluded from such legal protection. Gross negligence is normally covered by worker's compensation statutes; in most cases these require proof of intentional wrongdoing to establish liability. Governmental immunity will sometimes protect a person from liability for gross negligence, but not for intentional torts or for violation of civil rights. A release executed by a plaintiff after the incident, usually pursuant to a settlement, may apply to actions based on breach of contract, negligence, or intentional tort.

A third distinction among causes of action rests on the need for expert testimony. Most negligence cases and many contract cases require expert testimony that the defendant did not exercise the requisite care and skill. Expert testimony is not usually necessary, however, in proving an intentional tort or in certain contract actions.[119]

Another fact to consider in choosing a cause of action is that medical malpractice insurance does not cover all conduct commonly referred to as malpractice. A malpractice policy, for example, usually will not cover many of the intentional torts discussed above. For this reason, a plaintiff's attorney might choose a negligence or breach of contract theory so that damages will be collectible from the carrier of malpractice insurance. The Minnesota Supreme Court held that a physician's "professional liability and personal catastrophe" policy did not cover sexual assaults on several young patients during medical treatment at the doctor's clinic and once at the local hospital. The court found that the physician's sexual conduct involved neither the providing nor the withholding of professional services, and therefore the insurer's policy did not cover the plaintiffs' damages.[120] By contrast, the Wisconsin Court of Appeals held that a defendant psychiatrist's malpractice insurance covered a claim for damages resulting from the defendant's sexual acts with the plaintiff during the course of treatment. The court held that such conduct can constitute a failure to give proper treatment.[121]

Obviously, the availability of damages is important in the choice of possible causes of action. Damages are often classified as actual, nominal, or punitive. *Actual damages*, sometimes called *compensatory damages*, are the damages awarded to a plaintiff to compensate for past and future medical costs, past and future loss of income, physical pain, and mental anguish. *Nominal damages* are awarded to a plaintiff who proves the elements of a case but cannot prove actual damages. *Punitive damages*, also called *exemplary damages*, are designed to punish a defendant for conduct that the court considers willful or malicious. A plaintiff's right to recover any of the three types of damages will depend on the nature of the action. Table 3.1 shows the general rule regarding the types of damages that are recoverable in the various kinds of actions.

Actual damages, which are intended to compensate the victim for injury and loss, fall into two major categories: economic and noneconomic. *Economic damages* include expenses for medical care, rehabilitation, nursing care, child care, lost earnings, and so forth. Such damages are relatively easy to prove and are available in every kind of action. *Noneconomic damages* include injuries that are real but cannot easily be assigned a dollar value: pain and suffering and emotional distress, for example. Pain and suffering, which covers some of the nontangible damages accompanying physical injury, are allowed as an

Type of Action	Actual Damages	Nominal Damages	Punitive Damages	**TABLE 3.1**
Intentional tort[†]	Yes	Yes	Yes	Possible Types
Breach of contract	Yes	Yes	Rare	of Damage
Negligence	Yes	No	Rare	Recovery*

* These generalizations are ordinarily true, but some exceptions occur.

† In an assault and battery case, nominal and punitive damages can be recovered even if no actual damages were incurred.

item of damages in all but contract actions, but some states have enacted laws that place a dollar limit on such damages.

Courts vary in their allowance of damages for emotional distress, and this question is still unsettled. As a general rule recovery for emotional distress is allowed if the defendant has acted willfully or maliciously. Damages for mental distress are therefore usually allowed in suits for intentional tort. Such damages are also permitted by most courts in negligence actions if the emotional distress results from bodily injury; that is, if there was a physical impact. Courts are extremely reluctant, however, to allow damages for mental distress in a negligence action unless physical injury to the plaintiff occurred. Courts allow such damages generally only when the negligence constituted reckless disregard for the well-being of the plaintiff and the emotional distress was so great that it injured the plaintiff physically. Most medical malpractice cases do not show the willful malice or gross negligence needed to sustain a claim for damages for emotional distress in the absence of physical injury.

In some malpractice cases, however, the defendant's negligence is deemed so gross, willful, wanton, or malicious as to suggest an intent to harm or a reckless indifference to the consequences of the act. These are the cases in which damages for emotional harm may be granted by most courts even in the absence of physical injury.[122] Punitive damages may also be awarded in such cases. For example, in *Grimsby v. Samson* a husband brought suit against a hospital and physician because they allegedly failed to provide treatment for his dying wife. He claimed damages for the extreme mental distress he suffered as he watched his wife die. The Washington Supreme Court maintained its position of denying recovery for merely negligent infliction of mental anguish or emotional distress. It held, however, that the plaintiff had stated a cause of action for the intentional tort of outrage and could recover under that theory.[123] Outrage, because it is an intentional tort, is also an action under which punitive damages are available.

Punitive damages, while rare in malpractice actions, may be awarded if the defendant's conduct is judged willful, wanton, or malicious according to the state's standard.[124] For example, claims for punitive damages were permitted to go to the jury in a case in which the defendant injected liquid silicone in the plaintiff's breasts knowing that the silicone was labeled "not for human use,"[125] and also in which an anesthetist might have left the operating room without obtaining a qualified replacement.[126] Similar rulings were handed down in cases in which the defendant removed a patient's uterus without authorization,[127] and in which, according to the plaintiff, a physician opened the patient's abdomen inexpertly, removed some pus but made no attempt to remove a bowel obstruction, sewed up the wound, and sent the patient home in a hearse after telling her that she was going to die.[128] On the other hand, a claim for punitive damages was not allowed when a physician unknowingly operated on the wrong patient[129] and when a resident circumcised a baby against the wishes of the parents. In these cases the evidence established only negligence or inadvertence, according to the court, and not "that aggravated disregard of defendants' [professional] duties which has heretofore been considered by this court as a prerequisite in malpractice cases to the allowance of punitive damages for deterrent purposes."[130]

Countersuits by Physicians

A suit against a physician for malpractice is usually costly. Attorneys' fees and other costs of litigation must be paid, patients are lost, as is time from work, and malpractice insurance rates go up—all this in addition to mental anguish and the damage to reputation and even to health. If the physician wins the suit, is there any recourse against the plaintiff or his or her attorney for such damages? The answer in most cases is no unless the suit was completely frivolous, and even then it may be difficult to recover damages in some states.

The legal theories on which physicians have based countersuits in malpractice cases are:

- defamation;
- negligence;
- abuse of process; and
- malicious prosecution.

Defamation has not been successful because statements made in the course of legal proceedings are absolutely privileged, which means that the maker of the statement may not be sued for defamation.[131] Furthermore, courts have held that an attorney does not owe any duty to the adverse party (the physician) to investigate a malpractice claim to determine whether there is any basis for the plaintiff's claim before instigating suit. Attorneys are liable only to their clients for professional malpractice.[132] Abuse of process requires a showing that the plaintiff maliciously used a legal proceeding for some unlawful purpose; initiating a suit in itself does not constitute abuse of process. Probably because of the difficulty of showing a collateral motive on the part of the plaintiff, abuse of process has not been successful in countersuits by doctors.

Physicians have, however, successfully sued on the theory of malicious prosecution. In most states this tort requires that the following be shown: the malpractice suit must have been decided in favor of the physician; there was no probable cause to believe that the physician was liable; and the plaintiff or attorney acted maliciously in bringing the suit. The plaintiff's or attorney's motive of ill will, lack of belief of any possible success, or improper purpose may constitute malice. Most states also require a showing of actual damages. In some states special damages must be proved; for example, damages that arise from an arrest of the person or seizure of property.[133] Damages common to anyone involved in litigation, such as attorneys' fees, injury to reputation, and mental distress, are not considered special damages. Even an increase in rates for malpractice insurance has been considered insufficient to constitute special damages.[134]

In states not requiring a showing of special damages, physicians have had limited success in countersuing for frivolous malpractice actions. In one successful suit a patient authorized his attorneys to sue the manufacturer of an intramedullary rod that had broken after it was inserted in his leg to reduce a fracture, but he did not authorize the suit his attorneys brought against the physician. The court held that the physician stated a cause of action for malicious prosecution. Because the attorneys were not authorized to sue the doctor, this amounted to lack of probable cause. According to the court, it may be inferred that a suit filed without probably cause is filed with malice, especially if the attorneys have a large financial stake in the outcome as they did in this case.[135]

Reforming the Tort System

During the 1970s and '80s there was extensive talk, especially in the medical profession, of a "malpractice crisis." Whether in fact a crisis existed and, if so, what its cause was is a hotly debated topic, but it nevertheless seems clear that the tort system (like all human institutions) is imperfect. For this reason, many states have attempted in one way or another to reform the manner in which patients allegedly injured during the treatment process can have their claims adjudicated without undue expense or disruption to the medical profession.

Because a major reason for the early cries of "malpractice crisis" related to sharp raises in the cost of malpractice insurance, many states created joint underwriting associations to spread malpractice risks among the various insurance carriers. Some also established insurance plans to cover judgments beyond the limit of the primary insurance or authorized participation in a federal reinsurance program for the same purpose. Whether these reforms were effective or the so-called crisis ebbed of its own accord is uncertain. What is known, however, is that as we approach the end of the twentieth century and as more and more physicians are becoming employees of health systems and health plans, the issue of the cost and availability of individual malpractice insurance has subsided considerably.

Another attempt at reforming the system involved protecting the public from incompetent physicians through heightened licensing standards, mandatory continuing education, reporting of disciplinary actions, periodic recredentialing, and similar means. The federal government, for example, maintains the National Practitioner Data Bank, a resource that is intended to contain all disciplinary actions, license suspensions, malpractice settlements and judgments, and similar information for all physicians. A hospital's failure to query the NPDB during the medical staff privileges and credentials process, for example, could be construed as corporate liability for the organization; thus, providers are more closely monitoring the quality of care of the physicians on their medical staffs.

The third approach to reforming the system involves changing how injured patients are to be compensated. Four types of tort reforms are most common:

1. *Screening panels.* Although there are many variations, screening panels are basically committees of physicians and lawyers who review the merits of the case and advise whether evidence of negligence exists. Use of the panel is usually voluntary, although it has been mandated in some states as a prerequisite to filing suit.[136] Experience has shown that the panels find in favor of the patient about as frequently as courts do. When the panel finds in favor of the physician, patients seem less inclined to file suit.

2. *Procedural changes.* Various procedural changes have been proposed by those who want to reform the tort system. Use of mediation panels has been proposed as a way to reduce the backlog of malpractice cases, a circumstance that increases costs and frustrates all parties. Some states have prohibited use of the "ad damnum clause" (the specific dollar amount claimed in the plaintiff's original complaint) because it provides sensational headlines while typically being far in excess of what the plaintiff can reasonably expect to recover. Some have proposed to shorten the statute of limitations. Others have revised the standard for informed consent, *res ipsa loquitur*, or the locality rule to be more physician-friendly. Although all these types of reforms have been touted as partial solutions to the "malpractice crisis," none has seemed particularly effective in the grand scheme of things.

3. *Damage awards.* Another group of reforms relates to the damages that may be awarded to patients who have been injured by medical negligence. A few states specifically limit the size of a malpractice judgment; others only limit the amount of damages for noneconomic damages, such as pain and suffering. Some have passed laws reducing damage awards in medical malpractice cases by the amount the plaintiff received from collateral sources such as insurance (thus abrogating the traditional "collateral source rule," which held that the fact that the

individual was insured or received compensation from some other source was not relevant in his or her suit against the wrongdoer). Finally, many states have laws allowing periodic payments of a judgment in favor of a plaintiff, rather than a lump-sum payment.

4. *Contingency fees.* The common practice of a malpractice attorney being paid a percentage of the plaintiff's recovery has been the subject of much controversy. In reality, the contingency-fee system discourages many suits because responsible plaintiffs' attorneys are unlikely to take on cases that require many months of work with little likelihood of recovering an award. Nevertheless, several states have taken steps to limit the contingency fee by setting a maximum percentage that can be charged.

The various types of tort reforms have had mixed success, and it is clear that the system for adjudicating malpractice claims remains imperfect. For this reason, people have begun to look to alternatives to the traditional litigation process.

Alternatives to the Tort System

Arbitration has been proposed not only for pretrial screening of claims, but also as a system of resolving disputes. Other proposed alternatives to the tort system include no-fault compensation and problem solving by private contract rather than by public legislation.

Arbitration

Arbitration resolves disputes at a hearing before an impartial referee without involving the court system. Among the advantages cited for arbitration are these:

1. arbitration is speedier than the court system;
2. once the dispute is aired, arbitration saves the time of all parties;
3. matters under arbitration may be decided by an expert in the field;
4. the formalities and complex rules of court proceedings are relaxed;[137]
5. arbitration costs much less than a jury trial; and
6. arbitration proceedings allow greater privacy than court proceedings.[138]

Two major types of arbitration are relevant to malpractice disputes. First, *mandatory arbitration* may be imposed on the parties by statute or court rule. The second type of arbitration is voluntary, agreed to by the parties either when they initially enter into a contractual relationship or after the dispute arises in medical malpractice cases. *Voluntary arbitration* is not a recent development, having been introduced in some California health plans as early as the 1960s.

One of the major legal problems with arbitration provisions is that a court might consider them to be "contracts of adhesion" and therefore unenforceable. (A contract of adhesion is one entered into by a person whose bargaining position is weak because he or she cannot do without the other party's services. An obvious example would be an arbitration clause forced on a patient who urgently needs medical treatment.) Despite the possibility of adhesion problems, the California Supreme Court upheld an arbitration clause in the leading case of *Doyle v. Guiliucci,* which contested the arbitrator's decision in favor of the health plan and against the 3-year-old patient. The court decided that "the arbitration provision in such contracts is a reasonable restriction, for it does no more than specify a forum for the settlement of disputes."[139] However, a court might not order arbitration if a hospital or clinic has not manifested an intention to arbitrate the dispute. One clinic lost its chance to take a patient's claim to arbitration because it failed to demand arbitration immediately after suit was commenced and because even after making the demand it continued actively to litigate the case.[140]

Numerous arguments have been raised by patients attempting to avoid arbitration. In *Burton v. Mt. Helix General Hospital* the court considered and rejected several objections of a patient who had signed an arbitration agreement. First, the court decided that the patient's failure to read or understand the agreement did not make the agreement invalid. A person who signs a contract he or she is capable of reading and understanding is bound by its terms. Furthermore, the terms of the agreement were "clear and unmistakable." Second, the court found no evidence that the hospital defrauded the patient or exercised undue influence. Third, the court noted that arbitration is beneficial in that it provides an alternative to court litigation and thus saves both time and expense. Finally, the court decided that the arbitration agreement in question was not an adhesion contract; the court distinguished it from an earlier California case in which an agreement that relieved the hospital of all liability was offered as a condition of admission, and such a rule was held to violate public policy.[141]

The California experience has proven attractive to state legislators. A Michigan statute, for instance, provides that a hospital and almost all of the independent hospital staff must offer arbitration to patients. Physicians treating patients in their offices, however, are not required to offer arbitration. The arbitration agreement may not be offered as a prerequisite to treatment, and patients may revoke the agreement within 60 days after execution (or if it was signed on admittance to a hospital, within 60 days after the patient's discharge). Arbitration in Michigan is ordinarily conducted by an attorney, a physician, and a lay person, although a hospital administrator may be substituted for the physician if the claim is solely against a hospital.[142] The Michigan Supreme Court has held that this arbitration scheme does not deprive the patient of due process.[143]

The No-Fault Concept

No-fault systems, another proposed alternative to the traditional tort system, have existed in the United States for a number of years in other contexts.

One form of no-fault, worker's compensation, was first enacted into law in the early 1900s. More recently many states have adopted no-fault to replace to some extent the tort system in automobile accident cases. In its simplest terms, when an automobile owner purchases no-fault coverage and a person riding in the automobile is injured, the owner's insurance pays for the loss, no matter who caused the accident.

No-fault concepts are fairly adaptable to automobile accidents because it is usually clear when injury resulted from the accident. The concepts are more difficult to apply to medical injuries because the patients are to some degree ill or injured before receiving treatment. Thus in medical injuries a major problem with a true no-fault system is to prove that the physician caused the harm. The federal commission on malpractice recognized this difficulty:

> But what is a "medical accident"? A medical injury compensation system which is not fault-oriented presumably would authorize compensation for an injury which may be termed a "medical accident," an "untoward result," "a therapeutic misadventure" or some similar concept. All these phrases in substance describe an unanticipated event or result, and while they may be intelligible in the abstract, one is still faced in particular cases with the requirement to discover the causes of the compensable event.[144]

One alternative would be a private social security system with broader criteria for determining who is entitled to compensation.[145]

Some commentators suggest that healthcare providers could avoid malpractice suits by offering to compensate patients for economic losses from adverse medical occurrences.[146] Others suggest developing a list of "designated compensable events" that would be covered by insurance.[147] Injury caused by such an event would be covered by the insurer and the patient would be precluded from suing in tort. The insurance would be purchased by the healthcare provider, who would pass the costs on to patients. Some compensation for pain and suffering could be made, but there would be ceilings on such amounts.[148] Despite the various proposals, a workable no-fault plan for medical injuries has not yet been discovered.

Risk Management

An important consideration concerning the malpractice system is that the problem would not exist in the absence of adverse medical occurrences, many of which are caused by negligence. Risk management by those engaged in healthcare is preventive medicine. Avoidance of risk calls for identifying problems and forestalling incidents that lead to claims. It also includes dealing in a timely, reasonable manner with incidents that do occur. Physicians should exercise the required standard of care in treating the patients. Accurate medical records, essential in treatment, are also very important in risk management. Very often what is omitted from the record is more harmful to the physician than what is included. Finally, and perhaps most important, physicians should take a personal interest in each patient. Despite the impersonality often prevalent in our society, patients still have high expectations for sympathetic treatment when they visit their physicians. If they are disappointed,

> . . . there is a strong get-even, or revenge factor. I have heard plaintiffs' attorneys say that their clients did not really want to sue for money. What they really wanted was a chance to be alone in the room with the defendant doctor for about fifteen minutes. When a physician has maltreated you in a psychological sense, the revenge motive arises. If we ever had a tort in this country known as psychological malpractice we would not have enough courthouses to take care of all the cases.[149]

Notes

1. George J. Siedel III, J.D., wrote this chapter for the first edition of this book. It was revised for the second edition by Debora A. Slee, J.D.
2. 61 AM. JUR. 2d *Physicians and Surgeons* § 205 (1981). *See also* T. ROADY AND W. ANDERSEN, PROFESSIONAL NEGLIGENCE 70 (1960).
3. For a comparison of the standards imposed on general practitioners and specialists, see the section on the school rule, *infra*.
4. Baldo v. Rogers, 81 So. 2d 658 (Fla. 1955), *reh'g denied,* 81 So. 2d 661 (Fla. 1955); A. HOLDER, MEDICAL MALPRACTICE LAW 47 (2d ed. 1978).
5. DeFillipo v. Preston, 53 Del. 539, 173 A.2d 333 (1961).
6. Miller v. Toles, 183 Mich. 252, 150 N.W. 118 (1914).
7. Fiorentino v. Wenger, 272 N.Y.S.2d 557, 26 A.D.2d 693 (1966), *rev'd on other grounds,* 19 N.Y.2d 407, 227 N.E.2d 296 (1967) (decision against the hospital was reversed, however; the court of appeals decided that the hospital had no obligation to disclose or to make certain that disclosures were made unless it knew or should have known that informed consent was lacking and that the operation was not permissible under existing standards). Informed consent, which is often treated as a cause of action separate from negligence, is discussed in Chapter 11, "Consent for Treatment and the Withholding of Consent."
8. Locality can, of course, mean the same community or a wider area that is still in the general vicinity where the physician practices. The term is generally used in contrast to a national standard, discussed later in the chapter.
9. Faulkner v. Pezeshki, 44 Ohio App. 2d 186, 189, 337 N.E.2d 158, 162 (1975).
10. Only a few still adhere to the traditional locality rule. *See, e.g.,* Hunter v. Sukkar, 111 Ill. App. 3d 169, 66 Ill. Dec. 848, 443 N.E.2d 774 (1982).
11. Approximately 11 states adhere to the "same or similar" locality standard. *See, e.g.,* Lemke v. United States, 557 F. Supp. 1205 (D.C. N.D. 1983); McPherson v. Ellis, 305 N.C. 266, 287 S.E.2d 892 (1982); DeWitt v. Brown, 669, F.2d 516 (8th Cir. 1982).
12. Small v. Howard, 128 Mass. 131, 35 Am. R. 363 (1880), was overruled in 1968 by Brune v. Belinkoff, 235 N.E.2d 793 (Mass. 1968).
13. Zills v. Brown, 382 So. 2d 528, 532 (Ala. 1980).
14. *Id.* at 532.

15. At least 18 states have adopted a national standard. *See, e.g.,* Sullivan v. Henry, 160 Ga. App. 791, 287 S.E.2d 652, 659 (1982); Drs. Lane, Bryand, Eubanks & Dulaney v. Otts, 412 So. 2d 254 (Ala. 1982); Hall v. Hilburn, 466 So. 2d 856 (Miss. 1985).

16. 108 Idaho 743, 745, 702 P.2d 781, 783 (1985). *See also* Morrison v. MacNamara, 407 A.2d 555 (D.C. Ct. App. 1979); Ardoin v. Hartford Accident & Indemnity Co., 360 So. 2d 1331 (La. 1978), *reh'g denied,* July 26, 1978.

17. Drs. Lane, Bryand, Eubanks & Dulaney v. Otts, 412 So. 2d 254 (Ala. 1982).

18. Hall v. Hilburn, 466 So. 2d 856, 873 (Miss. 1985).

19. A Texas court noted that "[t]he circumstances to be considered include the state of medical knowledge *at the time the complained of treatment was performed.*" Guidry v. Phillips, 580 S.W.2d 883, 887–88 (Tex. Civ. App. 1979, *writ ref'd n.r.e.*).

20. J. WALTZ AND F. INBAU, MEDICAL JURISPRUDENCE 54 (1971).

21. *See, e.g.,* Dolan v. Galluzzo, 77 Ill. 2d 279, 396 N.E.2d 13 (1979) (podiatrist held to standards of podiatrists; M.D. testimony excluded).

22. Nelson v. Harrington, 72 Wis. 591, 40 N.W. 228 (1888). *See also* Hansen v. Pock, 57 Mont. 51, 187 P. 282 (1920) (herbologist held to standards of surgical and medical practice in the absence of a school of practice).

23. Spead v. Tomlinson, 73 N.H. 46, 59 A. 376 (1904).

24. 25 Wash. App. 158, 607 P.2d 864 (1980). *See also* Kelly v. Carroll, 36 Wash. 2d 498, 219 P.2d 79 (1950), *cert. denied,* 340 U.S. 892 (1950) (naturopath liable for patient's death from appendicitis; must know when treatment is ineffective and when medical care is needed).

25. Pittman v. Gilmore, 556 F.2d 1259 (5th Cir. 1977). *See also* Lewis v. Soriano, 374 So. 2d 829 (Miss. 1979) (general practitioner had duty to refer complicated fracture to orthopedic specialist).

26. Mata v. Albert, 548 S.W.2d 496 (Tex. Civ. App. 1977, *writ ref'd n.r.e*).

27. *See, e.g.,* Sinz v. Owens, 33 Cal. 2d 749, 705 P.2d 3 (1949) (physician who did not use skeletal traction in treating a double comminuted fracture of a patient's leg would be held to the skill of a specialist only if he should have known that greater skill than a general practitioner's was necessary); Reeg v. Shaughnessy, 570 F.2d 309 (10th Cir. 1978) (physicians held to that degree of care commensurate with their training and experience).

28. *See, e.g.,* Lewis v. Soriano, 374 So. 2d 829 (Miss. 1979).

29. 245 So. 2d 751 (La. App. 1971).

30. 144 So. 2d 544 (La. App. 1962).

31. 83 Wash. 2d 514, 519 P.2d 981 (1974).

32. This case has been the subject of much controversy and commentary. The medical community assailed it as judges telling doctors how to practice medicine. And studies have shown that the diagnostic test for glaucoma results in a high number of false positives, which require further, expensive testing. Coupled with the fact that glaucoma treatments are often ineffective, the question arises whether the result in *Helling* is good public policy in the long run.

33. WASH. REV. CODE § 4.24.290 (1975, as amended 1983).

34. 92 Wash. 2d 246, 595 P.2d 919 (1979).

35. 102 Mich. App. 47, 300 N.W.2d 727 (1980), *appeal dismissed,* 335 N.W.2d 1 (1982).

36. The girl gave birth to the child but said she would have had an abortion if she had known earlier about the pregnancy. The damages awarded were reduced for the comparative negligence of the girl and her parents.

37. Clapham v. Yanga, 102 Mich. App. At 55, 300 N.W.2d at 731.

38. Keogan v. Holy Family Hosp., 95 Wash. 2d 306, 622 P.2d 1246 (1980).

39. In Faulkner v. Pezeshki, 44 Ohio App. 2d 186, 193, 337 N.E.2d 158, 164 (1975), the court noted: "Locating an expert to testify for the plaintiff in a malpractice action is known to be a very difficult task, mainly because in most cases one doctor is reluctant and unwilling to testify against another doctor. Although doctors may complain privately to each other about the incompetence of other doctors, they are extremely reluctant to air the matter publicly."

40. For this reason attorneys have on occasion named a physician as a defendant in a suit solely for the purpose of obtaining testimony. In one such instance the physician so named successfully sued the attorney for malicious prosecution. *See* Carlova, *"Shotgun" Malpractice Suits Suffer a Costly Setback,* 58 MEDICAL ECONOMICS 29 (1981). Physicians' countersuits are discussed later in this chapter.

41. *See, e.g.,* Callahan v. William Beaumont Hosp., 400 Mich. 177, 254 N.W.2d 31 (1977).

42. *See, e.g.,* Siirila v. Barrios, 398 Mich. 576, 248 N.W.2d 171 (1976).

43. *See, e.g.,* Ferguson v. Gonyaw, 64 Mich. App. 685, 236 N.W.2d 543 (1976).

44. *Id.* In this case, the D.O. and his instructor were the only practicing D.O. neurosurgeons in all of Michigan. The court rejected the plaintiff's argument that they should not be permitted to set their own standards. A growing number of states have overruled the school rule when standards of different schools are similar.

45. 106 Mich. App. 35, 307 N.W.2d 695 (1981).

46. 15 N.Y.2d 20, 203 N.E.2d 469 (1964), *aff'd,* 278 N.Y.S.2d 209, 224 N.E.2d 717 (1966). *See* WALTZ AND INBAU, *supra* note 22, at 82.

47. Hearsay is an out-of-court statement offered into evidence to prove the truth of the matter asserted in the statement. Hearsay, as defined, is not admissible, but there are some notable exceptions, such as the business record exception, which makes medical records admissible under some circumstances. Out-of-court statements are admissible if offered for purposes other than to prove the truth of the statement, for example, to impeach the credibility of the witness.

48. The law tries to encourage settlements and will not allow into evidence an offer of settlement if the case goes to court. If the offer of settlement includes an admission of negligence, however, the admission itself can be used as evidence.

49. Scacchi v. Montgomery, 365 Pa. 377, 380, 75 A.2d 535, 536 (1950).

50. Wickoff v. James, 159 Cal. App. 2d 664, 324 P.2d 661 (1958). Both of these cases are discussed in Long, THE PHYSICIAN AND THE LAW 28–30 (1968).

51. Discrediting the testimony of a witness is called impeachment.

52. Bergen, *Medical Books as Evidence,* 217 J.A.M.A. 527 (1971).

53. Burnside v. Evangelical Deaconess Hosp., 46 Wis. 2d 519, 175 N.W.2d 230 (1970).

54. 33 Ill. 2d 326, 211 N.E.2d 253, 14 A.L.R.3d 860 (1965), *cert. denied,* 383 U.S. 946 (1966).
55. Darling v. Charleston Community Memorial Hosp., 33 Ill. 2d 326, 211 N.E.2d 253 (1965). This topic will be covered in greater detail in Chapter 10.
56. *See, e.g.,* CAL. EVID. CODE § 669 (1985 Supp.) (raises a presumption of negligence under these circumstances but permits the defendant to rebut the presumption by showing that he did what a "person of ordinary prudence," who desired to comply with the law, might do under similar circumstances).
57. 17 Cal. 3d 399, 131 Cal. Rptr. 69, 551 P.2d 389 (1976) (cause of action for negligence in failing to diagnose the syndrome was also stated by the complaint).
58. *See, e.g.,* Sinz v. Owens, 33 Cal. 2d 749, 205 P.2d 3, 8 A.L.R.2d 757 (1949).
59. 7 N.Y.2d 376, 380, 165 N.E.2d 756, 757 (1960). *See* Long, *supra* note 52, at 74–75.
60. 2 H. and C. 722, 159 Eng. Rep. 299 (1863).
61. This is a simplified description of the operation of the doctrine. Actual application varies from state to state. In some states the doctrine raises only a permissible inference of negligence; in some it creates a presumption of negligence to shift the burden of rebutting the presumption over to the defendant; in still others the defendant has the burden of persuasion. *See* W. PROSSER, LAW OF TORTS 244, 258–59 (5th ed. 1984). For a more thorough discussion, see Podell, *Application of Res Ipsa Loquitur in Medical Malpractice Litigation,* 44 INS. COUNSEL J. 634 (1977).
62. W. PROSSER, HANDBOOK OF THE LAW OR TORTS § 39, at 244 (5th ed. 1984).
63. Jamison v. Debenham, 203 Cal. App. 2d 744, 21 Cal. Rptr. 848 (1962).
64. 77 F. Supp. 706 (Md. 1948), *aff'd,* 178 F.2d 518 (4th Cir. 1949), *aff'd,* 340 U.S. 135 (1950).
65. 137 Cal. App. 3d 910, 187 Cal. Rptr. 357 (1982).
66. WALTZ AND INBAU, *supra* note 22, at 100.
67. 25 Cal. 2d 486, 154 P.2d 687 (1944).
68. *Id.* at 493, 154 P.2d at 691. Ybarra v. Spangard has been followed in California; *see, e.g.,* Hale v. Venuto, 137 Cal. App. 3d 910, 187 Cal. Rptr. 357 (1982); it has also been cited to with approval in various jurisdictions. *See* D. LOUISELL AND H. WILLIAMS, MEDICAL MALPRACTICE ¶ 14.02, at 14–18 (1984).
69. 158 P.2d 579 (Cal. App. 1945), *rev'd on other grounds,* 27 Cal. 296, 163 P.2d 860 (1945).
70. Alternatives to allocating loss on the basis of fault are discussed at the end of this chapter under "Alternatives to the Tort System."
71. *See* RESTATEMENT (SECOND) OF TORTS § 402A.
72. *See, e.g.,* Perlmutter v. Beth David Hosp., 308 N.Y. 100, 123 N.E.2d 792 (1954). Many states have dealt with this issue by legislation; *see, e.g.,* WIS. STAT. § 146.31(2) (West Supp. 1986) (precludes application of warranty or strict tort liability in cases involving contaminated blood).
73. *See, e.g.,* Carmichael v. Reitz, 17 Cal. App. 3d 958, 95 Cal. Rptr. 381 (1971) (doctor not liable for injury caused by prescribed drug); Barbee v. Rogers, 425 S.W.2d 342 (Tex. 1968) (optometrists not liable on strict liability theory for injuries from improper fitting of contact lenses, even if optometrists were considered sellers of lenses, because alleged injuries resulted from the exercise

of professional skill and judgment and were not attributable to the lenses themselves); Dubin v. Michael Reese Hosp. and Medical Center, 83 Ill. 2d 277, 415 N.E.2d 350 (1980) (x-radiation was not unreasonably dangerous per se; plaintiff's injuries did not result from the x-radiation itself but rather from an alleged error of professional judgment, to which a negligence standard, not strict liability, applied).

74. 79 Wis. 2d 444, 256 N.W.2d 379, 100 A.L.R.3d 1184 (1977).

75. *Id.* at 460, 256 N.W.2d at 387. The plaintiffs' argument in *Hoven* was based in part on Greenfield, *Consumer Protection in Service Transactions—Implied Warranties and Strict Liability in Tort,* 1974 UTAH L. REV. 661.

76. Cooper v. Sisters of Charity of Cincinnati, Inc., 27 Ohio St. 2d 242, 272 N.E.2d 97 (1971).

77. *Id.* at 247, 272 N.E.2d at 101.

78. 386 S.W.2d 879 (Tex. Civ. App. 1964).

79. Mehigan v. Sheehan, 94 N.H. 274, 51 A.2d 632 (1947).

80. *See, e.g.,* Cornfeldt v. Tongen, 295 N.W.2d 638 (Minn. 1980); Hanselmann v. McCardle, 275 S.C. 46, 267 S.E.2d 531 (1980); Hiser v. Randolph, 126 Ariz. 608, 617 P.2d 774 (Ct. App. 1980); *Cooper,* 272 N.E.2d 97.

81. *See, e.g.,* Hamil v. Bashline, 481 Pa. 256, 392 A.2d 1280 (1978); McBride v. United States, 462 F.2d 72 (9th Cir. 1972).

82. Herskovits v. Group Health Cooperative of Puget Sound, 99 Wash. 2d 609, 614, 664 P.2d 474, 476 (1983).

83. *Herskovits,* 664 P.2d 474. *See also* Glicklich v. Spievack, 16 Mass. App. 488, 452 N.E.2d 287 (1983), *appeal denied,* 454 N.E.2d 1276 (1983) (diagnosis of breast cancer delayed for nine months; jury verdict for plaintiff upheld).

84. *Herskovits,* 99 Wash. 2d at 614, 664 P.2d at 477.

85. While economic losses can be fairly accurately demonstrated, it can be difficult to attach dollar values to pain and suffering. Nevertheless, juries do assign dollar amounts to these noneconomic injuries, sometimes in very large amounts. For this reason some of those who argue for reform in the tort system suggest limitations on recovery for pain and suffering, and in fact several states have enacted statutes limiting these damages. One such statute was recently upheld as constitutional. Mansur v. Carpenter, 273 Ind. 374, 404 N.E.2d 585 (1980).

86. 349 F. Supp. 827 (S.D. Tex. 1972), *aff'd,* 493 F.2d 408, *cert. denied,* 419 U.S. 845. This case is discussed in greater detail in the chapter on the consent for treatment. *See also* HOLDER, *supra* note 4, at 306–9.

87. Champs v. Stone, 74 Ohio App. 344, 58 N.E.2d 803 (1944).

88. 166 Wis. 561, 165 N.W. 292 (1918). *See also* Heller v. Medine, 377 N.Y.S.2d 100, 102, 50 A.D.2d 831, 832 (1976) ("A patient's failure to follow instructions does not defeat an action for malpractice where the alleged improper professional treatment occurred prior to the patient's own negligence. Under such circumstances, damages are reduced to the degree that the plaintiff's negligence increased the extent of the injury").

89. Schuster v. St. Vincent Hosp., 45 Wis. 2d 135, 172 N.W.2d 421 (1969).

90. 60 Cal. 2d 92, 32 Cal. Rptr. 33, 383 P.2d 441 (1963). *See* 61 AM. JUR. 2D *Physicians, Surgeons* § 164 (1981).

91. 43 Ohio St. 2d 53, 54, 330 N.E.2d 678, 679–80 (1975).

92. *See, e.g.,* Ellis v. Bitzer, 2 Ohio 89 (1925).

93. Whitt v. Hutchison, 43 Ohio St. at 61, 330 N.E.2d at 684 (1975). *See also* Berger v. Fireman's Fund Ins. Co., 305 So. 2d 724 (La. Ct. App. 1974) (child injured in a school yard by a piece of wire thrown by a lawn mower. The surgeons either punctured her kidney or failed to discover a wound already there, and the child died the next day. The parents settled with the school board and executed a release, then brought a wrongful death action against the hospital and physicians. An appellate court ruled improper a summary judgment in favor of the defendants, because neither the release nor any testimony established negligence by the school board. Thus a factual issue remained: whether the school board and physicians were joint tort-feasors who could be released by a single release).

94. *See, e.g.,* VT. STAT. ANN. TIT. 12, § 519(b) (1973).

95. VT. STAT. ANN. TIT. 12, § 519 (1973); MINN. STAT. ANN. § 604.05 (as amended 1984) (West Supp. 1985).

96. Some have questioned the need for Good Samaritan statutes. Given that negligence is judged according to a standard of care *under the circumstances*, it is hard to see how anything but gross negligence could lead to liability for rendering care in an emergency situation. Indeed, research fails to reveal any cases in which Good Samaritan statutes have been applied to traditional emergency situations, such as when a physician happens upon the scene of an automobile accident.

97. See notes 23 to 25 and the accompanying discussion in Chapter 2, "Breach of Contract and Intentional Tort."

98. 144 Mich. App. 272, 375 N.W.2d 365 (1985).

99. *See also* Missouri *ex rel.* Eli Lilly and Co. v. Gaertner, 619 S.W.2d 761 (Mo. App. 1981) (administration of medication [sodium amytal] does not call for high-level, public-policy decision, hence no immunity from malpractice litigation existed for physicians employed in a mental institution).

100. *See, e.g.,* Pangburn v. Saad, 326 S.E.2d 365 (N.C. Ct. App. 1985) (immunity for state hospital personnel was qualified and did not extend to gross negligence and intentional torts; thus, the rule may not apply in a case in which the plaintiff's brother was released by the defendant after an involuntary psychiatric commitment and less than a day later attacked and stabbed the plaintiff. According to the court, the plaintiff could maintain an action for negligent release, distinct from a "classic medical malpractice" action; negligent release would be based on a general duty to the public not to create an unreasonable risk of harm at the hands of a psychiatric patient, such duty being independent of the physician-patient relationship).

101. *Id.,* citing Estelle v. Gamble, 429 U.S. 97, 106 (1976), *reh'g denied,* 492 U.S. 1066.

102. See notes 81 and 82 and accompanying text in Chapter 2, "Breach of Contract and Intentional Tort."

103. A summary of statutes of limitations may be found in A. MORITZ AND R. MORRIS, HANDBOOK OF LEGAL MEDICINE 212–14 (1970).

104. Or certain other specified, licensed healthcare providers. CAL. CIV. PROC. CODE § 411.30 (as amended 1984) (West Supp. 1985).

105. FLA. STAT. ANN. § 95.11(4) (b) (West 1982).

106. MORITZ AND MORRIS, *supra* note 104, at 211; Hill v. Hays, 193 Kan. 453, 395 P.2d 298 (1964).

107. Cates v. Baol, 54 Mich. App. 717, 221 N.W.2d 474 (1974).

108. 1970 WIS. L. REV. 915, 918; 6 AKRON L. REV. 265, 267–68 (1973).

109. Barrier v. Bowen, 63 N.J. Super. 225, 164 A.2d 357 (1960).

110. 261 Ind. 698, 310 N.E.2d 867 (1974).

111. Hubbard v. Libi, 229 N.W.2d 82 (N.D. 1975).

112. *See, e.g.,* Thompson v. Brent, 245 So. 2d 751 (La. App. 1971) (physician liable because a medical assistant in his employ was negligent in removing a cast with a Stryker saw).

113. Honeywell v. Rogers, 251 F. Supp. 841 (W.D. Pa. 1966). Vicarious liability is discussed in greater detail under Borrowed-Servant and Captain-of-the-Ship Doctrines in Chapter 5, "Liability of the Healthcare Institution."

114. Morrill v. Komasinski, 256 Wis. 417, 41 N.W. 2d 620 (1950). *See* WALTZ AND INBAU, *supra* note 20, at 119–21.

115. Kelsey-Seybold Clinic v. Maclay, 456 S.W.2d 229, *aff'd*, 466 S.W.2d 716 (Tex. 1971).

116. OHIO REV. CODE ANN. § 2305.06 – .11 (Baldwin 1984).

117. Apparently the Ohio statute is intended to cover all malpractice actions except those based on written consent. 42 OHIO JUR. 2D *Physicians & Surgeons* § 132 (1960). A similar decision was reached under a Maine statute in Merchants National Bank v. Morriss, 269 F.2d 363 (1st Cir. 1959). See the earlier discussion in this chapter regarding statutes of limitations.

118. The plaintiff may not be successful, however. In Steel v. Aetna Life & Casualty, 304 So. 2d 861 (La. Ct. App. 1974), *appeal denied*, 315 So. 2d 861 (1975), the parents of a child injured during surgery attempted to bring an action for breach of contract after the statute of limitations for malpractice had run, claiming that the physicians had expressly or impliedly agreed to treat their daughter with a high degree of professional skill and care. The court held that because the physicians had not warranted or promised a particular result, no contract action existed.

119. Holder, *Abandonment: Part I,* 225 J.A.M.A. 1157 (1973).

120. Smith v. St. Paul Fire and Marine Ins. Co., 353 N.W.2d 130 (Minn. 1984).

121. L.L. v. Medical Protective Co., 122 Wis. 2d 455, 362 N.W.2d 174 (1984).

122. A recent case permitted damages for a mother's emotional distress when a prescription for her infant daughter was improperly filled; the pharmacist's act was labeled "willful and wanton misconduct." Lou v. Smith, 285 Ark. 249, 685 S.W.2d 809 (1985).

123. 85 Wash. 2d 52, 530 P.2d 291 (1975) (court adopted the requirements for outrage as defined in RESTATEMENT (SECOND) OF TORTS § 46, including the necessity for the plaintiff to be an immediate relative of the victim and present at the event).

124. Many states, however, will either restrict or not allow punitive damages in a wrongful death action. *See, e.g.,* Tarasoff v. Regents of Univ. of Cal., 17 Cal. 3d 425, 131 Cal. Rptr. 14, 551 P.2d 334 (1976) (recovery of punitive damages barred in actions for wrongful death).

125. Short v. Downs, 36 Colo. App. 109, 537 P.2d 754 (1975).

126. Medveca v. Choi, 569 F.2d 1221 (3d Cir. 1977) (applying Pennsylvania law).

127. Pratt v. Davis, 118 Ill. App. 161, *aff'd*, 224 Ill. 300, 79 N.E. 562 (1905).

128. Morrell v. Lalonde, 45 R.I. 112, 120 A. 435 (1923), *appeal dismissed*, 264 U.S. 572 (1924).

129. Ebaugh v. Rabkin, 22 Cal. App. 3d 891, 99 Cal. Rptr. 706 (1972).

130. Noe v. Kaiser Found. Hosps., 248 Or. 420, 435 P.2d 306 (1967).

131. Huene v. Carnes, 121 Cal. App. 3d 432, 175 Cal. Rptr. 374 (1981).

132. *See, e.g.*, Friedman v. Dozorc, 412 Mich. 1, 312 N.W.2d 585 (1981); Hill v. Willmott, 561 S.W.2d 331 (Ky. App. 1978).

133. Ohio is one of the states requiring special damages. *See* Dakters v. Shane, 64 Ohio App. 2d 196, 412 N.E.2d 399 (1978); New York is another, Berlin v. Nathan, 64 Ill. App. 3d 940, 381 N.E.2d 1367 (1978), *cert. denied*, 444 U.S. 828, *reh'g denied*, 444 U.S. 974 (1979). The American Medical Association has recommended that the special injury requirement be eliminated in physician countersuits for malicious prosecution and also that the physician be permitted to recover costs in a frivolous suit. *Professional Liability in the '80s*, American Medical Association Special Task Force on Professional Liability and Insurance, Report 3, p. 14, March 1985.

134. Moiel v. Sandlin, 571 S.W.2d 567 (Tex. Ct. App. 1978)

135. Huene v. Carnes, 121 Cal. App. 3d 432, 175 Cal. Rptr. 374 (1981). In Harrell v. Joffrion, 73 F.R.D. 267, 268 (1976), a federal court assessed court costs and, under 28 U.S.C. § 1927, the jurors' mileage and per diem costs against an attorney, who was also a physician, because he "deliberately and 'vexatiously' had expended the time, attention, and efforts of the Court and jury over a three-day period in presenting a case which [the attorney] knew—or, as a medical doctor, certainly should have known—was totally frivolous."

136. *See, e.g.*, IND. CODE ANN. § 16-9.5-9-7 (West 1984).

137. U.S. Department of Health, Education, and Welfare, REPORT OF THE SECRETARY'S COMMISSION ON MEDICAL MALPRACTICE, Washington, D.C., U.S. Government Printing Office, App. at 215 (1973).

138. Bergen, *Arbitration of Medical Liability*, 211 J.A.M.A. 176 (1970).

139. Doyle v. Guiliucci, 62 Cal. 2d 606, 610, 43 Cal. Rptr. 697, 699, 401 P.2d 1,3 (1965).

140. Gunderson v. Superior Court, 46 Cal. App. 3d 138, 120 Cal. Rptr. 35 (1975).

141. Cal. Ct. App. 4th Dist., Div. 1 (Feb. 24, 1976). This case, originally certified for publication, was later decertified and thus does not stand as precedent. *Burton* and related cases are discussed in greater detail in Chapter 9, "Admission and Discharge."

142. MICH. COMP. LAWS ANN. §§ 500.3053 – .3061 (West 1983) and §§ 600.5041 – .5044 (West Supp. 1985).

143. Morris v. Metriyakool, 418 Mich. 423, 344 N.W.2d 736 (1984).

144. U.S. Department of Health, Education, and Welfare, *supra* note 136, at 101.

145. Keeton, *Compensation for Medical Accidents*, 121 U. PA. L. REV. 590 (1973).

146. *See* Moore and O'Connell, *Foreclosing Medical Malpractice Claims by Prompt Tender of Economic Loss*, 44 LA. L. REV. 1267 (1984). For other no-fault proposals see Havighurst and Tancredi, *Medical Adversity Insurance—A*

No-Fault Approach to Medical Malpractice and Quality Assurance, INS. L.J. 69 (Feb. 1974); Carlson, *Conceptualization of a No-Fault Compensation System for Medical Injuries,* 7 LAW & SOC'Y REV. 329 (1973); Switzer and Reynolds, *Medical Malpractice Compensation—A Proposal,* 13 AM. BUS. L.J. 65 (1975).

147. The American Bar Association Commission on Medical Professional Liability studied the feasibility of developing a list of compensable events and concluded that it was possible. Boyden and Tancredi, *Part III: Identification of Designated Compensable Events (DCEs),* in Commission on Medical Professional Liability, Designated Compensable Event System: A Feasibility Study (1979).

148. Havighurst and Tancredi, *Medical Adversity Insurance—A No-Fault Approach to Medical Malpractice and Quality Assurance,* INS. L.J. 69 (Feb. 1974).

149. MEDICAL MALPRACTICE 4 (D. McDonald, ed. 1971).

4

THE ORGANIZATION AND MANAGEMENT OF A CORPORATE HEALTHCARE INSTITUTION

Most hospitals and other institutional providers of healthcare are corporations; this chapter will focus on the fundamental nature of the corporate form of organization. It is important to note, however, that healthcare can be provided by sole proprietorships—a rare form today—and partnerships. In a *sole proprietorship*, an individual (such as a family physician) assumes all possible organizational roles: employer, employee, and owner. The proprietor will usually retain any profits, or suffer any losses, and will bear the full risks of the enterprise. If the proprietor is joined in this venture by someone who will share in the rewards and risks (as contrasted with an employee who receives a salary and is not responsible to other parties for debts incurred in the venture) a partnership exists.

Partnerships are governed by state law and an agreement between the parties,[1] and the parties have great latitude to develop an agreement that will suit their needs.

The simplest kind of partnership is a *general partnership*. General partners can agree to undertake different tasks and duties, and they may agree to receive unequal shares of profits or losses, but in most cases general partners are entitled to equal voting rights and are *personally liable* for the debts of the venture.[2] Upon the death of a partner, the partnership is automatically dissolved but the business operation is not necessarily terminated.[3] A business under a general partnership is ordinarily controlled by the owners, acting in consensus. As the volume of business and number of partners increase, however, many owners transform the business into a limited partnership or a corporation.

A *limited partnership* is a statutory form of business organization that provides limited liability to some persons who invest in the organization.[4] A limited partnership requires one or more general partners who have the managerial powers and unlimited liability that that status implies. Limited partners, on the other hand, have no right to participate in the day-to-day management or control of the business; in turn they are not liable to third-party creditors for debts of the partnership. To create a limited partnership a certificate of partnership must be filed with a designated public officer, typically the local county recorder or the secretary of state. The certificate will contain all the information about the business that is deemed essential for protection of the public and third parties. In a very real sense a limited partnership has some of the characteristics of a general partnership and some of a corporation with respect to both formation and operation.[5]

A *joint venture* is a special form of partnership created by contract to accomplish an identified, specific purpose: for example, operation of a free health screening service for the poor. A joint venture will usually exist for a limited period. Each participant will ordinarily share in management; profits and losses will be shared in accordance with the agreement; and liability is unlimited. Two or more corporations may create a joint venture.[6] Joint ventures have become popular in the healthcare industry. The rest of this chapter will focus on corporations, the predominant form of healthcare organization.

The Formation and Nature of a Corporation

A corporation is "an artificial being, invisible, intangible, and existing only in contemplation of law. Being the mere creature of the law, it possesses only those properties which the charter confers upon it, either expressly or as incidental to its very existence."[7]

Accordingly, a corporation is purely a creation of the legislature and can exist only by virtue of a statute providing for its formation and the grant of a franchise or charter. In both England and the United States the early corporations were ecclesiastical, educational, charitable, or even governmental in purpose and were usually created by special act of the legislature. The modern corporation came into prominence in the latter part of the nineteenth century with the state-by-state passage of general statutes for incorporating businesses. In effect these laws allowed any group of persons, or even a single individual in some states, to incorporate an enterprise for any lawful purpose, as long as statutory requirements were met. Thus, they eliminated the former need for special legislative action each time a corporation was created.

Legislation characterized as "general business corporation acts" provides for the formation and operation of the customary business corporations organized for profit and embracing a wide range of enterprises such as manufacturing, wholesaling, and retailing. Some states have no separate corporate statute for not-for-profit organizations, such as hospitals, but most have a not-for-profit corporation statute.

Many states also have separate incorporation statutes governing the creation and operation of particular types of business, such as banking and public utilities. Most states also have special statutes that allow practitioners of law, medicine, accountancy, and other licensed professions to incorporate their practices.

In any event, it is important for the executives of a corporation to know the relevant statute under which it is incorporated, for this statute will control the conduct of the corporation's affairs. Because a corporation is created by the legislature, the organization has only the powers granted to it by the charter and specified or implied in the relevant statute.

Implicit also in the definition of a corporation is the fact that it is an artificial person or legal entity separate and distinct from the individuals who created, own, or manage it. Accordingly, when a constitutional provision or statutory law uses the word "person," it is the general rule that the corporations are included. For example, the Fifth and Fourteenth Amendments to the U.S. Constitution provide that no "person" shall be deprived of "life, liberty, or property without the due process of law," and the Fourteenth Amendment provides that no state "shall deny to any person . . . the equal protection of the laws." It has long been held that corporations as well as individuals are protected by these fundamental doctrines of constitutional law.

On the other hand, a corporation is not a "person" under state licensure statutes governing the practice of the professions. A corporation, as an artificial person, cannot obtain a license to practice a profession because it cannot possess the educational requirements or meet the standards of personal character required for professional licensure. (This prohibition on corporate licensure must, of course, be distinguished from those statutes referred to above that sanction licensed individuals to incorporate their practice.) Similarly, a corporation is not a person within the meaning of the Fifth Amendment, which protects an individual against self-incrimination, because the purpose and intent of the provision applies only to people.

Although a corporation is generally a "person," it is not a citizen when that designation is used in written constitutional statutory provisions. Thus, it cannot as an entity vote in an election. More significantly, a corporation is not protected by the Fourteenth Amendment's provision that "no state shall make or enforce any law which shall abridge the privileges or immunities of citizens of the United States." Hence, a particular state can require that a corporation incorporated elsewhere pay special taxes, franchise fees, or other fees in return for the privilege of doing business within the state's borders. In other words, a natural person who is a citizen has freedom of mobility from state to state without special restrictions, whereas a corporation does not.

A corporation is a legal entity separate and distinct from those who created it, own it, or are employed by it. Hence, the corporation can acquire, own, and dispose of property (including stock in other corporations) in its own name. It can sue and be sued by an individual or corporate person, including its own shareholders, director, or officers. In short, a corporation is an independent entity with rights and responsibilities of its own.

A corporation is formed by filing articles of incorporation with the secretary of state or other designated official of the state in which incorporation is sought. As soon as these are approved by the authorized official, the corporate charter is said to have been issued. Although requirements regarding the proper form of the articles differ somewhat from state to state, the principal information in the articles includes the name of the corporation, the address of the corporation's office, the name of the registered agent authorized to receive service of process, the names and addresses of the incorporators, the duration of corporate existence (on which there is usually no limit), the purposes of the corporation, the names of the initial members of the board of directors, and the number and classification of shares of stock (in a profit-making corporation) or the designation of "members," if any (in a not-for-profit organization). The incorporators are those who prepare, sign, and file the articles of incorporation. Some states require a minimum number of incorporators, but many others permit a single individual to act as the incorporator.[8]

Advantages of the Corporate Form of Organization

The primary advantage of incorporation is *limited liability*. This means that normally the owners of a corporation are not personally liable for the corporation's contracts or torts. A shareholder of a profit-making corporation is not personally liable, with some few exceptions, for corporate debts beyond the extent of the investment in its stock. The magnitude of this advantage is easily appreciated if one considers how a catastrophic loss can affect a sole proprietor or partner. Limited liability, as has been appreciated for centuries, also encourages socially desirable ventures that may otherwise entail an unacceptable risk. Employees are also favored because those acting as agents of a corporation are not liable for corporate contractual obligations, so long as they act within the scope of delegated authority; the reason for this is that a corporate employer, as an entity, is legally capable of being responsible for the actions of its agents.

A second inherent advantage of the corporate form of organization is its *continuity of existence*. Unlike a sole proprietorship or partnership, a corporation's continued legal existence and its actual operational capabilities in most instances are not affected by the death or disability of an owner.

The third principal advantage of the corporation is the *free transferral of ownership interests*, at least if the corporation is organized as a for-profit. Shareholders in the organization can sell their interests either to fellow shareholders or the general public (unless special provisions are made and noted on the stock certificates). Free transferability is an important attribute because it increases the liquidity, and consequently the value, of corporate investments. In the case of a not-for-profit corporation, however, state statutes sometimes provide that membership interests may not be transferred unless the bylaws specifically provide for transferral.[9]

Fourth, a corporation is a *taxable entity* separate from its owners. That is, if the corporation has taxable income, the tax liability is that of the corporation rather than the individuals. The corporate tax rate is generally lower than the personal income tax. The persons who own the corporation are taxed only on any distributions of income (dividends) they receive, not on their share of the entire corporate profit.

Finally, the corporate form makes *raising outside capital* easier because third-party investors enjoy limited risks and an opportunity for reward. In a competitive market, access to equity capital, as distinct from borrowing and the creation of debt, is a major consideration when undertaking new or expanded ventures.

Powers of a Corporation

A corporation may act only within its corporate authority, which means that it possesses only those powers the state has expressly or implicitly granted through issuance of the charter and by virtue of the statute under which the corporation is formed. In this sense a *power* is the legal capacity to execute contracts or enter into transactions to carry out corporate purposes. The wording and language of the purpose clause in the articles of incorporation are therefore of utmost significance in determining the extent of corporate power.

There are two kinds of powers: express and implied. *Express powers* are those specifically designated by charter or statute. The relevant statute under which the corporation is formed will enumerate various express powers such as the power to buy, lease, or otherwise acquire and hold property and the power to make contracts to effectuate corporate purposes. *Implied power* flows directly from express powers and is defined most simply as the power to enter into those transactions that are reasonably necessary or convenient to carry out the express powers. The existence of implied power is generally determined by whether a transaction tends directly to further or accomplish the corporation's purposes and objectives.[10]

Any departure from express or implied corporate power is said to be *ultra vires*, or beyond corporate authority. Therefore, in planning for the future and in making commitments, the governing body of the corporation must keep a close eye on the corporate power to act, and legal advice regarding this issue is of utmost importance. For example, if a not-for-profit corporation makes a donation or transfers assets to another institution for a purpose not included in its own charter, the transfer would be *ultra vires*.

An *ultra vires* contract is usually void and can be challenged in a suit for an injunction. In an extreme situation the state could revoke the corporate charter; however, given the ease of amending the articles of incorporation and bylaws, *ultra vires* problems are relatively rare today.[11] One should note, however, that members of the governing body and corporate officers can be held personally liable for losses suffered by the corporation as a result of an *ultra vires* transaction in which they acted knowingly or without good faith. No personal liability will accrue, however, as long as they acted honestly and were simply mistaken in their judgment of the matter.

Typical transactions that directly raise the issue of corporate power or *ultra vires* are the following. A hospital corporation cannot ordinarily lend its credit or guarantee the debts of another corporation, because such a transaction would be outside the scope of a hospital's purpose. Similarly, it may not in general make loans to its own trustees, officers, or members. A corporation needs authority in its articles or from a statute before it can form a partnership with another corporation or an individual, because such a partnership requires sharing of control with another entity. Likewise a corporation needs statutory authority to consolidate or merge with another corporation, although two corporations could always dissolve and transfer their assets to a properly formed new corporate entity, as long as the transfer was consistent with the original purposes for which the property was held.[12] (Corporate consolidations and mergers will be discussed subsequently.)

The doctrine of *ultra vires* applies to governmental institutions as well as private corporations. For example, the attorney general of Florida issued an opinion in 1982 that a county hospital lacked authority in the absence of an express statutory provision to lease the hospital's facilities to a private corporation.[13] Similarly, a taxpayer in Georgia successfully challenged a public hospital's purchase and operation of a retail store that leased and sold medical equipment to the general public. When affirming the trial court's issuance of an injunction, the Georgia Supreme Court observed that a public hospital may not engage in independent private business enterprise without statutory authority.[14]

A few states place express statutory restrictions on the amount or type of property owned and held by a charitable corporation. These restrictions may be expressed in general terms. For example, a statute may provide that a charitable corporation shall hold only the amount of real estate or personal property that is "necessary" to accomplish its purposes. Other statutes are more restrictive, specifically limiting the monetary value of property held. In whatever way the restrictions are defined and interpreted, the holding of property in excess of the limitation may carry as severe a penalty as escheat (reversion of the property) to the state. As a safeguard, however, the donor or seller of the property exceeding the limit might have a legal right to rescind the transaction and recover the subject matter of the gift or sale.

Not-for-Profit Corporations

Of particular interest is the concept of a not-for-profit (a.k.a. nonprofit)[15] corporation as distinguished from a for-profit corporation. As previously noted, some states do not have general incorporation laws pertaining to not-for-profit corporations, and in these jurisdictions such enterprises are frequently incorporated under the general business corporation act. This situation is unfortunate, because the general business act will inevitably contain provisions that are inapplicable to not-for-profit enterprise; further, these acts may be silent on many matters that should be in a statute controlling the formation and operation of not-for-profit organizations.

To remedy this situation most states have enacted the Model Non-Profit Corporation Act[16] or a variation of it, thus codifying in a separate statute the corporate law of not-for-profit organization.[17] Before some of the major provisions of the model act are discussed, some general observations about a not-for-profit corporation will be useful.

The usual definition of a not-for-profit body is that no part of the income or profit of the organization can be distributed for private gain to shareholders, members, directors, trustees, officers of the corporation or other private individuals.[18] A profit-making corporation, as is well known, is owned by shareholders, who are entitled to and expect to receive dividends from the earnings of the corporation and to share in assets should the corporation be dissolved. Not-for-profit corporations are almost always prohibited by statute from issuing shares of stock, although the corporation may have voting members who are required to contribute capital and may then be given a "stock" certificate evidencing their membership.[19] They may not be paid dividends.[20] A not-for-profit corporation can, of course, earn income and actually make a profit without sacrificing its not-for-profit status, so long as it uses that profit or reinvests it for institutional purposes. Moreover it can, without question, pay a salary or wage to corporate members, trustees or other individuals who are actually employees or professional persons rendering actual service. As long as the compensation paid is reasonable, it is not "private gain" that would jeopardize the corporation's not-for-profit status.[21]

In sum, motive is important in determining not-for-profit status. In a not-for-profit institution, motives of ethical, moral, or social purposes predominate and profit is not fundamental to the purpose of the endeavor. A mere declaration of not-for-profit purpose in a corporate charter is never conclusive if in fact the entity is being used as an alter ego for private gain.[22] For this reason the purpose clause in the articles of incorporation of a not-for-profit corporation is usually quite restrictive. Although a not-for-profit corporation can be organized for any lawful purpose, the incorporators normally state a specific purpose such as establishing a hospital, a symphony orchestra, a museum of fine arts, and so on.

Not-for-profit status is a necessary first requirement for tax exemption, not only under the federal income tax statutes and regulations[23] but also under the various state statutes providing for taxes on income, real or personal property, and sales.[24] Aside from taxes, many state laws make significant distinctions between regulations governing not-for-profit and business organizations.

A not-for-profit corporation must be distinguished from a charitable corporation. Although charitable status demands not-for-profit organization and operation, a not-for-profit corporation need not have a charitable purpose. Many social clubs and similar organizations that provide services exclusively to members are organized and operated as legitimate not-for-profit corporations without being formed for charitable or benevolent purposes. Such corporations, therefore, will not qualify for the tax-exempt status that charitable corporations enjoy.[25]

In addition to the fact that a private business corporation has shareholders entitled to dividends and a not-for-profit corporation does not, there are other significant differences. Not-for-profit corporations may or may not have "members," depending on the provisions of the law under which they are incorporated. Members of a not-for-profit corporation are roughly equivalent to a business corporation's shareholders, but they are not entitled to receive dividends. Like shareholders, however, they are entitled to vote for members of the governing body and on other matters designated in the articles or bylaws.[26] In most states, members must meet at least annually to conduct business.

In addition to the membership type of not-for-profit corporation, certain states recognize what is termed a "nonstock directorship" form of organization.[27] A nonstock directorship is an appropriate form of organization in those situations in which a large number of persons contribute support to a not-for-profit activity and do not expect or desire to be involved in controlling the management or the purposes of the corporation. This form avoids possible misunderstandings about voting rights of members who are also directors, because a corporation with a nonstock directorship has no members. The board of directors is the sole governing authority, and it has the statutory power, for example, to amend the articles of incorporation and to approve a merger or dissolve the corporation.[28] In a corporation having membership, the members would normally have to approve such an extraordinary transaction.

Upon the dissolution or merger of a not-for-profit corporation, the assets of the corporation must be distributed in accordance with local law and the provisions of the articles of incorporation. Generally, the assets must be distributed to another corporation with a similar purpose. According to some cases, however, when a dissolution takes place, assets acquired by gift are to be returned to the donor; in others all assets are held to revert to the state; and in still others it has been ruled that members in a corporation with membership are entitled to the assets in certain circumstances.[29]

Internal Management of a Corporation

Corporate bylaws contain the rules for the internal management and governance of the corporation. Unless statutes or the articles of incorporation provide otherwise, the power to adopt and amend bylaws of the corporation lies with the membership or shareholders. In short, the governing body (board of directors or trustees) cannot adopt or amend corporate bylaws unless it has been specifically granted this power in the statute or charter. The bylaws define the rights and duties of the corporate members or shareholders among themselves and their relationship to the corporation, the powers and responsibilities of the governing body, and the rights and duties of the major corporate officers. Corporate bylaws are an internal document; hence, they need not be filed in any public office or otherwise made available for public inspection.

In a membership type of not-for-profit corporation, the bylaws will contain provisions for holding meetings of the members. Some of the statutes specifically require the members to conduct at least an annual meeting; and even if the relevant statute is silent on mandatory meetings, the assumption is that meetings will be held. Typically, a designated corporate officer will be responsible for giving proper notice of the meeting to the membership. If he or she should fail to schedule and file notice of the required meeting, the statutes will empower a member to do so. Notice of the meeting must also call attention to any extraordinary matter scheduled for vote. Failure to give proper notice will invalidate the meeting unless the members of the corporation waive their right to notice.

Extraordinary matters normally requiring the vote of members include decisions on accepting the charter as issued by the state, adopting or amending bylaws, electing board members, and amending the corporate charter. Members generally also vote on major transactions such as the sale or lease of real estate, significant grants to or contracts with other organizations (assuming that these would be embraced within corporate authority), voluntary bankruptcy or corporate dissolution, and any other transactions specifically mentioned in the bylaws as requiring the membership's decision. In other words, some major decisions are beyond the power of the governing body and must be dealt with by the membership. Proxy voting may or may not be permitted, depending on local law and provisions in the bylaws.

The Governing Board of a Healthcare Institution

The governing body of a healthcare institution has three major functions. The first is to develop policy and articulate plans for both short-range and long-range institutional goals. Second, the board is directly responsible for the appointment of staff, including the appointment of senior administrative officers and medical staff members and the delineation of individual clinical privileges. Third, the board has ultimate responsibility for reviewing and evaluating the professional performance of both lay administrators and the medical staff.

Committee Structure and Execution of Policy

To fulfill these three major functions properly, the board must ensure the proper organization of its own committee structure, the administrative committee structure, and the medical staff. For example, the board must be sure that its own executive committee is functioning and operating as it should in its role, which is to execute board policy between board meetings. This committee should not assume the power to make decisions that are legally reserved to the board as a whole or to the membership of a corporation. Moreover, the executive committee should not be permitted to delegate its responsibilities to any individual member of the committee.

Other major standing committees of a typical board are designated by the fields on which they focus:

- finance
- building and grounds
- personnel

- public relations
- education
- corporate compliance
- medical advisory activities

As its name implies, the finance committee is given authority for managing and investing hospital funds and for the overall supervision of fiscal policies. Similarly, the buildings and grounds committee generally oversees the physical plant; the personnel committee develops policies regarding salaries, wages, and fringe benefits for employees; the education committee recommends programs for the training of personnel; the corporate compliance committee ensures that measures are in place to enable compliance with legal standards; and the medical advisory committee or its like promotes mutual understanding between the lay board and the professional staff. Each committee's role is to offer recommendations and advice to the governing body, because the ultimate responsibility for all decisions must usually remain with the board.[30]

Having determined the policy for the institution, the board must make certain that the policy is effectively executed by its committees and the staff. As a board and as individual members, the trustees should not become involved in details of day-to-day management. Fundamentally the board delegates authority for formulating recommendations and executing policy to the hospital administration and to the medical staff by way of the chief executive officer. The board then periodically reviews performance and holds the corporation's agents accountable. It is elemental in law that whenever authority for implementing policy is delegated it can be and should be revoked if performance is unsatisfactory. The board must not abdicate its responsibilities by delegating responsibilities and not monitoring their execution. For example, any agreement by the board to place managerial authority in one person or in a particular group of persons without accountability is illegal. Similarly, any agreement expressed or implied for an individual trustee to be nominal is illegal. Accordingly, all corporate officers and the medical staff are in fact subordinate to the board.

As previously noted, the corporate bylaws govern the board's structure and the administrative structure of the hospital, control internal operations, and provide for management of corporate property. The bylaws define the powers, duties, and limitations of the board's responsibilities, always in accord, of course, with state incorporation statutes. In addition to corporate bylaws, the board is empowered to adopt bylaws for its own government. Special bylaws and rules and regulations govern and control the organization of the hospital's professional staff, its officers and committee structure, and its functions. These medical staff bylaws and subsequent amendments to them must be approved by the board of trustees and are incorporated by reference as a part of corporate bylaws.

Composition and Meetings of the Board

The size of the board is determined by the articles of incorporation or bylaws. Some corporate statutes provide for a minimum number of board members, usually three, while others allow as few as one board member.[31] In a membership type of not-for-profit corporation, the members of the corporation ordinarily elect the members of the governing body. Most statutes permit a nonmember of the corporation to be elected to the board. In a not-for-profit corporation without members, the board itself may select new members. This is called a "self-perpetuating" board. In some situations, such as a state or county hospital, some or all of the trustees or directors may be appointed by a public official. Terms of office and qualifications of the members of the board will be determined by charter or bylaw provisions drafted in accordance with statutory requirements. For example, local statutes may require that trustees be of majority age and that a certain number of trustees be residents of the state of incorporation.[32]

A West Virginia statute for hospital licensing requires that at least 40 percent of the members of governing boards of both local governmental and not-for-profit hospitals be composed of "consumer representatives." Such people are identified as those in small businesses, members of labor organizations, elderly persons, and low-income persons. Each of these groups is entitled to equal representation on each board. Women, members of racial minorities, and the handicapped are to be given special consideration when appointments or nominations are made for board membership. The statute may be enforced by an action for a court injunction initiated by any citizen or the state department of health.[33]

When the legality of this legislation was challenged, the Fourth Circuit Court of Appeals affirmed the district court's opinion to the effect that the law does not violate either West Virginia's or the U.S. Constitution.[34] Specifically, there was no violation of the equal protection clause because a rational basis existed for regulating local government and not-for-profit hospitals in this manner while excluding hospitals owned by the state and proprietary interests.[35] With respect to the due process clause the statute did not result in a taking of private property; furthermore, the law was rationally related to the goal of containing costs of healthcare, because representatives of consumer groups are likely to be more sensitive to such matters. Accordingly, the legislation was not unreasonable, arbitrary, or capricious.[36]

In addition, the court ruled that the law does not violate a religious society's right of association (some of the plaintiff hospitals were Catholic-sponsored), because it applies only to the governing boards of hospitals operated by a society and not to religious orders themselves or their governing bodies.[37] Finally, the statute was said to be consistent with Article I, Section 10 of the U.S. Constitution, which prohibits a state from impairing the obligation of contracts. Although a corporate charter is a contract entitled to protection, the state legislature can regulate corporations for the purposes of health, safety, and welfare in accordance with the state's police power as long as the regulatory statute does not interfere substantially with the corporation's purpose. In conclusion, the court observed that the healthcare industry is a highly regulated field and that the West Virginia law does not prevent the members of a corporation from selecting the individuals they prefer as board members. It only requires that those who govern corporate affairs be sensitive to consumers' interests.[38]

The West Virginia statute was enacted primarily to help control healthcare costs. There has been no subsequent evidence, however, that the presence of consumer representatives on healthcare organizations' boards has had an effect on reducing healthcare expenditures.

When vacancies on the governing board of a membership corporation are caused by the death, disability, or resignation of a member, they are filled by the members in a special election unless the statutes, the corporate charter, or corporate bylaws provide otherwise. Trustees can always be removed from their posts for legal cause or with justification, but generally this must be done by those possessing the power of election. To put the matter another way, the governing board of a not-for-profit membership corporation may not usually vote to remove a member of the board unless the statutes, charter, or bylaws provide for such action.[39] Depending on the circumstances and local statute, the removal of a board member sometimes requires court action or action of the state's attorney general. Regardless of who has the power of removal, the individual who is subject to the proceeding has a right to due process of law: a statement of the reasons of removal and an opportunity to hear and challenge evidence and cross-examine witnesses. One who has been the subject of an improper removal may bring an action in court for reinstatement.[40]

Members of the governing board usually cannot be paid or compensated for their services on that body unless local statutory law permits the corporate charter or bylaws to provide for compensation. The rule is particularly relevant to not-for-profit corporations because of the fundamental doctrine that members and trustees of such an institution must not derive any personal monetary gain from the corporation. Hence, salaries to board members or special financial benefits, such as a discount for hospital services rendered to board members and their families, are usually improper even if local corporate law would otherwise authorize such payments. This prohibition of course excludes salary paid to a corporate officer who is also a voting member of the board. For example, most healthcare organizations place the chief executive officer on the board; such an individual could be paid a reasonable salary for his or her executive services (although he or she may not participate in the board action that establishes his or her annual salary). Similarly, a hospital attorney who sits on the board may be paid reasonable fees.[41]

In managing the affairs of the corporation the board must act in a properly constituted, formal meeting. Independent action by one or even a majority of board members does not bind the corporation. Except for regular meetings provided for in the articles of incorporation or corporate bylaws, proper notice of a meeting must be given to each board member, usually in writing. Unless such notice is given, the meeting is invalid, except that if all members have actually attended the meeting, it can be said that they have waived the notice requirement. Even so, decisions made at a casual, unannounced gathering of the board may be ineffective. Moreover, unless the statutes provide otherwise, members must attend in person, and meetings conducted by telephone are not normally permissible. To an increasing extent, however, statutes are now recognizing the validity of formal conferences by telephone or even satillite.[42]

Needless to say, a written record (i.e., minutes) should be made of the action taken at each meeting of the board. Members who object to any proposed action should make certain that their dissents are noted in the record. The frequency of meetings depends on provisions in the charter or bylaws and on particular circumstances. Unless the local statutes, charter, or bylaws provide otherwise, the choice of the place of the board meeting may be at the discretion of the board. Meetings may even occur outside the state of incorporation, as long as the place selected is reasonably convenient.

The charter or bylaws will fix the number of board members necessary for a quorum. In the absence of a provision, the rule is that a quorum is a simple majority of the board and that a majority vote of those voting on an issue is sufficient to bind the corporation. Members of the board may not vote by proxy in the absence of a specific statutory or bylaw provision because each has a fiduciary duty to attend meetings personally and to exercise independent judgment.[43]

Accreditation Standards for Governing Hospitals

The foregoing general principles of corporate law are reflected in the 1998 Hospital Accreditation Standards published by the Joint Commission on Accreditation of Healthcare Organizations.[44]

Standard
GO.1 The hospital identifies how it is governed and the key individuals involved.

Intent of GO.1
The hospital has a document that shows how it is governed. This document includes lines of authority relative to key planning, management, operations, and evaluation of responsibilities at each level of governance.

Standard

GO.2   Those responsible for governance establish policy, promote performance improvement, and provide for organizational management and planning.

Intent of GO.2

The hospital's governing body or authority ultimately is responsible for the quality of care the hospital provides. To carry out this responsibility, the governing body or authority provides for the effective functioning of activities related to

- delivering quality patient care;
- performance improvement;
- risk management;
- medical staff credentialing; and
- financial management.

Standard

GO.2.1   The hospital's governing body or authority adopts bylaws addressing its legal accountabilities and responsibility to the patient population served.

Intent of GO.2.1

The governing body or authority provides coordination and integration among the organization leaders to

- establish policy;
- maintain quality patient care;
- provide for necessary resources; and
- provide for organizational management and planning.

At a minimum, the governing bylaws specify the

- organization's role and purpose;
- governing body's or authority's duties and responsibilities;
- process and criteria for selecting its members;
- governing body's or authority's organizational structure;
- relationship of responsibilities among those responsible for governing and any authority superior to the governing body or authority (if such exists), the chief executive offer, the medical staff, and other appropriate leaders;
- requirement for establishing a medical staff;
- requirement for establishing auxiliary organizations, if applicable; and
- definition of "conflict of interest."

Standards

GO.2.2   The hospital's governing body or authority provides for appropriate medical staff participation in governance.

GO.2.2.1 The medical staff has the right to representation (through attendance and voice), of one or more medical staff members selected by the medical staff, at governing body meetings.

GO.2.2.2 Medical staff members are eligible for full membership in the hospital's governing body, unless legally prohibited.

Intent of GO.2.2 Through GO.2.2.2
One medical staff contributes to the quality of care by coordinating their work with that of other leaders and those responsible for governing the organization. Through its participation in governance, the medical staff helps ensure that all medical staff members responsible for assessing, caring for, or treating patients are clinically competent and that clinical care rendered is appropriate. This participation also allows them the opportunity to contribute to the organization's planning, budgeting, safety management, and overall performance-improvement activities. The medical staff executive committee makes specific recommendations to the governing body for its approval (see MS.3.1.6 through MS.3.1.6.1.7 in Chapter 14, "Medical Staff Appointments and Privileges"). These recommendations relate to

- the medical staff's structure;
- the process designed for reviewing credentials and delineating individual clinical privileges;
- recommending delineated clinical privileges for each eligible individual;
- the organization of the medical staff's performance-improvement activities as well as the process designed for conducting, evaluating, and revising such activities;
- the process by which medical staff membership may be terminated; and
- the process designed for fair-heating procedures.

Standard
GO.2.3 The hospital's governing body or authority establishes a criteria-based process for selecting a qualified and competent chief executive officer.

Intent of GO.2.3
The chief executive officer has the knowledge and skills necessary to perform the duties required of the hospital's senior leader. Among other criteria, education and relevant experience are important qualifications. The chief executive officer may be selected by the governing body. Or, the governing body may approve a chief executive officer selected by corporate management or another group.

Standard
GO.2.4 The hospital's governing body or authority provides for compliance with applicable law and regulation.

Intent of GO.2.4
The intent of this standard is self-evident.

Standard
GO.2.5 The hospital's governing body provides for the collaboration of leaders in developing, reviewing, and revising policies and procedures.

Intent of GO.2.5
Because most policies and procedures address cross-functional, interdisciplinary, multidepartmental activities, they need to be developed collaboratively to be effective. The governing body or authority and other leaders collaborate to develop, review, and revise key policies and procedures. Such policies and procedures are written and appear in bylaws, rules, regulations, protocols, or other documents. Those affected by policies and procedures are aware of their content.
Policies and procedures address key items regarding

- nursing care based on nursing standards of patient care and nursing practice standards (for example, critical care protocols, discharge planning) and
- the medical staff's responsibility for developing, adopting, and periodically reviewing its bylaws and rules and regulations consistent with organization policy and applicable law and other requirements (see MS.3 through MS.3.1 in Chapter 14, "Medical Staff Appointments and Privileges").

Standard
GO.2.6 The hospital's governing body or authority provides for conflict resolution.

Intent of GO.2.6
The hospital has a system for resolving conflicts among leaders and the individuals under their leadership. Leaders regularly review the system's effectiveness, revising it as necessary.

Fiduciary Duties of a Governing Board

The members of the governing board of any for-profit or not-for-profit corporation are fiduciaries, and breach of a fiduciary duty can lead to personal liability. As previously pointed out, directors or trustees of a corporate entity are not agents of the corporation in their capacity as members of the board, nor are they principals or corporate employees. Hence, the directors or trustees are not personally and individually liable on corporate debts and contracts. Moreover, they are not personally liable for the negligence or torts of corporate employees under the doctrine of *respondeat superior*.[45] When corporations enter into contracts within their corporate authority, negotiated by their duly appointed agents acting within their authority, the corporation is the solely responsible party. If corporate employees commit a tort within the scope of their employment, both the corporation as the employer and the person who committed the tort are liable to the injured third party.

Notwithstanding these general principles of corporate law, the members of the governing board can be personally liable for their own breach of duty or failure to carry out their fiduciary role properly. The term "fiduciary" means simply, in its broadest sense, that one is in a position of great trust and confidence. Such a person is invested with rights and powers to be exercised solely for the benefit of others. The members of the governing board of a profit-making enterprise owe their fiduciary duties to the corporation and the stockholders. In a not-for-profit corporation the duties are owed to the corporation and members, if any. Thus, members of the governing board and corporate officers are personally liable for their own torts, even if these are carried out in the name of the corporation.

Members of the governing board of charitable corporations are frequently called "trustees." Strictly speaking, they are not trustees, however, because a trustee is vested with the title to property held and managed for the benefit of others. In a corporation the title to property is vested in the corporation itself. Under trust law the duty of a trustee is generally higher than the duty of a member of the governing body of a corporation. For example, the trustee of a trust may be liable for poor business judgments in the management of the property held for the beneficiaries' benefit. A governing board member, however, will generally be held liable only for actual negligence, willful disregard of duty, or wrongful acts. For most purposes the courts will apply the standards of corporate management when determining the duties of hospital trustees and will not apply the more stringent standards of trust law. Nevertheless, the trustees of a trust and the directors of a corporation have custody and control of property, which they must manage for the benefit of others, and accordingly they occupy a position of great trust and confidence.

Duty of loyalty

As fiduciaries the members of a corporate governing body have two paramount duties—loyalty and responsibility. Loyalty means that the individuals must put the interest of the corporation above all self-interest, a principle based on the biblical doctrine that no one can serve two masters. Specifically, no trustee is permitted to gain any secret profits personally, to accept bribes, or to compete with the corporation.[46]

The duty of loyalty also raises the question of whether a director can personally contract with the corporation. Can directors, for instance, sell their personal property or services to the hospital? In general, the answer to this question for a private, not-for-profit hospital is that a director may contract with the corporation if certain high standards are met. A director or trustee may usually contract with that corporation if the contract is fair, if full disclosure of all interest is made, and if utmost good faith is exercised.[47] To establish the fairness of the contract, competitive bidding should be used. Such a person should never vote or participate in the discussion, either directly or through an agent. The burden of proving the fairness of a contract and disclosure of interest is always on the individual director, and the court will closely scrutinize the transaction if the matter is challenged. It is therefore riskier for a director to buy from a hospital and then resell at a personal profit than to sell personal property or services to the institution at fair market value.[48]

A contract with a governing board member that does not meet the above standards is not void, but it is voidable. In *Gilbert v. McLeod Infirmary* the sale of hospital property to a corporation controlled by Aiken, a hospital trustee, was voided even though there was no actual fraud and in spite of the fact that Aiken had refrained from discussing the matter and had not voted on the transaction. However, the attorney for Aiken, who was also a member of the board, had favorably discussed the sale and voted in favor of the proposal. Moreover, Aiken had failed to carry his burden of proof to show fair and adequate consideration for the sale of the property.[49]

In some cases, however, especially if the hospital was at one time a charitable trust and was later incorporated, trust law may be applied to the issue of contracting with the corporation to carry out the original intent of the donor of the property. Trust law will dictate that a member of the governing board may not contract with the corporation, regardless of the fairness of the contract and the adequacy of consideration. It is also possible that a corporate hospital, even though it was never a charitable trust, may hold particular funds or property classified as trust funds. Thus, with respect to the management of these particular funds, the law of trusts will apply.

In a few jurisdictions there are specific state statutes pertaining to the matter of board members' entering into a contract with the corporation they serve. Wyoming's statute, for example, applicable to private hospital corporations, prohibits all officers and directors of not-for-profit corporations from receiving any direct or indirect pecuniary advantage.[50] Maryland's statute requires an officer or trustee of any not-for-profit institution to file an annual financial report if the person is also an employee, partner, or owner of any firm doing business amounting to more than $10,000 with the corporation.[51] The Maryland statute provides criminal penalties for violation. Other states have statutes that require filing conflict of interest statements with public authority in certain circumstances.

With respect to governmental hospitals, a strict rule is often applied as a result of statutes or on the basis of judicially declared public policy. The rule is that the officer or board member may not contract with the hospital in the sale or purchase of property, services, or supplies. Even if full disclosure is made and the contract is fair, the court will set it aside. Hence, in *Warren v. Reed*, a board member who agreed to furnish laundry services to the hospital and was in fact the lowest bidder could not enforce the contract, although the hospital did have to pay for the reasonable value of the services furnished prior to cancellation of the contract.[52]

The importance of local law is further illustrated by an opinion of North Carolina's attorney general interpreting a criminal statute of that state. The statute declares that it is a criminal act for public officers to contract for their own benefit.[53] The attorney general, in turn, has ruled that a trustee of a public hospital is absolutely prohibited from owning stock in a for-profit corporation selling goods or services to the hospital.[54] In these circumstances disclosure of the conflict of interest, abstention from voting, and good faith would not be enough to protect a member of a governmental hospital's governing board from liability in North Carolina.

Whenever members of a governing board wish to contract with the corporation they serve, it follows that they must seek careful legal advice based on local law. In addition to making certain that the letter of the law is followed, every hospital should carefully draft and closely follow appropriate policy declarations pertaining to both direct and indirect conflicts of interest. Of special concern are such indirect conflicts as that involving a board member who is an executive of a company from whom the hospital obtains goods or services. Although arm's length contracts bargained in good faith with such an independent firm (or bank) may be perfectly legal, they invite public charges of self-benefit to the hospital board member. Thus, each board member should be required to file a written declaration disclosing such possible conflicts of interest. Also of concern is acceptance by hospital officials of gifts, gratuities, and excessively lavish entertainment offered by companies or organizations doing business with the hospital, and this matter should be the subject of carefully drafted policy statements.

The fiduciary duty of responsibility means that members of the governing board must exercise reasonable care, skill, and diligence in every activity of the board. In other words, the trustees can be held personally liable for negligence, which can be an act of commission or omission. Reasonable care can be defined as the care that an ordinary, prudent director would exercise in similar circumstances. Good faith and honesty are the major tests in determining whether reasonable care has been exercised.[55] A few court cases make members of the board personally liable only for gross negligence or willful misconduct, but usually a member of the governing board of a not-for-profit corporation can be liable for ordinary negligence.[56] This is the same standard of care imposed on the director of a business corporation.[57]

Duty of responsibility

Embraced within this standard of responsibility is the notion that the trustees or directors of a corporation must actually direct the company. It is not enough merely to preserve corporate property as caretakers; they must employ corporate property to obtain corporate objectives. Any negligent loss or improper investment of assets can lead to liability. Trustees must also attend meetings of the board. Excessive absences can be treated as a negligent omission or nonfeasance. Moreover, as noted previously, trustees must personally vote on issues and cannot ordinarily vote by proxy.[58] Examples of activities that could lead trustees to be held personally liable for negligence are:

- distributing corporate assets to members of the corporation contrary to law or the articles;
- knowingly approving *ultra vires* transactions;
- improperly dissolving the corporation;
- making improper loans to trustees or officers; and
- failing to dissent when improper action occurs.[59]

Encompassed in the concept of fiduciary responsibility is the idea that directors and trustees must exercise reasonable care in selecting and appointing such corporate agents as the chief executive officer.[60] They must also use reasonable care in supervising the agents whom they appoint and in holding them accountable. Negligence in appointing and supervising hospital employees can lead to personal liability. Hence, directors have an individual duty to remove a chief executive officer whom they know or should have known to be incompetent.

There is clearly a corporate duty to exercise reasonable care in selecting and appointing individuals to the medical staff and in delineating their privileges. Moreover, the cases now make it clear that a corporate duty exists to restrict clinical privileges or terminate an appointment when the board knows or should have known of incompetence on the part of a medical staff member.[61] That is, there is corporate liability when the board knew of professional malpractice or when it should have known this from the medical staff committees or departments charged with reviewing each staff physician's clinical performance.

The cases involving the individual duty of trustees to remove an incompetent hospital administrator and the doctrine that trustees have a duty to act when they know of a breach of duty by a fellow trustee indicate that any member of the hospital board who knew that a doctor on the medical staff was incompetent and who failed to report it to the board for deliberation and decision could be personally liable. Nevertheless, the risk of personal liability is not considered serious as long as board members understand and support the institution's peer review process.

Board members may rely on written, documented reports, and recommendations from responsible professional sources such as medical staff committees, hospital accountants, and legal counsel. They need not verify all items in such reports if nothing arouses suspicion or question.[62] The risk of personal liability exists, however, if they fail to obtain documented professional advice when such a need is clearly apparent, for example, if they fail to obtain competent legal counsel when the hospital has a recognizable legal problem.

In general a trustee or director of a not-for-profit healthcare organization is not personally liable for honest errors in business judgment. This is consistent with the standard applicable to the directors of for-profit corporations and means simply that board members must exercise the judgment that reasonably prudent directors or trustees would be expected to exercise under similar circumstances. (An example of the lack of honest business judgment that could render a member of a governing board personally liable is permitting institutional funds to remain in a bank that the member knew or ought to have known to be in financial difficulty.[63])

Nature of Liability for Breach of Duties

If personal liability is successfully asserted against a board member or members, the liability is *joint and several.* This means that a plaintiff may sue one, several, or all members of the board. If the suit is successful, each of the defendants against whom a court judgment is obtained is fully liable for the amount of the judgment. As previously noted, certain breaches of fiduciary duty may be deemed by statutory law to create criminal liability as well as civil.

Suits asserting breaches of fiduciary duty can be brought by the corporation itself or by a stockholder or member of the corporation against the corporate director or officers.[64] An official of the state, usually the attorney general, having the power of regulating the corporation's affairs, can also initiate action. This has been the traditional legal means of enforcing charitable trusts and controlling the affairs of charitable corporations. With respect to governmental hospitals, a taxpayer probably has the requisite standing to bring suit.

In a leading case entitled *Stern v. Lucy Webb Hayes National Training School for Deaconesses and Missionaries,* the court first held that patients and prospective patients of the hospital have standing to bring a class action suit against hospital trustees individually and the hospital.[65] Alleged was breach of fiduciary duty because of fiscal mismanagement that resulted in unnecessary increases in hospital charges to the patients and the community it served. Among other allegations, the plaintiffs alleged that the trustees deposited large sums of hospital moneys in noninterest-bearing bank accounts while the hospital was paying interest on loans from the same financial institutions. Some of the defendant trustees were also directors or officers of the banks and savings and loan associations with whom the hospital conducted business.

The second principal allegation was that the defendants breached their fiduciary obligations with respect to management of the hospital funds. The defendant trustees were members of the board's executive committee, finance committee, and investment committee, some serving on more than one of these bodies. They had permitted the fiscal affairs of the hospital to be managed—virtually without governing board oversight—exclusively by two trustees and corporate officers.[66]

The *Stern* case is important not only because the court found that the trustees had breached their fiduciary obligations of responsibility and loyalty, but especially because it was ruled that trustees can be held personally liable for losses caused by negligent mismanagement or failure to manage hospital investments. The care required is ordinary and reasonable care, the same standard as that imposed on the directors of a business corporation. Certainly any failure of the finance and investment committee to meet and to supervise adequately the activities of the administrators constitutes a breach of this responsibility. As to loyalty, trustees must fully disclose any conflict of interest. Any contract with another enterprise in which a hospital trustee has an interest must be fair, and interested trustees must refrain from participating in the transaction whenever they or the other enterprise they serve contracts with the hospital or accepts a deposit of hospital investment funds. In other words, the court did not prohibit hospital trustees from serving as directors or officers of financial institutions with whom the hospital transacts business, but it clearly indicated that such interlocking directorships would be closely scrutinized.[67]

The *Stern* court did not hold the individual trustees liable for damages, nor did it issue an injunction removing them from the hospital board.[68] It did, however, issue an order declaring that trustees violate their fiduciary duties when they fail to use diligence in supervising the actions of corporate officers or of outside experts to whom investment decisions are delegated or when they engage in a business transaction with the hospital or with any other organization in which they are interested. They must not only perform all these duties honestly, in good faith, and with reasonable care and diligence, but they must also prepare a written policy statement governing investment of hospital funds and see that all investments conform to the guidelines developed in the policy statement.[69]

Protection Against Liability

Despite all that has been said here, the personal liability of hospital trustees is not a serious financial risk so long as they regularly attend meetings of the governing body, vote personally, avoid conflicts of interest, and exercise the utmost good faith and honesty. The best means of establishing good faith and honesty is a written record of all the board's deliberations, including the votes of individual trustees on individual transactions. Any member who dissents from majority action of the board should therefore make sure that the dissent is part of the written record.[70]

Individual trustees and corporate officers have two means of protecting themselves:

1. purchasing liability insurance; and
2. making sure that the corporation has appropriate indemnification provisions and procedures.

Because insurance may be expensive and not sufficiently comprehensive, many not-for-profit corporations favor indemnification plans or a combination of insurance and indemnity. Insurance for directors and officers may, for example, exclude coverage for gross negligence, for intentional acts, and for criminal activity. Indemnification means that if a trustee faces a civil suit alleging violation of fiduciary responsibilities or is prosecuted in a criminal action, the individual is entitled to be repaid by the corporation for personal expenses, including attorney's fees and perhaps even amounts paid as a result of the action. The hospital may in turn purchase insurance covering the costs of indemnification and perhaps for certain liabilities not indemnifiable under local and state law.

Most state laws authorize a corporation to provide for indemnification.[71] Many such statutes apply to directors or trustees and to officers of the corporation, and frequently they apply to both civil and criminal actions. The major point is that, depending on local and state law, the trustees and officers have the right to indemnification under certain circumstances. On this matter careful legal advice is necessary to ensure that the governing body understands the circumstances under which indemnification can or should be provided. It is also imperative that the corporate charter or bylaw provisions covering this matter be drafted with the utmost care.

Some statutes—those in New York, for example—are exclusive; that is, a corporation can have an indemnification agreement with its governing board and officers only to the extent precisely authorized by statute.[72] Most of these statutes, however, are permissive so that corporations may indemnify to a greater extent than the statutes provide. Delaware's is a prototype of this model.[73] In general, the statutes authorize indemnification plans for legal actions brought against trustees and officers by stockholders or by members on behalf of the corporation, as well as for actions by third parties, as in the *Stern* case previously discussed.

The Independent Hospital and Reasons for Change

The traditional corporate model of a hospital has been that of a single legal entity—one institution with a governing board—providing acute care for medical and surgical patients. All activities permitted by the corporate charter, including those not directly related to the care of patients, have been conducted by the single entity. More often than not, hospitals have benefited from not-for-profit status and have been exempt from local and federal taxes. Ownership of the not-for-profit institution has usually been vested in corporate members, a religious congregation, or a self-perpetuating governing board.

The independent hospital, whether not-for-profit or proprietary, has several advantages over alternative forms of corporate organization. A single corporate structure permits clear lines of authority for managing the enterprise. Because all activities are conducted by a single corporation, there is also more formal control over the institution and less chance of deviation from the corporate plan. Finally, a multicorporate structure may require formal contracts for business transactions between corporations within the organization, whereas transactions among departments or divisions of an independent enterprise call only for straightforward accounting entries.

Hospitals face numerous disadvantages in remaining independent, however. Because all activities are conducted by a single corporation, they are subject to a variety of governmental regulations affecting hospitals. Principal among these are state-mandated regulations for certificates of need (CON) limiting expenditures for capital improvements and any major change in services.[74] In addition, income earned by a hospital's profit-making activities is revenue of the corporation, and government or third-party insurers may reduce their reimbursements to the hospital accordingly. Income may also be subject to the federal unrelated business income tax as discussed in Chapter 6.

Independent corporations are also limited in their ability to expand or change their activities and to diversify. Hospital charters often limit the corporate purpose to inpatient care and directly related activities. In *Queen of Angels Hospital v. Younger*, for example, a religious order operating a general, not-for-profit hospital sought to lease its premises to a proprietary hospital, proposing to give up the operation of a general hospital and instead to use the rent generated by the lease to establish outpatient clinics in low-income neighborhoods that would serve indigent patients.[75] The state attorney general challenged the lease, considering the plan outside the purpose outlined in the corporation's charter. Although the charitable purpose of the proposed clinics was found admirable, the court nevertheless ruled that the charter contemplated continued operation of a general hospital. The outpatient clinics could therefore not be opened and the lease was canceled. As a final disadvantage the independent corporate form does not allow the sheltering of assets from legal liability. Because all activities are conducted by a single corporation, all corporate assets are at risk in both contract and tort litigation.

For these reasons, the single corporate entity for hospitals is becoming less and less common. The economic and political environment of recent years has induced healthcare institutions to make changes in their corporate form and engage in activities once considered quite inappropriate. As noted in the next section of this chapter, corporate reorganization or restructuring takes several different forms, the particular form being determined by the facts of each case.

To a significant extent, medical and hospital services in the United States have been transformed from a professional service to a business.[76] Dr. Eli Ginzberg called this transformation the monetarization of medical care, meaning that the "money economy" has penetrated "all facets of the health care system economy."[77] The developments that he says set "the stage for the explosive growth of for-profit medicine" include the decline in the role of philanthropy, increased needs for capital to expand and modernize institutions providing healthcare, the trend toward institutional employment of physicians, and the payment of stipends to medical house staff in training.[78] One can add to Dr. Ginzberg's list the pressure to control healthcare costs (brought about by governmental and business concerns), the advent of "managed care," changes in the Medicare and Medicaid payment systems, and a trend in the mid-1990s to develop "integrated delivery networks."

All these factors have led to a huge number of corporate reorganizations (and re-reorganizations) over recent years. In sum, the goals of corporate reorganization are to:

- diversify activity;
- maximize revenues;
- reduce cost;
- maximize market share;
- partner with physicians or other organizations; and
- (to the extent possible) obtain freedom from a variety of governmental regulations.

A multiorganizational system can substantially diversify the system's global operations. Collectively a corporate system can engage in a wide range of activities that a single institution could not undertake, because separate entities can provide special services or perform functions not related to healthcare without being hampered by certificate of need regulations, restrictive corporate law, and third-party reimbursement regulations.

Multihospital Systems and Corporate Reorganization

The terms "multihospital system" and "corporate reorganization" are generic and there is no single definition, model, or form that describes either concept. The term "system" has been applied to agreements to affiliate or to share services, consortiums of healthcare institutions, leases, contract management arrangements, and chains of institutions formed via consolidations, mergers, or acquisition of assets. Each of these relationships has quite different legal implications. Thus, the term "system" can apply to a mere contractual agreement, at one extreme, and to integrated corporate ownership and managerial control at the other. In any event, formation of a system is a linking together of existing and/or new legal entities.

The American Hospital Association (AHA) once defined a *multihospital system* as two or more acute care hospitals that are owned, leased, or contract-managed by a corporate office. This definition has become outdated, however, because many systems currently include skilled nursing homes and extended care facilities, ambulatory care centers, outpatient surgery, owned physician practices, home health agencies, managed care plans, and other healthcare organizations.

A *consortium* of healthcare institutions is simply a contractual arrangement in which several independent organizations join together to carry out specific programs or services and allocate resources. Each institution retains its own identity, ownership, and governing board. *Contract management* is an agreement between a healthcare institution and a professional managerial firm whereby the latter furnishes administrative personnel and resources for managing a department, a given service, or all of the services provided by the institution. In any event, the governing body of the institution retains the ultimate responsibility for fulfilling corporate purposes. Contract management and the formation of holding companies by consolidations, mergers, or the acquisition of assets of existing legal entities will be discussed later.

In contrast to the formation of a multihospital system a *corporate reorganization* is accomplished through an internal separation or division of units within an existing organization. Reorganization is usually undertaken to create separate corporate entities that will perform the medical and nonmedical functions formerly discharged by the single hospital corporation. This change in corporate structure is designed to focus the organization's activities, as much as possible, on its core business.

Some observers confuse a corporate reorganization with the formation of a multi-institutional system. Indeed, the end products, a multicorporate entity or a single corporate entity with multiple divisions, are often indistinguishable. The key distinction between these concepts is their origin. Corporate reorganization comes from within a single organization, while system formation is a collective response from two or more previously independent entities.

Multisystems may be not-for-profit or proprietary or a combination of both. For example, a not-for-profit corporation may own both not-for-profit and for-profit subsidiary corporations. A system may also be owned and managed by state or local government.

Whether composed of multicorporate entities or a single corporation with multiple divisions, all multi-institutional systems have a corporate office responsible for those activities that are best centralized. System management, corporate planning, and long-range financing, for example, lend themselves to such centralization. Some organizations may also centralize recruitment and training of personnel, risk management, quality assurance, and corporate compliance programs.

A multi-institutional system has several advantages. Organizations within the system are able to share services and thus secure economies of scale. Creation of a corporate management team enables specialization among administrative personnel. The cost of employing skilled personnel, such as analysts for long-range planning, can be spread over the multiple organizations. Senior corporate management can also be freed from routine administrative tasks and thus given more time to develop strategies for achieving long-term goals. Moreover, a system may not only improve the institution's access to capital funds, but it may make possible a relatively low rate of interest.[79]

Some evidence suggests, however, that multi-institutional systems use resources less efficiently than independent hospitals, earn lower rates of return on investment, and sometimes charge inpatients higher room rates.[80] The cost of supporting a corporate office may be a burden on an organization's resources, and the allegiance of individual hospitals may shift from the local community to the system at large in such a way that unneeded services are offered, or conversely that local services are inadequate. Independent hospitals should engage in a careful study of all relevant factors and probable outcomes before they make a commitment to form or join a multi-institutional system.

For institutions choosing to reorganize, many possible corporate structures may evolve. Two of the models that have met with the most success are the independent foundation and the holding company.

The Independent Foundation

During the 1970s some hospitals found it advantageous to transfer endowment services to a separate corporation called a foundation. As an independent entity, the foundation has its own corporate assets and governing body.

The primary motive for establishing an *independent foundation* was to free endowment income from being considered by third-party payors as an offset when calculating reimbursement. At one time Medicare, for example, required that costs of hospitalization be reduced by the amount of institutional income realized from activities other than the care of patients. Foundations can also shelter income from other forms of regulatory control such as rate setting by the state. States that set hospital rates will ordinarily take all available resources into account, including endowment income and revenue from activities other than directly caring for patients. Another advantage of the truly independent foundation is that their governing board and committees can be composed primarily of persons with more expertise in fund-raising and management of investments than most hospitals' governing bodies would possess.

The transfer of certain management services to a foundation is sometimes economically advantageous. The foundation can sell services to the hospital by contract at a profit, thereby increasing the portion of the foundation's revenue that is shielded from regulation.

There are, however, certain difficulties with the foundation concept. First, divestment of endowment funds held currently by the hospital might be hampered or even prevented by the specific terms of the gifts. Before existing assets are transferred to a foundation, the terms on which the hospital holds the funds must therefore be carefully reviewed. State law concerning the transfer of assets by a charitable corporation must also be followed. Further, if the foundation takes over any activity that required a state license, it is likely that a new license must be obtained.

If the hospital corporation is tax exempt, then a newly created foundation must also be a tax-exempt organization. Federal tax law prohibits the transfer of assets from a not-for-profit, tax-exempt entity to one conducted for profit. Healthcare foundations are generally organized under Section 509(a)(1) of the Internal Revenue Code and should be qualified as "non-private" foundations. If so, charitable donations to the foundation are fully tax-deductible by the donor and certain other tax advantages accrue. The tests that the organization must pass to qualify as a nonprivate foundation are reviewed in Chapter 6.

To shelter income from regulatory control, the foundation must maintain its operational independence from the hospital and must be governed by a separate board. The hospital and foundation boards must meet separately, maintain their own minutes, and assert their own corporate identity in all respects. Although some members may serve on both boards, the hospital must be cautious with respect to the number and influence of those who do so. Regulators, third-party insurers, and courts could treat the two corporations as a single unit unless they are convinced that independence is a reality.

The foundation should have a purpose clause that is sufficiently broad to avoid any suggestion that the hospital controls it. Restricting the bulk of the foundation's assets to the sole use of the hospital may, for example, be taken as evidence that the two corporations are dependent. Ideally the foundation should make grants to organizations other than the hospital to prove its independence.

The necessity of maintaining independence is the chief disadvantage of this form of reorganization. The foundation may develop goals different from, or even contradictory to, the goals of the hospital corporation. Although a degree of influence may be maintained by having some board members serve on both boards, the hospital must not dominate the board of the foundation.

In sum, although an independent foundation may provide benefits by sheltering hospital assets from certain regulatory constraints, hospitals should be cautious before yielding direct control over their assets to a foundation.

The Holding Company

A *holding company* consists of two or more corporations, a parent and at least one subsidiary. Activities that are not essential for hospital licensure may then be carried on by one or more separate corporations, which are then free from the regulatory controls applicable to hospitals. In this way the hospital restricts its activities to those that are legally essential while a broad range of services can be provided to the community through the related organizations.

Each subsidiary is a separate legal entity, with its own board of directors, assets, and financial statements. Each is a legal person, which can sue and be sued. The parent corporation is generally the sole corporate member or shareholder, an arrangement that allows the parent to elect members of the subsidiary's governing body. Accordingly, although a holding company involves multiple corporate entities, it can be considered a single organizational form.

The parent corporation can be created in a number of ways. For example, a new corporation can be formed by one or more hospitals, which then become subsidiaries. Or the members of two separate facilities can agree to join forces by creating a holding company to operate their previously independent organizations (see Figure 4.1). Obviously, there is a virtually infinite number of permutations on these models. The variations are limited only by the ingenuity of the lawyers, consultants, and planners involved in the transactions.

For maximum flexibility the parent of a charitable hospital should be organized as a tax-exempt corporation. This will allow the transfer of assets from the hospital to the parent without jeopardizing the tax-exempt status of the hospital. Exemption may be possible by certifying the hospital to be covered by Internal Revenue Code Section 501(c)(3) or Section 501(c)(4), or by designating it a public foundation under Section 509(a)(3). In any event, the parent must not be merely a nominal, inactive corporation. It must conduct charitable programs or welfare activities of its own to prove its tax-exempt status. At the same time, however, the tax-exempt parent may own a profit-making subsidiary whose profits may then be taxable as business income unrelated to tax-exempt purposes.[81]

Holding companies offer significant advantages over the independent foundation. Principal among these is retention of control. As previously noted, an independent foundation may develop conflicts between the long-term goals of the hospital and those of the foundation, and these conflicts might be sufficiently strong to disrupt relations between the two entities. Such conflicts are not possible with a holding company. The parent exercises control over subsidiaries through its role as sole corporate member or shareholder of each

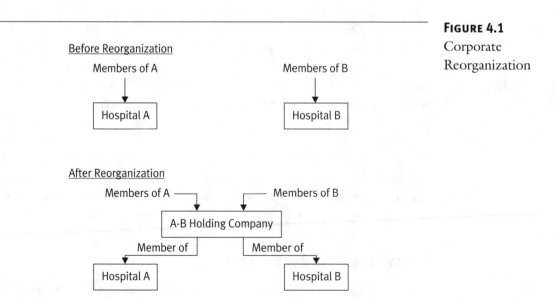

FIGURE 4.1
Corporate Reorganization

subsidiary, thereby ensuring that the overall corporate plan is followed.

Moreover, diversification of activities and the acquisition of other organizations are simplified when a holding company is the corporate form. The structure is already in place for subsidiaries to be added as need and opportunities arise. In addition, because subsidiaries are separately incorporated, newly acquired corporations can retain their own identity. This may make it more attractive for them to join a multi-institutional organization. Members of their boards may be retained or become part of an unofficial advisory board, and the move from independent status may therefore be more acceptable to both the community at large and the members of the acquired institution.

Most of the other potential advantages of the independent foundation, such as freedom from regulation, increases in reimbursement for patient care, and immunity of assets from legal liability, can be achieved through adoption of a holding company structure. A multiple holding company, by providing an additional step between the parent company's profit-making activities and its not-for-profit services, furthers the achievement of long-term goals.

The holding company structure has some disadvantages, however. Its creation involves significant organizational changes with the possibility of disagreement among the individual administrators who are reassigned among the various subsidiary corporations. Changing the viewpoint of the governing board to focus on a multiorganization structure instead of a hospital may be difficult, and changes in board membership are likely to be necessary. New managerial personnel may be needed if current employees cannot adapt to a diversified operation.

Communication within the organization may also become more difficult. Although each subsidiary is owned by the parent, each usually retains its own corporate identity. As subsidiaries are added, lines of communication become complicated and may become strained. Transfer of assets among corporations may also require formal contracts, and care must be taken that assets of tax-exempt companies do not benefit the taxable organizations.

Finally, some express concern that hospitals will lose their public-service orientation if they become members of multi-institutional organizations. A holding company moves the hospital away from center stage of the organizational structure. As this happens, the hospital may find itself being evaluated by the parent on the basis of its financial performance relative to other subsidiaries. To succeed in the long run a holding company must prove that this form of organization benefits the community at large; however, if the holding company brings economies of scale and enables provision of care across the continuum, the community can reap significant benefit from this organizational form.

Piercing the Corporate Veil

As previously discussed, a corporation is a legal entity that has rights and responsibilities of its own, separate and distinct from its owners. By constitutional and statutory provisions, it is an artificial person. A corporation may make and execute contracts, hold title to property, sue and be sued—all in its own name. The corporate owners, whether individuals or another corporation, enjoy limited liability from both tort and contract obligations because the corporation is solely responsible for its own commitments. In short, a corporation is a convenient legal fiction that, because it can provide limited legal and financial liability, has been an invaluable vehicle for encouraging investment in both for-profit and not-for-profit activities.

On the other hand, if a corporation is used to "defeat public convenience, justify wrong, protect fraud, or defend crime," the law will disregard the corporate fiction and place liability on the owners of the corporation.[82] This is known as "piercing the corporate veil." Most of the litigated cases in which the corporate veil has been pierced have concerned closely held corporations or corporate parent-subsidiary relationships.

For a court to pierce the corporate veil, three elements must normally be proved by the party challenging corporate existence:

1. there was complete domination of the corporation by its owner(s);
2. control of the corporation was used by the owner(s) to commit fraud or perpetrate a wrong, violate a statutory or other duty, or commit a dishonest or unjust act; and
3. corporate control was the proximate cause of the injury that is the subject of the suit.[83]

The burden of proving all three elements is on the party challenging corporate existence. Although as early as 1910 the United States Supreme Court noted a growing tendency to look beyond corporate form, courts remain reluctant to disregard the status of such an entity.[84] Accordingly, as a general rule all three elements must be proved to the satisfaction of the trier of fact.[85]

Complete domination of the corporation means domination of finances, business practices, and corporate policies to such an extent that the entity has no mind or will of its own.[86] Mere directorship of the corporation by a sole shareholder entitled to corporate profits is not enough to justify piercing the veil. Courts look on a case-by-case basis for unity of interest and ownership sufficient to destroy the separate identities of the owner or owners and the corporation. Evidence of this unity is found in such facts as:

- mingling of corporate assets with the owner's personal funds;
- neglect of business formalities such as filing separate tax returns, holding regular meetings of the board of directors, and keeping adequate corporate minutes;
- having a mere "paper" corporation with nonfunctioning officers and directors listed in the articles of incorporation; and
- insufficient capitalization of the corporation.[87]

The decision whether to disregard the corporate fiction, however, will not rest on a single factor. Rather, courts will most often look for several factors suggesting that the corporation and owner should be treated as one and the same.[88]

The case of *United States v. Healthwin-Midtown Convalescent Hospital* provides a good illustration of the doctrine.[89] Defendant Zide owned 50 percent of the stock of Healthwin, a convalescent center providing skilled nursing care and receiving payments for authorized services to Medicare patients. Mr. Zide also had a 50 percent interest in a partnership that held title to both the real estate occupied by Healthwin and the furnishings of the nursing home. From time to time Healthwin received estimated payments from Medicare, the exact amount due (or owed, in the case of overpayments) being determined by regular financial audits. Concluding that the nursing home had in fact been overpaid, the government brought suit against Healthwin and against Mr. Zide as an individual for the amount of the alleged overpayment. Mr. Zide defended the claim against him on the basis that the debt was solely the corporation's and that he was entitled to limited liability.

In rejecting his defense the court noted that Mr. Zide alone controlled the corporation's affairs. He was a member of the board, the president of the corporation, and the administrator of the nursing facility. He alone signed corporate checks without concurrence of another corporate officer. The board of directors did not meet regularly. Mr. Zide failed to maintain an arm's length relationship with the corporation by permitting Healthwin's funds to be "inextricably intertwined" with his personal accounts and other business transactions.[90] In addition, the corporation was seriously undercapitalized, having liabilities consistently in excess of $150,000 with an initial capitalization of only $10,000. Finally, the court noted that Mr. Zide diverted corporate funds to the detriment of creditors. In the court's opinion, these facts made it clear that Mr. Zide used the corporation to accommodate his personal business dealings. To allow him to escape liability in these circumstances, the court held, would produce an inequitable result. Accordingly, Mr. Zide was found personally liable for the amount due the federal government because the corporation was a mere alter ego or instrumentality of its principal shareholder.[91]

In addition to the various factors showing a unity of interest and ownership strong enough to outweigh the separate identity of the corporation and the owner or owners, for the corporate veil to be pierced limited liability must result in an inequity. Such an inequitable result is often found when a statutory duty has been violated or fraud or other wrongful action has been perpetrated. Two other cases that illustrate judicial application of the doctrine are *Woodyard v. Arkansas Diversified Insurance Co.*[92] and *Labadie Coal Co. v. Black.*[93]

In the *Woodyard* case the defendant, Arkansas Diversified Insurance Co. (ADIC), was a wholly owned subsidiary of Arkansas Diversified Services (ADS), which in turn was a subsidiary of Blue Cross and Blue Shield, Inc.

ADIC was established to write and sell group life insurance to Blue Cross–Blue Shield subscribers. Mr. Woodyard, the insurance commissioner for the state of Arkansas, denied ADIC's application for a certificate of authority to sell insurance, ruling that the statute enabling Blue Cross–Blue Shield to operate as a corporation restricted it to doing business as a not-for-profit hospital and medical service corporation.[94] In appealing the commissioner's ruling to the courts, ADIC argued that it was a separate entity. Although Blue Cross was clearly restricted by the enabling statute to the role of a medical service corporation, the statute did authorize Blue Cross to invest in a wholly owned subsidiary insurance corporation with the commissioner's consent.[95] A further argument in the appeal was that the commissioner had abused his discretion by denying ADIC authority to sell life insurance.

The Supreme Court of Arkansas upheld the commissioner of insurance. Noting that the president of Blue Cross was also the president of both ADS and ADIC, that other Blue Cross officers held positions in the two subsidiary corporations, that all the companies used the same location and similar stationery, that ADIC used Blue Cross employees to sell the life insurance, and that the underwriting of insurance for ADIC would be performed by ADS, the court determined that the three corporations were essentially the same and that the corporate veil should be pierced. The evidence also clearly showed that ADIC was not acting independently but was instead dominated in a manner that furthered the interests of Blue Cross. Because Blue Cross is a tax-exempt, not-for-profit corporation, it enjoyed an unfair advantage over its competitors in the life insurance business, thus producing an inequitable result. In view of these findings, the court would not overturn the administrative decision,[96] holding as a matter of administrative law that the insurance commissioner's decision was supported by substantial evidence and hence not arbitrary or capricious.

Labadie Coal Co. v. Black provides a concise, understandable description of the alter-ego doctrine and then itemizes the factors that determine whether the corporate veil should be pierced.[97] In the words of the court:

> 1. *The Purpose of the Veil*—The common purpose of statutes providing limited shareholder liability is to offer a valuable incentive to business investment. Although the greatest judicial deference normally is accorded to the separate corporate entity, this entity is still a fiction. Thus, when particular circumstances merit—e.g., when the incentive value of limited liability is outweighed by the competing value of basic fairness to parties dealing with the corporation—courts may look past a corporation's formal existence to hold shareholders or other controlling individuals liable for "corporate" obligations. Several factors have been identified as helpful in deciding when to pierce the corporate veil. . . .
>
> In evaluating the factors outlined below, it is helpful to group them under a two-prong test: (1) is there such unity of interest and

ownership that the separate personalities of the corporation and the individual no longer exist? and (2) if the acts are treated as those of the corporation alone, will an inequitable result follow? Relevant to the first question is the issue of the degree to which formalities have been followed to maintain a separate corporate identity. The second question looks to the basic issue of the fairness under the facts.

2. *Formalities*—Individuals who wish to enjoy limited personal liability under a corporate umbrella should be expected to adhere to the relatively simple formalities of creating and maintaining a corporate entity. In a sense, faithfulness to these formalities is the price paid for the corporate fiction, a relatively small price to pay for limited liability. . . .

    [I]t is clearly not necessary that all of these factors be present in a given case to justify piercing the veil.

    a. The nature of the corporate ownership and control. This court has previously suggested that a corporate form may be ignored whenever an individual so dominates his organization "as in reality to negate its separate personality."[98] . . .

    . . . the question before the court in a case like this is whether the corporation rather than being a distant, responsible entity, is in fact the alter ego or business conduit of the person in control. In many instances, the person "controlling" a close corporation is also the sole, or at least a dominant, shareholder. . . . The question is one of control, not merely paper ownership. . . .

    b. Failure to maintain corporate minutes or adequate corporate records. . . .

    c. Failure to maintain the corporate formalities necessary for issuance or subscription to stock, such as formal approval of the stock issue by an independent board of directors. . . .

    d. Commingling of funds and other assets of the corporation. . . .

    e. Diversion of the corporation's funds or assets to noncorporate uses such as the personal uses of the corporation's shareholders. . . .

    f. Use of the same office or business location by the corporation and its individual shareholders. . . .

(3) *The Element of Unfairness*—The court correctly observed that fraud is not a prerequisite in a suit to disregard a corporate fiction. . . .

    As the Supreme Court has observed, "The cases of fraud make up a part of the exception (which allows the corporate veil to be pierced). . . . But they do not exhaust it. An obvious inadequacy of capital, measured by the nature and magnitude of the corporate undertaking, has frequently been an important factor in cases denying stockholders their defense of limited liability."[99] . . .

[Undercapitalization] is only a single example of how the "unfairness" prong of the piercing test may be satisfied. There may be others. The "errant" party need not have willfully wronged the other party, nor need he have engaged in anything amounting to fraud in their relationship. The essence of the fairness test is simply that an individual businessman cannot hide from the normal consequences of carefree entrepreneuring by doing so through a corporate shell.[100]

Sufficiency of capitalization is measured from the time the corporation is formed. If, for example, initial undercapitalization of a bankrupt subsidiary corporation is evident along with the other relevant factors, the corporate entity of the subsidiary is disregarded and the parent is given an inferior position relative to other creditors.[101]

Finally, before the court will pierce the corporate veil, the third element of the alter-ego doctrine must be satisfied: control of the corporation must be the proximate cause of the injury or unjust loss to the complaining party. When courts evaluate the element of causation they are concerned with reality and not corporate form: how the corporation operated and the individual defendant's relationship to that operation.[102] This requirement is not met by simply alleging a pattern of transactions. There must be concrete proof that separate identities no longer existed between the owner or owners and the corporation when the transaction occurred.

Piercing the corporate veil must be distinguished from two other related legal doctrines that may result in shareholders' liability for corporate transactions. First, an owner of a corporation may become individually liable on a corporate obligation as a consequence of an express or implied contract. A parent corporation can, for example, agree by contract to be bound to transactions of its subsidiary, the parent's agreement being either as a primary co-obligor or as a guarantor of the subsidiary's debt.[103]

Second, the doctrine of *equitable estoppel* may result in shareholders' liability for a corporate obligation. The doctrine is a rule of last resort and rests on conduct by one party (the estopped party) that causes another party to change position and in turn results in injury or detriment to the latter. The following precise elements must be proven:

1. the estopped party's conduct consists of a false representation or concealment of material facts;
2. the estopped party has the intention or expectation that the false representation or concealment will be acted on by the third party; and
3. the estopped party has knowledge of the real facts.[104]

The party claiming the estoppel must lack knowledge or means of acquiring knowledge of the true facts, must rely in good faith on the conduct of the estopped party, and must be damaged or injured by a change of position.[105]

In *Washington Medical Center, Inc.*,[106] a bankruptcy proceeding, the medical center (WMC) established Doctor's Hospital, Inc. (DHI) as a wholly owned subsidiary. DHI entered into a participating hospital contract with Group Hospitalization, Inc. (GHI), the Washington, DC, area Blue Cross plan. The agreement provided that GHI would make advance payments to Doctor's Hospital based on estimates of amounts due for service to Blue Cross subscribers, with final liability to be determined at the end of each year following a cost audit. During most of the 1970s, Group Hospitalization annually overpaid DHI. Then, in 1979, both the Washington Medical Center and DHI filed petitions in bankruptcy, after which Blue Cross filed a claim for repayment against the former. The issue for the court was whether WMC, as the parent corporation, could be held liable for DHI's contractual obligation to refund the overpayments.

The U.S. Bankruptcy Court found that WMC was estopped (prevented) from denying liability. Soon after Doctor's Hospital contracted with GHI, an executive vice president of Washington Medical Center, H. C. Deyerberg, met with officers of GHI to "determine what WMC could do to prevent GHI from offsetting DHI's indebtedness for overpayments." At this meeting the officer of WMC, Mr. Deyerberg, indicated that GHI should deal with him. His company subsequently sent a check to GHI in partial payment of excess advances, stating in an accompanying letter that they would "send such a check every week until we have repaid whatever amount is finally agreed to *by the Washington Medical Center, Inc. and Group Hospitalization, Inc.*"[107] In further letters on WMC's stationery, the president of the medical center agreed with the determination of overpayments made by GHI for the year 1972, requested a waiver of an independent audit of Doctor's Hospital, proposed repayment of $150,000 from the sale of property by his center, and requested extensions of time for amounts owed by DHI to GHI.

Although the evidence fell short of providing a clear indication that Washington Medical Center intended to expressly contract with Group Hospitalization in an arrangement that was separate and distinct from the agreement between its Doctor's Hospital and Group Hospitalization, there was ample basis for applying the doctrine of equitable estoppel. Because all the essential requirements were present, WMC was estopped from denying that they implied that they were assuming their subsidiary's debt. Ultimate liability was assessed against the Washington Medical Center.[108]

Alternative Strategies: Contract Management, Consolidation, and Merger

Some hospitals, facing problems of fewer patients and reduced revenues and finding themselves unable to provide a full range of medical services, are looking to other organizations for aid. Purchasing specialized day-to-day managerial services from companies that specialize in healthcare has provided a means of increasing revenue while reducing costs and has given the institution access to highly trained and skilled administrative personnel that it would otherwise be unlikely to afford.

A contract with an independent firm to manage the hospital is perfectly legal and consistent with the corporate law, so long as the governing board does not abdicate its fiduciary duties. The board must:

- approve the appointment of the chief executive officer and other key managerial personnel furnished by the contractor;
- make certain that the terms set by donors of charitable funds are honored and that the hospital adheres to the corporate purpose clause and other legal constraints;
- approve any major changes in hospital services;
- review the contractor's performance regularly; and
- arrange for an annual independent financial audit.[109]

The term of the contract should be limited to two or three years, with appropriate provisions for renewal or termination by either party. If the hospital is a tax-exempt, charitable corporation the contractor should not be compensated on the basis of a percentage of income earned, because such a formula could constitute a private gain to the management firm and thus jeopardize the tax-exempt status of the hospital. The contract should contain detailed provisions regarding accountability of the contractor to the governing board.

The chief executive officer and other personnel furnished by the management company will be agents of the hospital as well as agents of the contractor. From the viewpoint of the hospital and third parties with whom it deals, the persons managing the hospital will possess the same express and implied authority as if they were in the direct employ of the institution. Implied authority will extend to all those transactions that are reasonably necessary to the operation of the hospital and customarily carried out by the agent in question. In describing, for example, the authority of the corporate president, a Delaware court once said:

> Corporations have assumed and acquired such a position in the business world that the office of president carries with it certain implied powers of an agency. [The president] is usually expressly or by implied consent made the chief executive officer, [and] without special authority or explicitly delegated power he may perform all acts of an ordinary nature which by usage or necessity or incidence of his office and by virtue of his office he may enter into a contract and bind his corporation in matters arising from and concerning the usual of the corporation's business.[110]

Particular economic and geographical circumstances may prevent contract management from being a viable solution for survival in a competitive environment. Some institutions thus find it advantageous to sell assets or stock to another corporation or to consolidate or merge with other entities.

The sale of a corporation's assets is a relatively straightforward trans-action, except that local law must be followed carefully when the seller is a charitable corporation. Normally the governing boards of both the buyer and the seller must approve the terms of the sale. The stockholders or members of the selling corporation must also approve the sale, because selling all or a substantial portion of assets constitutes an extraordinary transaction beyond the authority of the board acting alone.[111] After the sale is completed the selling corporation may dissolve and cease doing business or may continue to operate on a more restricted scale. If the seller is a charitable corporation, many local laws require that a designated state officer approve the final arrangement, because the state has the ultimate responsibility of enforcing terms of the charitable trust.

In a merger a given corporation is absorbed by another and ceases to exist. A consolidation, in contrast, is a transaction that creates a new corporation comprising two or more existing companies, both of which then dissolve.[112] Before engaging in a merger or a consolidation, each party must carefully scrutinize state corporation law and state statutes relevant to char-itable organizations, local certificate of need legislation, and perhaps other regulatory requirements.

Normally the governing boards of all the corporations involved and the shareholders or any members with voting rights must approve the plan. If an acquired corporation has issued bonds, the terms of the bond documents may require approval of the bondholders. The plan to merge or consolidate will of course contain a comprehensive explanation of the terms and conditions of the proposal. When the plan has been approved by all interested parties, articles of merger or consolidation are prepared and filed with the appropriate state officer responsible for enforcing the relevant corporate law, who then issues a certificate authorizing the transaction. Once this is issued, the new corporation owns all the property of those entities that no longer exist, has all their rights and privileges, and is also liable for all their debts.[113]

Consolidations and mergers of existing institutions frequently benefit the community at large and the institutions involved. Such arrangements not only improve the ability of a previously independent unit to diversify but enable the surviving corporation to provide a wider range of services. Quality assurance and risk management may be easier. Economies of scale can be realized and assets can be used more efficiently, with a consequent possibility of lowering the costs of healthcare. On the other hand, if market power is significantly increased, the merger may invite allegations that it violates antitrust laws. The antitrust aspects of asset acquisitions, consolidations, and mergers are thoroughly discussed in Chapter 7.

Joint Ventures with Physicians

In a competitive environment healthcare institutions and physicians' organizations often wish to develop contractual or business arrangements with each other in which both parties share the risks and rewards of the endeavor. These cooperative arrangements between healthcare institutions and physicians' organizations usually take the form of joint ventures, although they sometimes are incorporated. A *joint venture* is a special form of partnership, usually a general partnership, formed by two or more legal entities for a specific, single purpose and for a limited duration. A joint venture is thus one way of integrating two or more business organizations. In a true joint venture most of the rules of a general partnership normally apply:

- the parties have created more than a contractual relationship and owe fiduciary duties to each other;
- each has a right to participate in management;
- property is owned jointly;
- profits and losses are shared according to an agreement; and
- each participant has unlimited liability to third parties.

A joint venture differs from a general partnership, however, in that its participants are not agents of each other.[114]

In healthcare the term "joint venture" has been used more broadly to refer to a variety of legal relationships between institutional providers of care and physicians who have in many cases formed a corporation or a group practice. For example, the term may simply denote a contractual agreement between two legal entities, or a stock corporation created by physicians and others, or a limited partnership, as distinct from a general partnership. The participants may enter a contract with another or create a partnership or a corporation for a number of reasons:

- to diversify their activities;
- to provide new or additional services to the community;
- to seek capital from interested investors;
- to maximize their reimbursement from Medicare and other governmental healthcare programs; and
- to gain tax benefits.

Although numerous purposes are possible, joint ventures are usually formed for a single purpose. For example, a hospital and a physician's organization may establish a joint venture to provide ambulatory, surgical, or emergency care to outpatients; to create a health maintenance organization; to own and manage a nursing home, medical office building, clinical laboratory, laundry, or home nursing service; or to conduct utilization reviews.

In joint ventures the hospital and the physicians share the rewards and the risks while contractually agreeing on matters of ownership, control, and management. The sharing of risks has, in effect, been stimulated by a number of factors, primarily the government's adoption of the prospective payment system for Medicare beneficiaries. Although physicians decide treatments and the patients' length of stay, the hospitals receive a fixed, predetermined amount based on diagnosis. There are therefore good reasons for the hospital to share its financial risks with physicians. Doctors also find merit in a joint venture, because the growth of health maintenance organizations, preferred provider organizations, and group medical practices, coupled with the excess number of physicians in some parts of the country, have substantially reduced the attractiveness of solo practice. In short, physicians can gain competitive advantages by joining together with healthcare institutions.

Two other issues regarding joint ventures must be clarified. The first question is simply the true legal relationship between the parties. Is it merely contractual or have the parties formed a partnership, either general or limited? Each of these possibilities carries its own implications with respect to liabilities, tax law, local commercial law, federal antitrust laws, and the rules that determine Medicare payments.

The second issue flows from the first: for what purpose and in what context—that is, antitrust or tax laws—must legal advice or an opinion be sought? Healthcare executives and their counsel need to analyze carefully both the business arguments and the legal reasons for undertaking a particular venture before embarking on it. A complete legal analysis of each form of venture is beyond the scope of this chapter, but some of the tax implications of a joint venture will be mentioned in Chapter 6, and the antitrust aspects of various forms of joint action are analyzed in Chapter 7. Of unique importance and worthy of mention here is the possible effect of federal statutes that prohibit certain agreements concerning remuneration for medical services or the use of facilities.

As noted in Chapter 8, "Healthcare Fraud and Abuse," the Medicare-Medicaid legislation makes bribes, kickbacks, and rebates illegal whenever medical services or goods are to be paid for by a federal health program.[115] No one may receive or offer to pay any remuneration—directly or indirectly, overtly or covertly, in cash or in kind—to any person to induce such person to refer patients or to recommend the purchase of any medical services, goods, or facilities. Violation of the statutes constitutes a criminal act that can be penalized by large fines and imprisonment. Civil monetary penalties may also be imposed. The person who solicits and the one who receives the prohibited remuneration are both subject to prosecution (although, as all criminal laws decree, the criminal act must be committed knowingly or willfully). Because the language of the statute prohibits both direct and indirect as well as overt and covert remuneration, a conservative interpretation is that any economic reward for a referral or a purchase could constitute a violation. Joint ventures must therefore be closely scrutinized to make certain that a provider's economic benefits are related to substantive financial risks and not simply a payment intended to induce referrals. Clearly the substance, rather than the form, of a transaction or an agreement will determine the outcome of a given case. Designating a payment, for example, as a consulting fee when in reality it is a payment for referral of business will not save the transaction from being considered illegal.

There have been many cases involving payments that involved prohibited behavior. In *United States v. Universal Trade and Industries*, for example, the operator of a clinical laboratory was convicted of offering payment to a physician on the condition that the latter would use the laboratory exclusively for prescribed medical tests.[116] Similarly, a pharmacist who made regular payments to a nursing home in return for the opportunity to supply drugs to Medicaid patients there was found guilty of a criminal act.[117]

Another consideration is the prohibition on physician referrals to healthcare organizations in which the physician holds a "financial interest."[118] Known as the Stark self-referral law (named after its sponsor, Rep. Fortney "Pete" Stark of California), this statute is intended to remove the incentive to overuse healthcare services and thus drive up the cost of federal healthcare programs. It provides for fines and exclusion from Medicare and Medicaid participation of physicians who violate its complicated provisions. A joint venture between a healthcare organization and a physician or physician group may create a financial relationship that will trigger the self-referral statute.

In summary, joint ventures must be carefully designed and implemented lest the arrangement contravene congressional intent to prohibit transactions that provide remuneration for generating business. The participants in a venture must be certain that they have legitimate business reasons for adopting their agreement, that the terms comply with commonly accepted business practices, and that the venture does not increase the cost of federal or state healthcare programs.

Notes

1. Forty-nine states and the District of Columbia have adopted the Uniform Partnership Act (U.P.A.). Louisiana is the only state that has not adopted the U.P.A. 6 U.L.A. 1 (Supp. 1986) (table of jurisdictions).
2. *See generally* ALAN R. BROMBERG, CRANE AND BROMBERG ON PARTNERSHIP (1968) [hereinafter cited as CRANE & BROMBERG]. Personal liability of the owners is one of the most significant differences between partnerships and corporations.
3. UNIF. PARTNERSHIP ACT § 31 (4), 6 U.L.A. 394 (1969). *See* CRANE & BROMBERG, *supra* note 2, at 432–34; HAROLD G. REUSCHLEIN AND WILLIAM A. GREGORY, HANDBOOK ON THE LAW OF AGENCY AND PARTNERSHIP 368–70 (1979) [hereinafter cited as REUSCHLEIN & GREGORY].
4. Nineteen states and the District of Columbia have adopted the Uniform Limited Partnership Act of 1916 and 30 states have adopted the Revised Uniform

Limited Partnership Act of 1976. Louisiana is the only state that has not adopted either act. 6 U.L.A. 151, 201 (Supp. 1986) (tables of jurisdictions that have adopted the 1916 and 1976 acts).

5. *See generally* CRANE & BROMBERG, *supra* note 2, at 143–51; REUSCHLEIN & GREGORY, *supra* note 3, at 433–38.

6. *See generally* CRANE & BROMBERG, *supra* note 2, at 189–95; REUSCHLEIN & GREGORY, *supra* note 3, at 441–46.

7. Trustees of Dartmouth College v. Woodward, 17 U.S. (4 Wheat) 518, 636 (1819).

8. *See generally* HARRY G. HENN AND JOHN R. ALEXANDER, LAWS OF CORPORATIONS AND OTHER BUSINESS ENTERPRISES (1983) [hereinafter cited as HENN & ALEXANDER].

9. *Id.* at 130–32.

10. In Charlotte Hungerford Hosp. v. Mulvey, 26 Conn. Supp. 394, 225 A.2d 495 (1966), the court decided that where the corporate purpose clause provided for "maintaining and supporting a hospital" there was implied power to build, own, and maintain a medical office building for staff physicians, because such a facility would materially aid the hospital in carrying out its purposes. *Id.* At 397, 225 A.2d at 497.

    Similarly, the Missouri State Medical Association, a not-for-profit corporation, had the implied power to join with the Missouri Association of Osteopathic Physicians and Surgeons to form an independent corporation, Health Care Foundation of Missouri, for the purpose of conducting reviews of quality and costs of services rendered by physicians. Komanetsky v. Missouri State Medical Ass'n, 516 S.W.2d 545 (Mo. Ct. App. 1975). *Compare* Queen of Angels Hosp. v. Younger, 66 Cal. App. 3d 359, 136 Cal. Rptr. 36 (1977) (a charitable corporation formed to maintain and operate a hospital could not lease its premises, abandon hospital operations, and devote proceeds of the lease to operate medical clinics in low-income areas, regardless of the worthy purpose of the clinics, because this would constitute a violation of the hospital's articles of incorporation); *see also* Holt v. College of Osteopathic Physicians and Surgeons, 61 Cal. 2d 750, 394 P.2d 932 (1964) (where a corporate purpose clause provided for the establishment and conduct of an osteopathic medical and surgical college, the trustees could not make a decision to delete the word "Osteopathic" and convert the college to an allopathic medical school).

11. An *ultra vires* transaction should be distinguished from an illegal act. The latter is an absolutely void transaction; an example would be employment by the hospital of an unlicensed professional person. Tovar v. Paxton Memorial Hosp., 29 Ill. App. 3d 218, 330 N.E.2d 247 (1975) (a physician licensed in Kansas but not licensed in Illinois could not maintain an action for an alleged breach of an employment contract with an Illinois hospital).

12. *See generally* Oleksy v. Sisters of Mercy, 92 Mich. App. 770, 285 N.W.2d 455 (1979) (a private charitable hospital has statutory authority to convey its assets to another not-for-profit private hospital; the transaction is not *ultra vires*).

13. 82 Op. Fla. Att'y Gen. 44 (1982).

14. Tift County Hosp. Auth. v. MRS of Tifton, Ga., Inc., 255 Ga. 164, 165, 335 S.E.2d 546, 547 (1985) (quoting Keen v. Mayor of Waycross, 101 Ga. 588, 29 S.E. 42 (1897).

15. The terms "not-for-profit" and "nonprofit" are synonymous. The author prefers the former, however, because it emphasizes the essential point that the *purpose* of such a corporation is not to make a profit even though it may, and usually does, do so.

16. ABA-ALI Model Non-Profit Corp. Act (1964).

17. In 1983, for example, Michigan adopted a comprehensive Nonprofit Corporation Act, MICH. COMP. LAWS ANN. §§ 450.2101–450.3099 (West Supp. 1986).

18. *See generally* HOWARD L. OLECK, NON-PROFIT CORPORATIONS, ORGANIZATIONS AND ASSOCIATIONS § 3 (4th ed. 1980) [hereinafter cited as NON-PROFIT CORPORATIONS].

19. The Michigan statute recognized both stock and nonstock membership corporations. The statute generally treats the two organizational forms equally but does differentiate between the two forms in certain aspects. MICH. COMP. LAWS ANN. § 450.2302 (West Supp. 1986); *see generally* Darlow, *Michigan Nonprofit Corporations*, 62 MICH. B.J. 530 (1983). Darlow points out that a stock corporation is more appropriate for organizations that have varying property or economic rights, such as property-owner associations. A nonstock membership form is more appropriate for trade associations, garden clubs, or similar groups whose members participate actively in the affairs of the group. Darlow, *id*. at 533.

20. For example, the Michigan statute provides that a not-for-profit corporation may not "pay dividends or distribute any part of its assets, income, or profit to its shareholders, members, directors, or officer. . . ." The statute excludes, however, compensation for services, dissolution distribution, and distribution of member-paid fees from this provision. MICH. COMP. LAWS ANN. § 450.2301 (3)(a) to (e)-(4).

21. For example, the Michigan statute specifically states that a not-for-profit corporation "may pay compensation in *a reasonable amount* to shareholders, members, directors, or officers for services rendered to the corporation." *Id*. at § 450.2301 (3)(a) (emphasis added).

22. *See* NON-PROFIT CORPORATIONS, *supra* note 18, at 4. The author states: "Motive is the acid test of the right to nonprofit status, in most cases. When altruistic, ethical, moral, or social motives are the clearly dominant ones in an enterprise, that enterprise is nonprofit. Obviously, it is difficult to test for human motives in an enterprise. Abuse of nonprofit status, however, often is best tested by testing the motives of the organizers or officers of nonprofit organizations." *Id*. at 22.

23. *See* I.R.C. § 501 (1985); *see also* NON-PROFIT CORPORATIONS, *supra* note 18, at § 281 (general discussion of applicable federal tax code provisions).

24. *See* Jordan, *Trends in Tax Exemption*, ABA-ALI TRENDS IN NONPROFIT ORGANIZATION LAW § 11 (1977).

25. Charitable status is reviewed and explained in Chapter 6.

26. Typically, members vote on such decisions as those to merge or dissolve the corporation, amend articles and bylaws, appoint the chief executive officer, adopt budgets, and establish corporate philosophy, mission, and values.

27. *See, e.g.,* MICH. COMP. LAWS ANN. § 450.2302 (West Supp. 1986).

28. For example, Michigan statutes provide that "all matters which are subject to membership vote or other action in this act . . . shall be subject to duly

authorized action by the board of directors of a directorship corporation." *Id.* at § 450.2305.

29. *See generally* NON-PROFIT CORPORATIONS, *supra* note 18, at §§ 383–84. Generally, distribution problems arise in charitable organizations. Not-for-profit organizations that are not charitable generally distribute their free assets to members or, in some cases, transfer those assets to another organization depending on distribution procedures set up in their articles or bylaws.

30. There may be some exceptions to this general rule. For example, regarding the actual investment of financial resources, some states' incorporation statutes may authorize the corporate charter or bylaws to provide that investment of funds may be delegated by the board exclusively to the finance committee, thereby removing possible liability from other board members for improper investment. Investment of funds, however, must be distinguished from application of funds for hospital purposes. The board must always carry the responsibility for the latter on its own shoulders.

31. *See, e.g.,* OHIO REV. CODE ANN. § 1702.27 (A)(1) (page 1985). The Ohio Non-Profit Corporation Statute states: "The number of trustees as fixed by the articles or the regulations shall not be less than three or, if not so fixed, the number shall be three." *See, e.g.,* MICH. COMP. LAWS ANN. § 450.2505 (1) (West Supp. 1986). The statute states: "The Board shall consist of 1 or more directors. The number of directors shall be fixed by or in the manner provided by the bylaws, unless the articles of incorporation fix the number."

32. For example, a California statute prohibits anyone who owns stock or has any property interest in a private hospital or is a director or officer of a private hospital from serving as a director or officer of a public hospital servicing the same area. CAL. HEALTH & SAFETY CODE § 32110 (West 1973 & Supp. 1986). Accordingly, in Franzblau v. Monardo, 108 Cal. App. 3d 522, 166 Cal. Rptr. 610 (1980), the president of a not-for-profit private hospital was prohibited from serving as a director of the public hospital district.

33. W. VA. CODE § 16-5B-6a (1985).

34. American Hosp. Ass'n v. Hansbarger, 600 F. Supp. 465 (N.D. W. Va. 1984), *aff'd*, 783 F.2d 1184 (4th Cir. 1986), *cert. denied,* 107 S. Ct. 85 (1986).

35. 600 F. Supp. at 473–74. *See also* Pattie A. Clay Infirmary Ass'n v. First Presbyterian Church, 605 S.W.2d 52 (Ky. App. 1980) (private hospital's all female board does not violate the Fourteenth Amendment because there is no state action).

36. 600 F. Supp. at 476–78.

37. *Id.* at 474.

38. *Id.* at 479–80.

39. For example, the Ohio law permits a trustee of a not-for-profit corporation to be removed from office by any procedure that is provided for in the articles of incorporation or the bylaws. The remaining trustees may then fill any vacancy on the board by majority vote for the unexpired term, unless the articles or bylaws provide otherwise.

40. State *ex rel.* Welch v. Passaic Hosp. Ass'n, 59 N.J.L. 142, 36 A. 702 (1897) (director cannot be removed from office without fair notice and opportunity to be heard).

41. *See generally* HENN & ALEXANDER, *supra* note 8, at §§ 243–45. In a very few states, however, the statutes for not-for-profit corporations are so worded that they seemingly prohibit members of the governing body from receiving any compensation, making no distinction between ordinary and extraordinary services. In such jurisdictions salaried officers may not be able to sit as voting members of the governing board.

42. *See e.g.,* MICH. COMP. LAWS ANN. § 450.2521 (3) (West Supp. 1986).

43. *See generally* HENN & ALEXANDER, *supra* note 8, at § 209.

44. Joint Commission on Accreditation of Healthcare Organizations, 1998 HOSPITAL ACCREDITATION STANDARDS, 217–219 (1998).

45. Hunt v. Rabon, 275 S.C. 475, 272 S.E.2d 643 (1980) (trustees of hospital not personally liable when patient died as result of crossed oxygen and nitrous acid gas lines); *see generally* HENN & ALEXANDER, *supra* note 8, at § 234.

46. With respect to the duty of loyalty, see Patient Care Services, S.C. v. Segal, 32 Ill. App. 3d 1021, 337 N.E.2d 471 (1975) (a corporate officer and director who actively engaged in a rival and competing business to the detriment of a corporation must answer to the corporation for injury sustained. The defendant physician was an officer and director of the professional service corporation bringing the charge. He had established another professional service corporation to perform identical medical planning services for a hospital client, thereby attempting to seize an opportunity due the plaintiff corporation).

47. 18B AM. JUR. 2D *Corporations* § 1736 (1985).

48. *See* HENN & ALEXANDER, *supra* note 8, at § 238.

49. 219 S.C. 174, 64 S.E.2d 524 (1951); *accord* Fowle Memorial Hosp. v. Nicholson, 189 N.C. 44, 126 S.E. 94 (1925) (hospital corporation board member who leases property from corporation has burden to show fairness of transaction, adequacy of consideration, and that execution was not unduly influenced).

50. WYO. STAT. ANN. § 17-6-104 (1977).

51. MD. HEALTH-GENERAL CODE ANN. § 19-220 (1982).

52. 231 Ark. 714, 331 S.W.2d 847 (1960).

53. N.C. GEN. STAT. § 14-234 (1981 & Supp. 1983).

54. Public Officers and Employees; Conflict of Interest; Stockholder Subject to G.S. 14–234, 52 Op. N.C. Att'y Gen. 49 (1982).

55. *See generally* HENN & ALEXANDER, *supra* note 8, at § 234.

56. Stern v. Lucy Webb Hayes Nat'l Training School for Deaconesses and Missionaries, 381 F. Supp. 1003 (D. D.C. 1974). *But see* Beard v. Achenbach Memorial Hosp. Ass'n, 170 F.2d 859 (10th Cir. 1948) (trustees liable only for "gross or willful negligence").

57. The Michigan Corporation and Non-Profit Corporation Acts provide, for example, that a director shall discharge the duty of responsibility "in good faith and with that degree of diligence, care, and skill which an ordinarily prudent person would exercise under similar circumstances in a like position." MICH. COMP. LAWS ANN. §§ 450.1541 (1), 450.2541 (1) (West 1973 & Supp. 1986); see also CAL CORP. CODE §§ 309(a), 5231(a), 7231(a), 9241(a), 12371(a) (West 1977 & Supp. 1986); CONN. GEN. STAT. ANN. § 33–447 (d) (West Supp. 1986).

58. *See generally* HENN & ALEXANDER, *supra* note 8, at § 234.

59. Hill v. Hill, 79 N.J. Eq. 521, 82 A. 338 (1912) (liability was found when defendant trustee was aware that a co-trustee had acquired an interest adverse to the trust and did nothing about the matter; this case involved an actual trust).

60. *See* Reserve Life Ins. Co. v. Salter, 152 F. Supp. 868 (S.D. Miss. 1957).

61. See text and cases discussed in Chapter 5.

62. State statutes generally specify what items a trustee may rely on in discharging duties. *See, e.g.,* MICH. COMP. LAWS ANN. § 450.2541 (1) (West Supp. 1986) (a director may rely on "opinion of counsel for the corporation, upon the report of an independent appraiser selected with reasonable care by the board, or upon the financial statements of the corporation represented to the director or officer to be correct . . .").

63. *See* Epworth Orphanage v. Long, 207 S.C 384, 36 S.E.2d 37 (1945); *see also* Queen of Angels Hosp. v. Younger, 66 Cal. App. 3d 359, 136 Cal. Rptr. 36 (1977) (there was an improper exercise of sound business judgment or breach of fiduciary duties when the board of a not-for-profit charitable corporation compromised a $16 million claim by a religious order for past services rendered the hospital by members of the order. The settlement agreement provided that the hospital should pay the Motherhouse $200 per month for each Sister in the Order over 70 years of age, whether or not the particular sister performed services at the hospital, plus $200 per month "for each lay employee who had worked for the congregation for over 20 years, not to exceed ten lay employees at any on time." Although the claim was made in good faith and was not dishonest, the agreement was invalid and constituted a diversion of corporate assets, because there was no lawful obligation on the part of the hospital to pay for past services.).

64. In California, directors and officers of a hospital may bring suit against a director for self-dealing; the attorney general must be joined as a party. CAL. CORP. CODE § 5233(c) (West Supp. 1986).

65. 367 F. Supp. 536 (D. D.C. 1973) (Mem.) (patients could sue as a class for breach of trust to prevent additional injury to hospital but could not as a class recover personally).

66. Stern v. Lucy Webb Hayes Nat'l Training School for Deaconesses and Missionaries, 381 F. Supp. 1003, 1008–13 (D. D.C. 1974) (Supp. Opinion).

67. *Id.* at 1015.

68. *Id.* at 1017–20.

69. *Id.* at 1020–21.

70. For example, Michigan statute provides that board members are presumed to have concurred in a board action unless their dissent is entered in the minutes. Further, directors who are absent from meetings are presumed to have concurred with any board action unless they file a dissent with the secretary. MICH. COMP. LAWS ANN. § 450.2553 (West Supp. 1986).

71. *See, e.g., id.* at §§ 450.2561, .2562, .2563.

72. N.Y. NOT-FOR-PROFIT CORP. LAW § 721 (McKinney 1970); N.Y. BUS. CORP. LAW § 721 (McKinney 1986). The statute provides that no provision to indemnify directors or court-awarded indemnification "shall be valid unless consistent with this article." *See also* N.Y. NOT-FOR-PROFIT CORP. LAW §§

722–726 (McKinney 1970 & Supp. 1986) and N.Y. Bus. Corp. Law §§ 722–726 (McKinney 1986) (permissible indemnification provisions).

73. Del. Code Ann. tit. 8, § 145(f) (1983). The statute provides: "The indemnification provided by this statute shall not be deemed exclusive of any other rights to which those seeking indemnification may be entitled under any bylaw, agreement, vote of stockholders . . . "

74. The certificate of need (CON) program was established by the National Health Planning and Resource Development Act of 1974. CON required approval for acquisition of major medical equipment and expansion of clinical health services. *See* U.S.C. § 300m-6 (1982). States were compelled to administer this program via State Health Planning and Development Agencies or face loss of federal health allocation funds. Persons were compelled to comply with this law on penalty of fine, loss of license, or enjoinment from further activity. *See* 42 C.F.R. § 123.408 (1985).

The federal health planning program was terminated in 1986, although a significant number of states continue to have CON programs. CON approvals are usually costly, time, consuming, and, to some extent, political, which works to the detriment of small, independent hospitals. *See generally* Hamilton, *Barriers to Hospital Diversification: The Regulatory Environment,* 24 Duq. L. Rev. 425, 428–32 (1985) (Symposium: Current Developments in Health Law).

75. 66 Cal. App. 3d 359, 136 Cal. Rptr. 36 (1977).

76. Iglehart, *The Changing World of Private Foundations: An Interview with Dr. David E. Rogers,* 2 Health Affairs 5 (1983); Relman, *The New Medical-Industrial Complex,* 303 New Eng. J. of Med. 963 (1980).

77. Ginzberg, *The Monetarization of Medical Care,* 310 New Eng. J. of Med. 1162 (1984).

78. *Id.* at 1162.

79. Connors, *Multi-Hospital Systems Are Changing the Health-Care Landscape,* 32 Trustee 24 (July 1979).

80. Zuckerman, *Multi-Institutional Systems: Promise and Performance,* 16 Inquiry 291 (1979).

81. *See* I.R.C. §§ 511–513; *see also* I.R.C. § 501(b). However, an organization will not be regarded as tax exempt "if more than an insubstantial part of its activities is not in furtherance of an exempt purpose." Treas. Reg. 1-501(c)(3)–1(e)(1).

82. W. Fletcher, Cyclopedia of the Law of Private Corporations § 41 (perm. ed. 1983) [hereinafter cited as Fletcher].

83. *Id.* at § 43.10; *see also* Lowendahl v. Baltimore & Ohio R.R., 247 A.D. 144, 287 N.Y.S. 62, *aff'd,* 272 N.Y. 360, 6 N.E.2d 56 (1936).

84. J.J. McCaskill Co. v. United States, 216 U.S. 504, 515 (1910).

85. *But see* Church of Scientology v. Blackman, 446 So. 2d 190 (Fla. App.), *reh'g denied,* 456 So. 2d 1181 (1984); Dania Jai–Alai Palace, Inc. v. Sykes, 425 So. 2d 594 (Fla. App. 1983), *aff'd in part, rev'd in part,* 450 So. 2d 1114 (1984). In a succession of Florida appellate cases, the courts had held that total domination, by itself, justified piercing the corporate veil. However, on appeal of *Dania Jai–Alai Palace,* the Florida Supreme Court held that the corporate veil could "not be pierced absent showing of improper conduct." 450 So. 2d 1114, 1121

(Fla. 1984). Thus the almost universal rule that all three factors must be present to pierce the corporate veil.

86. *See* FLETCHER, *supra* note 82, § 43.10.

87. "In a sense, faithfulness to these [corporate] formalities is the price paid for the corporate fiction, a relatively small price to pay for limited liability." Labadie Coal Co. v. Black, 672 F.2d 92, 97 (D.C. Cir. 1982).

88. *See* Jabczenski v. Southern Pac. Memorial Hosp., 119 Ariz. 15, 579 P.2d 53 (1978) (mere existence of interlocking directorates between a not-for-profit and for-profit corporation was insufficient to justify disregarding the corporate identities).

89. 511 F. Supp. 416 (1981), *aff'd*, 685 F.2d 448 (1982).

90. *Id*. at 419.

91. *Id*. at 420.

92. 268 Ark. 94, 594 S.W.2d 13 (1980).

93. 672 F.2d 92 (D.C. Cir. 1982).

94. *See* ARK. STAT. ANN. § 66-4902 (1980).

95. *Id*. at §§ 66-4910(d), 66-2618.

96. 268 Ark. At 97, 594 S.W.2d at 16.

97. 672 F.2d 92.

98. *Id*. at 97 (quoting Quinn v. Butz, 510 F.2d 743, 758 (D.C. Cir. 1975)).

99. *Id*. at 99 (quoting Anderson v. Abbot, 321 U.S. 349 (1944) [citations omitted]).

100. *Id*. at 96–100 (footnotes omitted).

101. For an example of a hospital bankruptcy proceeding where the court held that the corporate veil should not be pierced between parent and subsidiary, see Washington Medical Center, Inc., 10 Bankr. 616 (1981), *infra* pp. 148–49; see also FLETCHER, *supra* note 82, at § 41.55

102. *See* FLETCHER, *supra* note 82, at § 43.10; *Lowendahl, supra* note 83, at 157, 287 N.Y.S. at 76.

103. *See* Washington Medical Center, Inc., 10 Bankr. 616, 623–24 (1981); *see also* 18 AM. JUR. 2D *Corporations* § 856 (1985).

104. 28 AM. JUR. 2d *Estoppel and Waiver* § 35 (1966).

105. *Id*.

106. 10 Bankr. 616 (1981).

107. *Id*. at 624 (emphasis added by the court).

108. *Id*. at 625–26.

109. *See generally* Brown, *Contract Management: Legal and Policy Implications*, 18 INQUIRY 8 (1981); A.H.A. TECHNICAL ADVISORY BULL., *Institutional Management Contracts* (1980); BLUE CROSS ASS'N., *Chain Organizations and Other Multiple Facility Groups* (1977).

110. Joseph Grenspon's Sons Iron & Steel Co. v. Pecos Valley Gas Co., 34 Del. 567, 570–71, 156 A. 350, 352 (1931).

111. *See* HENN & ALEXANDER, *supra* note 8, at § 341; *see, e.g.,* MICH. COMP. LAWS ANN. §§ 450.1753, 450.2753 (West 1973 & Supp. 1986).

112. *See generally* HENN & ALEXANDER, *supra* note 8, at § 346.

113. *See e.g.,* MICH. COMP. LAWS ANN. §§ 450.1701 – .1722, 450.2703 – .2722 (West 1973 & Supp. 1986); *see generally* HENN & ALEXANDER, *supra* note 8, at § 346.

114. *See generally* HENN & ALEXANDER, *supra* note 8, at § 49.
115. 42 U.S.C. § 1395nn(b) (Medicare), § 1396n(b) (Medicaid) (1982).
116. 695 F.2d 1151 (9th Cir. 1983); *see also* United States v. Hancock, 604 F.2d 999 (7th Cir.), *cert. denied*, 444 U.S. 991 (1979).
117. United States v. Ruttenberg, 625 F.2d 173 (7th Cir. 1980).
118. 42 U.S.C. § 1395nn.

LIABILITY OF THE HEALTHCARE INSTITUTION

During the 1940s and 1950s the doctrine that a private charitable corporation was immune from tort liability was abolished. Because the doctrine was originally developed by the courts as a common law rule, it was overturned by judicial cases on a state-by-state basis. The doctrine was discarded simply because the reasons for immunity no longer prevailed in a changing society.[1]

Some courts had originally adopted immunity because the assets of a charitable corporation constituted a trust fund available only to the beneficiaries and that trust would be violated by payment of tort claims. Others held that the beneficiaries of a charity impliedly waived their rights to sue in tort when accepting the benefits of charitable endeavor. Still others founded the rule simply on concepts of public policy, perhaps specifying that tort liability of an employer for the wrong committed by an employee would apply only to a profit-making enterprise.[2]

Whatever the rationale supporting charitable immunity, the reasons for the doctrine had evaporated by the 1950s. Certainly, the general public's perception of hospitals as not-for-profit, charitable organizations had changed. A hospital was no longer an almshouse. Insurance became available to cover costs of defense and to pay judgments resulting from personal injury litigation. The understanding grew that not-for-profit enterprises should be treated in the same manner as profit-making companies so far as third-party liability claims were concerned.

Following the decline of charitable immunity, healthcare became one of the most dramatically changing areas of personal injury law. This chapter will review the two legal theories of liability. The first of these is the doctrine of *respondeat superior*, which holds an employer liable to a third party who has been damaged by the tortious wrong of an employee committed within the scope of the latter's employment. The second theory of liability is characterized as *corporate liability* or *independent negligence*.

In the following discussion, attention will be called to the leading cases with an attempt to explain the reasons for each of the theories. The primary focus of the discussion is the private community hospital. Hospitals owned and operated by state or local government still enjoy immunity or partial immunity in some jurisdictions, although governmental immunity has been abrogated on a state-by-state basis similar to the fall of charitable immunity.

Liability Based on *Respondeat Superior*

Normally, the duty of an institutional provider of healthcare services is to possess and exercise, through its agents and employees, reasonable care practiced by similarly situated institutions in the same or similar communities.[3] There is the further rule that patients are entitled to such reasonable care and attention as their known condition requires. Some courts have extended the latter rule by saying that a healthcare organization must guard against conditions that it should have discovered by the exercise of reasonable care.[4] Accordingly, as a general matter, expert witness testimony is required to provide the jury with the legally expected standards of care. This is to say, to provide a breach of duty the plaintiff must normally introduce expert testimony regarding the practices of comparable institutions generally, at least when the particular case in litigation relates to the conduct of the institution's professional staff.[5] On the other hand, the testimony of expert witnesses may not be required when the conduct in question involves nonmedical or routine administrative care,[6] when a physician's order is violated,[7] or when the "common knowledge" rule is applicable.[8] Expert testimony is not required when laypersons by their common knowledge and experience are capable of determining that reasonable care was not exercised.

When liability is asserted on the basis of *respondeat superior*, there are essentially three questions:

1. Was a tort committed?
2. Was the person who committed the tort an agent or an employee of the defendant?
3. Was the tort committed within the scope of the agent's or employee's duties?

In short, the doctrine of *respondeat superior* simply states that an employer is liable to a third party for the tort that an employee has committed within the scope of employment. The employer answers for the employee's negligence but is not itself directly at fault. In this regard it differs from corporate liability. The employer in a *respondeat superior* case is not directly negligent, nor has the enterprise itself committed any personal, direct wrong to the third party. Rather, the justification for the theory in legal terms is the employer's right to control the means and methods of the employee's work. Presumably the imposition of liability will encourage the employer to develop and implement sound procedures for controlling employees' job performance.

In the final analysis the true basis for holding the employer vicariously liable is simply a matter of public policy: the employer is generally the entity with insurance coverage or with superior financial means of compensating for the damage caused by the employee's tort. Furthermore, an organization can only act through agents and employees; to hold the organization not liable for its individuals' actions would mean that the company could never be held responsible for decisions taken and acts committed in furtherance of institutional aims. Of course the employee who committed the tort can also be held individually and personally liable for the wrongful act or omission. Frequently both employer and employee are joined as defendants, although the employer-defendant is the primary target for recovery of damages because of its "deep pockets." Liability of the employer and employee is normally (unless abolished or modified by statute) joint and several, meaning that a successful plaintiff may collect the judgment in whole from one or in part from each of the defendants. If the plaintiff collects the judgment in whole or in part from an employer, the latter has a right of indemnification from the employee who committed the tort. In practice, employers rarely seek indemnification from their employees, although when the employer and employee are insured against liability by different insurance carriers there is incentive to do so.[9]

The alleged tort in a *respondeat superior* case may be an intentional tort (for example, assault and battery, false imprisonment, or an invasion of privacy) or it may be the tort of negligence. In most hospital liability cases negligence will be alleged. Negligence is the breach of a duty to conform to prevailing standards of care established to protect others against an unreasonable risk of harm. Breach of such a duty, if it is the proximate cause of damage to another, results in liability. Negligence can be an affirmative act or the failure to act when one should have acted.

Because the basis of the *respondeat superior* theory is the employer's right to control the means and methods of the employee's work, it follows logically that the employer is not liable vicariously for the tort or the negligence of an independent contractor. By definition an independent contractor is one who has sole control over the means and methods of the work to be accomplished, although the person who employs, hires, or appoints a contractor retains the right of control and power of approval over the final result of the work. (For example, if a person hires an independent contractor to build a house, the homeowner retains the right to determine specifications of the construction and the power to approve the final result.)

There are some long-standing and well-recognized exceptions to the general rule that one who engages an independent contractor is not liable to a third party for the independent contractor's tort. First, some duties of certain employers are *nondelegable,* and the employer may be liable vicariously despite the exercise of reasonable care. These nondelegable duties may be established either by statutes or by common law. In essence, where an enterprise owes duties to the public or the community at large, the performance of the duty cannot be delegated to an independent contractor. For example, the duty of a public or common carrier to exercise reasonable care in the transport of passengers is nondelegable.[10] Likewise the duty of a city to repair streets or other public facilities is nondelegable.[11] A third example is that of a landowner to refrain from obstructing an adjoining public way.[12]

A second exception to the general rule of nonliability is where the work to be performed by the independent contractor is inherently dangerous. Although the definition of "inherently dangerous" is not settled and is subject to interpretation on a case-by-case basis, the concept essentially means that the activity is dangerous to others even if all reasonable care is exercised. Examples are blasting with dynamite, use of fireworks, crop dusting, and excavations adjoining a public highway.[13] To date, medical or hospital care has not been considered an inherently dangerous activity.

In the field of hospital liability, a physician in private practice who is a member of the medical staff with certain delineated privileges has generally been considered an independent contractor. Accordingly, the hospital has not been liable to the third-party patient for the malpractice or negligence of the physician. For example, in the New Mexico case of *Cooper v. Curry*, suit was brought against both the hospital and a private surgeon.[14] Cataract surgery on both eyes during a single hospitalization resulted in the plaintiff's blindness. The patient had selected the surgeon, with whom she had discussed the need for cataract surgery prior to hospitalization. She had specifically requested that the surgical procedures be done on both eyes during the same hospital stay. Following the untoward results the plaintiff alleged, among other things, that the physician had failed to inform her adequately of the risks involved in the surgery and that the hospital had a duty to obtain her informed consent prior to the surgery. The majority of the court held that if the doctor had failed to inform the patient properly of the risks of the surgery, the negligence, if any, was the doctor's and the hospital was not liable for the tort or for the negligence of nonemployed physicians. A jury verdict finding the hospital not vicariously liable, pursuant to instructions from the court that the hospital was not liable for the negligence of an independent contractor, was affirmed on appeal.

In *Cooper* the plaintiff also alleged that the hospital could be liable on the theory that the institution and the doctor were engaged in a joint venture. When two or more persons are engaged in a joint enterprise, each is vicariously responsible for the wrong committed by the other(s) within the scope of the venture. The liability in such circumstances is the same as in a business or professional partnership. The trial judge in *Cooper*, however, rejected the plaintiff's requested instructions to the jury relative to the joint venture theory, and this ruling was upheld on appeal. The essential elements of a joint venture are lacking in the traditional hospital-doctor relationship—namely, a joint, community proprietary interest in the activity involved and a mutual right of control.

There are other cases recognizing a physician as an independent contractor.[15] In *Heins v. Synkonis*, a Michigan case, the hospital was not liable when the privately employed physician simply saw the patient in the hospital and the hospital merely provided facilities for the doctor's outpatient clinic.[16] The absence of either an actual or an apparent employment relationship resulted in the conclusion that the hospital was not liable for the alleged negligence of the doctor.

Various factors have, however, affected the independent contractor doctrine, and thus fewer situations now justify application of the defense. First, changing factual circumstances with respect to medical practice and hospital services have encouraged courts to expand the doctrine of *respondeat superior* by finding an employment relationship in situations in which none would have been found previously. Among these changing circumstances are the following. To an increasing extent patients no longer select their own private physician; rather, the hospital, an employer, or some other third party furnishes or provides a doctor. Patients use the hospital emergency room more frequently; it is not uncommon for a private physician to tell the patient to go to the emergency room on weekends or whenever the doctor is off duty. Healthcare institutions have increased the number of employed physicians on their staffs and in their clinics. Medical practice has become increasingly institutionalized and specialized. Finally, contracts with hospital-based specialists have dramatically increased in number and frequency. As these developments occur, *respondeat superior* expands. As *respondeat superior* expands, the availability of the independent contractor defense declines.

The Decline of Independent Contractor Status: Payment of Salary

The payment of a salary or wage to a physician employee will justify the imposition of vicarious liability on the hospital employer pursuant to the doctrine of *respondeat superior*. Even a physician on a part-time salary will be considered an employee of the institution. In *Niles v. City of San Rafael,* a part-time salaried director of a hospital pediatrics department was negligent in making only a cursory examination of a head injury and in sending the patient home with incomplete instructions for continued observation of the condition.[17] The doctor's negligence resulted in delayed diagnosis of intracranial bleeding, resulting in irreparable brain damage. Noteworthy is the fact that before being summoned to examine the plaintiff, the physician was in the hospital emergency room seeing a *private* patient and thus was not at the time serving in the *employee* role (director of the pediatrics department). Although it is not fully discussed in the court opinion, one apparent basis for finding the hospital liable was the fact that the physician was a part-time employee. To the same effect is the ruling in *James v. Holder*, where a private practicing physician was also a part-time employee and had seen a patient in the hospital in the role of employee. The hospital was held vicariously liable for the doctor's negligence.[18]

The hospital will also be liable for the negligence of interns, residents, and nurses performing their customary functions within and on behalf of the institution. As long ago as 1957 the New York Court of Appeals, in the landmark case of *Bing v. Thunig*, eliminated the distinction between administrative and medical acts, thereby settling the controversy over whether the professional status of an employee prevented the imposition of vicarious liability.[19] The frequently repeated quotation from *Bing* reads:

> The conception that the hospital does not undertake to treat the patient, does not undertake to act through its doctors and nurses, but undertakes instead simply to procure them to act upon their own responsibility, no longer reflects the fact. Present day hospitals, as their manner of operation plainly demonstrates, do far more than furnish facilities for treatment. They regularly employ on a salary basis a large staff of physicians, nurses and interns, as well as administrative and manual workers, and they charge patients for medical care and treatment, collecting for such services, if necessary, by legal action. Certainly, the person who avails himself of "hospital facilities" expects that the hospital will attempt to cure him, not that its nurses or other employees will act on their own responsibility.[20]

Both administrative and medical authorities of teaching hospitals must be particularly alert to the duties owed patients with respect to the role of resident physicians and interns. Clearly these persons are employees, and the hospital is liable for negligent acts committed within the scope of their employment.[21]

The Doctrine of Apparent Agency

Healthcare organizations frequently enter into contracts with medical specialists such as anesthesiologists, radiologists, pathologists, and specialists in emergency medicine, nuclear medicine, and other clinical specialties. The contract *for* service (akin to independent contractor status) is to be distinguished from an employment agreement or a contract *of* service. The contract for service may be an exclusive arrangement, thereby excluding from the hospital staff other qualified applicants practicing in the same specialty. It may also recite that the physician specialists are independent contractors, thereby attempting to establish that the hospital will not be liable to the patient for its tortious conduct. The document may further state that, if the hospital is ever held liable to a third party, full indemnity will be provided to the hospital by the physicians.

Where physicians are not, in fact, employed on a contract *of* service, hospitals have frequently asserted the defense of independent contractor in cases of alleged liability arising from the professional practice of the specialists. Generally this defense has not been successful because of expansion of the doctrine of *apparent agency* (sometimes termed "ostensible agency") or, under certain facts, *agency by estoppel*.[22] The essential elements of an apparent agency or an agency by estoppel are these:

- patients have been invited by the hospital to use the services of the medical specialists—indeed in many circumstances the patient has no choice but to use the specialists furnished by the hospital;

- a full-service hospital holds itself out as providing the complete range of medical care including all of the generally recognized specialties;
- patients rely on these representations; and
- this reliance justifiably permits them to conclude that the specialists are, in fact, employees or an integral part of the hospital.

Accordingly, it has frequently been ruled judicial error to grant a summary judgment in favor of a hospital on the basis that an allegedly negligent specialist was an independent contractor. The matter is often a question for the jury as to whether the patient was justified in "looking to" the hospital to provide treatment.

Two Delaware cases illustrate these principles. In *Vanaman v. Milford Memorial Hospital,* a private physician was on call to provide emergency service.[23] The court held that it was for the jury to decide whether the allegedly negligent doctor treated the patient in a private capacity or while fulfilling the hospital function of providing emergency care to the public. The hospital could be liable for the doctor's negligence if it represented the physician as its employee and the patient justifiably relied on the representation. To the same effect is *Schagrin v. Wilmington Medical Center,* where it was held proper to deny the hospital's motion for summary judgment.[24] A medical partnership staffing an emergency room may be an agent of the hospital and not an independent contractor depending on the degree of hospital control, the methods of paying the doctors, and the degree of patients' reliance on the hospital compared with their reliance on the physicians.[25]

Similarly, in *Hannola v. City of Lakewood* an Ohio appellate court provided two reasons for finding agency by estoppel, holding that the hospital could be liable for the malpractice of a physician member of an independent foundation operating an emergency room, regardless of any contractual arrangements: first, the hospital held itself out to the public as providing emergency care; second, the hospital governing body had control over appointments of physicians employed by the foundation.[26] In addition the hospital monitored the quality of care provided and had the power to revoke the privileges of individual emergency room doctors for justifiable cause.[27] Thus a hospital or other corporate institution cannot contractually insulate itself from liability to a patient by providing in its agreement with the independent specialist that the hospital will not be liable for their negligence. In fact, with increasing frequency the courts are inclined in these circumstances to find the hospital liable under principles of vicarious liability.

In *Beeck v. Tucson General Hospital* an Arizona court forthrightly held that there was an employment relationship between a hospital and a group of radiologists when:

- there was an exclusive arrangement for radiological services;
- the doctors were paid a given percentage of the department's gross revenue;

- the hospital owned the equipment and provided employed technicians;
- the hospital exercised control over the hours of work and vacation periods for the physicians; and
- the hospital reviewed professional standards of the department via a peer review evaluation process.[28]

It is significant that the court did not find it necessary to consider apparent agency or agency by estoppel in reaching its decision. Rather, it was simply willing to find an employment relationship based on the facts, even though there was no payment of a salary or a wage to the physicians.

As a Michigan case illustrates, the doctrines of apparent agency and agency by estoppel may be applied even if the allegedly negligent physician is not a medical specialist with an exclusive contract to perform a designated hospital service. In *Grewe v. Mt. Clemens General Hospital*, the plaintiff was taken to the hospital after suffering a severe electrical shock.[29] He was first seen by Dr. Gerald Hoffman, an internist. Dr. Hoffman consulted with Dr. Fagen, an orthopedic surgeon, who diagnosed a dislocated right shoulder. Dr. Fagen in turn designated an orthopedic resident to reduce the dislocation. The reduction was unsuccessful and a specialist in internal medicine was summoned to assist. Allegedly he did not view x-rays prior to his treatment of the patient, and his attempts to reduce the dislocation were also unsuccessful. Subsequently, the plaintiff claimed to have suffered a brachial plexus injury and fracture. Surgery was necessary to remove bone fragments.

The Supreme Court of Michigan held that if the "patient looked to the hospital to provide him with treatment," an agency by estoppel could be established, and it upheld a jury verdict in favor of the patient. The jury had found that the plaintiff had no previous physician-patient relationship with Dr. Katzowitz or the other physicians outside of the hospital setting; there was nothing to put the patient on notice that Dr. Katzowitz was an independent contractor distinct from being an employee of the hospital; the plaintiff had gone to the hospital expecting to be treated there; and accordingly all the physicians were ostensible agents of the hospital. Because the patient had not personally selected the physicians, he relied on the institution to provide care. Under the factual circumstances the hospital was estopped to deny the absence of an employment relationship with the physicians.[30]

It is therefore appropriate to conclude that the doctrines of apparent agency and agency by estoppel have contributed substantially to the demise of the independent contractor defense for the hospital. To be noted is that in *Grewe, Capan,* and similar cases the allegedly negligent doctor was neither an employee of the hospital nor the plaintiff's personal physician. The patients were entitled to jury trials on the issues of whether they had relied on the hospital to furnish care rather than on privately selected physicians and whether the hospital had held out the doctors as ostensible employees of the hospital by furnishing their services in the treatment of emergencies arising within the hospital.[31]

Decline of the Captain-of-the-Ship and Borrowed-Servant Doctrines

In recent years the courts have restricted the applicability of the "captain of the ship" and "borrowed servant" doctrines, thus further expanding hospital liability. The captain-of-the-ship doctrine was significant in a day when charitable hospitals were immune from tort liability. The concept presumed that the chief surgeon was the "captain of the ship" during surgery and therefore was vicariously liable for the negligence of any person serving as a member of the surgical team.[32]

In any vicarious liability case, the basis for liability is one's right of control over the negligent activities of another. As the number of persons on surgical teams has grown in size, and as anesthesiologists, nurses, surgical assistants, and others have been increasingly recognized as performing independent functions, the courts have realized that it is not sound legal doctrine to impose vicarious liability on the chief surgeon for the negligent acts of all surgical team members.

Numerous cases involving the miscount of surgical sponges or instruments illustrate this trend. In *Tonsic v. Wagner* the trial court applied the captain-of-the-ship doctrine to hold the surgeon liable when neither the scrub nurse, a circulating nurse, nor an intern counted the surgical instruments at the conclusion of a colectomy.[33] As a result a Kelly clamp was not removed from the patient. The court refused to permit the jury to consider whether the hospital could be liable for the alleged negligence of hospital personnel pursuant to the doctrine of *respondeat superior*. Accordingly, the jury returned the verdict against the surgeon. The trial judge felt constrained to follow the precedent set by the oft-cited Pennsylvania case of *McConnell v. Williams*, in which the captain-of-the-ship doctrine was articulated in 1949.[34] Despite this precedent, the trial judge's decision was reversed by the Pennsylvania Supreme Court, which noted that the law of agency generally applicable in business associations should likewise apply to hospitals and surgeons. Moreover, a negligent party may be the servant or the employee of two masters simultaneously even though the masters are not joint employers. In such situations both masters may be liable.[35] Accordingly, the plaintiff was entitled to a new trial in her suit against the hospital. It is a question for the jury whether the surgeon or the hospital was the sole controlling master, or whether there was joint control justifying imposition of liability on both the surgeon and the hospital for the negligent act of a member of the surgical team.

Similar facts were involved in *Sprager v. Worley Hospital*, where there was a failure to remove a surgical sponge from the patient.[36] In a suit against both the surgeon and the hospital the jury found that the surgeon was not personally negligent in failing to locate and remove the sponge. The jury further found that the surgical nurses were negligent in making an incorrect count of the sponges. Nevertheless, it refused to hold the defendant surgeon vicariously liable for the negligence of the nurses. A judgment was rendered against the hospital only. On appeal to the intermediate appellate court, this judgment was reversed and a judgment against the surgeon, on the basis of the captain-of-the-ship doctrine, was entered. On further appeal the Texas Supreme Court specifically disapproved the captain-of-the-ship doctrine and held that the determining factor was how much control the doctor actually had over nurses' activities. At a new hearing the original jury decision was reinstated.[37] In remanding the case for reconsideration the Texas Supreme Court pointed out that the nurses had been hired by the hospital, were assigned to surgery by the hospital, and were therefore the general agents of the hospital.

The mere fact that a nurse or other hospital employee carries out and executes the order of an attending physician does not establish that the employee is a borrowed servant of the doctor.[38] Thus in one case nurses in the intensive care unit of a hospital were not held to be servants of the surgeon whose orders they were carrying out.[39] And in another case x-ray technicians were not held to be employees of the physician under similar circumstances.[40] In these situations the doctor does not possess the actual right of control over the nurse or other professional who executes the orders for patient care, especially when the order is not executed in the presence of the physician.

The trend toward imposing vicarious liability on the hospital has been observable for nearly four decades.[41] When medical care is provided by a highly specialized, sophisticated team of professional individuals all working within an institutional setting, it is frequently difficult to determine who is exercising direct control over whom at any given time. When such difficulty in determination arises, it is only natural and logical that ultimate liability be placed on the corporate institution and not on the private physician.

The Doctrine of Corporate Negligence

Under the doctrine of *corporate negligence* it is the hospital itself as an entity that is negligent. This liability is not vicarious as it is under the doctrine of *respondeat superior*. Rather, it attaches directly to the corporation as a form of institutional or independent negligence. In other words, the hospital owes a defined legal duty directly to the patient, and this duty is not delegable to the medical staff or other personnel. A Connecticut court once defined corporate negligence in these words: "Corporate negligence is the failure of those entrusted with the task of providing accommodations and facilities necessary to carry out the charitable purpose of the corporation to follow in a given situation the established standard of conduct to which the corporation should conform."[42]

The primary legal question is this: What direct duties does the health-care organization owe the patient or other third party? To answer this query one must consider the corporate purposes of a community hospital or health system, whether owned and operated by a unit of government or by a private corporation. Is its role simply to furnish physical facilities and accommodations wherein private physicians care for and treat their patients? Or is the role of the modern healthcare organization broader in purpose? If a hospital is considered to be nothing more than a doctor's workshop, then institutional or corporate duties to the patient can justifiably be quite narrow and limited in scope. On the other hand, organizations with broader purposes and functions can be expected to have broader legal duties. As previously discussed, hospitals and health systems do more than provide physical facilities and accommodations for the practice of medicine. They are the focus for arranging, furnishing, and providing the community with an entire range of personal healthcare—preventative and curative, outpatient as well as inpatient. Hence the judicial and statutory duties and obligations of the institution have expanded in recent years.

Prior to the mid-1960s courts generally limited the corporate duties of hospitals to three arenas: exercise of reasonable, ordinary care with respect to the selection and retention of employees, the maintenance of buildings and grounds, and the maintenance and selection of hospital equipment.

Negligence in the maintenance of equipment may be premised on the continued use of equipment in the face of known or discoverable defects. Liability may also arise from misuse of the equipment[43] or negligent selection for the purpose intended.[44] The duty of reasonable care regarding the use of equipment and selection for an intended purpose also includes a duty to inspect the equipment systematically and regularly before use.[45] Rules and regulations of licensing authorities, accreditation standards, and instructional manuals supplied by manufacturers for the maintenance of equipment can be admitted at trial as evidence of expected standards of care. Failure on the part of hospital and medical personnel to comply with such standards would constitute evidence of breach of duty for the jury to consider.

It must also be kept in mind that under negligence theories a physician and, by analogy, hospitals or other institutional providers of care have a duty to warn a patient of known risks when a patient is furnished with a medical device. The duty to inform of risks that are known or should have been known at the time the device was furnished is embraced within the duty to obtain the informed consent of the patient. Moreover, courts are now extending the duty of the provider to inform patients of risks or dangers that become known after the device is furnished. Thus, if a heart pacemaker is implanted in a patient and the particular device is later determined by the manufacturer or the federal Food and Drug Administration to be defective and then recalled, there is a duty on the part of the physician who implanted the device to notify the patient if the doctor knew or should have known of the recall.

With regard to the availability of equipment and services, the rule has been that there is no duty on the part of a hospital to possess the newest and most modern equipment available on the market. Accordingly, in a Georgia case, *Emory University v. Porter*, it was proper to dismiss an action alleging that an infant was burned by an unshielded light bulb in an incubator not equipped with a thermostatic heat control.[46] There was no allegation that the incubator in use was defective or unfit for the purposes intended. Thus, as long as older models of such equipment were still in general use by similarly situated hospitals, there was no breach of duty. In the same fashion, a hospital's failure to have a cryostat for cutting tissue in its pathology department was not held to constitute negligence.[47] In place of an allegedly more sophisticated cryostat, which could cut thinner sections of tissue for more accurate diagnoses, the hospital used a freezing microtome process. There was no expert testimony to the effect that the microtome was an unsatisfactory instrument under the circumstances.

There is, however, a duty on the part of the institution to have available the usual and customary equipment and staff for any purpose, procedure, or service that the hospital undertakes to render. Accordingly, the failure to sterilize hypodermic needles by steam under pressure has been found to form the basis of liability.[48] Further, in *Garcia v. Memorial Hospital* a cause of action was stated against a hospital that did not have a pediatric endotracheal tube in the emergency room that might have saved a child's life.[49] The hospital operated an emergency room and held itself out as providing a full range of emergency services. In such circumstances it was held to be usual and customary to have a pediatric endotracheal tube available.

A third example of breach of duty to have proper and appropriate equipment available is provided by a Pennsylvania hospital that was found liable when its emergency room electrocardiograph became inoperative and no backup instrument was available.[50] An emergency patient then had to be given an electrocardiogram in another location, where he died. The court ruled that the issue of proximate cause was for the jury to determine.

By analogy then, if equipment is readily available, dependable, and useful, it might well be found to be a breach of the standard of care for a hospital to fail to have such equipment as computers, MRI machines, fetal monitoring equipment, and other new technology for diagnosis and treatment.[51] Of course, such a trend in the common law would contravene efforts to plan and rationalize facilities in the interests of containing costs of healthcare. A balance must be found by each community between costs of new, sophisticated equipment and adequate protection of the patient.

In part at least, the balance may be found by recognizing that liability would result if a hospital that did not have the equipment, facilities, and personnel reasonably necessary to treat the patient's case adequately failed to transfer or refer a patient to another center where adequate care could be provided. For example, in *Carrasco v. Bankoff*[52] a California hospital was liable when it failed to transfer a patient with third-degree burns; the defendant hospital did not have facilities for the "open method" of treating burns and the skin grafting the plaintiff's condition required. Noteworthy is the fact that liability was not based solely on the absence of facilities to treat third-degree burns. Rather, the fault of the hospital and its staff was premised on the failure to transfer the patient.

With regard to the duty of reasonable care in selecting and retaining employees, healthcare organizations have a corporate responsibility to exercise reasonable care in selecting and retaining employees. Accordingly, where the hospital violates its duty of reasonable care in the selection of employees, there can be liability to the patient or other third party who is injured as a result. Illustrating the breach of this duty is the Texas case of *Wilson N. Jones Memorial Hospital v. Davis.*[53] There the hospital's failure to investigate the background and references supplied by an applicant for the position of orderly resulted in an award of both compensatory and punitive damages to the patient. The hospital's normal procedure in hiring employees was to obtain four employment references and three personal references. Established policy was to verify at least one of the employment references and one of the personal references before hiring the applicant. In this case, the hospital's associate director of nursing employed the applicant as an orderly without checking or verifying any of the references on file. The reason later given for this action was that the hospital was confronted at the time with a critical need for orderlies. After the individual began work, an inquiry was directed to one of the employment references, which verified that the orderly had worked for them for approximately four months as a redress/rework operator. The former employer did not answer any of the other questions asked on the reference form, and the hospital failed to follow up on the matter. The applicant also represented that he had received his training as an orderly while in the U.S. Navy. No inquiry was sent to the Navy by the defendant for the stated reason that in such matters the hospital had unsatisfactory cooperation with the armed services in the past. Nevertheless, the plaintiff, who requested information from the Navy, promptly learned that the orderly had been expelled from the Navy Medical Corps School after a single month's training, that he had been diagnosed as having a serious drug problem, and that he possessed a criminal record.

At the time of applying for the position of orderly the applicant also listed three personal references, all of whom were shown to have had local telephone numbers and two of whom were residents in the same city as the hospital. There was only a single attempt by the hospital to reach one of these references, and this was unsuccessful.

Soon after employment by the hospital the orderly attempted to remove a Foley catheter from the patient's bladder without first deflating the bulb. This attempt resulted in serious injuries to the plaintiff. The hospital was held liable for both compensatory and punitive damages. The hospital's critical need for orderlies at the time did not justify the failure to exercise reasonable care in the selection of the employee. Moreover, the punitive damages awarded in the case were a result of "an entire want of care" and "conscious indifference to the rights, welfare, and safety of the patients in the hospital."

Violation of Rules and Failure to Adopt Rules as Corporate Negligence

Hospital bylaws, rules and regulations, and the accreditation standards of the Joint Commission on Accreditation of Healthcare Organizations are admissible in evidence at trial.[54] If violation of a hospital rule is the proximate cause of a plaintiff's damage, then liability can be premised on the fact that the rule provides evidence of an expected standard of care. Normally violation of a rule or written standard does not automatically constitute negligence, although it is possible for a court to find liability as a matter of law in such an instance. For example, in *Pederson v. Dumouchel* a hospital was liable as a matter of law when it permitted nonemergency dental surgery to be performed under a general anesthetic without the presence and supervision of a medical doctor in violation of a rule of hospital policy.[55]

Typically, however, the existence of a rule and evidence of its breach will be submitted to the jury as a factual matter. As would be expected, evidence that a rule has been violated is often persuasive in the minds of jurors. For example, a jury verdict for the plaintiff was affirmed in *Burks v. Christ Hospital,* holding that bed siderails be raised if the patient was restless, obese, or under sedation unless the attending physician had issued an order to the contrary.[56] The plaintiff sustained injuries when he fell from bed, and the jury was entitled to consider the violation of promulgated hospital standards as evidence of negligence.

It is not always clear from either the pleadings or court opinion whether these types of cases are founded on a theory of *respondeat superior* or corporate negligence. In *Polonsky v. Union Hospital* the hospital's policy required that bedrails be raised if patients were disoriented.[57] There, an 80-year-old patient was given Dalmane, a medication for aiding sleep. The drug package contained a warning that elderly patients might experience dizziness as a result of taking the drug. Nevertheless, the siderails were not raised, and when the patient climbed from the bed a fall resulted in injuries. The jury was permitted to infer that the nurse was negligent in failing to raise the siderails even though the plaintiff did not present any expert testimony with respect to professional nursing standards in this situation.

Another basis on which to predicate corporate liability is the violation of hospital licensure rules and regulations. In *Leroy Duchett v. North Detroit General Hospital* the patient's medical record failed to mention daily visits by a physician.[58] Yet a rule of licensure provided that all persons admitted to the hospital must be under the continuing daily care of a physician. The rule was admissible, and liability could follow if proximate cause of injury were established. An earlier Michigan case similarly noted that an administrative regulation requiring that hospitals have written policies regarding medical consultations and that consultations be recorded was intended to protect hospitalized patients.[59] Accordingly, the plaintiff was entitled to have the jury instructed on the purpose of this rule.

The failure to have and implement hospital rules professionally recognized as necessary for patients' safety may constitute corporate negligence. There was liability in *Habuda v. Trustees of Rex Hospital,* where the hospital had inadequate rules relating to the handling, storage, and administration of medications.[60] A similar decision was rendered in Indiana, where the state supreme court upheld a jury verdict for the plaintiff, who had been injected with a fluid labeled Novocaine when in fact the label was erroneous.[61] The court noted that the failure to implement proper instrumentalities and controls in the preparation, storage, and dispensation of medications constituted negligence. In another case a Texas hospital was held liable for failing to employ a licensed pharmacist in violation of standards established by the Joint Commission on Accreditation of Healthcare Organizations and the American Hospital Association.[62] Similarly, when a Michigan hospital failed to maintain adequate records regarding the medical history of prospective cornea donors for transplant, thereby violating professional standards regarding acceptability of donated cadavers, there was liability based on a theory of independent or corporate negligence.[63]

Another variation of corporate neglect is a hospital's failure to have and to implement adequate rules for the communication of vital information on patient care to others who are or will be responsible for treatment of the patient. For example, in *Keene v. Methodist Hospital* an injured patient was seen by a physician on duty in a hospital emergency room on Christmas Eve and sent home following the taking of x-rays.[64] Early Christmas morning the radiologist detected a possible skull fracture and suggested further x-ray studies. The physician dictated a tentative diagnosis and recommendations into a mechanical dictating device without further communication to the attending physician, the patient, or hospital administrators. Apparently as a result of the Christmas holiday the dictation was not transcribed for two days. During this period the patient lost consciousness, was returned to the hospital for emergency surgery, and died as a result of a fractured skull and hemorrhage. On presentation of evidence that the patient's life could have been saved by more timely and appropriate care, the hospital was held liable as a corporate institution for its failure to transmit the radiologist's report promptly to the treating physician or, in his absence, to hospital administrators. This factual situation is characterized properly as a corporate negligence because it is the duty of the hospital to have a system for prompt transcription of dictated communications as a component of its responsibility for maintenance and transmission of the patient's medical record.

Thus the failure to have proper rules, regulations, or systems in place when indicated by recognized professional standards, as well as the violation of such rules or established hospital policies can result in liability.[65] Sometimes this liability will be predicated on the theory of corporate negligence, particularly where the failure relates to administrative responsibility for patient care. In other factual contexts a failure to act or an omission on the part of a hospital employee will be indicative of a *respondeat superior* case. This is the liability theory of choice whenever the omission is recognized as a violation of generally recognized standards of practice by a healthcare professional. Nevertheless, because it is becoming increasingly difficult to distinguish between administrative responsibility and individual responsibility for patient care in an institutional setting, it is correspondingly difficult to determine whether the applicable legal theory is one of corporate negligence or *respondeat superior*. Just as in *Bing v. Thunig*,[66] which in 1957 eliminated any distinction between the administrative and professional negligence of nurses for the purposes of *respondeat superior*, the distinction between the vicarious liability (*respondeat superior*) and direct liability (corporate negligence) of hospitals and other institutional providers has nearly disappeared for all practical purposes.

In many circumstances the distinction is not at all clear, and as hospitals and other institutions assume a more active role in coordinating and arranging for patient care, the lines of demarcation blur even further. In any event, hospital rules, standards of accreditation, and licensure regulations must be realistic, known to all affected persons, capable of implementation, and consistently enforced. Further, the rules must be regularly and systematically reviewed; if they are not realistic and workable, then they should be eliminated.

Negligence in Selection and Retention of Medical Staff

Judicial and statutory law on a state-by-state basis now recognizes that a corporate healthcare institution has a duty to its patients to exercise reasonable care in the selection and retention of medical staff. The corporation may be liable if it knows or should have known that an individual physician was not competent to perform the permitted clinical procedures. This doctrine began to emerge as the result of the 1965 landmark case of *Darling v. Charleston Community Memorial Hospital*.[67] In that litigation the Illinois Supreme Court held that a hospital could be liable if nurse employees failed to notify medical and hospital administrators when they knew that a patient was receiving inadequate medical care from a private physician (*respondeat superior*), or if the hospital failed to review and monitor treatment rendered to the patient by the private physician and failed to enforce the medical staff bylaws requiring attending physicians to obtain medical consultation in certain cases (corporate negligence). The private physician was a general practitioner who had been permitted by the hospital to practice orthopedic medicine and whose clinical competence had not been reviewed during more than three decades of practice.

Significantly, *Darling* also established that standards set forth in medical staff bylaws, as well as those promulgated by the Joint Commission on Accreditation of Healthcare Organizations and by state licensing authorities, may be considered by the jury in determining negligence. The then relevant accreditation standards and hospital licensing regulations required a hospital to have an organized medical staff accountable to the governing board for the quality of clinical practice of individual physicians granted hospital privileges.

Moreover, the case abolished the "locality rule" regarding the standards of care to which a hospital must adhere. In short, the hospital could no longer fully defend itself by asserting that other local hospitals did not enforce their medical staff bylaws or review the professional clinical performance of members of the medical staff.

The Illinois court rejected the view that a hospital undertakes simply to procure nurses and doctors to act on their own responsibility. Such a role no longer reflects current hospital management. In fact, a hospital undertakes to treat the patient and to act through its nurses and doctors, even if the latter are not employees.[68] Following the *Darling* decision, one commentator wrote:

> Even in the absence of an employer-employee . . . relationship . . . there now appears to be some chance . . . to impose liability on the hospital on the theory of *independent negligence* in failing to review, supervise, or consult about, the treatment given by the physician directly in charge, if the situation indicates that the hospital had the opportunity for such review but failed to exercise it, or that its servants (usually nurses or residents) were negligent in failing to call the attention of the proper hospital authorities to the impropriety or inadequacy of the treatment being given [emphasis added.][69]

Case law has now established that hospital administration and medical staff have a joint role with respect to the clinical performance of individual practitioners. The governing body of the hospital has the responsibility to adopt corporate and medical staff bylaws providing for an organized medical staff accountable to the board for a systematic process of ensuring the credentials of the medical staff. Medical staff appointments, delineation of privileges on an individual basis, and reappointments are made by the governing body on receiving appropriate recommendations from duly constituted medical staff committees. In ruling on these recommendations, the board must be satisfied that the peer review process is in fact working and must avoid simply rubber-stamping recommendations that are submitted by medical staff. The responsibility of the governing body is nondelegable; the board does, however, delegate to medical staff the authority to implement the credentialing process and to prepare recommendations for appointments and reappointments to staff. To carry out its role properly the board should have some physicians as voting members. Moreover, medical staff committees engaged in the review could well benefit from having lay representatives, at least as liaison agents.

Since 1965, a number of other leading cases have recognized the corporate duty of a hospital to exercise reasonable care in the selection and retention of medical staff. A 1971 Georgia case, *Joiner v. Mitchell County Hospital Authority*, held that members of the medical staff making recommendations to the governing body of the hospital for appointment of physicians were agents of the hospital.[70] In considering these recommendations the governing body must act in good faith and with reasonable care when it makes appointments to staff.[71] A similar institutional duty was recognized by Nevada's supreme court in a medical staff privileges case entitled *Moore v. Board of Trustees of Carson-Tahoe Hospital*.[72] There the court stated:

> Today, in response to demands of the public, the hospital is becoming a community health center. The purpose of the community hospital is to provide patient care of the highest possible quality. To implement this duty of providing competent medical care to the patients, it is the responsibility of the institution to create a workable system whereby the medical staff of the hospital continually reviews and evaluates the quality of care being rendered within the institution. The staff must be organized with the proper structure to carry out the role delegated to it by the governing body. All powers of the medical staff flow from the board of trustees, and the staff must be held accountable for its control of quality. . . . The role of the hospital vis-à-vis the community is changing rapidly. The hospital's role is no longer limited to the furnishing of physical facilities and equipment where a physician treats his private patients and practices his profession in his own individualized manner. . . . licensing [of physicians], *per se*, furnishes no continuing control with respect to a physician's professional competence and therefore does not assure the public of quality patient care. The protection of the public must come from some other authority, and that in this case in the Hospital Board of Trustees. The Board, of course, may not act arbitrarily or unreasonably in such cases. The Board's actions must be predicated upon a reasonable standard.[73]

In *Gonzales v. Nork*, an unsuccessful and allegedly unnecessary laminectomy and spinal fusion was performed by Dr. Nork on a 27-year-old man who had been injured in an automobile accident.[74] Various complications developed that substantially reduced the plaintiff's life expectancy. Evidence was presented showing that the surgeon had performed more than three dozen similar operations that were either negligently done or unnecessary. The trial court issued a lengthy opinion recognizing that the hospital owed a duty of care to the patient with respect to the delineation of surgical privileges extended to private surgeons. The court stated forcefully that this duty included the obligation to protect the patient from acts of malpractice by an independently retained doctor if the hospital knew or should have known that such acts were likely to occur. Even though the hospital had no actual knowledge of Dr. Nork's propensity to commit malpractice, its demonstrated lack of a workable system for acquiring such knowledge justified a finding of negligence. Following a verdict against both the surgeon and the hospital, the hospital settled the claim before final judgment. There was accordingly no appeal of the verdict against the hospital.

A landmark Wisconsin case took a particularly enlightened view of the role of a hospital in its relations with the medical staff. In *Johnson v. Misericordia Community Hospital* the plaintiff alleged that the hospital was negligent in granting orthopedic surgical privileges to Dr. Salinsky.[75] During surgery to remove a pin fragment from the patient's right hip, the doctor severed the femoral artery and nerve, causing permanent paralysis of the right thigh. The plaintiff settled his malpractice claim against the physician for $140,000 and then proceeded to trial in a suit against the hospital. The Wisconsin Supreme Court affirmed a jury verdict for the plaintiff on the basis that the hospital had failed to inquire into the physician's professional background and qualifications prior to granting a staff appointment. Further, the hospital had failed to adhere to its own bylaw provisions and to Wisconsin statutes pertaining to medical credentialing. The court held that it was proper for the trial judge to instruct the jury that "a hospital has a duty to exercise due care in the selection of its medical staff."[76]

Important facts of the case follow. When Dr. Salinsky had earlier filed an application for a medical staff appointment at Misericordia Community Hospital, the hospital was licensed as a general hospital although the institution was not accredited by the Joint Commission. On the application form the physician claimed to be an active staff member of Doctors Hospital in Milwaukee with full orthopedic surgical privileges. He further claimed membership on the consulting staff at two other area hospitals and that his privileges at these, and for that matter any other institutions, had never been suspended, revoked, or reduced. The application was incomplete, however, to the extent that the doctor failed to answer questions relating to his malpractice insurance coverage and claims experience. He represented in his application that he was requesting privileges only to the extent that he was qualified by certification and granted the hospital permission to contact his malpractice insurance company and all hospitals with which he had been associated for information relative to his professional, moral, and ethical qualifications.

In actuality, Doctors Hospital had severely restricted Dr. Salinsky's surgical privileges less than two months before he filed his application with the defendant hospital. Two years earlier, St. Anthony Hospital had denied the physician all privileges. Eight years prior to that, Mt. Sinai Hospital had restricted Dr. Salinsky's surgical activities and transferred him to courtesy staff. Finally, there was no record of his consulting status at the two hospitals Dr. Salinsky named as having granted that privilege. Moreover, he was neither board certified nor board eligible in orthopedic surgery. In addition, had the hospital inquired, it would have learned that numerous malpractice suits had been filed against Dr. Salinsky in the Circuit Court for Milwaukee County.

Hospital records indicated that the lay administration of the hospital recommended Dr. Salinsky's appointment and that approval of the appointment was endorsed by Dr. Salinsky himself rather than by the chief physician of the relevant department. The record also disclosed that the doctor was given the position of chief of staff soon after his appointment. No duly constituted medical staff credentials committee had reviewed his application for appointment and surgical privileges because none was functioning at the time. Further, no investigation was made by anyone in hospital administration of any of the assertions made in the application. Additionally, there was no clear evidence that the medical staff executive committee even considered the matter of Dr. Salinsky's appointment.

At trial of the case there was undisputed medical expert testimony to the effect that the procedure used by the doctor to remove the pin fragment from the right hip of the plaintiff was not consistent with acceptable orthopedic surgical practice. The jury's finding that Dr. Salinsky was negligent was not challenged by the hospital on appeal. Because the surgeon was not an actual or apparent employee of the hospital, however, the doctrine of *respondeat superior* was not an appropriate theory on which to base hospital liability.

In addressing applicability of the theory of corporate negligence, however, the Wisconsin court clearly identified and articulated four principal elements. The first involves the existence of a duty on the part of the hospital to exercise reasonable care in the selection of its medical staff and the granting of specialized surgical privileges. This is a question of law for the court—not a factual question for the jury—and the clear answer of the court was in the affirmative. In accordance with long-standing tort law, a duty is established when there is a foreseeable risk of harm presenting an unreasonable risk of danger to another person. Whether the hospital owed a duty to the plaintiff depended then on whether it was foreseeable that the failure to scrutinize the physician's credentials and qualifications could have caused an unreasonable risk of harm to someone. The court observed that the failure to scrutinize credentials of applicants for appointment to the medical staff could foreseeably lead to the appointment of unqualified applicants, thereby creating an unreasonable risk of harm to patients.

In arriving at this conclusion the court cited the public's perception of the modern hospital as well as an extensive array of judicial decisions in other jurisdictions. It rejected an argument by defense counsel that Wisconsin law created only a moral duty to exercise care in selecting staff physicians. In this regard the Wisconsin Administrative Code provides in part:

> (d) Staff appointments shall be made by the governing body, taking into account recommendations made by active staff.
> > 1. The governing body shall have the legal right to appoint the medical staff and the moral obligation to appoint only those physicians who are judged by their fellows to be of good character and qualified and competent in their respective fields.[77]

Further, a state statute recognizes that "each individual hospital shall retain the right to determine whether the applicant's training, experience, and demonstrated competence [are] sufficient to justify the granting of medical staff privileges."[78] In rejecting the hospital's contention that this legislation created only a moral duty to exercise care, the court observed that the statute and the administrative code read together do not negate recognition of a common law duty owed patients; further, the very purpose of the enabling statute for the Wisconsin Administrative Code is to "promote safe and adequate care and treatment of patients in such hospitals."[79] Evaluation and review of medical staff applicants and a continuing peer review program are essential to promote quality care.

The Wisconsin Administrative Code further provides that the governing body of a hospital is legally responsible for the conduct of the hospital as an institution and has the ultimate responsibility for appointment of medical staff; an organized medical staff is responsible to the governing body for quality of care and for ethical and professional practices of staff physicians; the medical staff shall have a system to evaluate applicants for appointment, based on workable standards; and criteria for selection of medical staff shall include individual character, competence, training, experience, and judgment.[80] The court observed that such a statutory pattern creates mandatory, not optional, obligations and that medical staff bylaws providing for a credentialing procedure are admissible in evidence for the jury to consider in determining whether the hospital complied with statutory standards.

After establishing the duty owed to patients as a matter of law, the Wisconsin court stated that the second element in a corporate negligence action involves the standard of care that a hospital must exercise in discharging its duty and whether the hospital failed to exercise that standard of care. The standard required is ordinary care under the circumstances.[81] An act or omission that a person of ordinary intelligence and prudence should reasonably foresee as subjecting others to an unreasonable risk of injury breaches the duty. For the defendant hospital to be liable there must be a finding that it failed to exercise that degree of care and skill required of a hospital under like or similar circumstances.[82] Breach of the duty is a question of fact for the jury to determine.

In the *Johnson* case it was not necessary for the plaintiff to show that Dr. Salinsky was actually incompetent and that the hospital actually knew of his incompetence prior to the appointment. All the plaintiff was required to prove was that the defendant hospital "did not make a reasonable effort to determine whether Salinsky was qualified to perform orthopedic surgery."[83] Expert testimony was necessary and readily available to establish the procedures used by other hospitals in like circumstances to evaluate applicants. Here the hospital conducted no investigation whatsoever of Dr. Salinsky's qualifications, training, and experience despite at least constructive knowledge of his poor reputation in the medical community.[84] The average hospital would certainly have investigated the doctor's background. In sum, "a jury's finding of negligence . . . will not be set aside when there is any credible evidence that under any reasonable view supports the verdict."[85] Records at other hospitals relevant to Dr. Salinsky's difficulties were admissible in evidence as an exception to the hearsay evidence rule because they were maintained in the ordinary course of business by those hospitals.

The third essential element in a corporate negligence action is causation, which is also a question of fact for the jury. In this regard it was established by the intermediate court of appeals that the defendant hospital's acts or omissions need not be the sole or even the primary factor in causing the plaintiff's injuries; cause can be established if the hospital's negligence is a substantial factor contributing to the plaintiff's harm. The defendant is liable for all natural and probable consequences of its negligence.

The final element of the cause of action for corporate negligence is the establishment of damage or injury. Under Wisconsin law, when several defendants are involved, the jury may award damages proportionately. The jury assessed 80 percent of the causal negligence to the hospital, awarding $315,000 damages for personal injuries and $90,000 for loss of earning capacity. The court of appeals affirmed the award, finding that the apportionment was supported by the evidence and not based on speculation or conjecture; further, the size of the award was not excessive in view of the facts. The supreme court agreed.

The Wisconsin Supreme Court concluded its opinion by noting that hospitals, at a minimum, should require answers to all questions on a physician's application for privileges. Moreover, the hospital should verify all information provided by the doctor. It should also obtain information from the physician's peers with respect to education, training, experience, health, competence, and ethical character, and it should inquire into the doctor's current license to practice, malpractice losses, if any, current memberships in professional organizations, and medical staff privileges at other hospitals. The hospital then will have fulfilled its duty of exercising ordinary care under the circumstances.[86]

None of the case decisions since *Darling* have endeavored to imply a supervisory role for lay hospital administrators or trustees over physicians' clinical activities. Only physicians can practice medicine and exercise clinical judgment for proper care and treatment of patients. Accordingly, it is the duty of the governing board of the hospital and the administration to be certain that an organized medical staff is periodically reviewing the clinical behavior of staff physicians. The authority for the review and evaluation function is delegated by the governing board to the professional staff. In turn, the staff is accountable to the board for its recommendations.

The process of medical staff credentialing has three major components:

1. evaluation for staff membership;
2. delineation of specific medical or surgical privileges that may be exercised by individuals granted staff membership; and
3. systematic monitoring or review of the individual's continuing competence.

It is the medical staff's role to develop reasonable criteria and fundamentally fair procedures for evaluation, appointment, and delineation of privileges; information and data must be gathered and forwarded to the governing body in support of recommendations. The board, in turn, approves both the criteria and procedures for appointment, the delineation of privileges, and the renewal of appointments. It then acts on the medical staff's recommendations after making certain that all supporting information is complete.

Consistent with these responsibilities, hospitals must also develop a credentialing process for the increasing number of professional persons working within the institution who are neither hospital employees nor practitioners of medicine.[87] To an increasing extent physician's assistants, nurse practitioners, podiatrists, and others are being granted permission to provide services within an institutional setting. It is clear that the qualifications of these individuals must be evaluated by the hospital as must be done for members of the medical staff. Moreover, procedures must be developed to review periodically the performance of each of these persons. The scope of their clinical activities is a matter for the medical and nursing staff to develop according to local licensure laws and professional custom and usage.

Two Theories Have Become One

The recent Arizona case of *Fridena v. Evans* illustrates the confusion that has arisen between the doctrines of *respondeat superior* and corporate negligence as a result of the simultaneous development and expansion of both theories of liability.[88] Dr. Fridena, an osteopathic-orthopedic surgeon and the chief operating surgeon of the hospital, inserted a pin into a young woman's right hip and leg following the patient's involvement in an automobile accident. The operation caused the right leg to be one and a half inches shorter than the left leg.

A second operation was undertaken to lengthen the right leg. The attempt, however, was unsuccessful. Suit was brought against the estate of Dr. Fridena, an assistant surgeon, and the hospital on allegations that the second operation was negligently performed. The assistant surgeon and the hospital were both granted a summary judgment by the court prior to trial. On appeal the judgment was affirmed for the assistant surgeon but reversed regarding the hospital. As the cause of action went to trial, the hospital then moved for a directed verdict on the ground that the surgeon was not an agent or an employee of the hospital.

In denying the hospital's motion for a directed verdict, the trial court ruled as a matter of law that the evidence showed the relationship between Dr. Fridena and the hospital to be such that the doctor's negligence would also be the negligence of the hospital. The jury thereupon returned a verdict against the estate of Dr. Fridena and the hospital and awarded $300,000 in damages.

Dr. Fridena was the hospital's chief surgeon, the chairman of the board of trustees, the medical director, and the controlling stockholder. These several roles—except that of stockholder—certainly evidenced the physician to be an agent of the corporate hospital. The doctor had responsibility for enforcing medical policy and was actually the ultimate person in control. Accordingly, judgment against the hospital on the straightforward basis of *respondeat superior* would have been justified and consistent with traditional legal doctrine. Under the circumstances the hospital should not have been permitted to prevail on the argument that the doctor was an independent contractor in the role of operating surgeon. Thus, the trial judge was correct in denying the motion for a directed verdict.

The issue raised on appeal, however, was whether the trial court erred in finding the hospital liable for the negligent supervision of Dr. Fridena. This query is consistent with a corporate negligence theory, not vicarious liability. The court proceeded to answer the question in the negative and affirmed the judgment against the hospital. Relying on law review articles as well as case precedent in Arizona, the court held that a hospital can be liable for its negligence in failing to monitor and review medical services being provided within the institution.[89]

From this point of reference the court stressed that the liability of the hospital must be based on actual or constructive knowledge of allegedly negligent procedures by members of the medical staff. On the facts and circumstances here presented, the hospital had constructive knowledge on the basis that Dr. Fridena's awareness of his own professional inadequacies would be imputed to the hospital. The court said, "There is a well established rule in the law of agency that a corporation is bound by the knowledge acquired by, or notice given to, its agents or officers which is within the scope of their authority and which is in reference to a matter to which their authority extends."[90] Thus a theory of agency law was used to place direct, corporate liability on the hospital for negligent supervision by Dr. Fridena of the care Dr. Fridena provided to hospital patients.

The *Fridena* case illustrates and confirms the confusion and overlap that have developed in the application of the two theories of hospital liability. The law of agency and *respondeat superior* should not be employed to explain liability based on a violation of a corporate duty. It should rather be acknowledged that in the hospital setting there is no longer a viable distinction between the rules of *respondeat superior*, on one hand, and corporate or independent negligence, on the other. Essentially, the two theories have become one.

Liability of Managed Care Organizations

The emphasis on efficiency and cost savings that characterized the 1980s and 1990s led many to question whether the healthcare system was neglecting the quality of the care being provided. Issues arise when managed care organizations (MCOs) (health maintenance organizations and other prepaid health plans) make decisions not to admit or to discharge patients and those decisions adversely affect the medical outcome.

Some argue that irrespective of whether the MCO concurs and assumes financial responsibility, the decision to admit patients or extend their stay is a medical one that only a physician can make. Indeed this was the key point in *Wickline v. California*,[91] one of the first cases to attempt to assert liability against an MCO (in this case, the state's Medi-Cal program) when a utilization review (UR) decision forced a patient's early discharge. Although the court wrote, "Third party payors of health care services can be held legally accountable when medically inappropriate decisions result from defects in the design or implementation of cost containment mechanisms . . .", it also held that the physician had the final responsibility to make the medical decision whether to discharge. Because the physician in question had not appealed the UR decision and should have done so, the physician and not the MCO was held liable.

A later California case found otherwise, however. In *Wilson v. Blue Cross of Southern California*,[92] a physician requested a 30-day admission for a depressed psychiatric patient. The request was denied by UR and the patient later committed suicide. The court found that Blue Cross's refusal to pay for the admission was a "substantial factor" in the patient's death and added, "The language in *Wickline* which suggests that civil liability for a discharge decision rests solely within the responsibility of a treating physician in all contexts is dicta." Thus, the MCO was held liable.

There are substantial challenges for plaintiffs who wish to hold MCOs responsible for decisions that adversely affect patient care. The most imposing hurdle is ERISA, the Employee Retirement Income Security Act of 1974,[93] which preempts "any and all State laws insofar as they . . . relate to any employee benefit plan." Numerous cases have held that medical malpractice claims against managed care organizations are barred by the ERISA preemption provisions.[94] To date there has been no congressional action to amend ERISA and explicitly provide for MCO liability for UR decisions, but some related action has been taken at the state level.

Texas, for example, allows an individual to sue an MCO for injuries caused by negligent treatment decisions. The act provides, in relevant part, as follows:

(a) A health insurance carrier, health maintenance organization, or other managed care entity for a health care plan has the duty to exercise ordinary care when making health care treatment decisions and is liable for damages for harm to an insured or enrollee proximately caused by its failure to exercise such ordinary care.

(b) A health insurance carrier, health maintenance organization, or other managed care entity for a health care plan is also liable for damages for harm to an insured or enrollee proximately caused by the health care treatment decisions made by its:
  (1) employees;
  (2) agents;
  (3) ostensible agents; or
  (4) representatives who are acting on its behalf and over whom it has the right to exercise influence or control or has actually exercised influence or control which result in the failure to exercise ordinary care.[95]

This statute was upheld in *Corporate Health Insurance, Inc. v. Tex. Dept. Of Ins.,*[96] in which the court wrote, "Claims [such as malpractice claims] challenging the quality of a benefit . . . are not preempted by ERISA. . . . Claims based upon a failure to treat where the failure was the result of a determination that the requested treatment wasn't covered by the plan, however, are preempted by ERISA." The court held that the Texas statute addresses the quality of benefits actually provided and that its effect on ERISA plans was too tenuous to constitute an improper imposition of state law liability on them.

Notwithstanding the Texas case, until Congress or the Supreme Court speaks definitively, the question of whether ERISA provides immunity to MCOs for their financially motivated treatment decisions will continue to be the subject of much litigation.

Conclusion

It has become quite evident that insofar as the doctrine of *respondeat superior* is concerned, the defense of independent contractor has lost its vitality. In the hospital and healthcare industry there is a continually diminishing number of factual situations that justify successful use of the defense. Moreover, the captain-of-the-ship and the borrowed-servant rules are faltering, if not entirely obliterated, as meaningful defenses for institutional providers of healthcare. These twin doctrines will no longer insulate the hospital from liability and place the burden on the physician. In the delivery of healthcare services in an institutional setting, it is increasingly difficult to determine factually who is in control of whom. As allied health care professionals proliferate and are accorded a greater degree of independence from the direct supervision and control of the attending physician, the matter of the right to control another's actions becomes a very difficult question both as a matter of fact and of law. It therefore becomes necessary to place either sole or joint liability on the institution that, in the final analysis, is ultimately responsible for arranging, providing, and coordinating the activities of a host of professional persons, all of whom must work together in the care of patients.

The law of hospital liability has come full circle. In the 1930s and 1940s most charitable hospitals were immune from tort liability. After charitable immunity was overruled, courts began to apply the doctrine of *respondeat superior* to the hospital setting—timidly, at first. A distinction was clearly drawn between an employee and an independent contractor. A further distinction was made between an employee's administrative negligence and professional negligence. This latter distinction was readily abolished when it was recognized as unworkable in the hospital setting. Then emerged the concepts of apparent agency and agency by estoppel, together with the decline of the captain-of-the-ship and borrowed-servant doctrines. The apparent-agency notion has expanded to the point that the independent-contractor defense is no longer viable or desirable as a matter of substantive tort law in the field of hospital liability.

More significant, the expanded doctrine of corporate or independent negligence—the nondelegable responsibility of reviewing and evaluating clinical practices—has obliterated the distinction between vicarious and direct liability, as illustrated in the cases discussed here.

The rise of managed care in the 1980s and 1990s has led to questions about whether efforts to control costs compromise quality of care. This facet of liability promises to be the subject of scrutiny into the foreseeable future.

Notes

This chapter has been adapted, updated, and reprinted with permission from Arthur F. Southwick, *Hospital Liability: Two Theories Have Been Merged*, 4 JOURNAL OF LEGAL MEDICINE 1 (1983).

1. For a landmark case abolishing charitable immunity, see President & Directors of Georgetown College v. Hughes, 130 F.2d 810 (D.C. Cir. 1942).
2. The origin of immunity in the United States is generally attributed to the often-cited McDonald v. Massachusetts Gen. Hosp., 120 Mass. 432, 21 A. 529 (1876).
3. Foley v. Bishop Clarkson Memorial Hosp., 185 Neb. 89, 173 N.W.2d 881 (1970); Kastler v. Iowa Methodist Hosp., 193 N.W.2d 98 (Iowa 1917); McGillivray v. Rapides Iberia Management Enterprises, 493 So. 2d 819 (La. Ct. App. 1986). Additionally, Lamont v. Brookwood Health Services, Inc., 446 So. 2d 1018 (Ala. 1983) held that the standard of care for hospitals was determined by the national hospital community.

4. *Foley*, 185 Neb. at 95, 173 N.W.2d at 885.
5. *E.g.*, Reifschneider v. Nebraska Methodist Hosp., 222 Neb. 782, 387 N.W.2d 486 (1986) (when semiconscious patient was placed on cart in hospital emergency room without use of restraints, expert testimony was required to establish expected standard of care); Rosemont, Inc. v. Marshall, 481 So. 2d 1126 (Ala. 1985) (standard of care with respect to observation and supervision of patient's ambulatory status requires expert testimony).
6. *E.g.*, Keeton v. Maury County Hosp., 713 S.W.2d 314 (Tenn. App. 1986) (where hospital staff knew or could foresee that patient would likely be endangered by moving about unassisted, neither expert testimony nor violation of a physician's order is necessary to establish breach of duty); Bossier v. Desoto Gen. Hosp., 442 So. 2d 485 (La. App. 1983) (adherence to orders of physician does not excuse failure to exercise reasonable care with respect to supervision of patient undergoing intensive drug therapy); Roettger v. United Hosps. of St. Paul, Inc., 380 N.W.2d 856 (Minn. App. 1986) (where patient was assaulted and hospital was on notice that trespassers had been observed previously in patient care areas, expert testimony is not necessary to support jury verdict that defendant failed to provide adequate security).
7. *Reifschneider*, 387 N.W.2d at 489 (violation of physician's order that patient be attended at all times presented a *prima facie* case of negligence).
8. Hastings v. Baton Rouge Gen. Hosp., 498 So. 2d 713 (La. 1986) (violation of hospital bylaws constitutes breach of duty and eliminates need for expert testimony); Therrel v. Fonde, 495 So. 2d 1046 (Ala. 1986) (where facts establish a significant delay in treatment, expert testimony is not necessary to support jury verdict that defendant failed to provide adequate security).
9. There is no right of indemnification unless the claim is based on derivative or vicarious liability. Thus, one who is active and primary in committing a tort does not have a right of indemnification from another tortfeasor. Joint or multiple tortfeasors may, however, be entitled to contribution or apportionment of damages between themselves. *E.g.*, Williams v. St. Claire Medical Center, Inc., 657 S.W.2d 590 (Ky. App. 1983) (hospital that violated its own rules has no right of indemnification from a negligent noncertified nurse anesthetist); Salonia v. Samsol Homes, Inc., 507 N.Y.S.2d 186 (N.Y. App. Div. 1986) (contractor-owner of construction site who obtained release of claim from injured worker has no right of indemnification from physician whose treatment aggravated the injury; the right of contribution was waived when release was obtained); Brochner v. Western Ins. Co., 724 P.2d 1293 (Colo. 1986) (hospital as joint tortfeasor has no right of indemnification from staff neurosurgeon, and hospital's settlement of plaintiff's claim precludes right of contribution).
10. Dixie Stage Lines v. Anderson, 222 Ala. 673, 134 So. 23 (1931).
11. *See, e.g.*, Prowell v. City of Waterloo, 144 Iowa 689, 123 N.W. 346 (1909).
12. *See, e.g.*, Veazie v. Penobscot R.R. Co., 49 Me. 119 (1860).
13. *See, e.g.*, City of Chicago v. Murdock, 212 Ill. 9, 72 N.E. 46 (1904); Blue Grass Fair Ass'n v. Bunnell, 206 Ky. 462, 267 S.W. 237 (1924); Thomas v. Harrington, 72 N.H. 45, 54 A. 285 (1903).
14. 589 P.2d 201 (N.M. App. 1978); *see also* Fiorentino v. Wenger, 19, 19 N.Y.2d 407, 227 N.E.2d 296, 280 N.Y.S.2d 373 (1967) (duty to inform of surgical risks

is the physician's); *accord* Roberson v. Menorah Medical Center, 588 S.W.2d 134 (Mo. App. 1979).

15. *E.g.*, Mayers v. Litow & Midway Hosp., 154 Cal. App. 2d 413, 316 P.2d 351 (1957); Zelver v. Sequoia Hosp. Dist., 7 Cal. App. 3d 934, 87 Cal. Rptr. 79 (1970); Dickinson v. Mailliard, 175 N.W.2d 588 (Iowa 1970).

16. 58 Mich. App. 119, 227 N.W.2d 247 (1975).

17. 42 Cal. App. 3d 260, 116 Cal. Rptr. 801 (1974).

18. 34 A.D.2d 632, 309 N.Y.S.2d 385 (1970). *See also* Gilstrap v. Osteopathic Sanitorium Co., 224 Mo. App. 798, 24 S.W.2d 249 (1929); Newton County v. Nicholson, 132 Ga. App. 164, 207 S.E.2d 659 (1974).

19. 2 N.Y.2d 656, 143 N.E.2d 3, 163 N.Y.S.2d 3 (1957).

20. *Id.*, 2 N.Y.2d at 666.

21. With respect to hospital liability for negligence of residents and interns, see Waynick v. Reardon, 236 N.C. 116, 72 S.E. 2d 4 (1952); City of Miami v. Oates, 152 Fla. 21, 10 So. 2d 721 (1942); Klema v. St. Elizabeth's Hosp., 170 Ohio St. 519, 166 N.E.2d 765 (1960); Wright v. United States, 507 F. Supp. 147 (E.D. La. 1980) (resident staffing emergency room held to standards of physicians specializing in emergency medicine); Scott v. Brookdale Hosp. Center, 60 A.D.2d 647, 400 N.Y.S.2d 552 (1977).

22. An apparent or ostensible agency is created by estoppel, meaning that it is an agency imposed by law where a principal's conduct or method of business operation has estopped (prevented) him from denying an actual agency.

23. 272 A.2d 718 (Del. 1970).

24. 304 A.2d 61 (Del. Super. Ct. 1973).

25. *See, also* Mduba v. Benedictine Hosp., 52 A.D.2d 450, 384 N.Y.S.2d 527 (1976); Mehlman v. Powell, 281 Md. 269, 378 A.2d 1121 (1977); Rucker v. High Point Memorial Hosp., 20 N.C. App. 650, 202 S.E.2d 610 (1974); Paintsville Hosp. Co. v. Rose, 683 S.W.2d 255 (Ky. 1985); Barrett v. Samaritan Health Servs., Inc., 735 P.2d 460 (Arix. App. 1987).

26. 68 Ohio App. 2d 61, 426 N.E.2d 1187 (1980). *See also* Arthur v. St. Peter's Hosp., 169 N.J. Super. 575, 405, A.2d 443 (1979). *Contra* Pogue v. Hospital Auth., 120 Ga. App. 230, 170 S.E.2d 53 (1969) (member of a medical partnership under contract with a hospital to staff the emergency room ruled an independent contractor).

27. Other leading cases illustrating application of the doctrines of apparent agency or agency by estoppel are: Seneris v. Haas, 45 Cal.2d 811, 291 P.2d 915 (1955) (anesthesiologist); Lundberg v. Bay View Hosp., 175 Ohio St. 133, 191 N.E.2d 821 (1963) (pathologist); Kober v. Stewart, 148 Mont. 117, 417 P.2d 476 (1966) (radiologist). *See also* Griffin v. Matthews, No. CA 86-09-127, unreported, Butler County, Ohio Ct. App. (May 11, 1987) (representations by a full-service hospital establish an agency by estoppel even in absence of reliance by plaintiff); Smith v. Baptist Memorial Hosp. Sys., 720 S.W.2d 618 (Tex. Ct. App. 1986) (factual issues determine application of ostensible agency doctrine, and a hospital may not contractually disclaim liability for negligence of physicians employed by a professional association); Sztorc v. Northwest Hosp., 146 Ill. App. 3d 275, 496 N.E.2d 1200 (1986), *reh'g denied*, Sept. 8, 1986 (hospital's radiation therapy department staffed by group of private physicians represented

as intgral part of hospital precludes summary judgment for defendant hospital). *Cf.* Greene v. Rogers, 147 Ill. App. 3d 1009, 498 N.E.2d 867 (1986) (in the absence of representations by hospital and reliance by patient, a summary judgment for hospital is proper).

28. 18 Ariz. App. 165, 500 P.2d 1153 (1972) (consent form signed by the patient purporting to recognize radiologists as independent contractors was of no legal effect).

29. 404 Mich. 240, 273 N.W.2d 429 (1979).

30. *See also* Capan v. Divine Providence Hosp., 410 A.2d 1282 (Pa. Super. Ct. 1979). *See also* RESTATEMENT (SECOND) OF TORTS § 429 (1965). One who employs an independent contractor to perform services for another which are accepted in the reasonable belief they are being rendered by the employer is liable for physical harm caused by negligence of the contractor. *Cf.* Nicholson v. Memorial Hosp. Sys., 722 S.W.2d 746 (Tex. Ct. App. 1986) (mere referral of patient to a private physician by a hospital employee does not establish an ostensible agency relationship).

31. A physician who is on call for emergencies within the hospital may be personally liable as the result of a failure to respond, Hizer v. Randolph, 126 Ariz. 608, 617 P.2d 774 (1980). The hospital may also be liable. In Michigan, however, a Good Samaritan statute immunizes physicians from personal liability for ordinary negligence as distinct from willful or wanton misconduct when they treat emergency patients within the hospital setting in circumstances where the physician had no previous relationship with the patient and where it was not the doctor's duty to respond. Matts v. Homsi, 106 Mich. App. 563, 308 N.W.2d 284 (1981). *See also* McKenna v. Cedars of Lebanon Hosp., 93 Cal. App. 3d 282, 155 Cal. Rptr. 631 (1979) (resident doctor not personally liable in light of California Good Samaritan statute when he responded to an in-hospital emergency when not on call and in the absence of a previous relationship with the patient). Good Samaritan legislation, however, does not immunize on-call physicians from liability for negligence. Colby v. Schwartz, 78 Cal. App. 3d 885, 144 Cal. Rptr. 624 (1978); Guerrero v. Copper Queen Hosp., 112 Ariz. 104, 537 P.2d 1329 (1975). *See also* Hamburger v. Henry Ford Hosp., 91 Mich. App. 580, 284 N.W.2d 155 (1979).

32. The borrowed-servant doctrine is a similar concept applicable in a wider variety of situations. It is the rule that one who is normally an employee of the hospital serving a hospital function may be temporarily borrowed by a private physician, thereby becoming a servant or an employee of the physician and thus rendering the physician vicariously liable for the negligence of the hospital employee.

33. 458 Pa. 246, 329 A.2d 497 (1974).

34. 361 Pa. 355, 65 A.2d 243 (1949).

35. *See* RESTATEMENT (SECOND) OF AGENCY § 226 (1958).

36. 547 S.W 2d 582 (Tex. 1977).

37. 552 S.W.2d 534 (Tex. 1977). *Accord* Truhitte v. French Hosp., 128 Cal. App. 3d 332 (1982); City of Somerset v. Hart, 549 S.W.2d 814 (Ky. 1977); Grant v. Touro Infirmary, 254 La. 204, 223 So. 2d 148 (1969); Buzan v. Mercy Hosp., 203 So. 2d 11 (Fla. App. 1967); Miller v. Tongen, 281 Minn. 427, 161 N.W.2d 686 (1968). *Contra* Swindell v. St. Joseph's Hosp., Inc., 161 Ga. App. 290

(1982) (hospital employees' negligent act during performance of myelogram imputed to physician).

38. Honeywell v. Rogers, 251 F. Supp. 841 (W.D. Pa. 1966); Bria v. St. Joseph's Hosp., 153 Conn. 626, 220 A.2d 29 (1966); Burns v. Owens, 459 S.W.2d 303 (Mo. 1970); Bernardi v. Community Hosp., 166 Colo. 280, 443 P.2d 708 (1968); Dessauer v. Memorial Gen. Hosp., 628 P.2d 337 (N.M. App. 1981).

39. Variety Childrens Hosp., Inc. v. Perkins, 382 So. 2d 31 (Fla. App. 1980).

40. Simpson v. Sisters of Charity, 284 Or. 547, 588 P.2d 4 (1978).

41. This trend was anticipated and forecast by Professor Southwick as early as 1960 when he wrote: "The third trend in the law of hospital liability is the most significant. It is the increasing tendency . . . to impose vicarious liability on facts where none would have been imposed heretofore. By some leading decisions it no longer follows that a professional person using his own skill, judgment and discretion in regard to the means and methods of his work is an independent contractor. . . . Gradually, the test of hospital liability for another's act is becoming simply a question of whether or not the actor causing injury was a part of the medical care organization." Southwick, *Vicarious Liability of Hospitals,* 44 MARQ. L. REV. 151, 182 (1960).

42. Bader v. United Orthodox Synagogue, 148 Conn. 449, 453, 172 A.2d 192, 194 (1961).

43. Shepherd v. McGinnis, 257 Iowa 35, 131 N.W.2d 475 (1964); Ardoin v. Hartford Accident & Indem. Co., 350 So. 2d 205 (La. App. 1977).

44. Phillips V. Powell, 210 Cal. 39, 290 P.2d 441 (1930); Milner v. Huntsville Memorial Hosp., 398 S.W.2d 647 (Tex. App. 1966).

45. South Highlands Infirmary v. Camp, 279 Ala. 1, 180 So. 2d 904 (1965); Nelson v. Swedish Hosp., 241 Minn. 551, 64 N.W.2d 38 (1954).

46. 103 Ga. App. 752, 120 S.E.2d 668 (1961).

47. Lauro v. Travelers Ins. Co., 261 So. 2d 261 (La. App. 1972). *See also* Kujawski v. Arbor View Health Care Center, 132 Wis. 2d 178, 389 N.W.2d 831 (Wis. Ct. App. 1986) (in absence of a physician's order and expert testimony with respect to standard of care required, it was proper to dismiss complaint alleging that failure to provide a seatbelt in wheelchair was breach of duty).

48. Peck v. Charles B. Towns. Hosp., 275 A.D. 302, 89 N.Y.S.2d 190 (1949).

49. 557 S.W.2d 859 (Tex. 1977).

50. Hamil v. Bashline, 224 Pa. Super. 407, 307 A.2d 57 (1973).

51. One article includes mention of the settlement of a lawsuit against the District of Columbia General Hospital alleging negligence for failure to have available a CAT scanner for a patient suffering from a head injury, and settlements in cases where high risk, pregnant patients were not examined by fetal monitors. T. J. Hooper, 60 F.2d 737 (2d Cir. 1932). *See generally* 6 MED. LIABILITY ADVISORY SERVICE (Dec. 1981) and *New Technology-Related Areas of Liability for Hospitals and Physicians,* ISSUES IN HEALTH CARE TECH., May 1982.

52. 220 Cal. App. 2d 320, 33 Cal. Rptr. 735 (1963).

53. 553 S.W.2d 180 (Tex. App. 1977). *See also* Hipp v. Hospital Auth., 104 Ga. App. 174, 121 S.E.2d 273 (1961); Garlington v. Kingsley, 277 So. 2d 183 (La. App. 173), *rev'd on other grounds,* 289 So. 2d 88 (La. 1974).

54. Darling v. Charleston Community Memorial Hosp., 33 Ill. 2d 326, 211 N.E.2d

253, *cert. denied*, 383 U.S. 946 (1966). There are many other cases in accord, some which are cited *infra*.

55. 70 Wash. 2d 73, 431 P.2d 973 (1967).

56. 19 Ohio St. 2d 128, 249 N.E.2d 829 (1969). *See also* Haber v. Cross County Hosp., 37 N.Y.2d 889, 340 N.E.2d 734, 378 N.Y.S.2d 369 (1975) (violation of rules regarding use of bedrails is evidence of negligence); Griggs v. Morehead Memorial Hosp., 82 N.C. App. 131, 345 S.E.2d 430 (1986) (failure to make a nurse-patient assignment for patient in intensive coronary care unit in violation of hospital policy is evidence of negligent deviation from standard of care); Schneider v. Kings Highway Hosp. Center, 67 N.Y.2d 743, 490 N.E.2d 1221, 500 N.Y.S.2d 95 (1986) (patient who fell from bed establishes *prima facie* case by proof that rule requiring raised siderails for patients over 70 was violated).

57. 418 N.E.2d 620 (Mass. App. 1981).

58. 84 Mich. App. 426, 269 N.W.2d 626 (1979).

59. Kakligian v. Henry Ford Hosp., 48 Mich. App. 325, 210 N.W.2d 463 (1973).

60. 3 N.C. App. 11, S.E.2d 17 (1968).

61. Ball Memorial Hosp. v. Freeman, 245 Ind. 71, 196 N.E.2d 274 (1964).

62. Sullivan v. Sisters of St. Francis, 374 S.W.2d 294 (Tex. App. 1963).

63. Ravenis v. Detroit Gen. Hosp., 63 Mich. App. 79, 234 N.W.2d 411 (1975).

64. 324 F. Supp. 233 (N.D. Ind. 1971).

65. Hospitals owe a duty to exercise such reasonable care as the patient's known condition requires *and* to guard against conditions that should have been discovered by the exercise of reasonable care. Foley v. Bishop Clarkson Memorial Hosp., 185 Neb. 89, 173 N.W.2d 881 (1970). Moreover hospitals are held to standards and practices prevailing generally, not only in the local community, but in similar or like communities in similar circumstances. Dickinson v. Mailliard, 175 N.W.2d 588 (Iowa 1970).

66. 2 N.Y.2d 656, 143 N.E.2d 3, 163 N.Y.S.2d 3 (1957).

67. 33 Ill. 2d 326, 211 N.E.2d 253, *cert. denied*, 383 U.S. 946 (1966).

68. In support of its position, the court cited Bing v. Thunig, 2 N.Y.2d 656, 143 N.E.2d 3, 163 N.Y.S.2d 3 (1957).

69. 14 A.L.R.3d 873, 879 (1967).

70. 125 Ga. App. 1, 186 S.E.2d 307, *aff'd*, 229 Ga. 140, 189 S.E.2d 412 (1972).

71. The New York courts have also recognized that the hospital has a duty to the patient to select and retain staff physicians with care. *See* Fiorentio v. Wagner, 19 N.Y.2d 407, 227 N.E.2d 296, 299, 280 N.Y.S.2d 373, 378 (1967), where the court stated: "More particularly, in the context of the present case, a hospital will not be liable for an act of malpractice performed by an independently retained healer, unless it has reason to know that the act of malpractice would take place." There was no liability in negligence, however, when hospital permitted surgeon who was not certified by the American Board of Otolaryngology to operate in this specialized area. Thomas v. Solon, 121 A.D.2d 165, 502 N.Y.S.2d 475 (1986).

72. 88 Nev. 207, 495 P.2d 605, *cert. denied*, 409 U.S. 879 (1972).

73. *Id.*, 495 P.2d at 608. Readers will recognize that this language of the Nevada court is a paraphrased summation of Southwick, *Hospital Medical Staff Privileges*, 18 DePaul L. Rev. 655 (1969). *See also* Pedroza v. Bryant, 101 Wash. 2d

226, 677 P.2d 166 (1984) (hospitals owe independent duty to patients to use reasonable care in selection and retention of medical staff; duty does not extend to patient of physician who allegedly committed malpractice in private office practice).

74. No. 228566 (Super. Ct. Cal., Sacramento County, 1973), *rev'd on other grounds*, 60 Cal. App. 3d 728 (1976). Another widely publicized trial court case is Corleto v. Shore Memorial Hosp., 138 N.J. Super. 302, 350 A.2d 534 (1975). There the court ruled that the corporate hospital, the medical staff as an unincorporated association, and all individual members of the medical staff and board of trustees could be joined as defendants and be liable if they knew or should have known of a surgeon's incompetence. New Jersey statutes permit an unincorporated association to be sued as an entity. After the trial court denied a motion to dismiss the action, the surgeon's insurance company settled the case. Accordingly the merits of the liability claim against the hospital and members of the medical staff were never reviewed by an appellate court. Despite this judicial development in New Jersey, it would seem clear that individuals on the medical staff not participating in a peer review function would not be subject to individual liability.

75. 99 Wis. 2d 708, 301 N.W.2d 156 (1981). The opinion of the intermediate court of appeals is reported at 97 Wis. 2d 521, 294 N.W.2d 501 (1980).

76. 99 Wis. 2d at 723.

77. WIS. ADMIN. CODE § H24.04(1)(d)(1).

78. WIS. STAT. § 50.36(3) (1975).

79. *Id.* at § 50.34 (1975)..

80. WIS. ADMIN.CODE §§ H24.02(1), (1)(E).

81. 301 N.W.2d at 163, 171.

82. *See* Payne v. Milwaukee Sanitarium Found., 81 Wis. 2d 264, 260 N.W.2d 386 (1977); Shier v. Freedman, 58 Wis. 2d 269, 206 N.W.2d 166, 208 N.W.2d 328 (1973) (rejecting the locality rule in medical malpractice actions).

83. 301 N.W.2d at 172.

84. With respect to a hospital's failure to act and the doctrine of constructive knowledge, see Tucson Medical Center v. Misevch, 113 Ariz. 34, 545 P.2d 958 (1976).

85. 301 N.W.2d at 174.

86. *See also* Elam v. College Park Hosp., 132 Cal. App. 3d 332, 183 Cal. Rptr. 156, *modified*, 133 Cal. App. 3d 94a (1982).

87. *See* Policy and Statement, Privileges and Quality Assurance for Health Practitioners Other Than Medical Staff members and Employees, American Hospital Association, Chicago (1980).

88. 127 Ariz. 516, 622 P.2d 463 (1981).

89. *See* Kahn, *Hospital Malpractice Prevention*, 27 DePaul L. Rev. 23 (1977). In Tucson Medical Center, Inc. v. Misevch, the same court had said that if a medical staff is "negligent in supervising its members the hospital itself would be held negligent." 113 Ariz. 34, 545 P.2d 958 (1976); *see also* Purcell v. Zimbelman, 18 Ariz. App. 75, 500 P.2d 335 (1972).

90. 622 P.2d at 466. *See also* Joiner v. Mitchell County Hosp. Auth., 125 Ga. App. 1, 186 S.E.2d 307, *aff'd*, 229 Ga. 140, 189 S.E.2d 412 (1972).

91. 239 Cal. Rptr. 810 (Ct. App. 1986).

92. 271 Cal. Rptr. 876 (Ct. App. 1989).

93. 29 U.S.C. § 1001 *et seq.*

94. *See, e.g.,* Corcoran v. United Healthcare, Inc., 965 F.2d 1321 (5th Cir. 1992) *and* Rodriguez v. Pacificare of Tex., Inc. 980 F.2d 1014 (5th Cir. 1993). *But see,* Dukes v. U.S. Healthcare, 57 F.3d 350 (3rd Cir. 1995) *and* Pacificare of Oklahoma, Inc. v. Burrage, 59 F.3d 151 (10th Cir. 1995).

95. Tex. Civ. Prac. & Rem. Code Ann. § 88.002.

96. Civ. No. H-97-2702 (U.S.D.C., S.D. Tex., Sept. 18, 1998).

TAXATION OF HEALTHCARE INSTITUTIONS

A tax-exempt corporation or organization is one that is formed and operated exclusively for religious, scientific, educational, charitable, or similar purposes and is operated in a not-for-profit manner. (See the discussion in Chapter 4 regarding the difference between for-profit and not-for-profit corporations.) It is important to recall that not-for-profit status and tax-exempt status are determined by different criteria: the former by state corporation law, and the latter by federal and/or state tax law. To determine eligibility for tax-exempt status, one must generally look not only at the declaration of purpose in the corporate charter or other organizational document but also at the actual facts of the organization's operation.

The Nature of a Charitable Corporation

In a few states a charity must be incorporated. In others, however, incorporation is not required and other forms of business organization may be used: an unincorporated association of individuals, a trust, a community chest, or a foundation. As a practical matter most charitable healthcare institutions are incorporated.

Some states require that a charitable corporation be incorporated in the state where tax exemption or other preferred status is sought. Hence, foreign corporations (those incorporated in states other than the one where charity status is claimed) cannot successfully assert such a claim.

There is no single, all-inclusive definition of a charity. For example, for federal income tax exemption, the qualifications a charitable corporation must meet are determined by the wording of the Internal Revenue Code, by regulations promulgated by the Internal Revenue Service, and by court decisions interpreting the statutory law and regulations. Further, the various state constitutions and statutes providing for exemption from local taxes often differ from each other and from the federal requirements, and local courts may differ in their interpretations of constitutional or statutory provisions. Some state laws, for example, will exempt organizations described as "public charities" from local real estate taxation or other local taxes such as income taxes, sales and use taxes, or taxes on personal property. Other states omit the word "public" from tax exemption requirements. Accordingly, the advice of local legal counsel is crucial in a situation involving any specific taxation issue. State taxation of real estate owned or occupied by a hospital or other healthcare institution will be discussed in greater detail later.

First it is important to view the nature of a charity or charitable corporation and identify the major issues that may determine a decision in a particular situation. *Charity* in general refers to benevolent or eleemosynary aims and to public service for the benefit of an indefinite number of persons. Hence, a charity exists to promote the welfare of persons more or less at large or the welfare of a "community." Although benefits may be restricted to a particular class of beneficiaries—for example, the blind, children, the aged—the class must usually contain an indefinite number of persons to be served. To put the matter another way, a charity must normally be open to the public and not restricted to a privileged few. Accordingly, public service organizations must often be distinguished from social service and not-for-profit organizations generally. All charitable corporations are not-for-profit corporations, but not all not-for-profit organizations are charitable. As pointed out earlier, countless not-for-profit corporations—for example, social clubs, fraternal organizations, and labor unions—may provide a significant degree of social service, but they do not exist and operate for charitable purposes as that expression is defined in tax law.

This general definition of a charity raises the issue of whether benefits may be restricted to certain segments of a community. In all jurisdictions, and for both federal and state purposes, hospitals or other healthcare institutions that serve, for example, only children or women or mentally ill individuals are clearly considered "charitable" as long as they meet the other relevant requirements. In other words, confining the activity to a special purpose and restricting benefits to a particular age or sex group or to the treatment of a particular illness do not jeopardize charitable status, nor would restrictions necessitated by a lack of specialized staff and facilities. The class of persons to be served is "indefinite," notwithstanding such restrictions.

May the benefits of a charity be restricted to the members of a particular church, lodge, labor union, or fraternal order, or to the employees of a particular company? Here the answer may be more difficult to determine and depends on local law and the precise issue at stake in a given situation. Especially if local law requires tax-exempt organizations to be "public charities," it follows that the beneficiaries usually may not be restricted to the members of a given church, fraternal order, or similar group. A leading case, mentioned here solely by way of illustration, is *Philadelphia v. Masonic Home*, which denied real estate tax exemption to a home for aged Masons.[1] This is probably the majority rule for tax exemption from local state real estate taxes, although in many jurisdictions there is no precise authority. In contrast, by court interpretation of the law of Kansas, which does not require a charity to be "public," organizations serving, for example, only Masons, Methodist clergymen, or Roman Catholic nuns are categorized as charitable and hence exempt from local taxes.[2] The definition of and limitations on the class of persons to be served by a "charity" thus depend on local law and are still open questions in many jurisdictions. As noted elsewhere, federal income tax law (Section 501(c)(3) of the Internal Revenue Code) does not permit tax exemption to organizations catering only to a closed group of members.

A few states have attempted to require that a charity restrict its benefits to residents of the state where the organization's property is located or its services performed, denying charitable status to organizations that serve nonresidents to any significant degree. Such a restriction is, of course, highly unrealistic and should be considered contrary to public policy in an era of population mobility. No authoritative case support has been found to thoroughly uphold such residential requirements. In construing a Colorado statute, that state's supreme court permitted charitable status and tax exemption for an organization that served nonresidents, so long as the *primary* benefits were extended to Colorado residents.[3] In contrast and perhaps illustrating the general rule, a charity incorporated in New York does not jeopardize its status by doing most of its work outside the state and with nonresident beneficiaries.[4]

It is frequently said that a charitable corporation or organization may not restrict its services because of a patient's inability to pay. This matter also requires careful analysis of the particular facts relating to the question at issue. For federal income tax exemption and for most state real estate exemptions, as discussed elsewhere, the statement means as a minimum that a general acute care hospital, for example, with facilities for emergency service may not summarily reject a patient who seeks emergency care on the basis of inability to pay. (This point is discussed in more detail in Chapter 10, "Emergency Care.") Naturally, however, and in accordance with sound economics and the needs of particular communities, not all hospitals, even general hospitals, are required to provide emergency services.[5] The point is more obvious with respect to highly specialized institutions, such as hospitals that care only for patients with a particular disease or disability. Charitable status is therefore not lost by restricting benefits according to the institution's ability to serve, given its purpose, facilities, and staff.

Even though a charity may not generally restrict its emergency care to those able to pay, the question still remains whether the organization must render some amount of free care to maintain its status. A few state courts, in cases involving hospitals or other institutions seeking charitable status, have required the rendering of at least some free care to those unable to pay.[6] Most state courts, however, and the federal government have not required that a charitable institution provide a given amount of free care to maintain charitable status.[7]

For exemptions from state taxes and for determining charitable status as a matter of local law, the majority rule clearly indicates that a healthcare institution need not prove that it provides a specific amount of free care. This is a broader and more liberal view of the nature of a charity: that relief of poverty is not an absolute prerequisite.[8] As long as there is no private gain or profit, promotion of health is usually considered a valid charitable purpose in and of itself. Accordingly, the institution can be self-supporting and earn a profit as long as the profits are used for institutional needs and not distributed directly or indirectly to individuals. Profit can be invested in physical facilities or added to the organization's endowment. Many state court decisions follow this approach, and the philosophy was well stated by the New York court in *Doctors Hospital v. Sexton* as follows:

> Hospitals which are devoted to the care of the sick and injured, which aid in maintaining public health and which make valuable contributions to the advancement of medical science are rightly regarded as benevolent and charitable. A hospital association not conducted for profit which devotes all of its funds exclusively to the maintenance of the institution is a public charity and this is so irrespective of whether patients are required to pay for the services rendered.[9]

The view that care of the indigent is not a necessary condition for charitable status is justified on the grounds that both the wealthy and the poor are appropriate beneficiaries of charity whenever they are the victims of illness or injury, that a requirement of free care is difficult to define in terms of amount and extent, and that social welfare programs of government today should be designed to care for those unable to pay for medical and hospital services.

Finally, although promotion of health per se may be a valid charitable purpose for many organizations, such as research institutions and specialized hospitals, a general community hospital must actually benefit the community if it is to retain charitable status—hence the requirements that the hospital must admit patients without regard to race or creed and must welcome emergency room patients, assuming available facilities and staff.[10] In short, a community hospital must not turn away emergency patients on the basis of either their wealth or their poverty.[11] Some voluntary community hospitals have been known to instruct police and ambulance companies to take indigent emergency patients to public institutions, but such a policy would violate their status as a charity.[12] Some authorities, including the late Wilbur Cohen, former Secretary of Health, Education, and Welfare, have suggested that all charitable hospitals should be required to accept some patients eligible for Medicaid benefits.[13] Systematic refusal of admission or services to such persons may show an unwillingness to serve the community at large. In the final analysis each case will be decided on the particular facts in the context of a particular issue, and the ultimate inquiry will always be whether the hospital is serving the community, as defined by state law or by federal tax law.

Federal Taxation of Income

To be exempt from federal income taxation under Section 501(c)(3) of the Internal Revenue Code, a private corporation must be "organized and operated exclusively for religious, charitable, scientific . . . or educational purposes . . . no part of the net earnings of which inures to the benefit of any private shareholder or individual."[14] One should especially note that hospitals, nursing homes, and other healthcare institutions are not specifically named as exempt from tax. Nevertheless, they can qualify for exemption by meeting the two primary requirements of the Internal Revenue Code set forth above and by following the regulations of the Internal Revenue Service for implementing the code.

Requirements for Tax Exemption: Charitable Purpose

The first basic requirement of the code is that the tax-exempt organization must be both organized and operated for a purpose recognized as charitable. The second requirement is that there must not be monetary gain or inurement to private persons or private interests.

Further, the public service concept of a charity embraces these rules: services may not be restricted on the basis of race or creed;[15] a hospital's emergency room services may not be withheld because of inability to pay; and a hospital may not restrict the use of its facilities to a small, particular group of physicians, thereby excluding other qualified persons from membership on the medical staff.[16] It is recognized, of course, that a particular hospital may not have the facilities or the need to extend membership to all physicians who apply for admission to the medical staff; accordingly, under such circumstances a private hospital may reject an application from even a competent and well-qualified physician without losing its tax-exempt status. Under the law relating to medical staff privileges, however, the hospital is obligated to review physicians' applications fairly and carefully, provide them with an opportunity for a hearing if the application is rejected, and state the reasons for rejection.[17]

An organization exempt from federal income taxation under Section 501(c)(3) is prohibited from devoting a "substantial part" of its "activities" to lobbying and "influencing" legislation.[18] As an aid in defining and quantifying a "substantial part," the legislation permits public charities, except churches and certain religious organizations, to file an election with the Internal Revenue Service indicating an intent to engage in lobbying activity (defined as activity intended to influence the outcome of pending legislation). The statute then provides for certain limitations, expressed in both percentages and absolute monetary amounts, based on the charity's annual "exempt purposes" budget. To be distinguished from lobbying, however, are (1) publishing nonpartisan research data; (2) providing testimony to a legislative body regarding pending decisions that will affect the charity; and (3) sending communications to a nonlegislative governmental official. None of these activities is considered to be lobbying or "influencing" legislation.

Also to be distinguished from lobbying are active campaigning and electioneering on behalf of or in opposition to a particular candidate or candidates for political office. A Section 501(c)(3) organization is strictly prohibited from engaging in such partisan political activity, directly or indirectly. According to the usual rules of the law of agency, when the tax-exempt entity impliedly authorizes or ratifies the political activity of an employee or member, the individual's activities will be imputed to the organization. In contrast, a for-profit corporation, including a subsidiary of a Section 501(c)(3) organization, it may sponsor a political action committee with the power to receive funds from designated persons and may also expend those funds on behalf of particular political candidates.[19]

Certain tax-exempt organizations formed under other subsections of Section 501(c), such as trade associations, are not subject to the statutory restrictions on either lobbying or campaigning. The Supreme Court has held that such disparate treatment among exempt organizations does not violate either the First Amendment or the equal protection clause of the U.S. Constitution.[20]

Requirements for Tax Exemption: No Monetary Gain or Inurement

The second primary Internal Revenue Code requirement for tax-exempt status is that there not be private monetary gain or inurement to private persons.[21] This requirement goes hand in hand with the concept of public service or benefit. Each case must be decided on its own merits because persons' ingenuity with respect to activity through the corporate form of business is nearly limitless. No single factor or set of factors will decide the issue and hence determine the status of a given institution. Rather, the court in any given case will look to the facts of the operation, applying one criterion or more to determine whether a corporation claiming tax-exempt status is a shield for attaining private gain or whether the charity is conferring a gain on proprietary interests.

One authority identifies several factors that the courts will consider, most of which flow from or relate directly to corporate control.[22] When control of a corporation rests exclusively with a small group of individuals, especially physicians who once practiced in partnership or who owned a proprietary hospital and who subsequently incorporate as a nonprofit corporation, the facts raise doubts about their motives and invite close scrutiny. Private gain is indicated by such specific factors as the division of profits among trustees, members, or officers of a corporation,[23] the private use of corporate funds or facilities, exclusive privileges to admit or treat patients, and failure to provide services to those unable to pay.[24] Even if tax-exempt status is granted without requiring free care, the charity record of a hospital is evidence of a willingness to serve the public. To put the matter another way, the absence or near absence of charity work is evidence, depending on all the other factors noted above, of private gain.

Contracts between a hospital and a medical specialist under which, for example, a pathologist or radiologist receives a defined percentage of departmental revenue, gross or net, have raised the issue of private benefit. As long as the contract is negotiated at "arm's length," as long as the specialist's income is "reasonable" compared to that of other similar specialists in similar or typical circumstances, and as long as the physician has no significant ownership or control over the hospital, the arrangement does not constitute private gain that would jeopardize the hospital's tax status.[25] The hospital may legitimately furnish space, supplies, equipment, and personnel, and it may fix the charges for service jointly with the doctor and then bill the patients. (Note, however, that such arrangements as those discussed in this section may implicate state or federal "anti-kickback" and "self-referral" laws, as discussed in Chapter 8, "Healthcare Fraud and Abuse." The instant discussion concerns only the effect of such arrangements on an organization's tax status.)

To an increasing extent, especially since the advent of prospective payment mechanisms, hospitals have been developing economic incentive plans to attract physicians to the medical staff and encourage admissions of patients while simultaneously intensifying the use of hospital facilities and thus reducing costs. As long as the doctor's compensation is reasonable and is beneficial to the charitable purpose of the institution, the tax-exempt status is not jeopardized by such programs.[26] This means of course that the institution must receive measurable value in return for the incentives granted the doctors.

In addition to the traditional approach to private inurement and private benefit discussed above, the Taxpayer Bill of Rights 2 ("TBOR2"), signed into law on July 30, 1996, and codified at 26 U.S.C. § 4958 dramatically affects the manner in which the Internal Revenue Service will address the issue. The act imposes sizable financial penalties on persons who receive "excess benefits" and on the organizational managers who approve excess benefit transactions. The law makes it advisable for tax-exempt organizations to develop compensation and conflict of interest policies that will ensure the propriety of transactions with corporate insiders. Failure to abide by such policies places the insiders and corporate managers at substantial monetary risk.

As discussed earlier, it is a maxim of federal tax law that the net earnings of tax-exempt organizations may not inure to the benefit of private individuals. This provision is meant to ensure that the earnings of a tax-exempt organization remain dedicated to the organization's exempt purposes. In recent years, however, there have been a few highly publicized scandals involving self-dealing and excessive compensation in exempt organizations. These cases caused Congress to question whether the IRS needed additional measures to enforce the ban on private inurement. Passage of TBOR2 was the result.

Prior to the enactment of TBOR2 the IRS had only one method of enforcing the prohibition on private inurement: revocation of the organization's tax-exempt status. Revocation was viewed as such an extreme measure that the IRS was reluctant to invoke it except in the most egregious cases. TBOR2, however, gives the IRS the power to levy "intermediate sanctions"—significant financial penalties—on (1) insiders who benefit unduly from financial arrangements with tax-exempt organizations and (2) the corporate managers who approve such arrangements. Interestingly, no taxes are levied against the organization itself, and thus the payment of excessive benefits may not jeopardize the company's tax-exempt status unless the traditional private inurement standards are deemed to have been violated. In that case, the IRS's lone sanction remains the "death penalty" of exempt status revocation.

TBOR2 imposes a penalty excise tax on "disqualified persons" and "organization managers" of tax-exempt corporations who engage in "excess benefit transactions."[27] These three terms are defined as follows:

- "Disqualified persons" (hereafter referred to as "insiders") are (1) individuals who, at any time during the five-year period ending on the date of the transaction, were in a position to exert substantial influence over the tax-exempt organization's affairs, (2) family members of such individuals, and (3) entities in which such individuals have at least a 35 percent control interest. Physicians, officers, directors, trustees, and employees are insiders if they can exercise substantial influence; others may be considered insiders if they are able to exert the same degree of influence even if they hold no position with the organization.
- "Organization managers" are the organization's officers, directors, and trustees (as well as any individuals with similar powers and responsibilities regardless of title).
- "Excess benefit transactions" are transactions in which an economic benefit is provided by a tax-exempt organization, directly or indirectly, to or for the use of any insider and in which the value of the benefit exceeds the value of what the organization receives in return. This includes, for example, excessive executive compensation and purchase or sale of property at other than fair market value.

The act applies a two-tiered system of penalty taxes. The first tier addresses the excess benefit transaction itself, and the second tier focuses on the parties' willingness to correct the wrongful conduct. Under the first tier, the insider who enters into an excess benefit transaction is assessed a tax equaling 25 percent of the excess benefit. For example, if an insider physician's practice is purchased by a tax-exempt hospital for $200,000 and the fair market value of the practice is only $125,000, the excess benefit is $75,000. The physician is subject to an excise tax of $18,750 (25 percent of $75,000). In addition, each of the organization managers who participate in the transaction is subject to a 10 percent tax up to a maximum of $10,000. In the previous example, each organization manager of the hospital who knowingly participated in the practice purchase would be assessed a tax of $7,500 (10 percent of $75,000). The law provides an exception for an organization manager whose "participation is not willful and is due to reasonable cause," such as when a legal opinion had been obtained to the effect that the transaction did not constitute an excess benefit.

Under the second tier of TBOR2's penalties, insiders who do not "correct" the excess benefit transaction before a notice of tax deficiency is mailed or a tax is assessed will pay an additional 200 percent tax on the amount of the excess benefit received. Using the previous example, the insider physician who fails to correct the transaction is subject to an additional $150,000 tax penalty ($75,000 × 2), making the physician's total penalty $168,750. To correct the excess benefit transaction means "undoing the excess benefit to the extent possible" and taking other steps to restore the organization to the financial position it would have occupied had the insider adhered to "the highest fiduciary standards." Presumably, "undoing the excess benefit" means repaying it, but it is unclear how the IRS and the courts will determine whether the other measures to make the organization whole were sufficient.

The committee report accompanying TBOR2 states that transactions regarding insider compensation or purchase or sale of insiders' property are to be presumed reasonable if certain conditions are met. The arrangement in question must have been approved by a board of directors/trustees (or a committee thereof) that:

- was composed entirely of members unrelated to the insider and not under his or her control;
- gathered and used data for the purpose of comparing the transaction in question with similar transactions between other parties; and
- adequately documented the basis for its determination.

If these three requirements are met, penalty taxes are to be imposed only if the IRS can overcome the presumption with significant evidence that the transaction was unreasonable.

The committee report notes that these standards of reasonableness do not necessarily require individuals to accept less compensation simply because services are rendered to a tax-exempt, as opposed to a taxable, organization; however, an economic benefit will not be treated as compensation unless the organization clearly so indicates *at the time*. If this is not done, the IRS will not consider the benefits to be compensation and no presumption of reasonableness will be available.

According to the report, transactions entered into after September 13, 1995, and before January 1, 1997, are entitled to the presumption of rea-sonableness if the above criteria are satisfied within a reasonable time after the benefits are realized. For transactions occurring after December 31, 1996, the requirements must be met *before* insiders realize any excess benefits or, as provided in regulations, within a reasonable time period thereafter.

It is important to emphasize that the provisions relating to a presumption of reasonableness are not part of TBOR2 itself but are contained in the House Committee Report. A committee report—part of a bill's "legislative history"—does not carry the force of law; it merely provides guidance for regulatory and judicial interpretations regarding congressional intent. Whether the forthcoming IRS regulations and eventual court interpretations of TBOR2 preserve the presumption of reasonableness as described above remains to be seen.

Intermediate sanctions apply to many exempt entities, to these entities' successor organizations, and to taxable subsidiaries if the parent organization directs the subsidiary to engage in an excess benefit transaction. Intermediate sanctions may be imposed *retroactively* on benefit transactions occurring on or after September 14, 1995. The act does not apply to written agreements binding on September 13, 1995, even if benefits were realized later, so long as the terms of the transaction were not materially altered after the cut-off date. The IRS has authority to abate the penalty taxes if it determines that an excess benefit transaction was a result of reasonable cause, was not because of willful neglect, and was corrected in a timely fashion.

Because TBOR2's sanctions are levied on the individuals involved rather than the organization, the question of whether a tax-exempt entity could indemnify an organization manager for these taxes may well arise. The answer depends in part on applicable state law and the indemnity provisions of the organization's articles of incorporation and bylaws. In addition, however, because a finding of willful conduct is required to levy intermediate sanctions against organization managers, and because many state statutes preclude indemnification in the case of willful misconduct, it seems unlikely that indemnification would be possible.

If indemnification is prohibited, state law will determine whether it is permissible to insure against the risk. If an exempt entity could obtain coverage for taxes imposed under TBOR2, the law would likely treat such insurance itself as an excess benefit. This would require the organization manager to pay the insurance premium unless the premiums were intended as compensation, in which case the amount of the premium would need to be considered in determining the compensation package's excessiveness or reasonableness.

It is unlikely, although not inconceivable, that intermediate sanctions would be levied in conjunction with revocation of tax exemption. The law's legislative history indicates that intermediate sanctions are intended to be the sole penalty when the excess benefit transaction does not compromise the organization's tax-exempt status. In practice, revocation of tax-exempt status, with or without sanctions, should occur only in those cases in which the wrongful conduct is so egregious that it calls into question the tax-exempt nature of the organization.

In addition to the provisions dealing with intermediate sanctions, the act also imposes on exempt entities significant reporting and document disclosure requirements. For tax years beginning after September 30, 1996, the act provides that any excise penalties paid must be reported in the exempt organization's annual Form 990. These forms must include the amount of the fines, the nature of the transaction, and identification of all parties involved.

In addition, penalties paid for excess lobbying expenditures, disqualifying lobbying expenditures, and political expenditures must also be reported and detailed. The IRS will likely also require organizations to report changes in their governing board and accounting firm, information regarding professional fundraising fees, and aggregate payments of more than $100,000 by related entities to the highest-paid employees of the organization.

The act also provides for greater public availability of Form 990s, tax-exempt applications, and certain supporting documentation. All tax-exempt organizations are required to provide these documents when they are requested in person *or in writing,* subject only to reasonable copying and mailing expenses. (With respect to Form 990, this requirement only applies to the organization's three most recent tax years.) Exceptions to the document disclosure requirements may be made when the requests for documents amount to harassment or when the documents have already been made widely available. In addition to the new reporting requirements, penalties for failure to file complete and timely annual tax returns and failure to make documents available for public inspection have been substantially increased.

As the above review shows, the provisions of TBOR2 are complex and onerous. Worse still, they are ambiguous and open to interpretation in a number or areas. Nonetheless, some steps can be taken to ensure a maximum degree of protection from the new law. The following are some of the recommended preventive measures:

- Inform all corporate officers, directors, trustees, and other influential persons about their potential tax exposure under TBOR2.
- Review conflict of interest policies to ensure that they meet the three-part test for the presumption of reasonableness. At a minimum, these policies should require that:
  - interested persons disclose financial interests and material facts relating to any potential excess benefit transaction;
  - a determination be reached as to whether an interested person's financial stake results in a conflict of interest;
  - the conflict of interest be properly addressed by a disinterested, uninfluenced board or committee thereof;
  - actions taken to address conflicts be properly documented;
  - officers, directors, trustees, and other individuals with substantial influence over the organization receive, read, and promise to abide by the conflict of interest policy; and

- the conflict of interest policy be applied to compensation committees.
- Require that all transactions with insiders (including compensation and sale/purchase of property) be reviewed and approved by the organization's board or a committee thereof that:
  - is composed *entirely* of persons unrelated to and not controlled by the insider;
  - use adequate comparability data in its review of the reasonableness of the transaction; and
  - adequately documents the basis for its decision.
- Implement a policy of clearly identifying all benefits paid or provided to insiders as compensation and ensure that those benefits are promptly recorded and reported on appropriate tax forms.
- Review all potential excess benefit transactions entered into after September 13, 1995, and take steps to ensure that the three-part test for the presumption of reasonableness is satisfied for each one.

The issue of private gain or inurement must also be addressed when a tax-exempt institution enters into a joint venture with physicians or other proprietary interests. As defined and explained in Chapter 4, a joint venture is a special form of partnership formed for a limited or particular purpose. For a variety of reasons, in recent years hospitals and other healthcare institutions have created joint ventures that own or manage medical office buildings, treatment centers for alcoholism and substance abuse, home care agencies, CAT and MRI equipment, clinical laboratories, and even health spas. Because all partners to a venture generally contribute property or services as capital and then share profits and losses in accordance with their agreement, the question arises whether the tax-exempt participant has conferred a gain on private interests.

The operative facts of each situation will be closely examined by the Internal Revenue Service to determine whether the tax-exempt status of a participating party remains justifiable. The status of the tax-exempt participant is in jeopardy if the organization sells or leases property to the joint venture at less than fair market value, makes loans on terms that are considered commercially unreasonable, receives an inadequate return for capital contributions or services rendered to the endeavor, or agrees to allocate a disproportionate share of profits and losses to the proprietary participants.[28] In short, the terms of the joint venture agreement must provide evidence of a genuine, arm's length business agreement with a proportionate, equitable sharing of risks and rewards. These conclusions are derived from a series of private letter rulings issued by the Internal Revenue Service approving particular joint venture agreements. (Although a private letter ruling can be relied on by the taxpayer who requested it, a ruling does not bind the service in the future and cannot be cited as a precedent.)

Illustrative of the agency's approach is a ruling that approved a venture to form a 50-bed residential center for treating alcoholics and patients dependent on drugs. The two participants in the venture were a tax-exempt entity of a nonprofit, multicorporate healthcare system and a taxable subsidiary of another hospital. Because each of the participants contributed 50 percent of the initial capital and agreed to share profits and losses in the same ratio as their individual capital contributions, no inurement or private gain to the proprietary party jeopardized the tax status of the exempt participant.[29] Income received by the tax-exempt organization, however, may or may not be taxable as unrelated business income, a matter that will be discussed in the following section of this chapter.

A significant advantage of federal tax-exempt status is that donors to the organization may deduct the value of their gifts from their federal income tax liability. This is not the case for organizations exempt from income tax liability under Section 501(c)(4) of the code, which grants preferred tax status to certain groups or corporations whose purpose is to promote social welfare rather than to dispense charity. Some prepaid group practice plans or health maintenance organizations may therefore not qualify for exemption under 501(c)(3) because they may be in essence a closed group of persons who have agreed to associate for their own self-interest and private benefit rather than for the public or community interest.[30] Thus, if a health maintenance organization, even one organized as a not-for-profit corporation, has a closely controlled governing body, if participation is limited, for example, to members of a particular labor union or the employees of a particular employer, or if all members prepay the full costs of services rendered and patients do not represent an economic cross section of the community, the organization may be denied exemption from taxation under Section 501(c)(3).[31] Because it is exempt from federal tax under section 501(c)(4), the donors of grants or gifts to the organization could not deduct the value of the grants from their own taxes. This fact understandably inhibits the financing of group plans for prepaid medical care.

In a leading tax court case, however, a staff model health maintenance organization achieved charitable status by providing clinical services to non-members on a fee-for-service basis, by furnishing emergency medical care to all regardless of ability to pay, by subsidizing a portion of membership dues for those unable to pay the full amount, and by serving a significant number of Medicaid patients. When operating in this fashion, the health maintenance organization met the requirement that a charity must serve the welfare of the community at large.[32]

Akin to the noncharitable health maintenance organization is the preferred provider organization, which as a rule cannot qualify for Section 503(c)(3) status. As usual, there are exceptions to the general rule. In *Fraternal Medical Specialists Services Inc. v. Commissioner*, the U.S. Tax Court held that a medical and dental referral service was entitled to exemption as a charity when it served both members and the general community.[33] A directory of available healthcare services, together with information regarding costs of care and possible discounts, was furnished to members who paid a modest annual fee. Beyond the membership, the service promoted health by presenting programs to the general community, by sponsoring a health fair, and by publishing a newsletter. In the particular circumstances there was no prohibited private benefit or inurement.

Federal tax legislation distinguishes between public charitable foundations and private charitable foundations. Public charities are granted preferred status with respect to donations because these are fully deductible by the donor. To establish status as a public charity the organization must file a notice with the IRS and obtain a letter certifying exemption under Section 501(c)(3). Failure to file the notice of claim as a public charity results in a presumption that the organization is a private foundation.[34] The purpose of this provision is to encourage donations to public charities and to discourage the accumulation of excessive tax-exempt funds in the hands of private, family-controlled foundations. Private foundations are therefore subject to controls and scrutiny by the Internal Revenue Service that public charities are not. For example, donors of funds to private foundations receive less favorable tax treatment, additional disclosures of financial condition and operation are required,[35] and an excise tax on net investment income is levied.[36]

In 1968, Congress affirmed the merit and value of a plan under which several healthcare institutions would join together to form a separate corporation (often referred to as a "shared services" or "group purchasing" organization) organized to supply goods or services to the participating institutions. By virtue of Section 501(e) of the Internal Revenue Code, such a corporation can itself be tax exempt under Section 501(c)(3) if four requirements are met:

1. The service corporation must be organized and operated on a cooperative basis evidenced by appropriate bylaws or agreement.
2. If it is a stock corporation, all the stock must be owned by participating institutions, and all earnings must be paid to the members according to the volume of service they used.
3. All participating institutions must themselves be tax exempt or governmental hospitals providing medical care as distinct from custodial care of patients.
4. The services or goods supplied must be one or more of the following 12 specifically named in the code: data processing, purchasing, warehousing, billing and collection, food, industrial engineering, laboratory work, printing, communications, record keeping, personnel, and clinical. Such service organizations are thus recognized in the code as organized and operated exclusively for charitable purposes.

Notably absent and deliberately omitted from this list are laundry and management services. The income of a separately incorporated central laundry or cooperative is therefore taxable, because it cannot qualify as an exempt entity under Section 501(e). In *HCSC-Laundry v. United States* the Supreme Court reviewed the legislative history of the statute, construed the intent of Congress, and concluded that Section 501(e) constituted the exclusive means for a cooperative hospital service organization to achieve tax-exempt status.[37] A separately organized, central laundry service cannot therefore qualify as a charity on its own merits under Section 501(c)(3).

A tax-exempt parent corporation may own and control a for-profit subsidiary corporation without loss of its exempt status so long as the profit-making of the subsidiary does not constitute a "substantial part" of the parent's activities. In accordance with general principles of corporate law, the parent corporation and its subsidiaries are separate entities for tax purposes. As discussed in Chapter 4, however, each profit-making subsidiary must have a bona fide business purpose and a separate, distinct existence to avoid the risk that the Internal Revenue Service might pierce the corporate veil and treat the two corporations as a single unit.[38] The income of the for-profit subsidiary may be taxable, however, as being unrelated to the charitable purpose of the parent.

Taxability of Unrelated Business Income

When a charity that is exempt from income tax under Section 501(c)(3) derives income from various sources, it must face the issue of whether any income source is an "unrelated" trade or business (that is, one that is unrelated to a charitable purpose). Because allowing profits from a noncharity-related line of business to remain untaxed would give charitable organizations an unfair competitive advantage, such income is taxed, just as income is taxed for any individual or corporation engaged in profit-making endeavors. The tax-exempt status of the charity itself is not lost, however, as long as the unrelated activities do not become the organization's "primary" activity or constitute a "substantial" part of the charity's work.[39] The taxability of income from an unrelated trade or business is provided for by Sections 511–514 of the Internal Revenue Code.[40]

It must be noted that investment income consisting of dividends, interest, and annuities, as well as income from research, is not taxable as unrelated to charitable purposes;[41] however, income derived from the operation of regularly conducted gift shops, restaurants, parking lots, hospital pharmacies, physicians' offices, residences for interns, nurses, or other staff, and other facilities owned and operated by an exempt organization does present the question of unrelated trade or business taxation. The mere fact that all income from such activities is devoted to hospital or charitable purposes does *not* exempt the income from taxation. The reason for this general rule is that a hospital enterprise such as a pharmacy or a parking lot that charges its customers and is open to the general public should not be permitted an unfair competitive advantage over private businesses.

The general test of a particular income-producing activity is therefore whether it is "substantially related" to the charitable purpose of the tax-exempt institution.[42] In other words, is the pharmacy, restaurant, or parking lot furthering the purpose of the charity? To help answer these questions the Internal Revenue Code provides the "convenience rule," which states that the income is not taxable if the exempt entity can demonstrate that the activity is conducted primarily for the convenience of the institution's staff, patients, and visitors, in contrast to an enterprise selling goods and services to the general public.[43]

There is an exception to the substantial relationship test. Even if an activity does not meet that test, the income it produces is free from tax if most of the workers producing the income are volunteers or if the profits come from merchandise donated to the tax-exempt organization.[44] This rule permits a hospital, for example, to engage in fundraising supported by volunteer workers and donations, even if the efforts are carried out regularly. A volunteer is defined as a person who provides services without compensation.[45] Compensation is, in turn, defined by the courts as the receipt of benefits that would not have otherwise been granted. For example, although the brothers of a religious order were provided food, clothing, shelter, and medical care by virtue of their status while they performed more than 90 percent of the necessary labor on a large farm owned by the congregation, the income received from sales of the agricultural products was not taxable as unrelated income to the tax-exempt religious organization.[46] This is because as members of a religious order with a vow of poverty the brothers would have received the purported "compensation" irrespective of whether they worked at the farm.

If diversified enterprises are separately incorporated rather than owned and operated by the hospital, the income might be taxable because separate incorporation suggests a motive for operation beyond mere convenience for institutional patients and staff. The reason is that such a separate entity might be deemed a "feeder organization" under Sections 501 and 502 of the Internal Revenue Code. By definition a feeder organization is a separate business conducted for profit and not an integral part of the hospital.[47]

To protect the legitimate interests of commercial business, the income of a feeder organization may be taxable if the primary purpose is to earn profit and if the organization is in competition with private commercial enterprise (thus having no substantial relation to the conduct of the charitable healthcare institution). As previously indicated, the mere use of profits or earnings for charitable purposes is not in itself enough to establish the activity as related trade or business. Each case will be judged on its own facts. For example, a corporation organized to provide specialized purchasing and consulting services to several hospitals was free from the unrelated business income tax because the facts established that it was not effectively in competition with private interests.[48]

Income derived from property owned by a tax-exempt entity and rented to others is specifically excluded in the Internal Revenue's Code's definition of unrelated business income unless the property is "debt financed."[49] Generally, therefore, rent received from all real estate that is not debt-financed is exempt from taxation. On the other hand, rental income from debt-financed property is generally taxable in proportion to the amount of the debt. A mortgage loan, of course, is the most common example of a debt to finance the acquisition or the improvement of property.

There are significant exceptions to the general-rule taxing income from debt-financed property or from business leases of more than five years. If the rental income is derived from using the property in a way that is substantially related to charitable purposes, then it is free from federal tax. Hence, the rent from a medical office building built by a hospital on adjacent land and leased only to medical staff physicians for terms longer than five years was considered nontaxable in an Internal Revenue ruling.[50] The ruling properly recognizes that proximity of physicians' offices to a hospital increases efficiency, encourages fuller use of the hospital's facilities, and improves the quality of patient care.

As a general rule, income derived from sales of goods and services to the patients and staff of a healthcare institution will not be treated as taxable unrelated income. A liberal definition of "hospital patients" is usually recognized; it includes outpatients, persons seen in the emergency department, discharged inpatients returning to the hospital pharmacy for refills of prescriptions, patients in an extended-care facility owned by the hospital, and patients enrolled in a program of home care sponsored by the hospital.[51] As a means of applying the statutory standard that requires revenue-producing activity to be substantially related to the charitable purpose to be free from taxation, this interpretation of the "convenience rule" means that sales to persons who are neither patients nor staff members will normally be subject to taxation.

Because the sale of services to others is inhibited if the revenue is considered taxable, the foregoing approach to the issue of unrelated business income is clearly in conflict with an economic and political environment in which healthcare institutions are urged to rationalize their resources to serve the whole community. In recognition of this dilemma Congress responded in 1976 by enacting Section 513(e) of the Internal Revenue Code, which provides that sales of certain specified services to certain specifically identified buyers will be permitted as nontaxable transactions.

Section 513(e) specifies services that an institution may sell without their being treated as sources of unrelated business income. They are the same as those listed in Section 501(e), which relates to the tax-exempt status of a separately incorporated central service organization and was discussed earlier: data processing, purchasing, warehousing, billing and collection, food, industrial engineering, laboratory services, printing, communications, record keeping, personnel (selection, training, and education), and clinical. Management and laundry services are still excluded. For the sales to qualify under Section 513(e), however, the buyers must be tax-exempt hospitals with fewer than 100 beds. This very restrictive provision excludes sales not only to many other general hospitals but also to nursing homes and similar institutions providing long-term care. Finally, the sales must further the charitable purpose of the seller and prices must be at cost, although cost may include depreciation and a reasonable return on capital investment.[52] In summary, Section 513(e) has not significantly altered the general approach that sales to nonpatients will be considered unrelated business income, because the statute is so restrictive.

From time to time, however, quite aside from Section 513(e) of the Internal Revenue Code, the courts have been willing to expand the convenience rule and thereby shield revenue from the unrelated business tax. In *St. Luke's Hospital of Kansas City v. United States,* for example, the court held that a tax-exempt teaching hospital could sell laboratory services to the patient-physician community generally because such services were likely to benefit the teaching and research functions of the hospital and accordingly bore a "substantial relationship" to the hospital's charitable purpose.[53] Such sales were also considered to be for the "convenience" of those physicians who were in fact members of the hospital's medical staff. In *Hi-Plains Hospital v. United States* a federal circuit court approved sales of prescription drugs to patients of staff physicians even though some of the buyers had never been patients of the hospital.[54] The drug sales were not advertised to the general public, and in the particular circumstances the court concluded that the sales were consistent with the convenience rule. The court noted specifically that the hospital was located in a rural community and had difficulty in attracting physicians to the community. Notwithstanding these cases, however, revenue from sales to persons who are patients of private fee-for-service physicians but have never been patients of the hospital will not as a general rule be nontaxable income, even if the doctors are members of the medical staff.[55] This follows from the fact that physicians practicing in their private capacity are not considered to be "members, officers, or employees" of the hospital.

The Internal Revenue Service has sometimes lessened the impact of the patient-nonpatient rule by recognizing that in certain special circumstances sales to others will be treated as activities related to the seller's charitable purpose in promoting community health. For example, IRS private letter rulings have approved the sale of both managerial and electrocardiograph services that were not otherwise available in the particular communities involved and that enabled the seller to fulfill the community's needs in accordance with its charitable purpose.[56] Future application of the "special circumstances" rule is, however, highly uncertain, and only time will reveal the direction of administrative policies in interpreting the uncertain statutory language.

State Taxation of Real Estate and Personal Property

Real estate and personal property owned by federal or local governmental hospitals are exempt from taxation by the state and local government; the exemption is created by specific provision of the relevant state constitution or by statute. In some states ownership and control of the property standing alone is sufficient to establish exemption. Other states add the requirement that the public property be in use "exclusively for a public purpose" to justify exemption.[57]

In a Minnesota case a medical clinic owned and operated by a municipal hospital was not exempt from taxation when it was staffed by physicians practicing essentially on a fee-for-service basis. The board of the hospital and the physicians agreed annually on the fees to be charged patients. Each doctor then received 60 percent of his or her gross accounts receivable. Noting that the issue hinged on whether the primary use of the facility was for public purposes or for private gain, the state supreme court held that the tax court's decision to deny exemption was not unreasonable.[58] In the circumstances the facility was not being used exclusively for a public purpose.

With respect to privately owned healthcare institutions, the real estate that they occupy or own, as well as their personal property, may or may not be tax-exempt, depending on a number of factors. The first requirement of note is that the institution must qualify as a charity, a matter defined by local state law and discussed previously. Hence, real estate owned by a proprietary hospital, or one operated for profit, is fully taxable, just as the property of any other business is taxable. When the tax is based on the value of property it is characterized as an *ad valorem* tax.

Qualifying as a Charity

In some states a *mandatory* constitutional provision, as illustrated by the Utah constitution quoted below, is the source of exemption for real estate and other property owned or occupied by a public or charitable healthcare institution. The legislature of the state could not terminate such an exemption, and neither could the courts, although the courts have the power to interpret the constitutional language. Other states' constitutions contain *permissive* tax exemption provisions for charitable organizations, and a few state constitutions are entirely silent on the matter. In either of these situations, tax-exempt status will depend on legislative enactment. Hence, a permissive constitutional provision has the effect of granting the ultimate power of exemption to the legislature. The requirements of attaining tax-exempt status thus determined will be subject to court interpretation, however, especially with respect to legislative intent. The distinction between a mandatory constitutional provision and a permissive one or no provision at all—becomes significant in an era when local governments constantly need and are searching for additional revenue and when there is increasing political pressure to restrict or reduce the *ad valorem* tax exemptions.

It has already been mentioned that most state courts do not require an institution to render a certain amount of free care, or care below cost, and to be partly subsidized by public contributions before it can qualify as a charity and be exempt from taxation. At this point, however, it is important to consider this rule in the context of *ad valorem* taxation.

Illustrating the general rule that an undefined amount of free care is not necessary to qualify for state real estate tax exemption is the Nebraska case of *Evangelical Lutheran Good Samaritan Society v. County of Gage*.[59] A home for the aged was organized as a not-for-profit corporation. It required all residents to pay if they were able. The rates were nearly the same as those charged by proprietary homes, and the home operated at a profit in some years and at a deficit in others. The court held the real estate to be exempt, ruling in effect that "charity" should be defined in broader terms than almsgiving and relief of poverty.

In *Central Board on Care of Jewish Age, Inc. v. Henson* the Court of Appeals of Georgia ruled that a home for the elderly was exempt, saying:

> For the appellant to be tax exempt it must be purely charitable and public. . . . "A familiar meaning of the word 'charity' is almsgiving, but as used in the law it may include substantially any scheme or effort to better the condition of society, or any considerable part thereof . . . 'charity,' as used in tax exemption statutes, is not restricted to the relief of the sick or indigent, but extends to other forms of philanthropy or public beneficence, such as practical enterprises for the good of humanity, operated at moderate cost to the beneficiaries, or enterprises operated for the general improvement and happiness of mankind."
>
> Neither would the fact that the residents paid rent according to their ability destroy the charitable nature of the institution. . . .
>
> The purpose of the home is to care for the aged and provide for their physical and mental welfare. As is stated in *Bozeman Deaconess Foundation v. Ford:* "The concept of charity is not confined to the relief of the needy and destitute, for aged people require care and attention apart from financial assistance, and the supply of this care and attention is as much a charitable and benevolent purpose as the relief of their financial wants."[60]

In the *Henson* case the home provided medical and nursing services to elderly persons of the Jewish faith. The residents' average age was nearly 83, and each paid a monthly charge based on financial ability, the maximum being $450. No applicant was ever refused admission because of inability to pay, and at all times a few residents were permitted to remain without paying. Deficits in annual operating expenses were covered by contributions from time to time by the Jewish Welfare Fund or by individuals.

Subsequent cases have confirmed this broad definition of "charitable" for *ad valorem* tax purposes. For example, in 1981 the Massachusetts Supreme Judicial Court wrote:

> However, we recognize too that major changes in the area of health care, especially in modes of operation and financing, have necessitated changes as well in definitional predicates. The term "charitable," as applied to health care facilities, has been broadened since earlier times when it was limited mainly to almshouses for the poor. As a result, the promotion of health, whether through the provision of health care or through medical education and research, is today generally seen as a charitable purpose. [Citations omitted.] Such a purpose is separate and distinct from the relief of poverty and no health organization need engage in "almsgiving" in order to qualify for exemption. [Citations omitted.][61]

The prevailing view expressed by these cases can perhaps be identified as the "community benefit" rule.[62] In sharp contrast to the community benefit rule, however, is the majority opinion in *Utah County v. Intermountain Health Care, Inc.*[63] The litigation arose when the local county government assessed *ad valorem* taxes on the property of Utah Valley Hospital and American Fork Hospital. Both of these hospitals were components of Intermountain Health Care, Inc., a multi-institutional system which at the time of the controversy owned or leased 21 hospitals and also owned other subsidiary corporations, including a for-profit organization. Intermountain, the parent corporation, is not-for-profit, has no stock, and pays no dividends to individuals. It has a governing board whose members were without pay, and its corporate documents recite that no private gain will inure to any private person upon dissolution of the corporation.

With respect to taxation of property, the Utah Constitution provides that "the property of the state, counties, cities, towns, school districts, municipal corporations and public libraries, [and] lots with the buildings thereon used exclusively for either religious worship or charitable purposes . . . shall be exempt from taxation."[64] Legislation intended to clarify this constitutional provision recites: "Any property whose use is dedicated to . . . charitable purposes including property which is incidental to and reasonably necessary for . . . charitable purposes, intended to benefit an indefinite number of persons is exempt from taxation if all of the following requirements are met. . . ."[65] The statute then identifies the requirements necessary for tax exemption. Essentially these specific requirements simply state the classical definition of not-for-profit enterprise: the corporation using the property must not be organized to produce a profit; use of the property, earnings from the assets, and any distributions upon dissolution of the corporation shall not inure to the benefit of any private person. However, another section of the statute contained the following provision: "Property used exclusively for religious, *hospital*, educational employee representation, or welfare purposes . . . shall be deemed to be used for charitable purposes within the exemption provided for in [the Utah] Constitution. . . ."[66] Utah County conceded that both of the hospitals met these statutory requirements for exemption but took the position that the quoted provision was an unconstitutional expansion of the concept of "charitable purpose," as expressed in the state constitution.

The majority of the Utah Supreme Court agreed with the position of Utah County and reversed a decision of the state tax commission, which had granted tax exemption. Noting at the outset that both constitutional and statutory provisions are to be strictly construed and that the burden of proof is on those claiming exemption, the court went on to rule that the facts did not demonstrate conformance with Utah's concept of charitable purposes. Basically the court rejected the "community benefit" approach adopted in most states. Instead it required that an actual gift be made to the community as proof that the private organization was either alleviating a burden of government or providing a substantial amount of uncompensated services to the community at large. This theory requires a degree of almsgiving, at least to the extent of establishing that the hospital has provided a significant volume of unreciprocated services. The majority noted that in today's economic and political environment, nonprofit status is increasingly irrelevant to the provision of charitable services,[67] that multihospital systems accumulate and invest capital much in the same fashion as investor-owned healthcare organizations, and that this capital may not be returned to the local communities.[68] More specifically, the current operating expenses of the two hospitals involved in this appeal appeared to be nearly covered by revenues from charges. The court observed that

> [n]either of the hospitals in this case demonstrated any substantial imbalance between the value of the services it provides and the payments it receives apart from any gifts, donations or endowments. The record shows that the vast majority of the services provided by these two hospitals are paid for by government programs, private insurance companies, or the individuals receiving care. Collection of such remuneration does not constitute giving, but is a mere reciprocal exchange of services for money . . . . every effort was made to recover payment for services rendered.[69]

In sum, in the view of the Utah court, tax exemptions are subsides from government, and proof of a charitable purpose requires that there has been a genuine and quantifiable quid pro quo. Accordingly, a private charity must establish that it is performing functions that the state would otherwise perform. Providing a benefit to the community is not enough.

In two separate dissenting opinions it was vigorously maintained that the majority had departed sharply from traditional principles and thereby introduced "confusion and mischief" into judicial law,[70] that there are in fact fundamental differences between the operations of not-for-profit corporations and those for profit,[71] and that the majority had disregarded the factual findings of the state tax commission relative to the volume of care the two hospitals rendered to indigent persons and the subsidies they furnished patients under Medicaid, Medicare, and worker's compensation.[72] The case sharply illustrates contrasting views about healthcare in the current economic environment, conflicting perceptions of the role of not-for-profit corporations in this environment, and differing opinions on what public policy should be.[73]

Ownership of Exempt Property

In general, every parcel of land owned or occupied by a hospital claiming tax exemption as a charitable institution must separately qualify for such exemption. Normally, each parcel must also meet two tests: ownership by the hospital and use for a charitable purpose. The test of ownership is not as simple as it might first appear. Real estate law recognizes various types of estates in land as well as leasehold interests in land owned by another. All states, so far as the ownership test is concerned, grant exemption to land owned by a charity when the organization holds "fee simple" (i.e., complete) legal title. Nearly all likewise grant exemption to ownership in the form of equitable title. (An example of an equitable title is the purchase of land on an installment contract under which the seller retains legal title until the purchase price is paid in full or until the buyer has reached a certain amount of equity in the property and refinances the balance by mortgage.) A few states will deny exemption to a charity holding equitable title.

A larger number of states will deny real estate tax exemption to the owner of land who leases it to a charitable corporation. Here, clearly, the land is not owned by the charity, which has obtained by the lease the right of possession and use but which has neither legal nor equitable title. On the other hand, some states will exempt such property from taxation because according to past experience it is sound public policy to reduce the operating costs of charitable organizations. Competition in the healthcare industry may lead public policy to the opposite conclusion, as illustrated by the majority opinion in *Utah County v. Intermountain Health Care, Inc.* discussed above. This matter, of course, is resolved by the individual states according to judicial interpretations of constitutional and statutory requirements.

Use for a Charitable Purpose

Most states require that tax-exempt property of a charity be held for the "exclusive use . . . for charitable purposes." Note carefully that this contemplates actual use or occupancy of the property itself, and property owned for investment income would therefore not qualify for exemption. In other words, the *use* of the property determines the tax-exempt status and not the use of income derived from the property. Moreover the word "exclusive" in these provisions raises issues about property rented to or occupied by such others as medical staff members who practice as private physicians, hospital interns, residents, and nurses. The usual approach to these situations, which are decided case by case and state by state, is to examine how closely the use of the property relates to the primary purpose of the hospital and to analyze the relative benefits to the respective parties.

In general, property will be subject to real estate taxation if it is rented to private physicians or others who pay a rental, based on its market value, that allows the hospital a profit in excess of overhead.[74] This follows either from an express statutory provision forbidding rental of property held by a charity or from judicial interpretation of the "exclusive use" provision. A few states, however, allow exemption for property rented to medical staff physicians for their private offices or to hospital personnel for their residences if rental covers only the overhead cost or if no rent at all is charged.[75] The rationale would be that the hospital and its patients benefit by having the staff close at hand at all times, and public policy should hence serve the interests of the charity unless there is an express provision forbidding any rental. On the other hand, some courts will deny exemption to facilities such as physician's offices or residences for staff, even if rental does not exceed the costs of maintenance and amortization of investment. They do so either on the ground that the primary benefit is a private benefit, not a charitable one, and therefore the "exclusive use" test is not met or on the ground that local statutes allow tax exemption only on land occupied by the hospital itself.[76]

A frequently cited New York case illustrates the issues of public policy that come into play with respect to the lease of hospital-owned real estate.[77] Genesee Hospital constructed an office building adjacent to the hospital for lease to private physicians. Rent paid by the doctors was set at currently competitive prices, but at first the rents did not cover operating costs. The hospital is a teaching institution with a full-time staff of salaried physicians, together with resident physicians and interns. The private attending staff participate actively with the house staff in patient care and medical education. As in many other states the New York statute requires that "real property owned by a corporation or association organized or conducted exclusively for . . . hospital . . . purposes . . . and used exclusively for carrying out . . . such purposes . . . shall be exempt from taxation."[78] Further, however, the statute provides that "if any portion of such real property is not so used exclusively to carry out . . . such purposes but is leased or otherwise used for other purposes, such portion shall be subject to taxation and the remaining portion only shall be exempt."[79] At issue, then, was whether the office building was used exclusively for hospital purposes.

The trial court rendered an opinion favorable to the hospital and held that the building was exempt from taxation. Rather than applying a literal interpretation of the word "exclusively," the court, citing precedent, applied the standard of whether the office building was "reasonably incident to the major purpose" of the hospital. Because the evidence clearly established that the hospital's concern was to maintain a "first-rate" medical center for both patient care and medical education rather than to benefit the private physicians personally, the trial court judge concluded in essence that the hospital, its house staff, and patients benefited relatively more from the use of the building than the private physicians did.[80] The public policy involved was made evident when the trial court concluded that the community views a modern hospital building to be an important investment if it enables a highly trained staff of attending physicians to work together.

On appeal, however, the decision was reversed, and the space leased to the private practicing physicians was held to be subject to taxation. The appellate court recognized that a professional building was an admirable addition to the community and doubtless enhanced the patient care and teaching functions of the hospital. Nevertheless, the facility was in direct competition with privately developed professional office buildings serving an identical function of providing space for the private practice of medicine. Accordingly, the leased space did not qualify for exemption under the language of the New York statute.[81]

Issues similar to those relating to physicians' offices and nurses' residences are sometimes raised regarding cafeterias, gift shops, pharmacies, parking lots, and the like that a hospital owns and operates. Again, the legal issue is whether these activities are consistent with the requirement of "exclusive use for charitable purpose." If such an activity is not conducted for commercial profit, and if it takes place in a part of the hospital building or the immediate premises not open to the general public, the granting of tax-exempt status is likely.

Under the limited circumstances noted, the standard of primary purpose or use may simply be whether the activity is reasonably necessary or reasonably incident to the fulfillment of the functions of the hospital or healthcare institution. Hence, recreational areas for employees, housing for interns, residents, nurses, and other personnel, and land used for a nurses' training school were all exempt in a frequently cited California case.[82] In the same case, however, a building under construction for housing student nurses and property occupied by a thrift shop where donated merchandise was sold were held to be taxable. In Ohio and Maine, hospital parking lots limited to staff and visitors, where all the fees were devoted to maintenance or recovery of capital investment, were held to be exempt.[83] On the other hand, if any of the criteria noted above are violated, if the facility is operated by an independent organization through a lease that enables the hospital to earn a profit,[84] or if the property in question is actually owned by another corporation in a multihospital system, then legal questions arise that could jeopardize tax exemption.[85]

If tax-exempt status for a cafeteria, gift shop, parking lot, or similar facility cannot be maintained, the hospital must then determine whether the local and state statutes permit split-listing of property for tax purposes, because the related activity frequently takes place in some part of an institutional building. Split-listing means essentially that the local tax authorities will list as taxable only the space that is not exempt, allowing exemption on the remainder of the hospital building. In most jurisdictions split-listing is permitted.[86] Some states do not allow it, however, and in those states it is especially important to seek competent legal advice regarding uses such as those named above.

Many healthcare institutions own vacant land or recreational land for the use of employees, and often this is located away from the hospitals themselves. With respect to vacant or unoccupied land there is a diversity of judicial opinion, depending on the exact language of local state statute and judicial interpretation of that language. For tax exemption some states may provide that the land must not only be "used" for charitable purposes but must also be "occupied." Even if being occupied for a charitable purpose is not a statutory requirement, one must determine the meaning of "used." Vacant land that is held simply for possible use in the indefinite future and for which no plans for development exist would normally be taxable.[87] On the other hand, if plans for construction and development are well along, fund-raising is under way, and actual bids have been received for construction, then the land, although not yet in actual use, is exempt in some jurisdictions.[88] Some states, however, may require actual use and occupancy before granting exemption.

Finally, it should be observed that to an increasing extent healthcare institutions are choosing to lease rather than purchase equipment and other types of personal property. Just as in a number of states where the owner of land who leases it to a charity must pay real estate taxes on the property, as mentioned earlier, leased personal property may also be subject to *ad valorem* taxation. In an Alaska case a hospital's lease of beds, television sets, and x-ray equipment did not qualify the property for exemption. The exemption provisions did not apply because the lessor was presumably earning a profit and thus the property was not being used "exclusively for non-profit, religious, charitable . . . purposes" as required by the state constitution and the relevant statute.[89]

Notes

1. 160 Pa. 572, 28 A. 954 (1894); *accord* Missouri Pac. Hosp. Ass'n v. Pulaski County, 211 Ark. 9, 199 S.W.2d 329 (1947) (hospital owned by a railroad employees association and open only to railroad employees not exempt).
2. *See* Kansas Masonic Home v. Board of Commissioners, 81 Kan. 859, 106 P. 1082 (1910); *accord* Fitterer v. Crawford, 157 Mo. 51, 57 S.W. 532 (1900) (in *Crawford* home denied tax exemption for other reasons).

3. Young Life Campaign v. Board of Commissioners, 134 Colo. 15, 300 P.2d 535 (1956).

4. People *ex rel.* Near East Found. v. Boyland, 201 Misc. 855, 106 N.Y.S.2d 736 (1951).

5. Rev. Rul. 157, 1983-42 C.B. 9–10 (tax-exempt hospital need not provide emergency services, although it will be expected to serve community at large in other ways, for example, by serving Medicaid and Medicare patients).

6. *See, e.g.,* Cleveland Osteopathic Hosp. v. Zangerle, 153 Ohio St. 222, 91 N.E.2d 261 (1950); Vicksburg v. Vicksburg Sanitarium, 117 Miss. 709, 78 So. 702 (1918).

7. It is of historical interest that prior to 1969 the federal government did require a tax-exempt hospital to furnish an undefined amount of service below costs. Rev. Rul. 185, 1956-1 C.B. 202. This ruling was changed by Rev. Rul. 545, 1969-2 C.B. 117.

8. Bromberg, *The Charitable Hospital*, 20 CATH. U.L. REV. 241-44 (1970).

9. 267 A.D. 736, 48 N.Y.S.2d 201, 205 (1944), *aff'd*, 295 N.Y. 553, 64 N.E.2d 273 (1945). *See also* Bishop & Chapter of the Cathedral of St. John the Evangelist v. Treasurer of the City and County of Denver, 37 Colo. 378, 86 P. 1021 (1906) (hospital may charge fees to all patients, and amount received may exceed expenses).

10. Bromberg, *supra* note 8, at 248–51.

11. Hart v. Taylor, 301 Ill. 344, 133 N.E. 857 (1921); Natchez v. Natchez Sanitorium Benevolent Ass'n, 191 Miss. 91, 2 So. 2d 798 (1941) (*Hart* involved the validity of a charitable testamentary trust).

12. Bromberg *supra* note 8, at 250.

13. Bromberg *supra* note 8, at 249–250.

14. 26 U.S.C. § 501(c)(3).

15. Bob Jones Univ. v. United States, 461 U.S. 574 (1983) (Internal Revenue Service has administrative authority to deny exemption to educational institution practicing racial discrimination); *cf.* Allen v. Wright, 468 U.S. 737 (1984) (parents of black children in public schools lack standing to sue in a class action to challenge Internal Revenue Service's grant of tax-exempt status to private schools allegedly practicing racial discrimination); *cf.* Abortion Rights Mobilization, Inc. v. Regan, 544 F. Supp. 471 (1982), *motion for certification denied*, 552 F. Supp. 364 (1982), *renewed motion to dismiss denied*, 603 F. Supp. 970 (S.D.N.Y. 1985) (individuals and organizations favoring abortion have standing to challenge Internal Revenue Service's grant of tax-exempt status to a Roman Catholic church overtly engaged in electioneering and lobbying activities allegedly contrary to charitable status).

16. Rev. Rul. 185, 1956-1 C.B. 202. The ruling cited here restated the two code requirements and the necessity of an open medical staff.

17. See Chapter 14.

18. I.R.C. § 501(h)(1982).

19. *See generally* Hastings, Oldaker, and Kerman, *Tax-Exempt Hospitals and Electoral Politics*, HOSPS. August 1, 1984, at 80–82.

20. Regan v. Taxation With Representation of Washington, 461 U.S. 540 (1983).

21. I.R.C. § 501(c)(3).

22. Bromberg, *supra* note 8, at 252–53.

23. For example, a contract with an outside firm to manage a healthcare institution should not compensate the firm on the basis of a percentage of earnings or gross receipts. *See* E.S.T. of Hawaii v. Commissioner, TAX CT. REP. DEC. (P-H) ¶ 71.96 (Apr. 6, 1979).

24. *See, e.g.,* Sonora Community Hosp. v. Commissioner, TAX CT. REP. DEC. (P-H) ¶ 46.51 (Aug. 19, 1966), *aff'd,* 397 F.2d 814 (9th Cir. 1968); Lorain Ave. Clinic v. Commissioner, TAX CT. REP. DEC. (P-H) ¶ 31.19 (Oct. 31, 1958).

25. Rev. Rul. 383, 1969-2 C.B. 113.

26. *E.g.,* I.R.S. Priv. Ltr. Rul. 8610050 (CCH) (Dec. 10, 1985) (an "efficiency index" based on average length of patients' stay and use of the hospital's ancillary services for each physician admitting a certain number of patients per year may be used as a method of allocating the hospital's annual cost savings among the physicians); *see Quarterly Tax Report,* 9 HEALTH L. VIGIL (AM. HOSP. ASS'N) No. 7, at 4 (Apr. 11, 1986); I.R.S. Priv. Ltr. Rul. 8419071 (CCH) (Feb. 10, 1984) (guarantee of loan to private physician to establish radiation therapy facility does not constitute private gain); I.R.S. Priv. Ltr. Rul. 8422130 (CCH) (Feb. 29, 1984) (guarantee of minimum gross income to private physician for one year is payment of income and reportable on information return). *Compare* I.R.S. Gen. Couns. Mem. 39498 (April 24, 1986) (hospital's guarantee of annual income for two-year period to recruited physician was disapproved because there was no requirement to repay, insufficient evidence of value of physician's services to the hospital, and insufficient evidence of "reasonableness"); *see Physician Recruiting Programs,* 9 HEALTH L. VIGIL (AM. HOSP. ASS'N) No. 13, at 8–10 (July 4, 1986).

27. The law applies to § 501(c)(3) charitable organizations (other than private foundations), and § 501(c)(4) social welfare organizations.

28. *1985 Annual Tax Wrap-Up,* 9 HEALTH L. VIGIL (AM. HOSP. ASS'N) No. 1, at 5 (Jan. 17, 1986); I.R.S. Priv. Ltr. Rul. 8534089 (CCH) (May 31, 1985) (home care services); I.R.S. Priv. Ltr. Rul. 8504060 (October 30, 1984) (nuclear magnetic resonance system); I.R.S. Priv. Ltr. Rul. 8531069 (May 10, 1985) (ambulatory surgery center).

29. I.R.S. Priv. Ltr. Rul. 8521055 (CCH) (Feb. 26, 1985). *See generally* Bromberg and Teplitzky, *Tangling With Tax Law,* HOSPS. Mar. 1, 1983, at 69–78.

30. Rev. Rul. 185, 1956-1 C.B. 202.

31. For example, an independent practice health maintenance organization could not qualify as charitable when it did not serve Medicare and Medicaid patients or those unable to pay, and there were no community representatives on the governing board. I.R.S. Gen. Couns. Mem. 39057 (Sept. 17, 1982).

32. Sound Health Ass'n v. Commissioner, TAX CT. REP. DEC. (P-H) ¶ 71.16 (Nov. 13, 1978).

33. 52 T.C.M. (P-H) ¶ 84,644 (Dec. 12, 1984). Similarly, a healthcare coalition achieved § 501(c)(3) status by making governing board positions available to all interested groups, including the general public and public agencies, by conducting health educational programs and by assessing participants only nominal dues. *I.R.S. Denial of 501(c)(3) Status Supports Broad-based Coalitions,* 9 HEALTH L. VIGIL (AM. HOSP. ASS'N) No. 9, at 9 (May 9, 1986).

34. I.R.C. § 508(b) (1982).

35. I.R.C. §§ 6033, 6104, 6685, 7207 (1982 & Supp. II 1984).

36. I.R.C. § 4940 (1982 & Supp. II 1984).

37. 450 U.S. 1 (1981).

38. I.R.S. Priv. Ltr. Rul. 8519037 (Feb. 12, 1985); I.R.S. Gen. Couns. Mem. 39326 (August 31, 1984); Hospital Corp. of Am. v. Commissioner, TAX CT. REP. DEC. (P-H) ¶ 81.31 (Sept. 21, 1983).

39. Currently the Internal Revenue Service may challenge the tax-exempt status of a charity if gross income from unrelated activities exceeds 50 percent of the charity's total revenue. It should also be noted that sales of goods or services by an exempt organization to private proprietary parties below cost may constitute conferring a private gain or inurement, thus jeopardizing the tax-exempt status of the seller.

40. *E.g.*, United States v. American College of Physicians, 106 S. Ct. 1591 (1986) (income received by medical organization from commercial advertisements in professional journal taxable as unrelated business income).

41. I.R.C. § 512(b).

42. I.R.C. § 513(a); Treas. Reg. § 1.513-1(a) (1967).

43. I.R.C. § 513(s)(2).

44. I.R.C. § 513(a)(1).

45. *Id.*

46. St. Joseph Farms of Ind. v. Commissioner, TAX CT. REP. DEC. (P-H) ¶ 85.2 (July 1, 1985).

47. *See* TAX CT. REP. DEC. ¶ 74.17 (May 6, 1980).

48. Hospital Bureau of Standard Supplies v. United States, 158 Supp. 560 (Ct. Cl. 1958) (disapproved in HCSC-Laundry v. United States, 624 F.2d 428 (3d Cir. 1980), *aff'd*, 450 U.S. 1 (1981).

49. I.R.C. § 512(b)(3), (4).

50. Rev. Rul. 464, 1969-2 C.B. 132. Pub. L. No. 591, § 514, 68A Stat. 3, 172 (1954) (amended 1969, 1976). Similarly income from the leasing of an adjacent office building to a medical group by a tax-exempt hospital is related income and not taxable. Rev. Rul. 463, 1969–2 C.B. 131; Gundersen Medical Found., Ltd. v. United States, 536 F. Supp. 556 (W.D. Wis. 1982) (lease of debt-financed property to for-profit medical clinic did not result in taxable income to tax-exempt medical educational foundation because use of property substantially related to educational research programs of foundation).

51. Rev. Rul. 376, 1968-2 C.B. 246.

52. *Quarterly Tax Report,* 9 HEALTH L. VIGIL (AM. HOSP. ASS'N) No. 7, at 4 (Apr. 11, 1986); 42 U.S.C. §§ 1395x (v)1(A), (B) (1982 & Supp. II 1984).

53. 494 F. Supp. 85 (W.D. Mo. 1980).

54. 670 F.2d 528 (5th Cir. 1982) (sales to persons who were not patients of either the hospital or staff physicians would be taxable).

55. Carle Found. v. United States, 611 F.2d 1192 (7th Cir. 1979), *cert. denied,* 449 U.S. 824 (1980) (revenue from sales to ambulatory patients of physicians' clinic taxable as unrelated income); I.R.C. § 513(a)(2); Rev. Rul. 85-109, 1985-30 I.R.B. 17 (sale of laboratory services prescribed by private staff physicians is unrelated business when persons receiving the services have never been patients

of hospital); *Quarterly Tax Report*, 8 HEALTH L. VIGIL (AM. HOSP. ASS'N) No. 16, at 7–8 (Aug. 9, 1985).

56. I.R.S. Priv. Ltr. Rul 8004011; I.R.S. Priv. Ltr. Rul. 8050059; *Compare* Rev. Rul. 85-110, 1985-30 I.R.B. 18 (sale of laboratory services by nonteaching hospital to private office patients of hospital's staff physicians is unrelated business if equivalent facilities are otherwise available). *See* O'Brien, *1982 Tax Wrap-Up* 6 HEALTH L. VIGIL (AM. HOSP. ASS'N) No. 1, at 4–5 (Jan. 7, 1983).

57. For example, OHIO REV. CODE ANN. § 5709.08 (page 1985) provides: "Real or personal property belonging to the state or United States used exclusively for a public purpose, and public property used exclusively for a public purpose, shall be exempt from taxation." *See* Carney v. Cleveland, 173 Ohio St. 56, 108 N.E.2d 14 (1962).

58. City of Springfield v. Commissioner of Revenue, 380 N.W.2d 802 (Minn. 1986).

59. 181 Neb. 831, 151 N.W.2d 446 (1967).

60. 120 Ga. App. 627, 629, 171 S.E.2d 747, 749 (1969) (citations omitted). Compare the reinterpretation of Georgia Constitution and Code requiring that a tax-exempt organization be "purely charitable and public." St. Joseph Hosp. of Augusta v. Bohler, 229 Ga. 577, 193 S.E. 2d 603 (1972) (when hospital's costs were borne by patients who were encouraged to pay and its policies were not directed toward persons destitute and without economic means, it was not exempt from taxation even though its emergency room was open at all times to general public, its available annual surpluses were used to improve facilities, and during some years hospital operated at a deficit). The *Bohler* court made no reference to the *Henson* decision.

61. Harvard Community Health Plan, Inc. v. Board of Assessors, 384 Mass. 536, 542–43, 427 N.E.2d 1159, 1163 (1981) (citations omitted).

62. *See* South Iowa Methodist Homes, Inc. v. Board of Review, 173 N.W.2d 526 (Iowa 1970); Vick v. Cleveland Memorial Medical Found., 2 Ohio St. 2d 30, 206 N.E.2d 2 (1965); Community Memorial Hosp. v. City of Moberly, 422 S.W.2d 290 (Mo. 1967); Scripps Memorial Hosp. v. California Employment Comm'n, 24 Cal. 2d 669, 151 P.2d 109 (1944); Bozeman Deaconess Found. v. Ford, 151 Mont. 143, 439 P.2d 915 (1968); State *ex rel.* Cook v. Rose, 299 S.E.2d 3 (W. Va. 1982) (patients may be required to pay in accordance with their means); West Allegheny Hosp. v. Board of Property Assessments, 500 Pa. 236, 455 A.2d 1170 (1982) (can use patient revenues to finance repairs to property and costs of acquisitions that further charitable purposes). *Cf.* Presbyterian Homes v. Division of Tax Appeals, 55 N.J. 275, 261 A.2d 143 (1970) (home for elderly not exempt when it reserved right to terminate residence of persons who could not continue to pay monthly care); Passavant Health Center v. Board of Assessment and Revision of Taxes of Butler County, 502 A.2d 753 (Pa. Commw. 1985) (retirement cottages located on hospital property not exempt when residents were required to pay lump sum upon entrance and furnish evidence of ability to pay monthly service fee and charges for future medical care).

63. 709 P.2d 265 (Utah 1985).

64. UTAH CONST. art. XIII, § 2(c) (1895), *amded by*, UTAH CONST. art. XIII, § 2 (1982).

65. U.C.A. § 59-2-30.

66. U.C.A. § 59-2-31.
67. 709 P.2d at 271.
68. *Id.* at 275.
69. *Id.* at 274.
70. *Id.* at 294.
71. *Id.* at 290.
72. *Id.* at 284–85.
73. *See also In re* Doctor's Hosp., 414 A.2d 134 (Pa. Commw. 1980) (podiatric hospital not a public charity when it renders no free care and receives no significant contributions from public, and where equivalent professional services are readily available elsewhere).
74. Greater Anchorage Area Borough v. Sisters of Charity, 553 P.2d 467 (Alaska 1976) (building leased at commercial rentals to staff physicians practicing privately is taxable even though the facility was reasonably necessary to functions of community hospital).
75. Aultman Hosp. Ass'n v. Evatt, 140 Ohio St. 114, 42 N.E.2d 646 (1942) (residence for nurses exempt); Sisters of Saint Mary v. City of Madison, 89 Wis. 2d 372, 278 N.W.2d 814 (1979) (rent-free residence provided for full-time hospital chaplain was exempt); Oakwood Hosp. Corp. v. Michigan State Tax Comm'n, 374 Mich. 524, 132 N.W.2d 634 (1965) (housing for interns and residents exempt).
76. *E.g.,* Milton Hosp. v. Board of Tax Assessors, 360 Mass. 63, 271 N.E.2d 745 (1971); Medical Center of Vt., Inc. v. City of Burlington, 131 Vt. 196, 303 A.2d 468 (1973) (case remanded to determine facts of whether physician's use of offices at noncommercial rental was primarily for hospital purposes or private purposes); White Cross Hosp. Ass'n v. Warren, 6 Ohio St. 2d 29, 215 N.E.2d 374 (1966) (offices leased to physicians not exempt); Doctors Hosp. v. Board of Tax Appeals, 173 Ohio St. 283, 181 N.E.2d 702 (1962) (housing for married staff paid stipend by hospital not exempt); City of Long Branch v. Monmouth Medical Center, 138 N.J. Super. 524, 351 A.2d 756 (1976) (housing for resident interns and nurses exempt; space rented to private physicians at less than commercial rates is taxable), *aff'd,* 73 N.J. 179, 373 A.2d 651 (1977).
77. Genesee Hosp. v. Wagner, 76 Misc. 2d 281, 350 N.Y.S.2d 582 (N.Y. Sup. Ct. 1973), *rev'd,* 47 A.D.2d 37, 364 N.Y.S.2d 934 (1975), *aff'd mem.,* 39 N.Y.2d 863, 352 N.E.2d 133, 386 N.Y.S.2d 216 (1976).
78. N.Y. REAL PROPERTY TAX LAW § 420-a(1)(a) (McKinney 1984).
79. N.Y. REAL PROPERTY TAX LAW § 420-a(2).
80. 76 Misc. 2d at 285–89, 350 N.Y.S.2d at 586–90.
81. Genesee Hosp. v. Wagner, 47 A.D.2d 37, 364 N.Y.S.2d 934 (1975). *Compare* Barnes Hosp. v. Leggett, 646 S.W.2d 889 (Mo. Ct. App. 1983) (teaching hospital's lease of space to part-time medical school faculty who also practiced privately does not destroy tax exemption because faculty provided free care to indigent hospital patients).
82. Cedars of Lebanon Hosp. v. Los Angeles County, 35 Cal. 2d 729, 221 P.2d 31 (1950).
83. Bowers v. Akron City Hosp., 16 Ohio St. 2d 94, N.E.2d 95 (1968); Maine Medical Center v. Lucci, 317 A.2d 1 (Me. 1974); Methodist Hosp. of Memphis

v. Assessment Appeals Comm'n, 669 S.W.2d 305 (Tenn. 1984) (parking lots provided without charge to hospital employees exempt). *Compare* State Teachers Retirement Bd. v. Kinney, 68 Ohio St. 2d 195, 429 N.E.2d 1069 (1981) (where free parking reserved exclusively to employees of the state was not shown to be essential to the agency's function, property was taxable because not being used "exclusively for public purpose").

84. Sisters of Charity v. Bernalillo County, 93 N.M. 42, 596 P.2d 255 (1979) (lease of property by charitable corporation to subsidiary charitable corporation does not destroy exemption).

85. St. Joseph's Health Center Properties, Inc. v. Srogi, 51 N.Y.2d 127, 412 N.E.2d 921 (1980) (ownership by separate corporation of real estate for housing hospital staff does not prevent exemption).

86. Sisters of Charity v. Bernalillo County, 93 N.M. 42, 596 P.2d 255 (1979) (pro rata taxation allowed when office building and parking structure used for both charitable and noncharitable purposes); Barnes Hosp. v. Leggett, 646 S.W.2d 899 (Mo. Ct. App. 1983) (constitutional provisions authorize exemption for portions of property used exclusively for charitable purposes).

87. *E.g.*, Oak Ridge Hosp. v. City of Oak Ridge, 57 Tenn. Ap. 487, 420 S.W.2d 583 (1967); Cleveland Memorial Medical Found. V. Perk, 10 Ohio St. 2d 72, 225 N.E.2d 233 (1967); Hillman v. Flagstaff Community Hosp., 123 Ariz. 124, 598 P.2d 102 (Ariz. 1979).

88. *E.g.*, Good Samaritan Hosp. Ass'n v. Glander, 155 Ohio St. 507, 99 N.E.2d 473 (1951); Cleveland Memorial Medical Found. v. Perk, 10 Ohio St. 2d 72, 255 N.E.2d 233 (1967).

89. Sisters of Providence in Washington, Inc. v. Municipality of Anchorage, 672 P.2d 446 (Alaska 1983); *Accord* Kunnes v. Samaritan Health Serv., 121 Ariz. 413, 590 P.2d 1359 (Ariz. 1979) (to be exempt from *ad valorem* taxation equipment must be owned).

ANTITRUST LAW

There are three principal federal antitrust statutes: the Sherman Act passed by Congress in 1890, the Clayton Act of 1914, and the Federal Trade Commission Act, also enacted in 1914. An amendment to the Clayton Act, the Robinson-Patman Act, added in 1936, prohibits certain practices that result in discriminatory pricing. A further amendment, relating to the Clayton Act's provisions concerning corporate mergers and known as the Celler-Kefauver Act, was added in 1950. These statutes, procedures for their enforcement, and their application to healthcare organizations, will be described in this chapter.

The Sherman Act

Most antitrust litigation in the healthcare industry involves allegations that the defendants have violated either Section 1 or Section 2 (or both) of the Sherman Act. Section 1, cast in very broad language, reads as follows:

> Every contract, combination in the form of trust or otherwise, or conspiracy, in restraint of trade or commerce among the several states, or with foreign nations, is hereby declared to be illegal. Every person who shall make any contract or engage in any combination or conspiracy hereby declared to be illegal shall be deemed guilty of a felony, and, on conviction thereof, shall be punished by fine not exceeding one million dollars if a corporation, or, if any other person, one hundred thousand dollars, or by imprisonment not exceeding three years, or by both said punishments, in the discretion of the court.[1]

In supporting the broad and comprehensive language of Section 1, Senator Sherman of Ohio spoke as follows during Senate debate on the bill:

> I admit that it is difficult to define in legal language the precise line between lawful and unlawful combinations. This must be left for the courts to determine in each particular case. All that we, as lawmakers, can do is to declare general principles, and we can be assured that the courts will apply them so as to carry out the meaning of the law.[2]

Much of what follows certainly confirms that courts are called on with increasing frequency, especially in healthcare cases, "to determine [unlawfulness] in each particular case."

Section 1 clearly proscribes contracts or combinations in restraint of trade. To have an agreement, combination, or conspiracy there must be joint or concerted activity between two or more persons or legal entities.[3] Normally, unilateral action by a single person or business enterprise does not violate this section of the Sherman Act. A corporation cannot combine or conspire with its own employees or with its own separate departments or divisions even if the divisions compete with each other in the marketplace.

In 1984 the Supreme Court took this line of reasoning one step further and held that a parent corporation could not agree or conspire with a wholly owned subsidiary corporation even though the two corporations would be considered separate legal entities for many other purposes.[4] This result, of course, "leaves untouched a single firm's anticompetitive conduct (short of threatened monopolization) that may be indistinguishable in economic effect from the conduct of two firms subject to Section 1 liability."[5] Yet the Court concluded that Congress intended this very result, observing: "Subjecting a single firm's every action to judicial scrutiny for reasonableness would threaten to discourage the competitive enthusiasm that the antitrust laws seek to promote."[6] Single business enterprises are, of course, subject to the statutory prohibitions relating to monopolization: Section 2 of the Sherman Act, Section 7 of the Clayton Act, and Section 5 of the Federal Trade Commission Act.

Two or more competitors in a given market may engage in conscious parallel conduct, especially in formulating policy with respect to the pricing of their products. Such behavior standing alone does not violate Section 1 of the Sherman Act because collective action is absent. However, parallel conduct of two or more independent businesses may furnish circumstantial evidence of an agreement between them, express or implied, and is admissible as evidence for the jury when deciding Section 1 cases.[7] Similarly, when competitors exchange price information pertaining to specific products in identified customer markets, and this may have the effect of stabilizing prices, there is sufficient proof of a violation of the Sherman Act.[8] In essence the presence of an illegal agreement, combination, or conspiracy in restraint of trade is often a factual question to be determined on a case-by-case basis.

Restraints of trade may be horizontal or vertical. *Horizontal restraints* result when competitors at the same level of the distribution chain in a given industry or market agree, for example, to fix or stabilize prices, divide or allocate markets, exclude others from a market, or refuse to deal with third parties. In contrast, *vertical restraints* of trade exist when two or more entities at different levels in a distribution chain act collectively to effect changes in the competitive environment. For example, if a manufacturer and a retailer agree that the latter will sell the former's products at a given price, such behavior would be characterized as resale price maintenance, and as a general rule it would violate the Sherman Act. Other examples of vertical restraints subject to scrutiny are these: agreements by a manufacturer and a retailer to limit the latter's geographical market, tie-in sales,[9] contracts for exclusive dealing, and contracts that provide that a buyer will purchase all "requirements" of a given item from a single source. All three of the antitrust statutes apply to the particular arrangements mentioned. Each statute, however, has its own standards of illegality.

In contrast to Section 1, Section 2 of the Sherman Act applies to unilateral action of a single firm or business enterprise and specifically prohibits monopolies, attempts to monopolize, or combinations with others to monopolize a market.[10] In a leading case the Supreme Court indicated that Section 2 is violated when sufficient monopoly power exists to control prices or exclude competition from a relevant market coupled with "the willful acquisition or maintenance of that power as distinguished from growth or development as a consequence of a superior product, business acumen, or historic accident."[11]

Accordingly, in a case of alleged violation of Section 2, a court must:

1. determine the relevant market, both geographically and for the product;
2. decide whether the evidence shows actual or inferential control of prices or the exclusion of competitors; and
3. determine whether this monopoly power was acquired or maintained willfully.

Inferential control of prices or exclusion of others from the marketplace can be shown by data that establish the defendant's share of the defined market. Proof of a specific intent to monopolize need not be advanced to meet the requirement that monopoly power was willfully acquired. Rather, proof of a general intent to monopolize is sufficient if the probable result of the defendant's activities is monopolization. "Attempts to monopolize," in contrast to actual monopolies, however, do require that the plaintiff prove a specific intent to monopolize and a "dangerous probability" that a monopoly will result.[12] Finally, a "combination or conspiracy to monopolize" requires concerted action with another party, specific intent to achieve a monopoly, and overt acts toward that end.

Litigation alleging violation of the Sherman Act, Section 2, will typically be resolved by applying a "rule of reason" analysis. The process to determine illegality evidences Congress's concern with the extent of economic power possessed by a given enterprise, how that power was obtained, and how it is used. Some monopolies may actually foster competition and thus be perfectly legal. Furthermore, a successful business that has a superior product or a management with unusual business acumen should not be condemned as monopolist simply on the basis of market dominance. In other words, a monopoly standing alone is not illegal per se, and the Sherman Act does not condemn large business enterprises as such. Nor does it apply when a market can reasonably support only a single source of supply for a particular item or service; that is, the single supplier will not be judged in violation of Section 2 solely by reason of market position. On the other hand, predatory or unfair practices undertaken to gain control of a market will violate principles of antitrust laws as expressed in the Sherman Act. For example, pricing below cost to defeat a competitor and achieve monopoly status has often been condemned.[13] Thus, the courts are continually drawing a line between firms that have obtained their dominance of a market by developing a superior product or possessing special skill and those whose business practices show an intention to acquire or misuse monopoly power.

The Clayton Act

The language of the Sherman Act is general and broad. In 1914 Congress therefore provided somewhat more specific guidance by enacting the Clayton Act. This legislation was primarily directed toward declaring illegal the situations described below.

Price Discrimination

Section 2(a) of the new act was concerned with discriminatory pricing practices. As amended in 1926 by the Robinson-Patman Act it reads:

> [It is unlawful] to discriminate in price between different purchasers of commodities of like grade and quality . . . where the effect of such discrimination may be substantially to lessen competition or tend to create a monopoly in any line of commerce, or to injure, destroy, or prevent competition with any person who either grants or knowingly receives the benefit of such discrimination.[14]

Note especially that the section applies not only to sellers who practice discriminatory pricing practices but to buyers who receive the benefits. Discriminatory pricing includes all terms of a sale, including credit terms. The statute, however, specifically allows price differentials based on "the cost of manufacture, sale, or delivery resulting from the differing methods or quantities in which such commodities are to such purchasers sold or delivered." The section applies only to sales of commodities and eliminates applicability of Section 2(a) to a lease or a license to use somebody else's product. Moreover, the term "commodities" refers only to tangible goods or wares and consequently does not embrace services or intangible items like patents, stocks and bonds, royalty rights, and healthcare. Differential prices may also be legal when the commodities sold are different in grade and quality and when tangibles are sold to certain nonprofit institutional buyers for their own use.

For example, in *Abbott Laboratories v. Portland Retail Druggists Association, Inc.*, the Supreme Court interpreted congressional intent in using the phrase "purchases of their supplies for their own use."[15] Several pharmaceutical manufacturers had sold products to certain not-for-profit hospitals in the Portland, Oregon, area at prices lower than those charged commercial pharmacists for like products. The question, of course, was whether the purchases by the hospitals were for their own use. As in many other cases involving restraint of trade, the Court first observed that exemptions and immunities from antitrust legislation are to be construed strictly: exceptions to applicability of the legislation are not to be extended by implication. By enacting the exemption, Congress did not intend to "give the [not-for-profit] hospital a blank check."[16] On the other hand the role and activities of not-for-profit community hospitals have changed and expanded significantly since the exemption was passed in 1938. The Court recognized that the "nonprofit hospital no longer is a receiving facility only for the bedridden, the surgical patient, and the critical emergency. It has become a place where the community is readily inclined to turn." The Court further observed that "some hospitals, indeed, truly have become centers for 'delivery' of health care."[17]

The Court then identified various dispensations under which the pharmaceutical products purchased by the not-for-profit hospitals at a discriminatory price could be allowed. The following were considered "[p]urchases . . . for their own use" and thus exempt:[18]

- products purchased for use in treatment of inpatients, emergency patients, and outpatients seen on the premises;
- take-home prescriptions for those three categories of patients to the extent that the prescriptions supplemented treatment rendered at the hospital and were to be used for a limited time; and
- drugs furnished to hospital employees, students, and members of the medical staff for their dependents' personal use.[19]

Excluded from the exemption were refills of a prescription drug to a hospital's former patients and sales to walk-in buyers except in emergencies when there was no other source of supply.[20] Clearly, exempting refills of prescriptions for discharged patients and sales to the general public would give the hospital's pharmacy an unfair advantage over commercial pharmacies, and certainly Congress did not intend such a result. The Court also specifically stated that the exemption is not "to be applied and expanded automatically to whatever new venture the nonprofit hospital finds attractive in these changing days."[21] That statement, written in 1976, is particularly relevant today as not-for-profit hospitals are venturing more aggressively and widely into profit-making activity.

In addition to these statutory limitations of coverage and the general defense based on cost justification, Section 2(b) of the Clayton Act specifically provides that any price is lawful if promulgated in good faith to meet competition on either a customer-to-customer or a geographical basis. To assert this defense successfully, however, the seller must prove that the pricing policies in question were designed to *meet* competition, not drive it out. One should also note that discriminatory pricing may constitute an element of a monopoly or an attempt to monopolize, thus violating Section 2 of the Sherman Act, as previously discussed.

Tying and Exclusive Dealing Contracts

Section 3 of the Clayton Act specifically prohibits as unlawful a

> lease, . . . sale, or contract for sale of goods, wares, merchandise, machinery, supplies, or other commodities . . . on the condition, agreement, or understanding that the lessee or purchaser . . . shall not use or deal in the goods . . . or other commodities of a competitor . . . of the lessor or seller where the effect . . . may be to substantially lessen competition or tend to create a monopoly.[22]

Thus the legality of tie-in sales and exclusive dealing contracts is judged under both the Sherman Act, Section 1, discussed earlier, and Section 3 of the Clayton Act. More will be said later about these prohibited restraints of trade. As a point worth noting here, a careful reading of the statutory language makes it clear that Section 3 of the Clayton Act does not apply to contracts of service.

Corporate Expansion

Corporate mergers, consolidations, and acquisitions are the subjects of Section 7 of the Clayton Act. Thus Section 7 duplicates to a certain degree the prohibitions against monopolization and attempts to monopolize made illegal by Section 2 of the Sherman Act. Essentially the Clayton Act, as amended by the Celler-Kefauver Act in 1950, reads:

> "No person . . . shall acquire, directly or indirectly, the whole or any part of the stock . . . and no person subject to the jurisdiction of the Federal Trade Commission shall acquire the whole or any part of the assets of another person . . . where . . . the effect of such acquisition may be substantially to lessen competition, or to tend to create a monopoly."[23]

To be in violation of Section 7 a merger or acquisition must produce an anticompetitive effect in a relevant product and geographic market.[24]

The Federal Trade Commission Act

In 1914, the same year that the Clayton Act was enacted, Congress passed the Federal Trade Commission Act, which established the Federal Trade Commission (FTC). The FTC is an administrative agency with broad powers to conduct investigations, promulgate rules and regulations, and enforce statutory provisions prohibiting unfair competition and trade practices.

The commission's broad mandate is governed by the substantive provisions of Section 5, as amended, reading as follows: "Unfair methods of competition in or affecting commerce, and unfair or deceptive acts or practices in or affecting commerce, are hereby declared unlawful."[25] Pursuant to this language the agency is empowered as a practical matter to enforce both the

Sherman and Clayton acts because some activities of business will violate all three statutes.

Aside from enforcement of antitrust statutes, a careful reading of Section 5 reveals that the FTC is empowered to regulate trade practices that are "unfair or deceptive" to consumers. For example, the FTC has brought numerous cases to court charging commercial advertisers with unfair or deceptive practices:

- failure to reveal material facts about a product;
- making false claims and misrepresentations;
- offering misleading prices;
- disparaging a competitor's product by misleading or untrue assertions;
- announcing unsupported personal endorsements by well-known persons;
- presenting advertising that is intended to attract a customer who will then be switched to a higher-priced product;
- conducting contests where very few prizes are actually awarded;
- sending unsolicited merchandise; and
- using overbearing methods in door-to-door sales.

Interstate Commerce

Congress normally bases its power to regulate business activity on the commerce clause of the Constitution. Article I, Section 8, Clause 3 of the Constitution grants Congress the power to "regulate Commerce with foreign nations and among the several states." Congress may therefore regulate interstate commerce, but purely *intrastate* activities are beyond the jurisdictional reach of federal regulation when the power to legislate is based on the commerce clause.

The Supreme Court has defined antitrust jurisdiction rather broadly. In essence, the Court has said that Congress may regulate even local activities so long as they have a substantial and harmful effect on interstate commerce.[26] Nevertheless, for many years it was widely assumed that medical practice and the provision of health services, including the operation of hospitals, were beyond the jurisdictional reach of the federal antitrust statutes. A significant 1976 case proved that these assumptions were quite erroneous. In *Hospital Building Co. v. Trustees of the Rex Hospital* the Supreme Court reversed a decision of the Fourth Circuit Court of Appeals.[27] According to the Court an alleged conspiracy among a not-for-profit hospital, an individual trustee of the hospital, the hospital's administrator, and the executive secretary of the local health planning agency to prevent the relocation and expansion of plaintiff hospital had a "substantial effect" on interstate commerce, thus stating a cause of action under the Sherman Act.[28] According to the plaintiff's allegations a significant portion of the hospital's medicines and supplies, some of its patients, much of its revenue, and the contemplated financing for its planned expansion were all derived from out-of-state sources. In the view of the Court, these factors demonstrated an effect on interstate commerce sufficient to satisfy the jurisdictional issue.[29]

It is not necessary to show that the defendants' conduct directly affected commerce or that the defendants intended such an effect. The "substantial effect" test is met even if market prices are unaffected and the financial stability of out-of-state suppliers is not threatened.[30] Thus, most cases now hold that a nexus between the overall business of the defendant and interstate commerce is enough to find antitrust jurisdiction and that there need not be a connection between commerce and the particular activities alleged to be unlawful.[31]

On the other hand, a minority of courts in some factual contexts, especially in some of the cases regarding medical staff privileges, have adhered to the view that the facts alleged by the plaintiff must sufficiently support an inference that the defendants' challenged activities could have a "not insubstantial" effect on commerce.[32] In essence, these courts will not accept a mere allegation that the defendant's general business affects interstate commerce, and they will not presume that a nexus exists between the challenged activity and interstate commerce.

There remains some doubt, therefore, concerning the precise allegations that a plaintiff must make to withstand a motion to dismiss the action on the jurisdictional issue of interstate commerce. Several district and circuit courts continue to differ in their approach, notwithstanding the Supreme Court's decisions on the matter. In general, however, defendants in the healthcare industry will not be able to avoid scrutiny of their activities by claiming that their conduct has less than a substantial effect on interstate commerce.

Applicability to the Professions

Because the Sherman Act applies only to restraints of trade or commerce it was frequently asserted or assumed until the 1970s that principles of antitrust law did not apply to the practice of a profession. Such assertions were based on arguments akin to the jurisdictional defense of intrastate commerce discussed in the previous section.

In the landmark case of *Goldfarb v. Virginia State Bar Association*, however, the Supreme Court ruled that a state bar association's minimum fee schedule for attorneys amounted to a violation of Section 1 of the Sherman Act as an illegal price-fixing arrangement.[33] In so doing, the Court rejected the defendant's position that the antitrust laws do not apply to the so-called "learned professions." Similarly, in *National Society of Professional Engineers v. United States*[34] the Court held that a professional code of ethics prohibiting engineers from submitting price information to prospective customers constituted an unreasonable restraint of trade despite an argument that the standards were intended to improve professional service and hence benefit the public.[35]

As will be seen later, however, healthcare—although subject to the antitrust laws—is sometimes treated differently than other industries in the "rule of reason" analysis.

Exemptions from Antitrust Legislation

Neither the Sherman Antitrust Act nor the Clayton Act expressly provides for any statutory exemptions. From time to time commentators have suggested that the health industry should be expressly exempt from antitrust legislation as a matter of public policy. Congress, however, has not taken these suggestions seriously. As a matter of fact, public policy has narrowed drastically the exemptions often recognized by the judicial system.

There are five possible exemptions to the federal antitrust statutes in addition to the threshold jurisdictional issues previously discussed. Three of these exemptions—implied repeal, state action, and the Noerr-Pennington doctrine—were created by court decision and thus are subject to substantial modification from time to time on a case-by-case basis. The fourth exemption, established by Congress when the McCarran-Ferguson Act was passed in 1924,[36] exempts the "business of insurance" from federal antitrust concepts, provided that the defendant's conduct does not amount to a "boycott, coercion, or intimidation."[37] The final exemption relates to collective bargaining agreements between a labor union and business management.

Implied Repeal

When the federal antitrust laws are in irreconcilable conflict with a federal regulatory statute, the doctrine of "implied repeal" may be invoked to create an exemption or immunity from antitrust liability. To put the matter another way, by enacting a regulatory scheme applicable to a particular industry or set of factual circumstances, Congress may have intended to repeal antitrust legislation even in the absence of an express repeal or an express exemption.

The doctrine has been discussed in a number of antitrust cases involving the healthcare industry, primarily in litigation highlighting the conflicts between advocates of a free, competitive market and persons engaged in regional planning of health facilities and services. Conflict between the legal principles of antitrust law and the provisions of the National Health Planning and Resources Development Act of 1974 (NHPRDA) has also been seen.[38]

The NHPRDA, commonly referred to as Public Law 93-641, specified four legislative goals:

1. improving the health of residents;
2. increasing the accessibility, acceptability, continuity, and quality of health services;

3. restraining increases in the cost of health services; and
4. preventing unnecessary duplication of health resources.[39]

A fifth goal, added in the 1979 amendments to the act, was to preserve and improve competition in the health service arena.[40] The amendments, however, recognized that with respect to certain sectors of the health services industry, "such as inpatient health services and other institutional health services, for which competition does not or will not appropriately allocate supply," health planning agencies should "take actions . . . to allocate the supply of such services."[41]

The 1974 act established a system of regulatory controls and health planning agencies. Health system agencies (HSAs) were created as advisory bodies responsible for planning and rationalizing health facilities and services in local communities. Each HSA was charged with the primary responsibility of achieving "effective health planning . . . and the promotion of the development . . . of health services, manpower, and facilities which meet identified needs, reduce documented inefficiencies, and implement the health plans of the agency."[42] These local agencies were not, however, given regulatory authority over the providers of healthcare.

In turn, the health planning and development agency of each state was given the responsibility of integrating regional plans into a statewide plan and was further granted regulatory authority to implement a certificate of need program calling for state approval before constriction of new institutional healthcare facilities could begin. Legislation establishing a certificate of need program had to be passed before federal funds could be received. Each state also created a statewide health coordinating council with the power to review the regional plans submitted by HSAs, review and revise the state plan from time to time, and make recommendations to the health planning and development agency.[43]

The significant case of *National Gerimedical Hospital and Gerontology Center v. Blue Cross of Kansas City* arose in this environment.[44] Although the state of Missouri had not enacted a certificate of need statute at the time of the events that led to litigation, the local HSA had accumulated data showing a surplus of hospital beds in the Kansas City area and had announced that it would not approve the plans of any institution to expand the supply of acute-care beds. Joining in the widespread efforts to contain the costs of hospital care, Blue Cross had also announced that it would bar participating status to any new hospital unless it met "a clearly evident need . . . in its defined service area."[45] Nevertheless, National Gerimedical Hospital proceeded with the construction of a community hospital, obtained a license from the state, and opened its doors in 1978. The hospital then sought a contract with Blue Cross of Kansas City as a participating institution but was refused because construction at the facility had not been approved by the local planning agency.

The hospital then filed an antitrust suit against the Blue Cross plan and the national Blue Cross Association alleging violations of both Sections 1 and 2 of the Sherman Act and seeking money damages and an injunction requiring the health plan to award it a contract. The defendants promptly responded by moving to dismiss the complaint, maintaining that the NHPRDA had impliedly repealed the antitrust legislation as it applied to the admitted facts. The trial court granted the motion for dismissal, because it found that conduct that conformed to the requirements of NHPRDA is exempt from the operation of the antitrust laws. The court of appeals affirmed.[46]

The Supreme Court disagreed with both the district court and the court of appeals in a unanimous decision. It reversed and remanded for a trial on the merits of plaintiff's claim. Citing precedent and quoting prior opinions on the doctrine of implied repeal, the Court made these important points: "The antitrust laws represent a 'fundamental national economic policy' "[47]; " 'Implied antitrust immunity is not favored, and can be justified only by a convincing showing of clear repugnancy between the antitrust laws and the regulatory system' "[48]; and " 'Repeal is to be regarded as implied only if necessary to make the (subsequent law) work, and even then only to the minimum extent necessary.' "[49] Even governmental regulation does not provide evidence of congressional intent to repeal the antitrust laws.[50]

The standard then for applying the implied repeal doctrine is simply this: there must be a "clear repugnancy" between the two conflicting statutory provisions. Because the conduct by Blue Cross of Kansas City was "neither compelled nor approved by any governmental regulatory body," there was clearly no repugnancy on the facts between NHPRDA and the Sherman Act.[51] Blue Cross's refusal to contract with National Gerimedical was a purely voluntary decision by a private corporation in response to announcements of a planning agency acting in an advisory role. Hence, the Supreme Court forthrightly rejected the view of the court of appeals that voluntary cooperation among entities within the healthcare industry was necessary to make regional planning effective.

State Action

Local and state governments regulate various private business and economic activity in the interest of promoting public health, safety, and the general welfare. Sometimes state regulation restricts or restrains competition, however, thus generating apparent inconsistencies between state governmental regulation and antitrust legislation.

The state action doctrine, developed by the courts, grants immunity from antitrust sanctions whenever the defendants' anticompetitive conduct is the consequence of governmental regulation. The first landmark case establishing the exemption was *Parker v. Brown*.[52] During a period of economic recession, especially in agriculture, the state of California had passed laws controlling the production of raisins and thus restraining competition among the producers and increasing the market prices. When a raisin producer challenged this program, the Supreme Court of the United States held that the state officials administering the law were exempt from antitrust claims because the program "derived its authority and efficacy from the legislative command of the state."[53] For 32 years following *Parker* the courts and commentators generally interpreted the doctrine to mean that an exemption would be recognized whenever conduct restraining trade was contemplated, authorized, or approved by the state or its officers and agencies pursuant to statute.

Beginning in 1975, however, various significant decisions narrowed application of the exemption in two respects and thus had a major effect on the health services industry. First, the Court has rejected the assumption that if actual or contemplated anticompetitive behavior by private enterprise was authorized by state government or its agencies, such approval was sufficient to grant an exemption from scrutiny on the merits. Second, the Court has confined definition of the "state" to the state itself as a sovereign government and has refused to regard regulation by cities, other local government units, and administrative agencies as being within the realm of state action justifying exemption from antitrust legislation.

In both *Goldfarb v. Virginia State Bar* and *Cantor v. Detroit Edison Company*,[54] the Court refused to grant an exemption or find immunity in the absence of a showing that the defendants' anticompetitive conduct had been compelled or mandated by the state. Although the Virginia State Bar Association, a private organization, was supervised by and subject to the rules of the Supreme Court of Virginia, the court had not compelled the association to enforce a minimum-fee schedule promulgated by a county bar association. Thus, the doctrine of state action did not provide a defense to plaintiff's allegations that the fee schedule violated the Sherman Act. In the Court's words: "It is not enough that . . . anticompetitive conduct is 'prompted' by state action; rather, anticompetitive activities must be compelled by direction of the State acting as sovereign."[55]

In similar fashion the *Cantor* case held that approval by the state's public utilities commission of a private electric utility company's program dispensing free light bulbs to residential customers was not exempt from antitrust scrutiny. Essentially the light-bulb program and the accompanying tariff had been initiated by the company, and the state utilities commission had simply acquiesced in the proposal by approving the tariff arrangement. The cost of acquiring and dispensing the light bulbs was, of course, built into the rates charged customers and approved by the commission. In short, the state agency had not required the program as a matter of regulatory policy.[56]

In summary, with respect to the state-action doctrine, the cases have arrived at this point: to be exempt, the regulation must be an activity of the state itself acting in its sovereign capacity or—by a local government, an agency of the state, or a private party—must be conducted pursuant to a "clearly articulated and affirmatively expressed" state regulatory policy. Further, the state itself must then actively supervise the local government or private party engaged in the regulating.

The degree of state action required to meet the standard of a "clearly articulated and affirmatively expressed state policy" remains somewhat open to question. Even if anticompetitive action by local governments, state agencies, or private parties is clearly articulated by state policy, the conduct must continue to be actively supervised by the state to be exempt.

When the challenged conduct is that of the state itself as sovereign, the issues of clear articulation and active supervision need not be addressed. A recent decision on this point held that the supreme court of a state is in the same position as the legislative branch in the exercise of sovereign powers. Accordingly, when a court appointed a committee to use standards promulgated by the court, the decisions were not subject to the federal antitrust laws.[57]

Noerr-Pennington Doctrine

The Noerr-Pennington doctrine recognizes that activities to influence legislation are exempt from antitrust restraints. The doctrine originated in and is named for two Supreme Court decisions; it is based on the First Amendment to the Constitution, which guarantees freedom of speech and the right to petition government. The exemption thus has constitutional support. It is also a logical companion to the state-action doctrine discussed previously. If action by private parties pursuant to a clearly articulated governmental policy is exempt, then private activity to persuade or influence governmental action should also be exempt.

The doctrine was first announced in the case of *Eastern Railroad Presidents Conference v. Noerr Motor Freight, Inc.* in 1961.[58] Several railroads had cooperated in publishing materials to promote legislation potentially harmful to their competitors in the trucking industry. The Supreme Court, in reversing the trial court and the court of appeals, held that the collective activity of the railroads was exempt from antitrust analysis, saying "the Sherman Act does not prohibit two or more persons from associating together in an attempt to persuade the legislature or the executive to take particular action with respect to a law that would produce a restraint or a monopoly."[59] Even though the railroads had demonstrated an intent to harm the trucking industry, used unethical methods in their publicity campaign, and actually injured their competitors, the constitutional dimensions of the doctrine were sufficient to protect the defendants' activities from scrutiny under the antitrust laws.[60]

Several years later the Court had an opportunity to explain the doctrine further. The United Mine Workers labor organization combined with several of the larger coal producers to convince the Secretary of Labor that he should set a minimum-wage scale applicable to all coal producers selling coal to the Tennessee Valley Authority (TVA), a quasi-governmental corporation producing electric power. The goal of the union and the large producers was to make it more difficult for the small coal companies to compete for TVA contracts. In granting an exemption from restraint of trade legislation, the Court said: "Joint efforts to influence public officials do not violate the antitrust laws even though intended to eliminate competition. Such conduct is not illegal."[61] Thus, Noerr-Pennington applies to attempts to influence not only officials in the executive branch of government and administrative agencies, but also legislative bodies.

There are, however, limitations to the doctrine. An exemption will not be recognized if the conduct of the defendants constitutes a violation of a valid statute or if the intent is to prevent competitors from influencing or gaining equal access to governmental officials or agencies.[62] In such circumstances and perhaps others, the claim of exemption will be labeled a sham and accordingly denied.

The Noerr-Pennington defense was used successfully by a national trade association of pharmacists that encouraged the pharmaceutical licensing boards of various states to increase the regulation of mail-order suppliers of pharmaceutical products.[63] Similarly, in a case where the subsidiaries of two competing hospitals in Arizona formed a joint venture to seek a certificate of need for construction of a new hospital and opposed a similar application from another institution, the conduct of the defendants, even if anticompetitive, was protected activity so long as the participation in the adjudicatory process was in good faith and not frivolous.[64]

Exemption under the McCarran-Ferguson Act

In 1944 the Supreme Court ruled that the sale of insurance constituted interstate commerce; accordingly, the business of insurance became subject to the antitrust laws.[65] Prior to this decision it was generally assumed that insurance companies did not do business in interstate commerce and need not concern themselves with the Sherman Act and other statutes relating to restraints of trade.

There are valid reasons for considering the insurance industry to be unique and not subject to customary antitrust analysis. A completely free market characterized by open competition would naturally cause some companies to issue some policies at low rates that do not reflect actual risk. The consequences might well be inability to pay legitimate claims and, therefore, financial failure. Sound public policy therefore requires that government be concerned for the financial solvency and integrity of insurance carriers.

Because a freely competitive environment is not appropriate for the insurance industry, it follows that certain cooperative efforts among insurance companies are legitimate and perhaps should be encouraged by regulatory authority, even if they are anticompetitive. For example, companies may benefit by sharing information on the various risks in any given line of business and exchanging data on price and loss ratios. Cooperation in fixing actual rates for insurance has also been thought to be consistent with desirable public policy. In the words of a Senate committee studying the matter in 1944:

> For these and other reasons this subcommittee believes it would be a mistake to permit or require the unrestricted competition contemplated by the antitrust laws to apply to the insurance business. To prohibit combined efforts for statistical and rate-making purposes would be a backwards step in the development of a progressive business.[66]

Congress enacted the McCarran-Ferguson Act (MFA)[67] in respose to these views and following the Court's decision in *United States v. South-Eastern Underwriters*,[68] which specifically held that Congress did not intend to exempt the business of insurance from the operation of the Sherman Act. The MFA established in statutory form the previously assumed exemption of the insurance industry from federal antitrust laws:

> [A]fter June 30, 1948, the Act of July 2, 1890, as amended, known as the Sherman Act, and the Act of October 15, 1914, known as the Federal Trade Commission Act, as amended, . . . shall be applicable to the business of insurance to the extent that such business is not regulated by State Law.[69]

The MFA also provided, however, that the exemption would not apply "to any agreement to boycott, coerce, or intimidate, or act of boycott, coercion, or intimidation."[70] To this extent Congress recognized that insurance companies were capable of abusing an exemption and that engaging in a concerted refusal to do business with another or compelling a particular result by force should not be condoned.

Subsequent events and changing perceptions of sound public policy have caused doubts about the wisdom of continuing the McCarran-Ferguson Act's exemption. Some have criticized the broad statutory grant of immunity, suggested that particular practices in the insurance industry were actually anticompetitive, and questioned whether the regulatory goals of the various states were being attained and whether the insurance industry was functioning effectively and improving its products.[71] In particular there has been concern about provider control of the Blue Cross-Blue Shield plans and other third-party arrangements for financing healthcare.

Despite these criticisms, there has been no major legislative effort to repeal the MFA. Rather, through a series of decisions the courts have consistently narrowed the application of the legislation, thus restricting substantially the number of factual situations previously considered exempt from antitrust analysis. The result, of course, is to increase the number of cases that require a decision on the merits of the plaintiff's allegations.

There are three related issues for judicial decision in determining whether the act grants an exemption on a given set of facts. All three are derived from the statutory language quoted previously.

1. First, do the activities of the defendants alleged to be in violation of an antitrust statute constitute the "business of insurance"?
2. If the answer is yes, the next question is whether such activities are regulated by state law to a degree that justifies an exemption.
3. Finally, even if the conduct of the defendants constitutes the business of insurance regulated by state law, do the facts indicate a boycott or business practices amounting to coercion and intimidation?

In general, contractual agreements between a third-party payor and a provider of healthcare do not constitute the business of insurance. The terms of the contract, the formation of the agreement, and refusals of the third-party payor to contract with particular providers are accordingly all subject to antitrust analysis on the merits of each particular case. The leading decision holding that agreements involving provider reimbursement do not enjoy an exemption from antitrust legislation is *Group Life and Health Insurance Co. v. Royal Drug Co.*, decided in 1979.[72]

In *Royal Drug* several small, independent, and nonparticipating pharmacies challenged the terms of the third-party reimbursement contract for prescriptive drugs between Blue Shield of Texas (also known as Group Life and Health) and participating pharmacists. The plaintiffs alleged that the terms of the agreement constituted price fixing. All licensed pharmacies within Blue Shield's service area were offered participating status and were promised direct reimbursement by Blue Shield for the actual cost of the drug prescribed by the patient's doctor, plus a flat dispensing fee of two dollars paid by the subscriber as a deductible. If a Blue Shield subscriber obtained a prescribed drug from a nonparticipating pharmacy, the contract required payment of the actual retail price of the item to the pharmacist, then application for reimbursement from Blue Cross. In such circumstances Blue Cross reimbursed the subscriber for 75 percent of the difference between the price paid and the two-dollar deductible.

The purpose of these arrangements with the pharmacists and the subscribers was to have a measure of control over Blue Shield's costs, and in turn, over the subscriber's premium. The effect, however, was to encourage subscribers to obtain their prescriptive medicines only from participating pharmacies. Some pharmacies, especially small independent stores, claimed that they could not operate economically on the basis of the two-dollar dispensing fee; hence, they alleged that the participating contract amounted to a conspiracy to fix prices in violation of the Sherman Act.

The majority of the Supreme Court decided that the McCarran-Ferguson Act did not create an exemption from the Sherman Act for Blue Shield. In a 5–4 decision, the Court affirmed the Fifth Circuit Court of Appeals' decision that the provider reimbursement agreement did not constitute the business of insurance as contemplated and intended by Congress.

After tracing the legislative history of the MFA and noting further that exemptions from antitrust legislation are to be narrowly construed, the court found that not all of the business activities of insurance companies are exempt merely because the company is in the insurance business.[73] Interpreting the statutory language literally, the "business of insurance" applies only to spreading and underwriting risks.[74] Because the agreement concerning participating pharmacies did not involve the acceptance or spreading of risks it was not embraced within the "business of insurance." Rather, the arrangement was simply a contract by Blue Shield to purchase goods and services on behalf of its subscribers.[75] Further, the challenged contractual relationship in *Royal Drug* was between Blue Shield and a provider of healthcare, not between an insurance carrier and an insured person. Participating pharmacies are entities outside the insurance industry, and the legislative history of the MFA fails to reveal any congressional intent to exempt from antitrust law contractual arrangements between an insurance company and an entity outside the industry.[76] In sum, the Court interpreted the "business of insurance" to embrace only relationships between an insurer and the insured.

Another significant decision, *Union Labor Life Insurance Co. v. Pireno*, concerned an arrangement between a commercial insurance company and a committee of professional persons.[77] The committee was to review retrospectively the necessity of the healthcare furnished insured persons and the reasonableness of the fees charged by the provider. The Supreme Court held that no MFA exemption applied. The majority of the Court noted that the challenged activity involved an organization outside the insurance industry, was above and beyond the contract of insurance with the policyholder, was conducted long after the insured's risk had been transferred to the insurance carrier, and was more than simply a claims adjustment process within the company. Further, the role of the professional committee was advisory only, and opinions rendered in the context of particular insurance claims were not binding on the company.

In contrast to the narrow interpretation of the business-of-insurance as a requirement for an exemption, judicial decisions have traditionally given the state-regulation requirement of the MFA a broad meaning, although the Supreme Court has not definitely ruled on the issue. The lower courts have said that a state need not be engaged in detailed regulation of the particular activity alleged to violate antitrust statutes and that there need be no judicial finding of irreconcilable conflict between the state's regulation of insurance and antitrust statutes, or even a finding that a state's authority to regulate was actually being enforced.[78] In short, the courts have been willing to find that the MFA's requirement that the business of insurance be regulated by state law is fulfilled by the mere existence of any regulatory apparatus pertaining to the defendant's insurance enterprise. Interestingly this judicial attitude is in sharp contrast to recent interpretations of the state-action doctrine, which were discussed previously in this chapter.

Recall that the McCarran-Ferguson exemption does not apply if the challenged activity of an insurance company constitutes an "agreement to boycott, coerce, or intimidate, or act of boycott, coercion, or intimidation."[79] Prior to the Supreme Court's decision in *St. Paul Fire & Marine Insurance Co. v. Barry*,[80] the courts had held that this statutory exception to an exemption from antitrust applied only to conduct among insurance companies or their agents and did not apply to company activity that affected policyholders.[81] *St. Paul* changed that interpretation drastically, broadening application of the boycott exception and consequently narrowing the availability of an exemption. The facts of the case need to be examined briefly to appreciate the court's more expansive definition of the statutory language relating to boycott and coercion.

In response to a perceived increase in the number of medical malpractice suits, the St. Paul Fire and Marine Insurance Company announced that it was changing its malpractice insurance policy from an "occurrence" basis coverage to a "claims-made" basis. Under claims-made coverage the company agrees to defend only against claims filed against the insured during the actual term of the policy, regardless of when the alleged cause of action arose. In contrast, an occurrence policy covers liability for events that occur during the term of the policy. Because medical events may not lead to a lawsuit until many years later when the term of the policy has expired, a claims-made policy favors an insurance carrier: its obligation to defend a claim ends with the expiration of the insurance contract.

Following this managerial decision, a group of physicians who were insured by St. Paul brought an antitrust action alleging that the company had conspired with certain other carriers of malpractice insurance to decline applications by the plaintiffs for occurrence coverage. Allegedly, the defendant's motive was to force the plaintiffs to renew their existing coverage with St. Paul but to accept the claims-made type of policy. When St. Paul defended the suit, claiming that the MFA granted an exemption from the alleged antitrust violations, the Supreme Court held that the complaint stated a claim because of the boycott exception to the business-of-insurance exemption.[82]

The Court interpreted the concept of boycott liberally, saying that the intended meaning of the word for the purposes of the McCarran Act included concerted refusals to deal with another party as well as conduct designed to persuade others not to deal with identified parties.[83] To deny exemption the Court did not need to find that the conduct in question amounted to a per se antitrust violation, in contrast to conduct that would be analyzed under the rule of reason, a distinction to be discussed later in this chapter. The Court said that the term "boycott" in the McCarran Act means all anticompetitive conduct that would be recognized as an illegal boycott under the Sherman Act.[84]

Just as with claims for other exemptions, the denial of a McCarran Act exemption is not equivalent to a finding of illegal conduct. Courts will analyze the facts of each case on their merits, employing either a rule of reason or per se analysis, and then determine whether the challenged activity amounts to a "boycott, coercion, or intimidation." These concepts will be discussed further in relation to third-party reimbursement agreements with providers of healthcare and the denial of a hospital's medical staff privileges to a physician or allied health practitioner.

Exemption for Labor-Management Activities

Because healthcare benefits for employees are among the mandatory subjects for collective bargaining under the provisions of the National Labor Relations Act of 1935,[85] as amended, it follows that the mutually negotiated provisions of a contract between an employer and a labor union should be exempt from attack on antitrust grounds.[86]

Illustrating the controversy that can arise in healthcare is *Michigan State Podiatry Ass'n v. Blue Cross and Blue Shield of Michigan.*[87] In their 1979 labor contract the United Auto Workers and Chrysler Corporation agreed that under the healthcare plan for employees certain designated surgical procedures on the foot would be covered if a professional peer review produced certification that the proposed procedure was both medically necessary and appropriate. The Michigan State Podiatry Association challenged the terms of this predetermination program on the grounds that peer review constituted an unreasonable restraint of trade. The court dismissed the action, however, stating that arm's length collective bargaining between a labor organization and management is recognized as exempt from the concepts of antitrust law.

Sanctions and Enforcement of Antitrust Statutes

The Sherman Act provides for both civil and criminal sanctions.[88] As a criminal statute it declares that violations constitute a felony and may be punished by a fine or imprisonment or both. The maximum fine for individual defendants is $350,000, and the maximum prison term cannot exceed three years for each offense. Corporate defendants are subject to a maximum fine of $10 million for each violation.[89] Criminal prosecutions are initiated by the Department of Justice and filed in the relevant federal court by a U.S. attorney. The relevant court would be that of the district having jurisdiction over the alleged criminal activities of the defendants.[90]

The Department of Justice is also empowered to bring civil actions enforcing the Sherman Act.[91] In such proceedings the remedy sought is an injunction ordering the defendants to cease the illegal activity. Where an illegal monopoly is found, a breakup or divestiture of the monopolistic position can be decreed. Further, a state's attorney general may seek an injunction for alleged violation of the Sherman Act. Civil litigation may be terminated by a "consent decree," an agreement among the parties in which the defendants agree to eliminate the alleged illegal behavior without admitting guilt.[92] Because it may be less costly to modify business practices than to continue defending the matter in court, consent decrees are frequently perceived as mutually beneficial to all interested parties. Failure to abide by a consent decree or an injunction can result in a daily fine of $10,000.[93] This formidable economic burden provides a strong motive for defendants to comply with a resolution ordered by the court. Additionally, the attorney general of each state is authorized to enforce the federal law because local and state officials may be more aware of possible antitrust violations than governmental agencies farther from the scene.[94]

Finally, and most significant of all, private parties may bring causes of action alleging violations of the Sherman Act and obtain triple the amount of their actual damages.[95] They may also obtain an injunction, either as an alternative or as an additional remedy. The statute further authorizes the court to assess defendants for the plaintiffs' attorney fees.[96] This provision encourages private litigation and can result in considerable economic cost to defendants in an antitrust action because attorneys' fees in a major suit can amount to several million dollars. The provisions for recovering treble damages and allowing attorneys' fees are based on the idea that defendants in a meritorious antitrust action should be punished and that punishment will deter others from committing the same or similar acts. As a practical matter, enforcement of the Sherman Act is in the hands of private enterprise to a very significant extent, and private civil actions seeking damages occur much more frequently than either civil or criminal actions initiated by the government.

Among the private parties who may bring suit under the Clayton Act are individual healthcare consumers. In the 1982 case of *Blue Shield of Virginia v. McCready* the issue was whether a Blue Shield subscriber enrolled in a group plan had standing on behalf of all such patients to challenge Blue Shield's refusal to reimburse for certain psychotherapy treatments.[97] Blue Shield refused to pay a clinical psychologist unless the professional fee was billed through a physician although the plan directly reimbursed psychiatrists for psychotherapeutic services. According to the plaintiff's claim Blue Shield had conspired with the Neuropsychiatric Society of Virginia, Inc., in denying the psychologist direct reimbursement, and such conduct amounted to an unlawful refusal to deal and a boycott in violation of the Sherman Act, Section 1. In the plaintiff's view the reimbursement mechanism was injurious because it put economic pressure on Blue Shield subscribers to seek services from physician-psychiatrists rather than the psychologist. Both Blue Shield and the Neuropsychiatric Society were named as defendants in the suit.

The Supreme Court upheld the argument of the plaintiff and declared that a consumer of healthcare services does have standing to bring suit and possesses a private right of action alleging violation of the antitrust laws. To have standing it is not necessary to show that plaintiffs were actual targets of the defendants' conduct.[98] The absence of restrictive language in the Clayton Act, Section 4, indicates that Congress intended to provide a private right of action, and the "remedy cannot reasonably be restricted to those competitors whom the conspirators hoped to eliminate from the market."[99] Because the harm to the plaintiff was foreseeable, the financial injury to the plaintiff's business or property was direct and not so remote as to deny a remedy.

Unlike Sherman, the Clayton Act is not a criminal statute.[100] The civil remedies, however, are identical: an injunction or consent decree can be sought by the U.S. Department of Justice; the office of attorney general of a state may seek an injunction or damages; and private parties may sue for treble damages or an injunction, or both.

The Federal Trade Commission Act of 1914 is enforced only by the Federal Trade Commission (FTC).[101] There is no private right of action, nor is the Department of Justice involved. Moreover, the act provides for only civil remedies and sanctions. Protection of the consumer is the sole responsibility of the Federal Trade Commission. The commission also has statutory power to enforce Sections 2, 3, 7, and 8 of the Clayton Act, discussed above, and does indeed do so from time to time.[102] Because several of the activities that violate Section 1 of the Sherman Act also violate certain sections of the Clayton Act and Section 5 of the Federal Trade Commission Act, the FTC can thus be said to enforce all three of the antitrust statutes.

For many years, however, it was assumed that the FTC had no jurisdiction with respect to not-for-profit entities because Section 7 of the Clayton Act states that its prohibitions apply to persons "subject to the jurisdiction of the Federal Trade Commission,"[103] and the Federal Trade Commission Act only applies to for-profit organizations.[104] However, in a series of cases beginning with *U.S. v. Rockford Memorial Corp.*,[105] courts have since held that the FTC does have jurisdiction over not-for-profit companies.

As explained in *Rockford Memorial,* Section 11 of the Clayton Act assigns responsibility for that Act's enforcement to various agencies—each with respect to the industry it regulates—and to the FTC "where applicable to all other character of commerce."[106] As the court explained,

> We believe that the force of the . . . provision in section 7 is, therefore, merely to exempt mergers in the [enumerated] regulated industries
> . . . . Those industries do not include the hospital industry. The Clayton Act evinces a purpose of limiting the Federal Trade Commission's jurisdiction vis-à-vis that of other federal agencies charged with enforcing the Act in the industries that they regulate, but it evinces no purpose of exempting non-profit firms in industries within the domain that the Act bestows on the Commission ("all other character of commerce").

Based on this line of reasoning, most courts now agree that the FTC has jurisdiction to enforce the Clayton Act with respect to not-for-profit hospitals,[107] and in fact the agency has been actively investigating and pursuing possible antitrust violations in many healthcare-related areas such as mergers and acquisitions, physician-hospital joint ventures, and others.

Rule of Reason Analysis and
Per Se Violations

Contracts, combinations, or conspiracies in restraint of trade are illegal only if they are deemed unreasonable. Otherwise *all* contracts and joint activity between two or more persons would violate the Sherman Act, Section 1.[108] Thus in most cases the courts apply a "rule of reason" analysis, a time consuming (and expensive) case-by-case consideration of a series of factually complex issues. The relevant markets—geographical, product, and service—must be determined; the nature of the particular industry, product, or service must be examined; and the reasons for adopting the challenged restraint must be explored. Most significant, the court must assess the condition of the particular industry both before and after imposition of the restraint, thus weighing and balancing the negative and positive effects of defendant's conduct. In all this the focus is on the restraint's actual effect on competition and the counterbalancing justifications for the restraint.

Although the rule of reason is "the standard traditionally applied for the majority of anticompetitive practices challenged under Section 1 of the [Sherman] Act,"[109] some behavior is so clearly anticompetitive that a full-scale analysis of all the relevant factors and economic consequences of any restraint of trade is neither necessary nor wise. Accordingly, the courts have developed over time a "per se" standard of analysis best expressed in these words:

> [T]here are certain agreements or practices which because of their pernicious effect on competition and lack of any redeeming virtue are *conclusively presumed to be unreasonable* and therefore illegal without elaborate inquiry as to the precise harm they have caused or the business excuse for their use . . . . Among the practices which the courts have heretofore deemed to be unlawful in and of themselves are *price fixing . . . division of markets . . . group boycotts . . . and tying arrangements.*[110]

When the per se standard of analysis is applied, the plaintiff need not prove the restraint's actual or quantitative effect on competition in a particular market. The rule of reason, by contrast, places the burden on plaintiff to show the actual anticompetitive effects of the challenged activity.

The courts have traditionally identified the following as subject to per se analysis:

- horizontal price fixing among competitors;
- horizontal market divisions;
- group boycotts;
- joint refusals to deal; and
- tie-in sales arrangements.

Especially in the healthcare industry, professional and economic relations have become so complex that it is now impossible—or at least unwise—to label a given factual situation as a "group boycott" or "joint refusal to deal" and proceed to label it unreasonable per se. Even price fixing is difficult to identify and categorize without a thorough investigation of the complex business arrangements involved in most of the cases brought to court. The result has been an accelerating volume of expensive litigation that only increases the general uncertainty.

Applications to Healthcare

Concern about the high cost of healthcare in the United States has led some economists and government officials to assert that increasing competition will help control inflationary increases, despite some observers' concerns that healthcare is fundamentally different from other industries. Additionally, some argue that increased healthcare competition may actually increase costs through duplication of services, overbidding, and similar factors.

Nevertheless, antitrust enforcement has continued throughout the 1980s and '90s to encourage competition. Some of the specific activities by healthcare institutions that raise antitrust issues include:

- health planning;
- shared services;
- utilization review;
- medical staff privileges;
- reimbursement for providers;
- managed care organizations; and
- mergers and consolidations

These topics are summarized in the following sections.

Health Planning

As discussed earlier, amendments to the National Health Planning and Re-sources Development Act of 1974 provided limited immunity to the members and employees of health planning organizations.[111] The planning legislation did not, however, exempt from application of the antitrust laws the local activities of private parties who cooperate with each other or with health planning agencies to rationalize resources and make care more accessible. Further, the Supreme Court has held that Congress did not impliedly repealed the antitrust statutes when it enacted the planning legislation,[112] and the state action exemption is not applicable to local planning activities in the absence of a clearly expressed state policy and active supervision by state government.[113]

For these reasons, persons must exercise care that their actions do not amount to a contract, combination, or conspiracy with their competitors. For example, one effort to control healthcare costs has been the creation of local "business coalitions"—private collections of interested individuals who gather to achieve a stated purpose relating to healthcare. Coalitions' activities may include some or all of the following:

- educational programs to promote healthful living;
- educating members as to the causes of and possible remedies for rising healthcare costs;
- review of the quality of care;
- collection, analysis, and dissemination of data on costs, prices, and availability of services; and
- programs to improve access to care and encourage alternative, cheaper methods of healthcare delivery.

Because coalition members often include local business and healthcare leaders, the potential for joint activity by competitors is high. Of particular concern is the collection of price and cost information, because any agreement respecting such matters is a per se antitrust violation, as previously discussed. In addition, any voluntary cooperation and community-wide planning to rationalize and coordinate health services—no matter how well-intentioned— could well be considered a violation (e.g., a division of markets or group boycott) when the merits of particular cases are evaluated.

In general, however, a coalition can carry on the following activities:

- collect and publish data—including on prices, costs, and utilization—if the data are aggregated and delivered in such a way that identification of individual institutions is not possible;
- make recommendations and promote cost containment measures to the community of providers;
- study the community's access to healthcare;
- review standards of practice and quality of care;
- educate the public with respect to health and prevention;
- educate hospital trustees, administrators, physicians, and other professionals with regard to cost-effective measures; and
- petition government for legislation to contain costs.

Shared Services

Among the services often shared by hospitals and other healthcare institutions are laundry, data processing, purchasing, food service, accounting, industrial engineering, communications, printing, recordkeeping, and clinical laboratory services. Depending on the organizational format used, when healthcare providers enter into joint agreements regarding these activities, several antitrust concerns can be raised.

In the context of the Sherman Act, Section 1, for example, a non-member of a purchasing cooperative could allege that a group boycott has occurred, particularly if the group's members obtain a competitive advantage such as a lower price that is not available to nonmember competitors. To avoid the finding of group boycott, all eligible applicants should be invited to join the organization.[114] (The organization may have reasonable, objective membership standards, however. For example, eligibility rules based on tax-exempt status or location within a reasonable geographic boundary should be acceptable.)

Another legal risk inherent in shared services and group purchasing arrangements arises from the statutory provisions that make it unlawful for a seller of commodities to grant a discriminatory price and for the buyer to knowingly benefit from such a price. This statute—commonly referred to as the Robinson-Patman Act[115]—prohibits price discrimination "between different purchasers of commodities of like grade and quality" if the effect is to lessen competition substantially or tend to create a monopoly.[116] The statute provides an exemption for "schools, colleges, universities, public libraries, churches, hospitals, and charitable institutions not operated for profit" in the purchase of supplies for their own use. Thus, a group-purchasing entity created by not-for-profit hospitals would be exempt from the Robinson-Patman Act, but one created by for-profit or governmental institutions would not be.

When the statutory exemption is unavailable, group purchasing entities can assert one of two defenses to a Robinson-Patman charge:

1. that the discount is based on a corresponding saving in the cost of manufacture, sale, or delivery; or
2. that the price differentials were granted in good faith to meet competition and were not intended to eliminate competitors.

Utilization Review

An essential component of cost containment programs is retrospective review of individual cases to determine the medical necessity and appropriateness of the care rendered. The process is known as "utilization review" or sometimes "peer review," and it necessarily involves input by professional peers because the judgment of other practitioners is required to appraise the appropriateness of the diagnosis, length of state, type of test ordered, and so on. Moreover, data are needed from professionals regarding the fees they consider customary and reasonable for particular services. The inherent nature and requirements of this activity raise potentially serious antitrust concerns.

As discussed earlier, for some years the courts were divided on the question of whether utilization review was exempt from antitrust scrutiny by virtue of the McCarran-Ferguson Act. It is now established, however, that utilization or peer review is not exempt from antitrust analysis by virtue of the McCarran-Ferguson Act. Nevertheless, utilization review programs can survive antitrust scrutiny if properly structured. First, if the program is mandated by federal or state government or is conducted according to a clearly stated governmental policy and supervised by public agencies, it will be exempt under the "state action" doctrine of *Parker v. Brown*.[117] Accordingly, review of claims filed in connection with the Medicare and Medicaid programs or similar government health systems are not likely to be subject to antitrust challenges.

Second, a series of advisory opinions from the Federal Trade Commission in the early 1980s laid out standards that provide significant protection from antitrust scrutiny.[118] According to the FTC'S view, utilization or peer review is not legally objectionable if the sponsors of the program have no intent to hamper competition, do not engage in coercion, and limit practicing professional persons to an advisory role.

Medical Staff Privileges

The hospital as a legal entity is ultimately responsible for the standard of care exercised by its entire professional staff. The hospital's governing board has a duty to exercise reasonable care in appointing and retaining independent physicians on its medical staff. Failure to do so can result in liability. In the exercise of this duty, however, hospital trustees (or directors, as they are sometimes called) encounter numerous antitrust issues.

For example, exclusive service contracts granted to physicians in certain specialties (such as anesthesiology, nuclear medicine, and emergency medicine) have been challenged by physicians who are unable to obtain medical staff privileges because of the exclusive arrangements. The excluded physicians have argued that the contracts amount to a group boycott or concerted refusal to deal, both violations of the Sherman Act. Indeed, the entire process by which hospitals assess the credentials of the medical staff, whether under an exclusive service contract or otherwise, can trigger allegations of restraint of trade. However, most challenges against exclusive service contracts and the denial or revocation of staff privileges have not been successful.

Some unsuccessful cases have been dismissed on the jurisdictional point that interstate commerce is not affected. Most courts, however, will accept jurisdiction and analyze the merits of each case. A significant decision concerning the legality of a hospital's exclusive contract for specialized services is *Dos Santos v. Columbus-Cuneo-Cabrini Medical Center.*[119] The plaintiff, an anesthesiologist, had once been employed by a group of physicians who were under contract as exclusive providers of anesthesia services at the defendant medical center. When her employment by the group ended, the medical center refused to grant her an appointment to the medical staff as an individual. The court found the market for the services of an anesthesiologist to be broader than the geographical service area of the medical center. Additionally, the court suggested that the true purchaser of anesthesia services is the hospital and not the patient.[120] Accordingly, the plaintiff was not entitled to an injunction granting her privileges. The Seventh Circuit Court of Appeals remanded the case to the District Court of Northern Illinois with instructions to decide the matter on the merits. On remand, the court concluded that the contract did not have a significant adverse effect on competition in the relevant market and upheld the contract as reasonable.[121]

The only major case to cast doubt on the legality of a properly structured exclusive contract was *Hyde v. Jefferson Parish Hospital District No. 2*, decided by the Fifth Circuit Court of Appeals in 1982.[122] This court held that an exclusive contract for anesthesiology was a tying arrangement, or tie-in sale, and thus a per se violation of Section 1 of the Sherman Act.[123] The court found that the purchase of anesthesia services was improperly tied to the use of the hospital's surgical facilities because the patient had no choice in purchasing the services of a anesthesiologist and no alternative source of supply. This then becomes a per se violation of the Sherman Act because the seller was thought to have sufficient market power in the tying product, the surgical facilities, to force the purchase of the tied product, the anesthesia services. The Fifth Circuit's opinion was thus based on the finding that the hospital in question had a substantial degree of monopolistic power in the relevant market for surgical facilities.

On review, however, the U.S. Supreme Court unanimously reversed the Fifth Circuit and held that the exclusive contract in question did not constitute a violation of antitrust laws under either a per se or rule of reason analysis.[124] The Court rejected the view that the defendant hospital had enough market power in the circumstances to force patients into buying the services of the anesthesiologist because several other hospitals were available in the area.[125] Thus, a per se analysis did not apply, and under the rule of reason the restraint was reasonable because hospitals clearly have the right to control medical staff privileges as long as their reasons are legitimate.[126]

Clearly the reach of the antitrust laws will not inhibit suspending or revoking hospital privileges when the evidence shows that a physician is deviating from generally recognized professional standards. For example, in *Pontius v. Children's Hospital,* a pediatric cardiovascular surgeon was denied reappointment after evidence revealed that the mortality rate among his patients exceeded acceptable standards, that the surgeon transgressed standard medical practices, that he had engaged in unprofessional conduct with patients, and that he had demonstrated an inability to work with other members of the medical staff.[127] The surgeon failed in a suit alleging that the hospital's decision denying renewal of privileges violated the Sherman Act.

Quite aside from factual situations like *Pontius,* the cases involving medical staff privileges have not applied a per se standard of analysis, and allegations that denial or restriction of clinical privileges constitutes a group boycott or joint refusal to deal have not been successful. Several of the cases suggest that except for price fixing, restraints in the healthcare industry that are responses to obligations of public service may justify a somewhat different policy in antitrust enforcement.[128]

Because the rule of reason applies, and also because Section 1 requires that two entities must conspire or combine together to restrain trade, the courts will not find a violation unless physicians participating in the hospital's examination of credentials intend to lessen competition. The ultimate decision to appoint, deny an appointment, or restrict privileges is the hospital's, as has already been emphasized, and it is most important that it be made by the governing body of the institution (even though recommendations must be obtained from the medical staff and other professional sources). Courts have been realistic in understanding the need for professional advice, and they are hesitant to find a conspiracy to restrain trade unreasonably.[129]

The hospital can thus successfully defend cases involving medical staff privileges by providing ample documentation of the purpose and reasons for decisions adverse to the claimant. Only when evidence of intentional anticompetitive behavior is rather clear will an antitrust claim be successful.[130] Quite another situation arises, however, when an institutional policy excludes an entire class of practitioners from clinical privileges without providing cogent reasons and procedures for fairly evaluating their credentials and the institution's need for their services. Such a policy may well violate constitutional law, state common law, state statutes, or antitrust legislation, depending on the particular facts and the jurisdiction.

As an example of constitutional doctrine, a court in Texas held that a county hospital could not require all staff physicians to have postdoctoral training accredited by the Accreditation Committee on Graduate Medical Education.[131] Such a rule excluded osteopathic doctors, even those with the postdoctoral training accredited by the American Osteopathic Association that was acceptable for medical licensing in Texas. Hence, the rule was arbitrary and violated the Fourteenth Amendment to the Constitution. Similarly, the Sherman Act has been used as a legal vehicle to restrain the hospital and its medical staff from impeding the access of osteopathic doctors to the institution. There was, for example, an antitrust violation when a plaintiff established that a hospital had used different standards in deciding on appointments for osteopathic and allopathic physicians.[132]

An institution's policy of withholding clinical privileges from healthcare practitioners who are not physicians presents similar issues. State licensing laws usually recognize some or all of the following as limited practitioners (or "allied health professionals"): podiatrists, nurse-anesthetists, nurse-midwives, nurse-practitioners, physicians' assistants, clinical psychologists, and chiropractors. Depending on the state, statutes recognize that these types of professionals have a right to practice within a legally permissible scope. In the past, allied health professionals, except dentists, were granted neither membership on the hospital medical staff nor clinical privileges, but consumers and insurers in increasing numbers are demanding the services of the nonphysician allied practitioners because their services are less costly than a physician's and generally are of equal quality for treatment of common maladies.

Constitutional law,[133] state statutes,[134] or antitrust considerations[135] require a hospital to evaluate allied health professionals fairly and objectively. Decisions must apply only to individuals and must be made only after evaluation of each applicant's training, experience, and current competence, with due regard for the institution's needs and goals. Such an evaluation process does not of course require the hospital to grant medical staff membership privileges in individual instances.[136]

In 1984 the Joint Commission on Accreditation of Healthcare Organizations (then the Joint Commission on Accreditation of Hospitals) issued revised Medical Staff Standards that recognized that the medical staff of a hospital may include persons other than licensed physicians who are "permitted by law and the hospital to provide patient care services independently." This standard remains in effect today.[137] A careful reading of the standard reveals that no hospital is required to accept limited practitioners as staff members or grant them clinical privileges, but any hospital may appoint them to membership or grant clinical privileges consistent with the local licensure law and the individual's training, experience, and demonstrated competence. The standard also allows hospitals to limit admitting privileges to members of the medical staff.

As indicated throughout this discussion, a hospital can restrict the clinical privileges of any member of its professional staff for good reason. Moreover, the JCAHO standard does not change most hospitals' policy of making all new appointments provisional for a certain period, nor does it change judicial and statutory law making the corporation ultimately responsible for the quality of care. As stated when the standard first appeared in the early 1980s, a hospital that denies applications either from an individual or from "a category of practitioners" must base its decision "on the exercise of independent judgment under appropriately developed and adequately documented criteria, pursuant to a mechanism adopted by the hospital governing body."[138]

Some of the economic and social realities that prompted a change in organized medicine's prior reluctance to recognize the professional status of allied health care providers include the emphasis on cost reduction, the oversupply of physicians in many localities, and the fact that physicians' and limited practitioners' practices frequently overlap. (Consider, for example, podiatrists and orthopedic surgeons; clinical psychologists and psychiatrists; nurse midwives and obstetricians.) In light of these facts, allegations founded on constitutional doctrine, local and state law, or federal antitrust legislation may well succeed on proof that a defendant hospital, with its medical staff in an advisory role, has arbitrarily excluded an allied practitioner. In the context of an antitrust analysis, it would be easier for a plaintiff to establish a conspiracy among competitors resulting in a group boycott or refusal to deal, a traditional per se violation, when an entire class of practitioners is excluded. Even under the rule of reason analysis, anticompetitive interests and effects are easier to prove when a blanket exclusion exists.[139] The message to hospitals and other such institutions from several sources of legal doctrine is clear: decisions with respect to medical staff appointments and clinical privileges for individuals must be reasonable and supported by documented evidence.

Reimbursement for Providers

Third-party payors (government health plans and traditional insurance carriers) ordinarily contract with an employer or an individual patient to reimburse healthcare providers for services furnished the insured person. This contract, customarily referred to as the *subscriber contract*, guarantees service to the patient for which the third-party payor will agree to reimburse the providers of care directly. The providers may be hospitals, nursing homes, clinics, ambulatory care facilities, physicians, allied health practitioners, or similar entities and individuals. The contracts reciting the terms of reimbursement between the third-party carrier and the providers are usually referred to as *participating provider agreements.*

Antitrust law has sometimes been used to challenge the validity of participating provider agreements on the theory that they constitute possible price fixing, amount to a group boycott, or result in an illegal monopoly. Although it is clear that a participating provider agreement is not exempt from federal antitrust legislation,[140] most of these suits have failed. As long as the arrangement is preceded by proper and careful negotiation and then implemented consistently with the contractual terms, the contract will survive antitrust scrutiny.[141]

In one case, however, a *prima facie* case of per se illegal price fixing and joint refusal to deal was established by a "contracting," nonparticipating hospital upon evidence that participating hospitals had formed an "association" and then joined with Blue Cross to govern the reimbursement program. The arrangement called for different rates of reimbursement to participating hospitals from those received by contracting and nonparticipating institutions. Moreover, the participating hospitals contracted to underwrite the solvency of Blue Cross and were entitled to elect a certain number of persons to its governing board. All participating hospitals were not-for-profit institutions and were reimbursed for their services to Blue Cross subscribers on the basis of their "necessary and proper charges." Although nonparticipating, contracting hospitals could be proprietary, for-profit institutions, they were not given voting rights and were under no contractual obligation to underwrite Blue Cross's solvency. Blue Cross reimbursed the contracting hospitals for 100 percent of their charges to the patient, unless these exceeded the average per diem payment to participating hospitals for a similar illness or hospital stay. In effect, the nonparticipating hospital was required to forfeit a measure of profit on Blue Cross patients unless it could collect additional charges from the patients themselves. The plaintiff therefore alleged that the development and negotiation of the provider reimbursement contract, together with its implementation, constituted an illegal price-fixing scheme and group boycott or joint refusal to deal. The court found the evidence sufficient to support a treble damage claim and remanded the matter for trial.[142]

Similarly, it has been held that if an insurer's reimbursement program for nonparticipating providers is controlled by competitors who enjoy participating status, the arrangements could amount to illegal price fixing and boycott. In *Glen Eden Hospital, Inc. v. Blue Cross and Blue Shield of Michigan* the Court of Appeals for the Sixth Circuit reversed a summary judgment for the defendant and held that the plaintiff should be allowed to continue pretrial discovery to support allegations of an antitrust conspiracy.[143] In this instance the Blue Cross reimbursement contract granted participating hospitals the right to veto recommended changes in the terms of reimbursement to providers who were nonparticipants.

As long as competing providers do not control the terms of the reimbursement contract, however, courts have generally sustained agreements that require participating providers to accept the insurer's reimbursable amount in full payment and thus prohibit any collection of a "balance due" from the subscriber-patient. As noted earlier, the agreements may also provide that when subscribers obtain services from a nonparticipating provider the third-party insurer will not reimburse the provider directly. Instead the subscriber must usually pay the provider the price of goods or the fee for service and then seek a contractually specified, limited indemnification from the insurer. The purpose of such provisions is, of course, to encourage subscribers to seek services from participating providers and to induce institutions and professional practitioners to participate. Both the prohibition on balance billing and the refusal to reimburse nonparticipating providers were upheld in *Pennsylvania Dental Association v. Medical Service Association*.[144] Neither provision constituted an illegal vertical or horizontal price-fixing agreement, nor did the relevant market and the terms of this particular plan constitute an illegal monopoly or boycott. The patients were free to seek service from a nonparticipating provider, and the providers were equally free to enter similar participating contracts with other third-party insurers.[145]

In summary, various cases hold that it is not illegal to bargain unilaterally for a price, even if the buyer has sufficient market power to lower prices, as long as the pricing policy is not predatory. The courts are not in a position to supervise price bargains or to declare that a given price is "measurable." Although agreements to fix prices at any level are prohibited, where there is no horizontal agreement among competitors, or any vertical price fixing or resale price maintenance, there is no antitrust violation.

The relevance of antitrust legislation to the reimbursement of participating providers is an important matter for executives of third-party financial entities. They should make decisions unilaterally, without influence from competing providers and never as a result of an implied agreement among them. They also need to offer the same contractual terms to all qualified or eligible providers of healthcare, to allow patient-subscribers to seek care from a nonparticipating provider, and to have documentary evidence that the decisions were justified by legitimate business principles and a concern for efficiency and the quality of healthcare. Perhaps the most important reminder of all is that the current economic environment requires healthcare managers to record in full the reasons for their business decisions.

Managed Care Organizations

In recent years third-party payors and healthcare providers have developed various kinds of managed care organizations (MCOs) as a means of controlling the costs of care and in response to the competitive environment. MCOs include health maintenance organizations (HMOs), preferred provider organizations (PPOs), exclusive provider organizations (EPOs), independent practice associations (IPAs), point-of-service plans (POS plans), and various hybrids of the above. MCOs typically offer health services at a discount, compared to traditional fee-for-service plans, in return for a larger (or at least more predictable) patient load. There is usually a negotiated price schedule for services, a closed or limited panel of providers, and a mechanism for controlling utilization. Commonly there are economic incentives to choose the services of the MCO's physicians, but patients may or may not be required to do so.

Several antitrust issues relate to MCOs: the possibility of horizontal or vertical price fixing, concerted refusals to deal, monopolization or attempted monopolization of a relevant market, illegal division of markets, and predatory pricing. Nevertheless, as history has proven, these potential legal pitfalls can be avoided through proper structuring of the organization followed by careful attention to its implementation and administration.

The primary concern is that negotiated prices may constitute price fixing. As is now well known, *Arizona v. Maricopa County Medical Society* prohibits competing physicians from agreeing on prices for a given service and on a reimbursement schedule from a third-party payor.[146] The court held that a medical foundation composed of practicing physicians could not establish a maximum fee schedule for insurance reimbursement; such activity was a per se violation of the Sherman Act. A physician-controlled managed care organization that contracts with doctors for services would therefore be likely to constitute a per se price-fixing violation unless the MCO was truly an economic entity separate from the physicians. An economic entity (such as a multispecialty group practice) created by physicians could negotiate fees without violating the antitrust principles expressed in *Maricopa*.

In similar fashion, an MCO, controlled by a hospital or group of hospitals, that negotiates prices with other hospital providers would be likely to violate antitrust laws. Moreover, independent hospitals may not jointly agree on prices to be charged to a preferred provider organization.

In contrast to the foregoing prohibitions, however, a third-party payor is perfectly free to negotiate prices individually with each available provider, as long as the payor offers the same terms to each provider and the provider is free to serve patients other than the payor's subscribers.[147]

Maricopa left open the possibility that several providers could enter into a joint-venture arrangement, sharing capital risk in organizing and operating a preferred provider organization.[148] If a true joint venture is undertaken, a rule of reason analysis would apply rather than the per se ruling of *Maricopa*.

The facts in each case will determine, of course, whether a genuine joint venture has been created.[149] Important factors in judging the arrangement and applying the rule of reason are the degree of financial risk to the joint participants, whether the fee schedule agreed on is "reasonably necessary to achieve legitimate goals of the venture" and whether the venture will favor or hinder competition in particular markets.[150]

In summary, price-fixing issues can be avoided when a managed care organization is developed and operated by a third-party insurer or by an independent employer or entrepreneur; when it is a genuine joint venture; or when it represents a single institutional provider that unilaterally determines terms of reimbursement and contracts individually with other providers or purchasers of care. The crucial point is to avoid express or implied agreements among competitors.

Group boycotts have also been alleged by plaintiffs challenging MCOs. In general a *group boycott* exists when two or more entities join in refusing to deal with a targeted party or parties. The validity of a claim of illegality rests on a finding of a conspiracy or concerted action among competitors. A unilateral, independent decision to refrain from contracting with another is not an antitrust violation.[151]

In a few cases involving healthcare, courts have found the requisite degree of concerted action and have ruled that a claim exists. In *Virginia Academy of Clinical Psychologists v. Blue Shield of Virginia* a claim was stated against a Blue Shield plan controlled by physicians that refused to reimburse clinical psychologists unless their charges were billed through a physician.[152] Similarly, a refusal by Blue Shield to reimburse chiropractors presented a possible claim based on boycott.[153] In contrast, an agreement between a health maintenance organization and a clinic whereby the HMO agreed not to contract with any other similar clinic was not considered a group boycott.[154]

When a claim is stated the court must determine whether to apply a per se or rule of reason analysis. In the commercial world most litigated cases have used a per se analysis when the facts indicated a group boycott or concerted refusal to deal. In healthcare, however, the courts have usually applied a rule of reason analysis, even in decisions following *Arizona v. Maricopa County Medical Society*,[155] thereby recognizing that the healthcare industry should receive different treatment from that applied to industrial enterprises when restraints of trade other than price fixing are being evaluated.[156]

In sum, to avoid charges of violating antitrust laws, MCOs should observe the following fundamental principles of organizational structure and implementation. First, hospitals, physicians, and other participating health practitioners should not control the process of setting fees and reimbursement schedules. Second, the MCO should offer the same reimbursement terms to all providers who are proved eligible by objective criteria and then negotiate individually with each one. These negotiations and the resulting reimbursement contract should not be permitted to create monopolistic situations that will discourage the formation of competing groups in a relevant market.[157] Finally, to forestall claims of prohibited exclusive dealing, providers should be free to contract with other payors and to serve other patients.[158] Patients should also be free to seek care from hospitals or physicians who have chosen not to contract with the MCO. Patients who voluntarily seek care elsewhere can then be subjected to a deductible provision, a coinsurance clause, or other measures that provide economic incentives to choose a certain hospital or professional practitioner. If patients seeking care from a noncontracting provider are not to be reimbursed at all, then they should be able to choose voluntarily from a variety of prepaid healthcare plans with varying premiums. When all of these circumstances are present, MCOs in fact favor competition rather than hinder it, and they will survive scrutiny under both state and federal antitrust laws.[159]

Mergers and Consolidations

In general   Corporations grow and diversify by acquiring the stock of another corporation, purchasing the assets of another firm, merging with one or more other corporations, or consolidating. These four different transactions need to be distinguished for purposes of both corporate and antitrust legal analysis.

When a corporation or an investor wishes to acquire the stock of another corporation, the acquiring organization simply tenders an offer to the latter's shareholders to buy their stock at a named price. To the extent that these shareholders decide to sell, the investor acquires shares and, perhaps eventually, voting control of the corporation. Where federal jurisdiction applies, these tender offers are subject to regulation by the Securities and Exchange Commission.

The purchase of assets of another firm is usually a straightforward transaction. If both the purchaser and the seller are existing corporations, the sale usually requires the approval of both governing bodies. Whenever a firm disposes of a substantial portion of its assets, the corporate law of most states also requires that the shareholders or corporate members of the selling corporation approve the transaction. When a corporate seller has sold most of its assets, the firm may cease to do business and dissolve, although dissolution is not necessarily an inevitable consequence. If assets remain or if new assets are later obtained, the selling organization may well continue as a viable enterprise.

A merger results when an acquired firm discontinues its business operations and dissolves as a corporation. The business entity acquiring the assets of the dissolved corporation assumes the latter's liabilities and normally continues its business operations in the same or modified fashion. Corporate mergers are regulated extensively by the corporate law of the relevant state. Typically the board of directors and the majority of shareholders of both corporations must approve the transaction, although some statutes allow the boards alone to act if the corporate articles permit.

A consolidation differs from a merger in that a new corporate entity is created by two or more existing corporations. These organizations transfer all of their assets to the new corporation and then dissolve. Again, state law controls the procedures in a consolidation.

The terms "merger" and "consolidation" are frequently used interchangeably and indeed are also sometimes applied to a straightforward acquisition of another firm's stock or assets. Because corporate statutes and other legal pronouncements distinguish among the four methods of corporate expansion, it is preferable to refer to a combination rather than a merger in a general discussion of organizational changes in the corporate world.

Four different antitrust statutory provisions have relevance to mergers, consolidations, and acquisitions of stock or assets of another firm. All have been described previously.[160] For reasons that will be explained, Section 7 of the Clayton Act is by far the most significant.[161] Business combinations can also be challenged, however, under the Sherman Act, Sections 1 and 2[162] and Section 5 of the Federal Trade Commission Act.[163] A few observations about the Sherman and Federal Trade Commission Acts are in order here before going on to a more extensive discussion of the Clayton Act. **Applicable provisions**

As discussed earlier, Section 1 of the Sherman Act prohibits unreasonable contracts, combinations, or conspiracies in restraint of trade by two or more business entities acting in concert. Because business combinations have not been treated as per se violations, anyone who challenges a combination or conspiracy must show that the restraint results in an actual and substantial lessening of competition. The courts have recognized that some business combinations, mergers, and joint ventures may in fact increase business efficiency and thus favor competition. A plaintiff who must show an actual anticompetitive effect carries a heavy burden; hence, Section 1 is a less attractive legal vehicle for those challenging the decision of separate business entities to combine. Section 1 also requires that two or more persons agree to restrain trade and does not apply to unilateral action.

In contrast, Section 2 of the Sherman Act is applicable to unilateral action by single firms and prohibits their engaging in monopolies, attempts to monopolize, and conspiracies to monopolize.[164] The three essential elements of a Section 2 allegation require a case-by-case analysis:

1. proof of market power (the ability to fix or control prices above the competition);
2. definition of the relevant geographic and service markets; and
3. proof that the defendant has achieved or is maintaining monopoly power "willfully" or "unfairly."

These concepts, considered together, make it plain that mere size and the absence of competition do not constitute an illegal monopoly. Rather, what is prohibited is the willful and intentional acquisition of monopoly power to control prices or exclude competitors. Predatory pricing policies such as pricing below cost, or other unfair business practices may therefore be evidence of prohibited activities. In contrast, a dominant position in the market is not a violation in and of itself. Some firms achieve a dominant position or even sole dominance by supplying a quality product or service efficiently or simply because the market can support only a single enterprise. In a leading 1966 case it was ruled that "growth and development as a consequence of a superior product, business acumen, or historic accident" does not violate Section 2 of the Sherman Act.[165] Invention and innovation in a rapidly changing technological world encourage competition, and success does not by itself violate the principles of antitrust law.[166]

For a number of reasons, therefore, the provisions of the Sherman Act are difficult to enforce and are relatively ineffective in controlling monopolistic mergers and acquisitions. Although the statute remains in effect and is certainly a factor to be considered when evaluating the antitrust aspects of corporate reorganization, Section 7 of the Clayton Act is the preferred and most important means of challenging the legality of a newly created or proposed business combination.[167]

Section 7 prohibits mergers and acquisitions that "tend to create a monopoly." The relevant portion of the law, as amended, reads as follows:

> No person engaged in commerce . . . shall acquire, directly or
> indirectly, the whole or any part of the stock or other share capital
> and no corporation subject to the jurisdiction of the Federal Trade
> Commission shall acquire the whole or any part of the assets of
> another person engaged also in commerce . . . where in any line
> of commerce . . . in any section of the country, the effect of such
> acquisition may be substantially to lessen competition, or to tend to
> create a monopoly.[168]

As a matter of jurisdiction the Clayton Act applies only to mergers or acquisitions "in commerce." This test is more stringent than the standard employed in evaluating the jurisdictional reach of the Sherman Act, which applies to activity that "substantially affects commerce" or, as restated in *McLain*, activity that has a "not insubstantial" effect on commerce.[169] In contrast, the standard of "in commerce" rules out transactions that merely affect interstate commerce: the Clayton Act applies only to the actual production or distribution of goods or services in interstate commerce. The Clayton Act did not apply, for example, where an out-of-state corporation doing business nationally acquired two firms supplying local janitorial services in southern California because the companies acquired were not engaged in interstate commerce.[170]

Defining and Appraising Markets

A Clayton Act analysis first requires definition of the relevant product or service market and the geographic market and then appraisal of the proposed combination's effect on competition. In defining the product market, one must identify items that compete with each other as well as interchangeable substitutes. If buyers are prone to substitute a different, interchangeable product when the price of a hitherto preferred product increases, the substitute must be included in the market. On the other hand, if the evidence shows that purchasers do not substitute a comparable item when a given product increases in price, the conclusion may well be that the targeted product stands alone as a market. The term used in appraising this factor is "cross-elasticity of demand."

Each case must be considered on its own facts. For example, in a leading decision the majority of the Supreme Court held that cellophane was in competition with other forms of flexible packaging materials. Because the defendant possessed only 18 percent of the market for packaging materials, an antitrust violation had not occurred, even though the defendant company had nearly 75 percent of the cellophane market.[171]

In the healthcare arena, a prime example of this concept of case-by-case market analysis can be seen in two significant hospital merger cases. In *United States v. Carilion Health System,* the U.S. Justice Department brought suit to prevent the merger of two hospitals in Roanoke, Virginia.[172] The parties included Carilion Health System, which owned three not-for-profit hospitals in the state—including 677-bed Roanoke Memorial Hospital—and managed six others, and Community Hospital of Roanoke Valley, a 400-bed facility. Roanoke Memorial (staffed to operate 609 beds) and Community (staffed for 220) wished to merge. A third hospital in the Roanoke area, which operated about 335 beds, was not involved in the merger. All three hospitals provided primary, secondary, and tertiary care, although Community provided the least tertiary services.

In considering the geographic market, the court pointed out that Roanoke Memorial drew 27 percent of its patients from three West Virginia counties and eleven Virginia counties outside the Roanoke area. It also noted that the hospital drew at least 100 patients per year from each of six other counties. Community drew about 18 percent of its patients from eight counties outside of Roanoke. In this geographic area about 20 other hospitals provided primary and, in some cases, secondary care. Based on this analysis, the court concluded that the two merging hospitals compete with the various hospitals in those surrounding counties. Furthermore, noting the increase in the number of conditions that are treated on an outpatient basis rather than in an acute care hospital setting, the court found, "certain clinics and other providers of outpatient services compete with the defendants' hospitals to treat various medical needs" and that "the number of problems treated on an inpatient basis has declined steadily in recent years and can be expected to continue to fall."

Noting that the hospitals wanted to merge to improve their efficiency and competitive positions, the court held that the combination would not be an unreasonable restraint of trade and "would probably improve the quality of health care in western Virginia and reduce its cost and will strengthen competition between the two large hospitals that would remain in the Roanoke area."

In contrast, the following year a U.S. Court of Appeals decided *United States v. Rockford Memorial Corporation.*[173] This case involved the proposed merger of the two largest hospitals in Rockford, Illinois. It was estimated that the two facilities, if allowed to merge, would control between 64 percent and 72 percent of the inpatient services market and that they and the third largest hospital (which was not party to the merger talks) would control 90 percent. The court refused to consider healthcare services provided in nonhospital settings as relevant to the service market: "If a firm has a monopoly of product X, the fact that it produces another product, Y, for which the firm faces competition is irrelevant to its monopoly. . . . For many services provided by acute-care hospitals, there is no competition from other sorts of providers."[174]

Having concluded that the relevant product market was inpatient, acute-care services, the court turned to the geographic market analysis. Accepting (somewhat reluctantly, it appears) the trial court's finding that the service area was a ten-county area of northern Illinois and southern Wisconsin centered around Rockford, the appellate court noted that 87 percent of the hospitals' admissions come from Rockford, the rest of the county it is located in, and "pieces of several other counties." Although the service area contained six hospitals in all, "90 percent of Rockford residents who are hospitalized are hospitalized in Rockford itself." The court wrote that it was "ridiculous" to think "Rockford residents, or third-party payors, will be searching out small, obscure hospitals in remote rural areas if the prices charged by the hospitals in Rockford reside above competitive levels." "[F]or the most part hospital services are local," the court concluded, and it upheld the trial court's injunction prohibiting the merger.

The Rockford court's analysis has since become the majority view: that the relevant service market in hospital merger cases is general acute-care hospital services. Nevertheless, the Rockford and Roanoke cases illustrate the difference that geography and demographics can make in the "rule of reason" analysis that must be undertaken. They also illustrate why the outcome of hospital antitrust cases is extremely difficult to predict: "[T]hese decisions require factual judgments regarding what the future may hold in an industry undergoing revolutionary change. Like pilots landing at night aboard an aircraft carrier, courts are aiming for a target that is small, shifting and poorly illuminated."[175]

After both the relevant product or service market and the geographical market have been determined, the competitive effect of a merger or acquisition must be evaluated. The goal here, of course, is to determine whether the combination, in the words of the statute, "may be substantially to lessen competition or tend to create a monopoly."[176] Among the important factors to consider are whether competing firms or potential competitors have been eliminated from the market, whether an acquisition of a relatively small but locally dominant firm by a larger organization makes the acquired company even more dominant, whether the merger may lead the firms to buy each others' products and thereby harm competitors, and what in fact has happened to the competitive environment in situations in which the merger has already occurred.

In any event the focus is on the future and the potential adverse effects on competition. Challenges to a combination can occur long after the actual transaction because the statute of limitation does not begin to run until anticompetitive effects are apparent.[177] Because the statute itself does not provide either a quantitative or qualitative test for changes in competition, each merger or acquisition has to be viewed functionally in the context of the particular industry.

Horizontal mergers, as distinct from vertical combinations and conglomerates, are likely to have the most immediate adverse effects on competition. To appraise this effect in a given situation, the court will gather evidence of the merged firm's share of the market; the number of firms supplying the market, known as the concentration ratio; and the frequency of mergers within the market, known as concentration trends. To explain governmental policy in enforcing both the Clayton and the Sherman Acts the Department of Justice in 1982 issued revised "Merger Guidelines" announcing a mathematical formula known as the Herfindahl-Herschman Index (HHI) that would be used to measure market concentration. According to the formula, each firm's market share is squared and a total of the squares is calculated. Postmerger scores of less than 1,000 are considered evidence that the market is not seriously concentrated. Accordingly, the government is not likely to challenge these combinations. On the other hand, scores over 1,800 represent highly concentrated markets and may trigger a departmental investigation of all other relevant factors as a prelude to a possible antitrust proceeding. Moderately concentrated markets are those that have scores between 1,000 and 1,800.[178] To illustrate the calculation: if ten firms compete in a market and each has 10 percent of the market, the HHI is 1,000. On the other hand, if each of three firms has 30 percent of the market, and a fourth has 10 percent, the score is 2,800 ($30^2 + 30^2 + 30^2 + 10^2 = 2,800$) and a highly concentrated market exists. As would be expected, the Department of Justice is interested in index scores before and after mergers because such data are evidence of the anticompetitive effect of a given transaction. The HHI is of course only a starting point for analysis and investigation. Depending on the score in a given instance the department may or may not review other factors and determine whether the legality of a merger of acquisition is likely to be challenged. The ultimate decision rests with the courts, which will look for "an undue percentage share of the relevant market" resulting in "a significant increase in the concentration of [firms]."[179]

Unlike a horizontal business combination, a *vertical merger*, or acquisition, does not eliminate a competitor. Rather, it unites a customer with a supplier and is a means of ensuring availability of supplies, increasing retail sales of a manufacturer's product, or enabling more profitable marketing of products. When firms unite vertically the primary questions are these: Has the transaction deprived a competitor of a source of supply? Has it closed a competitor's or potential competitor's access to the market?[180] Illustrating these concepts is the acquisition of Autolite by the Ford Motor Company. Autolite manufactured spark plugs, an essential component for automobiles. Because the acquisition eliminated Ford as a potential spark plug manufacturer and removed Ford from the market as a significant buyer of these products, a violation of the Clayton Act had occurred.[181] A court evaluating the anticompetitive effect of a vertical arrangement will weigh the capital costs of entry into the market, concentration of buyers and sellers, the trends toward vertical integration, the nature and economic purpose of the transaction, and the intent of the parties.[182]

A *conglomerate* does not normally have a direct effect on competition because it simply combines different corporate entities that conduct business involving different products or services or operating in unrelated geographical areas. By definition, the acquired firm is not a competitor, a customer, or a supplier of the parent organization. Yet the courts have recognized that in given circumstances a conglomerate may have anticompetitive effects and that the Clayton Act applies to this type of combination.

In a leading case, *Federal Trade Commission v. Procter and Gamble*, the Supreme Court held that the defendant's acquisition of Clorox Chemical Company violated the statute.[183] Procter and Gamble Company, prominent producer of household detergents, did not manufacture liquid laundry bleach. Rather than expanding its product line internally, the company purchased the assets of Clorox, which commanded nearly half of the national market. The Federal Trade Commission sought divestiture, and the Supreme Court agreed that uniting an enterprise of the defendant's magnitude with the dominant producer of liquid bleaches was likely to make it more difficult for new firms to enter the market and for much smaller existing firms to compete.

It was noted, for example, that Procter and Gamble's ability to promote and market the product would inhibit smaller firms and "may substantially reduce the competitive structure of the industry."[184] As in the *Ford Motor* case the acquisition foreclosed the possibility that Procter and Gamble would become a new entrant in the liquid bleach market. In all probability, however, the litigation would have produced a different result had Clorox been a relatively minor manufacturer of bleach. On such facts, expansions of product line and territory have been permitted because the transaction does not promote an oligopoly characterized by a small number of companies controlling a product or service in a given market.

Still another form of business combination, quite prevalent in the healthcare arena, is the *joint venture*, in which two or more entities create an association specifically meant to accomplish a defined economic goal. In many respects a joint venture has the legal attributes and features of a partnership, but a joint venture normally has a limited life span because the association terminates when the economic goal is accomplished. A joint venture is subject to scrutiny under Section 7 of the Clayton Act, and the courts will evaluate all relevant factors in deciding whether a venture is likely to lessen competition substantially.[185] In general a joint venture will be approved if the defined goal of the agreement is legitimate and if the market share of the combination is relatively small.

To summarize: under the current judicial approach to enforcement of the Clayton Act, Section 7, the plaintiff bears the burden of proving the defendant's share of the market and the market's concentration ratios. The plaintiff must also show that a merger or acquisition is likely to have a anticompetitive effect.[186] This standard of proof in turn requires a rather broad and expansive factual inquiry on a case-by-case basis beyond a mere statistical showing of market share. The rule of reason analysis, then, permits the use of subjective judgment in evaluating facts presented in court and their effects. Finally, the courts are requiring that all relevant economic factors and probabilities be considered when the Clayton Act is used as the basis for challenging a merger or acquisition. Among these factors are such matters as ease of entry into a market, the economic health of the particular industry, characteristics of the products involved, availability of substitute products, the nature of consumer demand, and characteristics of the firms in question.

In certain circumstances both parties to a proposed merger or acquisition must report the pending transaction to the Department of Justice and the Federal Trade Commission.[187] Such notice enables the government to review the implications of an agreement or an offer to merge before the transaction is completed. If the department having jurisdiction in the case concludes that the transaction may constitute an antitrust violation, the government is authorized to seek a preliminary injunction in court.

Reporting to the government

The prior notice requirement applies to publicly announced offers to acquire the stock of another firm and to privately negotiated transactions whenever one of the firms has sales or assets of $10 million or more and the company acquiring the stock or assets of the other firm receives $15 million in value or 15 percent of the assets or voting control. In most situations the required period of advance notice is 30 days, although if an investor makes a cash offer for the stock of a publicly traded company the period is reduced to 15 days. If the government needs additional information to complete its review, it may extend the waiting period for the parties wishing to combine. These statutory requirements are of course consistent with the Clayton Act's purpose of preserving a competitive environment from the potentially harmful effects of a proposed combination, and noncompliance renders the parties liable for monetary penalties. Also important to note is that if advance notice of a merger or acquisition is given and the government fails to respond, such an omission does not bar later legal action under the substantive provisions of the antitrust statutes.

Affirmative defenses   Defendants may successfully contradict a plaintiff's allegations concerning the relevant market and dispute evidence of the probable competitive effects of a merger or acquisition. They may also succeed by asserting one of the affirmative defenses, a defense that by definition justifies an otherwise illegal transaction. Successful assertion of such a defense requires that the defendants carry the burden of proof.

One type of affirmative defense is that the company being acquired is failing financially: acquisition of a company actually about to go out of business will have no measurable anticompetitive effects. Because the argument is not readily accepted by either governmental agencies or the courts, and the substantive requirements will therefore be strictly construed, the defense should be applied cautiously. Typically the courts will require evidence that the allegedly failing company is indeed on the verge of bankruptcy with no reasonable prospect of paying its creditors, that reorganization is not likely to be successful, and that a firm acquiring the company is probably the sole suitor, as evidenced by good-faith efforts to find other potential purchasers.[188]

Another defense sometimes available is known as the "inadequate resources" or "weak competitor" defense. This defense is possible if the company being acquired lacks resources to compete effectively and its acquisition does not therefore substantially lessen competition. The defense is most applicable when an industry or a particular market is undergoing fundamental structural changes. An example is the coal-mining industry, which experienced massive dislocations and restructuring during the 1950s when natural gas became a dominant source of fuel in many areas of the country.[189]

A third possible defense, although of limited and infrequent application, is based on the motive prompting an acquisition of stock. When one corporation purchases the stock of another "solely for investment" purposes, as distinguished from bringing about the substantial lessening of competition, the Clayton Act, Section 7, does not apply.[190] The purchased stock may not be voted or otherwise used in competitive activity. Because the required proof is difficult to establish and most acquisitions are not solely for investment purposes, the defense is not often asserted.

The courts have frequently said that administrative efficiency, economies of scale, and other allegedly beneficial effects standing alone do not justify a merger or acquisition. Thus such arguments have not been recognized as a defense of an otherwise illegal combination.[191] On the other hand, however, courts and the enforcement agencies themselves have begun to consider such factors in their rule of reason analyses. For example, in *Federal Trade Comm'n v. Butterworth Health Corp.*,[192] a federal district court approved the merger of the two largest hospitals in Grand Rapids, Michigan, at least in part because the hospitals showed that the merger would result in cost savings. In addition, the court concluded that not-for-profit hospitals (as these hospitals were) operate differently than for-profit facilities (specifically, that they do not tend to raise—and may even lower—prices in a concentrated market), that their community-based boards were committed to providing low-cost services, and that their written, binding "community commitment" would benefit healthcare consumers in the area.

Other courts gave not-for-profit hospitals the benefit of the doubt in merger cases in the mid-1990s. In *Federal Trade Comm'n v. Freeman Hospital*,[193] both the district court and the court of appeals upheld the merger of the two smallest of three hospitals in Joplin, Missouri. (The largest hospital had 331 beds, and the other two had 158 and 96, respectively.) In denying the FTC's challenge of the combination, the trial court judge wrote,

> [A] private, nonprofit hospital that is sponsored and directed by the local community is similar to a consumer cooperative. It is highly unlikely that a cooperative will arbitrarily raise its prices merely to earn higher profits because the owners of such an organization are also its consumers.[194]

Other factors, of course, contributed to the final result, but the deference given to the hospitals' not-for-profit status is noteworthy.

The same year a district court refused to enjoin the merger of the only two hospitals in Dubuque, Iowa.[195] Although the case turned primarily on the judge's rather generous market definition and did not accord any special significance to not-for-profit status in and of itself, the court did note that the hospitals' board members "are serious about obtaining optimum efficiencies from the merger and will do everything within their power to achieve all the potential efficiencies that may result. . . ."[196] In addition, the court found that the current board members "have only the highest motives in proposing this merger. It is clearly their intent to provide high quality and efficient healthcare to the Dubuque community."[197]

The "Statements of Antitrust Enforcement Policy in Health Care" (Statements) issued by the Department of Justice and the Federal Trade Commission in 1996 recognize the relevance of the efficiency and economy of scale arguments in hospital mergers.[198] The Statements establish nine "safety zones" that "describe conduct that the Agencies [the Department of Justice and the FTC] will not challenge under the antitrust laws, absent extraordinary circumstances." Briefly summarized, these safety zones are:

- mergers involving a small hospital;
- joint ventures for expensive or high-technology equipment;
- joint ventures to provide specialized services;
- efforts to provide medical data;
- arrangements to provide fee information to purchasers of health services;
- surveys regarding prices, wages, salaries, and benefits;
- joint purchasing arrangements;
- exclusive and nonexclusive physician network joint ventures; and
- multiprovider network arrangements.

In the last category the Statements provide,

In accord with general antitrust principles, multiprovider networks will be evaluated under the rule of reason, and will not be viewed as per se illegal, if the providers' integration through the network *is likely to produce significant efficiencies that benefit consumers, and any price agreements (or other agreements that would otherwise be per se illegal) by the network providers are reasonably necessary to realize those efficiencies.*[199]

The Statements' safety zones are narrowly drawn so as not to foreclose agency action unnecessarily. For example, the hospital merger safety zone only applies to mergers of two hospitals where one has fewer than 100 beds and an average census of fewer than 40 patients. Nevertheless, the Statements are careful to note, "The inclusion of certain conduct within the antitrust safety zones does not imply that conduct falling outside the safety zones is likely to be challenged."[200] For example, in the commentary on mergers the Statements provide:

Hospital mergers that fall outside the antitrust safety zone are not necessarily anticompetitive, and may be procompetitive . . . .

Applying the analytical framework of the Merger Guidelines [issued in 1992] to particular facts of specific hospital mergers, the Agencies often have concluded that an investigated hospital merger will not result in a substantial lessening of competition in situations where market concentration might otherwise raise an inference of anticompetitive effects. Such situations include transactions where the Agencies found that: (1) the merger would not increase the likelihood of the exercise of market power either because of the existence post-merger of strong competitors or because the merging hospitals were sufficiently differentiated; (2) *the merger would allow the hospitals to realize significant cost savings that could not otherwise be realized*; or (3) the merger would eliminate a hospital that likely would fail with its assets exiting the market.[201]

Conclusion

The rapid changes seen in healthcare during the 1990s are expected to continue into the next decade. Mergers, consolidations, acquisitions, divestitures, network integration, new structures for care delivery—these and other activities hardly imagined yet will continue to occur in response to various social and economic pressures. As the healthcare field attempts to adapt, it will remain under the close scrutiny of federal and state agencies charged with antitrust enforcement.

As exemplified by certain court cases and the joint Statements of the Department of Justice and the Federal Trade Commission, the federal antitrust agencies are beginning to recognize that healthcare *is* somewhat different from other industries. Nevertheless, the basic premise of the antitrust laws remains: competition is to be encouraged. Healthcare executives must be constantly aware of the possible pitfalls and must be willing to seek competent antitrust counsel as developments occur.

Notes

1. 15 U.S.C. § 1.
2. 21 Cong. Record 2460 (1890).
3. United States v. Colgate & Co., 250 U.S. 300 (1919).
4. Copperweld Corp. v. Independence Tube Co., 467 U.S. 752 (1984).
5. *Id.* at 775.
6. *Id.* at 775.
7. Theatre Enterprises v. Paramount Film Distributing Corp., 346 U.S. 537 (1954).
8. United States v. Container Corp., 393 U.S. 333 (1969).
9. A tie-in sale is a sale of given merchandise on the condition that the buyer purchase a second product or service. Requiring a buyer to purchase the second item (the tied product) to obtain the item desired (the tying product) violates Section 1 of the Sherman Act whenever the seller has sufficient market power to force the buyer to take the unwanted product or service. The arrangement is only illegal, however, if the seller enjoys a monopolistic market position for the tying product. If the sale involves tangible goods, wares, or commodities, a tying arrangement may also violate Section 3 of the Clayton Act. Tying arrangements, however, have not been found in healthcare antitrust cases.
10. 15 U.S.C. § 2.
11. United States v. Grinnell Corp., 384 U.S. 563, 570-71 (1966).
12. Swift and Co. v. United States, 196 U.S. 375, 396 (1905).
13. Standard Oil Co. of N.J. v. United States, 221 U.S. 1 (1911).
14. 15 U.S.C. § 13(a).
15. 15 U.S.C. § 13c; *see* Abbott Laboratories v. Portland Retail Druggists, 425 U.S. 1 (1976), discussed *infra*.
16. 425 U.S. 1 (1976).
17. *Id.* at 11.
18. *Id.* at 14.

19. *Id.* at 14–17.
20. *Id.* at 15, 17–18.
21. *Id.* at 13.
22. 15 U.S.C. § 14 (1982).
23. 15 U.S.C. § 18.
24. Another section of the Clayton Act, Section 8 (15 U.S.C. § 19), proscribes certain interlocking corporate directorships in circumstances in which the companies involved are competitors. For various reasons, Section 8 has not played an important role in antitrust enforcement proceedings, and relatively few cases have alleged violations of the provision.
25. 15 U.S.C. § 45(a)(1).
26. *See, e.g.,* Heart of Atlanta Motel, Inc. v. United States, 379 U.S. 241 (1964) in which the Court wrote: "If it is interstate commerce that feels the pinch, it does not matter how local the operation which applies the squeeze." *Id.* at 258 (quoting United States v. Women's Sportswear Mfrs. Assn., 336 U.S. 460, 464 (1949)).
27. 425 U.S. 738 (1976), *reversing and remanding,* 511 F.2d 678 (4th Cir. 1975). As noted previously, the Sherman Act prohibits "[e]very contract, combination . . . or conspiracy, in restraint of trade or commerce among the several States." 15 U.S.C. § 1 (1982 & Supp. II 1984). The act also forbids the monopolizing of "any part of the trade or commerce among the several States." 15 U.S.C. § 2.
28. 425 U.S. at 744.
29. *Id.* at 746–47.
30. *Id.* at 745–46.
31. Hyde v. Jefferson Parish Hosp. Dist. No. 2, 513 F. Supp. 532 (E.D. La. 1981), *rev'd,* 686 F.2d 286 (1982), *aff'd,* 52 U.S.L.W. 4385 (1984); Feldman v. Jackson Memorial Hosp., 509 F. Supp. 815 (S.D. Fla. 1981), *aff'd,* 752 F.2d 647 (1985), *cert. denied,* 472 U.S. 1029 (1985); Robinson v. Magovern, 521 F. Supp. 842 (W.D. Pa. 1981), *aff'd,* 688 F.2d 824 (1982), *cert. denied,* 459 U.S. 971 (1982).
32. Furlong v. Long Island College Hosp., 710 F.2d 922 (2d Cir. 1983); Crane v. Intermountain Health Care, Inc., 637 F.2d 715 (10th Cir. 1980); Wolf v. Jane Phillips Episcopal-Memorial Medical Center, 513 F.2d 684 (10th Cir. 1975); Cardio-Medical Ass'n, Ltd. v. Crozer-Chester Medical Center, 536 F. Supp. 1065 (E.D. Pa. 1982).
33. 421 U.S. 773 (1975). *See also* Boddicker v. Arizona State Dental Ass'n, 549 F.2d 626 (9th Cir. 1977), *cert. denied,* 434 U.S. 825 (1978); American Medical Ass'n v. Federal Trade Comm'n, 638 F.2d 443 (2d Cir. 1980). Some state courts have ruled that state antitrust statutes do not apply to the professions. *See, e.g.,* Moles v. White, 336 So. 2d 427 (Fla. Dist. Ct. App. 1976); Willis v. Santa Ana Community Hosp. Ass'n, 26 Cal. Rptr. 640, 376 P.2d 568 (1962).
34. 435 U.S. 679 (1978).
35. *Id.* at 692–96; Federal Trade Comm'n v. Indiana Fed'n of Dentists, 106 S. Ct. 2009 (1986) (rule of dental association prohibiting members from submitting x-rays to insurers was unreasonable and could not be justified on quality of care arguments).

36. 15 U.S.C. §§ 1011–1015.

37. 15 U.S.C. § 1013(b).

38. 42 U.S.C. §§ 300k–300n-6; Pub. L. No. 99-660, § 701 (a), 100 Stat. 3799 terminated the federal health planning program. Nevertheless, the text discussion is relevant to the doctrine of implied repeal because the precedent established may be applied to other federal regulatory programs.

39. 42 U.S.C. § 3001-2(a).

40. 42 U.S.C. § 3001-2(a)(5).

41. 42 U.S.C. § 300k-2(b)(2).

42. 42 U.S.C. § 3001-2(a).

43. 42 U.S.C. § 300m-3(c).

44. 42 U.S.C. § 300m-3(c).

45. *Id.* at 381. By the terms of the reimbursement contract participating hospitals were paid directly the full costs of covered services rendered subscribers. Nonparticipating institutions were not paid by Blue Cross for care provided subscribers, although such persons were reimbursed to the extent of 80 percent of the hospital's costs. *Id.* at 380.

46. 479 F. Supp. 1012, 1029 (W.D. Mo. 1979), *aff'd*, 628 F.2d 1050, 1057 (8th Cir. 1980).

47. 452 U.S. at 388 (quoting Carnation Co. v. Pacific Westbound Conference, 383 U.S. 213, 218 (1966)).

48. 452 U.S. at 388 (quoting United States v. National Ass'n of Securities Dealers, 422 U.S. 694, 719–20 (1975)).

49. 452 U.S. at 389 (quoting Silver v. New York Stock Exch., 373 U.S. 341, 357 (1963)).

50. 452 U.S. at 389.

51. 452 U.S. at 389–90.

52. 317 U.S. 341 (1943).

53. 317 U.S. at 350.

54. 428 U.S. 579 (1976).

55. 421 U.S. at 791.

56. 428 U.S. at 593–95.

57. Hoover v. Ronwin, 466 U.S. 558, 570–74 (1984).

58. 365 U.S. 127 (1961).

59. *Id.* at 136.

60. *Id.* at 138–45.

61. United Mine Workers v. Pennington, 381 U.S. 657, 670 (1965). The Court also held that the UAW was not exempt from antitrust legislation on the basis of the labor exemption, discussed *infra*, because the union had acted jointly with nonlabor entities. *Id.* at 665–66.

62. California Motor Trans. Co. v. Trucking Unlimited, 404 U.S. 508 (1972).

63. Federal Prescription Serv., Inc. v. American Pharmaceutical Ass'n, 663 F.2d 253 (D.C. Dir. 1981), *cert. denied*, 455 U.S. 928 (1982).

64. Phoenix Baptist Hosp. & Medical Center v. Samaritan Health Serv., 688 F.2d 847 (9th Cir. 1982), *cert. denied*, 462 U.S. 1123. *See also* St. Joseph's Hosp. v. Hospital Corp. of Am. 795 F.2d 948 (11th Cir. 1986) (Noerr-Pennington

applies to activities opposing competitor's application for a certificate of need, although presentation of misinformation and baseless claims are within the "sham" exception).

65. United States v. South-Eastern Underwriters Ass'n, 322 U.S. 533 (1944).

66. REPORT OF SUBCOMMITTEE ON FEDERAL LEGISLATION TO EXECUTIVE COMMITTEE ON NATIONAL ASSOCIATION OF INSURANCE COMMISSIONERS, 90 CONG. REC. A4405 (1944); *see generally* M. THOMPSON, ANTITRUST AND THE HEALTH CARE PROVIDER 173–176 (1979).

67. 15 U.S.C. §§ 1011–1015.

68. 322 U.S. 533 (1944).

69. 15 U.S.C. § 1012(b).

70. 15 U.S.C. § 1013(b).

71. Antitrust & Trade Reg. Rep. (BNA) No. 897, Special Supp.

72. 440 U.S. 205; *cf.* Frankford Hosp. v. Blue Cross, 554 F.2d 1253 (3d Cir. 1977), *cert. denied*, 434 U.S. 860 (1977) (Blue Cross-hospital reimbursement contract was entitled to McCarran Act exemption; there were other circuit and district court opinions in the 1970s to the same effect).

73. *Id.* at 220.

74. *Id.* at 221. *See* Securities & Exch. Comm'n v. National Sec., Inc., U.S. 453 (1969); Securities & Exch. Comm'n v. Variable Annuity Life Ins. Co., 359 U.S. 65 (1959) (a variable annuity contract is not insurance).

75. 440 U.S. at 214.

76. 440 U.S. at 214.

77. 458 U.S. 119 (1982).

78. Manasen v. California Dental Serv., 424 F. Supp. 657 (N.D. Cal. 1976), *rev'd on other grounds*, 638 F.2d 1152 (1979); Crawford v. American Title Ins. Co., 528 F.2d 217 (5th Cir. 1975).

79. 15 U.S.C. § 1013(b).

80. 438 U.S. 531 (1978).

81. *See e.g.,* Addrisi v. Equitable Life Assurance Soc'y, 503 F.2d 725 (9th Cir. 1974), *cert. denied.*

82. 438 U.S. at 552–54.

83. *Id.* at 541–46.

84. *Accord* Virginia Academy of Clinical Psychologists v. Blue Shield of Va., 624 F.2d 476 (4th Cir. 1980), *cert. denied*, 450 U.S. 916 (1981); Ballard v. Blue Shield of S.W. Va., 543 F.2d 1075 (4th Cir. 1976), *cert. denied,* 430 U.S. 922 (1976).

85. 29, U.S.C. §§ 151–69 (1982 & Supp. II 1984).

86. Local 10, Amalgamated Meat Cutters v. Jewel Tea Co., Inc., 381 U.S. 676 (1965); American Fed'n of Musicians v. Carroll, 391 U.S. 99 (1968).

87. 1982-2 Trade Cas. (CCH) ¶ 64,801 (E.D. Mich. 1982).

88. 15 U.S.C. §§ 1–7.

89. 15 U.S.C. § 2.

90. 15 U.S.C. § 4.

91. *Id.*

92. 15 U.S.C. § 16(b).

93. 15 U.S.C. § 18a(g).

94. 15 U.S.C. § 15c.

95. 15 U.S.C. § 15(a). There is no provision in the federal antitrust statutes for contribution among multiple defendants found liable in a civil action for damages. Accordingly, a given defendant paying a judgment may not recover proportionately for a co-conspirator. Texas Industries, Inc. v. Radcliff Materials, Inc., 451 U.S. 630 (1981).

96. 15 U.S.C. § 15(a).

97. 457 U.S. 465 (1982).

98. *Id.* at 478–79.

99. *Id.* at 479.

100. 15 U.S.C. §§ 12-27.

101. 15 U.S.C. §§ 45(1)-(m), 50.

102. 15 U.S.C. § 46.

103. 15 U.S.C. § 18.

104. *See, e.g.,* Community Blood Bank, Inc. V.F.T.C., 405 F.2d 1011 (8th Cir. 1969) *and* U.S. v. Carilion Health Sys., 707 F. Supp. 840 (W.D. Va. 1989).

105. 898 F.2d 1278 (7th Cir. 1990).

106. 15 U.S.C. § 21.

107. *See, e.g.,* F.T.C. v. Freeman Hospital, 69 F.3d 260 (8th Cir. 1995).

108. 15 U.S.C. § 1.

109. Continental T.V., Inc. v. GTE Sylvania, Inc. 433 U.S. 36, 59 (1977).

110. Northern Pac. Ry. Co. v. United States, 56 U.S. 1, 5 (1958) (emphasis supplied, citations omitted).

111. 42 U.S.C. § 3001-(b)(4)(A).

112. National Gerimedical Hosp. & Gerontology Center v. Blue Cross, 452 U.S. 378, 388-93 (1981).

113. See discussion under "State Action," above.

114. Associated Press v. United States, 326 U.S. 1(1945) (restrictions on membership in a shared service organization are similar to restrictions imposed by trade or professional associations.)

115. 15 U.S.C. § 13-13b.21(a).

116. 15 U.S.C. § 13(b).

117. 317 U.S. 341 (1943).

118. *See* Iowa Dental Assn., 99 F.T.C. 648 (1982), *In re* Rhode Island Professional Standards Review Org., 101 F.T.C. 1010 (1983), *and* Federal Trade Commission Advisory Opinion (Aug. 19, 1983) rendered to the American Podiatry Association.

119. 684 F.2d 1346 (7th Cir. 1982) (on remand, No. 81 Civ. 4296 (N.D. Ill., Oct. 25, 1983)). *See also* Cardio-Medical Ass'n, Ltd. V. Crozer–Chester Medical Center, 721 F.2d 68 (3d Cir. 1983) (antitrust jurisdiction applies to medical center's exclusive contract for specialized services), *rev'g in part and aff'g in part,* 552 F. Supp. 1170 (E.D. Pa. 1982); Smith v. Northern Mich. Hosps., 703 F.2d 942 (6th Cir. 1983) (exclusive contract for emergency room service is to be judged by rule of reason).

120. 684 F.2d at 1352–54.

121. No. 81 Civ. 4296.

122. 686 F.2d 286 (5th Cir. 1982), *rev's,* 466 U.S. 2 (1984).

123. 686 F.2d at 291–92.

124. Jefferson Parish Hosp. Dist. No. 2 v. Hyde, 466 U.S. 2 (1984). *See also* Griffing v. Lucius O. Crosby Memorial Hosp., No. 5-83-0254 (D. So. Miss. 1984) (exclusive contract for radiological services not an illegal tie-in sale); Gonik v. Champlain Valley Physicians Hosp. Medical Center, 561 F. Supp. 700 (N.D. N.Y. 1983) (exclusive contract with group of anesthesiologists did not constitute conspiracy to fix prices or group boycott).

125. 466 U.S. at 36–29.

126. *Id.* at 29–32.

127. 552 F. Supp. 1352 (D.W.D. Pa. 1982). The Health Care Quality Improvement Act of 1986 (Pub. L. No. 99-660) provides civil immunity from federal antitrust liability for good faith hospital credentialing and peer review activities. 42 U.S.C.A. § 11111.

128. McElhinney v. Medical Protective Co., 549 F. Supp. 121 (E.D. Ky. 1982) (allegations that a hospital and doctors conspired to refuse patient referrals to plaintiff did not constitute a per se boycott or joint refusal to deal; insufficient evidence of actual anticompetitive effect to overcome motion for directed verdict); Everhart v. Stormont Hosp. and Training School for Nurses, 1982-1 Trade Cas. (CCH) ¶ 64, 703 (D. Kan. 1982) (denial of privileges was not a group boycott per se; rule of reason requires an examination of hospital's reasons for denial, evidence of competitive impact, and motive); Kaczanowski v. Medical Center Hosp. of Vt., 612 F. Supp. 688 (D. Vt. 1985) (grant of limited consulting privileges and denial of surgical or admitting privileges to two podiatrists did not constitute a per se group boycott).

129. Stone v. William Beaumont Hosp., 782 F.2d 609 (E.D. Mich. 1983) (no conspiracy between hospital, chief of staff, and professional corporation of cardiologists when an individual cardiologist was denied privileges; hospital policy was to prefer full-time persons for cardiology practice; part-time appointments given only to those physicians with associates readily available in an emergency). *See also* Williams v. Kleaveland, 534 F. Supp. 912 (W.D. Mich. 1983) (no conspiracy when there was evidence that doctor refused to adhere to reasonable hospital rules).

130. *E.g.*, United States v. Halifax Hosp. Medical Center, 1981-1 Trade Cas. (CCH) ¶ 64, 151 (M.D. Fla. 1981) (hospital denied privileges to physicians participating in a health maintenance organization that was competitive with hospital; consent decree prohibiting denial entered).

131. Stern v. Tarrant County Hosp. Dist., 565 F. Supp. 11440 (N.D. Tex. 1983). *See also* Griesman v. Newcomb Hosp., 40 N.J. 389, 192 A.2d 817 (1963) (private hospital as a matter of state common law, may not arbitrarily exclude osteopathic physician).

132. Weiss v. York Hosp., 548 F. Supp. 1048 (M.D. Pa. 1982), *aff'd in part, rev'd in part*, 745 f.2d 786 (3d Cir. 1984) (disparate standards constitute group boycott or concerted refusal to deal, violating Section 1 of Sherman; no violation of Section 2 because there was no evidence that hospital was willfully maintaining monopoly power; remanded for trial on claim for damages).

133. Shaw v. Hospital Auth. of Cobb County, 507 F.2d 625 (5th Cir. 1975) (when applying for privileges at public hospital, podiatrist was entitled to due process hearing).

134. Some state statutes prohibit hospitals from arbitrarily discriminating against persons practicing in certain enumerated allied health professions. *E.g.*, CAL. HEALTH & SAFETY CODE § 1316 (West 1979) (podiatrists) and § 1316.5 (West 1986) (clinical psychologists); NEV. REV. STAT. ANN. §§ 450.005, 450.430 (Michie 1986) (physicians, dentists, psychologists, podiatrists, practitioners of traditional oriental medicine); N.Y. PUB. HEALTH LAW § 2801-6 (McKinney 1985) (physician, podiatrist, dentist); D.C. CODE ANN. § 32-1307 (Michie 1985) (nurse anesthetists, nurse-midwives, nurse-practitioners, podiatrists, psychologists).

135. Bhan v. NME Hosps., Inc., 772 F.2d 1467 (9th Cir. 1985) (hospital's policy of permitting only M.D. anesthesiologists to administer anesthesia and denial of privileges to certified registered nurse anesthetists may violate antitrust because they are competitors in a relevant market).

136. Shaw v. Hospital Auth. of Cobb County, 614 F.2d (946) (5th Cir. 1980); Reynolds v. Medical and Dental Staff, 86 Misc. 2d 418, 382 N.Y.S.2d 618 (1976).

137. *See* JOINT COMMISSION ON ACCREDITATION OF HEALTHCARE ORGANIZATIONS, 1998 Hospital Accreditation Standards at 226 (1998).

138. ADJUNCT TASK FORCE, AMERICAN HOSPITAL ASS'N, AN ANALYSIS OF THE REVISED MEDICAL STAFF STANDARDS OF THE JOINT COMMISSION ON ACCREDITATION OF HOSPITALS 2 (1984).

139. Wilk v. American Medical Ass'n, 719 F.2d 207 (7th Cir. 1983) (jury verdict overturned and new trial ordered in antitrust case alleging conspiracy to induce physicians and hospitals to forgo contact with chiropractors when jury was permitted to consider defendants' generalized public interest motive as distinct from defendants' patient care motive; jury should be instructed to consider only effect of defendants' conduct on competition and patient care motive).

140. 15 U.S.C. §§ 1011–15. See discussion in the previous chapter.

141. *See, e.g.*, Royal Drug Co. v. Group Life and Health Ins. Co., 737 F.2d 1433 (5th Cir. 1984), *cert. denied* 469 U.S. 1160 (1985).

142. St. Bernard Gen. Hosp., Inc. v. Hospital Ser. Ass'n of New Orleans, Inc., 712 F.2d 1978 (5th Cir. 1983), *cert. denied*, 466 U.S. 970 (1984). In 1980 the Fifth Circuit had held that the provider contract was not exempt from antitrust by virtue of the McCarran-Ferguson Act, 618 F.2d 1140 (5th Cir. 1980); *see also* Reazon v. Blue Cross and Blue Shield of Kansas, 635 F. Supp. 1287 (D. Kan. 1986) (where Blue Cross of Kansas and certain participating hospitals met on several occasions before Blue Cross terminated participating status of Wesley Medical Center, a jury would be justified in finding an agreement to boycott in violation of Section 1 of the Sherman Act. Further, a per se analysis would be appropriate because there was evidence of an anticompetitive motive).

143. 740 F.2d 423 (6th Cir. 1984), *aff'g in part and rev'g in part*, 555 F. Supp. 337 (E.D. Mich. 1983).

144. 574 F. Supp. 457 (M.D.Pa. 1983), *aff'd*, 722 F.2d 733 (3d Cir. 1983), *cert. denied*, 471 U.S. 1016 (1985).

145. *See also* Kartell v. Blue Shield of Mass., 749 F.2d 922 (1st Cir. 1984), *cert. denied*, 471 U.S. 1029 (1985).

146. 457 U.S. 332 (1982).

147. An MCO controlled by nonproviders that negotiates individually with providers for a discount does not violate antitrust laws. Further, where providers pool capital and assume financial risk, a rule of reason analysis would apply and a discount price for services promotes rather than restrains competition because providers are given incentives to deliver efficient care. 17:2 Hosp. L., Feb. 1984 at 3, citing Op. Ohio Att'y Gen. (Nov. 17, 1983).

148. 457 U.S. at 356–57.

149. Where a group of anesthesiologists created a professional corporation and contracted with a hospital as a condition to the anesthesiologists' delivery of services, they fulfilled the requirements of a joint venture. Konik v. Champlain Valley Physicians Hosp. Medical Center, 561 F. Supp. 700 (N.D. N.Y. 1983), *aff'd*, 733 F.2d 1007 (2d Cir. 1984), *cert. denied*, 469 U.S. 884 (1984).

150. *See generally* presentation by L. Barry Costilo, Esq., Federal Trade Commission, American Bar Association, Forum Committee on Health Law (Feb. 3, 1984).

151. Barry v. Blue Cross of Cal., 805 F.2d 866 (9th Cir. 1986) (neither letters from physicians to defendant commenting on proposed preferred provider program nor existence of a physicians' advisory committee constituted evidence of an agreement to fix fees, refusal to deal, or group boycott).

152. 624 F.2d 476 (4th Cir. 1980), *cert. denied*, 450 U.S. 916 (1981). Normally, a conspiracy cannot be found when a corporation makes a decision acting through its governing body because a corporation is a single legal entity. Divisions or departments within a corporation are not entities capable of conspiring. *Virginia Academy*, however, found the requisite conspiracy where practicing physicians held majority control of the corporate board.

153. Ballard v. Blue Shield of S.W. Va., 543 F.2d 1075 (4th Cir. 1976), *cert. denied*, 430 U.S. 922 (1977).

154. Blue Cross of Wash. and Alaska v. Kitsap Physicians Serv., 1982-1 Trade Cas. (CCH) ¶ 64,589 (W.D. Wash. 1981).

155. 457 U.S. 332 (1982).

156. *See* Virginia Academy of Clinical Psychologists v. Blue Shield of Va., 624 F.2d 476 (4th Cir. 1980), *cert. denied*, 450 U.S. 916 (1981) (court applied rule of reason to determine whether policies requiring clinical psychologists to bill through physicians constituted an antitrust violation). *Cf.* Madden v. California Dental Serv., 1986-1 Trade Cas. (CCH) ¶ 67, 176 (Super. Ct. San Francisco, Cal., June 27, 1986) (in an analysis of state antitrust law, the rule of reason applies to the contract of a dental plan controlled by providers which requires participating dentists to charge the plan no more than they charge other purchasers of services).

157. Ball Memorial Hosp., Inc. v. Mutual Hosp. Ins., Inc., 784 F.2d 1325 (7th Cir. 1986), *aff'd*, 603 F. Sup. 1077 (S.D. Ind. 1985) (proper for trial court to deny preliminary injunction in suit alleging that preferred provider contracts between Blue Cross–Blue Shield constituted an unreasonable restraint of trade and illegal monopoly; although defendant had a large share of the market for medical insurance within the state of Indiana, it lacked market power to restrict output or raise prices because the financing of healthcare is a tangible product readily supplied by other suppliers; the rule of reason applies; case remanded for further proceedings).

158. *Id.*

159. Barry v. Blue Cross of Cal., 805 F.2d 866 (9th Cir. 1986) (preferred provider plan does not constitute price fixing, an unreasonable restraint, or illegal monopoly).

160. See discussion above at 197–215.

161. 15 U.S.C. § 18.

162. 15 U.S.C. §§ 1, 2.

163. 15 U.S.C. § 45.

164. 15 U.S.C. § 2.

165. United States v. Grinnel Corp., 384 U.S. 563, 571 (1966).

166. Berkey Photo, Inc. v. Eastman Kodak Co., 603 F.2d 263 (2d Cir. 1979) (there is no duty to disclose the introduction of new products in advance); ILC Peripherals Leasing Corp. v. International Business Mach. Corp., 458 F. Supp. 423 (N.D. Cal. 1978) (defendant's introduction of new technology at lower prices does not constitute monopolization).

167. 15 U.S.C. § 18.

168. 15 U.S.C. § 18.

169. 444 U.S. 232 (1980). See discussion in the previous chapter, *supra.*

170. United States v. American Bldg. Maint. Indus., 422 U.S. 271 (1975).

171. United States v. E.I. du Pont de Nemours Co., 351 U.S. 377 (1956); *cf.* United States v. Aluminum Co. of Am., 148 F.2d 416 (2d Cir. 1945) ("virgin aluminum ingot" manufactured from mined ore does not compete with reprocessed aluminum scrap, and control of 90 percent of market for virgin ingot constitutes an illegal monopoly).

172. 707 F. Supp. 840 (W.D. Va. 1989), *aff'd.* 892 F.2d 1041 (4th Cir. 1989).

173. 898 F.2d 1278 (7th Cir. 1990).

174. The court used kidney transplant, mastectomy, stroke, heart attack, and gunshot wounds as examples of the point. "If you need your hip replaced, you can't decide to have chemotherapy instead because it's available on an outpatient basis at a lower price," the opinion states.

175. Greany, *Night Landings on an Aircraft Carrier: Hospital Mergers and the Antitrust Laws*, 23 Am. J.L. & Med. 191 (1977). The author's thesis is that "courts deciding hospital merger cases are asked to make exceedingly fine-tuned appraisals of complex economic relationships." *Id.* at 192.

176. 15 U.S.C. § 18.

177. United States v. E.I du Pont de Nemours Co., 353 U.S. 586 (1957) (defendant's ownership of 23 percent of stock in General Motors Corp. could be challenged 35 years after the acquisition).

178. Merger Guidelines of Department of Justice—1982, Trade Reg. Reg. (CCH) ¶ 4500 (Aug. 9, 1982), revised and clarified in 1984 Guidelines, Trade Reg. Rep. (CCH) ¶ 4490 (Dec. 17, 1984).

179. United States v. Philadelphia Nat'l Bank, 374 U.S. 321, 322 (1963).

180. Fruehauf Corp. v. F.T.C., 603 F.2d 345, 352–54 (1979).

181. Ford Motor Co. v. United States, 405 U.S. 562 (1972).

182. 603 F.2d at 352–53.

183. 386 U.S. 568 (1967).

184. *Id.* at 578.

185. United States v. Penn-Olin Chem. Co., 378 U.S. 158 (1964).

186. United States v. General Dynamics Corp., 415 U.S. 486 (1974).

187. 15 U.S.C. § 18a.

188. Citizen Publishing Co. v. United States, 394 U.S. 131 (1969); International Shoe Co. v. F.T.C., 280 U.S. 291 (1930); Merger Guidelines of Department of Justice—1984, Trade Reg. Rep. (CCH) ¶ 4490 (Dec. 17, 1984).

189. United States v. General Dynamics Corp., 415 U.S. 486.

190. 15 U.S.C. § 18 (1982).

191. F.T.C. v. Procter & Gamble Co., 386 U.S 568 (1967); United States v. Philadelphia Nat'l Bank, 374 U.S 321 (1963).

192. 946 F. Supp. 1285 (W.D. Mich. 1996).

193. 911 F. Supp. 1213 (W.D. Mo. 1995), *aff'd.* 69 F.3d 260 (8th Cir. 1995).

194. 911 F. Supp. at 1222.

195. U.S. v. Mercy Health Services, 902 F. Supp. 968 (N.D. Iowa 1995).

196. 902 F. Supp. at 988.

197. 902 F. Supp. at 989. The court added, however, "[T]he fact remains that for antitrust analysis, the court must assume that new and different Board members can take control of the corporation, and that if there is the potential for anticompetitive behavior, there is nothing inherent in the structure of the corporate board or the non-profit status of the hospitals which would operate to stop any anticompetitive behavior." *Id. See also,* U.S. v. Long Island Jewish Medical Center, 983 F. Supp. 121 (E.D.N.Y. 1997) (holding that the not-for-profit status of the merging hospitals does not provide exemption from antitrust law but can be considered as a factor if supported by other evidence).

198. *Reprinted in* 4 Trade Reg. Rep. (CCH) ¶ 13,153 (Sep. 5, 1996). Documents such as these are also accessible by using the internet: *gopher@justice.usdoj.gov* or *www.usdoj.gov* or *www.ftc.gov.*

199. *Id.,* emphasis added.

200. *Id.*

201. *Id.,* emphasis added.

HEALTHCARE FRAUD AND ABUSE

The annual cost of healthcare in this country is more than $1 trillion, and the government estimates that as much as 10 percent of that amount may result from fraud (intentional deception) or abuse (unsound practices that result in increased costs).[1] Because the U.S. government is the largest single purchaser of healthcare, the elimination of fraud and abuse has been called the Department of Justice's number two law enforcement priority (second only to violent crime),[2] and ever more resources have been allocated to enforcement activities conducted by the Department of Justice (DOJ), United States attorneys, the Federal Bureau of Investigation, the Health and Human Services Department's Office of Inspector General (OIG), and other agencies. In addition, state attorneys general conduct their own investigations and prosecutions, often working closely with federal officials. Private citizens who have first-hand knowledge of fraud are even permitted to sue for the government and collect a percentage of the proceeds recovered, if any.

Verdicts and settlements in civil fraud cases can sometimes be hundreds of millions of dollars, and offenders who are prosecuted for criminal offenses can receive massive fines and lengthy jail terms. One example of the severity of the penalties is *United States v. Lorenzo*,[3] in which a dentist billed Medicare for "consultations" on nursing home residents. Although Medicare does not cover dental services or routine physicals, Dr. Lorenzo billed the government for his cancer-related examination of each patient's oral cavity, head, and neck, all of which is standard dental practice. The government proved that Dr. Lorenzo had submitted 3,683 false claims, resulting in overpayment of $130,719.20. The court assessed damages of nearly $19 million, almost 150 times the amount of the overpayment. A second example is *United States v. Krizek*.[4] Among other things, Dr. Krizek, a psychiatrist, charged the government for a full session (45 to 50 minutes) regardless of whether he spent 20 minutes or two hours with a patient. He argued that in practice the time evened out and the government was not harmed. In one instance, however, it was shown that he submitted 23 claims for full sessions in a single day. Dr. Krizek was fined $157,000 and assessed $11,000 in court costs.[5] Other examples include criminal convictions and civil fines of more than $100 million each levied against Caremark International, Corning (Damon) Laboratories, Roche Laboratories, National Medical Enterprises, and National Health Laboratories, and a settlement in excess of $30 million with the University of Pennsylvania. (The National Medical Enterprises case resulted in criminal and civil fines totaling $379 million.)

In such a volatile climate, it is little wonder that prevention of fraud and abuse has become a serious topic for healthcare executives in the late 1990s and will continue to be so for the foreseeable future. A basic understanding of the major criminal and civil fraud statutes is therefore essential.

Some of the most common types of healthcare fraud and abuse are the following:

- Filing claims for services that were not rendered or were not medically necessary.
- Misrepresenting the time, location, frequency, duration, or provider of services.
- "Upcoding" (i.e., assigning a higher current procedural terminology code or diagnosis-related group code than the procedure or diagnosis warrants).
- "Unbundling" (the practice of billing as separate items services, such as laboratory tests, that are actually performed as a battery).
- Violation of the "72-hour rule" (the rule stating that outpatient diagnostic procedures performed within three days of hospitalization are deemed to be part of the Medicare DRG payment and are not to be billed separately).
- Payment of "kickbacks" to induce referrals or the purchase of goods or services.
- Billing for services said to have been "incident to" a physician's services but that in fact were not provided under the physician's direct supervision.
- Self-referral (the practice of physicians referring patients for services to entities in which they have a financial interest).

The major statutes that these kinds of activities may violate include the civil and criminal False Claims Acts, the "anti-kickback" law, and the "Stark I" and "Stark II" self-referral laws. Depending on the facts of the case, mail and wire fraud statutes, the Racketeer Influenced and Corrupt Organizations Act (RICO), money-laundering statutes, and laws relating to theft, embezzlement, bribery, conspiracy, obstruction of justice, and similar matters may also be implicated. This chapter will focus on the major healthcare fraud statutes and will not address the kinds of laws noted in the previous sentence. Readers should be aware, however, that myriad legal standards (both state and federal) apply to healthcare organizations. The importance of competent legal counsel and a process to prevent criminal activity cannot be overemphasized.

False Claims Acts

The major weapon in the federal government's arsenal in the war on fraud and abuse is the civil False Claims Act (FCA).[6] The law provides that a person is liable for penalties if he or she:

- "knowingly presents, or causes to be presented, to an officer or employee of the United States a false or fraudulent claim for payment or approval";
- "knowingly makes, uses, or causes to be made or used, a false record or statement to get a false or fraudulent claim paid or approved by the Government";
- "conspires to defraud the Government by getting a false or fraudulent claim allowed or paid"; or
- "knowingly makes, uses, or causes to be made or used, a false record or statement to conceal, avoid, or decrease an obligation to pay or transmit money or property to the government."[7]

Violations result in penalties ranging from $5,000 to $10,000 *per claim* plus three times the amount of damages sustained by the government, if any. The costs of bringing the action are charged to the defendant. If the claim was false, penalties and costs can be assessed even if the claim was not paid and the government suffered no damages.[8]

Interestingly, the FCA was enacted during the Civil War to stem the practice of certain suppliers overcharging the Union Army for goods and services. Because the issue of what constitutes a "claim" was apparently somewhat more straightforward then than it is now, the term is not defined in the statute. In healthcare, however, what amounts to a "claim" has been a matter of considerable dispute. For example, each CPT code on a HCFA 1500 form (the form used for Medicare Part B payments to physicians) could be considered a separate claim and, therefore, each false code could result in up to $10,000 in penalties. Twenty false CPT codes would, by this line of reasoning, allow a penalty of up to $200,000 to be assessed, plus damages and court costs.

This issue was addressed in the appeal of *Krizek*, in which the U.S. Court of Appeals for the D.C. Circuit held that each HCFA 1500 form was one "claim" irrespective of the number of false codes contained on it. The court felt that the form was merely one request for payment of the total sum it represented.[9] This result seems consistent with other cases defining a "claim" as "a demand for money or for some transfer of public property."[10]

The language of the statute, quoted above, requires the government to prove that the defendant acted "knowingly" in presenting the false claim or making a false record. For some time there was a question of whether this standard required proof of a specific intent to defraud the government. In 1986, however, Congress amended the FCA by stating that "no proof of specific intent to defraud is required" and that "knowingly" with respect to a claim means either (a) actual knowledge of its falsity, (b) deliberate ignorance of its truth or falsity, or (c) reckless disregard of its truth or falsity.[11] As stated in the committee report accompanying the 1986 amendments,

> The Committee is firm in its intentions that the act not punish honest mistakes or incorrect claims submitted through mere negligence. But

the Committee does believe the civil False Claims Act should recognize that those doing business with the Government have an obligation to make a limited inquiry to ensure the claims they submit are accurate.[12]

Krizek illustrates the application of this standard. Although Dr. Krizek was not personally involved in the billing process, the court found that he had submitted the claims "knowingly."

> These were not "mistakes" nor merely negligent conduct. Under the statutory definition of "knowing" conduct, the court is compelled to conclude that the defendants acted with reckless disregard as to the truth or falsity of the submissions.[13]

This standard places healthcare providers (and their top management and governing board members) in the position of having an affirmative obligation to have a mechanism for verifying the accuracy of their organization's claims. A further incentive to do so, if one were needed, is the fact that the government may exclude from participation in the Medicare and Medicaid programs any individual who (a) has a direct or indirect ownership or control interest in a sanctioned entity and has acted in "deliberate ignorance" of the information or (b) is an officer or managing employee of a convicted or excluded entity, *irrespective of whether the individual participated in the offense.*[14] Any excluded person who retains ownership or control or continues as an officer or managing employee may be fined $10,000 *per day.*[15] The threat of "exclusion"—the Medicare and Medicaid programs' equivalent of the death penalty—and the potential for criminal convictions and massive fines have been major impetuses in the move to adopt "corporate compliance programs" in healthcare organizations. (Corporate compliance programs will be discussed later in this chapter.)

FCA cases are usually investigated by OIG and brought by a U.S. attorney. An unusual feature of the statute, however, allows private citizens to sue on their own behalf and for the government to recover damages and penalties. These *qui tam* lawsuits (the name comes from a Latin expression meaning "he who brings the action for the king and for himself") have become an important factor in FCA enforcement because, if successful, the "whistle blower" plaintiff (called a "relator" in legal parlance) can share in the amount of the award.

Any person with information about healthcare fraud can be a *qui tam* plaintiff, and "person" is defined to mean "any natural person, partnership, corporation, association, or other legal entity, including any State or political subdivision of a State."[16] The plaintiff must file the complaint (which is immediately sealed and thus not made public pending investigation) and file a copy with the U.S. attorney general and the appropriate U.S. attorney. The government then has 60 days (plus extensions for good cause) in which to determine whether to pursue the case. If the government decides to take over the case, the relator will receive between 15 and 25 percent of the amount recovered. If the government declines to pursue the matter, the relator may do so and, if successful, will receive between 25 and 30 percent of the recovery.

The potential *qui tam* plaintiff must meet certain conditions to file suit. The plaintiff must be the first to file, there must not already be any government proceeding relating to the same facts, and the suit must not be based on matters that have been publicly disclosed (unless the relator is the "original source" of those disclosures). If these jurisdictional barriers are met and the facts of the case warrant recovery, the *qui tam* plaintiff can proceed to assist the government or pursue the case individually, often to significant financial advantage. Furthermore, federal law provides a remedy for whistle blowers who are discharged, demoted, harassed, or otherwise discriminated against because of their having filed a *qui tam* case.[17] Given the financial incentives and the protection against employment-related retaliation, the *qui tam* lawsuit has become a popular and effective means of combating fraud and abuse. Recent statistics show that the number of healthcare-related *qui tam* lawsuits increased from 14 in 1992 to more than 280 in 1997.[18] Additionally, "the threat of a FCA suit that may be brought by anybody (competitors, current and previous employees or patients) will be an effective deterrent against greed-motivated individuals who may be tempted to submit fraudulent claims."[19]

Occasionally, healthcare-related *qui tam* plaintiffs have argued that a claim involving a kickback or self-referral (described in more detail below) violates the FCA, even though the claim itself is not "false" on its face. The roots of such an argument can be traced to *United States ex rel. Marcus v. Hess,* a World War II-vintage case in which a government contractor's claims were held to be false because the contract under which they were submitted was entered into as a result of collusion.[20] Similarly, in *United States ex rel. Woodard v. Country View Care Center, Inc.,*[21] the defendants had submitted Medicare cost reports that included payments to "consultants" that were actually kickbacks. Not too surprisingly, because the defendant's reimbursement was based on the cost reports, the court held that the False Claims Act applied. *United States v. Kensington Hospital,*[22] filed after the advent of the prospective payment system, brought a new twist to the argument. The defendants asserted that because their Medicaid reimbursement was a set amount, the government could not have suffered any loss and the cost of the kickbacks did not make the claims false. Citing *Marcus* and other cases, the court disagreed, holding that the government was not required to show actual damages to prove an FCA violation.

In neither *Country View* nor *Kensington Hospital* did the plaintiffs specifically base their claim of FCA liability on the kickback or self-referral statute. Some subsequent cases, however, have done so and have survived initial scrutiny by the courts. For example, an Ohio federal court denied a motion to dismiss a *qui tam* suit involving alleged kickbacks to doctors who referred business to an imaging center. The government alleged that the claims were false even though there was no allegation that the procedures were unnecessary or that the claims misstated the facts regarding the services rendered.[23] And in *United States ex rel. Pogue v. American Healthcorp*,[24] a trial court refused to dismiss a FCA case based on violations of the kickback and Stark self-referral laws. The court agreed with the relator's contention "that participation in any federal program involves an implied certification that the participant will abide by and adhere to all statutes, rules, and regulations governing that program."[25] The court held in effect that Stark violations create prohibited financial relationships and that, therefore, the FCA applies.[26] In *United States ex rel. Thompson v. Columbia/HCA Healthcare Corp.*, however, an FCA case based on alleged violations of the kickback and Stark laws was dismissed by a federal district court because "[a]llegations that medical services were rendered in violation of Medicare anti-fraud statutes do not, by themselves, state a claim for relief under the FCA."[27]

In summary, the proposition that a False Claims Act case can be based solely on violation of the anti-kickback or self-referral laws seems to have gained some acceptance, but the ultimate resolution of the issue remains in doubt. Clearly, relators and the government will continue to make this argument until the point is conclusively established or rejected. In the meantime, it remains an ominous threat for healthcare organizations because the cost of litigating such cases is high and the potential exists for massive penalties. The resulting pressures to settle, rather than litigate, FCA cases may mean that the issue will remain unresolved for some time.[28]

In addition to the civil FCA, another provision of federal law makes false claims a criminal offense.[29] If convicted, an organization can be fined $500,000 or twice the amount of the false claim, whichever is greater. An individual can be fined the greater of $250,000 or twice the amount of the false claim and can be sentenced to up to five years in prison. The standards of proof are higher, of course, in criminal prosecutions than in civil cases. In a civil FCA action the standard is a "preponderance of the evidence." But in a criminal FCA case the government must prove *beyond a reasonable doubt* that the defendant knew the claim was false. Therefore, and because the penalties in civil actions are already quite severe, criminal false claims cases are brought less frequently than their civil counterparts.

The Anti-Kickback Statute

Concerned about the high cost of healthcare and the potential for overutilization of healthcare services, in 1972 Congress prohibited any person to solicit, receive, offer, or pay any form of remuneration in return for or to induce referrals for healthcare goods or services for which Medicare or Medicaid would make payment.[30] Effective January 1, 1997, the statute was amended to cover payment by *any* federal healthcare program.[31] Violations of the anti-kickback law are felonies punishable by criminal fines of $25,000 per violation or imprisonment for up to five years, or both. In addition, the OIG has the authority to exclude from the Medicare and Medicaid programs persons who have violated the act.[32] This action can be taken without criminal prosecution and using the more lenient "preponderance of the evidence" standard. Finally, a 1997 amendment provides for *civil* penalties of $50,000 per violation plus three times the amount of the remuneration involved in addition to the possible criminal sanctions noted above.[33]

The statute contains numerous exceptions to the prohibition of remuneration to induce referrals.[34] The prohibition does not apply to:

- properly disclosed discounts that are reflected in the cost reports;
- amounts paid by an employer to an employee to provide healthcare services;
- certain amounts paid by a vendor to agents of a group purchasing entity;
- waivers of coinsurance for Public Health Service beneficiaries; or
- certain remuneration through a risk-sharing arrangement (e.g., under capitation).

In addition, a 1987 amendment required the Department of Health and Human Services to promulgate regulations "specifying those payment practices that will not be subject to criminal prosecution [or] provide a basis for exclusion. . . ."[35] These regulations provide for certain "safe harbors"— categories of activities in which providers may engage without being subject to prosecution—but they are very technical and are interpreted quite narrowly. The safe harbors are as follows:

- investment in large, publicly traded entities and certain smaller entities, if numerous conditions are met;
- fair market value leases for rental of space or equipment;
- fair market value contracts for personal services;
- purchase of physician practices;
- payments to referral services for patients, so long as the payment is not related to the number of referrals made;
- properly disclosed warranties;
- properly disclosed discounts that are contemporaneous with the original sale;
- bona fide employment relationships;
- discounts available to members of a group purchasing organization;
- waivers of coinsurance and deductibles for indigent persons;
- marketing incentives offered by health plans to enrollees; and
- price reductions offered by providers to health plans.

As mentioned earlier, these regulations are quite technical, and an in-depth analysis of their provisions is beyond the scope of this chapter. It is sufficient to say that although the anti-kickback statute is one of the most important laws affecting healthcare today, it is also, unfortunately, one of the most complicated and ambiguous. Congress itself recognized this fact when it wrote in 1987: "[T]he breadth of the statutory language has created uncertainty among health care providers as to which commercial arrangements are legitimate, and which are proscribed."[36] Unfortunately, although the 1987 amendments that led to the safe harbors listed above were intended to provide guidance and clarity, the basic uncertainty persists.

The problem is illustrated by considering the meaning of the word "referral." Unfortunately, neither the statute nor its implementing regulations define the term, and we are left with considerable uncertainty regarding one of the statute's key terms. For example, is it a "referral" when one member of a multispecialty group practice sends a patient to another member of the same group? If the referring physician's compensation depends in part on the volume of services he or she orders from other group members, is he or she receiving, and is the group paying, remuneration for referrals? These questions have not been answered because no enforcement action has been taken to date regarding intra-group referrals, but a literal reading of the statute calls the practice into question. The creation of a group practice "safe harbor" under the Stark self-referral laws (discussed below) seems to suggest that regulators believe a referral has occurred under those circumstances. Because intra-group referrals will not be Stark violations, the government may refrain to take enforcement action under the anti-kickback law for the same behavior. Whether this proves to be the case remains to be seen, of course.

A similar situation is involved when a medical group owns a hospital. Under traditional indemnity insurance plans, the physicians will benefit financially if they admit patients to their own hospital, yet distribution of the hospital's profits to the physician-owners would appear to violate the literal language of the statute. A proposed regulatory safe harbor for such situations was abandoned in 1993. Thus, the issue remains unresolved.

Hanlester Network v. Shalala illustrates what amounts to remuneration as an inducement for referrals.[37] In *Hanlester*, physicians were limited partners in a network of three clinical laboratories, to which they referred their patients for laboratory work (see Figure 7.1). The laboratories contracted with Smith-Kline Bio-Science Laboratories (SKBL) to manage the facilities for a fee of $15,000 per month or 80 percent of the laboratories' collections, whichever was greater. (As it turned out, the 80 percent figure was generally higher than the fixed monthly fee.) Because performing the tests at SKBL's own laboratories was more economical, 85 to 90 percent of the Hanlester labs' testing was done at SKBL. Even though the cash payments under the arrangement flowed from the Hanlester labs to SKBL, the Ninth Circuit held, among other things, that the arrangement was a scheme by which SKBL in effect had offered a 20 percent discount (the prohibited remuneration) for the physicians' referrals to the SKBL labs. (Note that today the arrangement would also violate the self-referral laws, discussed below.)

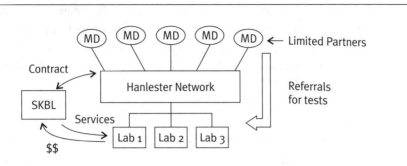

FIGURE 8.1
Hanlester
Network
Structure

Although neither the statute nor the regulations defines "remuner-ation," it is clear that the law reaches the provision of *anything* having a monetary value. The 20 percent "discount" in *Hanlester* is one example. Likewise, the provision of free goods or services has an economic benefit to the recipient and would be prohibited.[38] Furthermore, there is no exception for remuneration of a minimal nature. In one case, a physician was excluded from the Medicare program for having received a kickback in the amount of $30.[39]

Beyond prohibiting payment of remuneration to induce referrals, the anti-kickback law prohibits payment of remuneration to induce or in return for "purchasing, leasing, or ordering of, or arranging for or recommending the purchasing, leasing, or ordering of, any good, facility, service, or item for which payment is made in whole or in part by a federal health care program."[40] For example, it would clearly be illegal for a company that provides patient transportation to provide remuneration to the hospital employee who arranges for patient transportation to encourage that employee to choose that particular company. But query: Is it illegal for a hospital or clinic to provide free transportation to patients who are otherwise unable to come to the facility? In *United States v. Recovery Management Corp. III*, a psychiatric hospital pleaded guilty to an anti-kickback violation after it gave patients free air fares to and from the hospital as an inducement to choose the facility.[41] This case illustrates the fact that the anti-kickback statute applies even where no literal "referral" per se is involved (the referral in this case being the patient's choice of the facility), and it applies to the provision of anything of value that induces patients or providers to purchase or order services.

The practice of waiving coinsurance and deductible amounts is similarly prohibited as an inducement for referrals, except in limited circumstances. The 1996 Health Insurance Portability and Accountability Act (HIPAA; the Kassebaum-Kennedy Act) added civil money penalties that can apply to any person who "offers . . . or transfers remuneration . . . that such person knows or should know is likely to influence [the recipient] to order or receive [goods or services] from a particular provider, practitioner or supplier. . . ."[42] HIPAA defines "remuneration" to include:

the waiver of coinsurance and deductible amounts (or any part thereof), and transfers of items or services for free or for other than fair market value. The term remuneration *does not* include—

(A) the waiver of coinsurance and deductible amounts by a person if—

(i) the waiver is not offered as part of any advertisement or solicitation;

(ii) the person does not routinely waive coinsurance or deductible amounts; and

(iii) the person—

(I) waives the coinsurance and deductible amounts after determining in good faith that the individual is in financial need;

(II) fails to collect coinsurance or deductible amounts after making reasonable collection efforts; or

(III) provides for any permissible waiver as specified in section 1128B(b)(3) [of the Social Security Act] or in regulations issued by the Secretary;

(B) differentials in coinsurance and deductible amounts as part of a benefit plan design as long as the differentials have been disclosed in writing to all beneficiaries, third party payers, and providers . . . ; or

(C) incentives given to individuals to promote the delivery of preventive care as determined by the Secretary in regulations so promulgated.[43]

Thus the waiver of coinsurance and deductibles may be permissible in isolated instances meeting the criteria of HIPAA quoted above, but a practice of routinely waiving those amounts, and particularly of advertising that fact in the hope of stimulating business, would appear to violate the anti-kickback statute as an inducement for referrals.

The anti-kickback statute is one of the most important fraud and abuse statutes affecting healthcare today. Unfortunately, given the nearly infinite number of arrangements possible among healthcare-related organizations, it is also one of the most difficult to apply with any certainty. Because the penalties for violating the law can be extremely harsh, readers must be generally aware of its provisions and must be prepared to seek competent legal counsel whenever there is any question about the propriety of their conduct.

The "Stark" Self-Referral Laws

The Ethics in Patient Referrals Act (EPRA),[44] first enacted in 1989 and amended in 1993, was championed by Rep. Fortney "Pete" Stark of California. Its purpose, like that of the anti-kickback statute, is to discourage overuse of healthcare services and thus reduce the cost of the Medicare and Medicaid programs. As stated by HCFA:

Congress enacted this law because it was concerned that many physicians were gaining significant financial advantages from the practice of referring their [Medicare and Medicaid] patients to providers of health care services with which they (or their immediate family members) had financial relationships. For example, if a physician owns a separate laboratory that performs laboratory tests for his or her patients and shares in the profits of that laboratory, the physician has an incentive to overuse laboratory services. Similarly, if a physician does not own any part of an entity but receives compensation from it for any reason, that compensation may be calculated in a manner that reflects the volume or value of referrals the physician makes to the entity.

The reports of 10 studies in the professional literature, taken as a whole, demonstrate conclusively that the utilization rates of medical items and services generally increase when the ordering physician has a financial interest in the entity providing the item or service. These self-referrals generate enormous costs to the Medicare and Medicaid programs and jeopardize the health status of program beneficiaries.[45]

The provisions of the EPRA—commonly referred to as "Stark I" and "Stark II" (or simply "Stark")—are extremely complicated, and their application must be analyzed on a case-by-case basis. The law can, however, be summarized as follows.

In general, Stark prohibits a physician (a medical doctor, doctor of osteopathy, dentist, podiatrist, optometrist, or chiropractor) from referring Medicare or Medicaid patients for certain "designated health services" to entities with which the physician or an immediate family member has a financial relationship. "Financial relationship" is defined as a compensation arrangement or an ownership or investment interest (such as through equity or debt). If such a relationship exists, the physician may not, unless an exception applies, refer patients to the entity for the following kinds of services:

- clinical laboratory services;
- radiology services (including MRIs, CAT scans, and ultrasound);
- radiation therapy services and supplies;
- physical and occupational therapy services;
- durable medical equipment and supplies;
- parenteral and enteral nutrients, equipment, and supplies;
- prosthetics, orthotics, and prosthetic devices and supplies;
- outpatient prescription drugs;
- home health services;
- outpatient prescription drugs; and
- inpatient and outpatient hospital services.

Violations of the Stark law can result in various sanctions, including denial of payment for the services, an obligation to refund any payments made, civil money penalties of up to $15,000 for *each* illegal referral, and possible exclusion from the Medicare and Medicaid programs. In addition, a physician or entity that enters into a cross-referral arrangement or other scheme to bypass Stark can be fined up to $100,000 for each such arrangement and can be excluded from the programs. Stark also imposes an obligation on each entity that provides designated health services to report the names and identification numbers of all physicians who have a compensation arrangement or an ownership or investment interest in the entity to the Secretary of Health and Human Services. Failure to do so can result in a civil money penalty of up to $10,000 for each day for which reporting was required. Unlike the anti-kickback law, which requires proof that the defendant acted "knowingly and willfully," making a prohibited referral is a per se violation of Stark and no proof of intent is required. The fact that a defendant acted in good faith or that he or she was unaware of the law is not a defense. The anti-kickback and Stark laws differ in one other respect: the former applies to *anyone*, whereas the latter applies *only* to physicians.

The basic provisions of Stark are extremely broad and complex, as HCFA recognizes:

> The law is . . . complex because it attempts to accommodate the many complicated financial relationships that exist in the health care community. The prohibitions are based on the general principle that if a physician has a financial relationship with an entity that furnishes items or services, he or she cannot refer patients to the entity. However, the law provides numerous exceptions to this general principle, and it is the exceptions that contain the most detailed and complicated aspects of the law. The exceptions are complicated because they attempt to achieve a balance that allows physicians and providers to maintain some of their financial relationships, but within bounds that are designed to prevent the abuse of the Medicare and Medicaid programs or their patients.[46]

As this quotation notes, Congress provided for certain exceptions to the self-referral ban because without them the law's sweeping language would have made many legitimate, laudable, and even necessary arrangements illegal. For example, the law excepts referrals for services provided by other physicians in the same group practice and most in-office ancillary services furnished "personally by the referring physician, personally by a physician who is a member of the same group practice . . . , or personally by individuals who are directly supervised by the physician or by another physician in the group practice. . . ."[47] Such in-office ancillary services must, however, be billed by the physician or the group practice,[48] and they must be provided in the group's building or in another building used by the group for the centralized provision of such services.[49]

Likewise, because the financial incentive for self-referral does not exist with prepaid health plans (HMOs, for example), the statute does not apply when a physician refers members of such plans for designated health services.[50] It also does not apply to referrals for services provided by a hospital in which the physician has an ownership or investment interest and at which the physician is authorized to perform services.[51] It is notable that physicians who are merely employed by a hospital rather than owners or investors cannot avail themselves of this exception; instead, a more detailed exception relating to employment relationships is provided later in the statute.[52]

In addition to the above exceptions, there are exceptions for certain kinds of financial relationships.[53] The financial relationships that will not trigger Stark can be summarized as follows:

- owning stocks or bonds in a large, publicly traded company or mutual fund;
- owning or investing in certain rural providers or hospitals in Puerto Rico;
- reasonable rent for office space or equipment;
- amounts paid under fair and bona fide employment relationships;
- reasonable payments for personal services provided to the entity or for other services unrelated to the provision of designated health services;
- compensation under a legitimate "physician incentive plan" (such as by withholds, capitation, or bonuses in managed care);
- reasonable payments to induce a physician to relocate to the hospital's service area;
- isolated transactions such as a one-time sale of property or a practice;
- an arrangement that began before December 19, 1989, in which services are provided by a physician group but are billed by the hospital; and
- reasonable payments by a physician for clinical laboratory services or for other items or services.

These exceptions to Stark are much more complicated than the simple list above implies. They have been the subject of much controversy and have generated many ambiguities. For example, it is unclear whether the "isolated transactions" exception would apply to the purchase of a physician's practice where payment for the practice is made in installments rather than in a lump sum. HCFA takes the position that the exception would not apply and that installment payments are prohibited. To avoid this interpretation, some have suggested making the payments not as installments but as an additional part of the physician's employment-related compensation. But the exception for employment relationships is limited to amounts paid for the provision of *services.* Thus, HCFA takes the position that the "employment relationships" exception is inapplicable as well. One can argue that *how* the physician is paid for the practice is irrelevant because in the employment relationship there is an inherent incentive to refer, and yet employment relationships are exempt from Stark. Nevertheless, HCFA persists in its interpretation, and because the question has not been litigated, it stands unresolved as an example of the law's ambiguity.

One can see another example of ambiguity in the case of plans for a patient's care by a home health agency (HHA). A physician employed by a hospital that owns a home health agency would presumably want to order home health services to be provided by the hospital's HHA. The question arises whether the physician's financial relationship with the hospital also constitutes a financial relationship with the HHA. HCFA opined privately in 1996 that it *does* and that, therefore, the physician cannot refer to the HHA. This opinion had not been the basis for enforcement action through the end of 1998, but proposed regulations issued in January 1998 seem to perpetuate this view. Specifically, in addressing the physician "ownership or investment interest" exception, the regulations indicate that the physicians may refer to hospitals in which they have an ownership or investment interest, but only for services provided *by the hospital.* They may not avail themselves of the "ownership or investment" exception with regard to services provided by the hospital-owned HHA. This interpretation, of course, raises a whole new set of ambiguities. What are "services provided by the hospital," for example? If the hospital uses a separate provider number to bill for some services (e.g., radiology), are those services to be considered provided by the hospital or by a separate entity?

As this example shows, each issuance of "guidance" and "clarifying" regulations—although helpful in some respects—adds new uncertainties, increases healthcare providers' uneasiness, and makes the practice of law in this area extremely difficult. Because of the ambiguities and complexities involved, the importance of expert legal counsel cannot be overemphasized.

Corporate Compliance Programs

As one can see from the above discussion, healthcare organizations must be sensitive to their potential for fraud and abuse or other criminal conduct. Violations of law can lead to convictions of the individuals involved and to monetary penalties levied against both the perpetrators and the organization, even if the crime occurred at the lowest levels and was contrary to express corporate policy. Not only are the perpetrators and the organization subject to prosecution, but officers and management can be convicted for the conduct of their subordinates under certain circumstances, even though they neither authorized the crime nor had knowledge of it. Under the "responsible official" doctrine, officers and managers may be held personally accountable if they deliberately or recklessly disregarded the possibility of the criminal conduct occurring. It is, therefore, clearly a mistake to believe "what I don't know can't hurt me."

One of the most effective tools to minimize an organization's and its board's and management's exposure is an effective corporate compliance program (CCP). This section describes the elements of a CCP and how one should be developed.

The CCP concept gained salience after the publication of the federal government's *Sentencing Guidelines for Organizations*,[54] which is used by federal judges during the sentencing phase of a trial when a corporation has been convicted of a violation of law. The *Guidelines* are intended to provide a measure of uniformity and predictability in federal criminal sentences. Although criminal violations can occur in many areas (such as antitrust, taxation, environmental, employment, and, in the case of healthcare providers, confidentiality of patient information), the most fertile ground for illegal activity in healthcare is, of course, fraud and abuse. As noted earlier, federal and state governments are cracking down on healthcare fraud because by some estimates up to 10 percent of the United States' annual healthcare spending may result from fraudulent activity. Enforcement activities have led to penalties in the hundreds of millions of dollars in individual cases, and fines of hundreds of thousands of dollars are common.

To protect against this frightening scenario, many providers have begun to implement corporate cmpliance programs—systematic efforts to prevent, detect, report, and correct criminal misconduct and provide ongoing review of policies, procedures, and operations. Properly structured, a corporate compliance program will address the healthcare organization's potential liability in all areas of law, not just fraud and abuse. If the CCP is effectively implemented and is supported and encouraged by its governing board and top management, the program becomes powerful evidence that the organization took steps to prevent criminal violations by its employees and agents. It also demonstrates good faith, a critical factor in determining what sentence will be assessed in the event of a conviction.

Without a CCP, a convicted organization will incur much stiffer penalties and will usually face a court-imposed compliance program more severe than the sentencing guidelines require. Under the *Guidelines*, however, an organization with an effective CCP will benefit from penalty reductions of up to 95 percent. The following example illustrates this point. Assume that two hospitals, each with 3,000 employees,[55] are convicted of defrauding Medicare through coding errors. Assume further that the frauds resulted in overpayment of $1,600,000 to each facility. Hospital A does not have a corporate compliance program, and, in fact, its management was found "willfully ignorant" of the existence of the fraudulent activity.[56] Hospital B, on the other hand, has an effective CCP, discovered the fraud, and reported it to the authorities immediately. According to the *Guidelines*, the potential penalties for the two hospitals will be computed as follows:

	Hospital A	Hospital B
Base fine (usually the amount of the overpayment)	$1,600,000	$1,600,000
Culpability score (determined from a table):		
Base score (identical for all defendants)	5	5
Willful ignorance factor (aggravating)	4	4
Effective CCP factor (mitigating)	0	−3
Self-reporting factor (mitigating)	0	−5
Total Culpability Score:	9	< 0
Culpability multiplier range (CMR) (from a table)	1.8 to 3.6	0.05 to 0.2
Minimum fine (low CMR × base fine)	$2,880,000	$80,000
Maximum fine (high CMR × base fine)	$5,760,000	$320,000

In addition to reducing the organization's criminal sentence in the event a violation occurs, an effective CCP may also provide early detection of conduct that could lead to civil enforcement efforts by the government, *qui tam* litigation, or other civil actions. The CCP's preventive activities allow management to take corrective action before suit is filed and to show due diligence if the matter goes to trial.

Notwithstanding the obvious benefits, CCPs do have certain drawbacks. One is their cost: depending on the size and complexity of the organization and the number of attorneys and consultants required, the direct expense involved in starting the program will be at least $250,000 and may easily exceed $1 million. When one factors in staff time, other fixed costs, and the cost of ongoing implementation efforts, a CCP appears to be an expensive proposition indeed. Another disadvantage is that during the CCP development phase the organization may uncover past criminal activities. If so, the offenders will have to be dealt with and the conduct may have to be reported to the proper authorities. A final negative consideration is that, like all internal policies, the CCP will be viewed as the organization's self-established "standard of care." If the CCP is not followed, that fact could be seen as evidence of negligence or recklessness and could increase the sentence or verdict if a case goes to trial. Despite these considerations, the benefits of a CCP far outweigh the potential disadvantages.

The elements of an effective CCP are as follows. First, it must contain established compliance standards and procedures. This requires management to publish for its employees standards of conduct outlining legal requirements in all areas that affect the organization's business operations. Such areas include antitrust, document retention, employment and employee benefits, environmental compliance, Medicare/Medicaid fraud and abuse, occupational safety, patient protection, and taxation. Second, the CCP must be overseen by high-level personnel. Most organizations assign the function (either as a collateral duty or a full-time position) to an individual who reports to the chief executive officer and also has a relationship with the governing board. Third, the CCP must provide that no discretionary authority in the organization may be vested in persons who are known to be (or *should* be known to be) likely to engage in criminal conduct. In effect, this means that the organization must have a mechanism (such as a policy requiring criminal background checks) to prevent the hiring of persons who, for example, have previously been convicted of healthcare offenses or who have been excluded from Medicare and Medicaid.

The fourth element of an effective CCP is the communication of the standards of conduct and CCP procedures to employees and agents of the organization. This means that the organization must educate all employees and agents about the requirements of the CCP (its standards and related procedures) and must continually publicize the topic in employee newsletters and similar media. In effect, the CCP must have the commitment and understanding of everyone in the organization, including not only the board and senior management, but also lower-level employees. Without this level of support, the CCP may be viewed as a sham, which could lead to harsher penalties being assessed. Fifth, the CCP must establish reasonable methods to achieve compliance with the standards of conduct. These methods should include ongoing monitoring activities, periodic audits of various operational departments, and encouragement to employees to report suspicious activities (for example, through "hotlines" or anonymous written reports). Sixth, the CCP must provide for and the organization must carry out appropriate and consistent discipline (including possible termination of employment) for those who violate the standards of conduct or fail to report violations. And seventh, there must be appropriate and consistent responses to violations that are detected, including necessary corrective action to prevent recurrence.

Conclusion

Healthcare organizations, including their governing boards and senior management, must take seriously the possibility that criminal violations (including fraud and abuse) may occur in the course of their business. Although the cost of developing a corporate compliance program is significant, the consequences of not having a CCP can be dire if criminal conduct occurs, and significant benefits may accrue in the form of reduced exposure to *qui tam* suits and other civil actions. Each healthcare organization should begin immediately to adopt and implement effective corporate compliance programs covering their entire operation.

Notes

Portions of this chapter appeared in Gunn, Goldfarb, and Showalter, *Creating a Corporate Compliance Program*, 79 HEALTH PROGRESS 60 (May–June 1998), and are reprinted here with permission.

1. General Accounting Office, *Report on Medicare Fraud and Abuse*, GAO/HR-95-8 (Feb. 1995).

2. U.S. Dept. of Justice, *Department of Justice Health Care Fraud Report, Fiscal Year 1994* (Mar. 2, 1995).

3. 768 F. Supp. 1127 (E.D. Pa. 1991).

4. 859 F. Supp. 5 (D. D.C. 1994).

5. 909 F. Supp. 32 (D. D.C. 1995) (memorandum opinion).

6. 31 U.S.C. §§ 3729-3731.

7. This last provision was added in 1986 to deal with "reverse false claims," situations in which a person attempts to avoid paying money owed to the government.

8. *See, e.g.,* Rex Trailer Co. v. United States, 350 U.S. 148 (1952) and Fleming v. United States, 336 F.2d 475 (10th Cir. 1964).

9. United States v. Krizek, 111 F.3d 394 (D.C. Cir. 1997).

10. *See, e.g.,* United States v. McNinch, 356 U.S. 595 (1958).

11. 31 U.S.C. § 3729(b).

12. S. Rep. No. 345, 99th Cong., 2d Sess. 7.

13. 859 F. Supp. at 13. *But see*, United States v. Nazon, No. 93-C5456m (N.D. Ill. Oct. 14, 1993).

14. Pub. L. No. 104-191, § 213, amending 42 U.S.C. § 1320a-7(b)(15).

15. 42 U.S.C. § 1320a-7a(a)(4).

16. 31 U.S.C. § 3733(l)(4).

17. 31 U.S.C. § 3730(h).

18. *See, Federal Enforcers Urge Healthcare Companies to Police Their Own Fraud*, Vol. 1, No. 12, HEALTH L. NEWS 4 (Dec. 1998). An organization known as Taxpayers Against Fraud reports that total *qui tam* recoveries of all kinds were approximately $1.5 billion from the time of the 1986 amendments through October 1996. Cases arising in the Department of Defense accounted for the largest number of *qui tam* cases filed, but the number of HHS-related cases has been increasing steadily. Of the cases pending in October 1996, "approximately 80% involve DOD or HHS, and they are equally divided between the two." Taxpayers Against Fraud, www.taf.org.

19. Paschke, *The Qui Tam Provision of the Federal False Claims Act: The Statute in Current Form, Its History and Its Unique Position to Influence the Health Care Industry*, 9 J.L. & HEALTH 163, 179 (1994–95).

20. 317 U.S. 537 (1943); *see also* United States v. Forster Wheeler Corp., 447 F.2d 100 (2d Cir. 1971) (invoices submitted on contract that was based on inflated cost estimates are false claims) *and* United States v. Veneziale, 268 F.2d 504 (3d Cir. 1959) (fraudulently induced contract may create liability when the contract later results in payment by the government).

21. 797 F.2d 888 (10th Cir. 1986).

22. 760 F. Supp. 1120 (E.D. Pa. 1991).

23. United States *ex rel.* Roy v. Anthony, 914 F. Supp. 1507 (S.D. Ohio 1994).

24. 914 F. Supp. 1507 (M.D. Tenn. 1996).

25. *Id.* at 1508-1509.

26. *Id.* at 1513.

27. 938 F. Supp. 405 (S.D. Tex. 1996). *See also* United States v. Oakwood Downriver

Medical Center, 687 F. Supp. 302 (E.D. Mich. 1988) *and* United States v. Shaw, 725 F. Supp. 896 (S.D. Miss. 1989) (holding, in a case involving bribes to a Farmers Home Administration official, "[t]he bare fact that bribes were involved . . . does not necessarily lead to the further conclusion that false or fraudulent claims were made in connection with each of the loan applications or preapplications." *Id*. at 900.).

28. At least one consent judgment has been entered in a case of this type. In 1994, a company that ran home infusion centers agreed to pay $500,000 in settlement of an FCA case because it gave physicians incentives to refer patients to the centers. United States v. T[su'2'] Medical, Inc., Ga. No. 1:94-CV-2549 (N.D. Ga. Sept. 26, 1994).

29. 18 U.S.C. § 287.

30. 42 U.S.C. § 1320a-7b(b)(1)(A) and (2)(A).

31. Pub. L. No. 104-191, § 204, 110 Stat. 1999, codified at 42 U.S.C. § 1320a-7b(a).

32. 42 U.S.C. § 1320a-7(b)(7).

33. 42 U.S.C. § 1320a-7a(a)(7).

34. 42 U.S.C. § 1320a-7b(b)(3).

35. 42 U.S.C. § 1320a-7b.

36. S. Rep. No. 109, 100th Cong., 1st Sess. 27.

37. 51 F.3d 1390 (9th Cir. 1995).

38. Office of Inspector Gen., U.S. Dept. of Health & Human Servs., Advisory Op. No. 97-6 (Oct. 8, 1997).

39. Levin v. Inspector General, No. CR343 (HHS Dept. App. Bd. Nov. 10, 1994).

40. *See* 42 U.S.C. §§ 1320a-7b(b)(1)(B) and (2)(B).

41. Unreported decision cited in "Psychiatric Hospital Firm Pleads Guilty to Violating Anti-Kickback Statute," 4 BNA's HEALTH L. REP. 687

42. 42 U.S.C. § 1320a-7a(a)(5).

43. 42 U.S.C. § 1320a-7a(i)(6) (emphasis added).

44. Codified at 42 U.S.C. § 1395nn.

45. HCFA Trans. No. AB-95-3 (Jan. 1995), *reprinted in* BNA's HEALTH L. & BUS. SERIES No. 2400 at 2400:3401, 3402 (1997).

46. *Id*. at 2400:3403.

47. 42 U.S.C. § 1395nn(b)(2)(A)(i).

48. 42 U.S.C. § 1395nn(b)(2)(B).

49. 42 U.S.C. § 1395nn(b)(2)(A)(ii).

50. 42 U.S.C. § 1395nn(b)(3).

51. 42 U.S.C. § 1395nn(d)(3).

52. 42 U.S.C. § 1395nn(e)(2).

53. *See generally*, 42 U.S.C. § 1395nn(c)-(e) and the discussion below.

54. 56 Fed. Reg. 22,762, 22,786 (May 16, 1991).

55. The size of the organization is a factor in the *Guidelines'* sentencing formula.

56. Willful ignorance is an aggravating factor in the formula.

ADMISSION AND DISCHARGE

The important questions to be considered initially in this chapter are whether a patient has the legal right to be treated and to be formally admitted to a hospital. Admission policies for each institution must be developed according to a number of different factors because the legal aspects of admitting and discharge depend on the facts of the particular situation.

Access to Healthcare and Formal Voluntary Admission

The Right to Care

First, one must distinguish between emergency patients and others. The right of patients to be treated or formally admitted and the corresponding duties of the hospital depend in part on whether the patient's condition is an emergency and whether the hospital has the facilities and staff to render necessary emergency care. The rights of the patient and duties of the hospital with respect to formal admission may also depend on whether the patient has previously received any treatment or service from the institution. Care of emergency patients is discussed in Chapter 10.

Second, ownership of the hospital may affect the right of the patient to be admitted. A governmental hospital is subject to different standards of conduct than those legally imposed on a private hospital, because local law may apply to particular governmental institutions in some states.

Finally, voluntary hospitals that received federal funding under the Hill-Burton Act have a certain duty to provide service for the indigent, as will be noted later.

It is a common-law maxim that a nonemergency patient has no legal right to be admitted to any voluntary or proprietary hospital or to most governmental hospitals.[1] Thus, most institutions can generally accept or refuse nonemergency cases with impunity as long as admission policies are not illegally discriminatory and the relevant Hill-Burton Act regulations are followed. Refusal to admit therefore does not ordinarily give the patient a cause of action or entitle the complainant to a court order changing hospital policies.

Contractual arrangements could create an exception to the general rule that a patient has no legal right to be admitted. A hospital that enters into a contract with a particular group of patients or with another party (such as an employer or a managed healthcare plan) for the benefit of a class of persons undertakes a legal obligation to admit group members for care and treatment whenever the need arises. Breach of this contractual obligation gives the other party or the intended beneficiary a right to sue for damages.[2]

The U.S. Constitution does not consider access to healthcare a fundamental legal right, and denial of nonemergency care based on an inability to pay for services does not violate principles of constitutional law. As has been mentioned elsewhere, the Fourteenth Amendment ensures equal protection of the laws and due process of law. The equal protection clause, however, does not guarantee that all persons will be treated equally; rather, the concept of equal protection simply means that persons in the same or similar circumstances will be treated equally *in like cases.* Moreover, the amendment applies only to state or governmental action and not to purely private conduct. In other words, "state action" denying equal protection or due process is unconstitutional, but private action is not. Accordingly, the Fourteenth Amendment simply prohibits impermissible classifications of persons by government or by a private organization acting in the name of or in the place of government. Thus, denial of admission because of inability to pay for healthcare does not create a constitutional issue.

As has been noted in varying contexts, classifications by government that have a rational or reasonable relation to a legitimate public purpose or governmental interest are permissible. Only when governmental action invades a fundamental human right or discriminates against a court-determined "suspect class" of persons is the action presumptively invalid. In this event the court will require government to show that a compelling interest justifies the regulation or classification. These issues have been raised in a number of cases challenging legislative decisions regarding allocations for governmental healthcare.

Because access to healthcare is not a fundamental right akin to voting,[3] freedom of speech, the right to counsel in a criminal trial,[4] or the right of travel,[5] governmental requirements basing eligibility for healthcare benefits on a person's income or assets have generally received limited scrutiny by the courts and have been upheld as rational with regard to legitimate governmental interests.

Neither has indigency been characterized as a suspect class justifying invalidation of a policy basing eligibility on ability to pay.[6] Although neither the definition of a "fundamental right" nor that of a "suspect class" is free from doubt, the latter term has been restricted to groups of persons who have traditionally been "saddled with disabilities, subjected to a history of unequal treatment, or relegated to such a position of political powerlessness as to command extraordinary protection from the majoritarian political processes."[7] Clearly classifications based on race, color, creed, or national origin meet these standards.[8] In contrast, classifications of persons by gender,[9] illegitimacy,[10] alienage,[11] and indigency have not been characterized as suspect and thus justifying strict scrutiny.[12]

Although the Supreme Court has ruled that state legislation requiring a year's residency to qualify for welfare benefits was unconstitutional (because the freedom of interstate travel is a fundamental right),[13] it has nevertheless granted wide discretion to government in determining eligibility for financial aid or services. Maryland, for example, was permitted to limit aid to families with dependent children to $250 per month regardless of the number of children in the family;[14] Connecticut could provide Medicaid funds for the birth of a child but deny payment for a nontherapeutic abortion;[15] and Congress could authorize the states to exclude Medicaid payments for a therapeutic abortion except where the life of the woman was threatened.[16] In all of these situations the standard of judicial review was the reasonable, rational basis test, and in each case the Court ruled that the legislation protected legitimate public purposes or interests.

There is thus no constitutional basis at present for asserting that an individual has a right to healthcare or payment for it from public funds.[17] Both the right of access and the right to payment depend on federal or state legislation.[18] Legislation, in turn, differs from jurisdiction to jurisdiction and in accordance with changing political and economic environments. Only the future will determine society's longer-range policies on medical care for the significant number of indigent persons who need such assistance. More will be said later in the book about local governments' statutory duties to pay for care furnished to indigent patients.

Right to Admission and Services

Despite the apparent freedom of most hospitals to refuse care to nonemergency patients, legal risks arise when a hospital asserts too vigorously the general rule that a patient has no right to be treated or admitted. These risks will be more apparent in the cases, discussed in the next chapter, where patients present themselves at the emergency room requesting treatment. Admission policies based on discriminatory criteria such as race or inability to pay raise serious legal issues and generate lawsuits. Even refusing treatment of difficult, disruptive persons whose presence may interfere seriously with the care of other patients is a matter of increasing concern, as illustrated by a California case already referred to in connection with the physician-patient relationship discussed in Chapter 2.

Brenda Payton, a patient suffering from permanent and irreversible loss of kidney function (chronic end-stage renal disease), needed regular, systematic hemodialysis. Both her physician and a clinic for dialysis treatment had stopped treating her as a consequence of her disruptive behavior, persistent failure to follow orders, and abusive use of alcohol and drugs. Because she was given adequate notice to enable her to locate other providers, the doctor and the clinic were legally entitled to withdraw their services.[19]

When she sought regularly scheduled outpatient care elsewhere, however, two private hospitals considered her unacceptable as a patient because of her past, well-documented behavior. Because no common law or statutory grounds could be found requiring the hospitals to accept her for continued treatment, the refusals by the hospital were upheld by a California court.[20] It was held that a California statute requiring licensed health centers with appropriate facilities and personnel to extend emergency care to persons in need did not create a legal right in the circumstances, because the legislation was intended to apply only when the patient was in imminent physical danger at a particular moment. The statute was thus irrelevant to a patient requiring continual, long-term care.[21] By way of dictum the court observed that institutions with unique or scarce medical resources should not refuse services without good cause, but it left the impression that such a cause was present in the *Payton* case. The judge also indicated that providers of care should have collective responsibility in the community to share the burden of treating disruptive and uncooperative patients. The court did not, however, say how this responsibility could be implemented.[22]

This case is mentioned again here because it touches on an important issue. The governing board and the administration of a hospital, rather than being concerned with the presence or absence of a patient's legal right to be treated or formally admitted, should be more concerned with the hospital's purpose and role in the community. Having defined this purpose and role, with proper reference to statutes in the case of governmental hospitals and relevant state licensure regulations, the board's task is then to provide adequate facilities, equipment, and staff to fulfill the purpose and carry out the role. If such policies are adhered to, the narrow legal question of the patient's right to care does not generally arise.

Governmental hospitals and duty to provide services

Governmental hospitals are created by statutes that specify the purpose of the hospital. Many state statutes refer to and define the people intended to be served by the hospital, classified according to their particular diseases, their financial status, or their place of residence. From such statutes one may at least infer that a patient who falls within the class has a right to be admitted to the hospital, although actual court cases on the matter are lacking. It would appear, however, that even if such a legal right exists it is not absolute; hence, not every patient who is refused has a cause of action. For instance, any legal right created by the statutes would still be subject to the ability of the hospital to care for the particular patient and the availability of bed space at the particular time of the patient's request for admission. Furthermore, admissions are still subject to the rules and regulations of the governing board, so long as these rules are within the statutorily delegated authority of the board. For example, the board might properly require proof of inability to pay when the hospital is statutorily set up to serve those who cannot pay for private care. On the other hand, even when a state statute indicates that the hospital's purpose is to care for those unable to pay, there is generally nothing to prevent a governmental hospital from admitting patients who are able to pay if facilities are available.

Residency requirements are found in many statutes pertaining to governmental hospitals. Sometimes the statutory definition is very broad and includes all persons who fall ill within a particularly defined geographical area, even though they do not reside within the area. Other statutes appear to require actual residence within a specified area. As noted previously, however, residency requirements based on periods of time as prerequisites for state welfare benefits are unconstitutional.[23] Even so, the governing board may promulgate the rules and regulations that permit the admission of nonresidents.

Like a private general hospital, a governmental institution functioning as a general hospital may usually exclude persons suffering from illnesses that it is not equipped to treat adequately. For example, a general hospital may ordinarily deny formal admission to a mental patient or to one afflicted with a contagious disease when facilities and staff are not available to care for such individuals. Such patients would have no cause of action for being refused admission, particularly if their admission would endanger other patients.

Governmental hospitals that are not protected by the doctrine of governmental immunity (as those in some jurisdictions are not) owe the same duty as other hospitals of exercising reasonable care with respect to patients who seek treatment from an emergency room, even though such persons are not among those statutorily defined as the primary beneficiaries of the institution. In other words, in the case of an emergency patient, a refusal of service, or a failure to exercise reasonable care once service is undertaken, cannot be justified on the basis that the patient was outside the classes of persons to be served by the governmental hospital.[24]

Aside from legislation creating government-owned hospitals and specifying the persons to be served, most states also have statutes providing for payment from public funds for certain medical services furnished to indigent individuals. Legislation differs significantly from state to state regarding the services covered, patients entitled to care, eligibility of the provider for payment, and where services are rendered. Typically the statutes require municipal or county governments to pay for emergency medical care given in any location to certain indigent persons. As a matter of constitutional law, these enactments have been held valid.[25] Administrators of healthcare facilities should therefore be aware of local statutes and judicial decisions that determine an institution's right to reimbursement.

Local government's duty to reimburse for care

In both Arizona and Nevada, counties are required to reimburse for "emergency" medical care furnished "indigent residents." In Arizona, if a patient meeting the specified standards of indigency were admitted to a private hospital in urgent need of care, the county's obligation to pay for the services would continue throughout the period of hospitalization, even after the emergency ended. In a 1984 Arizona case an indigent patient was admitted to a private hospital for emergency treatment. Later the agency responsible for payment of the medical expenses could have arranged a transfer of the patient to a county-owned health facility and thus terminated the obligation to reimburse the private hospital; but this was not done and the government was obliged to pay.[26] In Nevada the county has a duty to pay for emergency care whether rendered at the county's own medical center or elsewhere, and prior governmental consent is not required if the patient's condition threatens life or permanent impairment.[27] In similar fashion cities in Florida must pay for certain medical services needed by indigent residents. In that state the obligation normally applies only to treatment given within the county of the patient's residence. Where emergency care was rendered by a university hospital outside the patient's residential county, however, there was a statutory duty to reimburse the hospital.[28]

Also a matter of concern to the provider is reimbursement for health-care furnished to arrested persons in police custody, to prisoners previously convicted of a crime, and to persons injured by the police while being apprehended. In all jurisdictions, of course, most patients are personally responsible for payment simply as a matter of contract law, even if they did not expressly request the care. Even without an express or implied contract, the provider would nevertheless have a legal right to collect the customary charges on the basis that the services enriched the patient.[29] Obviously, however, the provider must look elsewhere for payment if the patient is indigent, and often government is viewed as a source for reimbursement.

In analyzing the obligations of government to persons detained by or apprehended by public authority, one must distinguish between the duty to provide or summon care and a duty to pay a third party for that care. Further, it may be necessary to distinguish between persons adjudged guilty of a criminal act, those under arrest awaiting trial, and those injured during the course of apprehension. Finally, three sources of law must be consulted: common law, local legislation, and constitutional law as interpreted by the courts.

As a matter of common law and in the absence of governmental immunity in tort, the failure to exercise reasonable care in obtaining medical assistance for a prisoner or person in custody can lead to liability for negligence. For example, an Indiana municipality was liable for the wrongful death of a person arrested for being drunk and disorderly on the grounds that the police knew or ought to have known that the person needed medical care.[30]

Constitutionally the Eighth Amendment prohibits "cruel and unusual" punishment, and this has been judicially interpreted as requiring government to provide convicted prisoners with adequate medical care.[31] The Eighth Amendment does not apply, however, to persons detained by police or under arrest, because they have not been adjudged guilty of a crime. The due process clause of the Fifth and Fourteenth Amendments nevertheless establishes the right of a person confined in a government institution to receive essential food, shelter, clothing, and medical care.[32]

On the other hand, a person not dependent on government has no constitutional right to medical care.[33] And, as will be seen, the right to seek or receive care is not necessarily accompanied by a right to have that care paid for by the government.

Some local laws or state statutes implement the right to receive care by expressly providing that public authority shall pay the cost of care furnished prisoners[34] or persons committed to custody.[35] The duty to pay may be limited to cases in which the government's institutional facilities are inadequate[36] or where the prisoner (or the family) is unable to pay.[37] Most state legislation, however, simply affirms a prisoner's right to receive medical care and is vague and ambiguous about government's duty to pay an outside provider of healthcare.[38] Moreover, the statutes may not apply to persons injured by the police at the scene of an alleged crime or while being apprehended, because such a person is not under arrest or in custody. Although the police probably have a duty in such circumstances to seek medical care for the injured person, government is not obligated by either common or constitutional law to pay the provider of care.

In the leading case of *City of Revere v. Massachusetts General Hospital* Patrick Kivlin attempted to flee from the scene of an alleged crime and was shot by a police officer.[39] The ambulance summoned by the police took Mr. Kivlin to the Massachusetts General Hospital, where he remained for nine days, meanwhile being arrested and held in custody. A month later he was again hospitalized, but the city of Revere refused to pay for either that or the earlier hospital confinement.

As a matter of common law the hospital could not collect from the municipality because a mere request from a third party for medical services to an injured person did not amount to an implied-in-fact agreement to pay. Moreover, even if the action of the police in summoning aid for the injured person could have been construed as a promise to pay for services, the officer did not have the authority as an agent to create a contractual obligation for the city to pay the hospital.[40]

Furthermore, the Constitution does not require the government to pay a third-party provider for healthcare rendered to a person in Mr. Kivlin's position, even if the patient was at the time dependent on public authority. Thus, just as the state may deny payment from public funds for an elective abortion[41] and the federal government may restrict Medicaid payments to medically necessary abortions,[42] the city of Revere was permitted to deny payment to Massachusetts General Hospital.[43] Even if the patient's constitutional rights to receive care were equivalent to those of a convicted prisoner or an involuntarily institutionalized person, local government had no duty to pay the hospital in the absence of state legislation.

Once patients are voluntarily admitted to a hospital, there is a duty to exercise reasonable care for their treatment unless some relevant doctrine of immunity for tort liability is present. Moreover, admission can occur and the duty to exercise reasonable care can arise without formal admission procedures, as

Reasonable care requirements and admission forms

the case of *LeJeune Road Hospital, Inc. v. Watson* illustrates.[44] In this case the hospital refused a bed to a minor suffering from appendicitis because his mother had not paid the required advance deposit, although staff members had already put a hospital gown on him and examined him. Surgery on the youth was delayed until his parents could locate an institution that would care for him. In a suit for damages the defendant hospital contended that formal admission had not occurred and that no duty to exercise reasonable care had been created. This argument was rejected. The court held that, even though the hospital had no positive duty to admit, admission had in fact occurred.

Once a decision is made to admit a nonemergency patient, certain formalities should be accomplished. In general, patients or authorized representatives should be asked to sign a form containing a number of different items. Admissions personnel should not suggest by act or language that this is a formal contract because patients might then consider bringing suit against the hospital alleging breach of contract if they suffered injuries while hospitalized even though negligence could not be proved. Rather, the form should simply provide evidence of an understanding between the hospital and the patient with respect to certain matters.

For example, the admissions form should expressly identify the person responsible for payment of the hospital bill and should contain language legally sufficient to establish this express obligation or otherwise identify the expected source of reimbursement. Persons responsible will usually be the patients themselves, but a third person could be named. If the patient is a minor, for example, the party responsible for payment would normally be the parents. Although a legal obligation to pay for services rendered an unemancipated minor does not require the parent's signature, it is wise and practical to obtain it. In cases in which a third party who is not legally responsible for supporting the patient undertakes to guarantee payment of the account, most states require that this party's promise to pay be in writing to satisfy the statute of frauds. The legal aspects of hospital credit and collections are beyond the scope of this discussion, but the major point is that at the time of the patient's admission to the hospital it is always better, even if not legally necessary, to obtain an express, written promise from the person who will pay the hospital bill or the balance of the bill in excess of insurance coverage.

Another matter to clarify at the same time is the patient's consent for routine medical treatment and diagnostic procedures.[45] As discussed in Chapter 11, "Consent for Treatment and the Withholding of Consent," patients or authorized representatives should be asked by the admitting office to sign a generalized consent statement. Although oral consent to treatment is legally effective if proved, a written consent filed as a part of the patient's record provides far better protection to the hospital in the event of later misunderstanding. It should be emphasized, however, that this statement of consent is not sufficient to provide evidence of informed consent for surgical procedures or many of the more sophisticated diagnostic tests. A special consent form is advised for surgery and extraordinary diagnostic procedures. The signature on such a special consent form should be obtained by the physician undertaking the procedure—not by admissions personnel—because only a doctor can explain the recommended treatment or procedure as required by the doctrine of informed consent.

The admitting form should also give notice to patients that the hospital has an organized system for safekeeping of any valuables they may bring with them. Patients should be invited to deposit these with the hospital and should be advised that the institution cannot normally assume responsibility for loss of money or personal property kept by the bedside. The particular language employed in the admitting form must, of course, be consistent with local and state law regarding hospital liability for loss or theft of patients' property. Normally the hospital would be considered a bailee of property relinquished by the patient for safekeeping and would accordingly be under a duty to exercise reasonable care.[46]

At the time of admission it is also wise to obtain the patient's consent to release medical information to certain identified and legitimately interested third parties such as insurance carriers or governmental agencies paying for services rendered to the patient. Hospitals often receive multiple requests for medical information regarding a particular patient. The hospital need not ask the patient for a separate release form for each request. A better understanding is achieved and administrative procedure simplified if consent for releasing information is obtained at the time of admission to cover the most frequent situations. Special requests for medical information—certainly those from parties whose interests are adverse to the patient's—should be handled separately as they are received.

Still other matters might be covered in the written admission form, depending on the advice of local legal counsel. Counsel might advise, for instance, a statement that the hospital does not routinely provide special duty nursing and that patients requiring or wishing such care must arrange for the special duty nurses, perhaps from a hospital roster of persons available for such service.

Arbitration agreements

Many states have statutes that recognize the validity of agreements for voluntary binding arbitration regarding any claims arising from hospital or medical care. Michigan's statute, for example, goes further by actually requiring insured hospitals to offer inpatients and outpatients the option of arbitration.[47] Physicians are free to choose whether to offer arbitration. Binding arbitration has the effect of removing claims of liability from the normal judicial process of court litigation, as is more fully discussed elsewhere in the context of malpractice reform legislation.[48]

It should be noted here, however, that regardless of statutory approval of arbitration as a substitute for court litigation, a fundamental legal issue is whether the agreement was truly voluntary. By definition a contract of adhesion is an agreement thrust on a person contrary to free will or without full understanding. Such a take-it-or-leave-it contract is unenforceable. Moreover, drawing on the analogy of the sales-of-goods provisions of the Uniform Commercial Code, courts have the judicial power to declare that a given agreement is "unconscionable" and contrary to public policy. An unconscionable contract, usually the result of gross disparity in bargaining power, is one so unfair or harsh that it "shocks the conscience." Depending on the facts and circumstances, either of these interrelated arguments could be used to invalidate an individual's agreement to arbitrate.

Normally such an agreement is obtained at the time of the patient's admission to the hospital. This is frequently a time of anxiety for patients, and hospital personnel are perhaps too busy or not well enough informed to explain arbitration adequately. For these reasons the likelihood of securing a voluntary agreement that a court will find valid is diminished.

As would be expected, judicial decisions on the matter differ according to the facts in each case. In some cases arbitration agreements have been found invalid because the patient was unaware of a purported agreement to arbitrate or did not fully understand the arrangement.[49] Persons who admit patients to hospitals or accept them for care in an outpatient clinic of physician's office must therefore be aware of both statutory and common law requirements governing the enforceability of agreements to arbitrate. They should be prepared to explain the essence of binding arbitration and to answer questions that may arise.

Sometimes an agreement to arbitrate malpractice claims is a feature of a group health plan negotiated by a third party on behalf of subscribers. This was the situation in *Madden v. Kaiser Foundation Hospital,* where it was held that the agreement between the board of administration of the California State Employees Retirement System and Kaiser Foundation Hospitals was not a contract of adhesion because the two parties were in positions of relatively equal bargaining power.[50]

Legislation Guaranteeing Equal Protection

In developing admission policies and practices, healthcare administrators must consider legislation by Congress, federal regulations, state statutes and regulations, and local ordinances designed to prohibit discrimination on the basis of race, color, creed, national origin, or other prohibited criteria. In addition, straightforward court decisions interpreting the Fourteenth Amendment prohibit discriminatory policies in admitting patients, furnishing services and facilities, and appointing hospital medical staff. This statutory and judicial law developed rapidly during the 1960s and unequivocally committed the United States to the concept that all persons are entitled to equal protection of law. This extremely significant body of law does not grant an affirmative right to the patient to be admitted to a hospital, but it does proscribe discriminatory practices and policies.

The major antidiscriminatory legislation is the federal Civil Rights Act of 1964. One section of this act (Title II) prohibits racial discrimination in designated places of "public accommodation"; another applies to publicly owned facilities, including governmental hospitals; a third (Title VII) relates to racial and sexual discrimination in employment opportunities and embraces both private and public hospitals. Most significant, Title VI of the act prohibits discrimination on the basis of race, color, or national origin by an institution receiving federal financial assistance (such as Medicare).[51]

Every federal agency or department administering a financial program is authorized by Congress to promulgate administrative regulations to effectuate the purpose of the primary legislation.[52] The Department of Health and Human Services has published such regulations with reference to hospitals.[53] Effective July 1, 1966, to be eligible for participation in Medicare, a hospital must comply with Title VI of the Civil Rights Act. Accordingly, a hospital receiving Medicare funds must not discriminate on racial or ethnic grounds in its admission policies, room assignments (although the patient's medical condition, age, and similar factors can be considered in assigning rooms), and the availability of hospital facilities and services.

The constitutional basis of the federal Civil Rights Act is the power of Congress to regulate interstate commerce. Presumably, matters of intrastate commerce are beyond the power of congressional action. However, as a result of numerous Supreme Court decisions dating back to the 1930s, nearly all economic relationships are legally classified as interstate commerce, and in any event the constitutionality of the sections of the act relating to public accommodations and federal financing as defined in the legislation and applicable to private enterprise has been specifically upheld.

Another important federal statute pertaining to discrimination is the Hospital Survey and Construction Act, known more simply as the Hill-Burton Act.[54] This act and later legislation replacing the original statute are discussed below.

In addition to federal legislative and administrative regulation articulating forceful policies against racial and sexual discrimination, there are state statutes and city ordinances to the same effect. Hence, in addition to federal law, hospital administrators must consult state and local law in developing policies relating to the admission and discharge of patients. Most states and many major cities have enacted statutes forbidding discrimination on racial or ethnic grounds by business and institutions serving the public. The applicability of such laws to a particular hospital and the criteria for defining prohibited forms of discrimination are determined, of course, by the precise wording and interpretation of the particular statute in question. Generally, however, these laws are applicable to all types of hospitals.

Some of these local civil rights statutes or ordinances specifically mention hospitals. Most, however, speak simply in terms of public accommodation, which in turn may be broadly defined as a place that offers goods, services, or facilities to the general public.[55] This concept embraces hospitals, even proprietary institutions, unless a specific exemption is provided. Extended care facilities and nursing homes may be subject to these state laws as well, although the laws must be carefully interpreted.[56]

Antidiscrimination provisions may also be found in state hospital licensure statutes. The Michigan statute on licensure reads that a "patient or resident will not be denied appropriate care on the basis of race, religion, color, national origin, sex, age, handicap, marital status, sexual preference, or source of payment."[57] Statutes or regulations pertaining to tax-exempt status may also proscribe discriminatory practices.[58]

In developing admission policies, hospital administrators must also consult local law prohibiting forms of discrimination other than racial. Montana, for instance, has a statute to the effect that a voluntary hospital may not discriminate between patients of licensed staff physicians and those of licensed doctors not on the staff.[59]

Quite aside from federal and state statutory law designed to prohibit discriminatory practices, the Fourteenth Amendment ensures equal protection of the laws and due process of law. Specifically, the relevant language reads: "Nor shall any State deprive any person of life, liberty, or property without due process of law; nor deny to any person within its jurisdiction the equal protection of the laws." The amendment therefore applies to state or governmental action, but not to purely private action. In other words, *state* action denying equal protection or due process is unconstitutional, but *private* action is not. Hence, racial and other types of discrimination by private individuals or private business are not prohibited by the Fourteenth Amendment, although local statutes or ordinances may properly regulate private conduct to attain justifiable social policies. State constitutions may also contain equal protection and due process clauses similar to those of the federal Constitution.

As a matter of federal constitutional law the issue becomes one of defining state action. Clearly ownership by government is not necessary to bring the Fourteenth Amendment into play. Under various facts and circumstances a private voluntary hospital may be so closely allied or associated with government that it becomes subject to the mandates of the Fourteenth Amendment with respect to admission policies, the availability of facilities and services, and medical staff appointments and privileges—to name only three major areas of concern. In and of themselves, acceptance of governmental financial aid or tax-exempt status do not convert a voluntary hospital into a public hospital, as many cases have held. Nevertheless, such support and reliance on government may make the Fourteenth Amendment applicable in several contexts.

Illustrating this point is a leading case decided in 1963, *Simkins v. Moses H. Cone Memorial Hospital.*[60] This litigation concerned two private, not-for-profit hospitals that were participating in the Hill-Burton program, thus cooperating in the planning function with state and federal governments and receiving public funds. Accordingly, the action of the hospitals was deemed to be state action, and the court held that the Fourteenth Amendment prohibited racial discrimination with respect to both admission of patients and appointments of medical staff.[61] The contact with government can be even less direct than in *Simkins*. In *Eaton v. Grubbs* the voluntary hospital was located on land that, by terms of the deed, was to revert to government if the corporation dissolved. Furthermore, the hospital had received financial aid from the local municipal government. These factors were sufficient to make the Fourteenth Amendment applicable to hospital admission policies.[62] It is significant that *Simkins* and *Eaton* involved allegations of *racial* discrimination, a context in which courts are more likely to hold that state action exists. As will be seen, state action is often not found when the alleged discrimination is of another kind.

Thus there are several sources of law that require nondiscriminatory policies with respect to admission of patients and availability of facilities and services: local city ordinances, state statutes, federal legislation, state and federal administrative regulation pursuant to delegated legislative authority, and finally judicial interpretation of constitutional law.

Hill-Burton Act and Mandated Free Care

The purpose of the Hospital Survey and Construction Act, enacted in 1946 and commonly known as the Hill-Burton Act, was to provide federal financing for the construction and modernization of publicly owned and not-for-profit hospital facilities.[63] The legislation did not contain any provisions for the financing of health services, however, and another 20 years passed before Congress enacted the Medicare legislation. To accommodate the proposals of President Truman for a comprehensive national health service, Hill-Burton required recipients of financial assistance to furnish a "reasonable volume" of services for persons unable to pay, unless the providers were financially unable to do so.[64] This provision became known as the hospital's "uncompensated care obligation." The statute also required that hospital facilities financed with federal funds be made available to all persons in the community, a duty commonly referred to as the "community service obligation."[65]

As is frequently done for political reasons, this program of federal funding was implemented through the states. The states were given responsibility for determining the need for facilities, establishing a statewide plan, and obtaining assurances from applicants for federal grants or loans that they would comply with the obligations regarding uncompensated care and community service.[66] Statutory responsibility for enforcement of these obligations was initially placed in the states.

The Hill-Burton Act thus potentially represented a means of providing healthcare to indigent persons. For many years, however, hospitals were allowed to neglect the intent of these provisions because the requirements were not effectively implemented. The initial administrative regulations did not actually require the states to ensure that financially assisted institutions were furnishing free care. They also failed to define a "reasonable volume" of services and to specify eligibility criteria for persons entitled to care. Early in the 1970s, however, the legislation became the basis for several class-action lawsuits contending that institutions that required cash deposits or evidence of adequate hospitalization insurance before admitting patients, and those that automatically billed patients without regard for ability to pay, were in violation of the Hill-Burton Act. The initial legal issue was whether the plaintiffs had standing to sue to enforce the provisions of the act and regulations; that is, whether a private cause action existed to require hospitals receiving Hill-Burton funds to provide a given volume of free care or care below cost. The issue was answered in the affirmative by the leading and most authoritative case on the matter, which held that a private cause of action did exist.[67] Subsequently the federal District Court for the Eastern District of Louisiana held that the Secretary of the Department of Health, Education, and Welfare (now the Department of Health and Human Services) had violated his statutory obligations to enforce the Hill-Burton assurances that various hospitals had given.[68] The court also issued an order requiring the hospitals to develop rules for implementing their obligations and to submit these for court review.[69]

Following these court decisions the Department of Health, Education, and Welfare promulgated new regulations effective in 1973. An institution that received Hill-Burton financing could presumptively meet the requirements of providing free care or care below cost by budgeting for such care 3 percent of its operating costs less Medicare and Medicaid reimbursement for a fiscal year or by budgeting 10 percent of the federal Hill-Burton assistance for such care, whichever was less. If they choose, however, they could simply certify that they did not refuse admission solely because of inability to pay. The latter option for compliance was sometimes referred to as the open-door policy.[70]

The community-service obligation was interpreted as requiring all hospitals operating with Hill-Burton funds to serve Medicaid patients[71] and to extend emergency care to any person residing or employed in the service area regardless of the patient's ability to pay.[72] All services had to be nondiscriminatory with regard to race, color, creed, or national origin. A patient denied charity care was also entitled to the essentials of procedural due process: adequate notice of eligibility criteria, written reasons for denial, and an opportunity to appeal an adverse decision to an impartial administrator.[73] When a hospital could not demonstrate compliance for particular years it could be required to remedy the deficits.[74]

The regulations established a 20-year period of obligation for uncompensated care dating from completion of construction (or, in the case of a loan, of a period equivalent to the term of the loan). They also delegated to state Hill-Burton agencies the task of identifying persons eligible for uncompensated care according to certain specified criteria and made states responsible for monitoring hospital compliance, applying sanctions in cases of noncompliance, and posting notices to patients that uncompensated care was available.[75] The 1973 rules, however, permitted hospitals to treat uncollectible debts as free care by allowing the determination of eligibility to be made after rendering the services and billing the patient. Factors considered under the 1973 regulations in determining eligibility for uncompensated care included insurance coverage, family income, size of family, state standards for Aid to Families with Dependent Children, and federal guidelines for determining poverty. The state agency also established for each healthcare institution the reasonable level of uncompensated services, which was not to exceed the presumptive compliance guidelines noted previously, after considering the institution's adopted budget, annual statement, the nature and volume of services, the need within the service area, and the ability of other nearby healthcare organizations to provide charity care.

Several lawsuits were subsequently filed challenging these regulations. The presumptive compliance guidelines were consistently upheld as reasonable and not arbitrary.[76] Likewise, the 20-year limitation on the obligation to furnish uncompensated care was said to be consistent with congressional intent.[77] On the other hand, the regulations permitting routine billing of patients and postponing the determination of eligibility for free care until services had been rendered were held to be invalid.[78] Subject to certain exceptions—including a medical emergency, for example—the subsequently amended rules required a written determination of a patient's eligibility before the rendering of services.

The National Health Planning and Resource Development Act of 1974 (Public Law 93-641) in effect terminated the original Hill-Burton program and substituted a somewhat more restrictive scheme of providing federal funds for modernizing healthcare institutions.[79] This legislation not only recognized the continuing obligation of hospitals to provide uncompensated care and community service, but mandated new regulations. Congress now acknowledged that Hill-Burton had never been effectively implemented by the state agencies, and the new act accordingly placed greater responsibility on the department then known as Health, Education, and Welfare to enforce the provisions for care of the indigent. The statute also provided that funding of projects under the new law would obligate the recipients to furnish certain uncompensated care and community service for an indefinite period. Because the new law was not retroactive, however, institutions that received funds prior to 1975 may still claim the 20-year limit on their commitment to furnish free care.[80]

Restraints on the federal budget during recent years have restricted appropriations of new funds for hospital construction. Many of the previous commitments with a 20-year limit have thus expired without being replaced. Healthcare administrators must, therefore, review their institutions' history of federal funding to determine their obligations under either the Hill-Burton law or the regulations (enacted in 1979) that implemented the health planning law. Because of the passage of time and other nondiscrimination statutes and regulations, these two measures are less salient than they once were. They may have some lingering viability for some institutions, however.

Admission and Treatment of Mentally Ill Patients

Upon admission to a hospital or other institution, the legal rights of a mentally ill or incompetent patient are determined by both constitutional law and state statutory law. Because both these sources of law are continually evolving, hospital management needs competent, current advice concerning emergency treatment, temporary detention, and formal admission of these persons.

As explained in Chapter 10 the refusal of a general hospital to extend emergency care to an incompetent or mentally ill patient could well lead to tort liability. On the other hand, a refusal to admit such a person formally to the hospital will not usually lead to liability, especially if the hospital is not staffed or equipped to house and treat psychiatric patients. Nevertheless, at the request of relatives, social welfare agencies, or the police an acute-care hospital may decide to admit temporarily an unwilling, incompetent patient for the patient's own safety or for the protection of others. Unless admission procedures carefully follow local statutory procedures, the hospital risks liability to the unwilling patient for the tort of false imprisonment as well as assault and battery.

To protect against possible liability, the hospital should make certain that only such force is used to detain the patient as is reasonable in the circumstances, that detention continues only for a reasonable time within statutory limits, and that it has the legitimate purpose of protecting the patient or third parties. Second, the express consent or authorization of the nearest relative must be obtained whenever involuntary detention or hospitalization is requested by such a relative. Third, and most significant, medical and administrative personnel must be certain that they are following statutory requirements regarding involuntary hospitalization of patients.[81] Finally, unwilling, incompetent patients should be admitted or detained only on the order of a licensed physician exercising professional judgment in good faith. When professional persons are acting in good faith and according to constitutional and statutory requirements, the risks of liability are minimal.[82]

Involuntary Commitment

Because detention in an institution represents a significant deprivation of liberty, state statutes governing the civil commitment of mentally ill persons must ensure that the patient is granted both substantive and procedural due process of law.[83] A person may not be committed or recommitted involuntarily unless mental illness presents a danger to the patient or to third parties.[84] Danger to self can be found if patients cannot provide the basic necessities of life or if there are indications that they may harm themselves. Unless persons are adjudged dangerous to themselves or others, indefinite confinement in a state mental hospital without treatment violates their right to due process, and the officials responsible for such confinement can be personally liable under the Civil Rights Act of 1871.[85]

When mentally ill patients are unable to care for themselves and accordingly present a danger to their own well-being, a state has a legitimate interest under its *parens patriae* powers to provide care.[86] If mentally ill patients present a danger to the community or to third parties, the state's police power to regulate matters of health, safety, and welfare justifies civil commitment of such persons.[87] To conform to these substantive constitutional standards many states require evidence of a timely overt act or threat of violence to show that the patient represents a danger. To meet such a standard, however, requires psychiatrists and other professionals to predict a patient's behavior, a task that may be scientifically or medically impossible.

Balancing the legitimate rights of patients with the recognized interests of society thus involves difficult questions of social policy as well as legal and medical judgments. The attempt to achieve such a balance creates a twofold risk: some patients properly diagnosed as not dangerous may be released when they nevertheless need further care; others may be misdiagnosed and thought to pose no risk and may later harm others.[88] The possibility of error is increased by the fact that the concept of "dangerousness" is ill-defined in both medicine and law, and in many commitment hearings the matter is left for the jury to decide on the basis of testimony from expert witnesses.

Local statutes typically allow involuntary detention in emergencies for a limited period ranging from 48 hours to several days, depending on the jurisdiction. Because patients suffering acute psychotic episodes may seek help from the emergency staff of a community hospital, the personnel must be especially aware of relevant provisions authorizing short-term detention of such persons. In essence, the statutes require that the patient be either discharged from the hospital following the emergency or granted a timely hearing as specified by the statute.

In a civil commitment the patient must receive a notice of the contemplated proceedings and a statement of the reasons for commitment. Such patients have the right to be present and to be represented by counsel at the hearing, the right to examine and cross-examine witnesses, the right of jury trial, and the right of appeal.[89]

Because psychiatric diagnosis is based on medical impressions and subjective analysis, due process does not mandate that civil commitment proceedings by the state rely on the standard of proof "beyond a reasonable doubt" that is required in criminal proceedings.[90] On the other hand, the standard necessitating a "preponderance of evidence," which is applicable to most civil litigation, does not conform to the substantive dimensions of due process because involuntary hospitalization deprives the patient of liberty, and the risks of an erroneous decision are grave.[91] The Supreme Court has therefore held that an intermediate standard of proof is most likely to balance the rights of the mentally ill with the legitimate concerns of society and is thus consistent with due process. This modified standard is often expressed as requiring "clear, convincing, and unequivocal" evidence of danger to self or others.[92]

With respect to the standard of proof, however, the Court has distinguished between civil commitment of a mentally ill person not charged with a criminal act and a person who has been charged. In *Jones v. United States* the defendant was acquitted in a criminal trial by reason of insanity and then placed in an institution for the mentally ill. The finding of insanity was based on the standard calling for preponderance of evidence, as distinct from that requiring clear and convincing proof. The majority ruling held that the less demanding standard was consistent with due process even if the period of hospital confinement should exceed the term of imprisonment applicable to the initial criminal charge.[93]

Standard of Care and Administration of Medication

Once committed, a patient is dependent on the state and has substantive constitutional rights not only to adequate food, shelter, clothing, and medical care[94] but also to safe physical conditions, reasonable freedom from physical restraints, and rehabilitation or training appropriate to the individual's diagnosis.[95] Officials of state hospitals that fail to implement these duties can be held personally liable.[96]

Minimally adequate medical care and treatment for mentally ill persons has been defined by one federal court as follows:

> In order to render effective care and treatment, a hospital for the mentally ill must not only hire qualified individuals, but must ensure the continuation of their training and education during their employment . . . the court finds there are four standards generally advanced by mental health professionals as essential for minimally adequate treatment: a humane and therapeutic environment; qualified staff in sufficient numbers; an individualized treatment plan for each patient; and planned therapeutic programs and activities. It is against these standards that the conditions at a psychiatric facility must be measured in order to determine whether those operating the facility have failed to provide treatment for those mentally ill individuals involuntarily confined for such purpose in violation of the Fourteenth Amendment of the United States Constitution.[97]

To be especially noted is the need to provide therapy and treatment plans based on the patient's diagnosis and individual needs.

With respect to conditions of confinement and the patient's right to rehabilitation and training, the Supreme Court has held that the Constitution

> only requires that the courts make certain that professional judgment in fact was exercised . . . the appropriate standard [is] whether the defendants' conduct [is] . . . such a substantial departure from accepted

professional judgment, practice, or standards in the care and treatment of this plaintiff, as to demonstrate that the defendants did not base their conduct on a professional judgment.[98]

In the view of the Court this standard "affords the necessary guidance and reflects the proper balance between the legitimate interests of the State and the rights of the involuntarily committed to reasonable conditions of safety and freedom from unreasonable restraints." Because the judiciary is not qualified to second guess experts and professional practitioners, decisions they make are presumptively valid and "liability may be imposed only when the decision by the professional is such a substantial departure from accepted professional judgment, practice or standards as to demonstrate that the person responsible actually did not base the decision on such a judgment."[99] The Court then qualified this standard of liability by observing that a professional practitioner would not be liable if budgetary constraints prevented implementation of customary professional standards.[100]

In several contexts courts have developed the principle that mentally ill persons should not be presumed incompetent and incapable of participating in certain decisions while under treatment. The commitment proceeding is not equivalent to a finding of incompetence. The legal concept of informed consent, discussed at length in Chapter 11, applies to many recommended treatment regimes including the patient's participation in experimental programs in medical research. All competent psychiatric patients, whether voluntary or involuntary, for example, have a right to refuse medication because certain antipsychotic drugs may have unpleasant or even serious side effects. The right of refusal is based either on the substantive constitutional right of privacy as embraced within the concept of due process, or more simply on the common law.[101] The right can be overcome and medications can be forcibly administered only when there are compelling reasons for doing so.

In all jurisdictions, unless an immediate danger or threat of violence exists the patient is entitled to an informal professional determination that medication is necessary, an evaluation of alternatives, and regular review of the recommended course of treatment.[102] In such cases a formal adversary hearing is probably not necessary before administering medication, at least so far as the federal Constitution is concerned. Nor will the Constitution or most states require a specific judicial order authorizing forcible administration of drugs, although a court determination of incompetency and the appointment of a guardian may well be required by local law.

Discharge from Hospital

For most patients, discharge from the hospital presents no significant legal issues. Most discharged patients are of sound mind and do not suffer from a contagious disease; hence, they represent no risk of harm to themselves or others. As soon as they are medically ready, most wish to be at home or at another institution better suited to their need for further care.[103]

It is elementary that patients should not be discharged without a written order from a licensed physician. It is also fundamental that unless the institution is protected by the doctrine of governmental immunity under local state law a hospital, like a physician, can be held liable for abandoning or discharging a patient who is in need of further medical care. The legal test is whether the healthcare provider acted reasonably in the particular case.[104] The standard for what is reasonable is whether the patient's condition is likely to be aggravated by discharge or transfer to another facility.[105] If an unreasonable risk was taken, it does not matter why the hospital discharged a patient still needing further care. Failure by a patient to pay a bill is certainly no justification for discharge. Whenever transfer of patients to a less costly institution is contemplated or encouraged by standards of utilization review, attending physicians must be certain that in their professional judgment the receiving institution is adequately equipped and staffed to care properly for patients given their physical and mental condition.

Several reported cases illustrate the prospect of tort liability when a hospital discharges a patient in need of further care. For example, in *Meiselman v. Crown Heights Hospital* there was liability when the defendant hospital discharged a minor while his legs were in casts and open wounds in the legs were draining.[106] Further professional care at home was known to be necessary, and this was to be arranged and supervised by the chief of the hospital's surgical staff. The home care proved to be inadequate, however, and the patient had to be sent to another hospital. Because the probable need for further care was foreseeable and there was evidence that the motive for discharging the patient was financial, the discharge was held to be unreasonable.

Although patients are to be discharged or given temporary leaves of absence only on the written order of a physician, the decision is not solely a medical matter. In fact the hospital owes the patient a direct duty to exercise reasonable care with respect to its discharge practices and procedures. In a relevant case a physician mistakenly diagnosed a diabetic patient who was near death, stating that the person was suffering from delirium tremens and calling for the sheriff's office to remove the patient. When the patient's estate claimed that premature release was the proximate cause of death it was ruled that the plaintiff was entitled to a trial on material issues of fact relating to breach of the hospital's duty.[107] In the words of the court, "We cannot agree that the hospital operates as a slavish handmaiden to the physicians on its staff it claims it has no responsibility for. Under Alabama law a hospital does have a duty of care to its patients."[108]

If a patient represents a known threat to third persons, the hospital and attending physician can be liable to any person injured by the patient. In a New York case, a patient released from Pilgrim State Mental Hospital assaulted two women on the day of his release. More than a month earlier the attending psychiatrist had convened a commission of three physicians who approved the patient's discharge after evaluating his condition. He was not actually released for more than 40 days, however, because housing and outpatient care had to be arranged for him. During this interval he behaved violently on several occasions and had to be placed under restraint but was nevertheless discharged without further medical evaluation. Because the hospital and the attending physician were on notice that the patient's mental state had apparently deteriorated after the commission approved his release, the failure to reevaluate his condition constituted negligence that was the proximate cause of the injuries suffered by the plaintiffs.[109] Note especially, however, that liability was not imposed simply because of an erroneous medical judgment; the known facts of violent and uncontrollable behavior immediately prior to discharge were the basis for the finding of negligence.

In *Semler v. Psychiatric Institute of Washington, D.C.* a man who pleaded guilty to a charge of abducting a young girl received a suspended prison sentence contingent on continued inpatient treatment at a psychiatric institution.[110] On the later recommendations of his physician and probation officer the court approved his transfer to day care, permitting him to live at home and commute daily to the hospital with his parents. Soon, however, he began living alone and working as a bricklayer's helper, all with the knowledge of his attending physician and the court probation officer but without approval of the court. He then murdered a girl. In a civil suit for damages, the psychiatric facility, the physician, and the probation officer all were liable for transferring the patient to full outpatient status without obtaining the court's approval. Because the court had not authorized the probation officer to approve the transfer, the institution was not protected from liability on the basis of the officer's approval. Further, the officer's unauthorized act constituted a ministerial not a discretionary decision, thus rendering him also personally liable.

Even if a hospital or mental health facility is found not negligent in discharging or temporarily releasing a potentially violent patient, there can be liability if a readily identifiable potential victim suffers foreseeable harm and was not warned of the danger. Depending on the particular circumstances and local tort law, some courts have drawn a distinction between breach of duty to the community at large (negligent discharge) and breach of duty to warn a third party at risk.[111] A more thorough discussion of the latter group of cases appears in Chapter 13.

Programs for home and ambulatory care require that each patient's medical and mental condition be properly evaluated and continually monitored in accordance with the individual's needs. Discharge of a patient to home care also requires that attending physicians and hospital personnel be reasonably careful to instruct the patient and family and to relay medical information to professional persons responsible for the program.[112] Failure to do so would constitute a breach of the hospital's duty. The hospital would also remain vicariously liable for the negligent acts or failures to act of those responsible for continuing care of the patient if they are hospital employees or apparent employees. If the patient's care and treatment are rendered under the jurisdiction of the court, the orders of the court must be strictly followed.

A problem is presented when patients of sound mind insist on leaving the hospital though still in need of care. They cannot be held in the hospital against their will because that would constitute the tort of false imprisonment.[113] Attending physicians should give such patients medical advice and encourage them to remain hospitalized. If they refuse to do so, they must be discharged. In that event the hospital should try to obtain the patient's signature on an appropriately worded release for the medical record. This form should state that the patient was fully aware of the medical reasons for remaining and had been advised not to leave the hospital, the discharge was solely on the patient's own responsibility, and the refusal to stay was a matter of the patient's own free will and volition. Patients of sound mind who insist on leaving the hospital against medical advice may of course refuse to sign the release. If so, they cannot be forced to sign, but the facts should be thoroughly explained in a signed statement by the attending physician, and such entries to the medical record should be witnessed by other competent medical personnel familiar with the situation.

Restraining patients of unsound mind from leaving a hospital has been found permissible if their departure would endanger their health or life[114] or the lives or property of others.[115] On the same grounds patients of sound mind who are suffering from a contagious disease may be detained to protect themselves and others. In fact the hospital has an affirmative duty to the community to refuse to discharge such patients. Restraint in preventing them from leaving the hospital must be reasonable according to the circumstances in each case. It is essential to provide competent medical evidence of the contagious disease or the mental instability of patients detained on either of these grounds.

A patient should never be held in the hospital for failure to pay a bill or required to stay until arrangements for settlement are complete. Such action, at least where force is used or threatened, constitutes false imprisonment and gives the aggrieved patient a cause of action against the hospital.[116]

Unemancipated minors below the age of discretion should be discharged only to their parents, or in the parents' absence to persons known by the hospital to be legally entitled to custody. If the whereabouts of the parents is unknown and there is no court-appointed guardian, steps should be taken to procure a guardian. Social welfare agencies should help the hospital in these situations. If the parents or the parent entitled to custody can be located but for some reason cannot come to the hospital, the patient should be discharged only to someone presenting a written order from the parent.

Emancipated minors old enough to consent for themselves—that is, minors who are earning their own living and are permitted by their parents to retain these earning for their own use—can be discharged from the hospital in the same manner as adults. Emancipation is a matter of agreement between the parent and child; it is a question of fact in each case and does not depend on whether the youth is or is not living at home. In some states emancipation results when a minor marries.

Generally it is legally sound to discharge the infant child of a minor mother to the custody of the mother. The hospital cannot prevent the mother from claiming her child, especially when she intends to retain custody and responsibility for raising the infant. Even if she intends to place the child for private adoption, most states recognize her legal right to do so in accordance with local limitations and restrictions. If the mother does not claim the child herself but requests discharge to a third party, the child should not be discharged except on the recommendation of an approved and legally recognized social service agency handling adoptions. Legal counsel should be consulted for advice consistent with local law.

Utilization Review, PROs, and Managed Care

The role and function of the utilization review committee is to make recommendations on the need and appropriateness of continued hospitalization of individual patients. Utilization review committees should not order the discharge of individual patients. Only the patient's attending physician can authorize discharge or transfer to another healthcare institution. If an in-house review committee should insist on discharge contrary to the professional judgment of the attending physician, and if the patient later suffers harm or injury as the proximate cause of premature release, then the hospital would probably be liable because the utilization review committee would have acted as the agent of the hospital. An attending physician who properly documents the exercise of reasonable care in resisting the committee's order of discharge would not be personally liable to the patient for premature discharge. On the other hand, if an attending doctor should act contrary to professional standards in consenting to a discharge, personal liability would be established.[117]

A review committee should consult with the patient's attending physician before making its final recommendations. Moreover, the impact of the committee's recommendations is primarily financial: when the committee finds that a patient's medical condition no longer warrants continued hospitalization, a third party paying for the care, such as Medicare or Blue Cross–Blue Shield, will frequently discontinue reimbursement for inpatient care. Utilization review is not only mandated by governmental programs financing healthcare but is also required for payment by many private third-party insurance carriers. This mandated review has of course resulted from the ever-increasing cost of care, and it is only one of several techniques for reducing the cost of healthcare.

When review committees find no need for continued hospitalization and recommend discharge or transfer to a less expensive place, patients must normally assume responsibility for payment of costs if they remain at the institution. Attending physicians must carefully explain all this to their patients and the family, and together they must then decide on the future course and place of care. As long as a committee functions within its defined role and exercises good faith consistent with a professionally acceptable utilization review program, individual members of the committee run no significant risk of legal liability for rendering a decision adverse to the patient.[118] In many states, local statutes specifically provide that the members of a utilization review committee shall not be personally liable for damages when they conduct their review in good faith within the confines of the committee's proper functions.

Patients whose medical condition justifies discharge from an acute-care hospital or transfer to a place providing less intensive care have no common law or constitutional right to refuse to leave. Such a patient is a trespasser, and a court of equity will issue an injunction to remove the person from the premises.[119] The courts have reasoned that general hospitals have a duty to reserve their beds and facilities for patients who genuinely need their special services and should not permit a patient to remain when adequate care could be provided elsewhere.

On the other hand, as discussed above, a hospital may not abandon or discharge a patient in need of further care without making appropriate arrangements for that care. Hence, one who needs continuing care—in a nursing home, for example—presents a dilemma for all the parties involved if no appropriate facility is available, especially if the patient is unable to pay continuing hospital charges.

The conflict between economic and human values in such circumstances is illustrated by *Monmouth Medical Center v. State*.[120] At issue were New Jersey's administrative regulations prohibiting reimbursement from the Medicaid program for indigent patients no longer in need of acute hospital care and awaiting transfer to a nursing home. Because of a shortage of beds in local nursing homes the state regulations required the hospital to absorb the cost of continuing care, which it was unwilling to do. Although the purpose of federal Medicaid legislation is to provide financial assistance only for "medically necessary" services, federal regulations require states to furnish services "sufficient in amount, duration, and scope to reasonably achieve [their purpose.]"[121] Given the federal regulations and circumstances that were beyond the hospital's control, the New Jersey Supreme Court held that the state regulations were arbitrary, capricious, and in conflict with the federal legislation. So long as the hospital exercised good faith and reasonable diligence in attempting to place patients in nursing homes, it was legally entitled to reimbursement from Medicaid. In essence the philosophy underlying this decision was that fairness in the particular circumstances required society to absorb the costs of continuing care even if the patient no longer needed the services of a general hospital.

In sharp contrast, however, a later case in the federal courts upheld the statutory right of the federal government to deny Medicare reimbursement to a hospital for a particular patient who no longer required either the care customarily furnished by a general hospital or skilled care in a nursing home.[122] Although beds in a nursing home providing custodial care were not available in the area, this fact was essentially irrelevant because Medicare does not reimburse providers of custodial care.

Payment for care by a public program does not by itself create a property interest protected by the Fourteenth Amendment. A nursing home patient whose care is supported by Medicare or Medicaid therefore has no substantive or procedural due process rights when transfer to another facility is proposed.[123] For example, if a nursing home is no longer certified to care for Medicare or Medicaid patients because it failed to comply with the conditions of participation, transfer of the patient to a certified home is necessary if public benefits are to continue. More frequently, transfer may be recommended when a utilization review determines that a particular patient's medical condition justifies transfer to less costly care. In neither case is the patient entitled to a due process hearing to review the reasons for these administrative and medical decisions.

The Peer Review Improvement Act of 1984, enacted as a part of the Tax Equity and Fiscal Responsibility Act, replaced previous legislation that had established regional Professional Standard Review Organizations (PSROs).[124] The responsibility of the PSRO as expressed in the earlier legislation was to review both the appropriateness and quality of care furnished by institutional providers to beneficiaries of Medicare, Medicaid, and Maternal and Child Health Care programs.[125] The 1984 legislation reaffirmed the need for peer review and created in turn professional review organizations (PROs) aimed at cost containment and implementation of the prospective payment system adopted in 1983 as the basis for reimbursing Medicare providers. Each area-wide PRO enters into a contract with the Department of Health and Human Services and is charged with reviewing the necessity, appropriateness, and quality of care furnished Medicare patients. The contract sets forth the cost-containment objectives for each PRO and specifies the criteria for the relevant quality of care. Because hospital admission patterns and standards of medical practice differ among geographical areas, the objectives of utilization review and the criteria for quality of care also differ from region to region.

In general the legislative goals are to reduce the number of unnecessary and inappropriate hospital admissions and to encourage ambulatory or outpatient care. Each PRO is expected to conduct review of admissions and identify groups of patients whose diagnosis or contemplated treatment indicates that they could be safely cared for as ambulatory patients. Each PRO is also empowered to target specific objectives for reducing inappropriate admissions in its geographic region and to identify unacceptable admission patterns in use by particular institutions and medical practitioners. PROs have the additional task of validating the diagnosis-related group (DRG) classification assigned to each hospital patient.

To measure the quality of care furnished Medicare patients the PRO has these specific responsibilities:

- ensuring that patients with certain diagnoses receive adequate medical services, especially where appropriate facilities are available but are often underused;
- reviewing hospital readmissions caused by previous substandard care;
- identifying instances of unnecessary surgery; and
- reducing the number of avoidable deaths.

To achieve these objectives PROs develop treatment protocols applicable to particular diagnoses and set specific, attainable statistical goals. In addition to performing these functions on behalf of the federal government, PROs are statutorily authorized to contract with other public and private third parties paying healthcare costs for the purpose of conducting similar studies of utilization and quality.

A PRO has the power to deny reimbursement to a Medicare provider for unnecessary or inappropriate care.[126] In certain circumstances the review organization may also recommend penalties to providers, ranging from monetary fines to exclusion from the Medicare program.

The increasing emphasis on cost control and reducing utilization of acute care hospitals was in large measure the impetus for development of managed care plans in the mid-1980s and their increasing popularity in the 1990s. Such plans use primary care physicians as "gatekeepers" to determine the appropriate point of service for the patient's particular condition. Preauthorization from the managed care plan (an HMO, for example) is generally required before a patient can be admitted. If admission is approved, the patient cannot remain hospitalized longer than a predetermined period set by the plan unless additional approval is obtained.

In addition, some managed care plans pay physicians by means of a "capitated" rate: that is, a set amount per enrolled individual per month. The physicians are then obligated to treat all enrolled persons who present for treatment, regardless of the cost that is incurred. Accordingly, the physicians in a capitated plan assume the risk that the costs of treatment of all patients in a month may exceed the sum of their capitated payment. In theory, such a system encourages wellness and prevention activities and treatment of illnesses in the most inexpensive manner possible (for example, as outpatients or by use of physician assistants and nurse practitioners).

As a legal matter, managed care plans give rise to significant issues when a patient is refused admission to a hospital or is discharged prematurely and injury results. As has already been discussed, it is ultimately the physician's responsibility to decide what is in the patient's best interest, and a number of cases have held the physician liable for admission or discharge decisions that were motivated by a managed care plan's cost control policies.[127] On the other hand, some courts have taken the view that if the managed care plan is in effect dictating whether and for how long a patient can be hospitalized, it must assume liability for decisions that have adverse effect on patient care.[128]

In addition, state legislatures have begun to consider bills that will hold managed care organizations liable for coverage denials and utilization review decisions that adversely affect patient care. Texas, for example, enacted a law in 1997 that allows beneficiaries of health plans to bring suit against plans that do not exercise "ordinary prudence" under the circumstances.[129] The law was immediately challenged, and although parts of it were held to conflict with the federal Employee Retirement and Income Security Act (ERISA), the portions relating to beneficiaries' lawsuits were upheld.[130]

As with the utilization decisions of managed care plans, the activities or PROs significantly affect the common law of malpractice liability for both medical care institutions and professional practitioners. In the first place, the prospective payment system (reimbursement on the basis of diagnosis-related groups) may encourage the premature discharge of an inpatient at the risk of the legal exposure.

Second, denying a person admission as an inpatient and performing surgery or certain medical procedures in facilities for ambulatory care may also increase the risks to the patient and accordingly the risk of claims for damages. Professional criteria and protocols for specific medical conditions and diagnoses may well be accepted by the courts as evidence of current professional standards. Proof of deviation from the PRO criteria and treatment protocols would therefore certainly encourage and aid the plaintiff in a malpractice case. On the other hand, adherence to the criteria will in most circumstances support the position of the defendants by evidencing conformance to contemporary professional standards.

It follows that careful documentation of adherence to the specified criteria should be in the medical record of each patient. For the same reasons any deviation from the criteria should be documented and explained. Reviews should then help to identify, for example, cases of unnecessary or inappropriate surgery as well as avoidable medical and surgical complications. Reducing the number of such cases by means of review would also help to reduce malpractice claims. Finally, managed care, PRO reviews, and other efforts toward reducing utilization should encourage institutions to improve their risk management and quality assurance programs. From the defendants' viewpoint, effective programs of this nature can have a beneficial effect with respect to malpractice liability.

Notes

1. Hill v. Ohio County, 468 S.W.2d 306 (Ky. 1971), *cert. denied*, 404 U.S. 1041 (1972) (a pregnant patient had no right to be admitted to a hospital when no

emergency was apparent); Fabian v. Matzko, 236 Pa. Super. 267, 344 A.2d 569 (1975); *Cf.* Federal legislation prohibits denial of services to persons needing emergency care and to those in active labor. 42 U.S.C. § 1395dd.

2. Norwood Hosp. v. Howton, 32 Ala. App. 375, 26 So. 2d 427 (1946).

3. Harper v. Virginia Bd. of Elections, 383 U.S. 663 (1966).

4. Douglas v. California, 372 U.S. 353 (1963).

5. Shapiro v. Thompson, 394 U.S. 618 (1969) (one-year residency requirement to establish eligibility for state welfare benefits is unconstitutional); Memorial Hosp. v. Maricopa County, 415 U.S. 250 (1974) (one-year residency in county to establish eligibility for nonemergency medical care at county's expense is unconstitutional).

6. San Antonio Indep. School Dist. v. Rodriquez, 411 U.S. 1 (1973).

7. *Id.*, 411 U.S. at 20.

8. Nixon v. Herndon, 273 U.S. 536 (1927); Nixon v. Condon, 286 U.S. 73 (1932); Brown v. Board of Educ. of Topeka, 347 U.S. 483 (1954).

9. Frontiero v. Richardson, 411 U.S. 677 (1973).

10. New Jersey Welfare Rights Org. v. Cahill, 411 U.S. 619 (1973).

11. Plyler v. Doe, 457 U.S. 202 (1982), *reh'g denied*, 458 U.S. 1131 (1982) (although free public education is not a "fundamental right" and alienage does not constitute a "suspect class," Texas law barring certain children from public schools is unconstitutional).

12. The cases cited in notes 8, 9, 10, and others, especially those dealing with classifications by gender, have seemingly used a "heightened" or "intermediate" form of scrutiny requiring that there be "a substantial relationship to an important governmental purpose" to pass constitutional muster. The precise differences between the standard of "minimal scrutiny" and "intermediate scrutiny" are not clear and are subject to debate among legal scholars.

13. Shapiro v. Thompson, 394 U.S. 618 (1969).

14. Dandridge v. Williams, 397 U.S. 471 (1970).

15. Maher v. Roe, 432 U.S. 464 (1977).

16. Harris v. McRae, 448 U.S. 297 (1980).

17. *See also* Brooks v. Walker County Hosp. Dist., 688 F.2d 334 (1982), *cert. denied*, 462 U.S. 1105 (1983) (proper to dismiss federal court suit by indigents contending that they were entitled to free healthcare services under Texas Constitution pending clarification of state legal issues).

18. Spivey v. Barry, Mayor, District of Columbia, 665 F.2d 1222 (1981) (closing a medical clinic serving indigents did not violate either statutory or constitutional rights).

19. A lawsuit challenging the terminations had been settled by a stipulated court order. The parties agreed that treatment would be continued so long as the patient conformed to certain conditions; however, the patient repeatedly failed to meet the conditions.

20. Payton v. Weaver, 131 Cal. App. 3d 38, 182 Cal. Rptr. 225 (1982).

21. CAL. HEALTH & SAFETY CODE § 1317 (West 1979). See discussion in Chapter 10, "Emergency Care."

22. *See also* Modla v. Parker, 495 P.2d 494, 17 Ariz. App. 54 (1972) (in absence of

proof that treatment was actively retarded or condition worsened, there was no breach of duty when hospital discharged disruptive patient).

23. Shaprio v. Thompson, 394 U.S. 618 (1969); Memorial Hosp. v. Maricopa County, 415 U.S. 250 (1974).

24. See discussion and case citations in Chapter 10, *infra*.

25. Idaho Falls Consol. Hosps., Inc. v. Bingham County Bd. of County Comm'rs, 102 Idaho 838, 642 P.2d 553 (1982).

26. St. Joseph's Hosp. and Medical Center v. Maricopa County, 142 Ariz. 94, 688 P.2d 986 (1984).

27. Washoe County, Nev. V. Wittenberg & St. Mary's Hosp., 676 P.2d 808 (1984).

28. Shands Teaching Hosp. & Clinics of the Univ. of Fla. v. Council of the City of Jacksonville, 398 So. 2d 907 (Fla. App. 1981).

29. RESTATEMENT OF RESTITUTION § 116 (1937). The right of a competent person in police custody or prisoner to reject treatment is beyond the scope of this discussion.

30. Brinkman v. City of Indianapolis, 141 Ind. App. 662, 231 N.E.2d 169 (1967). *See also* Hart v. County of Orange, 254 Cal. App. 2d 302 (1967); Porter v. County of Cook, 42 Ill. App. 3d 287, 355 N.E.2d 561 (1976).

31. Estelle v. Gamble, 429 U.S. 97, *reh'g denied,* 429 U.S. 1066 (1977) (Eighth Amendment is violated by "deliberate indifference to serious medical needs"). *See also* Bivens v. Six Unknown Federal Narcotics Agents, 403 U.S. 388 (1971) (persons subjected to constitutional violations by federal officials have right to recover damages against the official).

32. Youngberg v. Romero, 457 U.S. 307 (1982) (involuntarily committed mental patient entitled to medical care).

33. Maher v. Roe, 432 U.S. 464 (1977); Harris v. McRae, 448 U.S. 297 (1980).

34. *E.g.,* CONN. GEN. STAT. § 18-7 (Supp. 1985); *see also* Hillcrest Medical Center v. State of Okla., *ex rel.* Dep't of Corrections, 675 P.2d 432 (Okla. 1983) (county liable for medical expenses of convicted murderer injured in automobile accident while in county's custody).

35. Idaho Code § 20-209 (1979); *but see* Sisters of Third Order of St. Francis v. County of Tazewell, 122 Ill. App. 3d 605, 461 N.E.2d 1064 (1984) (county not liable for care furnished arrestee in custody of municipal police).

36. ALASKA STAT. § 33.30.050 (1982).

37. MD. ANN. CODE art. 27, § 698 (Supp. 1985). *See also* Fla. Stat. § 901.35, which establishes a hierarchy of responsibility for medical expenses provided to "any person ill, wounded, or otherwise injured during or at the time of arrest. . . ." The first tier of responsibility includes (1) insurance, (2) the patient, and (3) a financial settlement relating to the cause of the injury or illness; only if those sources are not available may the provider seek reimbursement from governmental authority. (Based on the "during or at the time of arrest" language, some law enforcement officials attempt to avoid governmental responsibility by not formally arresting the suspect until after treatment is rendered.)

38. *See* Comment, *City of Revere v. Massachusetts General Hospital: Government Responsibility for an Arrestee's Medical Care,* 9 AM. J.L. & MED., 361, 369–70 (1983–84).

39. 463 U.S. 239 (1983).

40. Massachusetts Gen. Hosp. v. City of Revere, 385 Mass. 772, 484 N.E.2d 185 (1982). *Cf.* Spicer v. Williamson, 191 N.C. 487, 132 S.E.291 (1926) (public has duty to pay for medical treatment rendered a prisoner).

41. *Maher, supra* note 33.

42. *Harris, supra* note 33.

43. City of Revere v. Massachusetts Gen. Hosp., 463 U.S. 239 (1983).

44. 171 So. 2d 202 (Fla. Dist. Ct. App. 1965).

45. Parr v. Palmyra Hosp., 139 Ga. App. 457, 228 S.E.2d 596 (1976) (Georgia statute requiring consent to medical and surgical treatment applies to hospitals as well as physicians; if the consent is in writing, it is "conclusively presumed" to be valid in the absence of fraudulent misrepresentation of material facts).

46. People & C. v. Watt, 462 N.Y.S.2d 389, 118 Misc. 2d 930 (1983) (hospital bailee had no authority to release patient's clothes to police without consent).

47. MICH. COMP. LAWS ANN. § 600.540 (Supp. 1985); MICH STAT. ANN. § 27A.5040.

48. See Chapter 3, pp 67–69, *supra*.

49. Wheeler v. St. Joseph Hosp., 63 Cal. App. 3d 345, 133 Cal. Rptr. 775 (1976); Burton v. Mt. Helix Gen. Hosp., Cal. Ct. App. 4th Dist., Div. 1 (Feb. 24, 1976) (opinion upholding arbitration agreement subsequently decertified for publication, thus nullifying case as precedent); Moore v. Fragatos, 116 Mich. App. 179, 321 N.W.2d 781 (1982) (hospital's motion for accelerated judgment should be denied when it fails to establish by clear and convincing evidence that patient was informed and understood arbitration agreement); Roberts v. McNamara-Warren Community Hosp., 138 Mich. App. 691, 360 N.W.2d 279 (1984) (neither minor patient nor mother was given the information brochure required by law).

50. 17 Cal. 3d 699, 131 Cal. Rptr. 882, 552 P.2d 1178 (1976); *see also* Doyle v. Guiliucci, 62 Cal. 2d 606, 43 Cal. Rptr. 697, 401 P.2d 1 (1965) (parent can bind minor to arbitrate where such is a condition to voluntary membership in group health plan).

51. 42 U.S.C. § 2000 a-e (1964).

52. 42 U.S.C. § 2000 d-1 (1964).

53. 45 U.S.C. §§ 80.1-80.13 (1997).

54. 42 U.S.C. §§ 291-291n (1944).

55. *E.g.,* N.M. STAT. ANN. § 28-7-1 (F) (1983).

56. For example, the Michigan Civil Rights Law, Mich. Stat. Ann. §§ 28.343–.344 (1962) applies to places of "public accommodation." The attorney general has ruled that this does not include private nursing homes. 1957–58 MICH. ATT'Y GEN. BIENNIAL REP. Vol. I, at 349.

57. MICH. COMP. LAWS § 333.20201 (Supp. 1985).

58. *See, e.g.,* OKLA. STAT. ANN. § 68-2405 (j) (1966).

59. MONT. REV. CODES ANN. § 50-5-105(2) (1985).

60. 323 F.2d 959 (4th Cir. 1963), *cert. denied,* 376 U.S. 938 (1964).

61. Similarly, in Flagler Hosp., Inc. v. Hayling, 344 F.2d 950 (5th Cir. 1965), the court enjoined the hospital, which had received a Hill-Burton grant, from denying patients admission on the basis of race, and it retained jurisdiction for

such further orders as might be shown necessary by actual experience or sound medical reasons with respect to separate rooms and other facilities.

62. 329 F.2d 710 (4th Cir. 1974). The *Simkins* and *Eaton* cases do not of course create a constitutional right in the patient to be admitted. They simply prohibit discriminatory conduct. *See* Stanturf v. Sipes, 335 F.2d 224 (8th Cir. 1964), *cert. denied*, 379 U.S. 977 (1965).

63. Pub. L. No. 79-725; codified as amended 42 U.S.C. § 291-(o)-1 (1982).

64. 42 U.S.C. § 291c (e) (1982).

65. *Id.*

66. 42 U.S.C. §§ 291c (a), (e) (1982).

67. Cook v. Ochsner Found. Hosp., 319 F. Supp. 603, 11 A.L.R.3d 677 (E.D. La. 1970). *Cook* relied on the earlier case of Gomez v. Florida State Employment Serv., 417 F.2d 569 (5th Cir. 1969), which had held that migrant workers had standing to enforce certain provisions of the Wagner-Peyser Act. To the same effect as *Cook* was Organized Migrants in Community Action, Inc. v. James Archer Smith Hosp., 325 F. Supp. 268 (S.D. Fla. 1971). *See also* Euresti v. Stenner, 458 F.2d 1115 (10th Cir. 1972); Saine v. Hospital Auth. of Hall County, 502 F.2d 1033 (5th Cir. 1974).

68. Cook v. Ochsner Found. Hosp., 61 F.R.D. 354 (E.D. La. 1972).

69. *Id.*

70. 42 C.F.R. § 53.111(d)(2) (1984).

71. Cook v. Ochsner Found. Hosps., 61 F.R.D. 354 (E.D. La. 1972).

72. 42 C.F.R. § 124.603(b) (1) (1984).

73. Newsom v. Vanderbilt Univ. Hosp., 453 F. Supp. 401 (M.D. Tenn. 1978).

74. *Id*; Newsom v. Vanderbilt Univ. Hosp., No. 75-126, slip op. (M.D. Tenn. 1979), *aff'd in part, rev'd in part, modified in part*, 653 F.2d 1100 (6th Cir. 1981).

75. 42 C.F.R. §§ 53.111(I), (j) (1984).

76. Cook v. Ochsner Found. Hosp., 559 F.2d 968 (5th Cir. 1977); Corum v. Beth Israel Med. Center, 373 F. Supp. 550 (S.D.N.Y. 1974); Newsom v. Vanderbilt Univ. Hosp., 453 F. Supp. 401 (M.D. Tenn. 1978).

77. *Cook, supra* note 76; Lugo v. Simon, 426 F. Supp. 28 (N.D. Ohio 1976); *Newsom, supra* note 76 (20-year limit on the uncompensated-care obligation dates, however, from final approval of federal funds rather than from completion of construction, while the community-service obligation is of indefinite obligation).

78. *Corum, supra* note 76.

79. 42 U.S.C. §§ 300o–300t (1982).

80. Cook v. Ochsner Found. Hosp., 559 F.2d 968 (5th Cir. 1977) (20-year limit on uncompensated care obligations is valid on projects funded prior to 1975).

81. *E.g.,* Lowen v. Hilton, 142 Colo. 200, 351 P.2d 881 (1960); Maben v. Rankin, 55 Cal. 2d 139, 10 Cal. Rptr. 353, 358 P.2d 681 (1961); Geddes v. Daughters of Charity, 348 F.2d 144 (5th Cir. 1965); Jillson v. Caprio, 181 F.2d 523 (D.C. Cir. 1950).

82. *See, e.g.,* Jackson v. Indiana, 406 U.S. 715 (1972); Humphrey v. Cady, 405 U.S. 504 (1972).

83. Lewis v. Donahue, 437 F. Supp. 112 (W.D. Okla. 1977) (patient released from state hospital and transferred to outpatient status may not be recommitted

without due process protections); *see also In re* Anderson, 74 Cal. App. 3d 38, 140 Cal. Rptr. 546 (1977).

84. People v. Paiz, 43 Colo. App. 352, 603 P.2d 976 (1979).

85. O'Connor v. Donaldson, 422 U.S. 653 (1975); 42 U.S.C. § 1983.

86. Addington v. Texas, 441 U.S. 418 (1979).

87. *Id.*

88. Misdiagnosis standing alone does not constitute negligence or malpractice. When a patient or third party alleges that a physician's negligent diagnosis was the proximate cause of damage the plaintiff must carry the burden of proof and show by expert witness testimony that the defendant departed from generally recognized standards of practice. *See* Tobias v. Manhattan Eye and Ear Hosp., 283 N.Y.S.2d 398, 28 A.D.2d 972 (1967), *aff'd,* 23 N.Y.2d 724, 296 N.Y.S.2d 368 (1968).

89. Lessard v. Schmidt, 349 F. Supp. 1078 (E.D. Wis. 1972), *vacated,* 414 U.S. 473 (1974), *on remand,* 413 F. Supp. 1318 (1976); Doremus v. Furrell, 407 F. Supp. 509 (D.C. Neb. 1975).

90. Addington v. Texas, 441 U.S. 418.

91. *Id.*

92. *Id.* Due process, however, does not require the states to use the same uniform standard of proof in civil commitment proceedings. Some states have, in fact, adopted the criminal-law standard by statute or judicial decision. To use a standard higher than constitutionally required is permissible.

93. 463 U.S. 354 (1983).

94. Youngberg v. Romero, 457 U.S. 307 (1982); Wyatt v. Stickney, 344 F. Supp. 387 (M.D. Ala. 1972); 344 F. Supp. 373 (M.D. Ala. 1972), *aff'd in part, remanded in part,* 503 F.2d 1305 (5th Cir. 1974), *enforcing* 325 F. Supp. 781 (M.D. Ala. 1971).

95. Youngberg v. Romero, 457 U.S. 307 (mentally retarded person).

96. *Id.*

97. Rome v. Fireman, 473 F. Supp. 92, 104, 119 (N.D. Ohio 1979); *see also* Ohlinger v. Watson, 652 F.2d 775 (9th Cir. 1980).

98. *Youngberg, supra* note 95, at 314, quoting and adopting the view of concurring Chief Judge Seitz, Court of Appeals, Third Circuit, 644 F.2d 147, 178 (1980).

99. *Id.* at 321.

100. *Id.* at 323; *see also* Chasse v. Banas, 119 N.H. 93, 399 A.2d 608 (1979) (by enacting statute granting mentally ill patients a right to adequate treatment the state waives claim of sovereign immunity).

101. Rennie v. Klein, 653 F.2d 836 (3d Cir. 1981), *vacated,* 458 U.S. 1119, *on remand,* 720 F.2d 266 (1983); Davis v. Hubbard, 506 F. Supp. 915 (N.D. Ohio 1980); Rogers v. Okin, 634 F.2d 650 (1st Cir. 1980), *vacated,* 457 U.S. 291; Goedecke v. State, 198 Colo. 407, 603 P.2d 123 (1979) (common law recognizes mental patient's right to refuse medication).

102. Rennie v. Klein, 653 F.2d 836 (3d Cir. 1981).

103. Discharges and transfers to other hospitals of patients who are brought to the emergency room entail particular legal hazards, however. See the following chapter.

104. Parvi v. City of Kingston, 394 N.Y.S.2d 161, 41 N.Y.2d 553, 362 N.E.2d 960

(1977) (city potentially liable in negligence when intoxicated persons attempting to cross New York Thruway were struck by car after being abandoned by police in rural area).

105. Modla v. Parker, 17 Ariz. App. 54, 495 P.2d 494, *cert. denied*, 409 U.S. 1038 (1972) (hospital entitled to summary judgment in suit alleging wrongful discharge where there was no evidence that release retarded treatment or worsened patient's condition).

106. 285 N.Y. 389, 34 N.E.2d 367 (1941); *see also* Anderson v. Moore, 202 Neb. 452, 275 N.W.2d 842 (1979).

107. Morrison v. Washington County, Ala., 700 F.2d 678 (11th Cir. 1983), *cert. denied*, 464 U.S. 864 (1983).

108. *Id.*, 700 F.2d at 683. See Chapter 14 for a discussion of staff physician as an independent contractor.

109. Homere v. State of N.Y., 370 N.Y.S.2d 246, 48 A.D.2d 422 (1975).

110. 538 F.2d 121 (4th Cir. 1976), *cert. denied*, 429 U.S. 827 (1976).

111. Chrite v. United States, 564 F. Supp. 341 (E.D. Mich. 1983) (Veterans Administration could be liable for failure to warn patient's mother-in-law of threats of violence). *Cf.* Leedy v. Hartnett & Lebanon Valley Veterans Admin. Hosp., 510 F. Supp. 1125 (1981), *aff'd*, 676 F.2d 686 (1982) (Veterans Administration owed no duty to warn plaintiff's family when discharged mental patient posed no greater damage to plaintiff than to community at large).

112. Kyslinger v. United States, 406 F. Supp. 800 (W.D. Pa. 1975), *aff'd*, 547 F.2d 1161 (3d Cir. 1977) (no evidence to support allegations that patient with polycystic kidney disease and spouse were given inadequate information and training in use of home hemodialysis unit at time of discharge from hospital).

113. Cook v. Highland Hosp., 168 N.C. 250, 84 S.E. 352 (1915); *see generally* False Imprisonment in Nursing Home, 4 A.L.R.2d 449.

114. Marcus v. Liebman, 59 Ill. App. 3d 337, 375 N.E.2d 486 (1978) (psychologically disturbed patient entitled to jury trial on issue of whether her suspicion that force was threatened was "reasonable" thereby constituting tort of false imprisonment); *see also* Rice v. Mercy Hosp. Corp., 275 So. 2d 566 (Fla. App. 1973).

115. Paradies v. Benedictine Hosp., 431 N.Y.S.2d 175 (1980), *appeal dismissed*, 435 N.Y.S.2d 982 (1980) (proper to dismiss action against hospital and physician when patient, voluntarily admitted to general hospital for psychiatric evaluation, left hospital contrary to medical advice and subsequently committed suicide; at time of discharge there was no apparent danger to patient or others).

116. Gadsden v. Hamilton, 212 Ala. 531, 103 So. 553 (1925); Bedard v. Notre Dame, 89 R.I. 195, 151 A.2d 690 (1959). *Cf.* Baile v. Miami Valley Hosp., 8 Ohio Misc. 193, 221 N.E.2d 217 (1966) (no false imprisonment when no threat of force against mother of infant patient existed and patient was unaware of detention).

117. Wickline v. State of Cal., 183 Cal. App. 3d 1175, 228 Cal. Rptr. 661 (1986), *reh'g granted*, 727 P.2d 753, 231 Cal. Rptr. 560 (1986) (patient's physician determines medically necessary course of treatment and duration of acute care hospitalization in accordance with prevailing professional standards).

118. *Id.*, 228 Cal Rptr. at 671 (third-party payors are "legally accountable when

medically inappropriate decisions result from defects in design or implementation of cost containment mechanisms . . .").

119. Jersey City Medical Center v. Halstead, 169 N.J. Super. 22, 404 A.2d 44 (1979); Lucy Webb Hayes Nat'l School v. Geoghegan, 281 F. Supp. 116 (D.C.D.C. 1967).

120. 80 N.J. 299, 403 A.2d 487 (1979), *cert. denied,* 444 U.S. 942 (1979).

121. 42 C.F.R. § 440.230(b) (1984).

122. Monmouth Medical Center v. Harris, 646 F.2d 74 (3d Cir. 1981).

123. O'Bannon v. Town Court Nursing Center, 447 U.S. 773 (1980) (patient has no protected constitutional property interest in receiving public benefits in a particular facility); *see also* Blum v. Yaretsky, 457 U.S. 991 (1982) (utilization review decisions are made by private physicians and nursing home administrators; thus there is no "state action" rendering Fourteenth Amendment inapplicable).

124. Social Security Amendments of 1972, Pub. L. No. 92-603, codified as 42 U.S.C.A. §§ 1320c–1320c-13 (1983 & Supp. 1987).

125. *See* Association of Am. Physicians & Surgeons v. Weinberger, 395 F. Supp. 125 (N.D. Ill. 1975), *aff'd,* 423 U.S. 975 (1975) (PROFESSIONAL STANDARDS REVIEW STATUTE is constitutional and does not violate due process clause of Fifth Amendment).

126. 42 U.S.C.A. § 1320c-3 (1983).

127. *See, e.g.,* Wickline v. State, 192 Cal. App. 3d 1630, 239 Cal. Rptr. 810 (1986) *and* Corcoran v. United Health Care, Inc., 965 F.2d 1321 (5th Cir. 1992), *cert. denied* 113 S.Ct. 812 (1992) (ERISA preempts a claim against the health plan when the plan's utilization review agent refused to certify the plaintiff's hospital stay).

128. *See, e.g.,* Bauman v. U.S. Healthcare Inc., 1 F. Supp. 2d 420 (D.N.J. 1998) *and* Murphy v. Arizona Bd. of Medical Exam'rs, 190 Ariz. 441, 949 P. 2d 530 (1997).

129. Tex. Civ. Pract. & Rem. §§ 88.001 *et seq.*

130. Corporate Health Ins. Inc. v. Texas Dept. of Ins., 12 F. Supp. 2d 597 (S.D. Tex. 1998).

EMERGENCY CARE

A s has already been mentioned, patients ordinarily do not have a legal
right to be admitted to a hospital, whether private and voluntary or
governmental, or to be seen and treated in an outpatient clinic. That is,
as a general rule the hospital has no common law or statutory duty to admit
or even serve all who apply for service, except in a medical emergency.

With respect to some hospitals owned and operated by government in
some jurisdictions, however, the local statutes may be construed as creating
a right among some classes of individuals to be served by and admitted to
the facility. Statutes creating certain governmental hospitals and specifying the
purposes to be accomplished by the hospital may define or designate groups or
classes of persons to be served: for example, the population of a given county or
patients suffering from a particular disease. From such statutes a duty to serve
emergency patients might well be implied. The preceding chapter reviewed
these statutes and the extent to which particular patients have the legal right
to be admitted in particular circumstances.

The general rule denying the patient a legal right to be admitted may
be changed if the hospital has voluntarily undertaken by contract to serve
a defined population. Such a contract could be between the hospital and
an identifiable class or group of patients or between the hospital and, for
example, an employer (the latter's employees being designated beneficiaries of
the undertaking).[1] Such contracts are becoming more prevalent in the current
climate of managed care, and an obligation created by an express contract
must be performed. A duty to serve emergency patients is included among
such obligations.

One route of attack on the rule that there is no duty to serve arises
from the maintenance and operation of the hospital's emergency room. It
is perfectly evident that the American public expects service from the nation's hospitals and their medical staffs. Initially through the mechanism of
private lawsuits, judicial decisions established that the hospital's emergency
department has a duty to evaluate all patients who apply for service and to
render emergency care to those in need. Subsequently, federal law codified this
duty in the Emergency Medical Treatment and Active Labor Act,[2] discussed
below. Hospitals and their staffs must thus be organized and prepared to meet
the public's expectations as expressed in the judicial decisions and the federal
statute to be reviewed here. Recent decisions of influential courts appear to
be consistent with the philosophy that healthcare at the time of an emergency
is a right and must be provided regardless of ability to pay.

Considered below are situations in which patients appear at the hospital, frequently at an emergency unit, requesting examination and treatment. Many such persons have no private physician on the hospital's medical staff, or they come when their private physicians are unavailable. The hospital's legal responsibilities to all patients seeking emergency treatment depend on whether the situation is governed by statutory or common law, whether the institution has an emergency department, and finally on the apparent condition of the patient at the time.

Initially the question is whether a hospital must maintain a facility for emergency care. If it must, or if it voluntarily maintains such a facility, the issue is then the extent of the institution's duty to the patient.

Necessity for Emergency Care Facilities

The common law does not impose a duty on a community hospital or health-care institution to provide treatment and care for emergency patients. This means that a hospital, whether governmental or private, generally need not have any special room, equipment, or personnel for the care of those who suddenly fall ill or who are victims of an accident.

Approximately half the states, however, have statutes that either directly or indirectly require certain categories of hospitals to maintain emergency care facilities or arrange for care. These requirements may be found in some states' hospital licensure statutes. A Wisconsin statute, for example, provides that county hospitals in counties having a population of 500,000 or more "may establish and maintain . . . an emergency unit or department for treatment . . . of persons in the county who may meet with accidents or be suddenly afflicted with illness not contagious. . . ."[3] There is an implied duty not only to maintain an emergency facility, but also to treat emergency patients, although the statute authorizes safe removal to the patient's home or another hospital and thus does not require formal admission of all such patients. Moreover, the statute permits the county to provide this emergency care by contract with a private hospital. The point is that the statute obliges local county governments of populous counties to provide emergency care either directly or by contract with some other capable agent.

In Illinois a statute, applicable to both private and governmental hospitals where surgery is performed, requires the hospital to extend emergency care.[4] All hospitals receiving payments from the Pennsylvania Department of Public Welfare must have at least one licensed doctor or resident intern on call at all times.[5] New York provides that operating certificates can be revoked for any general hospital refusing to provide emergency care.[6] In practical effect such statutes—and the rules and regulations of hospital licensure that attempt to ensure that emergency care will be available—require establishment and maintenance of an emergency room. Violation will be penalized according to the particular statute, perhaps by a criminal sanction, revocation of license, or both. Moreover, and this is more significant perhaps than the usual criminal sanction, violation of such a statute could be the basis of a private civil lawsuit for damages.

These statutes represent a trend toward requiring hospitals to establish and maintain facilities and staff for emergency care. The public expects ready and convenient access to a hospital emergency department, but it does not follow that *all* general hospitals should be legally required to maintain relatively expensive capabilities for emergency care.[7]

Duty to Treat and Aid

Under Common Law

By the traditional common-law rule, persons have no duty to aid another in peril unless their own activities have placed the other in danger. (It was sometimes said, "No one has a duty to stop a blind man from walking off a cliff.") This doctrine, even though contrary to the morals and ethics of the medical profession, has been applied to physicians and hospitals as well as to lay persons. Hence, a physician has no common-law responsibility to respond to a call for help in the absence of a preexisting physician-patient relationship.[8]

Illustrating the common law is the case of *Childs v. Weis.*[9] A pregnant patient presented herself at the hospital emergency room at 2 a.m. apparently suffering from bleeding and believing she was in labor. The nurse on duty examined her and telephoned the staff physician on call. The doctor, who was a private practitioner, told the nurse to have the patient telephone her private physician for advice. As a matter of policy the hospital did not require physicians on call to see and examine all emergency room patients. The nurse apparently mistook the message and told the patient to go to her private doctor, located some miles away. After she had left the hospital and was still en route the baby was born but lived only 12 hours.

In a suit against the physician the court held that dismissal of the action was proper because a doctor's duty to exercise reasonable care depended on a contract with the patient, and no such contract and hence no duty to treat existed here. In other words, no doctor-patient relationship had been established; accordingly, the physician was not liable for even an arbitrary refusal to respond to the call, nor was the doctor liable for the nurse's negligence, if any, and the hospital was also not liable because it was a county hospital performing a governmental function and was accordingly entitled to "sovereign immunity" by a Texas law in effect at the time. With respect to the personal liability of the nurse for negligence, however, certain factual questions justified submitting the case to a jury.[10] The decision dismissing the action against the doctor in *Childs* might well have been different had the hospital's bylaws or rules and regulations required the staff physician on call to evaluate the condition of patients presenting themselves at an emergency room. In that event the physician would have had a contractual duty to respond, which in turn would have been enforceable by the patient. The bylaws and contractual arrangements of most hospitals today accomplish that result.

As mentioned previously, the only common-law exception to the rule that in the absence of a contract there is no duty to aid another in peril is when the person who fails to aid was responsible for placing the victim in peril. In such circumstances failure to aid could result in liability for breach of duty. Some cases have found liability only when negligent conduct placed the plaintiff in danger; other cases have found defendants liable for failing to aid no matter how they had endangered the plaintiff.

Similarly, by application of the early common law, a hospital did not need to employ its facilities and staff to aid persons requesting diagnosis and treatment. Recent court cases and statutes, however, have changed this position, at least with respect to hospitals maintaining emergency departments.

Judicial Decisions

Numerous court decisions beginning in the 1960s began to establish a duty to aid under certain circumstances without benefit of statute. In *Williams v. Hospital Authority of Hall County*, for example, a Georgia appellate court held that a governmental hospital that had an emergency department must extend aid to an accident victim who had applied for treatment of a fracture.[11] The court stressed that the defendant hospital was a public, tax-supported institution, and it expressly rejected the argument that the hospital had an absolute right to refuse to provide emergency services. The judge described as "repugnant" a refusal to serve where emergency care was needed and available.

The Missouri Supreme Court extended the same philosophy to a private hospital. In *Stanturf v. Sipes* a patient with frozen feet was refused treatment and admission to a private hospital. The initial reason was the patient's inability to pay an advance cash deposit, but the hospital maintained its refusal even after friends offered the deposit. The hospital apparently was doubtful that further payment could be ensured. The delay in care necessitated the amputation of both feet. In the court's opinion it was an error for the trial court to grant summary judgment for the hospital on the basis of the traditional rule that the defendant could refuse to admit the plaintiff without assigning a reason.[12] Rather, the plaintiff was entitled to a trial on the factual issues of whether an emergency existed, whether aid had been undertaken, and whether reasonable care had been exercised. Likewise, in an Arizona case, *Guerrero v. Copper Queen Hospital*, it was ruled that a licensed private hospital with an emergency room must extend care.[13]

Even before the three cases, *Williams, Sipes,* and *Guerrero,* the Delaware Supreme Court had issued a landmark decision in *Wilmington General Hospital v. Manlove*.[14] In this case an infant had acute diarrhea, a high temperature, and had not slept for two nights. The parents, unable to locate the family pediatrician, took the child to a private hospital's emergency room. The nurse on duty refused to examine the baby or call another doctor, however, because the patient was already under the care of a private physician. The nurse did try to call the private doctor but was unsuccessful in locating him. The nurse then suggested that the parents bring the infant to the hospital clinic the next day if the doctor was still unavailable. They returned home, where the baby died four hours later.

In a suit for damages the hospital, although not considered to be a public or quasi-public institution, was not entitled to a summary judgment because the nurse had a duty to determine whether an "unmistakable" emergency existed and to extend aid if the patient's parents had relied on custom of the hospital to provide care. Hence, at a minimum, a nurse in an emergency room must exercise reasonable care to ascertain the patient's condition and act accordingly. Under the *Manlove* reasoning, a nurse's decision would not result in liability if it accorded with a professional judgment, made with reasonable care, that in the circumstances the patient did not need immediate medical treatment.

Conversely, whenever the emergency room nurse or an unlicensed intern determines that a patient's condition requires the attention of a physician, hospital policy should require that the person be seen, examined, and advised by someone licensed to practice medicine. The physician, exercising professional judgment, may then order formal admission, arrange a transfer to another institution, or allow the patient to return home. Diagnosis and advice by telephone is not recommended because a legally valid physician-patient or hospital-patient relationship can be established by telephone, thus creating a duty to exercise reasonable care and skill under all the circumstances. A doctor who relies on diagnosis by telephone may risk breach of this duty, especially one without prior knowledge of the patient's condition and medical history.[15]

In contrast to the common-law rule that a private person or institution has no duty to aid a stranger in peril, police officers, fire department personnel, and members of the publicly owned paramedical rescue units do have a duty to aid victims of accidents or other emergencies. Legislation normally specifies the responsibilities of such persons and the jurisdictional boundaries of their departmental operations. Conversely, in theory, a privately owned ambulance or rescue service is in the same position as a private physician or hospital and has no legal duty to respond to a call for aid in the absence of a contractual obligation. Because a privately owned ambulance service is not a common carrier regulated extensively by state law, it has no duty to serve all who apply for service.[16] Recent litigation suggests, however, that this view may change, perhaps on the theory that in the absence of a valid reason an ambulance company's refusal to serve constitutes the tort of outrageous conduct.

Very few, if any, actions have been brought against policy officers and fire department personnel alleging negligence in administering first aid after an accident or in a medical emergency. Somewhat more likely are lawsuits contending that injuries were aggravated or harm was done in transporting patients to hospitals or other places for care. Depending on evolving local law, individuals who serve in a public capacity may be immune from personal liability simply on the basis that in rendering care they are performing a "discretionary act" requiring personal decision and judgment. Traditionally governmental officers acting in a discretionary role, as distinct from a purely ministerial capacity, are not liable in a negligence cause of action. A full discussion of the distinction between discretionary and ministerial acts, however, and an appraisal of the trends in the local case law would go far beyond the scope of this chapter.

Statutory Requirements

As mentioned earlier, statutes in some states have for years required certain hospitals to provide emergency care. The refusal of emergency care or hospital admission on the basis of race, color, creed, national origin, or other prohibited category violates various federal and state civil rights statutes and regulations governing the Medicare and Medicaid programs. Beginning in the early 1980s, however, the U.S. Congress became concerned about reports of alleged "patient dumping," the practice of some hospitals transferring or refusing to treat patients who were uninsured and unable to pay for medical care. As a result, in 1985 Congress passed the Emergency Medical Treatment and Active Labor Act.[17] This law is an amendment to Title XVIII of the Social Security Act (Medicare) and was contained in the Consolidated Omnibus Budget Reconciliation Act of 1985; it is therefore sometimes referred to as "medical COBRA." (It is also known as the "anti-dumping act.") It will be referred to in this text as EMTALA.[18]

The full text of EMTALA is reproduced in Appendix 10.1 as an exercise in statutory interpretation. As can be seen, the law provides that when *any* patient[19] presents to the emergency department of a hospital that participates in Medicare (virtually every hospital in the United States), the hospital "must provide for an appropriate medical screening examination . . . to determine whether or not an emergency medical condition . . . exists."[20] Violations can result in civil fines and possible exclusion from Medicare.

From a clinical standpoint, what constitutes an "appropriate medical screening examination" varies from case to case. For instance, a quick history and physical may be enough for a child with fever and a cold, but another child with fever might require extensive diagnostic services if meningitis is suspected. Thus it is important to understand that EMTALA does not simply require a physical examination: it requires the exercise of good clinical judgment and the use of all indicated ancillary diagnostic techniques to determine whether an emergency in fact exists.

If the screening examination reveals that an emergency exists, EMTALA requires that the condition be treated until it has been stabilized, unless the patient requests transfer or it is determined that the medical benefits of transfer outweigh the risk.[21] When transferring the patient is appropriate, the transfer must be in the patient's best interests and must meet certain standards of care:

- The hospital must provide what treatment it can to minimize the risks involved.
- A capable hospital must be located that is willing to accept the patient.
- Medical records, or copies of them, must accompany the patient to the second facility.
- Qualified staff and proper equipment must be used to effect the transfer.[22]

Essentially, then, unless transfer is in the patient's best interests, EMTALA requires that all patients known to have emergency conditions be given medically proper care until their conditions are stable. This care need not result in eventual admission to the hospital, and once the condition is stable, discharge or transfer will not violate EMTALA. But the statute specifically states that stabilizing care may not be delayed for the purpose of determining the patient's "method of payment or insurance status."[23] This seems straightforward enough, but, as is usual in statutory interpretation, considerable ambiguity exists.

The first ambiguity concerns when the duty to stabilize arises. According to the statute, it arises when "the hospital determines that the individual has an emergency medical condition. . . ."[24] If the patient is in the emergency department, the hospital must conduct an "appropriate medical screening examination" to make this determination.[25] But EMTALA does not define the latter expression, so the distinction between an appropriate medical screening examination and an inappropriate one has been the subject of considerable litigation and commentary.

Appropriate medical screening

Consider the case of *Summers v. Baptist Medical Center Arkadelphia*,[26] which involved a man who fell from a platform in a tree while deer hunting. Complaining of popping sounds when he breathed and pains in his chest, he was taken to the emergency department of Baptist Medical Center. There a physician examined him and ordered x-rays of his spine, which showed only an old fracture. No x-rays of the chest were taken. After receiving injections of pain medication (on the belief that he was suffering muscle spasms), Mr. Summers rode home in a pickup truck (a five-hour drive). Two days later, when his pain became unbearable, he went to another hospital and was diagnosed with a broken thoracic vertebra, a broken sternum, and a broken rib. A physician classified these injuries as "life-threatening," according to the trial record.

To summarize, Mr. Summers was given a medical screening examination at Baptist. Based on that examination the emergency department physician determined in good faith—albeit perhaps negligently—that no emergency medical condition existed. He therefore refused to admit Mr. Summers to the hospital and did not stabilize his condition. Mr. Summers was also given a medical screening examination at the second hospital. Based on that examination the emergency was perceived and he was treated for his injuries.

Clearly, the examination at the second hospital was an appropriate one, and it triggered the obligation to stabilize Mr. Summers. But was the presumably negligent examination at Baptist Medical Center also an appropriate one under EMTALA?

At first blush it seems logical to conclude that if an appropriate *transfer* is one that is medically proper and serves the patient's best interests, an appropriate screening would be one that meets the same standard of care. If so, the negligent examination at Baptist would not be considered appropriate and would be deemed a violation of COBRA.[27]

Indeed, some authors argue forcefully for just such an interpretation.[28] They lament that although appropriate transfer is defined in terms of being medically adequate, appropriate medical screening has been interpreted merely to mean one that is *nondiscriminatory*.[29] If appropriate means medically adequate in one part of the statute, they assert, it means medically adequate in another.

> Based on the plain language of the statute . . . and the legislative history, Congress intended to require hospitals with emergency rooms to establish fitting, proper and suitable procedures, within the capability of the hospital, to medically screen indigent and non-indigent patients to determine whether their present symptoms are life- or limb-threatening if not properly treated. . . . In applying these principles to a given factual scenario the question becomes, would a "reasonable physician" consider the hospital's established screening procedures appropriate to determine, "more likely than not," whether the presenting symptoms are life- or limb-threatening[?][30]

Admitting that this is perhaps the "most natural" meaning of the term appropriate in the context of medical examinations,[31] the *Summers* court rejected this meaning and held that the screening examination at Baptist was appropriate. Although negligent, it was undertaken in good faith and it did not result in the physician or the hospital realizing that an emergency existed. Because the duty to stabilize does not arise until "the hospital determines that the individual has an emergency medical condition,"[32] the court in effect held that the hospital and the physician are not to be charged with constructive knowledge of a condition that they should have diagnosed but did not.

In rejecting the argument that a negligent examination is *ipso facto* inappropriate, the court pointed out that the purpose of the statute was to prevent patient dumping, not to create "a general federal cause of action for medical malpractice in emergency rooms."[33] Indeed, Mr. Summers' position, if adopted, would require the parties to conduct a miniature medical malpractice trial on the issue of appropriateness in every case where no diagnosis of "emergency medical condition" was made. The *Summers* court was not about to assume that by enacting EMTALA Congress intended this result.[34]

The *Summers* decision is consistent with a growing body of jurisprudence. For example, in *Gatewood v. Washington Healthcare Corp.*[35] a U.S.

Court of Appeals held that EMTALA "is not intended to duplicate preexisting legal protections, but rather to create a new cause of action, generally unavailable under state tort law, for what amounts to failure to treat."[36]

The article referred to earlier argued that EMTALA should be viewed as "a statute designed to protect the health of the consumers of emergency room services rather than an emergency room civil rights statute."[37] Unless this view prevails, the authors argued, "the effect will be to render EMTALA a serpent without fangs."[38]

It can be argued, however, that given our federal system of government this cobra has sufficient fangs for its intended prey. This was the point of *Summers* court when it wrote:

> Congress can of course, within constitutional limits, federalize anything it wants to. Whether it chooses to do so is a matter of policy for it to decide, not us. But in construing statutes that are less than explicit, the courts will not assume a purpose to create a vast new realm of federal law, creating a federal remedy for injuries that state tort law already addresses. If Congress wishes to take such a far-reaching step, we expect it to say so clearly.[39]

Other decisions addressing the medical screening issue seem to agree that EMTALA is essentially a civil rights statute.[40] It imposes on a hospital the duty to treat all individuals alike, to triage them consistently, and to treat those who are thought to have emergency conditions. It appears that the fact that some undiagnosed emergencies may go untreated is a matter for state medical malpractice law, not EMTALA.[41]

The second ambiguity relates to whether EMTALA applies only to persons in the emergency department or includes those with emergencies elsewhere on hospital property. According to the first paragraph of EMTALA, the cobra begins stalking when "any individual . . . *comes to the emergency department* and a request is made . . . for examination or treatment. . . ."[42] The second paragraph, however, states, "If any individual . . . *comes to the hospital* and the hospital determines that the individual has an emergency medical condition, the hospital must provide [stabilization or appropriate transfer]."[43]

Coming to the hospital

Cases have applied EMTALA to a patient with unstabilized depression who committed suicide the day after being discharged from a psychiatric unit[44] and to a patient in labor who was transferred to defendant hospital's labor room from another hospital.[45] Both cases involved presumably known emergency conditions outside the emergency department.

In contrast, *Baber v. Hospital Corporation of America*[46] involved a patient who was transferred to a psychiatric ward from another hospital and was not known to have an emergency condition. Because the patient was not in the emergency department, the court held that the medical screening obligation did not apply, and because the emergency condition was not discovered until fatal symptoms developed, no EMTALA liability was found.

The EMTALA regulations do not define "comes to a hospital," but they define "comes to the emergency department" to include anyone requesting examination or treatment on hospital property.[47] Additionally, according to the regulations, "hospital property" includes not only the building and grounds but also hospital-owned and -operated ambulances, wherever they may be located.[48] Persons in non–hospital-owned ambulances on hospital property are also considered to have come to the emergency department.[49] Finally, the regulations define "hospital with an emergency department" to mean one that offers emergency services, irrespective of whether it has a defined emergency department as such.[50]

In short, if the standards set forth in the regulations meet judicial approval, it would appear that with the possible exception of situations like those in *Baber*—where the patient is in the hospital but not in the emergency department, is not requesting examination or treatment, and has an undiagnosed emergency condition—the full range of EMTALA's obligations will apply throughout the hospital.[51]

Motive   The final vexing question is whether the patient's inability to pay must have motivated the defendant's decision for there to be an EMTALA violation. Despite some early district court cases holding that such an allegation is necessary,[52] the appellate courts seem to be in agreement that no particular motive need be alleged or proven. They reason that EMTALA achieves its purpose (to discourage the practice of "dumping" indigent patients) by requiring that all patients—insured, uninsured, and self-pay alike—receive uniform treatment. If one does not receive uniform treatment, the reason for the lack of uniformity is immaterial.

The issue was raised in *Cleland v. Bronson Health Care Group, Inc.*,[53] where the Sixth Circuit wrote:

> We can think of many reasons other than indigency that might lead a hospital to give less than standard attention to a person who arrives at the emergency room. These might include: prejudice against the race, sex, or ethnic group of the patient; distaste for the patient's condition (e.g., AIDS patients); personal dislike or antagonism between the medical personnel and the patient; disapproval of the patient's occupation; or political or cultural opposition. If a hospital refused treatment to persons for any of these reasons, or gave cursory treatment, the evil inflicted would be quite akin to that discussed by Congress in the legislative history and the patient would fall squarely within the statutory language.[54]

Some have read this passage as support for the position that liability can be found only if the hospital had an improper motive in providing the disparate treatment.[55] One can argue, however, that the *Cleland* court recognizes the fact that a bad motive of some kind is inherent in all disparate treatment and therefore need not be a specific element of an EMTALA offense.[56]

For example, if physicians, acting in good faith, diagnose no emergency and discharge the patient, they have acted, whether negligently or not, in accordance with what they believe to be the patient's best interests. If, however, the physicians know that an emergency condition exists and discharge the patient anyway, their decision must have been motivated by something other than the patient's best interests.

Congress chose to address the issue of patient dumping by creating a kind of "emergency room civil rights statute" that requires equal treatment for all. If inequality is found, a violation has occurred and it is not necessary to prove the motivation for the disparate treatment.

EMTALA has been a significant issue for years, and the cobra has struck many hospitals and physicians. Its venom is always painful,[57] especially given ambiguities in the statute and the fact that a violation can subject the offender to a civil fine of up to $50,000 and possible exclusion from Medicare. (The fine, incidentally, would not be covered by standard insurance.) The recent clarifications of three issues should at least help healthcare providers and their counsel know when the cobra's fangs are within range.

Conclusion

Beginning of Aid: Duty to Exercise Reasonable Care

Liability and Negligence

EMTALA considerations aside, there is a long-standing and well-accepted common-law rule that once care has begun there is a duty to exercise reasonable care under the particular facts and circumstances. The rule clearly applies to both physicians and hospitals. The slightest act of aid to or exercise of control over the patient may trigger the application of this judicial doctrine. To illustrate: in *Bourgeois v. Dade County* the police brought an unconscious patient to the hospital. The physician on emergency call conducted only a cursory examination without benefit of x-rays and decided that the patient was intoxicated. With the doctor's approval the patient was then removed to jail, where he died. It was later established that the patient had been suffering from broken ribs that had punctured his lung. The issue of negligence was one for jury determination.[58]

Many other cases have involved the same principles and have resulted in findings of liability. There is no need to discuss all these decisions in detail here, but the reader should be aware of such other important cases as *Jones v. City of New York Hospital for Joint Diseases,*[59] *New Biloxi Hospital v. Frazier,*[60] and *Methodist Hospital v. Ball.*[61] In *Jones, Frazier,* and *Ball* the facts were fundamentally the same. In all instances the victims of violence or accident were accepted into the emergency room, and the hospital staff failed to exercise reasonable care in diagnosing and treating the cases.

In *Jones* an intern of a voluntary hospital did no more than clean and dress a patient's stab wounds before ordering a transfer to a city hospital. The delay in further treatment caused death. In both *Frazier* and *Ball* the patients were unattended for a considerable time (45 minutes in the *Ball* case, an hour or more in *Frazier*), were given minimal attention and diagnosis from hospital nursing and medical staff, and then were transferred to other institutions with adverse results.

These cases emphasize the legal and moral necessity of exercising reasonable care in making a diagnosis and deciding the course (and place) of treatment.[62] They also show that it is essential for hospital employees to determine which patients need immediate attention. Delay cannot be excused because others were being treated.[63]

A healthcare provider can be liable for reasons other than the negligence of hospital employees. This fundamental principle is well illustrated by a South Dakota case, *Fjerstad v. Knutson*.[64] An intern on duty in the hospital's emergency room on the Fourth of July had examined a patient, ordered a blood test and throat culture, and given a prescription for an antibiotic. Unable to reach the on-call physician, the intern then released the patient, who died the following morning from asphyxia caused by a blocked trachea. In the case against both the intern and the hospital, the trial court instructed the jury that the hospital could not be held liable unless the intern was found negligent. The jury's verdicts were for both defendants, but the plaintiff's appeal succeeded to the extent of obtaining a new trial against the hospital. The judge's instruction to the jury was found to be erroneous. The appellate court observed that the jury would have been justified in finding the hospital independently negligent, even if the intern had not been negligent, because of its failure to have a physician available for consultation with the emergency room staff. The failure was a violation of the institution's own standards, which required interns to contact the on-call physician before treating emergency room patients and before prescribing drugs. Such alleged breaches are sufficient to create an issue for a jury. Further, on the issue of proximate cause the plaintiff had presented expert testimony at trial establishing that a person with the decedent's symptoms should have been hospitalized and that his life could probably have been saved.

Significant also in the *Fjerstad* case was the plaintiff's allegation that the intern practiced medicine without a license in prescribing medication and pretended to the title of "Doctor." The court ruled that these actions and the hospital's employment relationship with the unlicensed intern did not constitute negligence *as a matter of law*. Rather, negligence of an intern is to be determined on a case-by-case basis by reference to the standards of care applying to licensed physicians in similar localities under similar circumstances.

Hospital Admissions and Transfers

Obviously not all emergency room patients need to be admitted to the hospital. Transfer to another hospital is justified when the patient's condition has been stabilized, when it is reasonably and professionally judged that the transfer will not aggravate the patient's condition, and when it otherwise meets the standards of EMTALA. Indeed, a hospital is under a positive duty to transfer a patient to another institution if it does not have the appropriate facilities and staff to care for the patient properly.[65] The transferring institution also has a duty to forward with the patient the diagnosis and other appropriate medical information, and the receiving hospital has a duty to obtain this information.[66]

As these cases demonstrate, patients presenting themselves at a hospital's emergency room should never be turned away until they have been seen and examined by a licensed physician, who should determine the seriousness of the illness or injury and then order admission, a return home, or a transfer to another facility (if appropriate under EMTALA), depending on the particular facts. Undue delays should not be tolerated. These policies should be stated clearly in written rules that hospital personnel and emergency room physicians can readily carry out. Because ignoring or violating written rules can be evidence of negligence, it is extremely important that established hospital policies be followed meticulously once they are expressed in writing.

It is also important to comply fully with the standards of emergency care promulgated by public and private agencies and professional groups. Among the standards issued by public agencies are the rules and regulations of state departments and agencies responsible for hospital licensure. If the particular state has a licensure law, and if there are regulations pertaining to emergency care, a violation of these regulations could be evidence of negligence. Standards established by such private agencies as the Joint Commission on Accreditation of Healthcare Organizations have the same legal implications.

For example, the Joint Commission requires that "a licensed independent practitioner with appropriate clinical privileges [must determine] the scope of assessment and care for patients in need of emergency care." The intent of this standard is that "a qualified, licensed independent practitioner is available, and is responsible for determining, as quickly as possible, what assessments the patient requires to care for his or her needs."[67] A medical record is to be maintained for every emergency patient and incorporated into the permanent hospital record. A plan for emergency care must exist, and no patient whom the hospital is capable of properly caring for should be arbitrarily transferred to some other institution. The Medicare "Conditions of Participation for Hospitals" also contain standards for emergency care similar to those promulgated by the Joint Commission.

The most significant legal point is that governmental regulations and the standards of professional associations—together with a hospital's own policies and medical staff bylaws—can be evidence for a jury to consider in a liability suit for damages.[68]

In addition, professional standards require written medical records for all patients seen in the emergency room, including those not formally admitted to the hospital. Not only are such records mandatory in the interests of adequate medical care, but the hospital may be called on later to document in the courtroom the standards of care rendered to a particular patient, in which event a medical chart is indispensable. Records should include the instructions for continuing care given to the patient at discharge and the information furnished to an institution or physician to whom the patient is referred.

Staffing the Emergency Department

All of the foregoing suggests that the legal duty of reasonable care owed to emergency patients mandates a well-organized department, staffed with qualified personnel, and equipped with the physical means of ensuring prompt diagnosis, stabilization, treatment, or referral.[69] Persons in charge of the emergency department must be an integral part of the organization and must be accountable for the quality of care. Ultimately the governing body of the hospital is responsible for the professional standards of the emergency department, just as it is responsible for other clinical standards of the institution.[70] Medical staff privileges must be delineated for each emergency department physician, as they are for those in other departments.

For moderately sized and larger hospitals, staffing the emergency room with nurses and interns supported by medical staff only on a rotating on-call basis no longer meets the expectations of the public or satisfies the legal responsibilities required in malpractice cases. When physicians serve only on call, there is too much opportunity for error in diagnosis and delay in treatment, both of which lead to unfortunate situations and increase such liability problems.

It is ironic that liability is made more likely by the trend to specialization in medical practice. Emergency medicine has become a specialty of its own. Many physicians, including specialists in other disciplines, are not competent to deal with emergency cases and should not be on emergency duty. Neither should interns, physicians' assistants, and graduates of foreign medical schools who lack emergency training.

Hospitals that wish to furnish full-scale emergency services should have a department with a full-time staff of locally licensed, experienced physicians, nurses, and other personnel trained to handle emergency cases.

Hospitals have several alternatives for staffing the emergency department. In most states, not-for-profit institutions may employ doctors directly, the "corporate practice of medicine" rule having been abolished in most jurisdictions. (The prohibition on corporate practice of medicine was announced years ago as a means of discouraging commercialization and exploitation of the medical profession and to emphasize that the physician's individual loyalties belong solely to the patient. It was developed, however, in the context of the private, profit-making corporation and is believed to have little or no relevance to modern not-for-profit hospitals. In those few states that adhere to the "corporate practice of medicine" doctrine, or when an alternative to salary is desired, a fee-for-service arrangement can be used.)

More typical than direct employment of salaried or fee-for-service physicians for emergency department staff is a contractual arrangement with a corporation of physicians, or a partnership, whereby the physicians undertake to provide full-time coverage for emergencies. Nearly all states now permit professional individuals to incorporate their practice under authority granted by special statute. A contract with a professional corporation or partnership must be carefully drafted to make sure that the organization is obligated to provide the services contemplated by the hospital and that the hospital retains adequate control with respect to the privileges of the physicians in the emergency department and the standards of their practice. By entering into such an arrangement the hospital must not abdicate its ultimate responsibility for the quality of healthcare. The contract, among other provisions, must provide guidelines for the following responsibilities: full-time coverage, supervision of hospital nurses and house staff, maintenance of equipment and facilities, fees and billing, and referral of patients. The document must also specify the duration of the arrangement and contain provisions for renewal. Above all, the medical staff of the hospital must be involved in monitoring the standards of practice in the emergency service and delineating clinical privileges, even when service is contracted to an independent group of physicians. This medical staff function must be clearly articulated in the contract with the physicians' group. The emergency room group should also be required to carry adequate malpractice insurance and agree to indemnify the hospital if malpractice judgments arise from the negligence of any physician or employee of the corporation or partnership.

The financial arrangements between the hospital and the contracting group may legally allow two charges to the patient—one for hospital services and another for the physician's service. The group may bill the patient directly or assign the account to the hospital for collection.

Contracts for emergency department coverage give rise to questions regarding the hospital's liability for malpractice or negligence by any of the doctors. Contracts often recite that the physicians are "independent contractors." As common law under the doctrine of *respondeat superior,* an employer is not legally liable for the negligence or other tort of an independent contractor. The reason for this long-established rule is that employers have no right to control the means and methods of independent contractors' work, although ultimately controlling its overall specifications and quality.

By way of example, a Georgia court, adhering to this traditional legal concept, held in 1969 that the hospital was not liable for the negligence of a physician who was staffing the emergency department as a member of a

medical partnership under contract with the hospital. The court observed
that the hospital retained no control over the physicians' individual professional decisions and that the contract in this case expressly represented the
doctors as independent contractors. Identification of the partnership's general
responsibilities and surveillance of standards of practice by the medical staff
were not sufficient "control" to deny the hospital the defense of independent
contractor. Accordingly, dismissal of the action was proper.[71] These views of
"control" and the legal effect of a contractual clause reciting that emergency
room physicians are independent have been forcefully rejected in more recent cases.

A contrary result was reached by the Supreme Court of Delaware as
early as 1970. Even if the physician is an independent contract vis-à-vis the
hospital, the hospital can be held liable for the negligence of such a doctor if
the institution has "held out" or "represented" to the patient that the doctor is
its agent or employee. This is the doctrine of *apparent or ostensible agency* that,
when applicable, justifies holding the hospital liable for a wrong committed
by one who is not in fact an employee of the hospital. Under certain facts the
doctrine may be referred to as an *agency by estoppel*, meaning that an apparent
agency is imposed by law when a principal's conduct or method of business
operation has estopped the firm from denying an actual agency. In *Vanaman v.
Milford Memorial Hospital, Inc.* the patient had twisted her ankle and appeared
at the emergency room for treatment. The family physician was not available.
Because the patient and her mother indicated no preference with respect to
physicians, the staff doctor on call was summoned. This doctor's treatment
resulted in further injury to the patient. The trial court dismissed the suit
against the hospital on the general basis that the institution had not held itself
out as a "provider of medical care." On appeal, however, the state's supreme
court reversed, saying the jury must decide whether the doctor was acting in
a private capacity or as agent of the hospital.[72] The fact that the physician was
not paid directly by the hospital was relevant but not conclusive.

Subsequent to *Vanaman* the same court held that a hospital could
be liable for the negligence of a physician who was a partner in a medical
partnership under the contract to provide coverage of the emergency room.
Again the Delaware court denied the hospital's claim that the doctor was an
independent contractor, basing its decision on the "holding out" or apparent
agency doctrine. It was improper, the court said, to grant a summary judgment
for the hospital, and a new trial must be held to determine, in effect, whether
the patient relied on the hospital to provide medical service.[73] Consistent
with Delaware, most states now hold that a contractual clause reciting that
the emergency room physicians are to be considered independent contractors
would not be regarded as barring a plaintiff's action against the hospital.[74]

A New Jersey court expressed the doctrine of apparent agency this way:

> [P]eople who seek medical help through the emergency room
> facilities of modern-day hospitals are unaware of the status of the

various professionals working there. . . . Absent notice to the contrary, therefore, plaintiff had the right to assume that the treatment received was being rendered through hospital employees and that any negligence associated with that treatment would render the hospital responsible.[75]

Clearly it would be unreasonable to expect the patient to inquire whether persons who render care in the emergency room are employees of the hospital or independent contractors.

In similar fashion the Michigan Supreme Court has said: "In our view, the critical question is whether the plaintiff . . . was looking to the hospital for treatment of his physical ailments or merely viewed the hospital as the situs where his physician would treat him for his problems."[76]

The governing board of a hospital retains ultimate control over the appointment of physicians employed by a medical corporation or partnership, monitors the quality of care provided, and has the power to revoke the privileges of individual doctors for justifiable cause. An Ohio court emphasized that this responsibility justified finding an agency by estoppel in a suit against the hospital.[77] Similarly, an Arizona appellate court has also stressed that the right of control can be the basis for holding a hospital liable for negligence by a radiologist member of an independent group of physicians.[78]

The Good Samaritan Statutes

Most states have statutes commonly called "Good Samaritan" laws. From the public policy viewpoint their purpose is to encourage physicians and other professional persons to extend aid to strangers at the scene of an emergency in the absence of an existing physician-patient relationship. The essence of the legislation provides that a physician, registered nurse, or other professional person—or in some statutes, "any person"—is not to be held liable for ordinary negligence or malpractice when extending aid at an emergency scene, as long as the aid is extended in "good faith" or without "gross negligence" or "willful and wanton misconduct."[79] Many of the statutes require that the aid be extended "gratuitously." Although the applicability of each statute to designated persons and to particular situations depends on its precise language, several general observations are useful.

The statutes were really unnecessary as a matter of law and legal liability, and they can be further criticized for frequently limiting their coverage to certain persons aiding in an emergency. Professional or lay persons not specifically designated in the relevant local statute are not protected by the legislation, and such individuals are still held to the well-recognized common-law rule that the beginning of aid raises the duty to exercise reasonable care under all the facts and circumstances.

Some of the statutes extend immunity to professional persons licensed to practice in other jurisdictions. Others do not and thereby characterize such individuals as lay persons when they render aid outside the state of licensure.

Most of the original Good Samaritan laws did not apply to ambulance attendants or emergency service personnel, although many jurisdictions now have an entirely separate statute granting immunity from individual liability to such persons. For example, the Michigan statute protects ambulance attendants and emergency medical technicians, as well as physicians, communications personnel, hospital employees, and the employer of emergency personnel from liability when performing services outside a hospital consistent with the individuals' training, so long as their acts or omissions do not amount to gross negligence or willful misconduct.[80] Similar special legislation for emergency medical care was adopted in many states in response to a 1973 federal law that offered financial incentives and otherwise encouraged the development of local and regional emergency services by professional paramedics working outside a hospital or other medical care institution.[81] The federal statute has since been repealed, but the state Good Samaritan laws remain.

Very few, if any, lawsuits are on record against Good Samaritans who were allegedly negligent in aiding accident victims. Moreover, the refusal of a physician or other professional person to assist at the scene of an emergency has never posed a serious threat of liability as long as the person was not already under an established duty to act.[82] The fear of suit and liability that prompted the enactment of the Good Samaritan legislation was unfounded. Moreover, "reasonable care" in an emergency outside of a hospital would be a rather minimal requirement, because the common law would not expect a physician, for instance, to possess life-saving equipment or drugs at the scene of a highway accident or when treating a victim of sudden illness.

Finally, most of these statutes as enacted at present do not specify where the "emergency care" must take place to qualify for immunity from common law liability. There has been significant uncertainty in the various states regarding the applicability of their statutes to emergencies treated in hospitals. In some jurisdictions either the Good Samaritan statute or one covering emergency medical service specifically extends immunity from ordinary negligence to professional individuals who aid during an in-hospital emergency as long as the person had no preexisting duty to respond.[83] Hence, in a Michigan case a hospital staff physician not on call could invoke the statutory partial immunity when he was called to attend an accident victim at the hospital.[84] Similarly, courts have interpreted California's statute as granting immunity to physicians who voluntarily provide services to hospitalized patients in an emergency.[85]

When there is a preexisting duty to respond to a call for services in an emergency, the Good Samaritan legislation does not apply. In litigation involving the Michigan statute the court held that the hospital was not granted any immunity when a "Code Blue" team transporting an unconscious person allegedly permitted the patient's unsupported head to strike a guard rail.[86] Because there was a preexisting hospital-patient relationship the statute did not abrogate the usual common law with respect to hospital liability. Furthermore, a leading California case, *Colby v. Schwartz,* held that two surgeons on a hospital's emergency call panel could not claim immunity under the statute because they had a duty to respond and thus were not "volunteers."[87]

Extending immunity to in-hospital "emergency" treatment was one of several approaches to address issues relating to the costs and burdens of malpractice litigation; however, many argue that this is not the proper solution from the viewpoint of public policy. Further, the limited applicability of the statutes, their wide variation from state to state, and their many ambiguities have made the legislation more counterproductive than productive. An alternative approach would be to enact legislation requiring all persons, whether professional or lay, to render aid to any stranger in peril, as has been done in some states and in foreign countries that operate under the Napoleonic Code (the system based on French law). A grant of immunity from tort liability in the absence of gross negligence or willful or wanton misconduct would then be justified.

Appendix 10.1

The full text of 42 U.S.C. § 1395dd is as follows:

§ 1395dd. Examination and treatment for emergency medical conditions and women in labor.

(a) **Medical screening requirement.** In the case of a hospital that has a hospital emergency department, if any individual (whether or not eligible for benefits under this title [42 USCS §§ 1395 et seq.]) comes to the emergency department and a request is made on the individual's behalf for examination or treatment for a medical condition, the hospital must provide for an appropriate medical screening examination within the capability of the hospital's emergency department, including ancillary services routinely available to the emergency department, to determine whether or not an emergency medical condition (within the meaning of subsection (e)(1)) exists.

(b) **Necessary stabilizing treatment for emergency medical conditions and labor.** (1) In general. If any individual (whether or not eligible for benefits under this title [42 USCS §§ 1395 et seq.]) comes to a hospital and the hospital determines that the individual has an emergency medical condition, the hospital must provide either—

   (A) within the staff and facilities available at the hospital, for such further medical examination and such treatment as may be required to stabilize the medical condition, or

   (B) for transfer of the individual to another medical facility in accordance with subsection (c).

(2) Refusal to consent to treatment. A hospital is deemed to meet the requirement of paragraph (1)(A) with respect to an individual if the hospital offers the individual the further medical examination and

treatment described in that paragraph and informs the individual (or a person acting on the individual's behalf) of the risks and benefits to the individual of such examination and treatment, but the individual (or a person acting on the individual's behalf) refuses to consent to the examination and treatment. The hospital shall take all reasonable steps to secure the individual's (or person's) written informed consent to refuse such examination and treatment.

(3) Refusal to consent to transfer. A hospital is deemed to meet the requirement of paragraph (1) with respect to an individual if the hospital offers to transfer the individual to another medical facility in accordance with subsection (c) and informs the individual (or a person acting on the individual's behalf) of the risks and benefits to the individual of such transfer, but the individual (or a person acting on the individual's behalf) refuses to consent to the transfer. The hospital shall take all reasonable steps to secure the individual's (or person's) written informed consent to refuse such transfer.

(c) **Restricting transfers until individual stabilized.** (1) Rule. If an individual at a hospital has an emergency medical condition which has not been stabilized (within the meaning of subsection (e)(3)(B), the hospital may not transfer the individual unless—

(A) (i) the individual (or a legally responsible person acting on the individual's behalf) after being informed of the hospital's obligations under this section and of the risk of transfer, in writing requests transfer to another medical facility,

(ii) a physician (within the meaning of section 1861 (r)(1) [42 USCS § 1395x(r)(1)]) has signed a certification that, based upon the information available at the time of transfer, the medical benefits reasonably expected from the provision of appropriate medical treatment at another medical facility outweigh the increased risks to the individual and, in the case of labor, to the unborn child from effecting the transfer, or

(iii) if a physician is not physically present in the emergency department at the time an individual is transferred, a qualified medical person (as defined in section 1861 (r)(1) [42 USCS § 1395x(r)(1)]), in consultation with the person, has made the determination described in such clause, and subsequently countersigns the certification; and

(B) the transfer is an appropriate transfer (within the meaning of paragraph (2)) to that facility.

A certification described in clause (ii) or (iii) of subparagraph (A) shall include a summary of the risks and benefits upon which the certification is based.

(2) Appropriate transfer. An appropriate transfer to a medical facility is a transfer—

(A) in which the transferring hospital provides the medical treatment within its capacity which minimizes the risks to the individual's health and, in the case of a woman in labor, the health of the unborn child;

(B) in which the receiving facility—

   (i)   has available space and qualified personnel for the treatment of the individual, and

   (ii) has agreed to accept transfer of the individual and to provide appropriate medical treatment;

(C) in which transferring hospital sends to the receiving facility with all medical records (or copies thereof), related to the emergency condition for which the individual has presented, available at the time of the transfer, including records related to the individual's emergency medical condition, observations of signs or symptoms, preliminary diagnosis, treatment provided, results of any tests and the informed written consent or certification (or copy thereof) provided under paragraph (1)(A), and the name and address of any on-call physician (described in subsection (d)(1)(C)) who has refused or failed to appear within a reasonable time to provide necessary stabilizing treatment;

(D) in which the transfer is effected through qualified personnel and transportation equipment, as required including the use of necessary and medically appropriate life support measure during the transfer; and

(E) which meets such other requirements as the Secretary may find necessary in the interest of the health and safety of individuals transferred.

(d) Enforcement. (1) Civil monetary penalties. (A) A participating hospital that negligently violates a requirement of this section is subject to a civil money penalty of not more than $50,000 (or not more than $25,000 in the case of a hospital with less than 100 beds) for each such violation. The provisions of section 1128A [42 USCS § 1320a-7a] (other than subsection (a) and (b)) shall apply to a civil money penalty under this subparagraph in the same manner as such provisions apply with respect to a penalty or proceeding under section 1128A(a) [42 USCS § 1320a-7a(a)].

(B) Subject to subparagraph (C), any physician who is responsible for the examination, treatment, or transfer of an individual in a participating hospital, including a physician on-call for the care of such an individual, and who negligently violates a requirement of this section, including a physician who—

   (i)   signs a certification under subsection (c)(1)(A) that the medical benefits reasonably to be expected from a transfer to another facility outweigh the risks associated with the transfer, if the physician knew or should have known that the benefits did not outweigh the risks, or

(ii)   misrepresents an individual's condition or other information, including a hospital's obligations under this section, is subject to a civil money penalty of not more than $50,000 for each such violation and, if the violation is gross and flagrant or is repeated, to exclusion from participation in this title and State health care programs. The provisions of section 1128A [42 USCS § 1320a-7a] (other than the first and second sentences of subsection (a) and subsection (b)) shall apply to a civil money penalty and exclusion under this subparagraph in the same manner as such provisions apply with respect to a penalty, exclusion, or proceeding under section 1128A(a) [42 USCS § 1320a-7a(a)].

(C) If, after an initial examination, a physician determines that the individual requires the services of a physician listed by the hospital on its list of on-call physicians (required to be maintained under section 1866(a)(1)(I) [42 USCS § 1395cc(a)(1)(I)]) and notifies the on-call physician and the on-call physician fails or refuses to appear within a reasonable period of time, and the physician orders the transfer of the individual because the physician determines that without the services of the on-call physician the benefits transfer outweigh the risks of transfer, the physician authorizing the transfer shall not be subject to a penalty under subparagraph (B). However, the previous sentence shall not apply to the hospital or to the on-call physician who failed or refused to appear.

(2) Civil enforcement. (A) Personal harm. Any individual who suffers personal harm as a direct result of a participating hospital's violation of a requirement of this section may, in a civil action against the participating hospital, obtain those damages available for personal injury under the law of the Sate in which the hospital is located, and such equitable relief as is appropriate.

(B) Financial loss to other medical facility. Any medical facility that suffers a financial loss as a direct result of a participating hospital's violation of a requirement of this section may, in a civil action against the participating hospital, obtain those damages available for financial loss, under the law of the State in which the hospital is located, and such equitable relief as is appropriate.

(C) Limitations on actions. No action may be brought under this paragraph more than two years after the date of the violation with respect to which the action is brought.

(3) Consultation with peer review organizations. In considering

allegations of violations of the requirements of this section in imposing sanctions under paragraph (1), the Secretary shall request the appropriate utilization and quality control peer review organization with a contract under part B of title XI [42 USCS §§ 1320c et seq.]) to assess whether the individual involved had an emergency medical condition which had not been stabilized, and provide a report on its findings. Except in the case in which a delay would jeopardize the health or safety of individuals, the Secretary shall request such a review before effecting a sanction under paragraph (1) and shall provide a period of at least 60 days for such review.

(e) Definitions. In this section:

(1) The term "emergency medical condition" means—

  (A) a medical condition manifesting itself by acute symptoms of sufficient severity (including severe pain) such that the absence of immediate medical attention could reasonably be expected to result in—

    (i) placing the health of the individual (or, with respect to a pregnant woman, the health of the woman or her unborn child) in serious jeopardy,

    (ii) serious impairment to bodily functions, or

    (iii) serious dysfunction of any bodily organ or part; or

  (B) with respect to a pregnant woman who is having contractions—

    (i) that there is inadequate time to effect a safe transfer to another hospital before delivery, or

    (ii) that transfer may pose a threat to the health or safety of the woman or the unborn child.

(2) The term "participating hospital" means hospital that has entered into a provider agreement under section 1866 [42 USCS § 1395cc].

(3) (A) The term "to stabilize" means, with respect to an emergency medical condition described in paragraph (1)(A), to provide such medical treatment of the condition as may be necessary to assure, within reasonable medical probability, that no material deterioration of the condition is likely to result from or occur during the transfer of the individual from a facility, or, with respect to an emergency medical condition described in paragraph (1)(B), to deliver (including the placenta).

(4) The term "transfer" means the movement (including the discharge) of an individual outside a hospital's facilities at the direction of any person employed by (or affiliated or associated, directly or indirectly, with) the hospital, but does not include such a movement of an individual who (A) has been declared dead, or (B) leaves the facility without the permission of any such person.

(5) [Redesignated]

(6) The term "hospital" includes a rural primary care hospital (as defined in section 1861(mm)(1) [42 USCS § 1395x (mm)(1)]).

(f) **Preemption.** The provisions of this section do not preempt any State or local law requirement, except to the extent that the requirement directly conflicts with a requirement of this section.

(g) **Nondiscrimination.** A participating hospital that has specialized capabilities or facilities (such as burn units, shock-trauma units, neonatal intensive care unites, or (with respect to rural areas) regional referral centers as identified by the Secretary in regulation) shall not refuse to accept an appropriate transfer of an individual who requires such specialized capabilities or facilities if the hospital has the capacity to treat the individual.

(h) **No delay in examination or treatment.** A participating hospital may not delay provision of an appropriate medical screening examination required under subsection (a) or further medical examination and treatment required under subsection (b) in order to inquire about the individual's method of payment or insurance status.

(i) **Whistleblower protections.** A participating hospital may not penalize or take adverse action against a qualified medical person described in subsection (c)(1)(A)(iii) or a physician because the person or physician refuses to authorize the transfer of an individual with an emergency medical condition that has not been stabilized or against any hospital employee because the employee reports a violation of a requirement of this section.

Notes

1. Norwood Hosp. v. Howton, 32 Ala. App. 375, 26 So. 2d 427 (1946).
2. 42 U.S.C. § 1395dd.
3. Wis. Stat. Ann. § 46.21(2)(m) (West 1987).
4. Ill. Ann. Stat. ch. 111$^{1/2}$ ¶¶ 86, 87 as amended (Smith-Hurd Supp. 1987).
5. Pa. Stat. Ann. tit. 35, § 435 (Purdon 1977).
6. N.Y. Pub. Health Law § 2806(1)(b) (McKinney 1985). Tennessee also requires all general hospitals to provide emergency service. Tenn. Code Ann. § 68-39-301 as amended (1983).
7. Some states have statutes or regulations recognizing differing levels of emergency care service: "comprehensive," "basic," and "standby."
8. At least two states, Vermont and Minnesota, have enacted Good Samaritan statutes that affirmatively create a duty to aid another person in an emergency provided that aid can be given without peril to the "Samaritan" or third parties. More will be said later about Good Samaritan statutes in general. The legislation parallels the law of France and other civil-law jurisdictions. Vt. Stat. Ann. tit. 12, § 519 (1973); Minn. Stat. Ann. § 604.05 (West Supp. 1985).
9. 440 S.W.2d 104 (Tex. Ct. Civ. App. 1969).
10. Childs v. Greenville Hosp. Auth., 479 S.W.2d 399 (Tex. Ct. Civ. App. 1972).

11. 119 Ga. App. 626, 168 S.E.2d 336 (1969).

12. 447 S.W.2d 558, 35 A.L.R.3d 834 (Mo. 1969).

13. 22 Ariz. App. 611, 529 P.2d 1205 (1974), aff'd, P.2d 1329 (1975).

14. 54 Del. 15, 174 A.2d 135 (Sup. Ct. 1961). See also Carr v. St. Paul Fire & Marine Ins. Co., 384 F. Supp. 821 (W.D. Ark. 1974) (where a patient's condition made a medical emergency readily apparent, and hospital personnel failed to summon a physician, a jury verdict against the hospital was justified).

15. Compare the case of Childs v. Weis, 440 S.W.2d 104 (Tex. Ct. Civ. App. 1969), discussed previously, where the suit was against the physician on call for hospital emergency duty, the hospital's policy did not require the doctor to see patients personally at the emergency room, and the doctor gave no advice to the patient or nurse other than apparently telling the nurse to have the patient telephone her private physician.

16. Hollander v. Smith & Smith, 10 N.J. Super. 82, 76 A.2d 697 (1950); cf. Leete v. Griswold Post No. 79, Am. Legion, 158 A. 919 (Conn. 1932).

17. 42 U.S.C. § 1395dd.

18. "The avowed purpose of EMTALA was . . . to provide an 'adequate first response to a medical crisis' for all patients and 'send a clear signal to the hospital community . . . that all Americans regardless of wealth or status, should know that a hospital will provide what services it can when they are truly in physical distress.'" Baber v. Hospital Corp. of Am., 977 F.2d 872 (4th Cir. 1992) (quoting Sen. David Durenberger, 131 Cong. Rec. S13904 (Oct. 23., 1985)). See also, Vickers v. Nash General Hosp., Inc., 78 F3d 139 (4th Cir. 1996) and Correa v. Hospital San Francisco, 69 F.3d 1184, 1189 (1st Cir. 1995).

19. Courts have consistently held that despite its purpose, EMTALA applies to all individuals, not merely those who are uninsured and unable to pay for care. See, e.g., Cleland v. Bronson Health Care Group, Inc. 917 F.2d 266 (6th Cir. 1990); Gatewood v. Washington Healthcare Corp., 933 F.2d 11037 (D.C. Cir. 1991); Brooker v. Desert Hosp. Corp., 947 F.2d 412 (9th Cir. 1991); Collins v. DePaul Hosp., 963 F.2d 303 (10th Cir. 1992); and Summers v. Baptist Medical Ctr. Arkadelphia, 1996 U.S. App. LEXIS 19173 (1996). This is consistent with the statutory scheme because EMTALA requires that when "any individual . . . comes to a hospital and the hospital determines that the individual has an emergency medical condition, the hospital must [provide stabilizing treatment or an appropriate transfer to another facility]. 42 U.S.C. § 1395dd(b)(1). This must be done without delaying to determine "the individual's method of payment or insurance status." 42 U.S.C. § 1395dd(h).

20. 42 U.S.C. § 1395dd(a). "Emergency medical condition" is defined as one that, without immediate treatment, would jeopardize the individual's health or would cause serious harm to bodily functions or organs. If the patient is a woman in labor, "emergency medical condition" includes jeopardy to the health of the fetus and also means that there is inadequate time to transfer the woman before delivery or that transfer itself would threaten the health of the woman or the unborn child. See 42 U.S.C. § 1395dd(e)(1).

21. 42 U.S.C. § 1395dd(c)(1)(A).

22. 42 U.S.C. § 1395dd(c)(2).

23. 42 U.S.C. § 1395dd(h).

24. 42 U.S.C. § 1395dd(b)(1).
25. 42 U.S.C. § 1395dd(a). Regarding patients not in the emergency department, *see* "Coming to the Hospital," below.
26. *Supra* note 19.
27. EMTALA provides for stiff civil monetary penalties against hospitals and physicians who violate its provisions, and it allows an individual who suffers personal harm to obtain damages from the hospital (but not the physicians) concerned. 42 U.S.C. § 1395dd(d).
28. *See, e.g.*, Bosler & Davis, *Is EMTALA a Defanged Cobra?*, 51 J. Mo. Bar. 165 (May–June 1995).
29. *Id.* at 167–68.
30. *Id.* at 168 (footnotes omitted).
31. "One possible meaning, perhaps the most natural one, would be that medical screening examinations must be correct, properly done, [and] if not perfect, at least not negligent. It would be easy to say, for example, simply as a matter of the English language, that a negligently performed screening examination is not an appropriate one." 91 F.3d at 1138.
32. 42 U.S.C. § 1395dd(b)(1).
33. 91 F.3d at 1140.
34. 91 F.3d at 1141.
35. 933 F.2d 1037 (D.C. Cir. 1991).
36. *Id.* at 1041. During consideration of the EMTALA bill Senator Edward M. Kennedy commented, "Some states have laws which ensure that no emergency patient is denied emergency care because of inability to pay. But 28 states have no such law." 131 Cong. Rec. 28,569 (1985).
37. Bosler and Davis, note 28 at 168.
38. *Id.* The authors also argued that because of EMTALA hospitals should adopt "standardized treatment protocols" for use in emergency rooms. They cite as support for this proposition a 1990 standard of the Joint Commission on Accreditation of Healthcare Organizations, which indeed called for written emergency procedures. The JCAHO accreditation manual is revised annually, however, and the current manual does not contain the 1990 standard. Instead, the relevant standard today states, "The hospital provides for referral, transfer, or discharge of the patient to another level of care, health professional or setting based on the patient's assessed needs and the hospital's capacity to provide the care." JCAHO Accreditation Manual for Hospitals, CC.6 (1996). Although written protocols are still favored and are something an accreditation team will look for, they no longer are an absolute JCAHO requirement.
39. 91 F.3d at 1140–41.
40. *See* Cleland v. Bronson Health Care Group, Gatewood v. Washington Healthcare Group, and Summers v. Baptist Medical Ctr. Arkadelphia, note 3. *See also* Maryland General Hosp., Inc., 996 F.2d 708 (4th Cir. 1993); Baber v. Hospital Corp. of Am., 977 F.2d 872 (4th Cir. 1992); Eberhardt v. City of Los Angeles, 62 F.3d 1253 (9th Cir. 1995); Repp v. Auadarko Mun. Hosp., 43 F.3d 519 (10th Cir. 1994); and Holcomb v. Monahan, 30 F.3d 116 (11th Cir. 1994).
41. "EMTALA is implicated only when individuals who are perceived to have the same medical condition receive disparate treatment; it is not implicated

whenever individuals who turn out in fact to have had the same condition receive disparate treatment. The Act would otherwise become indistinguishable from state malpractice law." Summers v. Baptist Medical Ctr. Arkadelphia, 91 F.3d 1132, 1147 (1996).

42. 42 U.S.C. § 1395dd(a) (emphasis added).

43. 42 U.S.C. § 1395dd(b)(1) (emphasis added).

44. Helton v. Phelps County Regional Medical Ctr., 794 F. Supp. 332 (E.D. Mo. 1992) (denying a motion to dismiss for failure to state a claim).

45. Smith v. Richmond Memorial Hosp., 416 S.E.2d 689 (Va. 1992).

46. Note 38.

47. 42 C.F.R. § 489.24(b) (1995).

48. *Id.*

49. *Id.* In Johnson v. University of Chicago Hosps., 982 F.2d 230 (1992), an infant was being transferred to a hospital by a Chicago Fire Department ambulance. When it was only five blocks away, the hospital advised the ambulance by radio that its emergency room was overcrowded and that is should go instead to a certain other hospital. The Seventh Circuit held that the patient had not come to the emergency department within the meaning of EMTALA.

50. 42 C.F.R. § 489.24(b).

51. Whether the law would apply to a *hospital-owned* clinic on a separate campus is an open question. In King v. Ahrens, 16 F.3d 265 (8th Cir. 1994), the court held that EMTALA does not apply to a private physician practicing in his privately owned clinic. Because hospitals today frequently own clinic facilities staffed with employed physicians, this issue will undoubtedly be litigated in the next few years.

52. *See, e.g.,* Evitt v. University Heights Hosp., 727 F. Supp. 495 (S.D. Ind. 1989) *and* Steward v. Myrick, 731 F. Supp. 433 (D. Kan. 11990).

53. *Supra* note 18.

54. 917 F.2d at 272.

55. *See, e.g.,* Bosler & Davis, note 28.

56. Of course plaintiffs' lawyers would prefer to have evidence of an ulterior motive, but the lack of such evidence is not fatal to the case.

57. See discussion of penalties at note 27.

58. 99 So. 2d 575, 72 A.L.R.2d 391 (Fla. 1957).

59. 134 N.Y.S.2d 779 (Sup. Ct. 1954), *modified,* 286 A.D. 825, 143 N.Y.S.2d 628 (1955).

60. 245 Miss. 185, 146 So. 2d 882 (1962).

61. 50 Tenn. App. 460, 362 S.W.2d 475 (1961).

62. *See also* Barcia v. Society of N.Y. Hosp., 39 Misc. 2d 526, 241 N.Y.S.2d 373 (Sup. Ct. 1963) (inadequate examination and a decision by a hospital intern in the emergency room to send the patient home before results of throat culture were known); Heddinger v. Ashford Memorial Community Hosp., 734 F.2d 81 (1st Cir. 1984) (had medical standards been followed, patient's finger would not have required amputation; jury verdict awarding $175,000 was justified); Tatrai v. Presbyterian Univ. Hosp., 439 A.2d 1162 (Pa. 1982) (hospital employee being treated in employer's emergency room has cause of action in negligence; workers' compensation is not exclusive remedy).

63. To collect damages, of course, the plaintiff must prove, usually by expert testimony, that a delay in diagnosis and treatment, or a delay occasioned by transfer to another institution, was the proximate cause of death or a worsened condition. *See, e.g.,* Ruvio v. North Browad Hosp. Dist., 186 So. 2d 45 (Fla Dist. Ct. App. 1966), *cert. denied,* 195 So. 2d 567 (Fla. 1966); Cooper v. Sisters of Charity of Cincinnati, 27 Ohio St. 2d 242, 272 N.E.2d 97 (1971) (although physician was negligent in not adequately examining a minor struck by a truck, no proof was shown that an appropriate examination would have saved the patient; hence, neither the physician nor the hospital was liable). *Accord* Rosen v. Parkway Hosp., 265 So. 2d 93 (Fla. Dist. Ct. App. 1972). *Cf.* Martin v. Washington Hosp. Center, 423 A.2d 913 (D.C. App. 1980) (expert testimony is not required on issue of proximate cause when jury has enough information to enable factual inferences; jury's verdict for plaintiff was justified when hospital emergency personnel released patient suffering anxiety caused by drug abuse who died in automobile accident 12 hours later); Valdez v. Lyman-Roberts Hosp., Inc., 638 S.W.2d 111 (Tex. Ct. App. 1982) (when evidence creates a reasonable inference that patient's condition could have been stabilized with proper care, a jury question is presented on the issue of proximate cause).
64. 271 N.W.2d 8 (S.D. 1978).
65. Carrasco v. Bankoff, 220 Cal. App. 2d 230, 33 Cal. Rptr. 673, 97 A.L.R.2d 464 (1963).
66. Mulligan v. Wetchler, 39 A.D.2d 102, 332 N.Y.S.2d 68 (1972).
67. Joint Commission on Accreditation of Healthcare Organizations, 1998 Hospital Accreditation Standards 69.
68. Darling v. Charleston Community Memorial Hosp., 33 Ill. 2d 326, 211 N.E.2d 253, 14 A.L.R.3d 860 (1965).
69. A survey conducted in 1983 by the Institute for Health Policy Studies at the University of California Medical School and the American Hospital Association revealed that 96.5 percent of 3,788 hospitals responding to the survey provide emergency services. The vast majority of these furnish care only within the institution, although the number of freestanding facilities operated by hospitals is increasing as a consequence of the current competitive environment. Ninety percent of the hospitals furnishing services have a formally organized emergency department. *Survey Reflects Emergency Care Changes,* HOSPS., Oct. 1, 1984 at 65.
70. *Darling, supra* note 68.
71. Pogue v. Hospital Auth. of DeKalb County, 120 Ga. App. 230, 170 S.E.2d 53 (1969). *See also* Dumer v. St. Michael's Hosp., 69 Wis. 2d 766, 233 N.W.2d 372 (1975) (a hospital was not liable for alleged negligence of a physician who was a member of Physicians Emergency Service Corporation, under contract with the hospital). *Compare* Newton County Hosp. v. Nickolson, 132 Ga. App. 164, 207 S.E.2d 659 (1974) (the hospital will be liable for an emergency room physician's negligence when he is paid an hourly wage and his schedule is controlled by the hospital).
72. 272 A.2d 718 (Del. 1970). Cases with similar reasoning are Lundberg v. Bay View Hosp., 175 Ohio St. 133, 191 N.E.2d 821 (1963) (involving a pathologist), and Kober v. Stewart, 148 Mont. 117, 417 P.2d 476 (1966)

(involving radiologists). See Chapter 5 for additional discussion and case citations.

73. Schagrin v. Wilmington Medical Center, Inc., 304 A.2d 61 (Del. 1973). *See also* Mduba v. Benedictine Hosp., 52 A.D.2d 450, 384 N.Y.S.2d 527 (1976) (a physician in charge of the emergency room was an employee of the hospital despite contractual language to the contrary, because the hospital controlled the means or manner of achieving emergency care through rule and regulations; even if the physician was not an employee, the hospital was liable for his negligence, because it held itself out to the public as furnishing emergency care).

74. Mehlman v. Powell, 281 Md. 269, 378 A.2d 1121 (1977); Rucker v. High Point Memorial Hosp., Inc., 20 N.C. App. 650, 202 S.E.2d 610 (1974); Gilligan v. Richmond Memorial Hosp., N.Y.L.J., July 22, 1982, at 12, col. 3B (N.Y.S.C.); Adamski v. Tacoma Gen. Hosp., 20 Wash. App. 98, 579 P.2d 970 (1978); Paintsville Hosp. Co. v. Rose, 683 S.W.2d 255 (Ky. 1985).

75. Arthur v. St. Peters Hosp., 169 N.J. Super. 575, 405 A.2d 443, 447 (1979).

76. Grewe v. Mt. Clemens Gen. Hosp., 404 Mich. 240, 273 N.W.2d 429, 433 (1978).

77. Hannola v. City of Lakewood, 68 Ohio App. 2d 61, 426 N.E.2d 1187 (1980).

78. Beeck v. Tucson Gen. Hosp., 18 Ariz. App. 165, 500 P.2d 1153 (1972) (consent form signed by the patient purporting to recognize radiologists as independent contractors was of no legal effect).

79. For example, Michigan's statute protects a physician, registered nurse, or licensed practical nurse from liability, even if care is rendered nongratuitously at the scene of an emergency, if no gross negligence or willful and wanton misconduct occurred and no previous patient relationship existed. MICH. COMP. LAWS ANN. §§ 691.1501–.1502 (West 1987).

80. MICH. COMP. LAWS ANN. § 333.20737 (West Supp. 1987); *see also* Ohio Rev. Code Ann. § 3303.21 (Baldwin 1986) (licensed emergency medical technician or paramedic not civilly liable for administering care, unless conduct was willful or wanton); ILL. REV. STAT. ch. 111$^{1/2}$, § 5517 (1987) (any person, agency, or governmental body authorized by this act who provides life support services in good faith in normal course of duties or in an emergency is not liable unless conduct was willful or wanton); N.J. STAT. ANN. § 2A:53A-12 (West Supp. 1987) (no member of volunteer rescue or emergency squad, including members of National Ski Patrol, shall be liable if services rendered in good faith and conduct not willful or wanton; immunity does not extend to operation of motor vehicle).

81. Emergency Medical Services Systems Act of 1973 (Pub. L. No. 93-145), codified as 42 U.S.C. § 300d-d-3 (repealed Oct. 1, 1981).

82. Nevertheless, Idaho considered it necessary to provide affirmatively that a physician shall not be required to furnish medical care and shall not be liable for refraining. IDAHO CODE § 39-1391c (1985).

83. MICH. COMP. LAWS § 691.1502 (West 1987). *See also* HAW. REV. STAT. § 663-1.5(c) (1985).

84. Matts v. Homsi, 106 Mich. App. 563, 308 N.W.2d 284 (1981).

85. McKenna v. Cedars of Lebanon Hosp., 93 Cal. App. 3d 282, 155 Cal. Rptr. 631 (1979) (resident physician not on call and not a member of hospital rescue

team); Burciaga v. St. John's Hosp., 232 Cal Rptr. 75 (1986) (staff pediatrician responded to medical emergency by treating newborn infant at request of obstetrician attending mother); *see also* Markman v. Kotler, 52 A.D.2d 579, 382 N.Y.S.2d 522 (1976) (Good Samaritan statute applied on facts even though a previous doctor-patient relationship existed).

86. Hamburger v. Henry Ford Hosp., 91 Mich. App. 580, 284 N.W.2d 155 (1979).

87. 78 Cal. App. 3d 885, 144 Cal. Rptr. 624 (1978); *See also* Gragg v. Neurological Assocs., 152 Ga. App. 586, 263 S.E.2d 496 (1979) (surgeon who responded to emergency in hospital's operating room not protected by Good Samaritan statute); Guerrero v. Copper Queen Hosp., 112 Ariz. 104, 537 P.2d 1329 (1975) (Good Samaritan law does not apply to hospital staff).

CONSENT FOR TREATMENT AND THE WITHHOLDING OF CONSENT

I t is a fundamental principle in Anglo-American law that the consent of the patient, or of someone authorized to act for a legally incompetent patient, must be obtained before any medical or surgical treatment is undertaken, unless an emergency justifies treatment without consent. The reason for this is that any unpermitted, intentional touching of the patient's person constitutes the tort of assault and battery, even if the person touched is not harmed or injured in any way.[1]

The law of assault and battery emphasizes, of course, that a mentally competent adult is in control of his or her person. Generally, medical or surgical treatment cannot be forced on a patient without consent, regardless of the urgency of the situation, unless some especially strong social policy is called into play to protect the interests of others.[2] It can therefore be said that a competent adult has the "right to die." (As will be seen, however, courts have sometimes ordered that care be rendered even when a competent adult has expressly refused it.) Regarding minors or the mentally incompetent, the same generalization applies. Medical treatment cannot be rendered over the objection of the parents or guardian, although the courts often protect the patient in such situations. When the patient cannot speak voluntarily because of incompetency, the law demands that someone in the proper position of authority speak as surrogate.

The classic judicial statement supporting the foregoing general principles is by Justice Cardozo in *Schloendorff v. Society of New York Hospital*:

> Every human being of adult years and sound mind has a right to determine what shall be done with his own body; and a surgeon who performs an operation without his patient's consent commits an assault for which he is liable in damages. This is true except in cases of emergency, where the patient is unconscious and where it is necessary to operate before consent can be obtained.[3]

The tort of assault and battery must be carefully distinguished from malpractice. Malpractice is professional negligence, the failure to adhere to legally imposed professional standards. Liability is based on deviation from the standards of medical practice as determined by reasonably prudent practitioners of the art of medicine in the same or similar communities under similar facts and circumstances; sometimes it is based simply on lack of reasonable care. In contrast, assault and battery is an intentional tort, as distinguished from negligence, and the wrong can occur even if all established professional standards have been followed in a given case. Lack of care is not relevant to a determination of whether an assault and battery has occurred. Both the torts of assault and battery and of malpractice may result, however, from a failure to obtain proper consent.

Court decisions have emphasized that an effective consent must be an *informed* consent. To grant an informed consent the patient must possess reasonably complete information about the advised medical treatment or surgery. The courts have said that if a doctor fails to warn the patient adequately regarding the risks accompanying the contemplated treatment or surgical procedure, the acceptable alternate methods of treatment, and the contemplated benefits of the proposed course, the consent given is not "informed" and is hence ineffective. Thus such a failure by the physician would result in liability for damages.

Types of Consent and Recommended Procedure

Legally sufficient consent can be classified as either express or implied in fact. (The latter is sometimes referred to as voluntary submission.) The difference between an express consent and an implied consent is in the method by which the patient, or the one authorized to consent, manifests consent. *Express consent* is manifested by words, oral or written, while *implied consent* is manifested by acts on the part of the patient and by all the circumstances surrounding the rendering of medical or surgical treatment. Both types of consent, to be sufficient, require that the patient—or the one authorized to consent—be conscious, be legally capable of giving consent and competent to do so, and possess knowledge and understanding regarding the medical or surgical treatment that is about to occur. Lack of knowledge and understanding regarding the nature and extent of the medical care that is purportedly consented to can overcome either express or implied consent presumably given.

Legally, therefore, consent need not be in writing. Oral express consent, if proved, is adequate. Moreover, a completely evident situation of voluntary submission to treatment is clearly adequate to protect the physician, nurse, or hospital from allegations of nonconsensual touching. To illustrate, a routine physical examination of a mentally competent, adult patient in a physician's office, or of a minor accompanied by a parent, need not be fortified by an express oral or written consent. A further illustration of a voluntary submission, or consent implied in fact, is a patient in labor presenting herself at the maternity or emergency department of a hospital.

When physicians or hospitals rely on an oral consent or on implied consent, however, at least two very real related problems of proof arise. First is the question of whether the patient, or the one authorized to consent, in fact consented to any treatment at all. Consent may be difficult to prove if reliance must be placed on an alleged oral consent or on implication from the facts of the particular case. Second, even if consent of some sort is established, a further question is whether the one consenting had full understanding and knowledge regarding the nature and the extent of the treatment that was in fact rendered.

Even when a written consent is obtained, subsequent proof by the patient that he or she lacked knowledge and understanding of what in fact took place will negate the written consent. Hence, one should never use a written consent purporting in very general language to authorize the surgeon or physician to do any procedure deemed necessary as a matter of professional judgment for the welfare of the patient. Such vague, general consent forms are no better protection for the physician and the hospital than simple reliance on voluntary submission. To illustrate, in *Rogers v. Lumberman's Mutual Casualty Company* the patient signed such a general consent form. The defendant surgeon successfully performed a hysterectomy. Subsequently the patient established that she thought she was consenting to an appendectomy, and she had not understood that the operation was to be a hysterectomy. No evidence existed of an emergency demanding immediate action by the surgeon to preserve life or health, hence the written, generalized consent was worthless to the physician. The facts that the surgery was skillfully performed and that a hysterectomy was medically advisable were immaterial, because these reasons do not justify proceeding without consent.[4] In similar fashion, surgery by a person other than the surgeon named by the patient constitutes battery by the "ghost" surgeon; furthermore, the surgeon who failed to perform the operation could be charged with malpractice.[5]

Physicians and hospitals are therefore advised to use two different written consent forms. The first should be obtained at the time of the patient's admission to the hospital, perhaps by the person processing the admission. It should recite simply that the patient, or one authorized to act, consents to routine hospital care, nursing service, and diagnostic procedures. The form should name the attending physician, and the wording should recognize that others—nurses and laboratory technicians, for instance—will touch the patient during hospitalization. The form should recite that no guarantees of cure have been made to the patient and that the nature of the hospital care to be rendered is fully understood.

In addition to the consent form obtained at the time of admission, the hospital should obtain a separate, special consent form whenever any surgery is undertaken, any anesthesia is used, any radium or x-ray therapy is employed, or any special diagnostic procedures are indicated. Other situations may arise in which the special consent form should be employed. The guiding principle should be to use a special form whenever the in-hospital procedure or treatment is classified as something more than routine hospital care.

The signature on the special consent form should be obtained only after the attending physician, or an intern or resident physician associated with the case, has had a clear conversation with the one giving consent, has conveyed all information necessary (in language the person understands), and has answered all questions. This conversation must not be conducted by a nurse or some member of the hospital's administrative staff. The reason is that the patient must fully understand the nature and extent of the surgical or medical procedure about to be undertaken if a consent is to be effective. Only a physician can properly convey the required knowledge and understanding. The physician should make note of the conversation in the medical record.

Once the physician has discussed the matter with the person giving consent, the consent form should be signed and witnessed. The form should name and authorize the physician or surgeon to select assistants, list the procedures to be undertaken, recite that the patient understands the procedures, recite consent to the administration of anesthesia under the supervision of a named physician or nurse, and state that the patient has received an explanation of the contemplated procedures. In addition, the language should recognize that unforeseen conditions arising during the surgery may dictate additional or different procedures from those contemplated and that the patient realized this and consents to such additional or different procedures as may in the professional judgment of the surgeon of physician be advisable.

It is elementary of course that any consent obtained by fraudulent misrepresentation is no consent at all. Moreover, signatures obtained after the partial administration of anesthesia or while the patient is under the influence of drugs may be worthless in proving valid onset if the patient is able to show that conditions at the time of signing prevented full understanding of the consequences of the purported consent.[6]

Experience indicates that the tactful, professional use of consent forms has beneficial effects on the physician-patient relationship. Certainly for the hospital and for the medical profession the use of the recommended consent forms ensures inexpensive protection from claims, perhaps unjust claims, of nonconsensual surgery or medical treatment. From the viewpoint of the patient-physician relationship, the use of the forms increases the patient's understanding and improves communication between the parties. Tactful application of techniques that make for better communication between doctor and patient are always encouraged. These consent procedures are recommended for that reason, not as a matter of legalistic formality.

Consent in Medical Emergencies

In a medical emergency no consent at all is required. In the absence of a competent refusal, the law presumes that consent has been given, and the lack of an express or implied-in-fact consent will not justify an action based on assault and battery or negligence against a physician or hospital. This rule applies to all patients regardless of age and is sometimes called consent implied by law.

It is not always easy, however, to define a medical emergency. To justify medical treatment without consent, the defendant must show, first, that it was not possible at the time treatment was undertaken to obtain the consent of the patient or the consent of the person authorized to act in place of the patient. Because a conscious, competent adult is generally entitled to refuse medical aid, even if failure to receive immediate care is likely to result in death, treatment without consent is permissible only when patients or those authorized to act for them are unable to express either approval or disapproval of the proposed treatment.

Second, the traditional legal concept of a medical emergency demands a situation where there is an immediate threat to life or a threat of permanent impairment of health. The medical need for a prompt operation or treatment is not tantamount to an emergency. According to some judicial decisions, if delaying treatment while consent is obtained would not increase the hazards to the patient, the "emergency" is not sufficient to justify treatment without consent.[7] Some cases, however, have liberalized the traditional legal definition of an emergency by permitting treatment without consent whenever immediate action is necessary to alleviate pain and suffering, even though no threat of irreparable harm is present.[8] The Emergency Medical Treatment and Active Labor Act provides a now well-established minimum definition of "emergency."[9]

The doctor who treats without consent always has the burden to establish by the preponderance of the evidence that an emergency existed. Medical personnel who treat without consent should thus make every reasonable effort to document the circumstances of the situation. Adequate notes should be included in the medical record explaining the immediate threat to life or health. Consultation with other physicians, if they are available and time permits, is most wise and helpful in justifying the attending physician's action.

Akin to the medical emergency, where treatment can proceed without consent, is the discovery of unanticipated conditions during surgery. The legal question is whether the surgeon is justified in extending the surgery to correct the unanticipated or undiagnosed conditions. Certainly, if the patient who consented to a given procedure was competent and rational and specifically prohibited any extension of the procedure, then the surgeon must not perform any extension, even if life depends on such extension. Normally, however, there will not be any specific instructions from the patient prohibiting extensions of surgery. The traditional and older legal rule is that the surgeon must not engage in any extension of the contemplated procedure unless an unanticipated condition is found during surgery that is itself an emergency and must be corrected at once to obviate an immediate threat to life or a permanent impairment of health.[10] Under this traditional rule, in the absence of an intraoperative emergency the better procedure is to complete the original surgery and correct the discovered condition at a later time.

A few cases, however, have developed a more liberal legal rule: a surgeon may extend the originally contemplated surgery whenever an unanticipated condition becomes evident during surgery and makes it medically advisable to correct the condition immediately.[11] This liberalized approach, however, is not legal sanction to the surgeon to proceed without consent whenever it seems advisable. The courts will still insist that medical and surgical treatment is a matter for the patient to decide. To avoid the risk of a court later holding that extension of surgery was not justified, it is wise to include in the surgical consent form a statement that surgeons and surgical assistants may, in the exercise of their professional judgment, extend the originally contemplated procedure to correct or alleviate unanticipated conditions discovered during the course of the operation.[12] Such language in the consent form and the liberalized attitude of some courts are consistent with common sense and good surgical technique. Physicians realize, and patients should also realize, that a precise diagnosis is frequently difficult if not impossible prior to surgery. Physicians should adequately explain to the patient the frequent advisability of surgical extensions. With proper explanations of this kind before the surgery is undertaken, the surgeon has no need to fear that a medically justified extension will produce a claim by the patient alleging treatment without consent.

The Healthcare Institution's Role in Consent Cases

Most lawsuits alleging lack of consent are brought against the attending physician or surgeon. Any professional or nonprofessional person, however, could be the alleged wrongdoer, and hence all individuals having responsibility for patients must be familiar with the law protecting the patient from nonconsensual touchings.

Further, attorneys for the plaintiff often also bring assault and battery or negligence actions against the hospital or institution. In actions arising out of an assault and battery or negligence, the hospital or other institution can be liable on either one of two theories. First, it is liable vicariously for the torts of its employees committed within the scope of their employment. This is the doctrine of *respondeat superior*, which is translated as "let the master answer." The theory rests on the principle that an employer should be liable for the personal wrongs that employees commit while they are furthering the business.

The second theory, in contrast to the doctrine of *respondeat superior,* is based on the institution's own corporate neglect or fault in failing to see that treatment without proper consent does not take place on its premises. If a hospital knows or should know that a battery or negligence is about to be committed on its premises and does nothing to prevent the event, the hospital is quite likely to be liable in damages to the aggrieved patient because it has failed to perform a duty it owes directly to the patient.

When the patient proceeds against the hospital on the theory of *respondeat superior,* he or she must establish, first, that the individual committing the wrong was an employee of the hospital. In the hospital setting, all nonprofessional people, as well as nurses, x-ray technicians, physiotherapists, interns, and resident physicians are normally employees rather than independent contractors. As a result the hospital would normally be liable for torts committed by these individuals.[13] Having established that the individual committing the wrong was an agent or a servant, the patient must further establish that the wrong was committed within the scope of employment. This is done simply by showing that the tort was committed while furthering the employer's business. As we shall see, the doctrine of *respondeat superior* comes into play in other questions of hospitals' liability. Here it is mentioned to emphasize that it is applicable to cases alleging treatment without proper consent.

Staff physicians are generally not employees of the hospital but independent contractors. Normally therefore the hospital is liable for treatment by a staff physician without the patient's consent so far as the doctrine of *respondeat superior* is concerned, at least when the doctor has been privately employed by the patient.[14] In some states, however, the payment of a salary is considered sufficient to invoke this doctrine and thus to hold the hospital liable for battery or negligence by the physician. Moreover, some courts have developed the theory of "ostensible" or "apparent" agency to justify holding the hospital liable for the tort of one who is in fact an independent contractor. This theory rests on the notion that the hospital has acted to represent to the patient that a given physician is in its employ, such as when the hospital contracts with a group of emergency physicians to provide coverage for the emergency department.[15]

When the patient proceeds against the hospital on the theory that the institution has violated its direct duty to use reasonable care in ascertaining that batteries do not occur on the hospital premises, the plaintiff need not establish that the alleged wrongdoer was an employee of the hospital. It is only necessary, after establishing that a nonconsensual touching did occur, to show that the hospital knew or in the exercise of reasonable care should have known that a battery or negligence was about to occur and did nothing to prevent the act.[16]

Previous discussion has emphasized that consent must be an "informed consent" and that hospitals and their medical staffs should use two separate written consent forms. The first would be obtained at the time of admission to the hospital and would cover routine hospital care; the second would pertain to surgical procedures and extraordinary or high-risk diagnostic procedures. Also stressed was the principle that the patient's signature on the second consent form should be obtained by the attending physician and not by the hospital's administrative or nursing personnel because only a doctor is professionally qualified to see that the consent is "informed."

The issue then is: how far must a hospital go in making certain that its medical staff physicians are in fact obtaining the informed consent of their patients? If a hospital is to protect itself from liability for treatment or surgery without consent, the hospital must as a minimum have administrative rules and regulations regarding the procurement of a properly drafted written consent consistent with reasonable and prudent standards of hospital care, including standards promulgated by the Joint Commission on Accreditation of Healthcare Organizations. Having adopted rules and regulations, it must then devise procedures to ensure enforcement of the rules.[17] Operating room supervisors or the chief surgical nurse should be assigned the responsibility of checking on the patient's identity and making certain that no surgery is undertaken before proper consent is obtained. Do hospital personnel need to go even further and inquire whether the private attending physician or surgeon has explained the contemplated treatment or procedure well enough to meet the legal tests of informed consent? A New York court said no in *Fiorentino v. Wenger*.[18] In this case the hospital personnel had no reason to know that the doctor who asked the father of a minor patient to sign the written consent form for surgery had not adequately explained the procedure, nor was the hospital aware that the surgery itself constituted malpractice because the type of spinal surgery performed on the patient was not generally recognized in the medical profession as acceptable. The defendant surgeon himself had developed the procedure and was at the time the only surgeon using that technique. In the absence of proof that the hospital knew or should have known that the surgeon failed to furnish adequate information to the patient's father or that the surgery would be malpractice, the hospital was not held to be responsible.[19]

In conclusion, so far as the doctrine of informed consent is concerned, the hospital appears to perform its duty to the patient by making private staff physicians aware that they must properly inform patients and by insisting that adequate written documentation of patients' consent be placed in the medical chart. The hospital, in other words, need not be an actual party or participant in privately employed physicians' discussions with patients or with persons legally authorized to consent for them. However, if nursing or administrative staff of the hospital know or ought to have known that a private physician has not obtained a legally sufficient consent or has otherwise acted unreasonably, then the hospital has a duty to prevent the unauthorized surgery or treatment; liability could follow from a breach of this duty.

The Doctrine of Informed Consent

As we have seen, because the patient is in control of his or her person, unless the facts and circumstances of the particular situation indicate an overriding social policy to the contrary, consent granted for medical care or surgery must be *informed*. But how far must a physician go in explaining to the patient the status of the diagnosis, the nature of the recommended treatment or procedure, the alternatives available, the possible or probable risks involved, and the expected benefits or outcome of the contemplated care?

The cases on this question are of three types. In the first type, the issue is framed as whether the physician has misrepresented the nature or character of the treatment or surgery (either affirmatively or by silence). Such a factual pattern can be characterized as an intentional tort, either an assault and battery or fraud. Illustrative of this type is *Rogers v. Lumberman's Mutual Casualty Company*,[20] in which the patient understood that she was to undergo an appendectomy when in fact a hysterectomy was performed. The consent form, written in very general language and failing to name the surgical procedure to be performed, did not protect the doctor from liability because the physician failed to explain the nature of the contemplated surgery and the medical indications of the patient's condition. The fiduciary duty that exists between the doctor and the patient certainly requires, at a minimum, full disclosure of the nature of the diagnosed condition, all material or significant facts concerning the condition, and an explanation of the more probable consequences and difficulties inherent in the situation.

Corn v. French illustrates a doctor's affirmative misrepresentation of the surgery to be undertaken.[21] After examining the patient, the physician recommended that she submit to a "test" for a possible malignancy. The patient then asked her doctor if he intended to remove her breast. He apparently replied in the negative. She signed a written consent form indication that a "mastectomy" was to be performed but received no explanation of this medical term and did not, in fact, know what the word mastectomy meant. Clearly there was liability for an unauthorized operation, even absent proof of medical malpractice in departing form acceptable professional treatment.

The second type of case involving informed consent is based on the rule that the patient is entitled to know the inevitable risks or results of the contemplated surgery. To illustrate, in *Bang v. Charles T. Miller Hospital,* an elderly male patient expressly consented to a transurethal resection of the prostate. He was not told that because of the particular circumstances, including his age and the possibility of infection, this professionally acceptable surgical technique would render him sterile. Accordingly there was liability.[22] This case can also be cited as authority for the proposition that a patient is entitled to an explanation of the alternatives to treatment or surgical techniques. In this situation the surgeon should have explained to the patient that protecting his ability to father children might entail a substantial risk of infection.

The third type of case—and clearly the most difficult for both physicians and the courts—involves the duty to disclose the foreseeable risks of the proposed treatment. These cases in turn break down into subcategories (or at least express differing legal theories or underlying philosophies) depending on the particular facts and the jurisdictions in which they are decided.

Both *Natanson v. Kline* in Kansas and *Mitchell v. Robinson* in Missouri seem to speak in terms of liability based on negligence or malpractice for failure to disclose possibly serious risks. In *Natanson* the physician recommended cobalt radiation therapy following removal of the patient's breast for cancer. The therapy was skillfully performed. The patient was not, however, informed that the therapy involved substantial risk of tissue damage. The Kansas Supreme Court held that the patient was entitled to be told in advance of probable consequences or hazards known to the doctor and that the physician was obligated to make "reasonable disclosures" as determined by what a reasonable medical practitioner would make under the same or similar circumstances.[23] Similarly, in *Mitchell* the Missouri Supreme Court said that plaintiff, who was given electroshock and insulin therapy, had the right to be informed that 18 to 25 percent of such patients suffered convulsions as a result of the treatment. In this particular case a convulsion caused fractured vertebrae. Although there was no allegation or evidence of negligence in the diagnosis or treatment, the court held that a jury must decide the factual question of whether the defendant was negligent in failing to apprise the patient of the risks.[24] The duty was to make reasonable disclosure of significant facts and probable consequences.

When liability is based on a negligence theory, the plaintiff must generally establish by expert testimony what disclosures of risks and hazards a reasonable medical practitioner would make under the particular circumstances. The answer may in turn depend on the custom or generally accepted professional standards of practice in the local medical community. For example, in a Delaware case, according to expert evidence a risk of damage to the voice existed in only 2 percent of the competently performed thyroidectomy operations, and it was not the custom of the medical profession in the area to warn patients of this risk. The court ruled that the defendant physician had no legal duty to disclose the risk.[25]

On the other hand, the plaintiff in a negligence action need not *always* present expert medical testimony to establish liability because the court may rule as a matter of law that the physician had a duty to disclose. The Kansas court did so in *Natanson*, where the evidence was clear that there had been no explanation of risks at all. Nevertheless, the usual malpractice action does require expert testimony to establish deviation from recognized professional standards, as in the *DiFilippo* case and others.[26] This judicial approach to the physician's duty of disclosure has been characterized by some commentators as the "reasonable doctor" rule.

By this line of decisions, if the plaintiff presents no expert witness testimony whatsoever to show the prevailing standards of disclosure in the medical community, the court will rule as a matter of law for the defendant. On the other hand, if there is conflicting expert testimony, the matter usually becomes a question for the jury.

On the other hand, informed consent cases that proceed on an assault and battery cause of action do not require expert testimony to support a verdict for the plaintiff because the facts can be established by credible lay testimony. Further, in a battery action punitive damages might be available to a plaintiff who could establish an evil or malicious intent on the part of the defendant, whereas only compensatory damages for actual harm or injury are normally available in a cause of action based on negligence or malpractice.

In contrast to the traditional, "reasonable doctor" rule, recent cases involving informed consent reject the idea that the doctor's duty to disclose is based on the prevailing custom among similarly situated practitioners. This newer approach stems from the premise that the physician's fiduciary duty is to provide full disclosure of all facts and risks that are relevant to the patient's granting of informed consent, regardless of what other physicians customarily disclose. The issue may still be one for the jury to decide, but it will rest on lay testimony rather than expert evidence. The rule has been characterized as the "reasonable patient" rule, or sometimes as the "right to know" rule.

The traditional view—that the nature and extent of a doctor's disclosure of the risks of treatment are to be measured by the prevailing standards of practice among similarly situated practitioners, which normally requires the patient to present expert medical testimony to prove a departure from standards—is of course highly favorable to the medical profession. It permits physicians to establish their own disclosure standards, and it burdens the plaintiff with the task of obtaining expert witnesses in support of the suit. Accordingly, most courts now adopt some other criteria for disclosure than those of prevailing professional standards, and to eliminate the evidentiary requirement of expert testimony.

Rejecting the concept that a physician must disclose to the extent that peers disclose was a 1972 Rhode Island case, *Wilkinson v. Vesey*, in which a diagnosis of malignancy was made although no biopsy was conducted. Treatments by radiation resulted in severe radiation burns that required eight subsequent operations, and it was eventually determined that the patient had never suffered from cancer.

In a suit based on the absence of an informed consent (among other allegations) the Rhode Island Supreme Court reversed the trial court's directed verdict in favor of the defendant radiologists. The court ruled that the patient was entitled to be informed of all material information and significant risks and need not present expert testimony pertaining to prevailing practices of other practitioners and the extent to which they customarily disclose.[27] The question of what the medical profession "knows" about risks would require expert testimony, but what the patient needs to know to make an intelligent choice can be decided by the jury. "Materiality" was defined in terms of both the "dangerousness" of the treatment or surgery and any other matters that would be significant to a reasonable person. The statistical remoteness of a risk does not determine its materiality because even a very small chance of serious consequences can be significant to a reasonable person.

Similarly, the California Supreme Court in *Cobbs v. Grant* held that the extend and scope of disclosure is not to be measured by generally acceptable professional practices.[28] Rather, disclosure of known hazards, inherent risks, and untoward results must be based on matters that are material to the individual patient's needs and decisional process,[29] although to assert a successful claim the patient must prove to the satisfaction of the jury that a reasonably prudent person would have refused consent for the treatment or surgery if an objective inquiry so indicated. (This proof would establish that lack of sufficient information about the surgery was the proximate cause of the injuries suffered.) The physician need not disclose minor risks of common knowledge to the lay patient, nor must disclosure be made if the patient exhibits a desire not to be informed. Finally, disclosure is unnecessary if, in the physician's documented opinion, full revelation of material information would adversely affect the patient's rational decision about consenting to the recommended treatment.

In *Cobbs* the patient underwent surgery for a duodenal ulcer in the course of which an artery at the base of the spleen was severed. That organ had to be removed as a result. Still later a gastric ulcer required removal of 50 percent of the patient's stomach. Although the patient had consented to the initial surgery, he was not informed that injuries to the spleen occur in approximately 5 percent of such operations. At the trial court level the plaintiff made allegations against the hospital and the surgeon charging both malpractice and negligence: malpractice in the conduct of the surgery and subsequent care, and negligence in the failure to obtain an informed consent. The jury returned a verdict for plaintiff against the hospital for $45,000 and against the surgeon for $23,800.

When the surgeon appealed the verdict against him, the Supreme Court of California returned the matter for a new trial, saying that it could not determine whether the verdict against the surgeon was based on the theory of malpractice in the conduct of the surgery and care or the theory of negligence in failing to obtain an informed consent. If the former, the verdict was not justified because there was inadequate evidence to support a finding of malpractice in the conduct of the surgery. If, on the other hand, the judgment was based on an inadequate explanation to the patient of material collateral risks and hazards, then the decision in favor of the plaintiff was proper, as long as it was consistent with the judicial guidelines noted in the case.

The ruling in *Cobbs v. Grant* has been extended to a situation in which the patient rejected her family doctor's advice and refused to have a Pap smear, apparently because she was unable to afford the cost of the test. Over a six-year period the defendant physician had treated her for several routine conditions, rendered advice on family matters, and cared for the patient during her second pregnancy. On repeated occasions he had recommended a general physical examination, and in particular a Pap smear. Assuming that his patient knew the purpose of this diagnostic test for cancer, the physician had not apprised her specifically of the risk involved in failing to have the test performed. When cervical cancer was eventually discovered by a specialist, the tumor was too far advanced for surgical removal and alternate forms of treatment proved to be unsuccessful. On these facts the California Supreme Court held that the trial court erred by not instructing the jury that the physician had a duty to disclose all relevant and material information, including the risks of refusing recommended care.[30] It would then be the jury's responsibility to determine whether the duty had been breached and, if so, whether the breach was the proximate cause of the patient's death. (This has sometimes been called a cause of action for "informed refusal.")[31]

As these cases show, physicians must exercise "reasonable care under the circumstances." Unless they know that a patient is already aware of the risk or that a given risk would not have any apparent materiality to the patient's decision, or unless they can establish that disclosure would adversely affect the rationality of a patient's decision, they must provide all significant information to the patient to allow for an *informed* consent. All such matters are to be submitted to the jury for decision without requiring plaintiff to provide expert testimony showing materiality of the nondisclosure, although experts must of course be used to establish medical facts—for example, the risks associated with a given procedure and to show that the patient's current condition is a result of the surgery or care rendered. In summary, the decisions rendered in these major cases removed the need for plaintiff to present expert medical testimony with respect to the required extent and scope of disclosure, and they created judicial rules or criteria for disclosure in place of professional custom and practices.

Several states have attempted from time to time to modify the liberalized informed consent doctrine by enacting legislation intended to restrict the judicially imposed standards of care. Statutes may specify, perhaps in detail, or delegate to licensing authority the duty of specifying the extent of information to be given a patient and then recite:

1. that a written consent form in compliance with the statutory standards will be presumed to be valid and effective unless the person who obtained the consent was not acting in good faith;
2. that the signing of the consent form was induced by fraudulent misrepresentation of material facts; or
3. that the person signing the form was unable to understand the language in which the form was written.[32]

For example, legislation in Hawaii authorizes the board of medical examiners to establish reasonable standards, applicable to specific surgical and treatment procedures, for the information the patient must be given to be reasonably informed of probable risks. The measure also provides that these standards shall be *prima facie* evidence of the standards of care required.[33] There is no evidence, however, to support the view that the statutes are effective as a deterrent to malpractice claims. Although some courts have upheld legislative intent when interpreting a particular statute and have ruled that the statutory presumption of validity prevails,[34] other courts have reduced the intended effectiveness of legislation by applying a very strict interpretation of statutory language.

In a few unusual circumstances, the courts have recognized that the physician may limit or withhold information from the patient for sound therapeutic reasons.[35] For example, full disclosure might well complicate or hinder treatment, depending on the patient's emotional state or personal traits. Hence, to further the interests of the patient's welfare the physician may in the exercise of professional judgment provide a less than full explanation of collateral risks and hazards in the proposed treatment or surgery. The physician should of course document the reasons for limiting or withholding information by appropriate notations in the medical record. The privilege could not be successfully asserted if the facts indicated that a competent and rational patient would have declined treatment had there been disclosure.

As should be evident, it is especially important to obtain an informed consent for any innovative therapy and for medical research involving human subjects. Such consent must be evidenced with a specially drafted, written consent form. In methods of treatment not yet accepted by the medical profession as standard practice where the contemplated therapeutic benefits are unknown or uncertain, the facts as known and unknown to the physician become of material importance to the patient. In a malpractice case involving the well-known cardiologist and surgeon, Dr. Denton A. Cooley, and his colleague, Dr. Liotta, a soundly prepared consent form and clear testimony at trial resulted in a court-directed verdict for the physicians.[36] The estate of a deceased patient alleged that the physicians had failed to obtain informed consent for ventriculoplasty surgery.

There is a difference between innovative therapy and medical research or experimentation. Like standard medical practice, which is defined as "interventions that are designed solely to enhance the well-being of an individual patient" with "a reasonable expectation of success,"[37] innovative therapy is intended also to benefit the patient, even though the treatments or procedures undertaken during innovative therapy are unsupported by data showing a reasonable expectation of success. Medical research, in contrast (sometimes called experimentation), is a departure from standard practice that is untested but is intended to test a hypothesis or develop new knowledge.[38] Thus, innovative therapy focuses on benefit to the individual patient while research or experimentation is undertaken most frequently to prove or disprove researchers' hypothesis for the possible benefit of a large number of patients. Both differ from standard practice in that proof of efficacy is lacking and knowledge of relative risks and benefits may be uncertain.

Because the risks and benefits of both innovative therapy and medical research are uncertain, it is essential that the patient be fully informed and that written consent be evidenced by a specially drafted form. The duty to patients of physicians recommending innovative therapy is determined solely by the general principles of tort law and malpractice liability on a state-by-state basis.[39] The doctrine of informed consent is especially relevant, and the consent form should be drafted in appropriate language that the patient can readily understand.

On the other hand, when biomedical and behavioral research is financed by a grant or contract from the Department of Health and Human Services and the research involves human subjects, then both the common law and federal legislation govern the selection of subjects, the obtaining and documentation of an informed consent, and the monitoring of data to ensure the subjects' safety and privacy and to minimize the risks.[40] Research is defined in the federal regulations as "a systematic investigation designed to develop or contribute to generalized knowledge."[41] Exempt from the legislation are survey research projects that involve no risk to those persons surveyed and programs that collect pathological specimens without means of identifying individual patients. Each institution conducting research that is regulated must create an institutional review board consisting of at least five persons, which approves the program and ensures ongoing compliance with the regulations.[42] To ensure that participation in research is voluntary there are detailed regulations governing the obtaining of patients' consent.[43] These specify that the written consent form be approved by the institutional review board and be signed by the patient or a legally authorized representative. Specifically, the review board has the responsibility of determining that the "risks to subjects are reasonable in relation to anticipated benefits, if any, to subjects, and to the importance of the knowledge that may reasonably be expected to result."[44] Thus, the board has the responsibility of balancing the risks and benefits when approving biomedical and behavioral research projects. Especially noteworthy are the additional detailed provisions applicable to grants and contract supporting research involving a human fetus, pregnant women, and human in vitro fertilization.[45] Similarly, the regulations provide additional protection to prisoners[46] and children.[47] "Children" are persons who are not legally capable of granting their own consent for medical treatment as determined by local and state law. Finally, it should be noted that in addition to the regulation of research financed by the Department of Health and Human Services, the Federal Food and Drug Administration regulates the testing of experimental drugs when human subjects are involved. As in medical research regulations, approval and review of experimental drug programs by an institutional review board is required.[48]

Without doubt the doctrine of informed consent raises significant problems for the physician and surgeon. On balance the courts seem primarily interested in increasing communication between physicians and their patients and in emphasizing the competent individual's freedom of choice. Moreover, from the physician's point of view, a fully informed patient is much less likely to be surprised, disappointed, or angry when unexpected and perhaps unfortunate results do follow medical treatment, diagnostic tests, or surgery. Practices by physicians and hospital personnel that increase communication and foster mutual understanding are the best possible antidotes for misunderstanding and litigation on the part of the patient.

The major criteria for the physician deciding how much to tell patients should always be their welfare and needs. The physician should review such questions as the following:

1. Is the patient likely to be unaware of a known hazard or risk?
2. Would a reasonably prudent patient be likely to withhold consent if aware of the risk?
3. Is there any acceptable justification for failing to disclose?
4. Is the risk or hazard, however remote, material to the patient's decision?

Patients do not need to be given a medical school education. But they should be informed and have trust and confidence in those caring for them. There is now a clear-cut judicial attitude that physicians must practice the golden rule and do as they would be done by.

Consent of Spouse or Other Relative

If the patient is competent to consent, neither the spouse nor a relative is authorized to render consent. Marriage or blood relationship alone does not make one the agent of the other. Because a spouse's or relative's consent is not normally necessary, the only reason for discussing the patient's condition with a spouse or a relative would be to improve relations with the patient's family.[49] In one case the ruling was to the effect that when it was possible to obtain a patient's consent before administration of sedatives to the patient and this was not done, the spouse's consent to surgery would not protect the surgeon or the hospital from liability.[50]

In special circumstances, however, a spouse's consent may be mandatory or advisable as a legal matter even though the patient is competent. This occurs if the procedure to which the patient has consented involves, for example, artificial insemination, surrogate motherhood, or even some types of purely elective surgery adversely affecting the normal function of reproductive organs. For such treatment, elected by the patient, a spouse's consent is generally deemed advisable by conservative legal opinion because the spouse in his or her own right may otherwise have a valid common-law cause of action for damages, based either on the theory of unjustified interference with the marital relationship or on the legal right of consortium. Moreover, there are local statutory requirements on a state-by-state basis pertaining or relevant to artificial insemination and surrogate motherhood. A thorough discussion of these matters is beyond the scope of this chapter. Nevertheless, it should be noted here that frequently the statutes contain a specific requirement that both husband and wife must consent voluntarily to a heterologous artificial insemination. Similarly, when a married woman is in the role of a surrogate mother, the consent of her husband should be obtained to overcome the usual presumption that a married man is the father of a child born to his wife.

When the patient's health and well-being are at risk, even if reproductive capacity is adversely affected, the consent of the spouse is not necessary. An Oklahoma case has held that the husband, who had not consented to his wife's hysterectomy, had no cause of action for loss of consortium.[51] In short, the wife's right to health is paramount, and her decision alone, based on the professional advice of her physician, is controlling. A reading of this case indicates that "health of the patient" will be very broadly construed, and that modern courts will be extremely reluctant to recognize a separate right in a husband to a fertile wife or vice versa. Moreover, as we see in Chapter 12, "Family Planning," a husband has no right of his own to prevent the surgical procedure on his wife. Nevertheless, whenever surgery of any nature affects the reproductive capacity of the patient, it is wise to obtain the spouse's consent, if possible, in deference to sound physician-family relations. If a competent adult patient seeks and consents to such a procedure, however, and if the patient's physician can justify the surgery as necessary to the physical or mental health of the patient, or if the patient has a constitutional right to the procedure as in the case of an abortion, then consent of the spouse is not necessary.

It follows that if a competent adult has consented to treatment or surgery necessary to preserve his or her physical or mental health, including sterilization or other surgery likely to affect adversely the reproductive function, the refusal of a spouse's or relative's consent should not be honored to prevent treatment of the patient, nor should refusal prevent treatment considered necessary in any medical emergency involving a threat to life or health, where the patient had not previously expressed an opinion regarding treatment and is unable at the time to give an effective consent. The reason is that a spouse or relative has no legal right to bar treatment necessary to preserve the life or the health of the patient when the latter has consented or when an emergency exists and the law presumes that the patient would consent. To illustrate, in *Collins v. Davis* an adult patient who had sought medical attention became comatose and required surgery to save his life. The spouse refused to consent to surgery, whereupon the hospital referred the matter to an appropriate court and obtained an order permitting the operation.[52]

If the spouse's consent or that of the nearest relative is sought and refused, the best advice is to proceed in the attempt to preserve life solely on the basis of the patient's own consent, if obtainable, or on the basis of a medical emergency if the patient's consent is not obtainable. If the patient is not competent to consent and time permits, the hospital could consider obtaining a court order, but even in the absence of such an order the spouse would have no legal right to bar emergency care for the patient designed to preserve life and restore health. If the spouse or nearest relative has no right to refuse consent on behalf of the patient, a suit for damages by the spouse or relative is not likely to be successful.

If the question of consent concerns withholding or discontinuing treatment, or administering treatment that is of doubtful effectiveness or otherwise "extraordinary," consent of a relative to withhold care may not be sufficient. These special circumstances are discussed later in this chapter under "Consent for Treatment of Incompetent Adults" and "Consent for Treatment of Minors."

Refusal of Patient to Consent

Recall that an emergency eliminates the need to obtain consent because the law values the preserving of life and the prevention of permanent impairment to health. This rule, however, applies only when the patient is incapable of expressing consent by reason of unconsciousness, mental incompetence, or legal disability. It further applies only when the person legally authorized to consent to the incompetent patient is similarly incompetent or unavailable.

Hence, the philosophical and legal situation is quite different when a competent adult patient expressly refuses to consent to medical or surgical treatment, for whatever reason. The logic begins with the point, quite consistent with the need to obtain consent, that the patient's express refusal of treatment or withdrawal of consent to a continuation of treatment must be honored—even if death is the likely result. Accordingly, one frequently hears that there is a legally recognized "right to die" unless a compelling state interest overrides the rights of the patient.

If follows that there would be civil liability for treatment rendered contrary to the express wishes of the mentally and legally competent patient. It also follows that a court would normally not step in and order treatment for such a patient; personal rights of self-determination outweigh the interest of society in preserving life. There are several leading cases to this effect.[53] Moreover, the common law right to refuse medical care, expressed while competent and proven by clear and convincing evidence, must be honored if the patient later becomes incompetent. On such facts a court will not order continuation of treatment on the basis of society's *parens patriae* power (the power to stand in as a "parent" to protect the welfare of incompetent persons), nor will the "substituted judgment" rule, to be discussed, apply.[54]

It likewise follows logically that a physician will not be criminally liable for honoring a competent adult's wish to forgo treatment or withdraw from ongoing treatment. The physician's duty to render care (even "ordinary" care) ends when consent is refused, thus eliminating any possible criminal liability.[55] Of course, active euthanasia (affirmative steps, such as administering a lethal injection to end the patient's life) may be considered homicide, as the ongoing saga of Dr. Kevorkian clearly shows.

The test of mental competence is whether patients understand their condition, the nature of the medical advice rendered, and the consequences of refusing to consent. A patient's decision does not need to appear rational; that is, a questionable decision does not necessarily indicate incompetency. In one famous case, a 72-year-old man with extensive gangrene in both legs faced death within three weeks unless his legs were amputated; with surgery, his chances of recovery were good. The hospital petitioned the court for a determination of incompetency, appointment of a guardian, and authorization of amputation and other necessary treatment. The hospital argued that the man's refusal was "an aberration from normal behavior" and that the refusal amounted to suicide. The court held, however, that the man was competent and that in such an extensive bodily invasion the patient's right to privacy outweighed the state's interest in the preservation of life.[56]

Mental competence is, of course, a matter for physicians to decide in their professional judgment. If it is determined that the patient is incompetent and that refusal to consent is therefore not based on free choice, the matter should be referred to the appropriate court for a legal determination of incompetence and the appointment of a guardian. If there is no time for a court determination, and if the physicians have decided in their professional judgment that the patient is incompetent, then it is better to render treatment in the interest of attempting to protect life. The legal exposure is greater in a malpractice suit based on inaction than in one based on lifesaving treatment contrary to wishes, assuming of course that the doctors have fully documented their determination of incompetence. When a competent adult refuses consent or withdraws consent, the physician or hospital, or both of these, should obtain written acknowledgment of the refusal from the patient and a release of liability. The form should be filed in the patient's medical record. If the patient refuses to sign such a form, then full documentation of the refusal of treatment should be recorded in the chart by those who witnessed the patient refuse.

The patient's right to choose or refuse treatment has been based on common law, the right of self-determination on which the doctrine of informed consent is grounded, and the right to privacy first enunciated in the abortion decisions. In addition, some state statutes specifically give the patient the right to refuse treatment.[57] However, the right is not unlimited. The state is usually said to have four interests that may override the individual's freedom to decide:

1. the preservation of life;
2. the protection of innocent third parties;
3. the preservation of the ethical integrity of the medical profession; and
4. the prevention of suicide.

The interest most often promoted by courts ordering treatment over a patient's objections is the protection of third parties, usually minor children or the unborn fetus. For example, in *In re Application of the President and Directors of Georgetown College, Inc.* the court ordered a blood transfusion for a mother for the sake of her 7-month-old child, in spite of her refusal on religious grounds.[58] The survival of dependent children, however, is not always sufficient to override the patient's right of refusal. A court did not order a transfusion to save the life of a 34-year-old Jehovah's Witness, even though he had two young children. The judge was convinced that adequate provision had been made for the children's well-being.[59]

The state is also said to have an interest in "maintaining the ethical integrity of the medical profession by protecting physicians against the compelled violation of their professional standards and against exposure to the risk of civil or criminal liability."[60] Thus, the argument goes, physicians should not be forced to give (or withhold) treatment against their medical judgment or to assist in suicide or expose themselves to possible manslaughter charges or malpractice suits. This purported state interest, however, is no longer held to outweigh the patient's right to refuse treatment.[61] Rather, the courts and legislatures have attempted to provide legal protection for physicians who accede to their patients' wishes. For example, according to the "natural death acts" discussed below, healthcare providers who comply with the provisions of these acts are not subject to criminal prosecution or civil liability. It is also recognized that withholding or withdrawing life-sustaining treatment is in some instances consistent with medical ethics:

> [I]t is perfectly apparent . . . that humane decisions against resuscitative or maintenance therapy are frequently a recognized *de facto* response in the medical world to the irreversible, terminal, painridden patient, especially with familial consent . . . that physicians distinguish between curing the ill and comforting and easing the dying; that they refuse to treat the curable as if they were dying or ought to die, and that they have sometimes refused to treat the hopeless and dying as if they were curable. . . . [M]any of them have refused to inflict an undesired prolongation of the process of dying on a patient in irreversible condition when it is clear that such "therapy" offers neither human nor humane benefit.[62]

In recent years many courts have held that society's interest in preservation of life is not sufficient to prevent a competent adult from making his or her own decisions about treatment, at least when no third persons might be affected.[63] The less hopeful the patient's condition, and the more intrusive the therapy, the weaker is the state's interest in preserving life. Even when the prognosis for recovery is good, however, the patient's right is usually upheld.[64]

Because most courts have determined that forgoing medical treatment is not the equivalent of suicide but a decision to permit nature to take its course, the fourth interest, the prevention of suicide, is usually not relevant to decisions concerning termination of treatment. However, the line between actively taking life—suicide and euthanasia—and letting nature take its course is not always clear. Courts will not condone suicide or euthanasia, but they may differ on whether a given set of facts constitutes either of these.

For example, an 85-year-old resident of a nursing home was suffering from multiple ailments and deteriorating health. Although the man, a former college president, did not have a terminal illness, he was very discouraged about his future and decided to hasten his death by fasting. A court found that the man was competent and had the right to refuse food and that the nursing home was neither obligated nor authorized to force-feed him. The man was permitted to die of starvation.[65]

By contrast, a 26-year-old woman, severely handicapped by cerebral palsy since birth, checked herself into the psychiatric unit of a hospital and demanded that she not be fed but only given medication to relieve her pain. Her intent was to starve herself to death; she was not otherwise in need of hospitalization. When the hospital sought to force-feed her, she petitioned a court for an injunction to prevent it, asserting her constitutional right to privacy. The court refused the injunction, finding that the patient was not terminally ill and that society had no duty to help her end her life. The court found that her right of self-determination was outweighed by the state's interests in preserving life, maintaining the integrity of the medical profession, and protecting third parties, because other patients might be adversely affected if they knew the hospital was helping a patient to die.[66] However, three years later this woman's health had so deteriorated that she was in constant pain, and because she was totally unable to care for herself hospitalization in a public institution was necessary. There, after her physicians determined that she was not obtaining sufficient nutrition by being spoon-fed, a nasogastric tube was inserted despite her objections. A trial court denied the patient's request to have the tube removed but was overruled by the appellate court, which held that the patient, who was mentally competent, had a constitutional right of privacy and this included the right to refuse medical treatment. Hence, the decision was not to be made by either doctors or judges. This court further ruled that the decision to forgo nasogastric feedings was not equivalent to an election to commit suicide, and the patient's motives were immaterial.[67]

Consent for Treatment of Incompetent Adults

A patient may be unable to grant an effective consent for medical or surgical treatment by reason of mental incompetence or other disability. If the incompetence has been recognized by a court through the appointment of a guardian, it is absolutely necessary for the physician and the hospital to obtain the guardian's consent, unless the guardian is unavailable and a medical emergency as previously defined is present.

In the absence of a court-appointed guardian, the extent of incompetence as determined by a qualified physician will govern the question of obtaining consent. Even patients who are emotionally disturbed and suffering from mental illness may nevertheless be capable of understanding the need for treatment and the significance of granting consent.[68] In this event the patients' own consent is sufficient, because the legal test of a valid consent is always their knowledge and their understanding. If the physician doubts the ability of a patient to give consent, then a court should be asked to rule on the patient's competence before treatment is undertaken, if there is time to obtain a ruling without jeopardizing the patient's physician condition. If time does not allow a court to rule, then presumably a medical emergency exists and treatment without consent would be justified. As previously discussed, an emergency exists whenever the patient's life is in jeopardy or there is risk of permanent impairment of health. Even though the spouse's or relative's consent is unnecessary in such circumstances, it is prudent to obtain the consent of the family if readily accessible, simply in the interest of maintaining a sound physician-family relationship.

When the incompetent patient is not represented by a legal guardian and there is no medical emergency, the role of the spouse and family in granting consent is unclear. If the patient had unequivocally objected to treatment while competent, then clearly the spouse has no authority to grant consent. Further, a spouse is not an authorized agent of the other person solely by reason of marriage. However, in certain special circumstances as a matter of local law, courts have from time to time recognized the authority of a spouse or relative to grant consent for the treatment of an incompetent patient. For example, judicial interpretation of relevant statutes in California relating to the involuntary commitment of mentally ill persons led the court to conclude that the family could grant consent for treatment of a committed patient.[69] Similarly, where local law provides that named relatives have the financial responsibility for maintaining an incompetent person, the relatives may have a right to consent.[70] In still other individual cases the courts have recognized the authority of a spouse or relative to speak for an incompetent adult.[71] On the other hand, some state courts have implied that a spouse or members of the family have no right to grant consent in the absence of a medical emergency. Most of these cases, however, have involved factual situations where the patient was legally capable of granting his or her own consent.[72] Because of the uncertainty and differing opinions, healthcare institutions and physicians treating an unconscious or incompetent adult cannot entirely rely on a consent form signed by a spouse or relative, although obtaining consent from such persons frequently strengthens the doctor-patient relationship and in some circumstances provides a measure of legal protection.

Decision to Forgo Treatment for Incompetent Adults

As discussed above, competent adults have a right to decide what medical treatment they receive, and this includes the right to refuse treatment. Although the right exists whether the persons have become incompetent or have always been incompetent,[73] decisions about their treatment involve three troublesome questions that have troubled the courts in recent years:

1. Who should make the decision?
2. What standards should apply?
3. What procedures should be followed in arriving at such decisions?

The first landmark case dealing with these issues was *In re Quinlan*.[74] In 1975 Karen Quinlan, a 22-year-old patient who had sustained severe brain damage, perhaps as a result of consuming alcohol or drugs, became comatose and remained for several months in a persistent "vegetative" state. Attending physicians employed a mechanical respirator to aid her breathing. When the physicians and the hospital later refused to terminate this life-support system at the request of her parents, her father filed suit to be appointed guardian of his daughter's person and to have the court authorize discontinuation of the respirator. Prior to trial it was stipulated by all parties that the patient was incompetent and that she was not dead by either the classical medical definition of death—that is, cessation of the cardiac and respiratory functions—or by the criteria of "brain death" (permanent cessation of all brain functions, including those of the brain stem). It should also be noted that New Jersey did not have a statutory definition of death, nor had there been any prior litigation in the state involving the concept of "brain death."[75]

The New Jersey trial court denied Mr. Quinlan's requests,[76] but on appeal the decision was reversed. The New Jersey Supreme Court held that Mr. Quinlan was entitled to be appointed guardian of his daughter, could select a physician of his choice to care for her, and could participate with this physician and the hospital's medical ethics committee in a decision to withdraw the mechanical respirator. The legal basis for the decision was the patient's right of privacy, specifically her right to decline treatment under the circumstances of her situation, as noted in the "right to die" cases discussed earlier. Most significant, the New Jersey court went on to rule that where the patient is so incompetent that she cannot express her right of privacy on her own behalf, her father as guardian may do so under the doctrine of "substituted judgment."

To guard against misuse of the substituted judgment doctrine, especially in situations less worthy on the facts or when the family's motives are suspect, the court spoke approvingly of relying on the hospital's ethics committee; in fact, it required the guardian and the attending physicians to consult with such a committee, which would then review the medical evidence and render an opinion about the probability that the patient might emerge from her chronic comatose state. In summary the court ruled that on concurrence of the guardian, the attending physician, and the ethics committee, the life-support system could be withdrawn without the fear of civil or criminal liability.[77]

Perhaps the most difficult question involving incompetent patients is what standards should prevail in life-or-death decisions. It is clearly established that a competent adult can refuse treatment for any or no reason; the soundness of that person's judgment is not subject to question under the right to privacy and common-law right of self-determination. If the patient becomes incompetent, however, someone else must make and implement the decision, substituting his or her judgment. Under such circumstances the judgment is subject to legal scrutiny to protect the interests of the incompetent person.

The *Quinlan* court held that because it was the personal right of the patient to refuse treatment, only the judgment of the patient herself could prevail. Under the "substituted judgment" doctrine, however, the court held that the decision-maker substituting for the patient (in this case, the guardian) was to determine *what the patient herself would decide* under these circumstances. Theoretically the guardian was not to use his own judgment in determining what was best for the patient, but only to judge what the patient's own wishes would be if she were for a moment competent to decide:

> We have no doubt, in these unhappy circumstances, that if Karen were herself miraculously lucid for an interval (not altering the existing prognosis of the condition to which she would soon return) and perceptive of her irreversible condition, she could effectively decide upon discontinuance of the life-support apparatus, even if it meant the prospect of natural death.[78]

Many other courts have followed *Quinlan* and have adopted the substituted judgment doctrine. In *Superintendent of Belchertown State School v. Saikewicz* the doctrine was applied to the case of a 67-year-old man who had always been profoundly mentally retarded and who was suffering from acute myeloblastic monocytic leukemia for which chemotherapy was the indicated treatment.[79] The state institution where he was a resident petitioned the court for appointment of a guardian and a guardian *ad litem* to decide what treatment he should receive. His illness was incurable, and without chemotherapy he would die within weeks or months. With chemotherapy he had a 30 percent to 50 percent chance of a remission for two to thirteen months. The chemotherapy would not cure the illness. It would moreover require the cooperation of the patient and cause serious, painful side effects. The guardian *ad litem* recommended that not treating the patient would be in his best interests. He stated:

If [Saikewicz] is treated with toxic drugs he will be involuntarily
immersed in a state of painful suffering, the reason for which he will
never understand. Patients who request treatment know the risks
involved and can appreciate the painful side-effects when they arrive.
They know the reason for the pain and their hope makes it tolerable.[80]

The probate judge weighed the factors for and against chemotherapy for
Mr. Saikewicz and concluded that treatment should be withheld. In favor of
treatment was the fact that most people elect chemotherapy and that it would
offer a chance for a longer life. Weighing against it were the patient's age, the
probable side effects, the slight chance of a remission against the certainty that
the treatment would cause suffering, the patient's inability to cooperate with
those administering the treatment, and the "quality of life possible for him
even if the treatment does bring about remission."[81]

The appellate court, adopting the standard of substituted judgment
that was applied in *Quinlan*, held that

both the guardian *ad litem* in his recommendation and the judge
in his decision should have attempted (as they did) to ascertain the
incompetent person's actual interests and preferences. In short, the
decision in cases such as this should be that which would be made by
the incompetent person, if that person were competent, but taking into
account the present and future incompetency of the individual as one
of the factors which would necessarily enter into the decision-making
process of the competent person.[82]

The court approved of the probate judge's decision, convinced that it "was
based on a regard for [Saikewicz's] actual interests and preferences"[83] and
supported by the facts. Rejecting any analysis that would equate "quality
of life" with the value of a life, the appellate court interpreted the judge's
reference to the quality of life "as a reference to the continuing state of pain
and disorientation precipitated by the chemotherapy treatment."[84]

In cases of persons who have never been competent or who have never
expressed any desire regarding termination of medical treatment, the inherent
problem with the substituted judgment doctrine—by which the surrogate
decision-maker is to "don the mental mantle of the incompetent"[85]—is that
the decision-makers cannot possibly know what the incompetent person would
choose. In fact, the decision-maker must guess what the incompetent would
choose, or make a decision believed to be in the best interests of the patient.
Any such decision will be a subjective judgment based on the values, biases,
and prejudices of the proxy decision-maker. This seems in fact what happened
in *Saikewicz*. The fiction of "substituted judgment" in these instances does not
permit any control over the decision-making because it provides no guidelines
or standards for the decision other than what the patient would have wanted.
Thus the incompetent is left essentially without legal protection and is obliged
to depend on the good judgment and good faith of the decision-maker.

These inherent legal and ethical issues were recognized by a New York court which refused to authorize discontinuation of regularized blood transfusions being administered to a 52-year-old mentally retarded man suffering from terminal cancer.[86] In the circumstances the treatment was in accordance with acceptable, standard medical practice, and although the patient's life could not be saved by administration of blood the transfusions were necessary to avoid the probability of an earlier death. Because the mentally impaired patient had never been competent, the court drew an analogy with cases denying parents the right to withhold usual and customary medical care from their minor children. Moreover, the court based its conclusion simply on common-law principles, in contrast to the vaguely established constitutional right of privacy, and accordingly did not address the question of whether an incompetent patient has the same right to refuse medical care as a competent person.

The problem inherent in allowing surrogate decisions was finally addressed by the New Jersey Supreme Court in another landmark case, *Matter of Conroy*.[87] That case involved a legally incompetent resident of a nursing home, an 84-year-old woman with serious and irreversible physical and mental impairments and a limited life expectancy. Her nephew, who was her legal guardian, sought permission to remove a nasogastric tube, which was the principal means of feeding her. His petition was granted by the trial court, but her guardian *ad litem* appealed.[88] The intermediate appellate court reversed, holding that the right to terminate life-sustaining treatment for incurable and terminally ill patients cannot be based on the guardian's judgment unless the patient is brain dead, irreversibly comatose, or vegetative.[89] Alternatively the court ruled that the feeding tube was not treatment but rather a basic necessity of life and that withdrawal of nourishment would be active euthanasia. Although the patient in *Conroy* died pending the appeal, the New Jersey Supreme Court granted review and took the opportunity

> to determine the circumstances under which life-sustaining treatment
> may be withheld or withdrawn from an elderly nursing-home resident
> who is suffering from serious and permanent mental and physical
> impairments, who will probably die within approximately one year
> even with the treatment, and who, though formerly competent, is now
> incompetent to make decisions about her life-sustaining treatment
> and is unlikely to regain such competence. Subsumed within this
> question are two corollary decisions for incompetent patients, and
> what procedures should be followed in making them.[90]

Although the holdings in this case were strictly limited to such patients, the principles at issue could be more widely applied.

In *Conroy* the New Jersey Supreme Court reiterated the patient's right to privacy and self-determination stated in *Quinlan* and noted that the "goal of decision-making for incompetent patients should be to determine and effectuate, insofar as possible, the decision that the patient would have made if competent."[91] The court held that under this subjective test life-sustaining treatment may be withheld or withdrawn when it is clear that the incompetent patient would have refused the treatment under the circumstances. The court further recognized, however, that determining some patients' wishes may be difficult or impossible and that in such cases it is "naive to pretend that the right to self-determination serves as the basis for substituted decision-making."[92] The court therefore concluded that the state's *parens patriae* power provided the authority to decide on behalf of incompetent patients whose actual desires could not be clearly established; this authority allows withholding or withdrawing treatment if it is "manifest" that the action would be in the patient's best interests.

Natural Death and Power of Attorney Legislation

Because of the uncertainties involved in these issues, in the mid-1970s state legislatures began responding to the need for guidance. Twenty years later, most states had enacted "natural death acts" aimed at allowing terminally ill patients to "die with dignity." These laws vary from state to state both in their approach and in the situations covered, but they do offer assistance and some measure of protection for those who face these troubling situations.

In the years since *Quinlan* and *Conroy* numerous courts have adjudicated the question of terminating the use of artificial nutritional devices for incompetent, terminally ill patients. The nearly universal view now is that there is no significant difference between disconnecting a respirator, as in *Quinlan,* and discontinuing artificial nutrition and hydration, as in *Conroy.* Furthermore, the decisions have abandoned attempts to draw a distinction between what is "ordinary" and "extraordinary" medical care (as earlier cases had done); instead, the analysis is made today by weighing the benefits of the particular treatment against the burden that it places on the patient (or even, in some circumstances, the family). When the burden outweighs the benefit, the care is called "disproportionate" and, hence, it may be terminated.

In the years immediately following *Quinlan* many cases addressed the questions of who could make decisions for incompetent patients and whether the courts must be involved in all cases. The *Quinlan* court believed that routine involvement by the courts would be "impossibly cumbersome," and most other courts have agreed. Of course, where there is no family or guardian, or where family members disagree, the courts are proper forums for resolution of the matter.

The courts have also become involved when the family's and the health-care provider's views on the matter conflict. One such case, *Cruzan v. Director, Missouri Department of Health,*[93] was the occasion for the U.S. Supreme Court's first and, to date, only decision regarding termination of medical treatment for incompetent patients. In this case, a young woman (Nancy Cruzan) lay in a "persistent vegetative state" as a result of injuries suffered in an automobile accident. Although she could breathe without assistance, she required artificial means for providing nutrition and hydration. After it became obvious that she would never regain her mental faculties, her parents asked officials at the state hospital where she was being treated to remove her feeding tube and allow her to die. When the hospital refused, the parents filed suit to compel termination of the treatment. At trial evidence was presented that Nancy had "expressed thoughts at age twenty-five in somewhat serious conversations with a housemate friend that if sick or injured she would not wish to continue her life unless she could live at least 'half-way normally.'" Based on this evidence of substituted judgment, the trial court entered an order in favor of the parents and permitting the artificial feeding to be terminated.

The Missouri Attorney General appealed, and the Supreme Court of Missouri reversed the trial court's findings. Although it recognized a right to refuse treatment based on the common-law doctrine of informed consent, the court held that Missouri had a strong public policy favoring life over death and that, therefore, evidence of an individual's wishes regarding termination of treatment must be "clear and convincing." The court found that Nancy's "somewhat serious conversation" was not sufficient to meet this standard. On certiorari to the U.S. Supreme Court, the Missouri court's decision was affirmed on narrow grounds. Although no other supreme court besides Missouri's had set such a high standard for these kinds of treatment decision, and although it recognized that there is a common-law right (supported by a constitutional "liberty interest") to refuse medical treatment, the Supreme Court held that there is nothing in the U.S. Constitution that "prohibits Missouri from choosing the rule of decision which it did." Furthermore, the Court commented:

> The choice between life and death is a deeply personal decision of obvious and overwhelming finality. We believe Missouri may legitimately seek to safeguard the personal element of this choice through the imposition of heightened evidentiary requirements. It cannot be disputed that the Due Process Clause protects an interest in life as well as interest in refusing life-sustaining medical treatment. Not all incompetent patients will have loved ones available to serve as surrogate decisionmakers. And even where family members are present, "[t]here will, of course, be some unfortunate situations in which family members will not act to protect a patient." A State is entitled to guard against potential abuses in such situations. Similarly, a State is entitled to consider that a judicial proceeding to make a determination regarding an incompetent's wishes may very well not be an adversarial one, with the added guarantee of accurate factfinding that the adversary process brings with it. Finally, we think a State may properly decline to make judgments about the "quality" of life that a particular individual may enjoy, and simply assert an unqualified interest in the preservation of human life to be weighed against the constitutionally protected interests of the individual.

In our view, Missouri has permissibly sought to advance these interest through the adoption of a "clear and convincing" standard of proof to govern such proceedings.

Following the U.S. Supreme Court's decision, the *Cruzan* case returned to the trial court in Missouri. After hearing additional testimony, the trial judge ruled that the evidence was clear and convincing, and he again ruled that Nancy Cruzan's artificially supplied nutrition and hydration could be withdrawn. The state attorney general declined to appeal, the treatment was terminated, and Nancy died in a matter of days.

The *Cruzan* decision was the last major judicial pronouncement on the subject of termination of treatment for incompetent patients. No other state has set forth a "clear and convincing" standard, and most of these difficult, heart-rending decisions today are made by physicians, in consultation with the family, without the necessity of judicial approval.

California was the first to pass such a statute, and many states have modeled their laws after California's. The California natural death act provides that competent adults may execute a directive, commonly called a "living will," instructing their physician to withhold or withdraw life-sustaining procedures in the even of a terminal illness.[94] Such a terminal condition is defined as an incurable state that according to reasonable medical judgment will cause death with or without life-sustaining procedures. Life-sustaining procedures are those that "would serve only to artificially prolong the moment of death and where, in the judgment of the attending physician, death is imminent whether or not such procedures are utilized."[95]

The California statute concludes with a strong statement that the legislature does not in any way condone or approve mercy killing or "any affirmative or deliberate act or omission to end life other than to permit the natural process of dying as provided in this chapter."[96]

The strength of a statute such as this is that it clarifies the procedure that can be followed to forgo life-sustaining treatment for certain patients under certain circumstances. It avoids judicial involvement and permits the "substituted judgment" doctrine to be carried out according to the written desires of the patient. Competent adults who feel strongly that they do not wish to be kept alive artificially when death is imminent and the treatments offer no hope of recovery can by this means express their wishes with confidence that they will be fulfilled. The major problem with a "living will" statute is that too many difficult decision-making situations are not covered: cases in which patients do not have a terminal illness, but for whom life-prolonging of life-sustaining treatment may be considered to be futile or not in the best interests of the patient (*Quinlan* and *Saikewicz* both fit this class); and cases in which no directive has been executed, a category that includes most patients.

To remedy some of the shortcomings of the so-called natural death acts, many states have enacted a law providing for a "durable power of attorney for health care."[97] Under this type of statute persons can designate a proxy to decide matters of healthcare if they should become incompetent. Decisions by the proxy would be as valid as the patients' would be if they were competent. On behalf of the patient a proxy could consent to or refuse most treatments, although depending on the state perhaps not on such matters as placement in a mental health institution, electroconvulsive therapy, psychosurgery, sterilization, and abortion. Physicians who comply with the provisions of the statute and rely in good faith on the decisions of the proxy are usually provided immunity from civil and criminal liability and professional disciplinary action.

The proxy system eliminates the need for a court to be involved either by appointing a surrogate decision-maker or by making the decision itself, although judicial review is usually available.[98] The statute usually sets forth the standards to be used in proxy decisions; these are similar to those established by case law. The proxy is to make decisions consistent with the desires of the patient. The patient may, and probably should, express his or her wishes in the durable power of attorney. If the patient's desires are unclear or unknown, the proxy is to decide in the best interests of the patient.

All hospitals should have procedures to handle decisions for incompetent patients in accordance with the laws of their state. Whenever possible physicians should discuss questions of treatment with the patient and the family before a patient becomes incompetent, especially when the illness appears to be terminal. The physician can call the patient's attention to the living will or power of attorney if these are recognized in that state. Relevant discussions and decisions, advance patient directive, durable power of attorney, or any other such document should be made part of the patient's medical chart. Any revocation of such a document should also be in the chart. "No code" orders should likewise be documented.

If the hospital, physician, family, or anyone else involved in the decision on treatment doubts the propriety of the proposed course or the manner in which the decision is being made, a judicial determination should be sought. Some states of course will require a court hearing under certain circumstances. These circumstances should be enumerated in the hospital's written policies.

Consent for Treatment of Minors

Several questions arise in connection with obtaining sufficient consent for treatment of minors. Because of differences in the facts of each situation and state law, not all of these questions can be answered with legal certainty. On occasion, therefore, a physician and the hospital must rely on their best judgment in the particular circumstances.

Recall at the outset that no express or implied-in-fact consent at all is legally necessary when there is a medical emergency. As previously defined, an emergency usually involves an immediate threat to life or health where delay would cause permanent damage. Medical necessity for treatment, if delay to obtain consent would not permanently harm the patient, is not tantamount to an emergency.

Physicians and hospital staff should always as a general rule, even when they believe that the situation involving a minor constitutes an emergency, make a reasonable effort to reach the parents or the person standing in a parental relationship, if the patient's condition allows the effort. If there is opportunity to do so, the medical emergency should also be documented by professional consultation.

The case of *Luka v. Lowrie* illustrates an emergency where the patient was a minor.[99] A 15-year-old boy was hit by a train. Five physicians determined that it was necessary to amputate his foot, and they acted without obtaining the consent of his parents. Their action was held to be justified because in the physicians' professional judgment the patient's condition constituted a threat to his life or health unless immediate action was taken. The case shows the importance of consultation with other physicians before administering care.

Age of Majority

Proper consent for the treatment of minors when there is no emergency requires that physicians and hospital personnel first determine the age of majority in their particular jurisdiction. At common law the age of majority is 21 years. Majority is reached the day prior to the patient's birthday. This is still the law of some states. In many jurisdictions, however, by statute married persons are considered adults, regardless of age. Furthermore, many states have reduced the age of adulthood to 18 for all persons. In short, the statutory and case law of each particular jurisdiction must be consulted to determine the age of majority. Once the age is attained, the patient is of course considered an adult.

In the absence of a local statute, the mere fact that an individual is authorized by law to marry without parental consent, to vote, or to purchase alcoholic beverages does not confer capacity to enter into a binding contract as an adult or to grant an effective consent for medical treatment. Hence, a married minor is not, legally speaking, an adult, and the fact of marriage does not in and of itself authorize a minor to consent to medical treatment unless a specific statute so prescribes. Similarly, emancipation from parental financial control and support, which can occur with or without marriage, does not create adulthood. Physicians and institutions in those states that have no statute speaking specifically on the matter must therefore not arbitrarily rely on the sole fact of marriage or emancipation as making it legally safe to proceed on the basis of the minor's own wish without obtaining parental consent.

The fact of marriage or emancipation, even though it may not establish adulthood, may be most important, however, in determining the response to the next question: whether the patient, even though a minor, is legally capable of giving effective consent without the consent of a parent or guardian. The answer may be provided by local statutory law or by judicial decision.

Consent Granted by Mature Minors

It has often been arbitrarily stated that in the absence of an emergency the consent of the parent, or the person standing in a parental relationship to the minor, is necessary before medical or surgical treatment can be administered to the minor. Analysis of the cases and a review of statutory laws indicate that this statement is not always true.

Policies and practices of healthcare institutions should be workable and practical, and at the same time they should provide maximum legal protection. The easiest rule perhaps would be to insist on parental consent in all cases of medical treatment or surgery involving minors, except in medical emergencies or when a local statute specifically eliminates the need for the consent of parents. Yet such a policy is not practical. There are too many situations in which medical or surgical care for a relatively mature and knowledgeable minor is advisable but where the parent is not readily accessible or is perhaps completely inaccessible. Moreover, a mature minor may seek care and object to obtaining parental consent, especially for treatment of medical conditions relating to pregnancy or family planning, for example.

Analysis of the cases suggests that in most decisions the basis for the common law rule that a parent's consent is necessary for treatment is the belief that minors are incapable, by reason of their youth, of understanding the nature and the consequences of their own acts and must therefore be protected from the folly of their own decisions. If this is the true basis for requiring the parent's consent then there is nothing magical about the arbitrary age of 21 or the fact that the patient is emancipated or married. As a matter of fact, to the author's knowledge no judicial case has held a physician or a hospital liable in any of these circumstances when treatment was beneficial to the minor. The ultraconservative policy of always insisting on parental consent regardless of the minor's maturity or status in life is accordingly not justified.

Furthermore, when a minor seeks a legal abortion or contraceptive services, statutes in most states authorize such care on the basis of the minor's own consent. In addition, a number of statutes in the various jurisdictions clarify the law with respect to treatment of minors in particular situations and for particular medical conditions. No effort is made here to list or categorize all of the relevant statutes. As noted previously, however, statutes in quite a number of states specifically provide that emancipated or married minors, regardless of age, may give their own consent for any medical treatment. And most states have statutes providing that minors themselves may consent to treatment of conditions relating to pregnancy, family planning, venereal disease, and the use of drugs. It is important, however, for physicians and hospitals to analyze carefully each particular statute and to seek the advice of local counsel, because limitations based on age, marriage, or other factors may affect the ability of the minor to give legal consent.

Both judicial and statutory law have thus contributed to a strong public policy to permit mature minors to receive health services without having to reach the age of majority. In other words, the test of the validity of a minor's own consent should depend on maturity—as measured in part by age and ability to comprehend the nature of a decision—and not the particular chronological age of majority. This judicial view is called "the age-of-discretion" doctrine.

Several cases of long standing as well as the *Restatement of Torts* recognize the legal validity of minor's own consent and do not insist on the parent's consent, providing the minor is capable of understanding and appreciating the nature of the consent.[100] Reliance on minors' own consent, however, should be limited to situations in which the medical treatment or surgery is for their benefit, as distinguished from situations in which the procedure is primarily for the benefit of another.[101]

Moreover, as a matter of practicality the healthcare institution should establish some minimum age as an aid in determining whether the given patient is sufficiently mature to understand the consequences of giving consent.[102] A workable rule might well establish the age of 16 as a guideline with each patient then evaluated individually.

Another important factor in application of the age-of-discretion doctrine is whether the minor has living parents who are readily available to grant consent. For example, in 1971 the Probate Court of the District of Columbia held that an 18-year-old girl who was without parents and without a legally appointed guardian could consent to an abortion.[103] Another example occurs in *Younts v. St. Francis Hospital*, where a Kansas court held that a 17-year-old could consent to surgery on an injured finger. The patient's mother was herself hospitalized and semiconscious, and the father was unavailable.[104]

A strong judicial tendency is thus evident to permit minors to give an effective consent whenever they are mature enough to understand the nature of the contemplated treatment and the consequences of their action whenever the treatment clearly benefits the patient, and especially when the risk is low.

Even in a jurisdiction that has not yet clarified the law by judicial decision or statute, necessary medical treatment should never be withheld from a mature and knowledgeable minor solely because parental consent has not been obtained. The withholding of services may well create more legal risk from charges of malpractice or negligence than would be incurred by furnishing the services in situations that might involve a technical assault or battery or the invasion of parental rights. Simply put, damages for failure to treat might well be far greater than damages for treatment without consent. Accordingly, each provider of medical care should develop guidelines for the treatment of minors, based on local law and on recognized standards of clinical care.

It seems perfectly clear that married minors can give consent for the treatment of their minor children. This common law has been clarified by statute in some jurisdictions, for example in Pennsylvania and Mississippi, where the statutes read that any minor who has been married or who has borne a child may give effective consent to all health services for the child.

Note that these provisions authorize a married father or a married mother or an unmarried mother to give consent, but they do not authorize the unmarried father to give consent for the treatment of a minor child.

Several reported cases have considered the question of whether a parent or a court may authorize surgery performed on a minor for the benefit of another person. The typical example is the removal of a kidney for transplantation. Although a few courts have permitted kidney transplants to be performed on twins who were mature minors giving their own consent to the surgery, parental consent should be obtained when the surgery has as its primary purpose the benefit of another. The issues still remain, however, whether a parent is authorized to consent to such an operation and whether a court may grant consent, especially when patients are too young or otherwise unable to express their own wishes. The cases are split.

Concern has also been expressed in those cases that have held that the parent or guardian of a minor or an incompetent may not consent to a sterilization of the patient.[105] The basis for these cases has been generally that the interest of the patients must be protected until they are in a position to make an individual choice on such an important matter as reproductive capacity.

When it is determined that parental consent is necessary, an issue that frequently arises is whether both parents must consent. The answer is that the consent of either parent is sufficient if the parents are living together. If, on the other hand, the parents are divorced or voluntarily separated, then the consent of the parent having custody of the child should be obtained.

No individual having temporary custody of a minor child, whether a relative or not, is authorized at common law to give consent for treatment of the minor. Babysitters thus have no authority to consent to treatment of a minor unless given specific authority by a parent. In the absence of the parents or a legally appointed guardian, the legal test of an individual's authorization to consent to treatment of a minor is whether the person having custody stands in place of the parent. This requires more than a showing of mere temporary custody.

Refusal of Consent for Treatment of Minors

If the parent or guardian consents to treatment, but the minor patient possesses both maturity and understanding and refuses consent for treatment, the physician and the hospital should not proceed to render care. This policy is consistent with the thought that minors capable of understanding their own acts are capable of giving their own consent. Such cases should then be handled as if the youth were an adult who has refused or withdrawn consent.

Those who render care may encounter the reverse of such a situation: a mature and understanding minor may consent to treatment, and the parent or guardian may refuse consent. In this event one should rely on the mature minor's own consent, and treatment should proceed. In both these situations the minor's rights are generally recognized to be paramount. The practical aspect of the dilemma is also recognized; that is, invading the rights or interests of one who is not a patient entails less legal risk than a course of conduct that invades the interest of a patient.

If the parent refuses consent for treatment of a minor who lacks maturity and understanding or is otherwise legally incapable of expressing his or her own consent, the situation poses practical, ethical, and legal difficulties, especially when a medical emergency exists and the patient is likely to die if treatment is withheld. If the condition of the patient does not permit delaying treatment until a court order is obtained, the physician and the hospital should proceed with treatment despite parental objections. These are situations in which life is at stake, and humanitarian action to save life is preferable to inaction that may cause death, even if technically the parents may have a cause of action against the physician and the hospital. In most instances of this kind, the damages obtainable by the parents would be small.

If a professional medical opinion determines that the minor's condition will not be permanently harmed by a delay in treatment, then the physician or the hospital should seek a court determination of the matter. The delay may not be long; it would depend on local procedure and on the working relations that the medical personnel have developed with the court. Courts have been known to act quickly and at all hours.

Under the early common law—strangely, perhaps—parental denial of medical care was not parental neglect, and hence some doubted a court's power to order medical care for a minor over the objections of the parents. All the states now have statutes, however, that provide that the appropriate court has jurisdiction to protect the interests of dependent and neglected children. These protective statutes differ in their language and in the procedures specified to invoke the power of the court, but in general the state, a social agency, a hospital, a physician, and even other relatives of a neglected child may petition the court for an order removing the child from the parents' custody and placing custody in a court-appointed guardian. Most of these statutes also require that suspected child neglect or abuse be reported to the appropriate authorities. Thus the physician and hospital have an affirmative duty toward the child who needs medical care.

The statutes are clearly a valid exercise of the state's police power to protect the general health and welfare of society. Hence, they are constitutional, even when their application conflicts with or violates the parent's religious belief, at least when the life of a child may be at risk. In the leading case of *State v. Perricone* the New Jersey Supreme Court affirmed the trial court's order that a blood transfusion be administered to an infant child of parents who were Jehovah's Witnesses.[106]

With respect to the constitutional issue of the parents' religious freedom, the court said:

Thus the [first] amendment embraces two concepts—freedom to believe and freedom to act. The first is absolute, but, in the nature of things, the second cannot be.

The right to practice religion freely does not include the liberty to expose . . . a child . . . to ill health or death. Parents may be free to become martyrs themselves. But it does not follow they are free, in identical circumstances, to make martyrs of their children before they have reached the age of full and legal discretion when they can make that choice for themselves.

Decisions in these types of cases turn on the following factors: the precise statutory language and specifically whether the statute expressly provides that parental refusal to allow medical care is included in the definition of a "dependent and neglected" child; the medical condition of the child and the probable result if treatment is withheld; the age of the child and whether (even though a minor) his or her wishes have been considered; and finally the basis for parental refusal of consent.

In states with statutes that do not specifically provide that parental denial of necessary medical care is included in the legal definition of a dependent and neglected child, most of the cases have construed the statutes liberally to embrace situations in which parents have refused medical care, at least when a medical emergency existed and death or permanent impairment of health was probable. In such situations, where medical testimony has asserted that death or irreparable injury was likely, most courts have readily made a finding of neglect and have upheld orders of treatment, even if the specific statute did not precisely define parental denial of medical care as "neglect."[107] In *Jefferson v. Griffin Spalding County Hospital Authority* statutory protection was extended to the unborn when custody of a fetus was transferred to the state and its mother ordered to undergo a cesarean section and related procedures necessary to save the unborn infant's life. This was done over the religious objections of the pregnant woman.[108]

The legal result is less predictable where no emergency exists, however needed and desirable the recommended treatment may be. These are the cases in which all of the other factors noted above are weighed. In *In re Hudson* the Washington Supreme Court respected the mother's refusal of consent and reversed a trial court order, holding that it would not order nonemergency treatment of an 11-year-old minor.[109] Each of the following factors was probably of some significance: the statute granting the court "custody, care, guardianship and control" or "delinquent and dependent children" did not specifically provide that parental denial of medical care was encompassed within the meaning of "dependent" or "neglect"; the only medical treatment for the child's deformity was amputation of the arm, entailing considerable risk; and the mother's refusal of consent was apparently sincerely based on the genuine medical risk involved and on a desire to postpone surgery until her daughter might be mature enough to express her own wishes. Note that *In re Hudson* did not involve any such issues of constitutional law as freedom of religious belief. In a subsequent Washington case, in which the court refused to remove custody from a father who had failed to seek medical care for his child's speech impairment, the result was similar.[110]

In a like manner a New York court refused to order care for a minor needing correction of a harelip and cleft palate. The father possessed a fear of surgery and had apparently passed it on to his son. The influential factors in the trial court's opinion, which was upheld by the New York Court of Appeals, were that the child was old enough to have opinions of his own which should be respected and that the surgery, although likely to be highly beneficial and free from risk, could wait.[111]

On the other hand, in a number of other cases the factual situation, the particular statute involved, and the philosophy of the judges have led courts to order nonemergency medical or surgical care for minors deemed to be neglected. Illustrative are the Texas case of *Mitchell v. Davis*, involving a 12-year-old suffering from arthritis and rheumatic fever, and the 1972 case of *In re Sampson*, in which a New York court ordered surgery to correct a serious deformity in a 15-year-old who had not attended school for several years.[112]

When issues of constitutional law are introduced into situations of nonemergency care, the matter becomes somewhat more complicated and perhaps even more emotional. In the 1972 Pennsylvania case entitled *In re Green* the minor patient, 16 years of age, needed corrective surgery of the spine as a result of polio. The mother gave her consent to the surgery itself, but she refused permission to administer blood because she was a Jehovah's Witness. The superior court declared the minor to be neglected and appointed a guardian. This decision was reversed on the grounds that the state could not interfere with a parent's religious beliefs unless the patient's life was in immediate peril. Further, said the court, the lower court had not taken into account the minor's own wishes.[113] As in many such cases, there was a strong dissent this time by three judges, who argued that the only concern should be the health of the minor and that parents should not be permitted to make martyrs of their children.

In recent years cases have arisen involving the courts more closely in medical questions such as whether any treatment at all should be administered in certain cases, and if so, which among all the alternatives is in the best interests of the child. A Massachusetts case, *Custody of a Minor*, which came to nationwide attention in 1978, involved a boy approximately two years old who had been diagnosed as having acute lymphocytic leukemia.[114] Doctors recommended a course of chemotherapy as being the only possible cure, and his parents consented. Several months into the treatment the parents stopped administering the drugs, however, apparently because of concern about their effect on the child. Several months later the boy's physician discovered this halt in the treatment and when he could not persuade the parents to continue the drugs, he petitioned the court to order the renewal of the prescribed care. The trial court found that the chemotherapy offered a substantial hope of cure, that there was no evidence offered of any alternative consistent with standard medical practice, and that failure to provide the treatment constituted neglect. The court therefore placed the child in the custody of the state for purposes of ensuring chemotherapy would be continued. The appellate court affirmed, applying the substituted judgment doctrine enunciated in *Saikewicz*. According to the findings, the side effects of the chemotherapy were minor and the life-saving nature of the treatment, in contrast to the life-prolonging treatment at issue in *Saikewicz*, justified a ruling that the child's inability to understand his temporary suffering "could not overcome his long-term interest in leading a normal, healthy life."[115]

Six months or so later the parents petitioned for review of the case, and the trial judge continued the order for chemotherapy. He also ordered the parents to stop giving the child laetrile, large doses of vitamins A and C, enzyme enemas, and folic acid. The parents produced four expert witnesses, none of whom was licensed in Massachusetts and none of whom testified that these treatments had any curative effect on leukemia. They did testify that the treatments might have some palliative and placebo effect when used with chemotherapy. The trial judge found that these administrations were not only useless but also dangerous to the child's health. The appellate court affirmed.[116]

Withholding Treatment from Seriously Ill Newborns

Infants are in the same legal position as other minors. That is, the parents are authorized to consent or withhold consent to treatment as long as they are competent to do so and their actions do not constitute neglect of their child. However, modern technology is keeping newborn infants alive who just a few years ago would not have survived because of low birthweight or severe birth defects. Decisions to administer or withhold treatment for these impaired newborns can be extremely difficult. It is not always clear whether a decision to withhold or withdraw treatment constitutes neglect or is medically, ethically, and legally sound. Furthermore, the same questions that arise for incompetent adults arise also for infants: Who should make such decisions, and what standards should prevail?

If treatment is available that would clearly benefit an ill newborn—particularly if such treatment is necessary to save the child's life or prevent serious, permanent consequences—then those providing medical care should respond to the parents' refusal in the manner suggested in the previous section. If time permits, a court order should be obtained. In an emergency the child should be treated despite the parents' objections. A third alternative is to render sufficient treatment to keep the child alive pending judicial decisions about future treatment.

Infants with terminal, incurable illnesses or those in persistent vegetative states have essentially the same rights as incompetent adults with similar conditions. The courts have recognized this and generally applied the same principles in decisions about forgoing life-sustaining treatment. Ordinarily the parents or guardian may have treatment withheld or discontinued if it is clearly futile or inhumane in the light of the infant's condition. *In re L.H.R.* involved a terminally ill infant who was in a persistent vegetative state, and the court found that a life support system was prolonging the dying process rather than her life.[117] The court ruled that the right of a terminally ill person to refuse treatment was not lost because of the incompetence or the patient's youth. The parent or legal guardian could exercise the right on the child's behalf after the attending physician's diagnosis and prognosis were confirmed by two other physicians who had interest in the case's outcome. The court did not require review by either an ethics committee or a court.[118]

Newborns with serious birth defects or extremely low birth weights raise more difficult issues. For example, the proposed treatment may be beneficial, even lifesaving, but will leave the infant with a handicap. The handicap might be cause by the treatment: blindness from the administration of oxygen, for example. Or it might be a result of an existing condition, such as Down's syndrome or spina bifida. In other cases the proposed therapy might be neither clearly beneficial nor clearly futile: the child might survive with therapy but with only a dim chance of long life and meanwhile the likelihood of suffering and continuing to lose ground. In making these difficult decisions parents or other surrogates must be fully informed of the medical alternatives and the prognosis, and all means must be used to ensure that such children are protected from decisions that are clearly contrary to their best interests.

The well-publicized case of "Baby Doe" focused national attention on the manner of deciding whether to treat seriously ill newborns.[119] In 1982 a baby boy was born in Indiana with Down's syndrome. He also had a surgically correctable condition that prevented him from eating normally. His parents discussed his case with attending physicians and decided not to consent to the corrective surgery. Food and water were also to be withheld. Within days, following a petition alleging neglect, a hearing was held. The probate court found that the parents were not neglectful but had made a reasonable choice among acceptable medical alternatives. Before an attempted appeal could be processed, the baby died. Since then, the parents' decision has been widely criticized as being against the best interests of the child.

Also receiving national attention was the case of "Baby Jane Doe."[120] Born in October 1983, she was found to have myleomeningocele, commonly known as spina bifida, besides other serious disorders. Surgery is the usual corrective treatment in such cases as hers. After lengthy consultation with neurological experts, nurses, religious counselors, and a social worker, however, the parents chose to forgo surgery and adopt a more conservative course of treatment. Although the parents' decision was challenged in court, physicians testified during the hearing that the parents' choice was "well within accepted medical standards." The trial court found that surgery was required to preserve the infant's life and ordered it to be performed, but the appellate court reversed. According to the higher court, failure to perform the surgery would not "place the infant in imminent danger of death"; and although the surgery might decrease the risk of death, it could also result in serious complications. The appellate court concluded that this was "not a case where an infant is being deprived of medical treatment to achieve a quick and supposedly merciful death. Rather, it is a situation where the parents have chosen one course of appropriate medical treatment over another."[121]

Cases such as these have caused a great deal of discussion and legislative activity concerning medical treatment for impaired newborns. The major fear is that, as apparently happened with Baby Doe, treatment may be withheld or withdrawn solely because of the child's disability, not because the treatment is not medically indicated. Courts, legislatures, and commentators have attempted to develop safeguards for all who are involved in decisions affecting seriously ill newborns. Ideally parents and physicians should be allowed discretion and a certain amount of privacy in decision-making, but children must be protected from judgments regarding "quality of life" that discriminate against the handicapped[122] and decisions that may delay the moment of death at a cost of great suffering to the infant.[123]

The report of the President's commission on *Deciding to Forgo Life-Sustaining Treatment*[124] concluded that most decisions on treatment for seriously ill newborns are properly made and conform to both law and medical ethics. The commission noted two kinds of problems, however: "(1) parents receive outdated or incomplete information from their physicians and this limits their capacity to act as surrogate decision makers, and (2) in what appears to be a limited number of cases, inappropriate decisions are made without triggering a careful reevaluation."[125] The commission concluded that hospital should have explicit policies and procedures for deciding on the treatment of seriously ill newborns. The policies should provide for internal review, ranging from consultation to review by an ethics committee or other appropriate body, whenever the physician and parents decide to forgo life-sustaining therapy or when physicians and parents disagree on the course of treatment. Pending the review the child's life should be sustained if possible. If in the meantime the child should die, a retrospective review is still appropriate.

The Child Abuse and Neglect Prevention and Treatment Program Act was amended in 1984 to provide that before a state may receive grants under the act it must establish within its child protection system procedures and programs for responding to reports of medical neglect, including reports of withholding medically indicated treatment for disabled infants with life-threatening illnesses. Such withholding is defined as "the failure to respond to the infant's life-threatening conditions by providing treatment (including appropriate nutrition, hydration, and medication) which, in the treating physician's (or physicians') reasonable medical judgment, will be most likely to be effective in ameliorating or correcting all such conditions." Exceptions are allowed if the infant is irreversibly comatose, if the treatment would merely delay death, if it would not correct all of the life-threatening conditions or would otherwise do nothing toward saving the child's life, or if it would be virtually futile and, under the circumstances, inhumane.[126] The act requires agencies for child protection to see that individuals are designated by and within the healthcare facilities who must report suspected medical neglect to the agency, which is given authority to pursue appropriate legal remedies, including court action. The DHHS notes that the "basic principle inherent in the statute" is that "medical treatment decisions are not to be made on the basis of subjective opinions about future 'quality of life' of a retarded or disabled person."[127]

Various states have also enacted laws covering medical treatment for newborn and other children. An Arizona statute, passed in 1983, delineates standards of care for newborns (children less than one year old.)[128] It prohibits the withholding of nourishment from a newborn infant "with the intent to cause or allow the death of the infant for any reason" including the following:

1. The child was born with a handicap.
2. The infant is not wanted by the parent, parents, or guardian.
3. The infant is born alive by natural or artificial means.[129]

The statute also prohibits denying an infant "necessary lifesaving medical treatment or surgical care," but it allows parents to refuse care if it is not necessary to save the child's life, if it has a potential risk that outweighs the potential benefit, or if it is futile or will only prolong the dying process when death is imminent. The statute further provides that "reasonable medical judgments in selecting among alternative courses of treatment shall be respected."[130]

The Arizona statute also provides some procedural safeguards to ensure appropriate decisions. When improper withholding of medical care or nourishment is suspected, healthcare institutions with perinatal, obstetrical, or pediatric units have a duty to report such incidents to the child protection authority, and hospital employees are protected from disciplinary action if they make such reports.[131] The law also obliges such hospitals to inform parents whose infants are born with handicaps about available agencies to assist the family.[132] Finally, the statute encourages the creation of infant-care review committees, whose proceedings and reports are to be confidential and not discoverable or admissible in evidence, except to a restricted degree specified in the statute.[133]

Decisions concerning treatment for seriously ill newborns are clearly no longer immune from public scrutiny. Hospitals, physicians, and parents have positive duties to act in a child's best interests. Where once the hospital or physician could look the other way if a parent refused consent for necessary care, the law now imposes a duty to act. As in the case of incompetent adults, hospitals must ascertain with their attorneys the applicable state and federal laws and develop procedures for complying with those laws.

Tests Requested by Law Enforcement Officials

Healthcare institutions are frequently requested to draw blood or take samples of urine from or perform a breath-analysis test on a person in police custody or under arrest to determine whether the prisoner is intoxicated or otherwise under the influence of drugs. Two major legal issues are presented by such requests.

The first is a question of civil law: Does the taking of such a test constitute an assault and battery or an invasion of privacy? Clearly, as a matter of common law, it would be a battery if the person has not granted a proper consent as previously defined.[134] Even if consent was presumably granted it might well be ineffective if the person were intoxicated or so nearly unconscious as not to understand the nature and effect of the act. Unless a statute specifically authorizes such tests without consent, a civil action for assault and battery or some other tort could be brought against the physician, others who performed the test, or the hospital.

In most cases, however, no actual physical injury or harm results and as long as the test was conducted without negligence any damages recoverable in a civil action are only nominal. Nevertheless, the risk of legal liability requires that hospitals and their personnel refrain from administering these tests unless there is an adequate consent or the test is authorized by local law. This recommendation is particularly relevant to the withdrawal of blood, which of course necessitates physical contact with the person.

Although law enforcement officials may request hospital personnel to conduct blood tests or similar tests in a variety of situations involving alleged criminal activity, most of them concern driving on public highways. To help the police promote highway safety, nearly all states have enacted "implied consent" laws. Many of these statutes do not, however, deal adequately with the civil liability of the hospital or of the personnel who administer the tests without consent.

Implied consent statues differ considerably among jurisdictions, and the advice of local legal counsel about the effect of a particular law is absolutely mandatory. In general, however, the statues provide that by driving a motor vehicle on a public highway a person "impliedly consents" to the administration of any or all blood, urine, and breath tests if apprehended and charged with driving while intoxicated or under the influence of alcohol. Many of the statutes require that the driver be formally under arrest and officially charged pursuant to the relevant criminal statute before the implied consent law can be invoked by government.

However, the majority of the statutes provide that a driver may affirmatively refuse administration of the test or tests itemized in the statute and thus overcome the statutory implied consent. The state in turn is thereupon authorized to revoke or suspend the driver's license for a time without further criminal prosecution for alleged violation of the statutes pertaining to driving while intoxicated or under the influence of alcohol.[135] The person under arrest may thus choose between submitting to the test in the hope of demonstrating innocence or refusing the test at the cost of driving privileges.

From the viewpoint of medical personnel the main point is that even though the test is authorized by the implied consent statutes and performed at the request of police, it should not be given in the face of an express refusal or resistance by persons in custody if they have a statutory right of refusal, as is true in most states. On the other hand, if the person consents to the test, then the hospital should obtain the subject's approval in writing. Hospital and medical personnel must also be certain that the subject is in fact formally arrested and charged, if that is a requirement of the local implied consent law. Further, some statutes require that the request from the police be in writing and that only certain persons—a physician, a registered nurse, or perhaps a licensed medical technologist—may perform the test. Statutory itemization of professional personnel authorized to conduct the requested test is especially likely for administering a blood test. Nurses' aides and orderlies may not be authorized to withdraw blood.

Quite a number of the implied consent laws contain provisions granting immunity from civil liability for medical personnel, nurses, and others, including the hospital itself in some states, if the blood is withdrawn or the test conducted at the request of police. However, the immunity provisions of statutes may not apply if the driver has refused the test or if the test was done "improperly." Immunity may thus be more apparent than real, thereby emphasizing once again the importance of having local counsel's opinion concerning hospital policy about tests that involve persons in police custody.[136]

Additional questions arise when the test is administered to a driver who is dead, incapacitated by injuries, or unconscious. This person cannot exercise the right of refusal of an alcohol test. Some of the statutes provide that implied consent to the test is effective, yet they do not answer the precise question of possible civil liability of the hospital and its personnel. Unless local counsel advises otherwise on the basis of interpretation of a particular statute, a blood test for the sole purpose of determining alcoholic content should not be administered to an incapacitated or unconscious person. Medical care can and should be rendered according to needs and the general law of consent.

The second major legal issue in taking blood for alcohol and similar tests is whether subjects' constitutional rights have been violated. The concern arises from state and federal constitutional provisions that protect individuals from unreasonable searches and seizures, from being a witness against themselves, or from providing self-incriminating evidence in criminal trials, and that also guarantee due process of law to all persons charged with a crime. If a person's constitutional rights are violated there are two major possibilities:

1. evidence so obtained may not be admissible in a criminal action against the alleged offender; and
2. persons who act "under color of law" can be individually and personally liable for violating another's federal constitutional rights.[137]

Certainly police act under color of law;[138] healthcare personnel could be considered as acting under color of law whenever they conduct a test or examination at the request of police. The risk of personal liability for medical care personnel does not appear to be great, however, because good faith is a defense in actions that allege violation of an individual's constitutional rights.[139] Legal actions in the areas discussed here have been few, but the issue of admissible evidence has been the subject of considerable litigation in both state and federal courts and remains a matter of discussion.

The courts may order reasonable medical or surgical treatment over the objection of persons charged with criminal activity when it is deemed necessary to promote the legitimate interests of society. Nevertheless, law enforcement officials and medical personnel must be constantly alert to the general rule that an informed consent is necessary before rendering medical care or treatment, including treatment intended to help enforce criminal laws, unless the particular facts and circumstances show that the interest of the public outweighs the individuals' right to be secure in their person. A healthcare institution that provides care to persons in police custody should seek an attorney's advice concerning practices and policies that will be consistent with local, state, and federal law.

Notes

1. The law of assault and battery is discussed in more detail in Chapter 2, "Breach of Contract and Intentional Tort."
2. Buck v. Bell, 274 U.S.200 (1927) (compulsory eugenic sterilization statute held constitutional); Jacobson v. Massachusetts, 197 U.S. 11 (1905) (compulsory smallpox vaccination not a violation of a patient's constitutional rights).
3. 211 N.Y. 125, 129, 105 N.E. 92, 93 (1914).
4. 119 So. 2d 649 (La. Ct. App. 1960); *see also* Pegram v. Sisco, 406 F. Supp. 776 (D. Ark. 1976) (signed consent form in generalized language does not relieve surgeon from explaining nature of diagnosis, material elements, and risks of recommended treatment using radium implants, as well as alternative methods of treatment).
5. Perna v. Pirozzi, 92 N.J. 446, 457 A.2d 431 (1983).
6. An example is found in Demers v. Gerety, 85 N.M. 641, 515 P.2d 645 (Ct. App. 1973) (consent form signed when patient was under influence of nembutal was

not effective), *rev'd and remanded on procedural grounds,* 86 N.M. 141, 520 P.2d 869 (1974).

7. An example is Zoski v. Gaines, 271 Mich. 1, 260 N.W. 99 (1935) (surgeon held liable for removal of a minor's tonsils without parental consent). For a contrasting situation involving an immediate threat to life or health see Luka v. Lowrie, 171 Mich. 122, 136 N.W. 1106 (1912), discussed in the section on consent for treatment of minors.

8. Sullivan v. Montgomery, 155 Misc. 448, 279 N.Y.S. 575 (New York City Ct. 1935).

9. See Appendix to Chapter 10.

10. Mohr v. Williams, 95 Minn. 261, 104 N.W. 12 (1905); *see also* Tabor v. Scobee, 254 S.W.2d 474 (Ky. Ct. App. 1951) (during surgery surgeon discovered infected fallopian tubes; ruled that he might not extend operation and remove tubes without consent unless an immediate threat to life or health existed).

11. Bennan v. Parsonnet, 83 N.J.L. 20, 83 A. 948 (Sup. Ct. 1912).

12. Davidson v. Shirley, 616 F.2d 224 (5th Cir. 1980) (where patient signed consent form for cesarean section and also authorized "such additional . . . procedures as are considered therapeutically necessary on the basis of findings during the course of the operation," there was no liability when surgeon performed a hysterectomy because extension of operation was consistent with reasonable and prudent surgical practice).

13. *E.g.,* Inderbitzen v. Lane Hosp., 124 Cal. App. 462, 12 P.2d 744 (1932) (hospital liable for permitting medical students, who were under hospital control and hence employees, to examine a patient without her consent).

14. Cox v. Haworth, 283 S.E.2d 392 (N.C. App. 1981) (hospital not liable for staff physician's failure to reveal risks of myelogram); Cooper v. Curry, 92 N.M. 417, 589 P.2d 201 (1979) (hospital not liable for alleged failure of staff physician to obtain patient's informed consent for cataract surgery).

15. For a thorough discussion of principles of hospital liability see Chapter 5.

16. Roberson v. Menorah Medical Center, 588 S.W.2d 134 (Mo. App. 1979) (in absence of employment relationship of knowledge of physician's inadequate explanation of risks, hospital not liable).

17. Magana v. Elie, 108 Ill. App. 3d 1028, 439 N.E.2d 1319 (1982) (hospital must conform to reasonable and prudent conduct in light of apparent risk even when physician is an independent contractor); *see also* dissenting opinion, *Cooper,* 92 N.M. at 423, 589 P.2d at 207 (Sutin, J.) (physician's duty is to obtain patient's consent while hospital's duty is "to ascertain whether the doctor has obtained consent").

18. Fiorentino v. Wenger, 19 N.Y.2d 407, 227 N.E.2d 296, 280 N.Y.S.2d 373 (1967); *cf.* Parr v. Palmyra Hosp., 228 S.E.2d 596 (Ga. App. 1976) (Georgia statute providing that written consent to medical and surgical treatment be conclusively presumed valid in the absence of fraudulent misrepresentations of material facts applies to hospitals as well as physicians).

19. *Roberson,* 588 S.W.2d 134 (hospital has no duty to inquire into depth or extent of consent obtained by doctor); *accord* Cross v. Trapp, 294 S.E.2d 446 (W. Va. 1982) (as matter of law hospital not liable for physician's alleged inadequate explanation of risks of surgery). *Compare, Magana,* 108 Ill. App. 3d 1028, 439

N.E.2d 1319 (hospital's duty to conform to reasonable standards and breach of duty is a question of fact).

20. 119 So. 2d 649 (La. Ct. App. 1960); *see also* Darrah v. Kite, 32 A.D.2d 208, 301 N.Y.S.2d 286 (1969) (father of minor patient was told that "routine brain tests" and a "general work-up" were necessary; in fact, the surgeon opened the patient's skull and penetrated the brain itself; whether informed consent had been obtained was a question for the jury).

21. 71 Nev. 280, 289 P.2d 173 (1955).

22. 251 Minn. 427, 88 N.W.2d 186 (1958).

23. 186 Kan. 393, 350 P.2d 1093 (1960), *second opinion*, 187 Kan. 186, 354 P.2d 670 (1960).

24. 334 S.W.2d 11 (Mo. 1960), 79 A.L.R.2d 1017; 360 S.W.2d 673 (Mo. 1962) (retrial in this litigation resulted in a verdict for defendants as they satisfactorily proved that they had adequately informed the patient). *See also* Shack v. Holland, 389 N.Y.S.2d 988 (Sup. Ct. 1976) (absence of informed consent from mother with respect to risks, hazards, and alternative delivery procedures is malpractice and gives child born permanently deformed a derivative cause of action; the statute of limitations begins to run when child is 21 years old).

25. DiFilippo v. Preston, 53 Del. 539, 173 A.2d 333 (1961).

26. *See also* Bowers v. Talmage, 159 So. 2d 888 (Gla. Dist. Ct. App. 1964) (question of fact for jury whether neurologist fulfilled duty of disclosing risks of arteriogram to parents of 9-year-old patient where expert testimony of neurosurgeon established custom of practitioners to disclose a 3 percent risk of paralysis); Williams v. Menehan, 191 Kan. 6, 379 P.2d 292 (1963) (custom among practitioners is guide to how much information should be given and how transmitted to patient); Haggerty v. McCarthy, 344 Mass. 136, 181 N.E.2d 562 (1962); Kaplan v. Haines, 96 N.J. Super. 242, 232 A.2d 840 (App. Div. 1967) (expert testimony regarding disclosure of medical information required to present issue to the jury); Peterson v. Lynch, 299 N.Y.S.2d 244, 59 Misc. 2d 469 (Sup. Ct. 1969); Govia v. Hunter, 2 Wyo. 1, 374 P.2d 421 (1962) (plaintiff claiming she was not informed that vein-stripping operation would disfigure leg failed because of lack of proof that surgeon deviated from accepted practice of other competent surgeons).

27. 110 R.I. 606, 295 A.2d 676 (1972).

28. 8 Cal. 3d 229, 502 P.2d 1, 104 Cal. Rptr. 505 (1972); *accord* Riedinger v. Colburn, 361 F. Supp. 1073 (D. Idaho 1973); Berkey v. Anderson, 1 Cal. App. 3d 790, 82 Cal. Rptr. 67 (1969); Cornfeldt v. Tongen, 295 N.W.2d 638 (Minn. 1980); Scott v. Bradford, 606 P.2d 554 (Okla. 1979); Nixdorf v. Hicken, 612 P.2d 348 (Utah 1980); Trogun v. Fruchtman, 58 Wis. 2d 569, 207 N.W.2d 297 (1973).

29. Hunter v. Brown, 4 Wash. App. 899, 484 P.2d 1162 (1971), *aff'd* 81 Wash. 2d 465, 502 P.2d 1194 (1972) (patient was Asian; risks of adverse results of a dermabrasion procedure are greater for Asians than for others, and she was entitled to know the risks relating to her situation).

30. Truman v. Thomas, 27 Cal. 3d 285, 295–96, 611 P.2d 902, 907–8, 165 Cal. Rptr. 308, 313–14 (1980).

31. A similar major precedent was set in Canterberry v. Spence, 464 F.2d 772 (D.C. Cir.), *cert. denied,* 409 U.S. 1064 (1972).

32. *See* Ohio Rev. Code Ann. § 2317.54.

33. Hawaii Rev. Stat. § 671-3 (Supp. 1984).

34. Ritz v. Florida Patients' Compensation Fund, 436 So. 2d 987 (Fla. App. 1983) (written consent form meeting statutory requirements constitutes granting of informed consent where there is no expert testimony establishing a different standard), *review denied,* 450 So. 2d 488 (Fla. 1984); Young v. Yarn, 136 Ga. App. 737, 222 S.E.2d 113 (1975) (doctor not liable for failing to inform patient that plastic surgery carried risk of scars where statutory consent form was obtained from patient).

35. Lester v. Aetna Casualty Co., 240 F.2d 676 (5th Cir. 1957); Roberts v. Woods, 206 F. Supp. 579 (S.D. Ala. 1962); Nishi v. Hartwell, 52 Haw. 296, 473 P.2d 116, *reh'g denied,* 52 Haw. 296 (1970); Harnish v. Children's Hosp. Medical Center, 387 Mass. 152, 439 N.E.2d 240 (1982); Starnes v. Taylor, 272 N.C. 386, 158 S.E.2d 339 (1968).

36. Karp v. Cooley, 349 F. Supp. 827 (S.D. Tex. 1972), *aff'd,* 493 F.2d 408 (5th Cir.), *cert. denied,* 419 U.S. 845 (1974); *see also* Schwartz v. Boston Hosp. for Women, 422 F. Supp. 53 (S.D.N.Y. 1976) (hospital has responsibility to obtain informed consent when patient is participant in surgical research program.).

37. National Commission for the Protection of Human Subjects of Biomedical and Behavioral Research, U.S. Dep't of Health, Educ. & Welfare, Pub. No. 0012, The Belmont Research 2 [hereinafter The Belmont Report]. The Boundaries Between Biomedical or Behavioral Research and the Accepted and Routine Practice of Medicine, Pub. No. 0013, The Belmont Report 1-1-1-44 App. I (1978). *See* Cowan and Bertsch, *Innovative Therapy: The Responsibility of Hospitals,* 5 J. Legal Med. 219 (June 1984).

38. The Belmont Report, *supra* note 37, at 3.

39. An exception to the general assertion in the text is that new drugs and medical devices are regulated by the Food and Drug Administration, a subject beyond the scope of this discussion. 21 U.S.C. § 355-60k (1982).

40. National Research Act, Pub. L. No. 93-348, 88 Stat. 342 (codified in various sections of Title 42, U.S.C.). 45 C.F.R. § 46.111.

41. 45 C.F.R. § 46.102(e).

42. 45 C.F.R. § 46.107.

43. 45 C.F.R. § 46.116, 46.117.

44. 45 C.F.R. § 46.111(a)(2).

45. 45 C.F.R. § 46.201–.211.

46. 45 C.F.R. § 46.301–.306.

47. 45 C.F.R. § 46.401–.409.

48. 21 U.S.C. §§ 301–92; 21 C.F.R. §§ 50.3, 56.103.

49. Jeffcoat v. Phillips, 417 S.W.2d 903 (Tex. Civ. App. 1967) (husband's consent not necessary for surgery on his wife; jury found as fact that the patient had given effective consent); Rytkonen v. Lojacona, 269 Mich. 270, 257 N.W. 703 (1934) (wife's consent not necessary for operation on her husband; he had consented);

accord Karp v. Cooley, 349 F. Supp. 827 (S.D. Tex. 1972), *aff'd*, 493 F.2d 408 (5th Cir. 1974), *cert. denied*, 419 U.S. 845 (1974); Janney v. Housekeeper, 70 Md. 162, 16 A. 382 (1889) (husband's consent not necessary for surgical procedure on his wife).

50. Gravis v. Physician's and Surgeon's Hosp. of Alice, 427 S.W.2d 310 (Tex. 1968).

51. Murray v. Vandevander, 522 P.2d 302 (Okla. Ct. App. 1974).

52. 44 Misc. 2d 622, 254 N.Y.S.2d 666 (Sup. Ct. 1964).

53. *See, e.g.,* Satz v. Perlmutter, 362 So. 2d 160 (Fla. Dist. Ct. 1978), *approved*, 379 So. 2d 359 (Fla. 1980) (73-year-old man with Lou Gehrig's disease had right to have mechanical respirator disconnected); *In re* Quackenbush, 156 N.J. Super. 282, 383 A.2d 785 (Morris County Ct. 1978) (competent patient with gangrenous condition in both legs could refuse consent to amputation even though necessary to save his life); Kirby v. Spivey, 167 Ga. App. 751, 307 S.E.2d 538 (1983) (not malpractice for a physician to respect the refusal of a competent patient to seek recommended treatment); Erickson v. Dilgard, 44 Misc. 2d 27, 252 N.Y.S.2d 705 (Sup. Ct. 1962) (court refused to order a blood transfusion for a competent adult); Winters v. Miller, 446 F.2d 65 (2d Cir.), *cert. denied*, 404 U.S.985 (1971) (medication may not be administered to a mentally ill patient contrary to her wishes when she has not been declared legally incompetent); *In re* Estate of Brooks, 32 Ill. 2d 361, 205 N.E.2d 435 (1965) (a court may not order administration of blood contrary to a patient's wishes based on religious convictions); Palm Springs Gen. Hosp. v. Martinez, No. 71–12687 (Cir. Ct. Fla. 1971) (physicians and hospital not civilly liable for complying with a competent, terminally ill patient's wishes to withdraw treatment).

54. Eichner v. Dillon, 434 N.Y.S.2d 46, 420 N.E.2d 64 (1981).

55. *See* Foreman, *The Physician's Criminal Liability for the Practice of Euthanasia*, 27 BAYLOR L. REV. 54, 57 (1975).

56. *In re* Quackenbush, 156 N.J. Super. at 290, 383 A.2d at 789.

57. *See, e.g.,* MINN. STAT. § 144.651 (12) (Supp. 1985); MICH. COMP. LAWS ANN. § 333.20201 (2)(f) (West Supp. 1985).

58. 331 F.2d 1000, 118 App. D.C. 80 (1964); *see also* Raleigh Fitkin-Paul Morgan Memorial Hosp. v. Anderson, 42 N.J. 421, 201 A.2d 537, *cert. denied*, 337 U.S. 985 (1964) (blood transfusion ordered to preserve life of unborn child). Courts will also order treatment to protect the public's health. *See, e.g.,* Jacobson v. Massachusetts, 197 U.S. 11 (1905) (compulsory vaccination).

59. *In re* Osborne, 294 A.2d 372 (D.C. Cir. 1972).

60. *Eichner*, 73 A.D.2d at 456, 426 N.Y.S.2d at 537.

61. In John F. Kennedy Memorial Hosp. v. Heston, 58 N.J. 576, 279 A.2d 670 (1971), the court, in ruling that the state had a compelling interest to preserve the life of a 22-year-old competent adult, ordered blood transfusions over her refusal on religious grounds, giving great weight to the interests of the hospital, nurses, and physicians in carrying out their professional duties. *Heston* was expressly overruled in *In re* Conroy, 98 N.J. 321, 486 A.2d 1209 (1985).

62. *In re* Quinlan, 70 N.J. 10, 355 A.2d 647, 667, *cert. denied*, 429 U.S. 922 (1976); *see also* Leach v. Akron Gen. Medical Center, 68 Ohio Misc. 1, 426 N.E.2d 809 (1980).

63. Bartling v. Superior Court, 163 Cal. App. 186, 209 Cal. Rptr. 220 (1984)

(competent adult with serious illnesses that were incurable but not diagnosed as terminal had right to have life-support equipment disconnected); Tune v. Walter Reed Army Medical Center, 602 F. Supp. 1452 (D.C.D.C. 1985) (71-year-old woman with terminal adenocarcinoma had right to have respirator that sustained her life disconnected in spite of Army policy precluding the withdrawal of life support systems); Saltz v. Perlmustter, 379 So. 2d 359 (Fla. 1980) (73-year-old competent patient had right to have respirator removed where all affected family members consented).

64. *See, e.g., In re* Melideo, 88 Misc. 2d 974, 390 N.Y.S.2d 523 (Sup. Ct. 1976) (Jehovah's Witness was permitted to refuse blood transfusion, even though death was likely to result); Lane v. Candura, 6 Mass. App. 377, 376 N.E.2d 1232 (1978) (court would not order amputation of the gangrenous leg of 77-year-old competent woman over her objection).

65. *In re* Plaza Health & Rehabilitation Center (Sup. Ct., Onandaga County, N.Y., Feb. 4, 1984).

66. Bouvia v. Riverside County Gen. Hosp., No. 159780 (Super. Ct., Riverside City, Cal., Dec. 16, 1983).

67. Bouvia v. Superior Court (Glenchur), 179 Cal. App. 3d 1127, 225 Cal. Rptr. 297 (1986).

68. Barclay v. Campbell, 704 S.W.2d 8 (Tex. 1986) (mentally ill person entitled to be informed of risks from use of neuroleptic drugs).

69. Maben v. Rankin, 55 Cal. 2d 139, 358 P.2d 681, 10 Cal. Rptr. 353 (1961).

70. Ritz v. Florida Patients' Compensation Fund, 436 So. 2d 987 (Fla. App. 1983) (father, though not an official legal guardian, who consented to brain surgery for an adult incompetent daughter may not bring action alleging that the operation was unauthorized), *review denied,* 450 So. 2d 488 (Fla. 1984).

71. Lester v. Aetna Casualty Co., 240 F.2d 676 (wife authorized to consent for electroshock treatments for husband where reasonable under all the facts and circumstances to believe that it would harm patient to obtain a fully informed consent from him), *cert. denied,* 354 U.S. 923 (1957); Farber v. Olkon, 40 Cal. 2d 503, 254 P.2d 520 (1953) (parent that is not legally appointed guardian can consent for a mentally incompetent adult child); Smith v. Luckett, 155 Ga. App. 640, 271 S.E.2d 891 (1980) (suit by patient who did not object during preparation for surgical procedure did not succeed when spouse had consented, as authorized by statute); Pratt v. Davis, 224 Ill. 300, 79 N.E. 562 (1906) (physician liable when surgery was performed on incompetent wife without husband's consent); Steele v. Woods, 327 S.W.2d 187 (Mo. 1959) (when patient incompetent, physician has duty to advise husband or relative competent to speak for the patient).

72. Karp v. Cooley, 493 F.2d 408 (5th Cir.) (spousal consent of no significance when competent adult consented to experimental surgery), *cert. denied,* 419 U.S. 845 (1974); *Nishi,* 52 Haw. 188, 473 P.2d 116 (1970) (physician may withhold disclosure of collateral risk for therapeutic reasons); Beck v. Lovell, 361 So. 3d 245 (La. App.) (absent medical emergency, spouse cannot consent for surgery on competent adult), *cert. denied,* 362 So. 2d 802 (1978).

73. *See, e.g., In re* Torres, 357 N.W.2d 332 (Minn. 1984); Severns v. Wilmington Medical Center, Inc., 421 A.2d 1334 (Del. 1980); John F. Kennedy Memorial

Hosp., Inc. v. Bludworth, 452 So. 2d 921 (Fla. 1984), *aff'g* 432 So. 2d 611 (Fla. Dist. Ct. App. 1983); Superintendent of Belchertown State School v. Saikewicz, 373 Mass. 728, 370 N.E.2d 417 (1977); *In re* Quinlan, 70 N.J. 10, 355 A.2d 647, *cert. denied,* 429 U.S. 922 (1976); Eichner v. Dilon, 434 N.Y.S.2d 46, 420 N.E.2d 64 (1981); *In re* Storar, 52 N.Y.2d 363, 420 N.E.2d 64, 438 N.Y.S.2d 266, *cert. denied,* 454 U.S. 858 (1981); Leach v. Akron Gen. Medical Center, 68 Ohio Misc. 1, 426 N.E.2d 809 (1980); *In re* Colyer, 99 Wash. 2d 114, 660 P.2d 738 (1983).

74. 70 N.J. 10, 355 A.2d 647 (1976).

75. There is no legal or ethical duty to treat a dead person. *See, e.g.,* Lovato v. District Crout In and For Tenth Judicial Dist., 198 Colo. 419, 601 P.2d 1072 91979). Although this seems obvious, it has nevertheless been difficult in some situations to determine when a person is dead and life-support systems may be justifiably discontinued. The common law defined death as the cessation of life. Until recently death meant the cessation of respiration and circulation, but with the use of mechanical respirators and other modern medical devices life as previously defined may now be continued indefinitely. Thus many states have adopted as the legal standard of death brain death, defined as the compete cessation of all functions of the entire brain, including the brain stem. *See, e.g.,* IDAHO CODE § 54-1819 (Supp. 1985); IOWA CODE § 702.8 (1979); MICH. COMP. LAWS ANN. §§ 333.1021–.1023 (1980); WYO. STAT. § 35-19-101 (Cum. Supp. 1985). Some states have adopted the brain-death definition through judicial decisions; *see, e.g.,* State v. Fierro, 124 Ariz. 182, 603 P.2d 74 (1979).

76. *In re* Quinlan, 137 N.J. Super. 227, 348 A.2d 801 (Ch. Div. 1975), *modified,* 70 N.J. 10 (1976).

77. After Karen Quinlan was removed from the respirator, she continued to receive antibiotics to ward off infections and was fed a high-calorie diet through a nasogastric tube. She continued to breathe on her own until her death in 1985.

78. *In re* Quinlan, 70 N.J. at 39, 355 A.2d at 633.

79. 373 Mass. 728, 370 N.E.2d 417 (1977).

80. *Id.* at 750, 370 N.E.2d at 430.

81. *Id.* at 753–54, 370 N.E.2d at 432.

82. *Id.* at 752–53, 370 N.E.2d at 431.

83. *Id.* at 754–55, 370 N.E.2d at 432.

84. *Id.* at 754, 370 N.E.2d at 432. Other cases applying the substituted judgment doctrine include *In re* Hier, 18 Mass. App. 200, 464 N.E.2d 959 (1984). Probate court properly refused to order surgery necessary to supply nutrition to 92-year-old severely mentally ill woman; among other factors the appellate court found that the "expressions of opposition by Mrs. Hier, while those of an incompetent person, and thus not to be given legal effect, are nevertheless to be taken into consideration in applying the substituted judgment test because they are indicative of the burden that she feels in being subjected to advanced medical technologies." *See also* 18 Mass. App. at 208, 464 N.E.2d at 965; John F. Kennedy Memorial Hosp. v. Bludworth, 452 So. 2d 921 (Fla. 1984), *aff'd* 432 So. 2d 611 (Fla. Dist. Ct. App. 1983)("living will" executed by patient prior to his becoming terminally ill and comatose was given great weight by surrogate decision-maker who substituted his judgment on behalf of the incompetent).

85. *In re* Carson, 39 Misc. 2d 544, 545, 241 N.Y.S.2d 288, 289 (N.Y. Sup. Ct. 1962) (cited in *Saikewicz,* 373 Mass. at 752, 370 N.E.2d at 431).

86. *In re* Storar, 52 N.Y.2d 363, 420 N.E.2d 64, 438 N.Y.S.2d 266, *cert. denied,* 454 U.S. 858 (1981).

87. 98 N.J. 321, 486 A.2d 1209 (1985).

88. *In re* Conroy, 188 N.J. Super. 523 (N.J. Ch. Div. 1983).

89. *In re* Conroy, 190 N.J. Super. 453, 464 A.2d 303 (N.J. Super. A.D. 1983).

90. *In re* Conry, 98 N.J. at 342–43, 486 A.2d at 1219.

91. *Id.* at 360, 486 A.2d at 1229.

92. *Id.* at 364, 486 A.2d at 1231.

93. 497 U.S. 261 (1990).

94. Cal. Health & Safety Code §§ 7185–7195 (West Supp. 1985).

95. *Id.* at § 7187(c).

96. *Id.* at § 7195.

97. *See, e.g.,* Cal. Civ. Code §§ 2430–2443 (West Supp. 1985). *See also* 20 Pa. Cons. Stat. Ann. §§ 5601–5606 (Purdon Supp. 1985) (durable power of attorney for medical decisions).

98. Whether the court needs to be involved in the determination of incompetence is not clear. "The implication is that doctors will continue to have the major role in assessing incompetence. The efficiency of the law would be severely impaired if judicial review of competence were routinely requested. When the physician has doubts about the patient's ability to give informed consent, he or she may seek consent from both the patient and the agent—an approach that does not involved legal proceedings." Steinbrook and Lo, *Decision Making for Incompetent Patients by Designated Proxy,* 310 New Eng. J. of Med. 1598, 1599 (1984).

99. 171 Mich. 122, 136 N.W. 1106 (1912).

100. Bishop v. Shurly, 237 Mich. 76, 211 N.W. 75 (1926) (19-year-old could consent to administration of a local anesthetic); Gulf & S.I.R. Co. v. Sullivan, 155 Miss. 1, 119 So. 501, 62 A.L.R. 191 (1928) (17-year-old could consent to vaccination); Lacey v. Larid, 166 Ohio St. 12, 139 N.E.2d 25 (1956) (18-year-old girl could consent to surgical operation); Masden v. Harrison, II 68651 Equity Mass. 1957) (19-year-old twin could consent to a kidney transplant operation); Restatement (Second) or Torts § 892A, comment b (1979).

101. Bonner v. Moran, 126 F.2d 121, 139 A.L.R. 1366 (D.C. Cir. 1941) (15-year-old's consent to skin grafting operation was held to be insufficient).

102. Zoski v. Gaines, 271 Mich. 1, 260 N.W. 99 (1935) (9-year-old's consent was insufficient); Moss v. Rishworth, 222 S.W. 225 (Tex. Comm'n of App. 1920) (11-year-old).

103. *In re* Barbara Doe (unreported case D.C. 1971).

104. 205 Kan. 292, 469 P.2d 330 (1970).

105. *See, e.g., In re* Estate of Kemp, 43 Cal. App. 3d 758, 118 Cal. Rptr. 64 (1974); Holmes v. Powers, 439 S.W.2d 579 (Ky. Ct. App. 1968); *In re* Smith, 16 Md. App. 209, 295 A.2d 238 (1972); *In re* M.K.R., 515 S.W.2d 467 (Mo. 1974); Frazier v. Levi, 440 S.W.2d 393 (Tex. Civ. App. 1969). *Cf.* Melville v. Sabbatino, 30 Conn. Supp. 320, 313 A.2d 886 (1973) (minor committed to mental hospital by parents has right to leave).

106. 37 N.J. 463, 181 A.2d 751, *cert. denied,* 371 U.S. 890 (1962).

107. Leading decisions are State v. Perricone, 37 N.J. 463, 181 A.2d 751, *cert. denied,* 371 U.S. 890 (1962); Wallace v. Labrenz, 411 Ill. 618, 104 N.E.2d 769, 30 A.L.R.2d 1132, *cert. denied,* 344 U.S. 824 (1952); Maine Medical Center v. Houle, No. 74–145 (Me. Super. Ct. 1974) (parents who withhold medically necessary and feasible treatment are guilty of legal neglect even if physician's opinion is that the child is brain damaged and life not worth preserving).

108. 247 Ga. 86, 274 S.E.2d 457 (1981) (prior to birth, abnormal condition corrected itself and th cesarean was not necessary); *see also* Hoener v. Bertinato, 67 N.J. Super. 517, 171 A.2d 140 (Juv. & Dom. Rel. Ct. 1961) (blood transfusion ordered at time of birth); Raleigh Fitkin–Paul Morgan Memorial Hosp. v. Anderson, 42 N.J. 421, 201 A.2d 537 (1964) (court ordered a transfusion when the life of an unborn child was threatened). *See generally* Finamore, *Jefferson v. Griffin Spalding County Hospital Authority: Court-Ordered Surgery to Protect the Life of an Unborn Child,* 9 AM. J.L. & MED. 83 (1983–84); Baker, *Court-Ordered Non-Emergency Medical Care for Infants,* 18 CLEV.-MAR. L. REV. 296 (1969).

109. 13 Wash. 2d 673, 126 P.2d 765 (1942).

110. *In re* Frank, 41 Wash. 2d 194, 248 P.2d 553 (1952).

111. *In re* Seiferth, 309 N.Y. 80, 127 N.E.2d 820 (1955).

112. 205 S.W.2d 812, 12 A.L.R.2d 1042 (Tex. Civ. App. 1947); 29 N.Y.2d 900, 278 N.E.2d 918, 328 N.Y.S.2d 686 (1972).

113. 448 Pa. 338, 292 A.2d 387, 52 A.L.R.3d 1106 (1972).

114. Custody of a Minor, 375 Mass. 733, 379 N.E.2d 1053 (1978).

115. *Id.* at 754, 379 N.E.2d at 1066.

116. Custody of a Minor, 378 Mass. 732, 393 N.E.2d 836 (1979).

117. 253 Ga. 439, 321 S.E.2d 716 (1984).

118. *See also In re* Barry, 445 So. 2d 365 (Fla. App. 2d Dist. 1984) (court authorized parents to consent to withdrawal of life-support systems for terminally ill, comatose 10-month-old child on basis of child's right to privacy); *In re* Benjamin C., (Sup. Ct. Cal., Feb. 15, 1979) (parents could rely on physician's judgment in authorizing disconnection of life-support systems for 3-year-old auto accident victim who was comatose; this would be consistent with generally accepted medical standards); Custody of a Minor, 385 Mass. 697, 434 N.E.2d 601 (1982) (court applied the substituted judgment doctrine and authorized a "do not resuscitate" order for abandoned, terminally ill newborn; the medical testimony was that heroic efforts to resuscitate the infant would not be in the child's best interests and would "offend medical ethics").

119. *In re* Infant Doe, No. 1-782A157 (Ind. App., Apr. 14, 1982). The medical circumstances of "Baby Doe" are described in a letter from John E. Pless, M.D., to the editor of the NEW ENGLAND JOURNAL OF MEDICINE, entitled *The Story of Baby Doe,* 309 NEW ENG. J. OF MED. 664 (1983).

120. Weber v. Stony Brook Hosp., 95 A.D.2d 587, *aff'd,* 60 N.Y.2d 208 (1983).

121. *Id.* at 589.

122. *See* Note, *Withholding Lifesaving Treatment from Defective Newborns: An Equal Protection Analysis,* 29 St. Louis U. L.J. 853 (1985). "A determination that death is in an infant's best interest, because its life is not worth living, rests on

two basic assumptions: first, that it is possible to make an accurate judgment regarding another's quality of life; and second, that an abnormal life can be less acceptable or meaningful than a normal life to the point to justifying a choice of death. These are dangerous assumptions. They invite abuse and are highly susceptible to error." *Id.* at 864–65.

123. *See* Stinson and Stinson, *On the Death of a Baby,* 7 J. MED. ETHICS 5 (1981). A baby born 15½ weeks premature and weighing less than two pounds was "in a state of painful deterioration from the start"; his parents wanted him to be allowed to die a natural death. "He was, in effect, 'saved' by the respirator to die five long, painful, and expensive months later of the respirator's side effects." *See also* STINSON AND STINSON, THE LONG DYING OF BABY ANDREW (1983).

124. PRESIDENT'S COMMISSION FOR THE STUDY OF ETHICAL PROBLEMS IN MEDICINE AND BIOMEDICAL AND BEHAVIORAL RESEARCH, DECIDING TO FOREGO LIFE-SUSTAINING TREATMENT: A REPORT ON THE ETHICAL, MEDICAL, AND LEGAL ISSUES IN TREATMENT DECISIONS. Washington, D.C., U.S. Government Printing Office (1983).

125. *Id.* at 223–24. As an example of the first problem, one couple with a 4-year-old child with spina bifida, described by her parents as a "joy," say that they almost lost her because of inaccurate information. Doctors had informed the parents, incorrectly, that the child was paralyzed, mentally retarded, and would almost certainly never walk. *Saving Spina Bifida Babies,* NEWSWEEK, November 15, 1982 at 110.

126. 45 C.F.R. § 5103 (b)(2) (1982).

127. *Summary of the Final Rule,* 50 Fed. Reg. 72, 14879 (1985).

128. ARIZ. REV. STAT. ANN. §§ 36-2281–2284 (Supp. 1984–85); *see also* LA. REV. STAT. ANN. §§ 40:1299.36.1–.36.3 (West Supp. 1985) ("[I]nfants born alive and other children: nutritional and medical deprivation prohibited"). Indiana has specifically provided that a handicapped child who is denied nutrition or necessary medical treatment is a neglected child under its child protection statute. This provision includes handicapped children to 18 years of age, not just newborns. IND. CODE ANN. § 31-6-4-3(f), (g) (West Supp. 1985).

129. ARIZ. REV. STAT. ANN. § 36-2281(A) (Supp. 1984–85).

130. *Id.* at § 36-2281(B), (C), (D) (Supp. 1984–85).

131. *Id.* § 36-2282 (Supp. 1984–85).

132. *Id.* § 36-2283 (Supp. 1984–85).

133. *Id.* § 36-2284 (Supp. 1984–85).

134. Bednarik v. Bednarik, 18 N.J. Misc. 633, 16 A.2d 80 (Ch. 1940). In general, under common law, medical and hospital personnel are under no legal duty to honor a request or command by law enforcement officials to conduct blood alcohol or other tests for possible intoxication. If a physician, for instance, is in the employ of a law enforcement agency, however, a duty is created by the employment contract. (The case cited was overruled on other grounds, Cortese v. Cortese, 10 N.J. Super. 152, 76 A.2d 717 (App. Div. 1950)).

135. Mackey v. Montrym, 443 U.S. 1 (1979) (90-day suspension of driver's license without a presuspension hearing after a driver refused to take breath-analysis test does not violate constitutional due process); *see also, e.g.,* McNulty v. Curry, 42 Ohio St. 2d 341, 328 N.E.2d 798 (1975) (implied consent statute is

constitutional, and person accused of driving under influence of alcohol has no constitutional right to refuse to submit to chemical test).

136. One of the more comprehensive immunity provisions would appear to be New York's statute. It provides that no physician, registered nurse, laboratory technician, physician's assistant, or hospital employer shall be sued or held liable for any act done or omitted when withdrawing blood at the request of a police officer. N.Y. VEH. & TRAF. LAW § 1194 (7)(b) (McKinney Supp. 1978–79). Accordingly, there appears to be immunity from liability even if the test is administered without consent of the patient. But, as the text cautions, not all immunity provisions are as protective of hospitals and their personnel.

137. 42 U.S.C. § 1983 (1982).

138. Hill v. Bogans, 735 F.2d 391 (10th Cir. 1984) (city liable for violation of civil rights after police conducted unreasonable strip search of motorist arrested under outstanding bench warrant for speeding violation).

139. McGhee v. Draper, 564 F.2d 902 (10th Cir. 1977); Aristocrat Health Club of Hartford, Inc. v. Chaucer, 451 F. Supp. 210 (D. Conn. 1978).

12

FAMILY PLANNING[1]

Courts of law today are asked to decide many of society's most perplexing problems. The judicial system of this country is daily asked to apply Solomonic wisdom to virtually intractable social, moral, and ethical controversies, all of which are presented in the guise of legal principles. Although the system often seems imperfectly constructed to do so, it must make a decision in every justiciable case.

Much of the litigation involving these kinds of issues has arisen along with advances in scientific and medical technology. For example, as doctors developed advanced reproductive techniques such as in vitro fertilization, questions surfaced regarding parental and custodial rights. For lack of any alternative forums for such disputes, the questions often found their way into courtrooms. And as medical technology expanded, particularly in the area of prenatal and neonatal care and treatment, courts have been asked to reevaluate earlier precedents in light of those changing conditions. The extent to which such decisions can or should be modified remains a continuing source of judicial inquiry, particularly in the area of abortion.

As long as society needs to have family-planning matters resolved, and as long as reasonable alternative forums are not developed, these issues will continue to be heard in our country's courtrooms. The difficulty the judicial system has with such matters is reflected in this chapter, and the reader should understand the cases not only for their legal merit but also for the real-life dramas that underlie each situation.

Abortion

Before the nineteenth century, abortion was not prohibited by English or American law, at least in the early stages of pregnancy. Some scholars maintain that English law never regarded abortion of a quickened fetus (one that has had movements the mother can feel) as a criminal act. Others disagree. In view of the apparent uncertainty in England, it is not surprising that American courts deciding cases pursuant to common law reached differing conclusions. Some held that an abortion of a quickened fetus was criminal, at least a misdemeanor, but others ruled that an abortion, regardless of the stage of pregnancy, was not a crime.[2] In any event, the matter soon became a question solely of statutory law because a generally well-accepted principle in Anglo-American jurisprudence is that criminal law must be established by statute and not by common-law judicial decision.

The English Parliament enacted the first restrictive abortion statute in 1803.[3] It provided that a willful abortion of a quickened fetus was a capital crime and established lesser penalties for abortions performed during earlier stages of pregnancy. If the surgery was performed in good faith to preserve the life of the mother, however, no criminal act had been committed.[4]

American jurisdictions soon adopted this viewpoint by passing restrictive abortion statutes. Connecticut was the first state to do so when it passed a statute in 1821 that accepted the English distinction between a quickened and unquickened fetus. Similarly, an 1828 New York statute provided that an abortion after quickening was a felony—that is, manslaughter—but a misdemeanor prior to that point in the pregnancy. An exception was made to preserve the life of the mother.

By shortly after the Civil War nearly all states had enacted restrictive abortion statutes of some type, and most statutes in time abandoned the distinction between a quickened and unquickened fetus. In the 1950s and 1960s the various laws generally fell into the following categories. A few states banned all abortions regardless of the stage of pregnancy and regardless of the reason for the procedure. Most, however, permitted termination of pregnancy to preserve the mother's life while prohibiting termination under all other circumstances, and a few statutes permitted the surgery to preserve the mother's health. Some of the laws specifically required that only a physician could perform the surgery; some required the attending physician to consult with other doctors; and from state to state there were similar statutory safeguards intended to ensure that professional people were following the fundamental statutory prohibitions on abortion. Violation of these restrictive laws was, of course, deemed a criminal offense. Consent of the patient did not generally protect the one performing the illegal surgery from criminal prosecution.

During the 1960s a trend developed to liberalize these restrictive state laws, and by 1970 approximately one-third of the states had adopted a model abortion law that permitted a licensed physician to terminate pregnancy when there was "substantial risk that continuance of pregnancy would gravely impair the physical or mental health of the mother, or that the child would be born with grave physical or mental defects or that the pregnancy resulted from rape, incest, or other felonious intercourse."[5] Termination of pregnancy under circumstances other than those described was a felony of the third degree if performed prior to the twenty-sixth week, and of the second degree if performed after that time. The law further required that all abortions take place in a licensed hospital, unless an emergency existed and such facilities were not available, and that at least two physicians had to certify in writing the circumstances justifying the surgery. Some jurisdictions added additional requirements:

- that the patient be a resident of the state for a specified time prior to the surgery;

- that the attending physician obtain the concurrence of the hospital's medical staff committee; or
- that the hospital where the surgery was to be performed be accredited by the Joint Commission on Accreditation of Healthcare Organizations.

By the end of 1970, liberalization of the law in New York, Washington, Hawaii, and Alaska had gone much further than the model law. These states had adopted in essence the principle of abortion on demand, at least up to a statutorily designated stage of pregnancy. New York, Hawaii, and Alaska accomplished this change by statute, and the state of Washington did so by popular referendum of the people. These states imposed certain restrictions. For example, that the procedure had to be done by a licensed physician in a licensed or an accredited hospital or that the woman must establish a period of residency in the state before she would be eligible for an abortion.

Then came the landmark abortion cases of January 1973. These decisions addressed a broad, fundamental issue of constitutional law: Does a woman have a right to decide for herself, without governmental regulation, whether to bear a child?

The Wade *and* Bolton *Cases*

Roe v. Wade[6] concerned the constitutionality of a very restrictive Texas statute, while the companion litigation of *Doe v. Bolton*[7] raised issues relevant to more liberal Georgia legislation.

The Texas law permitted an abortion at any stage of pregnancy, but only to save the life of the mother. The issue presented to the court was whether the state had a sufficient "compelling interest" in the subject matter of regulation to justify the nearly total prohibition of abortion. To justify an exercise of the police power the state generally needs only to establish that the regulatory measure bear a rational relationship to legitimate governmental interests. When "fundamental" individual rights are involved, however, the state must convince the court that there is a "compelling interest" to justify the restraints. Because an individual's right of privacy is a fundamental right, the *Wade* and *Bolton* cases employed the compelling interest test when ruling on the constitutionality of the Texas and Georgia abortion statutes.

In *Roe v. Wade* the court held the entire Texas statute to be unconstitutional in violation of the due process clause of the Fourteenth Amendment. A "balancing of interests" between the state, acting on behalf of the general welfare, and the individual seeking an abortion led to the conclusion that the individual's rights of privacy are paramount to the interests that the statute sought to promote.

This does not mean that the state may not regulate abortion at all. The court recognized that the state had two legitimate interests that would justify regulating abortions: protecting the life and health of pregnant women and protecting the "potentiality of human life." These were the interests the court weighed against the woman's right of privacy to decide regarding an abortion. The court found that during the first trimester of pregnancy the risk to the woman's health was less from an abortion than from childbirth. Thus the state's interest in maternal and fetal health did not outweigh the right of privacy. For that reason states may only restrict abortions during the first trimester as they might restrict other surgical procedures: for example, by requiring that they be performed by licensed physicians.[8] Essentially the decision to perform an abortion during the first trimester of pregnancy is solely up to the patient and her physician.

During the second trimester, the court found, the risk to the woman is greater. Under the balancing test the state's interest in protecting the woman's health becomes compelling, and the state may place restrictions that protect her health, as long as these do not unreasonably interfere with the woman's right to make her own decision on abortion.

The court held that state's interest in protecting *potential* life, however, does not become compelling until the fetus is viable, that is, capable of surviving outside the mother. In 1973 this stage was reached about 28 weeks after conception. At that point the stage may proscribe abortions altogether, unless they are necessary to protect the life or health of the mother.

Note that the court in *Roe v. Wade* did not decide when life begins or when the fetus becomes a "person." Physicians, theologians, and philosophers have long debated these questions. Rhode Island legislation enacted after the landmark Supreme Court cases declared that life begins at conception and that accordingly abortion at any stage of pregnancy is criminal. This law was declared unconstitutional, even though the *Wade* case had sidestepped this particular question.[9] Hence, the constitutional right to have an abortion, as articulated by *Wade*, may not be avoided by a state statute expressing another philosophy or other grounds that attempt to circumvent individual rights.

In 1973, medical science allowed a relatively clear division of pregnancy: risk to the woman increased after the first three months and viability generally occurred after the end of the second three months. This trimester structure was used in determining when the state's interests outweighed those of the woman and therefore when the state could place restrictions on abortions. Nevertheless, there are those who criticize the soundness of this legal approach. As pointed out by Justice O'Connor:

> Just as improvements in medical technology inevitably will move *forward* the point at which the State may regulate for reasons of maternal health, different technological improvements will move *backward* the point of viability at which the State may proscribe abortions except when necessary to preserve the life and health of the mother. . . .

> The *Roe* framework, then, is clearly on a collision course with itself. As the medical risks of various abortion procedures decrease, the

point at which the State may regulate for reasons of maternal health is moved further forward to actual childbirth. As medical science becomes better able to provide for the separate existence of the fetus, the point of viability is moved further back toward conception. Moreover, it is clear that the trimester approach violates the fundamental aspiration of judicial decision making through the application of neutral principles "sufficiently absolute to give them root throughout the community and continuity over significant periods of time . . ." [Citation omitted.] The *Roe* framework is inherently tied to the state of medical technology that exists whenever particular litigation ensues.[10]

A companion case to *Wade, Doe v. Bolton*,[11] involved the constitutionality of Georgia's "liberalized" statute patterned after the model law discussed earlier. The law permitted termination of pregnancies by a licensed physician whenever continued pregnancy would endanger the woman's life or injure her health, when the baby was likely to be born with grave, permanent defects, or when pregnancy was the consequence of rape. In the interest of protecting the patient's health and well-being, however, the law required physicians to exercise their "best clinical judgment" when recommending an abortion. It also required that the procedure be carried out in a hospital accredited by the Joint Commission on Accreditation of Healthcare Organizations, that it be approved by an abortion committee comprising members of the hospital's medical staff, and that the judgment of the patient's physician be confirmed by two other independent physicians who had examined the patient. Further, the patient had to establish Georgia residency to be considered eligible for an abortion.

The Supreme Court upheld the statutory requirement that "best clinical judgment" of the patent's physician be exercised when the need for an abortion is evaluated. However, it invalidated the three procedural requirements and the residency requirement, holding that they unduly restricted the rights of doctors and patients to decide on the surgery needed by the patient and thus violated the Fourteenth Amendment. The court supported its conclusion regarding the procedural matters by noting that Georgia law did not require that other surgical procedures of similar risk take place only in hospitals accredited by the Joint Commission or that they be preceded by consultation with other physicians. The decision to conduct the surgery is left to the professional judgment and advice of the patient's own physician. Nevertheless, the court specifically recognized that that state might, if it wished, require that abortions after the first trimester be performed at licensed facilities and that the state might also promulgate reasonable standards consistent with its legitimate interest in protecting maternal health.[12] The residence requirement was said to be an invasion of the constitutionally protected right to travel, included in the privileges and immunities clause of Article IV of the U.S. Constitution, and hence no state could limit local medical care to its own residents.

The Georgia statute expressly provided that no hospital, physician, or employee of a hospital should be compelled to perform or participate in an abortion. In *Bolton* the court specifically approved this statutory language, at least by dictum (which means that the precise issue was really not directly involved in the litigation). The intent of this provision—often referred to as a "conscience clause"—is of course to protect the institution's and individuals' rights to adhere to their moral or religious convictions and to recognize in the law that not all hospitals are adequately equipped and staffed to perform abortions. Individuals had to state in writing their refusal to participate on moral or religious grounds, and such refusal could not form the basis of a claim for damages or other disciplinary action.

Insofar as such statutes pertain to individual physicians, nurses, and other health professionals, they are certainly constitutionally permissible. The individual's moral convictions should be upheld and protected, although at least the physician should be bound—and would be bound under the general judicial law of malpractice—to refer the patient to another competent practitioner willing to perform an abortion whenever such referral was medically indicated. Whether making hospitals and other healthcare institutions subject to such statutes is constitutional is discussed later in this chapter.

State Regulation of Abortion Since Wade and Bolton

In the years since *Wade* and *Bolton*, the Supreme Court issued further guidelines for judicial review of state abortion regulation. In *City of Akron v. Akron Center for Reproductive Health, Inc.* the Court held that regulations concerning first-trimester abortions are valid only if they have "no significant impact" on a woman's right to decide the question of abortion in privacy, and if they are "justified by important state health objectives."[13] Even then, such regulations "may not interfere with physician-patient consultation or with the woman's choice between abortion and childbirth."[14]

The Court in *Akron* also held that although the state may regulate abortions after the first trimester to protect the mother's health, the "health standards adopted must be 'legitimately related to the objective the State seeks to accomplish,'" and the regulations may not "depart from accepted medical practice."[15]

The constitutionality of various types of state regulation has been examined using the standards set forth in *Wade, Bolton,* and *City of Akron.* In *Planned Parenthood Association of Kansas City, Missouri, Inc. v. Ashcroft,* decided the same day as *City of Akron,* the Supreme Court held that to require submission of any tissue removed following an abortion, whether in a hospital or clinic, to a pathologist placed a "relatively insignificant burden" on a woman's decision on abortion.[16] Because the regulation was "reasonably related to generally accepted medical standards" and furthered "important health-related State concerns," the Court found it valid. Four justices, it should be noted, disagreed with this finding, doubting that the increased cost of up to $40 was insignificant and the pathologist's report was justified.

Requirements for record keeping and reporting, provided that they are not unduly burdensome, that they protect confidentiality, and that the facts are legitimately related to the state's health interest, have generally been upheld even though they apply to all phases of pregnancy.[17] For example, the Michigan Department of Public Health requires that in freestanding facilities for outpatient surgery a half-page "abortion report" must be completed for each abortion and signed by the attending physician. Upon challenge, the provision was held constitutional.[18] Also upheld was a Pennsylvania requirement that all abortion facilities file reports subject to public disclosure, because such disclosure would not "appreciably affect a woman's abortion decision."[19]

Onerous reporting requirements, however, have been struck down. The Pennsylvania Abortion Control Act required detailed reporting for each abortion performed at any stage of pregnancy. Physicians had to sign and file a report the following month identifying themselves and naming the hospital or clinic and the referring physician, agency, or service. The report also called for the woman's place of residence, her age, race, and marital status, the number of her prior pregnancies, the date of her last menstrual period, and the probably gestational age of the unborn child. The physician had to record the type of procedure performed and any complications, the "length and weight of the aborted unborn child when measurable," the basis for "any medical judgment that a medical emergency existed" and for the physician's determination "that a child is not viable." A physician who determined that a child was viable had to state the basis for concluding that the abortion was necessary "to preserve maternal life or health." The method of payment for the abortion had also to be reported. Physicians whose patients had complications from an abortion procedure were required to file another detailed report for each such patient.[20] The U.S. Supreme Court found that identification was the "obvious purpose of these extreme reporting requirements" and that they posed an unacceptable danger of deterring the exercise of the woman's right to choose to terminate her pregnancy by raising the "spectre of public exposure and harassment."[21]

City of Akron challenged an ordinance that required, among other things, that all abortions after the first trimester take place in a hospital. The Supreme Court found that the safety of second-trimester abortions had increased dramatically since *Wade* was decided and that the dilatation and curettage (D and C) procedure widely used for second-trimester abortions could be performed safely in an outpatient setting. Requiring a hospital locale greatly burdened the woman by increasing the cost and inconvenience of the abortion, and the facilities of a hospital were no longer considered a necessity according to acceptable medical practice. Thus, the Court found that the requirement "unreasonably infringes upon a woman's constitutional right to obtain an abortion."[22] Similarly, a Missouri statute requiring that second-trimester abortions be performed only in general acute-care facilities was held unconstitutional.[23] A Virginia statute, however, that required that second-trimester abortions be performed in licensed clinics was upheld as a reasonable means of furthering the state's compelling interest in maternal health.[24]

The Supreme Court in *City of Akron* also made it clear that it is unconstitutional for states to require any waiting period between the woman's consent to an abortion and the abortion itself. The Court found that no legitimate state interest was served by such a requirement; further, the "decision whether to proceed with an abortion is one as to which it is important to 'affor[d] the physician adequate discretion in the exercise of his medical judgment.' "[25] The state-mandated delay is an unconstitutional infringement on the woman's right to choose abortion.[26]

In 1976 the Supreme Court held that it was permissible for states to require written informed consent of the woman prior to an abortion.[27] According to the Court, informed consent meant only "the giving of information to the patient as to just what would be done and as to its consequences. To ascribe more meaning than this might well confine the attending physician in an undesired and uncomfortable straitjacket in the practice of his profession."[28] The Court noted in *City of Akron* that the physician is primarily responsible for seeing that a patient is properly informed according to her particular circumstances and that the state's interest "[would] not justify regulations designed to influence the woman's informed choice between abortion or childbirth."[29] In this same case the Court examined and found unconstitutional provisions in one of Akron's city ordinances, which stated that certain specific information must be given to the woman before obtaining her written consent. In the court's view, requiring a physician to inform a patient that "the unborn child is a human life from the moment of conception" was inconsistent with the following holdings in *Wade:* that a state could not adopt one theory of when life begins; that a detailed description of the "anatomical and physiological characteristics of the particular unborn child" would involve "at best speculation by the physician"; and that a statement that "abortion is a major surgical procedure" along with a description of a number of possible physical and psychological complications was a " 'parade of horribles' intended to suggest that abortion is a particularly dangerous procedure."[30] The Court concluded that "much of the information required is designed not to inform the woman's consent but rather to persuade her to withhold it altogether."[31] The Court also based an "equally decisive" objection to the ordinance on "its intrusion upon the discretion of the pregnant woman's physician." For example, physicians were required to recite risks even if they believed them nonexistent for their patients.[32]

Another portion of the informed consent provisions cited in *City of Akron,* however, was struck down although the Court had no objection to provisions that the woman must be informed of the particular risks associated with her pregnancy and of the abortion technique to be employed, and that she must be given instructions for care following the abortion. The Court did object to the requirement in this part of the ordinance that the information be given by the attending physician. The Court found that singling out the physician as the only one to counsel the patient served no vital need on the part of the state, although a state could establish minimum qualifications for those assigned to such counseling, and could require that the physician make sure the patient is properly informed prior to giving her consent.[33]

The Supreme Court in *Wade* held that a state could proscribe (and make criminal) all abortions after the fetus becomes viable, except those necessary to preserve the mother's life or health, because at that point the state's interest in protecting the "potentiality of human life" becomes compelling. The Court observed that "in the medical and scientific community, a fetus is considered viable if it is 'potentially able to live outside the mother's womb, albeit with artificial aid.'"[34] The *Wade* court stressed that the "abortion decision in all its aspects is inherently, and primarily, a medical decision," and "left the point [of viability] flexible for anticipated advancements in medical skill."[35] Some of these advances have occurred. In 1973 a fetus was considered viable at about 28 weeks; since then, medical science has made it possible to save the lives of infants born at 22 weeks or even earlier. Some abortions, however, such as those where genetic diseases or defects are diagnosed, cannot be performed before about 18 to 20 weeks after conception because amniocentesis, the procedure that reveals the disease or defect, is not always possible before that time. Some abortions performed during the second or third trimester result in live births, although a fetus that survives an abortion may not be capable of living more than momentarily outside the mother.

The question of viability thus raises a number of issues, not all of which have been (or are capable of being) addressed by the legislatures or courts. If abortions are criminal after viability, who determines viability? Who decides whether the abortion was necessary to protect the mother's life or health, and what does "health" encompass? Even if the abortion is medically necessary, must the physician use the method most likely to preserve the life of the fetus? What duty of care is owed to the fetus who survives an abortion?

Some of these issues were addressed by the Supreme Court in *Colautti v. Franklin*.[36] The Pennsylvania Abortion Control Act passed in 1974 provided that

> if the fetus was determined to be viable, the person performing the abortion was required to exercise the same care to preserve the life and health of the fetus as would be required in the case of a fetus intended to be born alive, and was required to adopt the abortion technique providing the best opportunity for the fetus to be aborted alive, so long as a different technique was not necessary in order to preserve the life or health of the mother.[37]

The Supreme Court, in reviewing this provision, reiterated the following principle:

Viability is reached when, in the judgment of the attending physician on the particular facts of the case before him, there is a reasonable likelihood of the fetus' sustained survival outside the womb, with or without artificial support. Because this point may differ with each pregnancy, neither the legislature nor the courts may proclaim one of the elements entering the ascertainment of viability—be it weeks of gestation or fetal weight or any other single factor—as the determinant of when the State has a compelling interest in the life or health of the fetus. Viability is the critical point. And we have recognized no attempt to stretch the point of viability one way or the other.[38]

The Pennsylvania statute imposed a duty on physicians that arises when the fetus "is" or "may be" viable. The Court found the provision unconstitutional on the grounds that it was ambiguous and confusing. "Viable" and "may be viable" appeared to refer to distinct conditions, one of which differed "in some indeterminate way from the definition of viability as set forth in Roe and in Planned Parenthood."[39] In addition to being unclear, the statute appeared to impose criminal liability without scienter: that is, even physicians who judge in good faith that a fetus is not viable could apparently be found criminally liable if it turned out that the fetus was in fact viable.[40]

In Colautti the Supreme Court also examined the requirement that if the fetus was viable the physician must choose the abortion method that would be most likely to preserve the life of the fetus unless another method was necessary to preserve the life or health of the mother. The Court found this provision also too vague because it did not specify whether the mother's health always prevailed over the life of the fetus if there was a conflict or whether "necessary" meant "indispensable" to the woman's health. Further, the phrase "life or health of the mother" did not necessarily imply "that all factors relevant to the welfare of the woman may be taken into account by the physician making the decision."[41] The Court emphasized that choosing an appropriate abortion method involved a complex medical judgment on which experts could disagree. This provision, like the determination of viability, also lacked a scienter requirement. The Court held that a state could not require a physician to trade off the health of the mother for that of the fetus.[42]

Some states seeking to protect the life of the viable fetus have imposed a requirement that a second physician be present to attend to the health of the fetus at all postviability abortions. This requirement was upheld by the Supreme Court in Planned Parenthood Association of Kansas City, Missouri, Inc. v. Ashcroft as reasonably furthering the state's compelling interest in protecting the lives of viable fetuses.[43] However, so that the mother's health is protected in cases of emergency, there must be an express or implied exception to the requirement calling for a second physician. In examining such a requirement in a Pennsylvania statute, the Supreme Court found that no exception covering emergencies could be implied from the language of the statue and so ruled the provision unconstitutional.[44]

Missouri was the focus of another landmark abortion case, *Webster v. Reproductive Health Services*,[45] decided in 1989. In *Webster* the Court addressed four provisions of a Missouri statute:

1. its preamble, which declared that life begins at conception and that "unborn children have protectable interests in life, health, and well-being";
2. a prohibition on the use of public facilities or employees to perform abortions;
3. a prohibition on public funding of abortion counseling; and
4. a requirement that physicians conduct viability tests prior to performing abortions.

The Supreme Court declined to wade into the philosophical quagmire of when life begins. Instead, it upheld the statute's preamble by holding that it was merely a value judgment favoring childbirth over abortion, a position that the legislature had the authority to express. The Court explained that "the extent to which the preamble's language might be used to interpret other state statutes or regulations is something that only the courts of Missouri can definitively decide." It added that Missouri already protected unborn children in the areas of tort and probate law and that the preamble "can be interpreted to do no more than that."

The Court also upheld the other provisions of the Missouri law. With regard to restrictions on the use of public facilities and employees for abortion, the opinion states, "Nothing in the Constitution requires States to enter or remain in the business of performing abortions. Nor . . . do private physicians and their patients have some kind of constitutional right of access to public facilities for the performance of abortions." Likewise the prohibition on the use of public funds to support abortions was held not to be an unconstitutional governmental obstacle for a woman who chooses abortion. Finally, the Court upheld the requirement that physicians test for fetal viability before performing an abortion procedure.

The significance of *Webster* was not so much its specific holdings but the language of the opinion, written by Chief Justice Rhenquist, that called *Roe v. Wade*'s trimester analysis into doubt:

> We think that the doubt cast upon the Missouri statute by these cases is not so much a flaw in the statute as it is a reflection of the fact that the rigid trimester analysis of the course of a pregnancy enunciated in *Roe* has resulted in subsequent cases making constitutional law in this area a virtual Procrustean bed. . . .
>
> In the first place, the rigid *Roe* framework is hardly consistent with the notion of a Constitution case in general terms as ours is, and

usually speaking in general principles, as ours does. The key elements of the *Roe* framework—trimesters and viability—are not found in the text of the Constitution or in any place else one would expect to find a constitutional principle. Since the bounds of the inquiry are essentially indeterminate, the result has been a web of legal rules that have become increasingly intricate, resembling a code of regulations rather than a body of constitutional doctrine. As Justice White has put it, the trimester framework has left this Court to serve as the country's "*ex officio* medical board with powers to approve or disapprove practices and standards throughout the United States."

In the second place, we do not see why the State's interest in protecting potential human life should come into existence only at the point of viability, and that there should therefore be a rigid line allowing state regulation after viability but prohibiting it before viability. . . .

Because no clear majority of justices was prepared to overrule *Wade*, however, the quoted language remains dictum. It is dictum, however, that greatly encouraged the antiabortion forces who awaited the day when *Roe v. Wade* would be overturned. The next great assault on *Wade* came in the 1992 case of *Planned Parenthood of S.E. Pa. v. Casey*,[46] which involved a Pennsylvania law containing numerous provisions the plaintiffs felt were obstacles to a woman's choice of abortion. These were:

1. a requirement that informed consent, accompanied by certain clinical information, be provided at least 24 hours prior to procedure;
2. parental or judicial consent for a minor's abortion; and
3. a narrow definition of "medical emergency" allowing the above requirements to be avoided in certain situations.

Supporters of the law, including the Commonwealth of Pennsylvania and the United States, not only asked that the statute be upheld but urged that *Wade* be overturned. A widely divided Supreme Court declined to do so. The Court upheld the first two provisions, stating that they did not constitute an "undue burden" on a woman's right to choose, but struck down the others as overly burdensome and too narrowly written.[47] In the course of announcing the decision, Justice O'Connor's lead opinion declared, "Liberty finds no refuge in a jurisprudence of doubt." From this strong reaffirmation of the principle of *stare decisis,* it went on to reaffirm *Wade*'s essential holdings:

- that a woman's right to choose an abortion before viability cannot be unduly interfered with by the State;
- after viability the State may restrict abortions except in the case of those to protect the mother's life or health; and

- all throughout pregnancy the State has legitimate interests in protecting the health of the mother and fetus.

But *Wade* did not escape unscathed. Justice O'Connor wrote, "We reject the rigid trimester framework or *Roe v. Wade.*" Instead of trimesters, the opinion focused on the concept of fetal viability: "[T]he concept of viability . . . is the time at which there is a realistic possibility of maintaining and nourishing a life outside the womb, so that the independent existence of the second life can in reason and all fairness be the object of state protection that now overrides the rights of the woman." The opinion continued on this point, "The woman's right to terminate her pregnancy before viability is the most central principle of *Roe v. Wade*. It is a rule of law and a component of liberty we cannot renounce."

It is important to note that the judgment of the Court was announced in an opinion authored primarily by Justices O'Connor, Kennedy, and Souter. Justices Blackmun and Stevens joined in portions of the opinion, thus providing the five votes necessary for the particular actions ultimately taken ("affirmed in part" and "reversed in part"), but these two justices also joined Chief Justice Rhenquist and Justices White, Scalia, and Thomas in dissenting to at least a part of the lead opinion. Furthermore, the latter four members of the Court would have reexamined *Wade*'s principle that abortion is a fundamental right, concluded that the choice of an abortion is not a constitutional right at all, and urged that the statute be upheld in its entirety.

Clearly, as these cases show, abortion is one of the most difficult and divisive issues the judicial system has ever faced, and it has been so for more than a quarter century. As stated by the dissent in *Webster*, it is "the most politically divisive domestic legal issue of our time." But, according to the majority in the same case, "the goal of constitutional adjudication is surely not to remove inexorably 'politically divisive' issues from the ambit of the legislative process, whereby the people through their elected representatives deal with matters of concern to them. The goal of constitutional adjudication is to hold true the balance between that which the Constitution puts beyond the reach of the democratic process and that which it does not."

In drawing the line at viability and using an "undue burden" standard (for judging "whether a state regulation has the purpose or effect of placing a substantial obstacle in the path of a woman seeking an abortion of a nonviable fetus") the Court has perhaps held true the balance the *Webster* opinion referred to.

Sterilization

Sterilization is a surgical procedure intended to terminate the ability to procreate. For the male the most common procedure is termed a vasectomy; the operation for the female is called a salpingectomy. In a legal analysis one should distinguish between voluntary and involuntary sterilizations and classify them according to their purpose. Voluntary sterilizations are those performed on patients who are competent to understand the nature of the procedure and have given a fully informed consent. Voluntary sterilizations fall into two groups: those performed for the patient's convenience—to prevent conception, for example—and those undertaken as therapeutic measures, where there are sound medical reasons for the procedure.

Involuntary sterilizations—that is, those lacking the informed consent of the patient—may occur because the patient is incompetent to consent or because the state has declared the sterilization to be compulsory. Some involuntary sterilizations, including those which are compulsory, are called "eugenic" because their purpose is to protect society from inheritable disability. Eugenic sterilizations are now rare; such procedures must be authorized by statute, and few states have eugenic sterilization statutes. Some states, however, permit the sterilization of incompetent persons for the benefit of the patient, as will be discussed.

Voluntary Sterilization

There are no legal issues of unique significance in connection with a procedure to preserve the life or health of the patient or the spouse that incidentally results in sterility. Such a procedure, such as hysterectomy or orchidectomy to treat cancer, should not even be termed a form of "sterilization," and all states permit such treatment. The term "therapeutic sterilization" should be reserved for surgery the primary purpose of which is to produce sterility.

All states permit therapeutic procedures that incidentally result in sterility. Contraceptive sterilization, however, has not always been lawful in all jurisdictions. At least two states—Connecticut and Utah—expressly prohibited sterilizations solely for purposes of contraception and made the procedure a criminal act. In Utah the statutory language prohibited all sterilizations except those dictated by medical necessity. An action for declaratory judgment challenged that statute in relation to voluntary sterilizations for convenience, however, and it was ruled that the statute was applicable only to institutionalized patients.[48] Voluntary sterilization of other patients was said not to be criminal. The court based this conclusion on the grounds that the statute is a part of the Utah code dealing with eugenic sterilization and is under the general statutory topic of "State Institutions."

Connecticut had a statute that prohibited use of contraceptives and giving advice or assistance in their use. Voluntary contraceptive sterilization was thus prohibited by implication. This sterilization was declared unconstitutional in the landmark case of *Griswold v. Connecticut,* in which the U.S. Supreme Court ruled that the statute invaded a "zone of privacy created by several fundamental constitutional guarantees" protected by the due process clause of the Fourteenth Amendment.[49] Another Connecticut statute, which purported to authorize only sterilizations pursuant to *statutory* provisions for eugenic sterilization, was repealed in 1971.

In most states, however, the law is and always has been silent on the matter of contraceptive sterilization.[50] The procedure is thus lawful, and neither criminal nor civil penalties may be assessed against the physician, the hospital, or the patient for a properly performed sterilization requested by the patient for personal reasons, although the usual rules of civil liability for malpractice, breach of contract, or lack of an informed consent would apply. In all states modern social mores and ideas about family planning have now firmly established voluntary sterilization as a matter of personal choice. There are thus now no significant legal barriers to contraceptive sterilization (sterilization for convenience) although there continues to be significant objection to it from some religious sources, particularly the Roman Catholic Church.

All cases of sterilization, however, raise special issues concerning informed consent. Sterilization is a serious and usually permanent operation, forever depriving the sterilized patient of the fundamental right to procreate. Patients, especially the young, may not always fully understand the consequences. Certain patients also—for example, those dependent on governmental assistance—may be misled intentionally or unintentionally about the nature of the operation, its necessity, or the effect of their decision on their eligibility for financial assistance. In such a sensitive matter voluntary, informed consent is particularly necessary not only to ensure that the patient fully understands the operation and its consequences, but also to make certain that no duress, coercion, or deception has been used and that the patient is voluntarily exercising his or her fundamental right of privacy.

In choosing to fund voluntary sterilizations, the federal government has provided lengthy and specific safeguards so that patients may fully understand the consequences and are not led to believe that sterilization is related in any way to their right to receive federal assistance. Federal regulations govern all sterilizations performed under federally financed programs.[51] These regulations permit sterilizations only of voluntarily consenting, competent individuals at least 21 years old and not institutionalized. They specify the information patients must be given before their consent is obtained: the nature of the procedure, the risks, the alternatives, and the uncertainty of reversing the sterilization procedure. Patients must also be told that they are free to withhold or withdraw consent and that this will not affect their future care or benefits. A 30-day waiting period is required between the written informed consent and the procedure, except in emergencies.

These regulations are detailed and specific. The government supplements them by providing the approved consent form as well as informative pamphlets for the patients. Because such regulations are subject to change, hospitals, physicians, and other healthcare providers involved in federally financed sterilizations should keep fully posted on the current federal regulations governing these procedures.

The immediate consequence of failure to comply with the federal requirements would be refusal by the federal government to finance the sterilization. It may be claimed, however, that the provisions regarding informed consent are evidence of the standard of care required for informing patient prior to sterilization. Further, if the consent is obtained under circumstances that give the patient grounds for fearing the withdrawal of public assistance or healthcare, the patient may claim that the consent was not voluntary because it was obtained under duress or coercion. In such instances patients may have a cause of action for medical malpractice based on lack of informed consent or on denial of civil rights.

In addition to the federal regulations, some states have laws governing voluntary sterilizations. For example, a Virginia statute makes it lawful for a licensed physician to perform sterilizations on competent individuals who are at least 18 years old.[52] The physician must fully explain the nature and consequences of the operation and describe alternative methods of contraception. The consent must be in writing, and patients who have never had or adopted a child must wait 30 days between the consent and the sterilization. Maine also has a statute requiring a physician to obtain and record the informed consent of the patient prior to a sterilization procedure.[53] If the patient is under 18 and not married or emancipated, under a guardianship, or in a state institution, or if the physician cannot obtain informed consent, the statute requires a court hearing to determine whether the patient is a capable of giving consent.

Sterilizations, like abortions, differ in some legal respects from other medical procedures. They affect the individual's constitutional "right of privacy," which encompasses the right to decide whether to procreate. Actions that deny or interfere with such rights, when they involve state action, may have legal consequences even if there has been no medical malpractice. Healthcare providers should in any case be fully aware of state and federal laws governing sterilizations, and they should set up procedures to ensure compliance. Even in the absence of applicable legislation, the provider's policies and actions should make certain that the patient's consent is both fully informed and voluntary whenever a surgical procedure will or may result in sterilization, regardless of the primary purpose of the surgery. If the competence or understanding of the patient is at all in doubt, judicial guidance is advised.

Eugenic Sterilization and Sterilization of Incompetent Persons

Eugenics is the science dealing with the influences that improve the hereditary qualities of a race or breed. Hence, the term "eugenic sterilization" denotes surgery on persons alleged to be unsound or unfit to be parents because of presumably inheritable disabilities.

To be legal, a true eugenic sterilization must be based on a state statute that is consistent with the protection of state and federal constitutional law. Approximately one-half of the states have never enacted statutes authorizing compulsory eugenic sterilization. Accordingly, the practice has never existed in those jurisdictions, except for an occasional attempt to use judicial authority to justify the surgery. In another dozen or so states laws permitting eugenic sterilization have been repealed either altogether or in part.

In the remaining states, provisions of the statutes on eugenic sterilization differ, but essentially the pattern is first to identify the persons subject to the law, and then to detail the procedures to be followed before the surgery. The typical operations that are statutorily permitted are male vasectomies and females salpingectomies.

Most of the authorized eugenic sterilizations are compulsory because the surgery can be performed without the consent of the patient or guardian, although the law requires proper recommendations and procedures. On the other hand, a few of the statutes permit only voluntary eugenic sterilization, which requires consent of the patient or of the patient's legal representative.

Some statutes apply only to persons confined in state or governmental institutions (such as hospitals for the mentally ill, training schools, or prisons), but some apply to other individuals as well. In any event, the statutes usually identify the persons subject to the law, using such terms as the insane, the feeble-minded, the epileptic, the habitual criminal, the mentally defective, the sexual psychopath, the incurably incompetent, and similar designations presumably meaningful to medical science.

The basic constitutionality of the statutes was established by the famous Supreme Court case of *Buck v. Bell*, decided in 1927.[54] Carrie Buck had been duly committed to the state colony for epileptics and the "feeble minded." She was the daughter of a "feeble minded" mother who had been confined to the same institution, and she herself had given birth to an illegitimate child alleged to be "feeble minded." Following statutory procedures, a circuit court in Virginia ordered the superintendent of the institution to have a salpingectomy performed on Carrie Buck. As in cases in which compulsory vaccination had been upheld, the statute was held to be constitutional under the police power of the state to regulate the general health and welfare. The law, in effect, was said to have a direct relation to public health. In writing the opinion validating the Virginia law, Justice Holmes spoke his often-quoted line, "Three generations of imbeciles are enough."[55]

In fact, neither Carrie's mother nor her daughter was mentally handicapped. The mother was only mildly retarded, and the daughter was only one month old when she was labeled "mentally defective" by a Red Cross nurse. The child died of the measles in 1932 and had by that time completed the second grade, where she was reported to be not only normal but very bright.

In contrast to *Buck*, the Supreme Court held unconstitutional an Oklahoma statute that authorized sterilization of "habitual criminals" but exempted individuals described as "embezzlers." The constitutional point of law was that the exemption resulted in an arbitrary, unreasonable classification and accordingly violated the equal protection clause of the Fourteenth

Amendment.[56] Substantive equal protection and due process require that statutory identification and classification of persons subject to eugenic sterilization be such that they can be applied without arbitrary or discriminatory bias. The Supreme Court in this case also recognized the right to procreate as a fundamental constitutional right, thus subjecting the statute to strict scrutiny regarding equal protection. *Buck v. Bell*, therefore, is no longer a valid precedent, although it has never been explicitly overruled.

To be constitutional the statutes must also provide procedural due process of law. Statutes differ in detail, but due process requires that certain elements of fundamental fairness be observed. In most instances either the superintendent of the institution that houses the patient or the parent or guardian will be empowered to initiate the proceedings for sterilization. The recommendation must ordinarily be supported by medical opinion, often that of a committee chosen from the hospital's medical staff. Formal notice must be given to patients and their guardian or next of kin no matter who initiated the proceedings, and a hearing must be provided by the statutorily designated public authority. Depending on the state of residence or the circumstances, this hearing may be conducted by a court or by an administrative board in the presence of the patient or proper representatives. Due process also requires a right of appeal from an administrative order. This may be to an appropriate court or from a trial court to an appellate court. If the statutory procedures for a eugenic sterilization are not minutely followed, criminal and civil liability would follow.

Eugenic sterilization statutes have been much criticized. One underlying premise for the procedure, that traits such as mental illness, retardation, and criminality are hereditary, has been largely discredited by the scientific community.[57] The legal support for the statutes has been attacked, and it is very unlikely that the laws could withstand constitutional scrutiny today.[58] The "right of privacy" is more and more accepted and is not to be infringed except to serve a compelling state interest. Even then, such infringement must be narrowly drawn and shown to be clearly necessary; if there is any other way of meeting the state's need, that way must be chosen instead. The Minnesota Court of Appeals has observed that sterilization must not be used as a "subterfuge for convenience and relief from the responsibility of supervision."[59] Finally the most disturbing premise behind the statutes, that society has the right to decide who will be born and who may become parents, has been discredited. According to the New Jersey Supreme Court:

> It cannot be forgotten . . . that public attitudes toward mental impairment and the handicapped in general have sometimes been very different. We must always remain mindful of the atrocities that people of our own century and culture have committed upon their fellow humans. We cannot adequately express our abhorrence for the kind of ideology that assigns vastly differing value to the lives of human beings because of their innate group characteristics or personal handicaps.[60]

Although eugenic sterilization is all but obsolete in present U.S. law, the sterilization of incompetent persons for other reasons can still take place. It is, however, increasingly regarded as the right of the incompetent person rather than the right of the state. Sterilizations to prevent procreation of "undesirables" and to protect the public pocketbook are thus generally prohibited.

At the same time, some sterilizations of incompetent persons may be morally and legally justified, such as those performed in the best interests of the incompetent person. Because the fundamental right of privacy allows competent persons to choose to be sterilized, that same right should be afforded the incompetent. This is the same reasoning used in decisions permitting the withdrawal of life-sustaining treatment for incompetent persons. As in "right to die" cases, however, the primary legal difficulties lie in the way such decisions are made, who makes them, and what standards serve as their basis.

It is not necessary to present a detailed analysis of the decisions in this area because they are relatively rare and each one turns on its own specific facts. Suffice it to say that if the issue presents itself, one must consult local law. A few states have statutes permitting sterilization of incompetent persons when it is in the person's best interests.[61] In others, case law permits sterilization under such circumstances. Healthcare providers would be well advised to seek legal counsel in such situations and to require a court order be obtained prior to performing the procedure.

Hospital's Role in Providing Services

The primary question raised here is whether a particular healthcare institution is legally required to make abortion and sterilization services available to potential patients, assuming that it has the facilities and staff for rendering such care.

As we have seen, specific state or federal statutes may contain a "conscience clause" like that in Georgia, which reads, "nothing in this section shall require a hospital to admit any patient . . . for the purpose of performing an abortion" and which was discussed by way of dictum in the case of *Doe v. Bolton*.[62] In the absence of such a clause, the legal issue to be judicially decided is whether the hospital that refuses to provide abortions or sterilizations is acting in the name of the state in denying the patient due process and equal protection of law—and thus violating the Fourteenth Amendment—or whether it is acting under "color or law" in denying statutorily established civil rights. In short, a state or any of its agencies, or an institution acting in the name of government, must not prevent an individual from exercising constitutional or statutorily protected rights. An individual or an institution with a duty to implement a right may not refuse to perform the duty. As emphasized repeatedly in various contexts throughout this book, however, the Fourteenth Amendment applies only to state action and not to private action.

It seems to be well settled that a hospital owned and operated by federal, state, or municipal government may not refuse to perform abortions and sterilizations that are lawful surgical procedures. Publicly owned hospitals clearly act in the capacity of government and are hence subject to the Fourteenth Amendment. A leading decision is *Hathaway v. Worcester City Hospital*.[63] In this litigation the patient's physician recommended that she undergo a therapeutic sterilization because additional pregnancies might well threaten her life. The court entered an order declaring that a hospital's policy that prohibited all sterilization procedures was a denial of the patient's constitutional right to equal protection of the law. Local statutes creating Worcester City Hospital and pertaining to its operation were silent regarding the provision of sterilization services. That is, the statute neither permitted nor prohibited such surgery. The decision assumes that the hospital had the facilities and staff necessary for the sterilization operation, and it rules, in effect, that restrictions may not be placed on sterilization, a legal surgical procedure, that are not placed on other surgery entailing similar risks.

Even prior to the abortion cases of *Wade* and *Bolton* a federal court had held that a public hospital basing its policy regarding sterilizations on a patient's age and the size of the existing family might well be open to a cause of action for damages. The arbitrary policy resulted in a denial of civil rights as expressed in federal statutes, the court held, although the statute relevant to this particular litigation did not, of course, specifically grant a right to sterilization.[64] In this case the patient had been denied a sterilization solely on the basis that her age and the size of her family did not meet the rules of the hospital regarding such surgery. Further, in *Doe v. General Hospital of the District of Columbia* a governmental institution was ordered to process applications for abortions if patients met its rules and regulations, which presumably accorded with the then existing law of legal abortions in the District of Columbia.[65]

Consistent with the *Hathaway* case is *Nyberg v. City of Virginia*, where it was held that a city-owned hospital may not prohibit its staff physicians from performing legal abortions.[66] Although there is no affirmative duty on the part of the hospital to provide staff and facilities for abortion, it may not arbitrarily ban surgery that is not contrary to the legal criteria established by the Supreme Court of United States. The plaintiffs in *Nyberg* were two staff physicians who were licensed to practice medicine, including the performance of abortions. It is assumed that there was no issue in this litigation relative to the doctors' professional competence to do the surgery.

The matter of whether the law should require a private, voluntary hospital to furnish family-planning services is more difficult. On the one hand, the moral and religious convictions held by the institution should certainly be respected. As a legal matter, however, private hospitals that have received Hill-Burton Act funds or other governmental funding in significant amounts have been made subject to the mandates of the Fourteenth Amendment in cases where "state action" has been found. As emphasized in the chapter on medical staff privileges, this result has been reached in several leading cases that have held that the physician is entitled to the constitutional rights of due process and equal protection with respect to staff appointment and clinical privileges. Accordingly, some lower court and early decisions held that a voluntary hospital may not refuse the patient a sterilization (and by analogy presumably an abortion) that has been recommended by the attending physician if the hospital had received Hill-Burton Act funds and no other hospital with adequate staff and facilities was available in the immediate vicinity.[67]

However, the weight of authority has reached an opposite conclusion: namely, that a private hospital need not provide abortion or sterilization services, even if it has been funded to a significant extent by Hill-Burton Act money and other governmental funds in addition to such benefits as tax-exempt status. The leading case asserting this position is *Doe v. Bellin Memorial Hospital*, decided by a federal circuit court of appeals in 1973.[68] As a private hospital Bellin Memorial could prevent its staff physicians from performing legally permissible abortions because no "state action" was involved. Similarly, relying on *Bellin*, *Allen v. Sisters of St. Joseph* held that a Catholic institution could ban a sterilization procedure requested solely to prevent future pregnancy.[69] It should be noted that hospital policy in the *Bellin* case prohibited abortion and continued to do so even after the *Wade* and *Bolton* cases, except to preserve the mother's life or health, to prevent the birth of an infant likely to be born deformed, or when the patient was a victim of rape. Further, in *Bellin* the stage of pregnancy made an out-of-hospital abortion inadvisable, and all three of the private general hospitals in Green Bay, Wisconsin, followed similar policies of refusing to admit patients for such surgery.

In another important case, *Watkins v. Mercy Medical Center*, a physician brought suit against a Catholic hospital that forbade both abortions and sterilizations.[70] The policy of the hospital was upheld by a federal district court, which said that state action was not involved by receipt of governmental monies, state licensure, or tax exemption. Significant in this decision was that Public Law 93-45, the Health Programs Extension Act of 1973, specifically provides that receipt of Hill-Burton money does not require a hospital to provide abortions or sterilizations as long as refusal is founded on institutional religious beliefs or moral conviction.[71] Although Mercy Medical Center was not required to permit the plaintiff physician to perform the desired surgical procedure, it could not terminate a medical staff appointment solely on the basis of the physician's personal beliefs. Unlike the situation in *Bellin*, it is interesting to note, in *Watkins* several other institutions within a reasonable distance pursued policies that permitted their medical staff to perform abortions.

In sum, most decisions pertaining to private hospitals have to date held that no "state action" is involved under the Fourteenth Amendment and voluntary institutions that prohibit abortion and sterilization do not act under "color of law" in denying civil rights established by federal civil rights statutes. This conclusion is based either on the grounds that receipt of governmental funds and other benefits does not require the hospital to recognize the constitutional rights of the patient, as in the *Bellin* case, or on the grounds that the Health Programs Extension Act of 1973 protects the religious and moral convictions that the hospital represents, as in *Watkins* and *Taylor*.[72]

As mentioned previously, many states have specific statutes that state that designated institutions and individuals need not participate in abortions and sterilizations against their moral or religious convictions. Most of these state laws relate only to abortions. They purportedly apply to all hospitals, governmental and private, but some are made applicable only to hospitals owned and operated by churches or religious orders. The provisions of the Georgia statute, quoted previously, were apparently approved as constitutional in the case of *Doe v. Bolton*.[73]

The Michigan "conscience clause" statute is perhaps typical.[74] It reads, in essence, that a hospital, clinic, teaching institution, or any other medical facility need not admit a patient for the purpose of performing an abortion. Moreover, a physician or any other person connected with the institution may refuse to perform or participate in a termination of pregnancy, and a statement of refusal based on professional, ethical, moral, or religious beliefs shall render the individual immune from any civil or criminal liability. A physician who refuses to give advice relative to an abortion shall not be liable to the hospital or other institution or subject to discipline from any institution with which he or she is associated; nor shall there be liability in malpractice as long as these doctors adequately inform their patients of their refusal. Notice, however, that the Michigan statute relates only to the refusal of an abortion and does not apply to sterilization. In that respect it is similar to the Georgia statute.

Even though the Supreme Court approved the "conscience clause" of the Georgia statute at least by dictum, further litigation is probable, especially with respect to statutes applicable to governmental institutions. The provisions pertaining to an individual's right of refusal to participate would seem clearly constitutional. Perhaps the same can be said of the statutes recognizing the moral and religious convictions of a private sectarian hospital because these are valuable rights to be protected in a free society.[75] The previously discussed judicial opinions based solely on judicial law would be additional grounds for approval of similar statutory pronouncements of public policy.[76] On the other hand, insofar as the statutes pertain to governmental hospitals serving the general community they are probably unconstitutional, although the U.S. Supreme Court may be called to rule precisely on the issue in the future.[77] In the final analysis, the Supreme Court is the ultimate decision maker with respect to constitutional interpretation of statutory law, and the decisions of the future may turn on the facts of individual cases. It is all a matter of balancing the various public policy issues involved.

A somewhat related issue is whether a state may deny Medicaid payments for either elective or medically necessary abortions rendered to indigent patients. The Hyde Amendment, the first version of which was passed in 1976 and which has been renewed annually every year since, denies federal funding of abortions except to save the mother's life or in cases of rape or incest. The Supreme Court has ruled that Title XIX of the Social Security Act (Medicaid) does not require a state participating in the Medicaid program to fund either elective nontherapeutic abortions[78] or medically necessary abortions[79] as a condition of participation.

Because a private hospital need not provide abortion services, hospitalized patients who are refused an abortion or sterilization should be fully informed of their condition and provided with sound medical advice indicating where proper and appropriate care can be obtained. If surgery is without question indicated for therapeutic reasons and transfer of the patient to another institution would foreseeably harm the patient's health, then liability would probably follow if the surgery were denied or the patient transferred. These observations are based simply on general principles of the law of hospital liability.

If abortion is denied in circumstances in which there is no threat to the mother's life or health, the matter of civil liability is unsettled. If the abortion is solely the personal choice of the mother, and the hospital has no duty to provide the service, then the hospital would not be liable. On the other hand, if an abortion is prompted by fear that the infant may be born deformed, for example, then failure to abort or failure to exercise reasonable care in advising the patient could lead to civil liability of the hospital or the attending physician, or both. This matter is discussed in the next section.

Additional legal issues concern hospitals that either choose to or must permit abortions and sterilizations. Most state statutes continue to declare that third-trimester abortions that are not necessary to preserve the life or health of the mother, and even earlier abortions under certain circumstances, are criminal acts. A hospital has a duty to prevent criminal acts from taking place on its premises; hence, counsel must carefully advise the hospital and its medical staff about the current legal status of pregnancy terminations. Administrative policies and procedures must be developed to make sure that the institution and staff perform their duty with respect to prevention of criminal acts.

In connection with a criminal abortion, the question can arise concerning the physician's civil liability in damages to the patient, or that of a layperson performing the criminal act. Numerous cases have dealt with this issue and judicial authority has differed. Quite a number of jurisdictions, probably most, have denied recovery of damages in the absence of proof of malpractice, simply on the basis that the patient consented to the procedure and hence is equally at fault in the performance of the crime.[80] Others have differed and allowed recovery of damages even when the patient freely and voluntarily consented. This latter view is founded on the philosophy that public policy should discourage criminal acts, and one way to do this is to allow a civil lawsuit for damages by the victim, even when she had consented.[81]

A second legal issue, which concerns hospitals and physicians even more in light of the greatly liberalized law of abortion, is obtaining the patient's informed consent before a legal abortion is performed. All of the previous discussion of consent in Chapter 11 is clearly applicable to any procedure designed to terminate a pregnancy. Indeed, there is probably more risk of a lawsuit claiming damages because informed consent was not obtained for abortions and sterilizations than exists in connection with many other surgical procedures. The hospital must insist that the attending physician explain the procedure and the risks to the patient and obtain a formal written statement from the patient as evidence that proper consent was obtained, although it should not take special steps for abortions that are not applicable to surgery of like risk.

Third, whether the abortion is or is not a criminal act, the physician, the attending personnel, and the hospital would be civilly liable for negligence or malpractice in the way the procedure was conducted or in the postoperative care. Hence, all the general principles of the law of hospital liability and professional negligence are relevant. This fact should be of particular concern to physicians performing abortions in their offices or in clinics not possessing the supporting equipment and trained personnel of a hospital.

In an institutional setting, quality assurance programs and medical audits of an individual doctor's competence to perform surgery are clearly necessary and legally supportable in connection with abortions, just as they are in connection with any surgery. In other words, not all medical staff physicians need to be allowed to perform this surgery. Privileges to perform abortions and sterilizations can be restricted pursuant to the substantive and procedural law reviewed in Chapter 14, "Medical Staff Appointments and Privileges." The judicial and statutory requirements for institutional peer review of medical staff performance have not been eliminated or diluted as a result of these abortion cases, as long as the review system does not single out abortion and impose restrictions not equally applicable to other surgical procedures of similar complexity and risk.

Liability for Wrongful Birth and Wrongful Life

Cases in which sterilizations or abortions do not achieve their purpose raise possibilities of suits against medical personnel and institutions. For example, a man suffering from neurofibromatosis, a disorder caused by a genetic defect, fathered two children, both of whom also had the disorder. Fearing that future offspring would be similarly afflicted, the couple decided that they should have no more children and that the husband should undergo a vasectomy, after which the doctor assured him that he and his wife could now resume sexual relations without contraceptives. Nevertheless, the wife became pregnant and sought an abortion. Although the physician performing the operation told her it was successful, she gave birth to a third child, a girl with neurofibromatosis. In such a case are the parents entitled to maintain a suit against the physicians who performed the operations? If so, what are their damages? May they recover the costs of raising the child? Would the amount of damages be different if the child had been born healthy? Does the child also have a right to recover?

The facts and issues set forth in this example were the basis of *Speck v. Finegold*.[82] As to the parents' cause of action, the court held that this was like any other malpractice action, and if negligence was proven the parents were entitled to recover their pecuniary expenses for the care and treatment of their daughter. The court denied the child's cause of action, however, holding that there was no legally cognizable injury because the alleged injury was that the child existed, and it is impossible to say that existence even with handicaps is worse than nonexistence. The court also denied the parents' claim for damages for emotional disturbance and general distress caused by the infant's birth.

Many courts before and since *Speck* have addressed similar issues in cases designated by the terms "wrongful birth" and "wrongful life."[83] These cases have greatly increased in the past 20 years, largely because of two simultaneous developments: the legal recognition of parents' right to decide whether to conceive or abort under certain circumstances and the great advances in medical science that make genetic testing and counseling, sterilization, and abortions commonplace medical practices. Legal actions have arisen from various circumstances:

- unsuccessful contraceptive measures, including negligently performed sterilizations;
- failure to provide genetic counseling or testing;
- failure to diagnose and inform the patient of pregnancy;
- failure to detect and warn the patient of diseases such as rubella or genetic defects early enough to permit abortion; and
- negligence in performing an abortion.

Births resulting from these failures may result in a healthy (but unplanned or unwanted) or a deformed, handicapped child.

The situations described above are all instances of tradition medical malpractice. The unique aspect of these plaintiffs' claims is that if the physician had not been negligent the child would never have been born. Rather than claiming an injury to an already existing person or in some cases one who would have been born healthy if there had not been negligence, these plaintiffs are claiming that the very existence of the child is the injury. Such cases have given the court great legal and philosophical difficulties.

To succeed in any malpractice claim the plaintiff must show the following: a duty of care to the plaintiff, a breach of that duty, an injury proximately caused by the breach, and legally recognized damages. In the cases charging wrongful birth and wrongful life the courts have had no difficulty in finding the duty. Courts in virtually all jurisdictions have held that physicians owe a duty of professional care to their patients and those who may foreseeably be injured by a lack of such care. The duty is therefore owed not only to a parent who is the doctor's patient, but also to the unborn child. This duty holds true in prenatal injury to a fetus, and it has also been extended to the unconceived child. For example, in *Turpin v. Sortini* the parents of a little girl were told she had normal hearing when in fact she was deaf from a hereditary condition.[84] Their next child was also deaf. The court held that the professional who tested the first child's hearing had a duty to the second child because it was foreseeable that the parents and their "potential offspring" would be directly affected by the negligence.

The physician's duty in these and other medical malpractice cases is to conform to the generally accepted standards of care exercised by other physicians in similar circumstances. The standard relates to the state of the art at the time of the alleged malpractice. For example, in 1969 a physician allegedly failed to tell his patients of the risk that their baby would be afflicted with cri-du-chat syndrome, a chromosomal disorder causing severe mental retardation, and did not perform amniocentesis. The parents sued for damages after their child was born with cri-du-chat syndrome, but their suit was rejected because "on the bases of the patient's medical history and the state of medical knowledge regarding the use of the amniocentesis test in 1969, the defendants' failure to perform the test was no more than a permissible exercise of medical judgment and not a departure from then accepted medical practice."[85] However, a physician who in 1974 failed to advise his 37-year-old pregnant patient of the increased risk of bearing a child with Down's syndrome in women over 35 and did not advise her of the availability of amniocentesis to detect the defect was held liable. The court reasoned that by then amniocentesis was an accepted medical practice, abortion was recognized as a patient's right, and genetic counseling had become customary.[86] In fact, because genetic testing can now reveal many types of birth defects, the standard of care requires that prospective parents who risk occurrence of the defect be given counseling and information about available tests and medical alternatives such as abortion, even if the defect cannot be cured and abortion is the only way to prevent the birth.[87] This duty is imposed although it may be against the physician's conscience or morals to recommend abortion. Courts have held that physicians are not required to recommend abortion, but they must inform patients of the facts and the available alternatives or at the very least, refer a patient to another practitioner early enough to allow a choice of solutions.

Regarding other types of negligence that may result in actions for wrongful birth, the physician's duty is likewise to exercise reasonable care and fully inform the patient. Tests, procedures, and diagnoses should be in accordance with accepted medical practice. For example, liability has not only been found for negligence in sterilizations and for unsuccessful abortions, but also in cases involving the following:

- a failure to diagnose rubella in a pregnant woman whose child was born with a handicap;[88]
- a failure to diagnose cystic fibrosis in the parents' first child thus leaving the parents unaware of the risk that a second child would be similarly afflicted;[89]
- the dispensing of tranquilizers instead of birth-control pills, a mistake resulting in the birth of a healthy but unwanted child;[90] and
- the failure to inform the patient that the drug she was taking to control her epilepsy could cause birth defects.[91]

Claims for wrongful birth may also be based on other legal theories, such as breach of warranty or contract. Mere failure to accomplish complete sterility, the intended result, would not normally be malpractice, and pregnancy following a sterilization of either spouse would not normally be proof of negligence because physicians and hospitals are not guarantors or insurers of a particular result.[92]

However, if the physician should expressly by words or action guarantee or promise sterility, a breach of contract has occurred if pregnancy follows. Several cases have alleged this theory as the basis of a cause of action and a few have succeeded. According to *Doerr v. Villate,* an Illinois decision, assurances that sterility would result from a vasectomy performed on the husband provided a cause of action in breach of contract when the wife later gave birth to a mentally retarded and physically handicapped child; it was further ruled that the contractual statute of limitations, which was longer than that for malpractice, would apply to the action.[93] In *Doerr* the wife had previously given birth to two retarded children; for this reason the parents had sought the vasectomy. On the other hand, a Kentucky case held that a doctor's statements that a vasectomy is a "sure thing," a "fool-proof thing, 100 percent" were merely the expression of a professional opinion and thus could not be the basis of a cause of action in contract.[94] Even when the court rules that the evidence of promise or warranty is sufficient to present a jury question, however, the plaintiff must convince the jury that the promise of sterilization was in fact made expressly, in words or at least by the physician's action. As noted above, this legal theory of action can in most cases be successfully defended if a carefully worded written consent form has been obtained from the patient and the spouse. This form would include a full explanation of the proposed surgery, the risks, and the probable outcome, and it should also state that there are no promises or guarantees of results.

Even if a plaintiff has a provable claim of malpractice, the suit must be brought within the applicable statute of limitations. Traditionally the statute for medical malpractice actions began to run at the time of the alleged malpractice (or breach of contract, if the jurisdiction recognizes breach of contract as a cause of action). Hence, the cause of action would be barred when the time, measured from the date of the alleged wrong, had expired. Because pregnancy and birth may occur years after the sterilization procedure, however, the tendency of recent decisions is to hold that the statute will run from the time the tort or beach of contract is discovered, or when in the exercise of reasonable care it ought to have been discovered. In other words, the statute runs from the time that the pregnancy was or ought to have been known.[95] Otherwise the plaintiff might be barred from action before the tort or breach of promise and the injury could be discovered. The application of the "discovery rule" to cases of wrongful birth follows the development of the rule in other malpractice situations. At least one court has held that the statute of limitations in a case involving a child with congenital birth defects begins to run from the date of birth.[96]

Although courts hearing cases of wrongful birth have had little difficulty with findings regarding duty, standard of care, and breach of the standard, the various jurisdictions have come to widely divergent conclusions regarding proximate cause, injury, and recoverable damages. On these matters they have differed specifically in their treatment of the parents' rights and the child's rights. Recently most courts have held in favor of the parents' cause of action, finding the requisite proximate cause in the fact that, but for the physician's negligence, the child would never have been born.[97] In at least one case, involving alleged negligence in performing a sterilization, the defendants claimed that the husband's sexual relations with his wife were an "intervening cause" of the pregnancy, thereby relieving the defendants of responsibility. The court was not persuaded.[98] Courts have also uniformly rejected the claim that the parents have a duty to mitigate damages by obtaining an abortion or placing the child for adoption.[99]

Although the courts recognize that the parents of unwanted or hand-icapped children have been harmed by professional negligence, they have had trouble determining the proper damages because public policy values the sanctity of life and generally views the birth of a child as a blessing. Virtually all courts recognizing a cause of action for wrongful birth have allowed parents to recover expenses for the pregnancy and childbirth, even when the child was healthy.[100] Other pecuniary damages such as lost wages have also been held recoverable.[101] Damages for the woman's pain and suffering as a result of the pregnancy and birth have been allowed,[102] as well as damages for the husband's loss of consortium.[103]

Damages for the parents' emotional distress is a matter on which courts disagree. When a child was born with a serious disease or disability, many courts have permitted compensation for the parents' mental suffering. For example, a man's blood was mislabeled and the couple did not discover that he was a carrier for Tay-Sachs disease until their child was born with the disease. Damages were allowed for the parents' emotional distress over the child's suffering and death.[104] In another case involving Tay-Sachs disease, however, the court denied damages for emotional harm, arguing that the injury was suffered by the child, not the parents.[105]

Claims for the expense of raising a child to majority arouse more controversy. Almost all jurisdictions view the birth of a child, even one with disabilities, as of some benefit and joy to the parents. A traditional rule of tort law, the "benefit rule," requires that any damages awarded to an injured plaintiff be reduced by the value of any benefit that the tortfeasor has incidentally bestowed upon the plaintiff. Most courts, even those allowing the costs of child-rearing, thus require the jury to offset the damages by the benefits to the parents of having the child.[106] Some courts, however, find that these benefits outweigh the costs of rearing the child as a matter of law, and therefore deny any child-rearing costs.[107]

In *Cockrum v. Baumgartner* a negligent sterilization failed to prevent the birth of an unwanted but healthy child.[108] The court recognized the parents' cause of action for wrongful birth because the decision not to have a child is a legally protected right, and as a matter of public policy its violation cannot be ignored. Noting that damage awards are an effective recognition of legal rights, the court allowed the costs of raising the child. It held that the benefit rule did not apply because it is applicable only if the benefit is to the same interest that was harmed. The court found that the emotional benefits of child-rearing are separate from the injured financial interests of the parents.

The extraordinary costs of raising a handicapped child—payments for institutional or other specialized care, medical expenses, and special education and training—have generally been allowed. These amounts are arrived at by identifying the extra expenses beyond what would be spent on a healthy child.[109] Even in these cases, however, some courts have held that the advantages of parenthood and the child's own life outweigh the burdens of child-rearing.[110]

A child's cause of action for "wrongful life" has been recognized to date in only a few states. No such action has been allowed on behalf of a healthy child who was unwanted or illegitimate because the courts have found that there was no injury to the child.[111] Even when the child is suffering from a grave disease or birth defect, courts have repeatedly refused to recognize a cause of action.[112] This refusal has been on several grounds: the professional negligence was not the cause of the disease or injury; life, even one that is impaired, cannot be seen as a legal injury; and damages for an impaired life, as opposed to no life, cannot be determined. The usual purpose of compensatory damages is to place plaintiffs as nearly as possible in the position they would have occupied had there been no negligence. In the case of wrongful life, that position would be nonexistence. The courts have held that no one can determine the value of nonexistence, and therefore such actions must fail, lacking the necessary requirements of proximate cause or legally compensable injury. Courts have also held that there is no fundamental right to be born healthy.[113] Some courts also believe that allowing a cause of action for wrongful birth would diminish the value of human life and be contrary to society's goal of protecting, preserving, and improving the quality of human existence.[114]

Nevertheless, a few states have rejected these arguments and recognized a cause of action for wrongful life. In *Curlender v. Bio-Science Laboratories, Inc.* the plaintiff was a child born with Tay-Sachs disease, allegedly as a result of negligent testing to determine whether the parents were carriers of the disease.[115] The child was mentally and physically disabled, with a life expectancy of only four years. The California Court of Appeals, finding a "palpable injury" to the child, held that the child could recover damages for pain and suffering during its limited life span, in addition to pecuniary loss because of the impaired condition. Costs of care were to be awarded only once, however, and not to both the parents and the child.

The California Supreme Court recognized another child's cause of action for wrongful life in *Turpin v. Sortini*, rejecting the argument that such actions were against public policy.[116] According to the court it was "hard to see how an award of damages to a severely handicapped or suffering child would 'disavow' the value of life or in any way suggest that the child is not entitled to the full measure of legal and nonlegal rights and privileges accorded to all members of society."[117] According to the court's finding, one could not say that as a matter of law an impaired life is always preferable to no life.

A California statute recognizes the fundamental right of adults to control medical decisions, including the decision to withdraw or withhold life-sustaining procedures.[118] The *Turpin* court found that parents in actions for wrongful life were prevented from making an informed and meaningful choice in considering whether to conceive or bear a handicapped child, and that such a choice is partly on behalf of the child. Although the court agreed with other opinions that general damages would be impossible to assess, it found that the extraordinary expenses of caring for an impaired child were not speculative, and that it would be illogical to permit the parents but not the child to recover for its own medical care. If the defendant's negligence caused the need for this extraordinary care, basic principles of liability hold the defendants liable for the costs of such care whether borne by the parents or child. Otherwise, the court stated, the child's receipt of necessary medical expenses would depend on whether the parents sued and recovered damages or whether the expenses were incurred when the parents were still legally responsible for the child's care.

The Washington Supreme Court also found that a child should have a cause of action for wrongful life. In *Harbeson v. Parke-Davis, Inc.* it held that imposing liability for wrongful life would promote such social objectives as genetic counseling and prenatal testing and would discourage malpractice.[119] The court had no difficulty finding the requisite proximate cause:

"It is clear in the case before us that, were it not for negligence of the physicians, the minor plaintiffs would not have been born, and would consequently not have suffered fetal hydantoin syndrome. More particularly, the plaintiffs would not have incurred the extraordinary expenses resulting from that condition."[120]

The distinction between parents' and children's causes of action is important to the determination of damages. Awards to the parents would only cover their expenses during the time they are legally responsible for the child—for example, until majority. The child's own damages, however, could continue throughout life, perhaps many more years beyond majority.

Some states have passed laws concerning actions for wrongful life and wrongful birth. In *Curlender,* discussed above, the California Court of Appeals said by way of dicta that children born with a birth defect should be allowed to sue their parents for their pain and suffering if they foresaw the defect and chose not to abort. The California legislature quickly responded with a statute outlawing such causes of action lest parents be placed under pressure to abort or prevent conception.[121] Minnesota went further with legislation prohibiting actions for wrongful birth and wrongful life in which it is claimed that but for the alleged negligence a child would have been aborted.[122] The statute does permit actions for failure of a contraceptive method or a sterilization procedure as well as for a failure to diagnose a disease or defect that could have been prevented or cured if detected early enough. Abortion may not be viewed as a prevention or cure, however, and neither the failure nor the refusal of anyone to perform or obtain an abortion constitutes a defense in any action or a consideration in the award of damages.[123]

More and more of the decisions in actions for wrongful birth and wrongful life demonstrate that as medical knowledge and technology expand, the duty of the physician also grows, not only to perform tests and procedures with the necessary care but also to fully inform patients of potential risks and available tests and treatments. In addition to performing all duties to a patient in the proper manner, physicians should for their own protection carefully document and preserve in the medical record any discussions with individual patients concerning possible genetic and other risks to the patient's unborn or unconceived children, as well as the availability of appropriate preconception or prenatal testing, therapies, and alternatives. The documentation should also cover the patient's decision concerning the risks, testing, and alternatives. Obtaining and recording informed consent for medical treatment is essential in any circumstance, but it is especially so in the humanly important and constitutionally protected matter of procreation.

Other Family-Planning Issues

Two other kinds of family planning cases deserve note: surrogate parenting and in vitro fertilization. Surrogacy is the practice of carrying a fetus to term for another woman, generally for a fee. (The surrogate mother is sometimes said to have "rented her womb.") The embryo from which the fetus grows may result from artificial insemination or in vitro fertilization, or it may have been conceived normally and transferred to the surrogate because the natural mother was known to be unable to continue the pregnancy without miscarriage. If either artificial insemination or in vitro fertilization (fertilizing the egg outside the uterus under laboratory conditions) is used, the sperm may or may not be that of the husband of the egg-bearing woman. In fact, the genetic "parents" (whose identities may or may not be known) can be different than the "parents" for whom the surrogate mother carries the child.

It is not difficult to conceive of how many complicated legal relationships may result from these various techniques. For example, in the 1988 case *In re Baby M,*[124] the Supreme Court of New Jersey was asked to determine parental status after a surrogate mother reneged on her contractual agreement to surrender the child after birth. The contract was between Mary Beth Whitehead and William Stern (whose wife was infertile). It provided that for a fee of $10,000, Mrs. Whitehead would be inseminated with Mr. Stern's sperm, would conceive a child and carry it to term, and then give the child to Mr. and Mrs. Stern for the latter to adopt. (Mr. Stern, having been the sperm donor, would be recognized as the natural father.) When Mrs. Whitehead failed to abide by the contract, the Sterns filed suit. Although the lower court determined that the surrogacy contract is valid, the New Jersey Supreme Court disagreed.

In reaching its conclusion, the court found that the contract conflicted with New Jersey laws prohibiting the use of money in connection with adoptions and with various other statutory provisions. "The contract's basic premise, that the natural parents can decide in advance of birth which one is to have custody of the child, bears no relationship to the law that the child's best interests shall determine custody." The court continued, "This is the sale of a child, or, at the very least, the sale of a mother's right to her child, the only mitigating factor being that one of the purchasers is the father. Almost every evil that prompted the prohibition on the payment of money in connection with adoptions exists here."

The court next needed to settle the issue of who should have custody of Baby M. Holding that the claims of the natural father and the natural mother are entitled to equal weight, the court determined that the child's best interests would be dispositive. Weighing the personalities, financial situations, and family lives of all the parties, the court concluded that the child's best interests called for custody to be given to the Sterns but that Mrs. Whitehead should be allowed visitation rights.

A 1986 Kentucky case appears to contradict *Baby M.* In *Surrogate Parenting Associates, Inc. v. Commonwealth* ex rel. *Armstrong,*[125] a company that assisted infertile couples by arranging surrogate motherhood was sued by the state attorney general. The suit alleged that SPA's activities violated a state statute prohibiting the sale, purchase or procurement for sale or purchase of "any child for the purpose of adoption." The court held that

SPA's activities did not constitute buying and selling babies because "there are fundamental differences between the surrogate parenting procedure in which SPA participates and the buying and selling of children as prohibited by [law]." The court wrote approvingly of SPA's services: "[W]e have no reason to believe that the surrogate parenting procedure . . . will not, in most instances, proceed routinely to the conclusion desired by all of the parties at the outset—a woman who can bear children assisting a childless couple to fulfill their desire for a biologically-related child." It is interesting to consider, in light of this precedent, what result the Kentucky court would have reached had the *Baby M* case been tried in Kentucky rather than New Jersey.

Another example of the kinds of disputes that arise from new family planning technologies was apparent in *Davis v. Davis*.[126] The case began as a divorce action in which the parties—appellee Junior Lewis Davis and his wife, Mary Sue Davis—agreed on all settlement terms except the disposition of seven frozen embryos that were the product of in vitro fertilization (IVF). Mrs. Davis had asked for custody of the embryos to become pregnant after the divorce. (She later change her mind and stated that she wanted to donate them to another couple for implantation.) Mr. Davis refused to agree. The trial court held that the embryos were "human beings" from the point of conception, and it awarded custody to Mrs. Davis. The court of appeals reversed, holding that Mr. Davis had a constitutional right not to beget a child in this manner and that the state had no compelling interest to overrule either party's wishes.

The Supreme Court of Tennessee began its consideration by addressing the issue of whether the embryos were "persons" or "property" in the eyes of the law. It concluded that neither Tennessee law nor the U.S. Constitution would consider them "persons," but it also found that the embryos deserved greater respect than that of mere property because of their potential to become human beings. Thus, the court set aside the persons/property issue to focus on the essential dispute of whether the Davises will become parents. In balancing the parties' interests, the court found that to grant Mrs. Davis's wish would possibly impose unwanted parenthood on Mr. Davis, "with all of its possible financial and psychological consequences." This, the court held, was a greater burden than Mrs. Davis's disappointment of knowing that the IVF procedures she underwent were futile and that the embryos would never become children, and judgment was entered in favor of Mr. Davis.

Notes

1. Debora A. Slee, J.D., wrote this chapter for the second edition of this book; it has been revised for the present edition by J. Stuart Showalter.
2. See citations in footnotes 27 and 28 of Roe v. Wade, 410 U.S. 113 (1973), *reh'g denied*, 410 U.S. 959 (1973). *Se also* Wasmuth and Chareau, *Abortion Laws: The Perplexing Problem*, 18:3 Cleveland St. L. Rev. 503 (Sept. 1969).

3. Lord Ellenborough's Act, 42 Geo. 3, ch. 58. Parliament reversed this position by enacting a liberal abortion bill in 1967.

4. The statutory language of "preserving the life of the mother" was liberally interpreted. In Rex v. Bourne (1939) 1 K.B. 687 (1938) a physician who induced an abortion for a 14-year-old rape victim was acquitted of criminal charges after the judge instructed the jury that a doctor was acting within the law to prevent the patient from becoming a mental or physical "wreck."

5. MODEL PENAL CODE § 230.3(2) (1962).

6. 410 U.S. 113 (1973).

7. Doe v. Bolton, 410 U.S. 179 (1973), *reh'g denied*, 410 U.S. 959 (1973).

8. Such a requirement is clearly constitutional. May v. State of Ark., 254 Ark. 194, 492 S.W.2d 888 (1973), *cert. denied*, 414 U.S. 1024 (1973). This decision was rendered after the *Wade* and *Bolton* cases. *See also* State v. Norflett, 67 N.J. 268, 337 A.2d 609 (1975). However, no other restrictions may be placed on a patient's right to terminate her pregnancy. For example, cancellation of an unmarried teacher's contract because she was pregnant was held to be an unconstitutional invasion of her privacy, because she had the right to decide whether or not to have an abortion. Drake v. Covington County Bd. of Educ., 371 F. Supp. 974 (N.D. Ala. 1974).

   A state or city may not enact local statutes or ordinances regulating clinics and other facilities for first-trimester abortions, even if such laws are intended to improve the care rendered. *See, e.g.,* Word v. Poelker, 495 F.2d 1349 (8th Cir. 1974) (The court invalidated a St. Louis ordinance requiring abortion clinics to obtain a city permit that called for disclosure of the names of the applicants, of all physicians using the facilities, and of nurses, with resumés of the qualifications of the personnel and a description of the space and equipment available. The basis of the decision was that similar permits or licenses were not required for other clinics or facilities in which surgery of like risk was performed on ambulatory patients, and thus the regulatory ordinance substantially limited the doctor's right to practice medicine and the patient's freedom of choice in seeking a first-trimester abortion.) *See also* Coe v. Gerstein, 376 F. Supp. 695 (S.D. Fla. 1974), *appeal dismissed and cert. denied*, 417 U.S. 279 (1974), *aff'd*, 517 F.2d 787 (5th Cir. 1975) (held unconstitutional a Florida statute requiring that abortions be performed in an "approved facility").

   However, a Michigan statutory scheme to regulate all freestanding surgical outpatient facilities (FSOFs) not connected to hospitals was upheld as constitutional because it applies to all such facilities, not just those performing abortions. The statute also withstood an attack that it violated the equal protection clause because it applied to FSOFs but not physicians' offices where abortions are performed. Certain staffing, structural, and equipment requirements of the Michigan scheme were held invalid, however, because compliance would involve expensive alterations and so increase the cost of first-trimester abortions. Also ruled unconstitutional was a requirement that post-first-trimester abortions may not be performed in an FSOF unless it is owned and operated by a hospital. Birth Control Centers, Inc. v. Reizen, 743 F.2d 352 (6th Cir. 1984) (MICH. COMP. LAWS ANN. §§ 333.1101–333.1117 (1980 & Supp. 1987)).

9. Doe v. Israel, 358 F. Supp. 1193 (D.R.I. 1973), *cert. denied,* 416 U.S. 993 (1974). Further, the *Wade* and *Bolton* decisions have been held to apply retroactively. A criminal conviction of a physician under an abortion statute now declared unconstitutional must be vacated even if it preceded the Supreme Court decision. State v. Ingel, 18 Md. App. 514, 308 A.2d 223 (1973).

10. City of Akron v. Akron Center for Reproductive Health, Inc., 462 U.S. 416, 456–58 (1983) (O'Connor, J., dissenting).

11. 410 U.S. 179 (1973).

12. This was taken by many to mean that states could require that second-trimester abortions be performed only in hospitals. However, such a requirement was later found unconstitutional. City of Akron v. Akron Center for Reproductive Health, Inc., 462 U.S. 416 (1983).

13. *Id.*

14. *Id.* at 430.

15. *Id.* at 431.

16. Planned Parenthood Ass'n of Kansas City, Mo., Inc. v. Ashcroft, 462 U.S. 476 (1983).

17. *See* Planned Parenthood of Central Mo. v. Danforth, 428 U.S. 52 (1976).

18. Birth Control Centers, Inc. v. Reizen, 743 F.2d 352 (6th Cir. 1984).

19. American College of Obstetricians v. Thornburgh, 737 F.2d 283 (3d Cir. 1984).

20. 18 Pa. Cons. Stat. Ann. §§ 3211(a), 3214(h) (Purdon 1983).

21. American College of Obstetricians v. Thornburgh, 106 S. Ct. 2169, 2182 (1986).

22. City of Akron v. Akron Center for Reproductive Health, Inc., 462 U.S. 416, 439 (1983).

23. Planned Parenthood Ass'n of Kansas City, Mo., Inc. v. Ashcroft, 462 U.S. 476 (1983).

24. Simopoulos v. Virginia, 462 U.S. 506 (1983).

25. City of Akron v. Akron Center for Reproductive Health, Inc., 462 U.S. 416, 450 (1983) (quoting Colautti v. Franklin, 439 U.S. 379, 387).

26. Waiting periods after a minor's parents have been informed of or have consented to their child's prospective abortion until the procedure may be performed have also been declared invalid. *See, e.g.,* Zbaraz v. Hartigan, 763 F.2d 1532 (7th Cir. 1985), *petition for cert. filed,* 54 U.S.L.W. 3311 (U.S. Oct. 16, 1985) (No. 85–673).

27. Planned Parenthood of Central Mo. v. Danforth, 428 U.S. 52 (1976).

28. *Id.* at 67, note 7.

29. City of Akron v. Akron Center for Reproductive Health, Inc., 462 U.S. 416, 444 (1983).

30. *Id.* at 445.

31. *Id.* at 444.

32. Similar requirements for informed consent were held invalid in American College of Obstetricians v. Thornburgh, 106 S. Ct. 2169 (1986). Required information included the "fact that there may be detrimental physical and psychological effects which are not accurately foreseeable"; the "probable gestational age of the unborn child at the time the abortion is to be performed"; the "fact that medical assistance benefits may be available for prenatal care, childbirth and

neonatal care"; the "fact that the father is liable to assist in the support of her child, even in instances where the father has offered to pay for the abortion"; the fact that the woman has the right to review certain printed materials, including a list of available agencies and services to assist a woman through pregnancy, and a statement that the "Commonwealth of Pennsylvania strongly urges you to contact [these agencies] before making a final decision about abortion"; and materials "designed to inform the woman of the probable anatomical and physiological characteristics of the unborn child at two-week gestational increments from fertilization to full term, including any relevant information on the possibility of the unborn child's survival." 18 PA. CONS. STAT. ANN. §§ 3205, 3208 (Purdon 1983).

33. A Michigan regulation requiring that abortion facilities "make available and offer appropriate counseling, interpretation and referral for subsequent indicated care" was recently upheld by a federal court of appeals, which found that the rule was "rationally related to a legitimate State interest in health" and that because the regulation did not mandate counseling, but only required that it be available, it had no significant impact on a woman's right to obtain an abortion. Birth Control Centers, Inc. v. Reizen, 743 F.2d at 362. MICH. COMP. LAWS ANN. §§ 333.1101–333.1117 (1980 & Supp. 1987).

34. Roe v. Wade, 410 U.S. 113, 160 (1973).

35. Colautti v. Franklin, 439 U.S. 379, 387 (1979) (quoting Roe v. Wade, 410 U.S. at 160, 166).

36. 439 U.S. 379 (1979).

37. *Id.* at 382.

38. *Id.* at 388–89.

39. *Id.* at 393.

40. *See also* Charles v. Daley, 749 F.2d 452 (7th Cir. 1984), *appeal dismissed sub nom.* Diamond v. Charles, 106 S. Ct. 1697 (1986) (statute which proscribed abortion after viability and prescribed standard of care was unconstitutionally vague).

41. Colautti v. Franklin, 439 U.S. 379, 400 (1979).

42. *See also* American College of Obstetricians v. Thornburgh, 106 S. Ct. 2169 (1986) (a statutory requirement that the method used to abort a viable fetus be the one most likely to preserve the life of the fetus unless that procedure would result in a "significantly greater" risk to the mother, was held unconstitutional because it failed to require that the mother's health be the paramount consideration).

43. 462 U.S. 476 (1983).

44. American College of Obstetricians v. Thornburgh, 106 S. Ct. 2169 (1986). The lower court in *Thornburgh* also upheld a provision that prohibits abortions after viability but provides a complete defense if the physician had "concluded in good faith, in his best medical judgment," that "the unborn child was not viable at the time the abortion was performed or induced," or that "the abortion was necessary to preserve maternal life or health." PA. CONS. STAT. ANN. § 3210(a). The court presumed that the Pennsylvania Supreme Court, if it construed the provision, would place the burden of proving lack of medical necessity on the prosecution once the defense is raised and would construe "maternal life or health" broadly to include factors that are "physical, emotional, psychological,

familial [as well as] the woman's age." *Thornburgh,* 737 F.2d 283, 299 (3d Cir. 1984), citing Doe v. Bolton, 410 U.S. at 192. This issue was not before the Supreme Court on appeal.

45. 492 U.S. 490 (1989).
46. 112 S. Ct. 2791 (1992).
47. In upholding the provision regarding minors, the court implicitly affirmed the general rule that a state may require parental consent for a minor's abortion if there is also an option for the minor to seek judicial approval if she does not wish to seek or cannot obtain a parent's consent.
48. Parker v. Rampton, 28 Utah 2d 36, 497 P.2d 848 (1972).
49. 381 U.S. 479 (1965). *See also* Eisenstadt v. Baird, 405 U.S. 438 (1972) (unmarried persons have the same constitutional right to privacy with respect to contraceptive measures as married persons do).
50. Although the law of most states was silent on the issue, fears and arguments were expressed that sterilization could be considered criminal mayhem, and many physicians refused to perform the surgery except for therapeutic reasons. In general terms, mayhem can be defined as an intentional or willful disfigurement of the body. Criminal statues frequently prohibit such act regardless of malicious intent of the agent or consent of the victim. At least two cases, however, although not directly on the point, do indicate by way of interpretation or dictum that a consensual voluntary sterilization is not a criminal act, the arguments being that criminal statutes prohibiting mayhem implicitly or explicitly require malicious intent or, more broadly, that public policy does not prohibit population control and family planning. Shaheen v. Knight, 11 Pa. D. & C. 2d 41 (Dist. Ct. of Lycoming County 1957) (a private contract between a patient and a physician for sterilization is not void as being against public policy, although an award of damages for alleged breach of contract if the normal birth of a normal child followed such surgery would be contrary to public policy). *See also* Christensen v. Thornby, 192 Minn. 123, 255 N.W. 620, 622 (1934).
51. 42 C.F.R. §§ 50.201–50.210 (1985).
52. CODE OF VA. § 54-325.9 (1982).
53. ME. REV. STAT. ANN. TIT. 34-B, § 7004 (1984).
54. 274 U.S. 200 (1927). During the 1920s and 1930s several state courts also handed down decisions that upheld the constitutionality of eugenic sterilization statutes. A more recent case, *In re* Cavitt, approved a statute as valid under the police power, 182 Neb. 712, 157 N.W.2d 171 (1968), *appeal dismissed,* 396 U.S. 996 (1970). In this situation compulsory sterilization was required before a retarded mother of eight children was released from a state hospital. *See also In re* Sterilization of Moore, 289 N.C. 95, 221 S.E.2d 307 (1976) (a statute permitting sterilization under certain circumstances of persons who are victims of "mental illness" or who are diagnosed as "mental defective(s)" is constitutional when applied to sexually active persons).
55. *See* Burgdorf and Burgdorf, *The Wicked Witch Is Almost Dead: Buck v. Bell and the Sterilization of Handicapped Persons,* 50 TEMPLE L.Q. 995 (1977).
56. Skinner v. Oklahoma, 316 U.S. 535 (1942).
57. *See, e.g.,* North Carolina Ass'n for Retarded Children v. State of N.C., 420 F. Supp. 451, 454 (1976), in which the court made a finding of fact that

"[m]ost competent geneticists now reject social Darwinism and doubt the premise implicit in Mr. Justice Holmes' incantation that ' . . . three generations of imbeciles is enough.' [P]revalent medical opinion views with distaste even voluntary sterilizations for the mentally retarded and is inclined to sanction it only as a last resort and in relatively extreme cases. In short, the medical and genetical experts are no longer sold on sterilization to benefit either retarded patients or the future of the Republic."

58. *See* Burgdorf and Burgdorf, *supra* note 55.

59. Matter of Welfare of Hillstrom, 363 N.W.2d 871, 876 (Minn. App. 1985) (sterilization was not warranted for a 41-year-old mentally retarded woman who was closely supervised and was not likely to engage in sexual intercourse).

60. *In re* Grady, 85 N.J. 235, 245, 426 A.2d 467, 472 (1981). *See also* Burgdorf and Burgdorf, *supra* note 55.

61. *See, e.g.,* N.H. STAT. § 464-A:25 I(c) (1983). *See also, In re* Penny N., 120 N.H. 269, 414 A.2d 541 (1980).

62. 410 U.S. 179, 197 (1973).

63. 475 F.2d 701 (1st Cir. 1973), *appeal for stay of mandate denied,* 411 U.S. 929 (1973), reversing the federal district court, which had held that the patient possessed no constitutional right to have a sterilization performed in a city hospital. 341 F. Supp. 1385 (D. Mass. 1972). The decision of the circuit court of appeals was rendered after the *Wade* and *Bolton* cases on abortion.

64. McCabe v. Nassau County Medical Center, 453 F.2d 698 (2d Cir. 1971).

65. 313 F. Supp. 1170 (D.D.C. 1970), 434 F.2d 423 (D.C. Cir. 1970).

66. 495 F.2d 1342 (8th Cir. 1974), *cert. denied,* 419 U.S. 891 (1974). *See also* Doe v. Hale Hosp., 369 F. Supp. 970 (D. Mass. 1974), *aff'd,* 500 F.2d 144 (1st Cir. 1974), *cert. denied,* 420 U.S. 907 (1975) (a municipal hospital that prohibited all elective abortions although permitting therapeutic abortions was subject to "state action," and hence the policy was in violation of the equal protection clause of the Fourteenth Amendment. The district court noted that virtually no other hospitals in the area provided elective abortions. The cause of action in *Hale* was brought by prospective patients who were in the first trimester of pregnancy). *Cf.* Poelker v. Jane Doe, 432 U.S. 519 (1977), *reh'g denied,* 434 U.S. 880 (1977) (city-owned hospitals do not violate the Constitution when they choose as a policy to provide publicly financed hospital services for childbirth without providing corresponding services for elective nontherapeutic abortions), *rev'g* Doe v. Poelker, 515 F.2d 541 (8th Cir. 1975).

67. Taylor v. St. Vincent's Hosp., 369 F. Supp. 948 (D. Mont. 1973), *aff'd,* 523 F.2d 75 (9th Cir. 1975), *cert. denied,* 424 U.S. 948 (1976). The federal district court issued a temporary injunction enjoining a private hospital from enforcing a ban on sterilization on the basis that receipt of governmental funds resulted in "state action." Subsequently the injunction was dissolved and the initial decision was thereby reversed, Taylor v. St. Vincent's Hosp., 369 F. Supp. 948 (D. Mont. 1973), thus upholding the hospital's policy of not permitting surgical sterilization. The basis of the reversal was, as in the *Watkins* case discussed later, that no violation of constitutional or civil rights was involved in light of congressional enactment of the Health Programs Extension Act of 1973, 42 U.S.C.A. § 300a-7 (1973), which specifically provides that receipt of

governmental funds under certain federal acts does not authorize any court or public official to require the facility to provide abortions or sterilizations when a policy of prohibition is based on religious belief or moral convictions. The district court's decision was upheld by the circuit court of appeal, 523 F.2d 75 (9th Cir. 1975) and the United States Supreme Court denied certiorari, 424 U.S. 948 (1976), thus upholding the Health Programs Extension Act of 1973. *Cf.* Doe v. Charleston Area Medical Center, 529 F.2d 638 (4th Cir. 1975), noted in note 104, *infra.*

68. 479 F.2d 756 (7th Cir. 1973).

69. 361 F. Supp. 1212 (N.D. Tex. 1973), *appeal dismissed,* 490 F.2d 81 (5th Cir. 1974). Moreover, the district court's decision is not now reviewable by the circuit court of appeals, because the patient in fact obtained a sterilization at another hospital. Allen v. Sisters of St. Joseph, 490 F.2d 81 (5th Cir. 1974).

70. 364 F. Supp. 799 (D. Idaho 1973), *aff'd,* 520 F.2d 894 (9th Cir. 1975).

71. Health Programs Extension Act, 42 U.S.C.A. § 300a-7 (1973). Where nothing in the record proves that a private hospital's policy of prohibiting abortions is based on institutional religious beliefs or moral convictions, the Health Programs Extension Act does not apply. Moreover, a private hospital is engaged in "state action" when it has received Hill-Burton and other governmental funds. Doe v. Charleston Area Medical Center, 520 F.2d 638 (4th Cir. 1975).

72. *See also* Chrisman v. Sisters of St. Joseph of Peace, 506 F.2d 308 (9th Cir. 1974) (Health Programs Extension Act, 42 U.S.C.A. § 300a-7 is constitutional). Greco v. Orange Memorial Hosp., 374 F. Supp. 227 (E.D. Tex. 1974), *aff'd,* 513 F.2d 873 (5th Cir. 1975), *cert. denied,* 423 U.S. 1000 (1975) (a private hospital is not engaged in "state action," even though it receives a significant amount of governmental funds; thus it may bar abortions. The denial of certiorari by the Supreme Court in effect permits conflicting decision on "state action" to remain, without resolving the issue on constitutional merits). *Cf.* Doe v. Bridgeton Hosp. Ass'n, Inc., 71 N.J. 478, 366 A.2d 641 (1976), *cert. denied,* 433 U.S. 914 (1977) (nonsectarian, private nonprofit hospitals may not deny first-trimester elective abortions when they permit therapeutic abortions, when staff and facilities are available, and when they are the only general hospitals in their respective communities. As "quasi-public" institutions, they must exercise fiduciary powers reasonably and for the public good. A statute that no hospital shall be required to provide abortion services cannot constitutionally be applied to nonsectarian institutions).

73. 410 U.S. 179, 197 (1973).

74. MICH. COMP. LAWS ANN. §§ 333.20182–.20183 (1980 & Supp. 1986).

75. Chrisman v. Sisters of St. Joseph of Peace, 506 F.2d 308 (9th Cir. 1974).

76. Doe v. Bellin Memorial Hosp., 479 F.2d 756 (7th Cir. 1973), apparently approved of a conscience clause statute pertaining to a private hospital, although no such statute was involved in that litigation and hence the approval would be considered dictum. *Cf.* Doe v. Bridgeton Hosp. Ass'n, Inc., 71 N.J. 478, 366 A.2d 641 (1976) (New Jersey conscience clause statute may not be constitutionally applied to private nonsectarian hospitals).

77. *See* Doe v. Mundy, 514 F.2d 1179 (7th Cir. 1975). In Roe v. Arizona Bd. of Regents, 23 Ariz. App. 477, 534 P.2d 285 (1975), a statute providing that no

hospital was required to admit any patient for an abortion was ruled overly broad and unconstitutional when applied to public hospitals; further, a statute providing that no abortions should be performed at any facility under the jurisdiction of the board of regents unless it was necessary to save the life of a mother could not be upheld. Subsequently the Arizona Supreme Court reversed the court of appeals, at least with respect to the ruling on the statute relevant to the university hospital. It was said to be constitutional in light of the institution's statutes as a teaching hospital and the availability of other public facilities for abortions. Roe v. Arizona Bd. of Regents, 113 Ariz. 178, 549 P.2d 150 (1976). *Cf.* Wolfe v. Schroering, 541 F.2d 523 (6th Cir. 1976) (an institutional conscience clause in a Kentucky statute is unconstitutional as applied to public hospitals and constitutional as applied to private hospitals, physicians, nurses, and employees).

78. Beal v. Ann Doe, 432 U.S. 438 (1977); moreover, the equal protection clause of the Fourteenth Amendment does not require a state participating in the Medicaid program to pay expenses of nontherapeutic abortions for indigent women even though it does pay expenses of childbirth, Maher, Comm'r of Social Servs. of Conn. v. Susan Roe, 432 U.S. 464 (1977).

79. Harris v. McRae, 448 U.S. 297 (1980), *reh'g denied,* 448 U.S. 917 (1980). The court also held that the Hyde Amendment does not violate due process, equal protection under the Fifth Amendment, or the Establishment Clause of the First Amendment.

80. *E.g.,* Miler v. Bennett, 190 Va. 162, 56 S.E.2d 217, 21 A.L.R.2d 364 (1949).

81. *E.g.,* Milliken v. Heddesheimer, 110 Ohio St. 381, 144 N.E. 264 (1924) (a patient who consented to a criminal act can nevertheless recover civil damages).

82. Speck v. Finegold, 268 Pa. Super. 342, 408 A.2d 496 (1979), *modified,* 497 Pa. 77, 439 A.2d 110 (1979).

83. The actions have generally been labeled "wrongful conception" or "wrongful pregnancy" if the alleged negligence occurred prior to conception; "wrongful birth" describes an action by the parents on their own behalf, and "wrongful life" an action brought on behalf of the child. Not all courts use the same terminology, and "wrongful birth" is often an umbrella term for all such actions.

84. 31 Cal. 3d 220, 182 Cal. Rptr. 337, 643 P.2d 954 (1982).

85. Johnson v. Yeshiva Univ., 42 N.Y.2d 818, 820, 396 N.Y.S.2d 647, 648, 364 N.E.2d 1340, 1341 (1977).

86. Becker v. Schwartz, 46 N.Y.2d 401, 413 N.Y.S.2d 895, 386 N.E.2d 807 (1978).

87. Examples of wrongful birth actions for negligence in genetic counseling, testing, or diagnosis include (among others) cases involving Down's syndrome, *see, e.g.,* Call v. Kezirian, 135 Cal. App. 3d 189, 185 Cal. Rptr. 103 (1982); Berman v. Allen, 80 N.J. 421, 404 A.2d 8 (1979); Azzolino v. Dingfelder, 71 N.C. App. 597, 322 S.E.2d 567 (1984), *review granted,* 327 S.E.2d 887 (1985); Phillips v. United States, 508 F. Supp. 537 (D.S.C. 1980), 508 F. Supp. 544 (D.S.C. 1981); and Tay-Sachs disease, *see, e.g.,* Curlender v. Bio-Science Laboratories, 165 Cal. Rptr. 477, 106 Cal. App. 3d 811 (1980); Goldberg v. Ruskin, 128 Ill. App. 3d 1029, 471 N.E.2d 530 (1984); Gildiner v. Thomas Jefferson Univ. Hosp., 451 F. Supp. 692 (E.D. Pa. 1978).

88. Dumer v. St. Michael's Hosp., 69 Wis. 2d 766, 233 N.W.2d 372 (1975).

89. Schroeder v. Perkel, 87 N.J. 53, 432 A.2d 834 (1981).

90. Troppi v. Scarf, 31 Mich. App. 240, 187 N.W.2d 511 (1971).

91. Harbeson v. Parke-Davis, Inc., 98 Wash. 2d 460, 656 P.2d 483 (1983).

92. *E.g.,* Lane v. Cohen, 201 So. 2d 804 (Fla. Dist. Ct. App. 1967); Peters v. Gelb, 303 A.2d 685 (Del. Super. Ct. 1973), *reh'g denied,* 314 A.2d 901 (1974).

93. 74 Ill. App. 2d 332, 220 N.E.2d 767 (1966).

94. Hackworth v. Hart, 474 S.W.2d 377 (Ky. 1971). *See also* Herrava v. Roessing, 533 P.2d 60 (Colo. Ct. App. 1975) (statements made by the doctor were opinions and not a guarantee of results).

95. Hackworth v. Hart, 474 S.W.2d 377 (Ky. 1971); Hays v. Hall, 488 S.W.2d 412 (Tex. 1972); Vilord v. Jenkins, 226 So. 2d 245 (Fla. Dist. Ct. App. 1969); Teeters v. Currey, 518 S.W.2d 512 (Tenn. 1974).

96. Blake v. Cruz, 108 Idaho 253, 698 P.2d 315 (1984).

97. In certain cases the plaintiff may have to prove that she would have had an abortion or chosen not to conceive. For example, if the plaintiffs blamed the wrongful birth on the defendants' failure to tell them that children born to mothers over 35 years of age risked Down's syndrome and that amniocentesis could detect the condition, they had to show that if they had been properly informed they would not only have undergone amniocentesis but would also have chosen abortion if the results were adverse. Becker v. Schwartz, 46 N.Y.2d 401, N.Y.S.2d 895, 386 N.E.2d 807 (1978).

98. Custodio v. Bauer, 251 Cal. App. 2d 303, 59 Cal. Rptr. 463 (1967).

99. *See, e.g.,* Jones v. Mailinowski, 299 Md. 257, 473 A.2d 429 (1984); Cockrum v. Baumgartner, 99 Ill. App. 3d 271, 425 N.E.2d 968 (1981), *cert. denied,* 464 U.S. 846 (1983), *rev'd on other grounds,* 447 N.E.2d 385 (1983). *Cf.* Sorkin v. Lee, 434 N.Y.S.2d 300, 78 A.D.2d 180 (1980) (although the mother had no obligation to have an abortion, it should be disproportionate penalty to impose child-raising costs on the physician who negligently performed a tubal ligation. Thus such parents may recover only costs of medical care, loss of consortium for husband, and pain and discomfort for the mother).

100. *E.g.,* Nolan v. Merecki, 88 A.D.2d 1021, 451 N.Y.S.2d 914 (1982).

101. *See, e.g.,* Troppi v. Scarf, 31 Mich. App. 240, 187 N.W.2d 511 (1971); Ziemba v. Sternberg, 45 A.D.2d 230, 357 N.Y.S.2d 265 (1974).

102. *See, e.g.,* Bushman v. Burns Clinic Medical Center, 83 Mich. App. 453, 268 N.W.2d 683 (1978); Sorkin v. Lee, 434 N.Y.S.2d 300, 78 A.D.2d 180 (1980).

103. *See, e.g., Bushman, supra* note 102; James G. and Lurana G. v. Caserta, 332 S.E.2d 872 (Sup. Ct. App. W. Va. 1985); Sorkin v. Lee, 434 N.Y.S.2d 300, 78 A.D.2d 180 (1980).

104. Naccash v. Burger, 223 Va. 406, 290 S.E.2d 825 (1982). Interestingly, the costs of the child's funeral and grave marker were deducted by the court from the damages awarded, because the death was caused by the disease and was not the fault of the laboratory personnel. Other cases permitting recovery for emotional distress include Berman v. Allen, 80 N.J. 421, 404 A.2d 8 (1979); Blake v. Cruz, 108 Idaho 253, 698 P.2d 315 (1984).

105. Howard v. Lecher, 53 A.D.2d 420, 386 N.Y.S.2d 460 (1976), *aff'd,* 42 N.Y.2d 109 (1977). *See also* Becker v. Schwartz, 46 N.Y.2d 401, 413 N.Y.S.2d 895, 386 N.E.2d 807 (1978) (damages for emotional harm would be too speculative); Goldberg v. Ruskin, 84 Ill. Dec. 1 (1984), *modified,* 128 Ill App. 3d 1029, 471

N.E.2d 530 (1984) (parents failed to allege that they suffered physical injury and therefore could not recover damages for emotional harm).

106. *See, e.g.,* Ochs v. Borelli, 187 Conn. 253, 445 A.2d 883 (1982).

107. *See, e.g.,* Rieck v. Medical Protective Co., 64 Wis. 2d 514, 219 N.W.2d 242 (1974) (failure to make a timely diagnosis of pregnancy). Other cases denying costs of raising a healthy child include Wilczynski v. Goodman, 73 Ill. App. 3d 51, 29 Ill. Dec. 216, 391 N.E.2d 479 (1979) (negligent performance of therapeutic abortion); Public Health Trust v. Brown, 388 So. 2d 1084 (Fla. App. 1980) (failed sterilization); Wilbur v. Kerr, 275 Ark. 239, 628 S.W.2d 568 (1982) (husband had not one but two unsuccessful vasectomies); Sorkin v. Lee, 434 N.Y.S.2d 300, 78 A.D.2d 180 (1980) (failed tubal litigation).

108. 99 Ill. App. 3d 271, 425 N.E.2d 968 (1981).

109. *See, e.g.,* Blake v. Cruz, 108 Idaho 253, 698 P.2d 315 (1984); Goldberg v. Ruskin, 84 Ill. Dec. 1 (1984), *modified,* 128 Ill. App. 3d 1029, 471 N.E.2d 530 (1984); Schroeder v. Perkel, 87 N.J. 53, 432 A.2d 834 (1981); Jacobs v. Theimer, 519 S.W.2d 846 (Tex. 1975).

110. *E.g.,* Berman v. Allen, 80 N.J. 421, 404 A.2d 8 (1979).

111. *See, e.g.,* Still v. Gratton, 55 Cal. App. 3d 698, 127 Cal. Rptr. 652 (1976); Zepeda v. Zepeda, 41 Ill. App. 2d 240, 190 N.E.2d 849 (1963), *cert. denied,* 379 U.S. 945 (1964); Williams v. State, 25 A.D.2d 906, 269 N.Y.S.2d 786 (1966).

112. *E.g.,* Elliot v. Brown, 361 So. 2d 546 (Ala. 1978); DiNatale v. Lieberman, 409 So. 2d 512 (Fla. App. 1982); Blake v. Cruz, 108 Idaho 253, 698 P.2d 315 (1984); Goldberg v. Ruskin, 84 Ill. Dec. 1 (1984), *modified,* 128 Ill. App. 3d 1029, 471 N.E.2d 530 (1984); Whit v. United States, 510 F. Supp. 146 (D. Kansas 1981); Eisbrenner v. Stanley, 106 Mich. App. 357, 308 N.W.2d 209 (1981); Berman v. Allen, 80 N.J. 421, 404 A.2d 8 (1979); Becker v. Schwartz, 46 N.Y.2d 401, 413 N.Y.S.2d 895, 386 N.E.2d 807 (1978); Gildiner v. Thomas Jefferson Univ. Hosp., 451 F. Supp. 692 (E.D. Pa. 1978); Phillips v. United States, 508 F. Supp. 537 (D.S.C. 1980), 508 F. Supp. 544 (D.S.C. 1981); Nelson v. Krusen, 678 S.W.2d 918 (Tex. 1984); Dumer v. St. Michael's Hosp., 69 Wis. 2d 766, 233 N.W.2d 372 (1975).

113. Becker v. Schwartz, 46 N.Y.2d 401, 413 N.Y.S.2d 895, 386 N.E.2d 807 (1978).

114. Blake v. Cruz, 108 Idaho 253, 698 P.2d 315 (1984).

115. 106 Cal. App. 3d 811, 165 Cal. Rptr. 477 (1980).

116. 31 Cal. 3d 220, 182 Cal. Rptr. 337, 643 P.2d 954 (1982).

117. *Id.* at 233, 182 Cal. Rptr. at 344–45, 643 P.2d at 961–62.

118. CAL. HEALTH & SAFETY CODE § 7186 (Supp. 1986). The court also cited Matter of Quinlan, 70 N.J. 10, 355 A.2d 647 (1976), *cert. denied,* 429 U.S. 922 (1976); Superintendent of Belchertown v. Saikewicz, 373 Mass. 728, 370 N.E.2d 417 (1977) in recognizing that an individual has the right to decide whether life is preferable to death under certain circumstances.

119. 98 Wash. 2d 460, 656 P.2d 483 (1983).

120. *Id.* at 483, 656 P.2d at 497. Other cases permitting a wrongful life action include Call v. Kezirian, 135 Cal. App. 3d 189, 185 Cal. Rptr. 103 (1982); Azzolino v. Dingfelder, 71 N.C. App. 289, 322 S.E.2d 567 (1984), *review granted,* 313 N.C. 327 S.E.2d 887 (1985); Procanik v. Cillo, 97 N.J. 339, 478 A.2d

755 (1984). These cases followed *Turpin* in permitting special damages for extraordinary expenses but denying general damages.

121. CAL. CIVIL CODE § 43.6(a) (1982): "No cause of action arises against a parent of a child based upon the claim that the child should not have been conceived or, if conceived, should not have been allowed to have been born alive."

122. MINN. STAT. ANN. § 145.424, subds. 1 & 2 (West Supp. 1986). In light of the constitutional right of reproductive freedom, this statute may not be constitutional.

123. MINN. STAT. ANN. § 145.424, subd. 3. The California statute has a similar provision, CAL. CIVIL CODE § 43.6(b) (1982).

124. 109 N.J. 396, 537 A.2d 1227 (1988).

125. 704 S.W.2d 209 (1986).

126. 842 S.W.2d 588 (Tenn. 1992).

MEDICAL RECORDS

This chapter will review the legal aspects of three major questions relating to the patient's medical record:

1. legal requirements for medical records;
2. access to medical record information; and
3. use of records in legal proceedings.

The primary purposes of a medical record are to serve the interests of the individual patient and facilitate medical care and treatment. A current and complete record is indispensable to the practice of medicine. Furthermore, records of patients compiled over an extended period can be subjected to study and analysis that will reveal standards and patterns of care for an institution and for the individual physician, thus documenting the hospital's and physician's quality of care. The medical records thus become an essential source of information for effective institutional peer reviews and quality assurance programs.

Additionally, the Medicare and Medicaid programs and private insurance carriers require documentation of both the necessity and quality of care as a precondition to reimbursement for services. An accurate record facilitates this process.

Legal Requirements

Form and Contents

In most states the legal requirements for maintaining medical records will be found in the rules and regulations promulgated by the administrative agency responsible for licensing healthcare institutions. Many of these regulations simply specify that an "adequate" or "complete" record be maintained. Some states provide by regulation or statute that the record contain certain minimum categories of information expressed in general language, leaving it to the professional judgment of physicians, nurses, and paramedical personnel to decide the details of its organization and content. For example, the Florida statute provides:

> Each hospital . . . shall require the use of a system of problem-oriented medical records for its patients, which system shall include the following elements: basic client data collection; a listing of the patient's problems;

the initial plan with diagnostic and therapeutic orders as appropriate for each problem identified; and progress notes, including a discharge summary.[1]

The licensure regulations of some states specifically authorize an automated medical record system that eliminates the need to prepare handwritten or typed documents, as long as the computerized system satisfies the substantive regulatory requirements relating to content. Maintaining medical information in computerized form has numerous advantages—such as greater accuracy and accessibility—but it also raises issues like confidentiality, accuracy, durability, and compliance with licensure requirements. As is so often the case, the law has not kept pace with the progress in the medical field. Laws relating to confidentiality and medical record content and retention, for example, were written when paper records were the universal standard. If those statutes have not been updated in a particular state, an electronic medical record system might be held not to comply with the law. It is important, therefore, to obtain a legal opinion regarding the acceptability of a computerized medical record before implementing such a system.

Physicians and hospital administrative personnel must be familiar with local statutes and licensure regulations governing medical records because violation of such provisions could lead to license suspension or revocation. The record-keeping policies of the institution and its staff must also meet current standards of professional practice. These standards will in most instances exceed the legal requirements.

The Joint Commission on Accreditation of Healthcare Organizations has promulgated standards for keeping medical records.[2] Failure to comply with them can result in the loss of accreditation and could be evidence of negligence if a patient brought a civil lawsuit against a hospital alleging injury or damage, the proximate cause being the institution's failure to adhere to recognized standards of care.[3] The standards of the Joint Commission provide that:

- An adequate medical record must be maintained for every person evaluated or treated as an inpatient, an outpatient, an emergency patient, or a patient in a hospital-based home care program.
- The record must contain sufficient information to identify the patient and to support the diagnosis and treatment, and it must furnish accurate documentation of results.
- The records shall be confidential, secure, current, authenticated, legible, and complete.
- The record department shall be adequately directed, staffed, and equipped, and it shall maintain a system of identification and filing to facilitate prompt location of each record.

Current interpretations of the Joint Commission's standards permit hospitals to develop and maintain a fully automated medical record system. Because some states accept accreditation as qualification for licensure, the commission's recognition of computerized systems may be a reason why formal regulations have not been brought up to date in many states. Whatever system is in use, however, the role of medical record personnel in evaluation of patient care must be defined.

In addition to the general legal requirements for compiling and keeping a clinical medical record, there are local laws that require certain information to be reported to public authorities for statistical purposes. State statutes commonly require hospitals and physicians to maintain records of births, deaths, autopsies, and similar events in which the public has an interest. Local statutes also require that records be kept and reports be made to appropriate public authority when patients are diagnosed as suffering from certain contagious diseases, when they may have been involved in crimes of violence, when child abuse is suspected, or when public health and welfare are otherwise at stake. Any failure to be aware of and comply with such public health laws can have grave consequences for medical personnel and hospitals. More will be said later about these implications.

Both legal regulations and professional standards of medical practice require that entries in the medical record be signed by the physician, nurse, or other provider. Hence, a physician's spoken order must be later recorded and signed. One physician may not sign for the responsible or prescribing doctor unless both share the responsibility for the patient's care. This general requirement is of course meant to provide proper authentication of the record. Together with the requirement that the record be written, it leads to the traditional rule that entries in the record must be manually authenticated, either by the actual handwriting of the doctor or by another form of signature, such as a printed or stamped name or initials. Depending on the specific language of a local statute or regulation, a "signature" does not necessarily have to be handwritten. In general, however, current law does require the production of a "signature," however that term is defined. Therefore, automated authentication of entries in a computerized medical records system is legally questionable in many states.[4] To be certain that the signature requirements are met, the medical staff bylaws and rules and regulations should contain provisions relating to proper authentication of entries in the patient's chart.

Similarly, the staff bylaws should require that the physician attending the patient keep the record up to date and that the record be completed within a reasonable time after the patient's discharge. The Joint Commission on Accreditation of Healthcare Organizations considers a medical record complete when the medical history, diagnostic and therapeutic orders, all reports of consultations and tests, progress notes, and a clinical resumé are entered and signed by the attending physician. Such a rule, like that of properly authenticating the record, is consistent with both local law and acceptable standards of practice. As noted in Chapter 14, "Medical Staff Appointments and Privileges," a physician found to have violated such a medical staff or hospital policy can be subject to appropriate disciplinary measures.

Failure to maintain complete, accurate, and current records can have severe adverse effects for a defendant in civil litigation. For example, failure of nurses to be systematic in keeping a patient under observation in accordance with his or her condition and in recording the observations without delay can be evidence of negligence for a jury to consider. Because medical records are generally admissible as evidence in a malpractice suit, the absence of appropriate entries in the chart—or the inclusion of inaccurate information—can be the basis for a jury's adverse verdict.[5]

In a New York case a patient was diagnosed as having suffered damage to the liver as a result of an adverse reaction to the anesthetic halothane, administered during foot surgery, but no record of this diagnosis was made in the chart. A month later the patient underwent surgery on the other foot and the same anesthetic was given. This time it caused the patient's death. The absence of a notation in the medical record was a persuasive factor in the jury's decision favoring the plaintiff.[6]

Corrections of inaccurate information or changes in diagnosis should also be entered in the medical record at once and in a proper fashion. Erasures or total obliteration of medical information in the patient's chart should never be permitted; instead, the person making the change should carefully draw a line through the original entry, leaving the writing legible, and authenticate the correction by signing the corrected entry. Alterations of information in the record should include the date and the reason for the change. The wisdom of adhering to such policies is illustrated by a Connecticut case in which the court held that the jury was entitled to know that an entry in the chart of a mental patient, who had been left unattended in a locker room for several hours, had been obliterated, rewritten, and falsified. A verdict in the amount of $3.6 million was upheld on appeal.[7]

The adverse implications of an incomplete medical record are seen in the case of *Carr v. St. Paul Fire and Marine Insurance Company*.[8] The patient came to the hospital's emergency room complaining of severe abdominal pains and vomiting but was examined only by a licensed practical nurse and two orderlies, who recorded the vital signs. Although hospital personnel tried unsuccessfully to reach the patient's personal doctor, they failed to summon another physician. After being allowed to return home, the patient died the same evening. The medical records compiled during the visit to the emergency room were then destroyed. In a subsequent lawsuit against the hospital's insurance company, the jury was allowed to know that the patient's records had been destroyed, contrary to acceptable hospital practice, and then to infer that the documents would probably have revealed a medical emergency necessitating attendance by a physician. The jury award on the grounds that hospital personnel had failed to exercise reasonable care under the circumstances was therefore justified.

One of the best possible defenses in malpractice litigation is therefore to present in evidence a medical record that completely and accurately documents the continued care and treatment of the patient. Such a record is frequently convincing evidence that the patient received reasonable care under all the facts and circumstances.

Information in the record must be readily available when the circumstances of the individual patient's case require it. To illustrate, in *Howlett v. Greenberg* the victim of an automobile accident was examined by a hospital staff physician, who dictated the results of an examination.[9] This information had not, however, been transcribed and affixed to the patient's chart when Dr. Greenberg performed nonemergency surgery on the patient's wrist, even though he knew that it should have been and that proceeding with surgery in these circumstances was contrary to hospital rules. Adverse results followed the surgery.

In such instances, if the patient can show that failure to have relevant medical information readily at hand was the proximate cause of injury or damage, liability of both the hospital and the operating surgeon can be established. The surgeon could be negligent by undertaking surgery with the knowledge that the patient's history and the report of the physician's examination were not part of the record, or in assuming that no history was taken and no physical examination performed. The hospital also could be liable for not having an effective system of compiling and ensuring the availability of required medical information whenever it is needed.

Incident and accident reports compiled in the course of a patient's care should not be included as a part of the medical record. The primary reason is that the medical record is generally available as evidence in a malpractice suit, as will be discussed more thoroughly. Incident reports are likely to contain factual information that might indicate fault of negligence on the part of physicians or hospital personnel. If such reports are incorporated as a part of the medical chart, they become available for consideration by a jury. Under some decisions, incident reports are subject to pretrial discovery proceedings and hence available to a plaintiff.[10] Even so, if they are separate from the medical record, they would not normally be admissible as evidence at trial. There are several reasons for this, including the fact that they constitute hearsay evidence. Moreover, a system for reporting incidents if maintained for educational purposes and to improve general standards of patient care and safety. To serve these ends there should be assurance that such reports will not be available to potential malpractice plaintiffs. On the other hand, accurate and factual information with respect to the diagnosis and treatment of a particular patient following an accident or an incident properly belongs in the medical chart.

Retention Requirements

Hospital policies regarding the length of time that medical records are retained in their original form and whether they should be preserved in other forms—

by microfilm or electronically, for example—will depend on local law and standards of professional care of patients in light of institutional purposes.

The latter point recognizes that the foremost purpose of maintaining and preserving the charts of patients is to provide a high quality of care from the point of view of both the individual patient and the institution. Accordingly, governing bodies of hospitals and other medical organizations must not only be familiar with local legal requirements respecting the length of time that records must be preserved; they must also analyze their own medical and administrative needs regarding future use of the records. Teaching hospitals, for example, and other institutions engaged in significant and continuous medical research will wish to retain records longer than other hospitals to facilitate retrospective review. Such organizations may wish to keep records for 75 years or more, for example. All institutions will need to retain records long enough to facilitate continuing programs of peer review and quality assurance.

The law regarding the length of time that medical records must be retained varies widely from state to state. Although a few states may have statutory law on the subject, most commonly the matter is found, if at all, in administrative rules and regulations bearing on licensing of healthcare organizations. Regulations range from a total absence of rules about retaining medical records to requirements that patients' charts must be kept "permanently." The latter would probably not effectively prohibit microfilming, and some regulations affirmatively permit it. In general, if local law says nothing about microfilming, the process is assumed to be permitted.

Medicare Conditions of Participation require records to be kept for at least five years.[11] Some states also provide for retention of records for a stipulated number of years: for example, 10, 15, or 25 years, dating from the discharge of the patient from the hospital or perhaps from the patient's known death. Regulations of this type may also permit microfilming, or they may permit certain items in the record, such as nurses' notes, to be destroyed earlier than others. Notes on a patient's progress are important in malpractice litigation, and it is hence suggested that nurses' notes be retained with the rest of the record, even if local law permits earlier disposal. Regulations regarding the preservation of records may provide that records of minors be retained in their original form or on microfilm for a stipulated period after the patient reaches adulthood.

Some states require approval of the licensure authority before records may be destroyed. Some licensure regulations say only that the period of retention shall be determined by state law pertaining to the statutory limitations on actions in contract and in tort. Such a provision means that hospital and medical personnel must know the relevant statutes of limitation and their judicial interpretations. Healthcare institutions are advised to consult legal counsel for current information on the length of time that the original records of patient care must be retained and on the legality of microfilm copies. In any event, when state statutes or regulations do not specify a longer period, the minimum period of retention should be determined by relevant statutes of limitations because the records may be necessary in defending any lawsuits that may arise.

In the absence of a statutory or administrative rule specifying the required period for record retention, there is apparently no affirmative common law duty to retain. When a patient sought x-rays for use as evidence in a pending malpractice action against a physician, the hospital where the x-rays were taken was not liable when it was unable to produce the films.[12] The court observed that there was no duty on the part of the hospital to preserve them and further that plaintiff had presented no proof of damages resulting from their unavailability. It should be observed, however, that other courts could make a distinction between written medical records and x-ray films, finding that there is a duty to retain the former. In any event, when a duty is found and the matter of breach of duty is sent to a jury, the absence of a record is quite harmful to the defendant.

Besides a statutory or common-law duty to retain records, one must consider the advisability of retaining records for defense of possible malpractice actions, as was mentioned earlier. To do so, one must factor in the length of the state's statute of limitations, the period of time within which a plaintiff must file the lawsuit. In many states the statute of limitations is two years from the time the alleged malpractice occurred; however, in most states that time period is "tolled" (suspended) until the malpractice is discovered or while the plaintiff is a minor or mentally disabled. Thus, for example, in the case of a newborn the two-year limitations period does not begin to run until the child reaches the age of majority. If the age of majority is 18 in the particular state, therefore, it would be wise to retain records of infants born in the hospital for at least 20 years. Some states have altered the common law "tolling" rules; Florida, for example, provides that "in no event shall the action be commenced later than four years from the date of the incident or occurrence out of which the cause of action accrued, except that this four-year period shall not bar an action brought on behalf of a minor on or before the child's eighth birthday."[13]

In summary, how long the clinical records of patients are retained and whether they are microfilmed will be determined by standards of professional practice, by the administrative and medical needs of the particular hospital, and by local law in each state. Institutional policies on these questions must be carefully developed and reviewed from time to time with the aid of legal counsel.

Many regulations provide that records be stored in fireproof or fire-resistant facilities. This requirement also emphasizes the need for medical and hospital personnel to be familiar with state administrative law. Because administrative regulations are subject to much amendment and modification, it is important to conduct frequent reviews of current requirements.

Private organizations such as the Joint Commission on Accreditation of Healthcare Organizations and the American Hospital Association have occasionally published statements of policy on retention and destruction of records. The current AHA policy statement recommends retaining records for at least 10 years.

Access to Medical Record Information

Ownership and Control of the Medical Record

Ownership of medical records rests with the hospital (or with the physician in the case of private patients). Similarly, x-rays, laboratory reports, reports of consultants, and other documents relating directly to the care of individual patients are owned by the hospital or by the physician who orders them in connection with a private practice.[14] The owner of the record has the right of physical possession and control.[15] As a general rule such owners should not permit removal of any chart from their control except by court order. Neither a patient nor an authorized representative has a right to a physical possession of the medical records. These principles are included specifically in the hospital licensure regulations of some states.

Ownership and right of physical control does not mean, however, that the patient and various legitimately interested third parties have no legal right of access to the medical record and the information it contains. Most jurisdictions affirm that patients have a right to view and copy their records and to appoint authorized representatives to examine the documents, as will be more fully discussed in the next section. Moreover, attending physicians may not prevent disclosure to hospitalized patients of information from the hospital record, with the possible exception of cases in which such disclosure might adversely affect a patient's physical or mental health.[16]

Physicians who retire from practice, those who have been replaced by other doctors selected by their patients, and the estates of deceased physicians are morally and ethically obligated to transfer the medical record or copies of it to the current physician when a patient so requests. Hence, in a New York case the court invalidated a provision in a deceased physician's will that all his professional records be burned by his executor.[17] At the same time the court recognized that the physical records belonged to the physician's estate and should not be delivered to the doctor's former patients.

Instead of delivering the entire original record to a newly chosen physician, a former doctor may wish to transfer a copy of the record or whatever excerpts or summaries are necessary for adequate treatment or diagnosis. This would be the normal procedure for hospitals when a patient is transferred to another institution or when a former patient seeks care elsewhere. When a hospital transfers a patient to another hospital—or when a private physician, for example, recommends a consultation with a specialist—the hospital or the physician has a legal and ethical duty to make available to the receiving institution or the consultant all medical information of record that is relevant to and necessary for the appropriate care of the patient.

The ethical and legal obligation to transfer information to succeeding practitioners or institutions may require some exceptions. If the patient requests transfer of the record or of information to a person known by the physician or hospital to be clearly unqualified or unlicensed, there is probably a duty to refuse the request. The physician or hospital, in the exercise of reasonable care consistent with recognized professional standards, should advise such patient that the proposed recipient lacks the proper qualifications.[18]

The Patient's Right to Medical Information

Most states recognize that the patient has a legal right to the information in the medical record, even in the absence of currently pending litigation. This right has been established in many jurisdictions by statute; in others it has been articulated by judicial decision. Accordingly, the long-held assumption that medical records are not to be inspected by the patient or an authorized representative is no longer valid: Physicians and hospitals should review and modify their traditional policies of not allowing records to be viewed by patients or their authorized representatives without a court subpoena.

As will be pointed out, however, the right of patients to view their records is qualified to some extent. Generally there must be a legitimate reason for inspection and patients must comply with reasonable safeguards established by the physician or hospital to ensure the physical safety of the record during the inspection. Perhaps also—at least in the opinion of some courts—the attending physician may deny any access to recorded information that would not be in the best interests of a patient's health, according to the good faith and professional judgment of the doctor.

Statutes giving the patient a right to receive medical information are illustrated by enactments in Connecticut, Massachusetts, Wisconsin, and Louisiana. The Connecticut statute, applicable to all hospitals that receive state aid, provides that a patient, his or her physician, or an authorized attorney may examine the medical record.[19] The right includes access to the patient's medical history, including bedside notes, charts, pictures, and plates. Copies may be made. In other jurisdictions the statute may extend the right of access only to written medical records and notes, thereby excluding x-rays. In still others the legislation does not specify the items that are to be accessible. In Massachusetts all hospitals except those under the control of the state's Department of Mental Health must make the records available for inspection by the patient or by an attorney having a written authorization from the patient.[20] As in Connecticut the patient or a representative is entitled to a copy of the record upon payment of a reasonable fee. Wisconsin's statute requires all physicians and hospitals that have custody of records and reports concerning care or treatment to make them available for inspection and copying by the patient or any authorized representative possessing written consent.[21] If the patient is deceased, the right is given to the beneficiary of an insurance policy on the patient's life or a personal representative (executor). Denial of the right renders the physician or hospital liable for the reasonable costs of enforcing the patient's right to discover. In Louisiana all general hospitals administered by the state's Department of Health and Human Resources are directed to furnish a "report," as distinguished from a copy of the record, to the patient's doctor, the patient, and the patient's heirs or attorney upon the written request of the doctor who made the referral to the hospital.[22] Such a report is to be available upon the patient's discharge from the hospital (or death) and shall include diagnosis, laboratory and x-ray findings, and treatment.

Most of the statutes do not specifically mention either the right of minor patients to obtain information from their medical records or their parents' right to the information. Logically, however, the minor would have the right whenever the relevant jurisdiction has recognized by either legislation or judicial decision that a mature minor can consent for treatment without parental consent. Accordingly, it might follow that a statute simply granting the patient access to information would not grant the parents a right to view the minor's records. On the other hand, if the minor is of tender years or cannot give legal consent for treatment, it would appear that parents should have the right to medical information contained in the minor's chart.

A few states allow the medical record to be available to the patient's attorney or representative but deny direct access by the patient.[23] The attorney must have the patient's written authorization, the consent of the parents or guardian of a minor patient unable to give his or her own consent, or the consent of the personal representative or heir of a deceased patient. In New Jersey when compensation or damages are claimed for an injury or death, the claimant may examine the pertinent hospital records.[24]

Most states thus recognize by statute that the patient or an authorized representative has a legal right to information contained in a medical record. Simultaneously the courts have been active in developing the right of access simply as a matter of local common law. For example, in *Cannell v. Medical and Surgical Clinic* an Illinois court held that the fiduciary relationship between the physician and the patient required the former to provide medical information on request.[25] The court also held that legal proceedings were not required.

As noted earlier, in the past physicians and hospitals customarily refused to allow patients access to the medical record. They often based this policy on the belief that records are technical and not understood by lay persons, that revelation of medical information might adversely affect the patient's health, and that the privacy of third parties who may be named in the chart should be protected. Clearly the first and third of the foregoing reasons are no longer supportable in the light of a growing social concern for individuals and their rights to information that directly affects health and welfare. The second reason is still recognized by several courts as valid and honorable as long as the denial is based on the attending physician's professional judgment that the patient's health might suffer and that judgment is properly documented.

Hospitals and their medical staffs must reevaluate their former policies in light of the new concern for patients' rights. An arbitrary policy of routinely denying a request to inspect the chart unless a court order has been obtained is no longer acceptable. Such a policy can only cause conflict with patients and their bona fide representatives, especially their attorneys.[26] Indeed, a policy of denying access may even encourage malpractice suits, for then the medical record will always be available to the attorney and the client.

As a starting point in developing administrative policies, hospitals and other institutions should generally make the medical chart available to a patient's attorney upon presentation of a current written authorization by the patient. In some communities, healthcare institutions and the local bar association have entered into agreements to this effect, thus improving the relations and the mutual understanding existing between the medical and legal professions. At the same time the provider can and should exercise reasonable control and supervision over inspection of the record and is also entitled to recover costs of the inspection.[27]

Although under the law an attending physician cannot arbitrarily deny a patient access to the record, the doctor should be consulted and should be asked to consent before the patient or a representative examines the record. Not only is this a matter of professional courtesy, it protects the patient, whose health or willingness to continue treatment may be adversely affected by revelation of certain information. Further, inspection of the record should be permitted only after the patient is discharged from the hospital and after the record has been completed.[28]

Especially important is the moral, if not legal, duty of a hospital or physician to make certain that the patient's consent is current and genuine whenever an attorney, insurance company, or other third party wishes to inspect the record. Although the prospect of liability for release of medical information without a patient's consent is not as great as is sometimes believed, a matter discussed in detail in the next section, there is a growing social and legal concern about the confidentiality of information. Healthcare personnel must therefore be sensitive to the validity and authenticity of documents that purport to be the patient's authorization to release information to third parties.[29]

Release of Information Without the Patient's Consent

To many persons the concept of confidentiality or privileged communication implies that private information entrusted to another shall not be divulged to a third party without the consent of the subject of the information. Because ethical considerations treat medical information as confidential, and because many states have privileged communication statutes pertaining to the physician-patient relationship, it is sometimes believed that the release of the information to a third party will constitute a civil wrong and give the patient a cause of action for damages unless the release is specifically ordered by a court or authorized by the patient. As the following discussion shows, this belief is an oversimplification of the law.

As a legal matter, confidentiality of private information is usually governed by state law. Accordingly, local statutes and judicial decisions must be consulted to determine reliable answers to the particular questions that continually arise concerning the release of medical information by an institution, physician, or other depository.

The U.S. Constitution does not afford individuals a right of informational privacy. That is, disclosure of personal information does not offend the Constitution.[30] Although the Supreme Court has recognized an individual's constitutional right to make certain personal decisions without interference by government or other third parties,[31] the right has not generally been extended to confidentiality of information.

Moreover, no federal statutes of general application exist to protect the confidentiality of medical or personal information. As noted elsewhere in this chapter, specific legislation or regulations apply in particular circumstances: for example, to providers participating in the Medicare program[32] or receiving funds pursuant to the Drug Abuse Office and Treatment Act.[33] No federal law, however, reaches the privately funded healthcare provider.[34]

The Freedom of Information Act provides for public access to certain types of information held by federal governmental agencies, but it excepts specific classes of information, including medical data the disclosure of which would constitute an unwarranted invasion of privacy.[35] The Privacy Act of 1974, in turn, counterbalances the Freedom of Information Act by limiting disclosure by the government of certain information in which individuals could be identified. Both of these federal statutes are discussed in detail subsequently, and neither has any significant effect on the general question of disclosing medical information without the patient's consent.

There are situations where third parties have a legitimate interest in medical information respecting a particular patient and where they have a legal right to obtain the information. In such instances the release of information by a physician or a hospital without the patient's express consent will not lead to liability in damages. Indeed, in some circumstances a hospital or a doctor has a positive legal duty to disclose medical information whether or not the patient has consented.

Court orders   A valid court order directing that medical records be made available to a given third party or revealed in a given circumstance must be honored, and the patient's consent is not required. Some typical situations where a court will order revelation are noted at the close of this chapter. Generally the legal process for obtaining medical record information is through a subpoena *duces tecum* ordering that a witness appear, together with records or documents specified by the subpoena, in a court or other duly constituted tribunal having jurisdiction over pending litigation.

Statutes also exist that require hospitals and medical personnel to report certain medical facts to public authority in particular circumstances. Such requirements differ from state to state, and those providing medical care must be familiar with local law. Virtually all states require reporting vital statistics. Usually deaths and births must be reported, and many states also require reporting of fetal deaths[36] and abortions.[37] The statutes are constitutional as a legitimate exercise of the police power to regulate public health, safety, and welfare.[38] Also typically required are reports on patients suffering from sexually transmitted and other contagious or infectious diseases as well as from wounds that may be the result of violent criminal acts.[39] Some of these statutes extend the reporting requirement to accidental or self-inflicted wounds. Abuse of drugs must be reported in California, Illinois, and some other states. All states require that treatment of infants who may be victims of child abuse or neglect must be reported. Failure to comply with the statutes and report such cases to the appropriate public authority may lead to civil liability in damages or to a criminal penalty.

Statutory reports

Quite apart from statutory duties to report certain medical information to public authority, if a physician or hospital knows that a patient's psychological condition represents a foreseeable serious risk to a third party, the institution or individual has a duty to disclose and warn of the danger. In a California case with a tragic outcome a male student was undergoing psychiatric treatment at a university hospital as a voluntary outpatient. Several psychotherapists employed by the hospital were aware that he had threatened to kill a particular individual. One of the psychologists determined that the student should be committed to a mental institution and requested the campus police to detain him, which they did. Later, however, the police released the student, who appeared to be rational, and subsequently the chief of the psychiatry department reversed the psychologist's order for detention.

Duty to warn third parties

Two months later the student did in fact kill his intended victim. In *Tarasoff v. Regents of the University of California,* a suit by the parents of the victim, the California court held that the duty of disclosure was superior to the duty of holding medical information confidential.[40] According to the court, the psychotherapists and their employer had a duty to exercise reasonable care to give threatened persons a warning that foreseeable dangers could arise from the patient's condition or treatment. Breach of the duty can result in liability for damages. In a case similar to *Tarasoff* a hospital operated by the federal government failed to disclose pertinent information about a mental patient at a trial court hearing to determine whether he should be discharged from the hospital. Following his discharge the patient killed his wife, and the hospital was held liable.[41]

The *Tarasoff* doctrine is limited to situations where the physician or psychotherapist knows or should know that the patient represents a serious or imminent threat to a readily identifiable victim. For reasons of policy there is no duty to warn an entire community or neighborhood in general terms of a person's unspecific threats to unspecified individuals. In a leading California case interpreting *Tarasoff,* the supreme court held that there was no duty to warn the community or the police that a juvenile delinquent released from governmental custody to the home of his mother had exhibited violent propensities toward young children.[42] Hence, there was no liability when the juvenile subsequently caused the death of a 5-year-old boy. In the absence of an imminent risk to an identifiable victim, the criminal act causing the death was not a foreseeable event.[43] Fundamentally, these limitations on the duty to warn third parties are the criteria for balancing an individual's right to confidentiality with a third person's right to know that a risk exists. The imminence and probability of the risks must be given weight along with identification of the probable victim to justify a conclusion that the third person's interests are paramount to those of the patient.[44] As a practical matter, the professional person who must balance these interests is in the unenviable position of having to predict violent behavior despite the fact that current medical knowledge has apparently not advanced to the point where self-injury or injury to others can be accurately foreseen.

Consistent with the traditional majority approach, the duty to exercise reasonable care in a given instance is typically a matter of law for the court to determine. If a duty of care to a third party is recognized, the further questions of breach of duty and proximate cause become matters of fact for a jury to resolve. Thus, foreseeability of harm in a given case is frequently a question for the jury. Hesitation to send this question to the jury may be the reason that some jurisdictions have apparently rejected the rule handed down in *Tarasoff,* or at least they have distinguished the case on its facts and have concluded in other cases that the physician-patient privilege establishing confidentiality of medical information prevails over a duty on the part of a doctor or therapist to warn others of danger.[45] Even California has declined to apply the principle of *Tarasoff* to a situation in which a psychiatrist was allegedly aware of a patient's suicidal tendencies and failed either to restrain the patient or warn the parents.[46]

Peer review statutes   "Peer review" is a vital activity under the Medicare statute intended to ensure the medical necessity, reasonableness, and quality of care given to Medicare beneficiaries. Under federal regulations,[47] to carry out their responsibilities peer review organizations (PROs) have the right to access patient records and other information. In turn, the PRO must hold the information in confidence and not disclose it except as authorized by law (for example, as aggregate data that does not identify an individual patient or healthcare provider).

A third party's legal right to receive medical information regarding a particular **Lien statutes** patient is further illustrated by hospital lien statutes, which exist in approximately one-third of the states. In simplest terms, the lien laws grant to the hospital a legal claim under which the cost of hospitalization is paid from damages that the patient recovers from a third party whose negligence or civil wrong caused the patient's hospitalization. In turn, the third party is entitled to access to the patient's medical chart without authorization by the patient.

Liability for Unauthorized Disclosure

Before undertaking a review of the legal theories on which a patient may sue for unauthorized disclosure of medical information, we should note the ethical and moral obligations involved. The Hippocratic oath requires physicians to hold inviolate and confidential all information entrusted to them by their patients. This ethical obligation may be incorporated in state rules and regulations governing the licensure of physicians and healthcare institutions, and its violation may be a cause for revoking or suspending a license. Whether violation of licensure regulations creates a civil cause of action for damages is, however, very much an open question legally.

At common law there was no doctrine of confidential or privileged communication between patient and physician. The common law recognized a doctrine of privileged communication in only three relationships: attorney-client, husband-wife, and minister/priest-parishioner. Accordingly, neither a doctor nor an institution was obligated under common law to hold medical information about patients confidential.

To correct this situation and establish a confidential relationship between physician and patient, the legislatures of most states have enacted laws known as "privileged communication statutes." Although these statutes differ somewhat in detail, the essence of the legislation is to declare that medical practitioners may not disclose any information that they acquire in attending patients in their professional capacity and that was necessary to the care and treatment of their patients. (As will be noted, a patient may waive this privilege; in that event the doctor is not prohibited from making such disclosures and could even be compelled by a court order to do so.)

It is important to note that the privileged communication statutes do not necessarily apply to out-of-court disclosures of medical information. They are applicable only to disclosures made in the course of judicial or quasi-judicial proceedings. Further, they do not apply to institutional providers of care. Hence an out-of-court disclosure of private medical information does not contravene the privileged communication statutes, and as a general rule an aggrieved patient may not base a civil cause of action for damages on an alleged violation of the statutes.[48]

Accordingly, a patient bringing an action against a physician or institutional provider, or both of these, for damages allegedly resulting from an unauthorized out-of-court disclosure of information must base the action on a common law tort or on a theory of contract law. There are three theories of action: defamation of character; invasion of privacy; or, as noted in some recent cases, breach of an implied contract to respect confidentiality.

Defamation   The tort of defamation arises from a written or oral communication to a third party of information about a living person that injures his or her reputation by diminishing the esteem, respect, or confidence in which the person is held or by exciting adverse or derogatory feelings against that person.[49] Traditionally a cause of action for defamation did not survive the death of a person whose reputation suffered damage. The modern trend, however, reverses the tradition, as illustrated by a federal court decision applying the law of New Jersey.[50]

A written communication injuring reputation is libel, and an oral communication is slander. In either event, the communication must be made ("published") to someone other than the aggrieved party. Accordingly, a physician's dictated letter addressed personally to a nurse suggesting that she may have committed a crime by administering a substitute for a prescribed medicine did not constitute libel.[51]

Although at common law some actions in defamation could succeed without proof of actual harm, the modern rule is that damage to reputation will not be presumed unless the defendant acted with malice or with "knowledge of falsity or reckless disregard for the truth."[52] This standard is particularly relevant to publications by newspapers or other media of communication to the public at large.

In the context of release of information from a medical record, however, the prospects of successful libel or slander suits against physicians and medical care institutions are slight indeed. In the first place, the truth of the published statement is a complete defense to either libel or slander in most jurisdictions, even in the absence of any legitimate motive or reason for its publication.[53] (Because this rule creates immunity regardless of motive and permits a morally indefensible dissemination of information, some states have modified the defense either by statute or case decision to provide that truth will be a defense only when the publication is made with a good motive or for a justifiable end.) The burden of proving the truth will normally be on the defendant. Even if not true, a published retraction by the defendant or evidence that a defamatory statement was published with a proper motive and a reasonable belief that it was true will generally provide a partial defense that can be considered in the reduction or mitigation of damages.

Even if a statement published about another without consent is quite untrue and adversely affects the subject's reputation, the law has long recognized two privileges that may afford a defense. There is an absolute privilege related to judicial proceedings and even proceedings by executive or administrative officers of government. Hence, when a hospital honored a court subpoena and disclosed a medical record indicating that plaintiff was under the influence of alcohol, a statement alleged to be false, there could be no liability based on defamation because the release was absolutely privileged.[54]

A qualified privilege exists where information is transmitted to a third party with proper motive or purpose and with the exercise of reasonable care that the information is true. Information may be published in good faith to protect or advance the legitimate interests of the publisher or to protect the interests of an individual recipient or of the public if persons publishing it reasonably believe themselves to be morally obligated to speak and make "fair comment" on matters concerning the public interest.[55] Specifically, a hospital or physician could normally release information to an insurance carrier, even without express consent of the patient, for the purpose of collecting hospitalization insurance benefits, without fear of being liable in damages for defamation. Similarly, governmental agencies having a legitimate interest in the care rendered a patient have a right to relevant information and a qualified privilege to release it. Even attorneys representing the patient's interest may be given medical information, although a better administrative practice would be to require an express consent from the patient before allowing an attorney access to the medical chart.

Hospitals and physicians may use information from medical records in their own defense when they are sued by a patient, or for internal administrative purposes.[56] The institution and the medical staff may use the charts of patients for medical research, for education, and for the proper implementation of peer review and quality assurance programs. In several jurisdictions the use of medical information for research is affirmatively approved by statute, and some statutes provide further that data can be shared with the state health commissioner or other public or private agencies engaged in research.[57]

In a Nebraska case, *Simonsen v. Swenson,* a physician disclosed to a hotel that his patient, a resident of the hotel, had a contagious venereal disease. In a suit alleging unwarranted disclosure of confidential information the court held that, even if the diagnosis was incorrect and hence untruthful, the defendant physician was protected from liability by reason of the qualified privilege delineated by the law of defamation. Because the information was transmitted in good faith without malice to a legitimately interested party, with a belief that there was a moral obligation to protect third parties, there could be no liability.[58]

Whether a publication was made in good faith with a reasonable belief and care respecting the truth may be a question for a jury to determine, as was held in a Utah case entitled *Berry v. Moench.*[59] A physician in Wyoming, acting on behalf of the parents of a young woman, wrote to the defendant physician asking about a young man who wished to marry her and who had been one of the defendant's psychiatric patients. Without authorization from the young man, the defendant wrote that the former patient had a psychopathic personality and suffered from depression. The patient's father had taken his own life. The patient himself had been married several times and had not supported his wives and children. He was in trouble with the authorities during World War II and was financially irresponsible. The Wyoming doctor passed this information on to the young woman's parents who refused their approval of the marriage and disowned the daughter when it took place.

These events gave rise to a suit founded upon libel in which the Supreme Court of Utah observed that the publisher of the facts had no interest of his own to protect, although a privilege might still exist to protect or advance the interests of third persons. However, a judgment for the defendant physician by the trial court was error as a matter of law because a factual issue was raised respecting the defendant's exercise of reasonable care to ascertain the truth of the communication. The physician had admitted some uncertainty about the source of all the transmitted information, having apparently relied to some extent on statements by a former wife of the patient. Accordingly, the possible failure to exercise care could be considered malice-in-law, a libelous publication without legal justification, and this issue was to be resolved by a jury. With respect to qualified privilege the court said:

> Where life, safety, well-being or other important interest is in jeopardy, one having information which could protect against the hazard, may have a conditional privilege to reveal information for such purpose. . . . But the privilege is not something which arises automatically and becomes absolute merely because there is an interest to protect. It has its origin in, and it is governed by, the rule of good sense and customary conduct of people motivated by good will and proper consideration for others. This includes due consideration for the subject being informed about as well as the recipient being protected.[60]

When a publication is motivated by spite or ill will (malice-in-fact), the publisher can be liable for punitive as well as compensatory damages. In a New Mexico case a physician who was examining a patient to determine the reason for her absence from school falsely reported to the school authorities that the 13-year-old girl was pregnant and refused to retract or correct the report after learning it was false. The refusal resulted in loss of privilege. Because a matter of alleged pregnancy is libelous per se when it is false, the plaintiff is entitled to compensatory damages without proof of actual monetary loss and is also entitled to punitive damages for malice-in-fact.[61]

In an action based on defamation, the question of malice justifying an award for punitive damages may be one for the jury, and the proper standard for the jury to consider is whether the publication was made with knowledge of falsity or with reckless disregard for its truth. In a Virginia case a pediatrician who had resigned from the medical staff of a hospital was quoted by a newspaper as saying that the reason for resigning was his inability to "condone the quality of gynecological and obstetrical medicine" at the hospital. The pediatrician denied making such a statement, and the newspaper editor had not verified the story. The two physicians remaining on the obstetrical staff brought suit against the newspaper for libel.[62] (Although a jury handed down a verdict for punitive damages, it was reversed because the jury had been improperly instructed by the judge, and a new trial was ordered.)

Because most hospitals and physicians uphold ethical standards and do not as a rule publish information that they know to be false or show a reckless disregard for the truth, the prospect of their being held liable for punitive damages is minimal.

Invasion of privacy

Separate from the tort of defamation is the civil wrong of invasion of privacy. Invasion of privacy as a tort was recognized and developed by the courts following publication of a famous law review article in 1890, which illustrates the profound influence that legal scholars can have on the process of judicial law-making.[63] The majority of courts have recognized the tort, although they have imposed certain limitations to discourage unwarranted litigation and to balance properly an individual's right to privacy with freedom of the press and of speech. A few states have recognized the right of privacy by enacting statutes that carefully delineate limitations to the cause of action.

Broadly defined, the right of privacy is the right to carry on one's personal affairs without unreasonable and serious interference that exceeds the limits of decent conduct and is offensive to persons of ordinary sensibilities. With respect to publication of private information to third parties or to the public, there is a legal wrong only when the recipient has no legitimate interest in the information.[64] In contrast to actions based on the law of defamation, the truth of an unwarranted publication is not necessarily a defense. On the other hand, of course, express consent to the publication is a defense.

An Ohio court, affirming the principle that an individual has a legally protected right of privacy, defined the right in the case syllabus as follows:

> An actionable invasion of the right of privacy is the unwarranted appropriation or exploitation of one's personality, the publicizing of one's private affairs with which the public has no legitimate concern, or the wrongful intrusion into one's private activities in such a manner as to outrage or cause mental suffering, shame or humiliation to a person of ordinary sensibilities.[65]

To succeed in an action for invasion of privacy it is not necessary for the plaintiff to prove monetary loss. Damages can be awarded for mental suffering. The right, however, is a personal one; the privacy of a deceased person cannot be invaded, and hence surviving relatives have no cause of action when the alleged tort occurs after death.[66] Nor does a person too young to be damaged by "mental distress" have any right of privacy that can be invaded. Similarly, in contrast to defamation, a corporation or a partnership cannot bring the action, although other legal theories will protect a business entity from unwarranted appropriation of its name or good will.[67]

Cases of invasion of privacy can be classified into four groups according to the factual situations. The first are those involving the unauthorized commercial appropriation of the plaintiff's name, personality, professional skills, or photograph. Most of these cases concern the use of plaintiff's name or picture without consent in connection with the commercial sale of defendant's product or for the promotion of a business. Some courts have extended the right of privacy to a second group of cases: the use of plaintiff's name or likeness for the defendant's own purposes or benefit, even thought the use was not commercial and even if the benefit to the defendant was not financial.[68] Perhaps in this category is the Pennsylvania trial court case of *Clayman v. Bernstein*.[69] A physician had photographed a patient's facial disfigurement for instructional purposes without consent. The plaintiff succeeded in preventing the use of the photographs to show the effect of the disability.

On the other hand, Ohio held that no relief could be granted when a magazine publisher and credit card company sold subscription lists to direct mail advertisers without the consent of the subscribers. The sale of mere names did not amount to an "appropriation" of "personalities."[70] Thus, not all of the cases involving the use or appropriation of a person's name or likeness can be reconciled. It seems clear that no wrong is committed by the mere mention of an individual's name, by reference to newsworthy public activities, or by merely gathering information about an individual.[71] Only when one seeks to take advantage of a person's reputation, prestige, or personal values does there appear to be an unwarranted appropriation of another's personality.

As already noted, however, professional healthcare personnel must exercise caution in their use of photographs obtained in caring for patients. Normally the mere taking of a photograph of a person is not an invasion of privacy, just as the mere mention of a name is not a civil wrong. When photographs are taken as a routine part of a patient's care, for the benefit of the patient and in accordance with acceptable professional standards, and when the photographs are then made a part of the medical record, no appreciable legal issue is presented. Like other parts of the record, such photographs can be used by the medical staff of the hospital in evaluating standards and patterns of care and for scientific or research purposes, at least when the patient's anonymity is preserved.[72] To prevent any possible risk of liability, however, in light of *Clayman* and other cases, it is sound administrative practice to have the patient consent expressly to the photography.

Photography of a kind that does not accord with professional standards of medical practice or photographing the patient without consent could constitute an invasion of privacy and be within the third category of cases, a physical intrusion into one's private affairs. Moreover, the unauthorized use and publication of the pictures might also fall within the fourth group of privacy cases: where private information is made public to those who have no legitimate concern or interest in the information.[73]

An unjustified and unwarranted physical intrusion into a person's private domain or affairs constitutes a well-recognized invasion of privacy.

Tapping a plaintiff's telephone wires and listening to conversations on a dictaphone have both been held to be actionable wrongs.[74] Similarly, entry into a woman's bedroom and a lay intruder's witnessing of a childbirth without the patient's consent constituted wrongful acts.[75] "Bugging" the apartment bedroom of a married couple by the landlord was said to be an intrusion on the plaintiff's right to physical and mental seclusion.[76] These litigated cases exemplify acts that cause mental suffering or humiliation to a person of ordinary sensibilities.

In healthcare such cases may arise when physicians or hospitals permit lay visitors to be present during surgery or diagnostic examinations of a patient. Such a practice is an invasion of patients' privacy, unless they are made aware of the visitor's presence and the reason for it and have consented to it. Teaching hospitals should make clear to patients that medical students may from time to time accompany house staff and physicians who are administering care and treatment, and it should be explained that the opportunity to observe is an integral part of the students' education.

Perhaps the most difficult privacy cases are those in the fourth group: where private information is revealed to individuals or the public without serving a legitimate concern or interest. The courts must delicately balance several related issues. In a general sense, the tort of invasion of privacy is founded on recognition of an individual's right to be let alone and to be free from unwarranted disclosure of private information, especially the mass dissemination of information. On the other hand, public policy frequently requires that information be made public to ascertain the truth and to promote justice. Ascertaining truth is particularly important in litigation and other adversary situations. The legitimate interests of the publisher may outweigh the interest of the individual who asserts an invasion of privacy. Issues of freedom of speech and of the press are frequently present in cases claiming an invasion of privacy, at least when medical information concerning an individual is published in a magazine or newspaper.

When publication of private information violates concepts or ordinary decent conduct and serves no legitimate purpose it is an invasion of privacy. In a leading case a newspaper, a hospital and a photographer were enjoined from publishing pictures of a deceased malformed child.[77] When a national magazine published a photograph and story of a young woman suffering from a metabolism imbalance that caused her to consume a fantastic amount of food there was an invasion of privacy.[78] A psychiatrist was liable for compensatory damages for publishing intimate, private information regarding the thoughts and emotional characteristics of a former patient, even though the plaintiff was not named specifically.[79] In a Kentucky case a store owner posted a large sign in the window announcing that the plaintiff had not paid a debt; this act of publication went beyond the limits of decent conduct and was held unreasonable and oppressive.[80]

On the other hand, a majority of courts have determined that a creditor may, without invading the employee's privacy, notify an employer that the employee has not paid a legitimate debt because the creditor has an interest in pursuing collection and the employer also may have an interest in the credit standing of an employee.[81] Minnesota's Supreme Court ruled that the plaintiff's privacy was not invaded when a clerk in the hospital's credit section demanded payment of an outstanding hospital bill in the presence of several others while the plaintiff was seeking to have a son admitted to the hospital.[82] In voicing the demand the hospital employee added that the debt had been included in a petition for bankruptcy filed in court by the plaintiff. The Minnesota court reasoned that the bankruptcy was a matter of public record, that only a few persons witnessed the demand, and that under the circumstances the behavior of the hospital's employee did not amount to undue or oppressive publicity.

Disclosure of private information may be privileged on the basis that revelation protects the interest of others. Release of medical information without the express consent of the patient to persons and organizations having a legitimate interest in the information would not ordinarily constitute an invasion of the patient's privacy, nor would a release of information to advance the legitimate interests of the hospital or attending physician.[83]

Individuals and organizations having such an interest include attorneys for the patient, insurance carriers, various governmental agencies, bona fide research personnel, and family members in some circumstances.[84] For example, during the marriage a husband is entitled to information relating to his wife's medical condition, and a subpoena seeking that information in connection with a pending divorce proceeding is proper.[85] In contrast, a New York court has held that a psychiatrist was not justified in disclosing a former patient's mental condition to the spouse unless lack of disclosure would present a danger to the patient, the spouse, or a third person.[86] In another example, *Iverson v. Frandsen,* a child suffered from claustrophobia so severe as to prevent her attendance at school. The mother took the child to a state institution, which administered an intelligence quotient test and reported the score to the child's school. In a suit against the state institution the court denied recovery.[87] There is also a common law to warn persons who may be exposed to or at risk of contracting contagious disease, including members of the patient's family and persons rendering care.[88]

In addition to these circumstances in which disclosure is permissible, actions by a patient may result in a waiver of any possible right to confidentiality of medical information. In a New York case a civilian employee of the U.S. Air Force who had been absent from work asked his physician to certify that he was ill. The physician did so on several occasions without revealing the diagnosis of the illness. When the Air Force requested additional information about the patient's condition, the doctor, after first notifying the employee, reported that the patient was an alcoholic. An action against the physician was unsuccessful on the basis that the patient had requested partial disclosure and thus was prevented from asserting any civil wrong when full disclosure was later asked for by the employer.[89] On such facts the patient had waived any right to confidentiality of the information, although the court apparently recognized that had there been no waiver the physician would have had a duty of confidentiality. This duty derives from New York's privileged communication statute respecting courtroom testimony and from the medical practice act providing that "unprofessional conduct" is a basis for disciplining a physician. Privileged communications statutes and their effect are more fully discussed below.

Persons who consent to publicity or who place themselves in the public eye through their activities and exploits—for example, authors, actors, or candidates for public office—waive their rights of privacy to the extent that the public has a legitimate interest in newsworthy events.[90] This principle applies also to persons who are not considered public figures but who voluntarily take actions or are victims of circumstances that put them temporarily in the public eye. Unless news stories and photographs exceed the bounds of ordinary decent conduct, as discussed earlier, persons cannot complain when, for example, the press reports an accident that they are involved in, when they commit a crime that is publicized, or when they figure in any other newsworthy event, so long as the publicity is not misleading or the facts misrepresented.

Illustrative of the public's interest in a newsworthy event is a decision by a 1981 federal court of appeals. In an article on medical malpractice and its causes, a magazine identified an anesthesiologist and mentioned that suits against the physician were pending. To illustrate a presumably typical failure of the corporate hospital and its medical staff to exercise proper discipline the article described the doctor's psychiatric and personal problems. All of the facts related in the article were true. Because professionals' actions or failures to act in self-disciplinary matters are newsworthy events, the plaintiff's suit for invasion of privacy did not succeed.[91]

Ordinarily a hospital's release of information acknowledging an individual's admission to the hospital, naming the physician, and describing in general terms a medical condition presents no legal risk of liability for invasion of privacy.[92] If, however, the mere fact of admission could reveal the presence of mental illness or a disease thought to be shameful and humiliating—as might occur, for example, when the institution in question was known to treat only alcoholics or those suffering from mental illness—then an announcement of admission could lead to liability, at least if the patient was not a public figure. Thus, a news story on surfing in a national sports magazine was not privileged to disclose bizarre details concerning a surfer's private life because freedom of the press and of speech does not extend to the publication of unnewsworthy and embarrassing private affairs.[93] As in many other cases of invasion of privacy, the truth of the published matters was not a defense to the action.

Another actionable invasion of privacy occurred when a newspaper story concerning a special education class in a public school included photographs in which pupils were named and described as "retarded" and "trainable mentally retarded." The children had not become "public figures" by merely being enrolled in the class, and hence the publication offended concept of ordinary decency.[94]

Publishers and others broadcasting newsworthy events to the general public—including hospitals that permit access to news reporters—must also be aware that they may be liable for the torts of defamation and invasion of privacy. It will be remembered that truth is a defense to a cause of action founded on defamation, but what legal duty does the publisher have to ascertain the truth before publication? Normally, as noted earlier in this chapter, truth is an affirmative defense and the burden of proof is on the defendant, However, in the publication of matters of public interest this rule has gradually been relaxed to make more meaningful the constitutional guarantees of freedom of the press.

Formerly the press was strictly liable for publishing false and defamatory statements, strict liability being found to exist regardless of a defendant's intent to injure the plaintiff's reputation and the standard of care exercised in ascertaining truth. In general a qualified privilege was not extended to newspapers and other media because the defendant's interest in publishing was deemed commercial in nature. Thus, the news media were legally in the position of being insurers of the truth of published materials.[95]

In 1964, however, the Supreme Court determined that the doctrine of strict liability represented an encroachment on freedom of the press as expressed in the First Amendment to the Constitution. Accordingly in *New York Times v. Sullivan,* a landmark case, the Court held that an elected public official could recover in a cause of action based on defamation only if there was proof that a false publication was the result of "actual malice,"[96] malice meaning that the defendant had "knowledge that [the statement] was false" or published "with reckless disregard of whether it was false or not."[97]

In connection with a plaintiff who is not a public figure, the Supreme Court has ruled that each state may determine for itself the standard of liability when a news source publishes allegedly defamatory statements, as long as the standard is not that of strict liability.[98] Some state courts have adopted the same criteria for private persons as expressed in *Sullivan* for public personalities;[99] others have modified the rules slightly by requiring a finding of gross negligence or irresponsibility.[100] The majority of the states, however, have applied a more stringent standard and now hold the defendant liable for ordinary negligence in failing to ascertain the truth of published material. Ordinary negligence means that the defendant knew or should have known that the statement was false or would create a false impression in some material respect.[101]

These decisions illustrate once more the conflict between opposing public policies in current society. On one hand, constitutional law encourages freedom of the press and the public's right to know. On the other hand is the duty to protect individuals' rights to keep their private affairs from being known. A proper balance must be struck, but in an open, democratic society this is not easy.

On the question of releasing recorded medical information without the consent of the patient, healthcare institutions and physicians run little risk of liability based on allegations of defamation or invasion of privacy when the release benefits the publisher in some way or when the third party has a legitimate interest in the information.[102] The patient's primary protection is derived from the ethical standards accepted by the medical community, not from the law of defamation or invasion of privacy.

Breach of contract

The relatively slight legal protection afforded the patient from the classical and traditional torts of invasion of privacy and defamation, the increasing array of third parties claiming access to medical records, the development of automated systems of record-keeping, and the growth of centralized computer data banks have occasioned much concern about the maintenance of confidentiality. Certainly the computer and the tremendously enlarged role of government and third parties in financing medical care have increased the risk of misuse and unjustified disclosure of private information. Current economics of healthcare and modern technology have thus combined to intensify the threat to individuals' privacy rights.

Hence the implementation of ethical standards regarding disclosure of confidential information—at least the implementation of institutional policies—needs to be strengthened to make certain that only legitimately interested third parties have access to medical information and that such parties use the information only for proper purposes. There is also a need to strengthen the patient's legal right to insist on confidentiality. It now appears that some courts are willing to take that step by developing a third theory to protect patients as distinct from the torts of defamation and invasion of privacy. Legislative bodies too are exhibiting a greater interest in protecting confidentiality, and examples of these legal developments will be noted. This third theory being developed by judicial law can be labeled liability for breach of the physician-patient contract.

As long ago as 1851 a court in Scotland held that an implied term of the physician-patient contract required the physician to retain the confidentiality of medical information obtained in treating the patient.[103] Until recently, however, no American cases provided such straightforward legal reasoning, in spite of the well-accepted ethical standards of the Hippocratic oath and the American Medical Association.[104] The Alabama Supreme Court broke new ground when it held in 1973 that a physician who furnished medical information to a patient's employer without consent could be liable for breach of contract when as a result of the disclosure the patient was dismissed from work.[105]

The basis for the decision by the Alabama court was simply that a mutual intent to maintain confidentiality arises from the doctor-patient relationship as a consequence of common understanding. Only a supervening public interest or significant private interest of the patient would override the contract and justify disclosure. The court also adopted the view that the physician-patient relationship is fiduciary in nature and, accordingly, the doctor has a duty to maintain confidentiality. In support of this view the court referred to the medical licensure statute, which states that willful betrayal of a professional secret forms a basis for revoking a physician's license to practice medicine.[106] Note that the traditional law of invasion of privacy would have undoubtedly insulated the doctor from liability by recognizing a privilege of disclosure, assuming that the employer could be recognized as a legitimately interested party. But if breach of contract is acknowledged as a basis for liability, no such privilege is granted. The same contractual principle could be applied to the hospital-patient relationship as well.

In *Hammonds v. Aetna Casualty and Surety Company* a federal district court found a physician liable for disclosure of information on a unique set of facts. A hospitalized patient was injured when a bed collapsed. The same insurance carrier had insured both the hospital and the patient's attending physician. When the patient filed a claim against the hospital, the carrier claimed that the physician was also to be sued, although this was not true, and prevailed upon the doctor to make a medical report on the patient's condition. Both the carrier and the physician were held liable for actual damages, the doctor's liability apparently being based on an implied contractual obligation to maintain confidentiality of the patient's medical record.[107] The court indicated that maintenance of confidentiality was more important as a matter of public policy than granting a privilege of disclosure based on the interests of the insurance carrier. In reaching this conclusion the court made reference to the ethical standards of the medical profession, to the Ohio Medical Practice Act, which requires licensed physicians to refrain from betraying a professional secret, and to the Ohio privileged communication statute, which precludes a physician from testifying in court with respect to confidential information.

As noted previously in this chapter, most courts in the past have said that violation of licensing statutes and of rules and regulations providing for confidentiality of medical information may justify suspending or revoking a license to practice medicine, but that violation does not form the basis of a private cause of action in favor of the patient.[108] The same has been said of the privileged communication statutes because they apply only to court or quasi-judicial proceedings. Further, even if a patient can base a private action for damages on a violation of licensure laws or privileged communication statutes, no liability for disclosure without consent results when the disclosure fulfills a more important moral or social duty to protect the interests of a third party or the public.[109] Both of these rules may be changed or significantly modified as additional decisions impose a contractual duty of nondisclosure on the doctor and the healthcare institution to maintain the confidentiality of medical records. This can be done simply by reference to professional ethical standards or to specific provisions of licensing statutes and regulations, or by implication from the privileged communication statutes. In that event privilege of disclosure, in the context of the defamation and invasion of privacy cases previously discussed, will be significantly curtailed. Such a result is especially likely when information is released to a third party adverse to the patient.[110]

Statutory Provisions Mandating Confidentiality

Physicians and hospital personnel must be familiar with local and federal statutes and regulations that create a positive duty not to release medical information in specific circumstances. For example, New York's mental hygiene law declares that officials of state mental institutions shall not make case records available except as provided in the law. Violation of this state statute created civil liability to a patient when a hospital director released the record to an adverse attorney.[111] The majority of states recognize that the records of the mentally ill are peculiarly sensitive and have accordingly enacted statutes protecting the confidentiality of medical information pertaining to patients treated in state mental hospitals.[112] Most of these laws, however, do not apply to the records of noninstitutionalized patients receiving mental health services elsewhere in the community. Each of the statutes also provides for various exceptions to the general prohibitions on disclosure. State legislation of this nature does not usually grant the patient access to the record, although some statutes do recognize that the patient has a right of access.[113]

The Illinois statute is an example of comprehensive legislation that grants mental patients or a parent or guardian access to the medical records and applies principles of confidentiality to all services related to mental health or developmental disability furnished by physicians, psychiatrists, psychologists, social workers, and nurses in the community at large.[114] The personal notes of a therapist are not held to be a part of the medical record,[115] but no information in the record itself can be disclosed without written consent of the patient, parent, or guardian[116] except to professional colleagues, peer review committees, and institutions having legal custody of the patient.[117] Furthermore, the statute includes detailed provisions relating to testimonial disclosures in judicial and quasi-judicial proceedings.[118] Violation of these mandated provisions is both a criminal and civil offense; the patient can sue for an injunction and may also seek damages, including recovery of attorney fees.[119]

Although most states protect to some extent the confidentiality of records relating to certain mentally ill persons, only a few jurisdictions have legislation designed to protect the information typically found in the medical record compiled by an institution or a professional practitioner for medical-surgical patients. Most states have simply not addressed the matter systematically and rely instead on the common law, ethical standards, and standards of the Joint Commission on Accreditation of Healthcare Organizations to protect patients' interests, as previously discussed.

Some states have adopted wholly or in part the model legislation recommended by the American Medical Association or the National Association of Insurance Commissioners.[120] Rhode Island's statute, for example, prohibits disclosures of information by a provider of healthcare without a patient's consent unless one of the several enumerated exceptions applies.[121] Among those authorized to receive information from a provider without the patient's consent are medical peer review committees, scientific researchers and program evaluators, financial auditors, third-party payors, state insurance regulators, other providers in an emergency, and governmental agencies as designated by mandated reporting laws. Further, providers possessing medical information may use it for their own administrative purposes—accreditation, risk management, reimbursement, and defense of legal actions. Violations of the statute give the patient a cause of action for actual and punitive damages. Determining actual damages is difficult, however, because the most common consequence of an unauthorized release of accurate medical information is simply embarrassment or mental anguish. Not often, for example, does a patient lose a job or suffer other serious loss solely as a result of disclosure of confidential data. To recover punitive damages the aggrieved party must further prove that the disclosure was made maliciously.

The most comprehensive statutory scheme attempted to date has been adopted in California. Like that in Rhode Island, California's Confidentiality of Medical Information Act applies to all records containing "medical information" relating to a patient's medical history, mental or physical condition, or treatment by any licensed or certified individual, group, or institutional provider of healthcare.[122] "Medical information," however, does not include the patient's name, address, age, sex, or the general reason for treatment and the general condition of the patient. A provider of care can therefore furnish this "nonmedical" information to a third party unless the patient has signed a specific written request to the contrary.[123]

Disclosures of medical information in the absence of written consent are prohibited unless compelled by court order, an administrative agency's authority, or some other legal process. The legislation lists other circumstances in which release of information is permitted without the patient's consent. Others serving the patient, such as insurance companies, third-party payors, and administrators of healthcare plans, as well as peer review committees and organizations, licensing and accreditation agencies, research groups, and in certain circumstances employers are all authorized to receive medical information.[124] The statute sets up certain criteria for the written consent form[125] and further provides that no recipients of information may disclose the information to others without a new authorization unless they are specifically permitted by law.[126] Redisclosures by insurance companies and governmental agencies are controlled by separate statutes.[127]

Violations of the Confidentiality of Medical Information Act constitute a criminal misdemeanor.[128] In a civil action a patient may recover both compensatory and punitive damages, the latter being limited to a maximum award of $3,000 plus attorney fees of $1,000 and costs of litigation.[129]

At the federal level the Medicare Conditions of Participation provide specifically that only "authorized" personnel shall have access to the record and that "the hospital must have a procedure for ensuring the confidentiality of patient records."[130] Breach of these conditions could lead to exclusion from the Medicare program.

Federal legislation such as the Comprehensive Drug Abuse Prevention and Control Act of 1970,[131] the Drug Abuse Office and Treatment Act of 1972,[132] and the Comprehensive Alcohol Abuse and Alcoholism Prevention, Treatment, and Rehabilitation Act Amendments of 1983[133] imposes stringent requirements for maintaining the confidentiality of records of patients receiving treatment for drug dependency and alcoholism under programs supported by federal funds. The legislation applies to all federally assisted healthcare providers, whether the assistance is direct for research on the abuse of drugs or alcohol or indirect through Medicare, Medicaid, or other governmental programs. Together, the statutes and attendant regulations[134] provide that medical information is to be disclosed only to those connected with the program. Family members, law enforcement officials, and courts have no access except as specifically provided, unless the patient has given express written consent to the disclosure. The consent form must contain certain detailed information, including the purpose of the disclosure, the name of the recipient, the precise nature of the information to be released, and the length of the time the consent is valid. Specially drafted consent forms are thus necessary for each disclosure of information. These requirements apply to the medical records for all patients receiving therapy for drug and alcohol abuse, whether minors or adults, and cover the patient's identify, the treatment provided, and the diagnosis and prognosis. Not even the parents or guardian of a minor can receive information without the minor's consent unless some physical or mental condition or a patient's very young age renders an independent decision impossible. Providers who violate these consent requirements are subject to a criminal fine.

Disclosures without a patient's consent can be made only to personnel in drug or alcohol programs, to other providers when a medical emergency arises, to organizations conducting research and evaluations as long as particular patients are not identified, and by special court order based on good cause.[135] Consequently, patients cannot be identified in any civil, criminal, or administrative procedure, and information cannot be released to law enforcement officials without a specific court order. The normal initiation of civil or criminal proceedings and the usual procedural rules for the issuance of a subpoena do not justify breach of the patient's right to confidentiality. Hospital and medical personnel must therefore develop policies to prohibit release of all medical information concerning drug or alcohol patients, including the identity of the patient, without a court order. In the course of granting such an order, the judge in effect determines what information should be released.

Courts have ordered release of information in proceedings to revoke criminal probation,[136] in connection with child neglect,[137] and in an investigation by the Internal Revenue Service.[138] In contrast, good cause for a disclosure was not established in a criminal proceeding to determine a person's potential for rehabilitation[139] and when the credibility of a witness was in question.[140] A New York court protected the confidentiality of photographs that had been taken in the waiting room of a methadone treatment clinic and were later sought by law enforcement officials in connection with the investigation of a murder.[141] Where the medical records of a patient in a drug abuse program contained information likely to exonerate a patient from involvement in an alleged crime, however, procedural due process would require disclosure.[142] A judicial *in camera* review is often necessary to determine "good cause" and what portion of the record should be released.

Underlying the stringent requirements is the thought that the assurance of nearly absolute confidentiality will encourage patients to seek help for drug and alcohol abuse. Such a position frequently overlooks other, contradictory statutory requirements based on conflicting public policies. Thus a balancing of interests and compromise is often necessary.

Contradictory goals of public policy, each legitimate standing alone, require compromise in some contexts. A Minnesota case illustrates the conflict between the federal alcohol abuse legislation and the mandatory reporting of child abuse required by state statute.[143] In a criminal proceeding the defendant had been charged with sexually abusing a 10-year-old stepdaughter and an 11-year-old niece. The state filed a motion for access to the defendant's medical records compiled under an alcohol abuse program maintained by a medical center. The defendant had been arrested and had then voluntarily entered the program before being charged with sexual abuse. Interpreted literally and standing alone the Comprehensive Alcohol Abuse and Alcoholism Prevention, Treatment, and Rehabilitation Act Amendments of 1974[144] would have prohibited the reporting of child abuse as required by state statute[145] if the report identified a patient as a drug or alcohol abuser. The federal law purports to preempt state law.[146] The Minnesota Supreme Court, however, quickly determined otherwise and held that the alcohol treatment act does not bar either the reporting of child abuse or the use of medical records in subsequent criminal proceedings to the extent permitted by state law. Because the same 1974 Congress enacted both the Alcohol Treatment Act and Federal Child Abuse Prevention Act of 1974,[147] which in turn required the states to pass mandatory reporting laws as a condition for receipt of federal funds in support of child abuse programs, Congress could not have intended to preempt the state statutes.[148]

Having disposed of that issue the court then identified the type of information that could be used in the criminal proceeding. This matter was determined by reference to both the statute mandating reports of child abuse[149] and the state's statute on privileged communication.[150] In the context of this case the question for decision was: does the reporting of child abuse totally abrogate patients' statutory privilege to maintain confidentiality of their medical records in judicial proceedings?

In the criminal proceeding the court answered that question in the negative and in accordance with the reporting law ordered disclosure of the identities of the abused children, their parents or guardians, and the persons who made the report, as well as the nature and extent of the injuries. The prosecution was not entitled, however, to medical information gathered by professionals treating such patients. Information acquired in group therapy sessions was also protected because those sessions were an integral part of the patient's diagnosis and treatment. To this extent the state's privileged communication statute prevailed. Three dissenting justices would have abrogated the evidentiary privilege completely, viewing the complete protection of children as paramount to a patient's statutory privilege of confidentiality.[151]

Federal Freedom of Information and Privacy Laws

The Freedom of Information Act, passed by Congress in 1966 and amended on several later occasions, is based on the premise that much government information should be available for public inspection and scrutiny. The legislation responded to well-articulated views that the processes of government should be open to the public and that regulatory agencies should be accountable to their constituencies.

Although the Freedom of Information Act contains specific exemptions to the government's duty to disclose, it was apparent by the early 1970s that the confidentiality of certain information in the hands of governmental agencies needed further protection. Thus the Privacy Act of 1974 was passed to restrict the disclosure of individually specific information. Several other federal statutes and accompanying regulations also address issues of confidentiality regarding particular classes of information: for example, information from the medical records of patients in Veterans Administration facilities, of those receiving care under federally supported alcohol and drug treatment programs, and of those whose expenses are reimbursed by the Medicare program, as discussed in the preceding section.

It should be emphasized that the federal freedom of information and privacy statutes do not apply generally to disclosure of information by private practitioners or providers of medical care. In such circumstances the matters of statutory or judicial privacy and confidentiality will usually be governed by state law. This fact may indicate that the general public and their elected representatives in Congress do not perceive lack of confidentiality to be a serious problem.

The Freedom of Information Act requires that "governmental agencies" disclose "agency records" to the public.[152] Federal district courts are authorized to enjoin an agency from withholding agency records and to order "the production of any agency records improperly withheld from the complainant." Requests for records can be made by any member of the public or by an organization with sufficient interest in the subject matter.

An agency's duty to disclose is tempered by several explicit statutory exemptions. Four express exemptions relate to healthcare:

- Exemption 3 relates to information "specifically exempted from disclosure by statute,"[153] provided that the statute in question grants no discretion on the issue or that it establishes particular criteria for withholding information;
- Exemption 6 pertains to "personnel and medical files and similar files the disclosure of which would constitute a clearly unwarranted invasion of personal privacy";[154]
- Exemption 5,[155] intended to cover the work product of an attorney, will occasionally be an issue in healthcare cases, as will
- Exemption 4[156] relating to trade secrets and privileged financial information.

The latter is particularly relevant to the pharmaceutical industry. As would be expected, the breadth and reach of these exemptions have been the subject of extensive litigation.

According to the statutory language the Freedom of Information Act applies to "governmental agencies," which immediately presents the question of defining an agency of government. For example, the 1972 amendments to the Social Security Act required that professional standards review organizations (PSROs) be established by professional groups to review the medical necessity, quality, and appropriateness of services provided Medicare and Medicaid beneficiaries. PSROs were private, not-for-profit organizations formed by statute with defined governmental powers and functions. Because Congress often delegates governmental functions to private organizations, the legislative intent behind the Freedom of Information Act must be ascertained in seeking definitions of both "agency" and "agency's records."

The Supreme Court has held that the receipt of federal funding does not make the recipient an agency of government.[157] Moreover, data and information in the hands of a research grantee and never in "possession" of the governmental grantor do not constitute the "records" of an agency, even if government relies on the data in its decisions.[158] In the formulation of these conclusions it was immaterial that the government had a right of access to the information. An essential prerequisite then to a duty of disclosure is that any agency of government have actual "possession and control" of the information sought.[159] Moreover, a private party may not force the government to retrieve documents removed from agency files without authority by an official.[160] Thus the Supreme Court has rather narrowly interpreted the related concepts of "agency" and the "possession" of records.

On the basis that the Supreme Court's decision in *Forsham v. Harris*[161] required extensive day-to-day supervision by government before an organization could qualify as a governmental agency, a district court held that a PSRO was not subject to the Freedom of Information Act.[162] A contrary decision had been rendered previously in another district court[163] and then reversed.[164] Certain documents and records originating with the PSRO were therefore not available to the party requesting the information. The precise issue with respect to the federal review program was rendered partially moot when Congress later enacted an express, although limited, exemption from the freedom of information requirements for records maintained by a professional standards review organization. An exemption from disclosure was granted for one year following a court order requiring disclosure, or on the final day of a congressional session in progress at the time the court order was entered, whichever was later.[165] The PSRO statute enacted initially in 1972 has now been replaced by new legislation establishing a somewhat different form of review organization with the simpler name of professional review organization.[166] Access to peer review data required by the federal government thus remains at issue, and the continuing judicial and legislative activity that it generates illustrates the difficulty of determining congressional intent when the philosophies of confidentiality, on one hand, and the right to know, on the other, conflict so dramatically.

Perhaps even better examples of conflicting philosophies are cases involving disclosure of cost reports prepared by providers participating in the Medicare program and then filed with the fiscal intermediary administering the reimbursement arrangements. These reports reveal a provider's detailed expenditures and financial position. So far as the Medicare regulations are concerned, disclosure of these reports to the public is permitted on receipt of a written request.[167] In conflict with these regulations, however, is exemption 4 of the Freedom of Information Act, which provides that "commercial or financial information obtained from a person and privileged or confidential" need not be disclosed.[168] This exemption is commonly referred to as the "trade secrets" exemption to the act, and it applies when disclosure is likely to cause substantial harm to the competitive position of the organization from which the information was obtained.

The Trade Secrets Act, in turn, imposes criminal sanctions on any employee of a federal agency who discloses confidential data on the profit or loss or on the expenditures of any person or business organization unless authorized by law.[169] The dilemma then is this: are the Medicare cost reports in the category of "trade secrets" the disclosure of which would be likely to harm the subject's competitive position? Or is the issue controlled by Section 1106 of the Social Security Act and the accompanying regulations authorizing disclosure in the public interest?

Prior to 1979 several lower courts had held that a provider's Medicare cost reports need not be disclosed, and in each of these cases the party seeking confidentiality prevailed.[170] In effect the courts took the view that exemption 4 of the Freedom of Information Act was paramount because disclosure of cost data would be likely to harm the provider's competitive position. Worth noting is that all of these cases denying disclosure involved proprietary hospitals, but the decisions were not based solely on that fact. In 1979, however, the Supreme Court held in *Chrysler Corporation v. Brown* that a private party who is required to provide information to the government has no private cause of action to force a governmental agency to invoke an exemption to the Freedom of Information Act and enjoin threatened disclosure.[171] In essence the Court held that Congress intended the act to be a disclosure law and that it permits but does not require the government to refuse third-party requests for disclosure of information. In short, refusal of information is discretionary, not mandatory. Accordingly, when the Social Security Act and Medicare regulations authorize disclosure of Medicare cost reports, there is no violation of Section 1905 of the Trade Secrets Act.[172] Where the public has an interest, as it certainly does in the financing of Medicare, public policy leans in favor of disclosure rather than confidentiality, even if the information sought is presumably subject to an exemption from the Freedom of Information Act.

The Privacy Act of 1974[173] is to be compared with and is related to the Freedom of Information Act. The purpose of the Privacy Act is to restrict disclosure of information held by the federal government and governmental contractors that can be identified with individual persons. Further, the legislation permits the individual subject to obtain information in governmental files and to correct any misinformation. Generally the individual's consent is required prior to release of information, but the statute itemizes 12 exceptions to the right of confidentiality that allow disclosure without the subject's consent. Among the excepted disclosures are those required by the Freedom of Information Act. In light of this exception the Privacy Act standing alone does not constitute legal authority for refusing a third party access to the medical information relating to a Medicare beneficiary.

With respect to medical information relating to an individual the two statutes need to be read together. Exemption 6 to the Freedom of Information Act pertains to "personnel and medical files and similar files the disclosure of which would constitute a clearly unwarranted invasion of personal privacy."[174] Using this exemption, the government in its discretion could decline to disclose medical information requested by either a third party or a patient. On the other hand, the Privacy Act would clearly require the patient's consent for the release unless one of the exceptions permitting disclosure without consent applied. With respect to the Privacy Act, disclosure to third parties without the patient's consent is permitted whenever the data are routinely used to further the purposes for which the information was collected, in statistical research, and in law enforcement.

The scope of exemption 6 and its relation to the Privacy Act are yet to be determined. The Supreme Court has interpreted the freedom of information exemption rather narrowly in the context of personnel records (as distinct from medical records) by noting that information is exempt from disclosure only if "disclosure . . . would constitute a clearly unwarranted invasion of personal privacy."[175] In doubtful cases the statute itself authorizes a judicial *in camera* inspection to determine whether particular records or portions thereof should be withheld.[176] In spite of the Supreme Court's narrow interpretation, a federal trial court in Florida applied exemption 6 to a request for public disclosure of the names of physicians providing services to Medicare patients and the amount of reimbursement received by each.[177] The court said in effect that the Privacy Act should control and thus prohibited disclosure of this particular information without the physicians' prior written consent.

The limited ability, however, of the two federal statutes to prevent release of private information is illustrated by a decision of the Ninth Circuit Court of Appeals in *St. Michael's Convalescent Hospital v. State of California*.[178] The plaintiffs were corporate providers of care to Medicaid patients who had been reimbursed for this care by the state of California. The California Department of Health Services and the state's Health Facilities Commission possessed certain cost information that the plaintiffs had been required to file to qualify for reimbursement. In a suit to enjoin the release of the cost data the court held that neither the Freedom of Information Act nor the Privacy Act provided a basis for enjoining disclosure because the federal statutes apply only to federal agencies and not to state governmental agencies; furthermore, federal regulation of the state-administered Medicaid program did not amount to sufficient day-to-day supervision to allow the state's activities to be considered equivalent to federal action. In addition, the court observed that the Privacy Act protects only "individual(s)" and not corporations. Accordingly, plaintiff corporations lacked standing to assert in court that the legislation required the subject's prior consent for disclosure of the information. The opinion recognized, however, that cost data may constitute a "trade secret" amounting to "property" as contemplated by the Fifth and Fourteenth Amendments to the U.S. Constitution. If so, then a release of the information without plaintiffs' consent could amount to a "taking" of the "property" without due process by law, and the plaintiffs were thus entitled to amend their complaint to plead a constitutional claim, as distinct from the statutory claim. A constitutional argument based simply on the personal right of privacy, however, was rejected because cost information is not related to a "fundamental" personal right akin to those recognized in prior privacy cases: the right of procreation, the right to seek an abortion and to marry, and the right of access to information about contraception. Clearly there are no ready and simple answers to the questions that arise when asserted rights of confidentiality conflict with the rights of others to know.

State Open-Meeting Laws

A majority of states have statutes requiring governmental agencies to open their meetings to the public and to make available the minutes of the meetings, as well as certain other records, for public inspection. Sometimes these statutes are referred to as "sunshine" laws, connoting that the public is entitled to have daylight shed on the conduct of government affairs and has a right to information on which governmental decisions are based.

To ensure compliance by officials, the statutes typically provide that a violation of the public's right to know constitutes a criminal offense punishable by a fine. More significant, members of the public can usually enforce their statutory rights by a civil action in court seeking a *writ of mandamus* that compels compliance or an injunction ordering appropriate relief. Depending on the particular provisions of a given statute and the circumstances of the case, a court may be authorized to declare governmental decision made in violation of the statute to be null and void. In some states the plaintiff's attorney fees can be assessed against the public agency named in the suit or even against individual members of a board or agency.

As is true of any legislation, there is always the question of whether the statute applies to a particular set of facts. Most often the concept of a governmental "agency" includes governmental hospitals and public hospital authorities.[179] Moreover, the statutes typically apply to all levels of government: state, county, and municipal. Thus a county-owned hospital in Florida was subject to that state's Public Records Act, and the institution's personnel records were considered to be "public records" subject to inspection.[180] The records were not protected by either a statutory exception or a common-law right of privacy. In similar fashion the Georgia Supreme Court has held that a county hospital authority is subject to that state's legislation and that a newspaper had the right to access the names, job titles, and salaries of all employees earning more than $28,000.[181] In Florida *Gadd v. News-Press Publishing Company, Inc.* held that a newspaper was entitled to view a public hospital's medical staff personnel files and its utilization review documents.[182] Again, the Florida public Records Act did not provide a specific exception or an exemption for the records of a medical peer review committee. Although another Florida statute exempts peer review records and proceedings in an action against a provider of health services from both pretrial discovery and admissibility in evidence during litigation,[183] the *Gadd* court held that the apparent inconsistency between the two statutory schemes was a matter for the legislature to resolve. These cases are examples of the typical judicial approach to interpret the "sunshine" statutes liberally in accordance with legislative intent.

Private corporations are not normally subject to the open meeting laws, even if they receive financial support or other forms of assistance from government. Accordingly, a charitable hospital created by the terms of a private individual's will was not governed by the Massachusetts open-meetings law even though municipal bonds had been issued to support the institution, hospital trustees were elected by local voters, and legal title to the hospital's property was vested in the town.[184] The circumstances of each individual case must be matched with the law of the relevant jurisdiction, however, before categorical conclusions can be drawn with respect to applicability of the statutes to private organizations that have associations or contracts with government.

When, for example, a private, not-for-profit medical center in Florida leased space from a governmental hospital authority, certain records of the medical center were accessible to the news media.[185] Moreover, whenever a governmental function is delegated to a private organization, the open-meetings statute may apply. For example, in *Seghers v. Community Advancement, Inc.*, a not-for-profit corporation administering a governmental antipoverty program and actually making policy decisions was subject to the Louisiana statute.[186] Similarly, a corporation operating a municipal electric utility system could not claim exemption as a private organization.[187]

Some of the statutes can be construed as applying to committees of the agency's governing board and to the minutes or records of those committees, as in Florida.[188] The matter in many jurisdictions is not free from doubt, however, and is likely to be an issue in future litigation.

The majority of the statutes provide for certain exceptions to the right of public access. Sometimes these exceptions are cast in very general language, while in other states the exceptions are more specific. A court may also create an exception whenever there is a persuasive reason for limiting the applicability of the legislation. Typically the statutes will except meetings and records relating to pending litigation, negotiations with labor unions, acquisition of capital, such as the purchase of real estate, and disciplinary action against governmental personnel. Illustrating the latter, a New York case held that certain records of patients and interviews with various persons, which were used in a statutory disciplinary proceeding against a physician, were exempt from access insofar as the state's freedom of information law was concerned.[189] Also in New York it was found that a county medical center need not disclose medical records of patients, even with identifying information removed, because they are embraced within a specific statutory exception.[190] A further basis for the latter decision was that the freedom of information statute must be reconciled with the patient's right to maintain confidentiality of information in the medical record. The court concluded that it must have been the intent of the legislature to recognize the patient's right as paramount. In California the state's Medi-Cal (Medicaid) agency was permitted to refuse disclosure of a fiscal audit manual sought by the plaintiff hospital. The court felt that the manual contained critical information relating to the state's audit of Medi-Cal providers and that the interest of the public was best served by nondisclosure.[191] Courts are thus continually called on to balance and reconcile competing interests when confronted with specific requests for information.

In contrast to the foregoing situations in which access to information was denied, a public hospital had to release the records of a patient who brought an action based on Washington's Public Disclosure Act, even though the statute exempted personal information from disclosure.[192] The survey report by the Joint Commission of a governmental hospital was also accessible in a Pennsylvania case.[193] Because these reports are often used by state government as evidence of qualification for licensure for private hospitals, the survey may be classified as a public record and subject to disclosure unless the particular hospital delivered the report to the state with the express understanding that the report would be held in confidence.[194] In Minnesota the Data Privacy Act allowed public access to the names of physicians who received payment for abortion services they provided to state-assisted indigent patients.[195] Neither the patient nor the doctor had a right of privacy or a property interest of sufficient magnitude to prevent disclosure of the doctors' names, the court held. In similar fashion a consumer advocacy group had not only standing to sue under the Michigan Administrative Procedure Act but also the right of access to field reports and facility evaluation reports compiled by the Michigan Department of Public Health in the course of granting licenses to nursing homes.[196]

As in other situations, the matter of gaining access to information in possession of the government or private organizations performing governmental functions involves balancing various interests in a particular set of circumstances. The result in such cases will depend on the language of the relevant statute, judicial understanding of legislative intent, the purposes or motives of the plaintiff who seeks access, and the countervailing interests of the defendant or third parties.

Medical Records in Legal Proceedings

As mentioned previously the common law did not recognize the physician-patient relationship as privileged; accordingly, medical information entrusted to or acquired by a doctor was not confidential under the common law.[197] The vast majority of the states, however, have enacted privileged communication statutes that prohibit the physician (and perhaps other professional medical personnel, depending on the particular statute) from disclosing information in judicial or quasi-judicial proceedings unless the patient has waived the privilege or has consented to the disclosure. A typical statute reads as follows:

> The following persons shall not testify in certain respects: . . . A physician, concerning a communication made to him by his patient in that relation or his advice to his patient, except that the physician may testify by express consent of the patient or, if the patient is deceased, by the express consent of the surviving spouse or the executor or administrator of the estate of the deceased patient and except that, if the patient voluntarily testifies . . . the physician may be compelled to testify on the same subject, or if the patient, his executor or administrator, files a medical claim . . . the filing shall constitute a waiver of this privilege with regard to the care and treatment of which complaint is made.[198]

Statutory Privilege of Confidentiality

In general, privileged communication statutes are applicable to pretrial proceedings, such as motions for inspection and discovery of records; they are also applicable to investigations conducted by state legislative bodies. Thus the privilege is not confined to actual courtroom trials. As a general rule the privilege of confidentiality continues after the death of the patient and may be asserted by a descendant's estate.[199]

To create a privilege of confidentiality a patient-physician relationship must exist, and the information acquired by the physician must relate to the care and treatment of the patient. No privilege will be recognized if either element is absent. In *State of Washington v. Kuljis* a hospital staff doctor who drew a sample of a patient's blood to test for intoxication, and did so at the request of the police and with the apparent consent of the patient, had not established a patient-physician relationship, nor had he obtained information for the purpose of treating the patient. Consequently, the results of the test were admissible in evidence in a criminal prosecution.[200] The effect of a privileged communication statute is to prevent a physician or other professional person possessing confidential information from disclosing it in court or in quasi-judicial proceedings if, as will be explained, the patient asserts the privilege.

Modern procedural law, however, generally encourages liberal pretrial discovery practices as a means of ascertaining all material and relevant evidence that may be admissible subsequently at trial. Accordingly the parties to a civil lawsuit can usually be required to make depositions on medical issues arising during litigation, and their medical records are normally subject to subpoena. Parties to a lawsuit will ordinarily be said to have waived the privilege of confidentiality. In contrast, the medical records of one who is not a party to a legal proceeding are not generally subject to pretrial discovery or admissible in evidence, although as will be explained there is a decided trend toward a liberalization of this traditional approach. In essence, the usual effect of the privileged communication statutes is to protect the confidentiality of the medical records of anyone not a party to a judicial or quasi-judicial proceeding or when medical issues are not material or relevant to the issue.

Admissibility of Medical Records

In states without a privileged communication statute, or when the privilege does not apply or cannot be asserted by the patient, medical records are generally admissible as evidence in litigation under one or more of the exceptions to the rule of evidence that prohibits hearsay testimony. Medical records are considered hearsay evidence for several reasons. First, the information contained in a medical chart is compiled by persons not under oath. Second, these persons are frequently not available to testify in person in a trial, and thus their recorded statements are not subject to cross-examination by the adverse party.

However, the law of evidence has long recognized statutory and judicial exceptions to the hearsay rule. The foremost exception is the "business record rule," which is recognized in the statutes of nearly all states and in federal law. These statutes provide that records compiled in the regular course of business, at or near the time of the act or event under scrutiny, and for the purpose that such records are intended to serve are admissible as long as their authenticity is properly established. Medical records maintained by a physician or a hospital have frequently been held to fall within the business record exception.[201] Medical records may also be admissible under a rule very similar to the business records rule, namely the shopbook rule (a shopbook being an original record kept by tradesmen or shopkeepers to indicate accounts due for work or service performed). A third basis for admitting medical records in evidence is the view that they constitute public or official documents.[202] This is especially relevant in states with statutes that require that particular forms of medical records be kept and that itemize the types of information to be recorded. Finally, a few states have statutes providing specifically that medical records of certain hospitals are admissible. If the original records have been microfilmed and then destroyed the microfilms would normally be admissible as evidence in accordance with the foregoing criteria. Computer printouts have also been accepted as evidence.[203]

But even if records or parts of records are admissible in court under one of the exceptions to the hearsay rule, their authenticity and reliability must be established. In other words, a proper foundation must be laid for admissibility, and normally this is done by having the medical record librarian or other custodian of the documents testify in court as to the procedures used in compiling and maintaining current medical information. To be admitted, evidence must meet the additional rules that all courtroom testimony be relevant to the issue at hand and that only a medical expert may state a diagnosis or an opinion regarding the patient's medical or mental condition. For example, a hospital patient's history that included the statement "hit by a truck that was passing properly on the right" is not admissible as evidence in personal injury litigation as a business record because the statement pertains to a cause of the accident and not to the medical or surgical treatment of the patient. Moreover, the statement is an opinion based on hearsay of a lay person.[204]

In some jurisdictions legal authority allows records or excerpts from records to be received as evidence only when the person who entered the information in the chart is not available to testify in person. It should also be noted that the parties to litigation may affirmatively agree or stipulate that medical records will be received in evidence. In that event the hearsay rule and exceptions to it become irrelevant.

It is sound public policy to admit records in evidence during litigation, subject to the safeguards of materiality and relevance, when no privileged communication statute exists or when the patient has waived the right of confidentiality. The fundamental purpose of litigation should be to ascertain the truth and accomplish justice between the parties in an adversary situation. Records maintained in the regular course of a patient's care will presumably help establish that truth. Because physicians, nurses, and hospitals do not ordinarily falsify information describing the diagnosis and care rendered a particular patient, courts and quasi-judicial bodies receiving medical records can be confident that the information accurately reports the facts and medical opinions regarding the case. In addition, the records are frequently more reliable than personal recollections. Witnesses may be forgetful or they may not be available to testify in person. Even if they are available, the entries may have been made by so many different persons that it would be extremely time consuming and expensive if they all had to appear as witnesses. To exclude medical records from evidence because they are hearsay would defeat the legitimate goals of the judicial process.

Privileged communication statutes are thus contrary to the policy that the purpose of litigation is to determine the truth. By providing that medical information is to be held confidential and that a physician shall not be permitted to testify, they deprive a court or quasi-judicial body of the opportunity to receive evidence that could be relevant and material to the issues being litigated. As will be noted shortly, however, the privileged communication statutes do have many exceptions that in effect recognize that disclosure is frequently preferable to confidentiality.

Extent and Applicability of Statutory Privilege

The privileged communication statutes differ in detail and sometimes in major respects from state to state. All, however, extend the confidential privilege only to the patient, and not to the physician.[205] In other words, the physician may not assert a refusal to testify for personal reasons. Further, as noted earlier, the statutes pertain only to judicial or quasi-judicial proceedings and do not generally prohibit a doctor from disclosing medical record information out of court. Further, according to the traditional view, such disclosure does not give the patient a cause of action for alleged violation of the privilege statute. Some modern decisions involving civil liability, however, have cited the privilege statute as providing one more reason why a contractual duty of confidentiality should be imposed on a physician (and by analogy a hospital) by implication.[206]

The use of confidential information in court contrary to the privilege statute gives rise to a civil cause of action against the medical practitioner who discloses it, in the view of the South Dakota Supreme Court. In *Schaffer v. Spicer* a divorced woman was successful in an action against her psychiatrist, at least to the extent of obtaining a decision that issues of civil liability were presented. The woman and her former husband were preparing to engage in custody proceedings, and the case arose because the wife's psychiatrist prepared an affidavit for the husband's attorney in which the doctor disclosed confidential information reflecting unfavorably on the wife's fitness as a mother. The affidavit was intended for use in the pending custody proceedings and had not been ordered by the court.

By a majority ruling the South Dakota Supreme Court held that the privilege statute had been violated because the information had been acquired by the doctor in the course of treating the patient and the patient had not consented to the disclosure or waived her right of privilege, even though she had stated in the divorce action that she had been treated by the psychiatrist.[207]

The court also ruled that the concept of privilege and confidentiality was paramount to the interests and welfare of the children who were the subjects of the pending custody hearing. Despite this ruling, however, the doctor could perhaps be called as a witness in the hearing of the dispute and be compelled to testify on matters affecting the children's welfare. This would be possible if it were held that by seeking custody of her children the patient had waived her privilege of confidentiality.[208]

Privileged communication statutes' applicability differs considerably according to the type of practitioner, the nature of the information considered to be privileged, and the court or tribunal in which the privilege is asserted. At least one state limits the privilege to the relationships between patients and psychiatrists or applied psychologists; no privilege applies generally to medical practitioners.[209] New Mexico requires a patient to submit a malpractice claim to a medical review commission before filing an action in court, grants the review panel access to all medical and hospital records pertaining to the matter, and provides for waiver of any claim of privilege during this review.[210] Some states exclude from privilege all proceedings before worker's compensation boards or other specifically designated administrative tribunals, while others recognize the privilege in such a context.[211] Pennsylvania permits a patient to claim privilege only with respect to medical information that may blacken character.[212]

Some states broaden the privilege by extending the patient's right of confidentiality to relationships other than those established with medical practitioners. The privilege may also apply to designated allied health care personnel, although applicability to these professional persons is certainly not the general or majority view.[213] In some states the privilege applies only to criminal cases.

Where it is otherwise applicable, the privilege generally applies to an institution's medical records on the grounds that they contain information acquired by the physician in the course of treating the patient.[214] However, because the privilege can be asserted only by the patient, the privileged status of hospital records is not directly relevant to the hospital in litigation between the patient and third parties. In other words, a hospital may not assert confidentiality of records on its own behalf when the court proceedings involve third parties, although it may claim confidentiality on behalf of a patient who is not able to assert a claim of privilege. In most cases between patients and third parties the matter of privilege must be determined by the litigating parties and the court.[215] On the other hand, if the hospital is one of the litigant parties, the statute directly concerns the hospital's position, for then the hospital cannot use the records as evidence if the patient asserts a proper claim to the privileged status of the information. As will be emphasized shortly, however, the patient will be deemed to waive a right of privilege by bringing suit against the hospital.

The privileged status of medical records is exemplified in a California case in which the plaintiff sought damages following an automobile accident allegedly caused by the defendant's negligence. During pretrial discovery, the plaintiff admitted to having been involved in an earlier automobile accident in 1969, to having attempted suicide in the same year, and to having been under the care of a psychotherapist. The defendant then obtained a subpoena for all of the plaintiff's medical records, but the supreme court held that under California's statute the records were privileged and not subject to discovery.[216] Plaintiff had not waived the right to confidentiality because the suit against the defendant raised no issue related to her mental health. In similar fashion, in a medical malpractice suit in which a father on behalf of his infant child alleged that the defendants were negligent in caring for the child during pregnancy and delivery, the complete and life-long records of the mother's medical and family history were not subject to pretrial discovery when the mother was not a party to the action and had not waived her privilege.[217] Because her medical condition during pregnancy was relevant to the issues to be litigated, however, records relating to the pregnancy were accessible on the basis of a waiver.

When a physician died in an automobile accident and his estate claimed accidental death benefits, the insurance company was unable to gain access to his medical records to establish—if possible—that the accident was a suicide. Because there was no evidence of suicide other than the accident, the privilege of confidentiality prevailed.[218] In another California case the plaintiff attempted to establish that a minor's parents were aware of their daughter's violent tendencies and sought her psychiatric medical records to support the claim. The court denied access, thus recognizing a privilege of confidentiality.[219]

Access to Medical Records of Third Parties

Many plaintiffs in lawsuits will seek by means of pretrial discovery to obtain information from the medical charts of other patients not parties to the litigation or from hospital documents that they believe will aid the preparation and trial of their case. As noted previously, the medical records of a patient not a party to litigation are generally not discoverable; however, depending on interpretation of local law, the type of information sought, and the issues raised by a plaintiff's motions for discovery, some actions seeking the records of third parties have been successful, as will be noted.

An Arizona case illustrates the traditional approach and an unsuccessful attempt to gain access to the charts of other patients. The plaintiff had filed a malpractice action against a hospital because complications had occurred during childbirth when her private obstetrician was absent from the delivery room though allegedly on the hospital premises. Arguing that under the circumstances the hospital had a duty to reach the physician, who was not a defendant in the action, plaintiff sought access to the hospital records of another patient to learn what they might reveal about the doctor's actions at the time in question. The trial court granted discovery of the records, but this decision was reversed by the intermediate court of appeals, which held that when neither the doctor nor the other patient was a party to the litigation the information was privileged.[220] Moreover, the court ruled that the hospital had a duty to assert the privilege on behalf of the absent patient.

Consistent with this view is an Illinois decision denying access to the medical records of nearly 800 persons who, along with the plaintiffs, had allegedly suffered injury following administration of an investigative drug. It was held that the hospital on behalf of its patients could claim the records to be privileged because it was highly probable that the individual patients could be identified even if their names were deleted.[221] The court further said that patients whose records were sought had not waived their privilege of confidentiality by authorizing release of information to third parties responsible for reimbursement of hospital charges.

In other cases illustrating the applicability of the privilege, however, the courts have held that certain printed records revealing information about third parties are not confidential and that a plaintiff is entitled to such information. For example, an Arizona court permitted a malpractice plaintiff to examine the medical records of 24 surgical patients who had received heart pacemakers, provided that the patients' names and other identifying information were removed.[222] Plaintiff's suit against the hospital alleged that implanting a pacemaker in this particular instance was unnecessary and that the institution had been negligent in failing to monitor the surgeon's privileges properly. Because an essential question was whether the hospital was aware or should have been aware of the surgeon's alleged deviations from acceptable professional standards, the records of other similarly situated patients were relevant to the plaintiff's claim.

A malpractice plaintiff has a right to discover the names of other patients who may possess information regarding the alleged negligence or malpractice, and their consent to such disclosure is not necessary.[223] Otherwise the hospital could seek witnesses favorable to its side while denying plaintiff a like opportunity. In itself, the release of the names of patients does nothing to reveal the nature of their illnesses or the treatment rendered. According to a New York suit against a hospital that allegedly failed to supervise dangerous patients, the victim of an assault by a hospitalized mental patient is entitled to records relating to prior assaults by the same patient.[224] Nonmedical data regarding other assaults by such a patient are clearly discoverable by a plaintiff, such disclosure not being a violation of either the privileged communication statute or New York's mental hygiene law, which provides that the medical records of patients of state mental institutions are confidential.[225]

Another issue was raised in the case of *Bremiller v. Miller,* in which a registered nurse was charged by the New York Department of Education with unprofessional conduct.[226] The question was whether the nurse could have access to the medical record of a mental patient who was alleged to have been assaulted by the nurse and who was the complaining witness. In seeking this patient's records, the nurse contended that they would show a pattern of aggressive conduct by the patient and thus aid the defense. On behalf of the Department of Education, the New York attorney general maintained that the mental hygiene law, which provided for confidentiality of medical records of patients in state mental institutions, prevented access to the records unless the patient waived the privilege. On the issue of waiver the New York court observed that because the patient's mental competency was questionable it could not rule for the nurse on the basis that the patient had waived the privilege.

Nevertheless, in the interest of fairness the use of the records in the nurse's defense was permitted. The ruling in effect recognized that sound public policy requires that a privilege of confidentiality should not be absolute to the detriment of persons having a legitimate interest in obtaining medical information pertaining to another. The pending disciplinary action jeopardized nurse's license to practice and thus her right to earn a living. In the view of the court the defendant had a right to question the credibility and capacity of the complaining witness. Further, the hearing procedure before the Department of Education was not a public hearing; thus, the patient's identity could be protected, and disclosures from the record could be limited to those matters that were material and relevant to the pending allegation of unprofessional conduct.

Patient's Waiver of Privilege

Patients who file suit for damages and thereby place their physical or mental health in issue have clearly waived the privilege of confidentiality, and their medical records will be available to an adverse party and admissible in evidence at trial, subject to the usual law of evidence as previously reviewed. When a person who claimed to have been injured in an automobile accident brought an action against both the state of Vermont and an individual alleging that the defendants' negligence caused the accident, the Supreme Court of Vermont affirmed the trial court's order permitting discovery of the medical records compiled by the treating physician.[227] In another suit, one alleging that a hospital was negligent in the maintenance of its property and thus caused plaintiff's fall, it was ruled that in bringing suit the plaintiff placed her physical condition in issue and fairness required the hospital to have access to all relevant medical information, including treatment for a preexisting complaint.[228] A further illustration of waiver occurred in New York, where the patient brought suit against the manufacturer of an intrauterine device. In this case the defendant was entitled to discover the patient's record of venereal disease on file with the city health department.[229]

Although a waiver of privilege in a given situation may depend on the particular wording of the state statute, a waiver by a patient can usually become effective in two ways: it may be made expressly by words or conduct, or it may be implied by acts of the patient or a legal representative.[230] In the majority of states, however, waiver only permits the adverse party to pursue formal discovery procedures and seek admissible evidence. That is, in most jurisdictions adverse counsel may not generally question or interview the patient *ex parte* (without the safeguards of a formal deposition under oath and the presence of the plaintiff's lawyer).[231] Other jurisdictions, especially those without privilege statutes, allow or even encourage informal, *ex parte* interviews to facilitate early evaluation and settlement of cases.[232]

In determining whether information contained in a medical record or possessed by a medical practitioner is subject to pretrial discovery proceedings or is admissible in evidence in judicial or quasi-judicial proceedings, a court must first interpret any local statute that relates to privileged communications and then apply it to the particular circumstances. If no statute exists or if the statute does not prevent access to medical information, the court must determine the admissibility of the information by application of the general rules of evidence respecting hearsay testimony and their exceptions and then evaluate the authenticity, reliability, credibility, materiality, and relevance of the record. In jurisdictions with privilege communication statutes, the public policy issue of balancing the patients' rights to confidentiality against the other parties' rights to ascertain the truth and protect their legitimate interests is a sensitive matter. As is evident through this discussion, the courts attempt to deal fairly with these conflicting interests on a case-by-case basis.

Government's Right of Access to Medical Records

There is no statutory privilege of confidentiality under federal law, nor do state statutes apply in cases involving a federal legal issue. Accordingly, when a federal agency seeks access to medical records the only grounds for denial is a constitutional claim based either on the individual patient's right of privacy or on an allegation that authorizing disclosure is unconstitutional. Because the federal government frequently has legitimate reasons for access to a patient's medical records to enforce fairly its various social welfare and regulatory laws, claims of unconstitutionality have not often been successful so far (and have been rarely asserted), although some cases have considered the matter.

Situations in which the federal government has been permitted to review medical records without consent of the patient are exemplified in cases initiated by the Internal Revenue Service (IRS) and the National Institute of Occupational Safety and Health (NIOSH). The IRS was granted access, for example, to the medical records of a deceased person to ascertain whether gifts or property during the patient's lifetime were made in contemplation of death and thus subject to the federal estate tax.[233] In another case the IRS was successful in obtaining the surgical records of a physician who had failed to file tax returns.[234] NIOSH may subpoena employees' medical records that employers must maintain under the Occupational Safety and Health Act.[235] In none of these situations did the state's privileged communication statute apply to protect the confidentiality of the records.

In a widely publicized 1983 case, the U.S. Department of Health and Human Services sought the records of a newborn, severely handicapped infant, contending that failure to perform surgery because the parents refused their consent constituted unlawful discrimination against a handicapped person in violation of the Rehabilitation Act of 1973. The federal district court denied the government access to the records, holding that honoring the parents' refusal in the circumstances would not violate the act.[236] The decision was later affirmed by a federal court of appeals but for different reasons. In the view of the appellate court the factual situation was beyond the contemplation and intent of Congress when the legislation prohibiting discrimination against handicapped persons was enacted, and therefore the statute was not relevant.[237] It is worth noting that the district court observed in its opinion that disclosure of the records would not have been barred by a state privilege of confidentiality because no statutory privilege exists when a federal question is being decided.[238] An argument that disclosure would offend the patient's constitutional right of privacy was deemed to be "extremely weak."[239]

In contrast, a few courts have recognized a constitutional right to maintain confidentiality of records in certain factual situations. For example, a district court has held that a federal grand jury investigating allegations that a mental hospital and a physician defrauded certain insurance companies was not entitled to inspect patients' medical records.[240] In this instance the court found a privilege of confidentiality, ruling that it was constitutionally based, and held that a physician could assert the privilege on behalf of patients. A similar conclusion was reached in Hawaii. In that state a statute authorized administrative warrants to search the files of psychiatrists who were caring for Medicaid patients upon a showing of probable cause. The purpose of the legislation, of course, was to aid in finding fraud and abuse by physicians receiving public funds. Nevertheless, the court issued an injunction prohibiting enforcement of the statute, thereby recognizing a constitutional right of privacy that cannot be interfered with in the absence of a compelling governmental interest.[241] Apparently the court felt that the state had not sufficiently demonstrated a compelling need to inspect the records.

On the other hand state authorities, like federal administrative agencies, have frequently been successful in gaining information that is necessary to enforce the law and to protect against fraud and abuse of third-party financing arrangements. The U.S. Court of Appeals for the Sixth Circuit has said, for example, that a psychotherapist may be required to disclose the names of patients and the dates of their treatment to a grand jury investigating an alleged scheme to defraud the Michigan Blue Cross–Blue Shield plan.[242] Similarly, a New York court permitted the state's Department of Social Services to review a psychiatrist's records of Medicaid patients when investigating the physician's billing practices.[243] The physician could not claim that the records were privileged. Further, neither the state's privileged communication statute nor a constitutional right of privacy prohibited the access to documents containing medical information relating to patients by a grand jury investigating a death in a hospital's intensive care unit.[244] In California and many other jurisdictions, as a result of either judicial decision or statute, the Board of Medical Quality Assurance, which is responsible for licensure, may review medical records when examining the professional conduct of a physician whose hospital privileges have been revoked, although local law may require that the names of patients be deleted.[245] Information in the hands of a state's medical licensure board is also frequently available to both state and federal agencies investigating possible criminal activities by physicians.

Although most courts have not recognized a constitutional right to privacy of information, and even if the common-law doctrine of qualified privilege protects medical personnel and institutions from civil liability in many instances in which medical information is released to law enforcement officials without the patient's consent, disclosures should not be made without such consent, some explicit statutory authority, or appropriate legal process. Institutions should distribute carefully stated guidelines that specify policies for relationships with the police and law-enforcement agencies. The principle behind such guidelines must be recognition of the need to balance the patient's rights to confidentiality with the community's legitimate interests in preserving public safety and general welfare.[246]

Notes

1. Fla. Stat. § 395.016.
2. Joint Commission on Accreditation of Healthcare Organizations, ACCREDITATION MANUAL FOR HOSPITALS. This manual is updated annually.
3. Darling v. Charleston Community Hosp., 33 Ill. 2d 326, 211 N.E.2d 253 (1965), *cert. denied*, 383 U.S. 946 (1966).
4. *See, e.g.*, Roach and Aspen Law Center, MEDICAL RECORDS AND THE LAW 172 (1994).
5. *See, e.g.*, Hansch v. Hackett, 190 Wash. 97, 66 P.2d 1129 (1937) (the hospital was liable for a nurse's negligence in failing to observe and record symptoms of eclampsia).
6. Goldstein v. Madison Ave. Hosp., No. 24212/76 (Kings County, N.Y., May 21, 1981).
7. Pisel v. Stamford Hosp., 430 A.2d 1 (Conn. 1980).
8. 384 F. Supp. 821 (W.D. Ark. 1974).

9. 34 Colo. App. 356, 539 P.2d 491 (1975).

10. Pretrial discovery proceedings must be carefully distinguished from the use of records as evidence at trial. Whether incident reports are subject to pretrial discovery is a matter of local and state law, and there is a conflict of authority. An example of a decision that incident reports are *not* subject to discovery is Sligar v. Tucker, 267 So. 2d 54 (Fla. Dist. Ct. App. 1972).

11. 42 C.F.R. § 482.24.

12. Hryniak v. Nathan Littauer Hosp. Ass'n, 446 N.Y.S.2d 558 (1982).

13. Fla. Stat. § 95.11(4)(6).

14. Pyramid Life Ins. Co. v. Masonic Hosp. Ass'n, 191 F. Supp. 51 (W.D. Okla. 1961).

15. McGarry v. J.A. Mercier Co., 272 Mich. 501, 262 N.W. 296 (1935); Flaum v. Medical Arts Center Hosp., 160:36 N.Y.L.J. 2 (Sup. Ct. 1968) (the court would not order the actual hospital x-rays to be sent to a physician); Cannell v. Medical and Surgical Clinic, 21 Ill. App. 3d 383, 315 N.E.2d 278 (1974).

16. Matter of Weiss, 208 Misc. 1010, 147 N.Y.S.2d 455 (Sup. Ct. 1955).

17. *In re* Culbertson's Will, 57 Misc. 2d 391, 292 N.Y.2d 806 (Sup. Ct. 1968).

18. Batty v. Arizona State Dental Bd., 57 Ariz. 239, 112 P.2d 870 (1941) (license to practice may be revoked if a dentist sends patients to unlicensed dental practitioners; according to the court the licensed practitioner who knows that a patient is about to undergo needed care by an unlicensed person has a duty to advise the patient).

19. CONN. GEN. STAT. ANN. §§ 4-104, 4-105 (West 1969); *see also* ILL. ANN. STAT. ch. 110, ¶¶ 8-2001–2004 (Smith-Hurd Supp. 1986) (patient, physician, or authorized attorney may examine medical records of every private and public hospital, except those of institutions under jurisdiction of Department of Mental Health and Developmental Disabilities).

20. MASS. GEN. LAWS ANN. ch. 111 § 70 (West Supp. 1975), amended 1985.

21. WIS. STAT. ANN. § 804.10(4) (West Supp. 1976); *see also* MISS. CODE ANN. § 41-9-65 (1972) (patients or representatives may have access to information in hospital records on showing of "good cause" and on payment of reasonable charges). Young v. Madison Gen. Hosp., 337 So. 2d 931 (Miss. 1976) (dismissal of bill of complaint was proper when request for access to information in medical records was made by mail; statutory right of access requires patient's or representative's personal appearance).

22. LA. REV. STAT. ANN. § 40:2014.1 (West 1977).

23. CAL. EVID. CODE § 1158 (West Supp. 1985); UTAH CODE ANN. § 78-25-25 (1977).

24. N.J. STAT. ANN. § 2A:82-42 (West 1976).

25. 315 N.E.2d 278 (Ill. App. 1974). *See also*, Emmett v. Eastern Dispensary and Casualty Hosp. 396 F.2d 931 (D.C. Cir. 1967). Courts often add that there is no duty to provide copies of records free of charge. *See, e.g.*, Rabens v. Jackson Park Hosp. Found., N.E.2d 276 (Ill. App. 1976).

26. The Secretary's Commission on Medical Malpractice recommended in 1973 that medical records should be available to patients through a duly authorized representative. U.S. Department of Health, Education, and Welfare, REPORT OF

THE SECRETARY'S COMMISSION ON MEDICAL MALPRACTICE, Washington, D.C., U.S. Government Printing Office, 75–77 (1973).

27. A charge of $1 per page for photocopying hospital records is arbitrary and unreasonable because the fee bears no relationship to the actual cost involved; $.25 per page plus a fee of $15 for retrieval would be reasonable. Matter of Hernandez v. Lutheran Medical Center, 193:22 N.Y.L.J. (Sup. Ct. 1985).

28. With respect to recommended administrative policies regarding inspection of patients' charts *see generally*, Horty, *The Patient's Right of Access to His Medical Record*, ch. 5, ACTION KIT FOR HOSP. L. (1974).

29. Thurman v. Crawford and St. Louis Univ. Hosp., 652 S.W.2d 240 (Mo. App. 1983) (hospital may take reasonable precautions to ascertain authenticity of patient's consent to release medical information and may refuse to honor consent when date has been altered).

30. Whalen v. Roe, 429 U.S. 589 (1977).

31. Griswold v. Connecticut, 381 U.S. 479 (1965) (state may not prohibit use of contraceptives of advice or assistance in their use); Roe v. Wade, 410 U.S. 113 (1973) and Doe v. Bolton, 410 U.S. 179 (1973) (abortion cases).

32. 42 C.F.R. §§ 401.101–.152.

33. 42 C.F.R. § 2 (1986).

34. *See* Winslade, *Confidentiality of Medical Records: An Overview of Concepts and Legal Policies*, 3 J. LEGAL MED. 497 (1982).

35. 5 U.S.C.A. § 552b(c)(6).

36. *E.g.*, IOWA CODE ANN. § 144.29 (West 1972).

37. MO. ANN. STAT. § 188.052 (Vernon Supp. 1987); N.Y. Pub. Health Law § 4160 (McKinney 1985); MINN. STAT. ANN. § 145.413 (West Supp. 1987).

38. Robinson v. Hamilton, 60 Iowa 134, 14 N.W. 202 (1882); Planned Parenthood of Central Mo. v. Danforth, 428 U.S. 52 (1976).

39. N.Y. PUB. HEALTH LAW § 2101 (McKinney 1985) (communicable disease); N.Y. PENAL LAW § 265.25 (McKinney 1980) (wounds); IOWA CODE § 147.111 (West 1972) (wounds resulting from criminal act).

40. 17 Cal. 3d 425, 551 P.2d 334, 131 Cal. Rptr. 14 (1976).

41. Hicks v. United States, 357 F. Supp. 434 (D.D.C. 1973), *aff'd*, 511 F.2d 407 (D.C. Cir. 1975).

42. Thompson v. County of Alameda, 27 Cal. 3d 741, 614 P.2d 728, 167 Cal. Rptr. 70 (1980).

43. Mangeris v. Gordon, 94 Nev. 400, 580 P.2d 481 (1978). *See also* Leedy v. Hartnett, 510 F. Supp. 1125 (M.D. Pa. 1981) (Veterans Administration Hospital had no duty to warn of discharged patient's propensity for alcohol-induced violence without a readily identifiable victim); Brady v. Hopper, 570 F. Supp. 1333 (D. Colo. 1983) (psychiatrist had no duty to warn because patient, John Hinckley, Jr., who attempted to assassinate President Reagan, had not threatened to shoot anyone); Soutear v. United States, 646 F. Supp. 524 (E.D. Mich. 1986) (physicians not negligent in releasing psychiatric patient and not warning parents when patient, who killed mother three months later, had never behaved violently).

44. Mavroudis v. Superior Court for County of San Mateo, 102 Cal. App. 3d 594,

162 Cal. Rptr. 724 (1980); McIntosh v. Milan, 168 N.J. Super. 466, 403 A.2d 500 (1979).

45. *E.g.,* Shaw v. Glickman, 45 Md. App. 718, 415 A.2d 625 (1980) (where estranged husband shot wife's male friend, psychiatrists not liable for failure to warn, even if patient had threatened to harm plaintiff); Cole v. Taylor, 301 N.W.2d 766 (Iowa 1981) (plaintiff who had been convicted of murdering her former husband could not maintain an action against her psychiatrist alleging negligence in failing to restrain her and warn victim); Case v. United States, 523 F. Supp. 317 (S.D. Ohio 1981); Hawkins v. King County Dep't of Rehabilitative Servs., 602 P.2d 361 (Wash. App. 1979).

46. Bellah v. Greenson, 81 Cal. App. 3d 614, 146 Cal. Rptr. 535 (1978).

47. 42 C.F.R. §§ 462.1–476.143.

48. *See, e.g.,* Noble v. United Benefit Life Ins. Co., 230 Iowa 471, N.W. 881 (1941) and Simonsen v. Swenson, 104 Neb. 224, 177 N.W. 831 (1920).

49. PROSSER AND KEETON, TORTS § 112 (5th ed. 1984); RESTATEMENT (SECOND) OF TORTS § 559 (1976).

50. MacDonald v. Time, Inc., 554 F. Supp. 1053 (D. N.J. 1983).

51. Farris v. Tvedten, 623 S.W.2d 205 (Ark. 1981).

52. Gertz v. Robert Welch, Inc. 418 U.S. 323, 349 (1974) (plaintiff may not recover presumed or punitive damages against press or broadcasters without proof of actual damage); France v. St. Clare's Hosp. and Health Center, 82 A.D.2d 1, 441 N.Y.S.2d 79 (1981) (written letter to a blood donor's coworker stating falsely that donor had venereal disease did not constitute libel when no actual damage was found and no malice or reckless disregard for truth could be shown). *Cf.* Hearst Corp. v. Hughes, 297 Md. 112, 466 A.2d 486 (Md. Ct. App. 1983) (defamation action may succeed with award of compensatory damages for negligence of television station broadcasting untruths about defendant's business though only emotional distress was proved).

53. Koudsi v. Hennepin County Medical Center, 317 N.W.2d 705 (Minn. 1982) (statement that plaintiff was a patient in hospital and had given birth was true and could not be defamation).

54. Gilson v. Knickerbocker Hosp., 280 A.D. 690, 116 N.Y.S.2d 745 (1952).

55. Griffin v. Cortland Memorial Hosp., Inc., 85 A.D.2d 837, 446 N.Y.S.2d 430 (1981) (notation on chart that outpatient was abusing drugs protected by qualified privilege).

56. Hyman v. Jewish Chronic Disease Hosp., 15 N.Y.2d 317, 258 N.Y.S.2d 397 (1965).

57. MICH. COMP. LAWS ANN. §§ 333.2631–.2638 (1980). *See also* Klinge v. Lutheran Medical Center of St. Louis, 518 S.W.2d 157 (Mo. Ct. App. 1974) (hospital medical staff committee may use medical records of a staff physician's patients without their consent to determine qualifications and competency of that physician).

58. 104 Neb. 224, 177 N.W. 831 (1920); *see also* Cochran v. Sears Roebuck, 72 Ga. 458, 34 S.E.2d 296 (1945) (no liability was held when a company nurse in good faith and without proved malice mistakenly told the supervisor that an employee had a communicable venereal disease, and the employee was discharged).

59. 8 Utah 2d 191, 331 P.2d 814 (1958).

60. *Id.* at 197, 331 P.2d at 817, 818.

61. Vigil v. Rice, 74 N.M. 693, 397 P.2d 719 (1964).

62. Newspaper Publishing Corp. v. Burke, 216 Va. 800, 224 S.E.2d 132 (1976).

63. Warren and Brandeis, *The Right of Privacy,* 4 HARV. L. REV. 193 (1890).

64. Smith v. Doss, 251 Ala. 250, 37 So. 2d 118 (1948).

65. Housh v. Peth, 165 Ohio St. 35, 36, 133 N.E.2d 340, 341 (1956). Posser and Keeton, Torts § 117 (5th ed. 1984) identifies four categories of cases: (a) appropriation, for defendant's advantage, of plaintiff's name or likeness; (b) intrusion on plaintiff's seclusion or solitude, or private affairs; (c) public disclosure of embarrassing private facts; and (d) publicity that places plaintiff in a false light in the public eye. The author's classification of cases will vary somewhat from these.

66. *But cf.* MacDonald v. Time, Inc., 554 F. Supp. 1053 (D. N.J. 1983) (when a living person is libeled, the claim survives death and is saved from abatement by New Jersey survival statute).

67. *Cf.* Chico Feminist Women's Health Center v. Butte Glenn Medical Soc'y, 557 F. Supp. 1190 (E.D. Cal. 1983) (California constitutional law gave abortion clinic cause of action for invasion of privacy, on behalf of women seeking its service, against hospital, physicians, insurance company, and medical society for statements and activities intended to force the clinic's closure; corporation did not have cause of action for invasion of privacy in its own right).

68. RESTATEMENT (SECOND) OF TORTS § 652C (1977).

69. 38 Pa. D. & C. 543 (1940). *See also* Estate of Berthiaume v. Pratt, M.D., 365 A.2d 792 (Me. 1976) (photographing a terminally ill patient for research when the patient objects invades the right of privacy).

70. Shibley v. Time, Inc., 45 Ohio App. 2d 69, 341 N.E.2d 337 (1975).

71. Nader v. General Motor Corp., 25 N.Y.2d 560, 255 N.E.2d 765 (1970) (applying District of Columbia law).

72. Commonwealth v. Wiseman, 356 Mass. 251, 249 N.E.2d 610 (1969).

73. *See* Vassiliades v. Garfinckel's, 492 A.2d 580 (D.C. App. 1985) (publication of photographs by physician without patient's consent may be a tort).

74. Rhodes v. Graham, 238 Ky. 225, 37 S.W.2d 46 (1931); McDaniel v. Atlanta Coca-Cola Bottling Co., 60 Ga. App. 92, 2 S.E.2d 810 (1939); Nader v. General Motors Corp., 25 N.Y.2d 560, 255 N.E.2d 765 (1970).

75. Byfield v. Candler, 33 Ga. App. 275, 125 S.E. 905 (1924); DeMay v. Roberts, 46 Mich. 160, 9 N.W. 146 (1881).

76. Hamberger v. Eastman, 106 N.H. 107, 206 A.2d 239 (1964).

77. Bazemore v. Savannah Hosp., 171 Ga. 257, 155 S.E. 194 (1930). *See also* Douglas v. Stokes, 149 Ky. 506, 149 S.W. 849 (1912) (publishing a photograph of nude bodies of twin children who were born joined together transgressed bounds of decency); Rinsley v. Frydman, 221 Kan. 297, 559 P.2d 334 (1977) (publicity placing plaintiff in a false light and being highly offensive to a reasonable man is invasion of privacy).

78. Barber v. Time, Inc., 348 Mo. 1199, 159 S.W.2d 291 (1942).

79. Doe v. Roe, 400 N.Y.S.2d 668 (Sup. Ct. 1977).

80. Brents v. Morgan, 221 Ky. 765, 299 S.W. 967 (1927).

81. Hawley v. Professional Credit Bureau, 345 Mich. 500, 76 N.W.2d 835 (1956); Gouldman-Taber Pontiac v. Zerbst, 213 Ga. 682, 100 S.E.2d 881 (1957).

82. Hendry v. Conner, 226 N.W.2d 921 (Minn. 1975). *Cf.* Biederman's of Springfield, Inc. v. Wright, 322 S.W.2d 892 (Mo. 1959) (invasion of privacy when a creditor's collection agent entered on several occasions the café where the debtor worked and announced loudly to customers that debtor and spouse refused to pay their bills and were "deadbeats").

83. Beth Israel Hosp. and Geriatric Center v. District Court in and for the City and County of Denver, 683 P.2d 343 (Colo. 1984) (physician may have access to medical records of his patients especially because case names and not patients' names were requested).

84. Knecht v. Vandalia Medical Center, Inc., 14 Ohio App. 3d 129 (1984) (a qualified privilege based on commonality of interest existed when mother employed by physicians told son that his friend was examined for venereal disease).

85. Pennison v. Provident Life and Accident Ins. Co., 154 So. 2d 617 (La. App. 1963). *See also* Curry v. Corn, 52 Misc. 2d 1035, 277 N.Y.S.2d 470 (1966) (a physician is privileged to reveal a patient's condition to the spouse).

86. MacDonald v. Clinger, 84 A.D.2d 482, 446 N.Y.S.2d 801 (1982).

87. 237 F.2d 898 (10th Cir. 1956).

88. *E.g.*, Edwards v. Lamb, 45 A. 480 (N.H. 1899); Jones v. Stanko, 118 Ohio St. 147, 160 N.E. 456 (1928); Davis v. Rodman, 227 S.W. 612 (Ark. 1921).

89. Clark v. Geraci, 29 Misc. 2d 791, 208 N.Y.S.2d 564 (1960); Orr v. Sievert, 162 Ga. App. 677, 292 S.E.2d 548 (1982) (mother waived possible common-law right to privacy in filing malpractice suit on behalf of minor son); Mull v. String, 448 So. 2d 952 (Ala. 1984) (physician treating patient for burns not liable in furnishing hospital and its attorney with copy of report when patient had suit pending against hospital).

90. *But see* Sinclair v. Postal Telegraph and Cable Co., 72 N.Y.S.2d 841 (Sup. Ct. 1935) (actors may insist on dignified public presentations of themselves and their work; hence, the defendant's presentation of an actor's picture presenting him in an undignified light, without permission, was wrongful).

91. Gilbert v. Medical Economics Co., 665 F.2d 305 (10th Cir. 1981); *see also* Strutner v. Dispatch Printing Co., 2 Ohio App. 3d 377 (1982) (publishing name and address of parents of suspect in a criminal case does not constitute actionable invasion of privacy); Zacchini v. Scripps-Howard Broadcasting Co., 47 Ohio St. 2d 224, 351 N.E.2d 454 (1976) (television station not liable for filming and broadcasting plaintiff's performance as a "human cannonball" at a county fair without consent).

92. Koudsi v. Hennepin County Medical Center, 317 N.W.2d 705 (Minn. 1982) (informing family member that plaintiff had borne a child in hospital did not violate any common-law or statutory right to confidentiality).

93. Virgil v. Time, Inc., 527 F.2d 1122 (9th Cir. 1975).

94. Deaton v. Delta Democrat Publishing Co., 326 So. 2d 471 (Miss. 1976).

95. *See* Hartmann, Solimine, Renas, and Kumar, *Relaxed Liability: A Proposed New Standard for Defamation by the Press,* 22 Am. Bus. L.J. 93 (1984).

96. 376 U.S. 254 (1964).

97. 376 U.S. at 279–80.
98. Gertz v. Robert Welch, Inc., 418 U.S. 323 (1974).
99. *E.g.,* Walker v. Colorado Springs Sun, Inc., 538 P.2d 450 (Colo. 1975).
100. Chapadeau v. Utica Observer-Dispatch, Inc., 38 N.Y.2d 196, 341 N.E.2d 569, 379 N.Y.S.2d 61 (1975).
101. Taskett v. King Broadcasting Co., 86 Wash. 2d 439, 546 P.2d 81 (1976).
102. *But see* Horne v. Patton, 291 Ala. 701, 287 So. 2d 824 (1973) (physician's unauthorized disclosure to a patient's employer of embarrassing and humiliating details of patient's illness may constitute invasion of privacy if no legitimate reason prompted disclosure).
103. A.B. v. C.D., 14 Sess. Cas. 2d 177 (1851).
104. Section 9 of the 1957 *Principles of Medical Ethics of the American Medical Association* reads: "A physician may not reveal the confidence entrusted to him in the course of medical attendance, or the deficiencies he may observe in the character of patients, unless he is required to do so by law or unless it becomes necessary in order to protect the welfare of the individual or of the community."
105. Horne v. Patton, 291 Ala. 701, 287 So. 2d 824 (1973).
106. *Cf.* Mull v. String, 448 So. 2d 952 (Ala. 1984) (patient initiating personal injury suit against hospital waives contractual right of confidentiality against physician who released medical information to hospital and its attorney without patient's specific consent).
107. 237 F. Supp. 96 (N.D. Ohio) (insurance carrier inducing breach of contract between patient and physician may be liable for consequences), *aff'd,* 243 F. Supp. 793 (N.D. Ohio 1965) (implied condition in a physician-patient contract is that confidential information acquired through the relationship will not be released without the patient's consent).
108. *E.g.,* Quarles v. Sutherland, 215 Tenn. 651, 389 S.W.2d 249 (1965) (the court also held that no contract existed between a customer injured on the store's premises an the physician examining the customer for the store; hence, when the doctor released a medical report to the store's attorney the customer had no cause of action for breach of contract).
109. Simonsen v. Swenson, 104 Neb. 224, 177 N.W. 831 (1920) (physician who disclosed to a hotel proprietor that a patient residing in the hotel suffered from venereal disease was not liable). *See also Clark, supra* note 89.
110. Alexander v. Knight, 197 Pa. Super. 79, 177 A.2d 142 (1962) (physician liable for breach of fiduciary duty when he released information to attorney adverse to patient).
111. Munzer v. Blaisdell, 183 Misc. 773, 49 N.Y.S.2d 915 (1944), *aff'd,* 269 A.D. 970, 58 N.Y.S.2d 359 (1945); N.Y. MENTAL HYG. LAW § 33.13 (McKinney Supp. 1987).
112. *See generally* Sloan and Hall, *Confidentiality of Psychotherapeutic Records,* 5 J. LEGAL MED. 435 (1984).
113. OHIO REV. CODE ANN. § 5122.31(E) (Baldwin 1987). Even without an express statutory provision granting the mental patient access, a court may rule that patient or a representative has a right to view the record. *E.g.,* Sullivan v. State, 352 So. 2d 1212 (Fla. App. 1977); N.Y. City Health and Hosps. Corp. v. Parker, 102 Misc. 2d 433, 423 N.Y.S.2d 442 (1980); Doe v. Commissioner of Mental

Health, 372 Mass. 534, 362 N.E.2d 920 (1977) (patient's father, an attorney, granted access); *but see* Matter of J.C.G., 144 N.J. Super. 579, 366 A.2d 733 (1976) (patient's mother denied access).

114. Mental Health and Developmental Disabilities Confidentiality Act, 1-17, ILL. ANN. STAT. ch. 911/2 ¶¶ 801–17 (Smith-Hurd 1987). *See* ¶¶ 804(a) and 802(9).

115. *Id. at* ¶ 802(7).

116. *Id.* at ¶ 805(a).

117. *Id.* at ¶ 809.

118. *Id.* at ¶ 810.

119. *Id.* at ¶¶ 815–16.

120. *See* Winslade, *Confidentiality of Medical Records,* 3 J. LEGAL MED. 497, 519–30 (1982).

121. R.I. GEN. LAWS § 5-37.3 (1986); *see also* MONT. CODE ANN. §§ 50-16-301–314 (1985); Ariz. Rev. Stat. Ann. §§ 20-2101–2120 (1986). CONN. GEN. STAT. §§ 38-500–523 (1983); ILL. ANN. STAT. ch. 73, ¶¶ 1065.701–.724 (Smith-Hurd Supp. 1987).

122. CAL. CIV. CODE § 56 (West Supp. 1987).

123. *Id.* at § 56.16.

124. *Id.* at § 56.10. Use of information by employers is governed by Sections 56.20–.245.

125. *Id.* at § 56.11.

126. *Id.* at § 56.13.

127. CAL. INS. CODE §§ 791–791.26 (West Supp. 1987) (insurance companies); CAL. CIV. CODE §§ 1798–1798.78.

128. CAL. CIV. CODE § 56.36.

129. *Id.* at § 56.35.

130. 42 C.F.R. § 482.24.

131. 42 U.S.C.S. § 242(a); 21 U.S.C.S. § 872 (c), (d).

132. 42 U.S.C.S. § 290ee-3.

133. 42 U.S.C.S. § 290dd-3.

134. 42 C.F.R. pt. 2.

135. 42 U.S.C. § 290ee-30(b)(2)(A-C). Information can also be exchanged between the armed forces and the Veterans Administration without violating the statute, 42 U.S.C. § 290ee-3(e).

136. United States v. Hopper, 440 F. Supp. 1208 (N.D. Ill. 1977).

137. Matter of Dwayne G., 97 Misc. 2d 333, 411 N.Y.S.2d 180 (1978).

138. United States v. Providence Hosp., 507 Supp. 519 (E.D. Mich. 1981) (involving IRS investigation of a physician who filed no taxes for several years).

139. United States v. Fenyo, 6 M.J. 933 (1979).

140. United States v. Graham, 548 F.2d 1302 (8th Cir. 1977).

141. People v. Newman, 32 N.Y.2d 379, 298 N.E.2d 651, 345 N.Y.S.2d 502 (1973), *cert. denied,* 414 U.S. 1163 (1973).

142. People v. Carr, 190 N.Y.L.J., Nov. 29, 1983, at 13.

143. State v. Andring, 342 N.W.2d 128 (Minn. 1984).

144. 42 U.S.C. § 290dd-3 (1985).

145. MINN. STAT. § 626.556 (1987).

146. 42 C.F.R. § 2.23 (1986).

147. 42 U.S.C. § 5101-(b)7 (1985).

148. 342 N.W.2d at 131.

149. MINN. STAT. § 626.556 (1987).

150. MINN. STAT. § 595.02 (1987). Statutes that create evidentiary privileges are explained and analyzed on pp. 524–35.

151. 342 N.W.2d at 135. *See also* Matter of Baby X, 97 Mich. App. 111, 293 N.W.2d 736 (1980) (probate court may admit mother's medical records of drug dependency case in alleging neglect of newborn child); Goldade v. State, 674 P.2d 721 (Wyo. 1983) (4-year-old patient's statements to hospital nurse and physician about beatings by mother are admissible as an exception to the hearsay evidence rule).

152. 5 U.S.C. § 552 (1984).

153. 5 U.S.C. § 552(b)(3) (1984).

154. *Id.* at § 552(b)(6).

155. *Id.* at § 552(b)(5). Exemption 5 exempts "inter-agency or intra-agency memorandums or letters which would not be available by law to a party . . . in litigation with the agency." *E.g.*, Federal Trade Commission v. Grolier, Inc., 462 U.S. 19 (1983).

156. 5 U.S.C. § 552(b)(4) (1984) exempts "trade secrets and commercial or financial information obtained from any person and privileged or confidential."

157. Forsham v. Harris, 445 U.S. 169 (1980).

158. *Id.* at 185.

159. Kissinger v. Reporters Comm. for Freedom of Press, 445 U.S. 136 (1980).

160. *Id.* at 148.

161. 445 U.S. 169 (1980).

162. St. Mary Hosp. v. Philadelphia Professional Standards Review Org., No. 78–2943 (E.D. Pa., June 25, 1980).

163. Public Citizen Health Research Group v. Department of Health, Educ., and Welfare, 477 F. Supp. 595 (D.D.C. 1979) (PSROs are agencies subject to the act, and none of the exemptions apply because identification of patients will be omitted when the records are disclosed).

164. Public Citizen Health Research Group v. Department of Health, Educ., and Welfare, 668 F.2d 537 (D.C. Cir. 1981).

165. Omnibus Reconciliation Act of 1980, codified as 42 U.S.C. § 1320(c) (1985).

166. 42 U.S.C.A. §§ 1320c–1320c-13 (1987).

167. 42 C.F.R. § 401.135 (1986) (Social Security Act, Section 1106, prohibits government's disclosure of information obtained in discharging its duties "except as the Secretary may by regulations prescribe." 42 U.S.C. § 1306 (1984)).

168. 5 U.S.C. § 552(b)(4) (1984).

169. 18 U.S.C. § 1905 (1982).

170. *E.g.*, Humana of Va., Inc. v. Blue Cross of Va., 455 F. Supp. 1174 (E.D. Va. 1978) (news reporter may not gain access to cost reports of proprietary hospitals); Parkridge Hosp., Inc. v. Blue Cross and Blue Shield of Tenn., 430 F. Supp. 1093 (E.D. Tenn. 1977).

171. 441 U.S. 281 (1979).

172. Doctors Hosp. of Sarasota, Inc. v. Califano, 455 F. Supp. 476 (M.D. Fla. 1978)

(the state's Department of Health and Rehabilitation Services may have access to hospital's cost reports); St. Joseph's Hosp. Health Center v. Blue Cross, 489 F. Supp. 1052 (N.D. N.Y. 1979); Cedars Nursing and Convalescent Center, Inc. v. Aetna Life and Casualty Co., 472 F. Supp. 296 (E.D. Pa. 1979).

173. 5 U.S.C. § 552a (1984).

174. 5 U.S.C. § 552(b)(6) (1984).

175. Department of the Air Force v. Rose, 425 U.S. 352, 353 (1976).

176. 5 U.S.C. § 552(a)(4)(B) (1984).

177. Florida Medical Ass'n v. Department of Health, Educ., and Welfare, 479 F. Supp. 1291 (M.D. Fla. 1979).

178. 643 F.2d 1369 (9th Cir. 1981).

179. The Mississippi statute, Section 25-41-3 (1986), effective in January 1976, however, grants a specific exemption to the boards, committees, and staffs of both "public and private hospitals."

180. Douglas v. Michel, 410 So. 2d 936 (Fla. App. 1982).

181. Richmond County Hosp. Auth. v. Southeastern Newspapers Corp., 311 S.E.2d 806 (Ga. 1984); see also Moberly v. Herboldsheimer, 345 A.2d 855 (Md. App. 1975) (newspaper may compel municipal hospital to disclose administrator's salary and fees paid to legal counsel).

182. 412 So. 2d 894 (Fla. App. 1982).

183. FLA. STAT. § 768.40(4) (1985).

184. District Attorney for N. Dist. v. Board of Trustees of Leonard Morse Hosp., 389 Mass. 729, 452 N.E.2d 208 (1983).

185. Cape Coral Medical Center, Inc. v. News-Press Publishing Co., Inc., 390 So. 2d 1216 (Fla. App. 1980).

186. 357 So. 2d 626 (La. App. 1978).

187. Raton Public Service Co. v. Hobbes, 76 N.M. 535, 417 P.2d 32 (1966).

188. News-Press Publishing Co., Inc. v. Carlson, 410 So. 2d 546 (Fla. App. 1982) (budget committee appointed by governing board preparing proposed budget is subject to open-meetings statute).

189. Matter of John P. v. Whalen, 54 N.Y.2d 89, 429 N.E.2d 117, 444 N.Y.S.2d 598 (1981).

190. Matter of Short v. Board of Managers of Nassau County Medical Center, 57 N.Y.2d 399, 442 N.E.2d 1235, 456 N.Y.S.2d 724 (1982).

191. Eskaton Monterey Hosp. v. Myers, 134 Cal. App. 3d 788, 184 Cal. Rptr. 840 (1982).

192. Oliver v. Harborview Medical Center, 94 Wash. 2d 559, 618 P.2d 76 (1980).

193. Patients of Philadelphia State Hosp. v. Commonwealth of Pa., 417 A.2d 805 (Pa. Commw. Ct. 1980).

194. Nassau-Suffolk Hosp. Council v. Whalen, 89 Misc. 2d 304, 390 N.Y.S.2d 995 (1977).

195. Minnesota Medial Ass'n v. State, 274 N.W.2d 84 (Minn. 1978).

196. Citizens for Better Care v. Reizen, 215 N.W.2d 576 (Mich. 1974).

197. Apparently the first exception to the assertion in the text was the appellate court case of Allred v. State. 554 P.2d 411 (Alaska 1976). The Supreme Court of Alaska recognized a common-law privilege respecting communications made in psychotherapeutic treatment by psychiatrists and licensed psychologists.

See also In re "B", Appeal of Dr. Loren Roth, 482 Pa. 471, 394 A.2d 419 (1978) (patient-psychiatrist relationship creates a privilege founded on patient's constitutional right of privacy).

198. OHIO REV. CODE ANN. § 2317.02(B).

199. Boggess v. Aetna Life Ins. Co., 128 Ga. App. 190, 196 S.E.2d 172 (1973).

200. 70 Wash. 2d 168, 422 P.2d 480 (1967). See also Conyers v. Massa, 512 P.2d 283 (Colo. App. 1973) (privilege does not apply to examinations for third party's benefit).

201. Weis v. Weis, 147 Ohio St. 416, 72 N.E.2d 245 (1947); Sims v. Charlotte Liberty Mutual Ins. Co., 256 N.C. 32, 125 S.E.2d 326 (1962); In re Estate of Searchill, 9 Mich. App. 614, 157 N.W.2d 788 (1968) (when the mental competence of deceased at the time a contested will was executed was at issue, a hospital's medical records are admissible under the Michigan Business Records Act); Rivers v. Union Carbide Corp., 426 F.2d 633 (3d Cir. 1970) (hospital records disclosing a history of alcoholism and intoxication at the time of an accident are admissible by virtue of Federal Business Records Act, 28 U.S.C. § 1732).

202. City of Bay St. Louis v. Johnston, 222 So. 2d 841 (Miss. 1969).

203. United States v. Russo, 480 F.2d 1228 (6th Cir. 1973), cert. denied, 414 U.S. 1157 (1973).

204. Dorsten v. Lawrence, 20 Ohio App. 2d 297, 253 N.E.2d 804 (1969); Ce Buzz, Inc. v. Sniderman, 171 Colo. 246, 466 P.2d 457 (1970) (hospital records antedating an injury in litigation by as much as five years are not relevant); Kelly v. Sheehan, 158 Conn. 281, 259 A.2d 605 (1969) (statement in the hospital records that a "16-year-old boy was driving the car" was not admissible, because the patient did not make the statement, nor did it relate to his medical care and treatment).

205. In re Lifschutz, 2 Cal. 3d 415, 467 P.2d 557, 85 Cal. Rptr. 829 (1970) (although psychiatrist-patient privilege exists under California statute, the psychiatrist may not assert privilege and refuse to disclose a relationship with a particular patient when sued by the patient for assault; the psychiatrist may be jailed for contempt of court if he refuses to honor a subpoena). See also People v. Williams, 39 Mich. App. 91, 197 N.W.2d 336 (1972) (the state may not claim privilege; in a criminal prosecution for statutory rape, where the victim testified for the prosecution that she became pregnant and gave birth after an alleged assault by defendant, the state could not prevent defendant from calling the victim's physician as witness); Klinge v. Lutheran Medical Center of St. Louis, 518 S.W.2d 157 (Mo. 1974) (although hospital records are within the physician-patient privilege, the hospital medical staff committee may examine medical records of staff physicians' patients without their consent to determine qualifications and competence of such physicians, because the privilege is that of the patient and not the physician).

206. See discussion supra, "Breach of Contract."

207. 215 N.W.2d 134 (S.D. 1974).

208. Cf. In re "B", Appeal of Dr. Loren Roth, 482 Pa. 471 (1978) (statutory privilege waived by mother who placed her mental health in issue in custody hearing, but psychiatrist may not be compelled to testify because patient has privilege founded

on constitutional right of privacy); Trans-World Investments v. Drobny, 554 P.2d 1148 (Alaska 1976) (in suit for personal injury plaintiff has waived privilege).

209. GA. CODE ANN. § 24-9-21 (1982) (psychiatrists); GA. CODE ANN. § 43-39-16 (1984) (applied psychologists).

210. N.M. STAT. ANN. § 41-5-15 (1986).

211. Skelly v. Sunshine Mining Co., 62 Idaho 192, 109 P.2d 622 (1941); Hamilton v. P.E. Johnson and Sons, 224 Iowa 1097, 276 N.W. 841 (1937); Acosta v. Cary, 365 So. 2d 4 (La. App. 1978); *see also* IOWA CODE ANN. § 85.27 (West 1984); *cf.* The State *ex rel.* Holman v. Dayton Press, Inc., 11 Ohio St. 3d 66 (1984) (Industrial Commission may not require claimant to waive physician-patient privilege as a precondition to consideration of worker's compensation claim).

212. PA. STAT. ANN. tit. 42, § 5929 (Purdon 1982).

213. The privilege of confidentiality in Ohio does not extend to dentists. Belichick v. Belichick, 37 Ohio App. 2d 95, 307 N.E.2d 270 (1973). The Ohio statute was quoted earlier in this section.

214. *But see* State of Iowa v. Bedel, 193 N.W.2d 121 (Iowa 1971) (blood-alcohol test with consent of hospitalized patient on request of arresting officer not privileged when not related to medical diagnoses and treatment); Unick v. Kessler Memorial Hosp., 107 N.J. 121, 257 A.2d 134 (1969). *See also Klinge, supra* note 205.

215. Hospitals are frequently innocent bystanders when the confidentiality of records is contested. In Nelson v. Grissom, 152 Colo. 362, 382 P.2d 991 (1963), an ex-husband brought an action to prevent his former wife from removing their children from the state. The woman had remarried, and plaintiff challenged the fitness of the stepfather to care properly for the children and sought access to medical records bearing on the stepfather's physical and mental condition. In such situations hospitals should not release the information without a court order; the court will decide the issue of privilege in accordance with local law.

216. Roberts v. Superior Court of Butte County, 9 Cal. 3d 330, 508 P.2d 309, 107 Cal. Rptr. 309 (1973).

217. Hughson v. St. Francis Hosp. of Port Jervis, 93 A.D.2d 491, 463 N.Y.S.2d 224 (1983); *see also* Williams v. Roosevelt Hosp., N.Y.L.J., Feb. 24, 1984, at 6, col. 3B (Sup., N.Y., Feb. 6, 1984) (mother who is not a party to action for her son's injuries at birth may assert that her own medical records are privileged).

218 Grey v. Los Angeles Superior Court, 62 Cal. App. 3d 698, 133 Cal. Rptr. 318 (1976).

219. Grosslight v. Superior Court of Los Angeles County, 72 Cal. App. 3d 502, 140 Cal. Rptr. 278 (1977).

220. Tucson Medical Center, Inc. v. Rowles, 21 Ariz. App. 424, 520 P.2d 518 (1974).

221. Parkson v. Central DuPage Hosp., 105 Ill. App. 3d 850, 435 N.E.2d 140 (1982).

222. Ziegler v. Superior Court in and for the County of Pima, 134 Ariz. 390, 656 P.2d 1251 (1982).

223. Connell v. Washington Hosp. Center, 50 F.R.D. 360 (D.D.C. 1970); King v. O'Connor, 103 Misc. 2d 607, 426 N.Y.S.2d 415 (1980) (name and address of patient possibly a witness to alleged malpractice is discoverable); Vanadio v. Good Samaritan Hosp., 85 A.D.2d 662, 445 N.Y.S.2d 215 (1981) (hospital must disclose names and addresses of patients sharing room with plaintiff); Lipari v.

Center for Reproductive and Sexual Health, Inc., 187 N.Y.L.J. No. 91, May 12, 1982, at 12, col. 5M (plaintiff is entitled to names, addresses, and records kept by physicians who examined or were consulted by him); Geisberger v. Willuhn, 390 N.E.2d 945 (Ill. App. 1979) (privilege does not apply to patient's name).

224. Mayer v. Albany Medical Center Hosp., 37 A.D.2d 1011, 325 N.Y.S.2d 517 (1971).

225. Katz v. State of N.Y., 41 A.D.2d 879, 342 N.Y.S.2d 906 (1973); Moore v. St. John's Episcopal Hosp., 89 A.D.2d 618, 452 N.Y.S.2d 669 (1982) (although medical records of a hospitalized patient are privileged in absence of waiver, hospital must disclose to malpractice plaintiff nonmedical information reporting prior assaults or violent behavior of another patient).

226. 79 Misc. 2d 244, 360 N.Y.S.2d 178 (1974).

227. Mattison v. Poulen, 353 A.2d 327 (Vt. 1976).

228. Sklagen v. Greater S.E. Community Hosp., 625 F. Supp. 991 (D.D.C. 1984).

229. Carr v. Schmid, 432 N.Y.S.2d 807 (Sup. Ct. 1980). *See also* Pennison v. Provident Life and Accident Ins. Co., 154 So. 2d 617 (La. Ct. App. 1963) (wife's medical records are subject to subpoena in divorce action if relevant to litigated issues).

230. 81 AM. JUR. 2d *Witnesses* § 268 (1976). *See also* Greuling v. Breakey, 56 A.D.2d 540, 391 N.Y.S.2d 585 (1977) (in malpractice action against physician, plaintiff must furnish defendant with medical records of treatment by other physicians; patient could not refuse access to these medical records when plaintiff's physical condition in issue).

231. Wenninger v. Muesing, 307 Minn. 405, 240 N.W.2d 333 (1976); Jaap v. Dist. Court of Eighth Judicial Dist., 623 P.2d 1389 (Mont. 1981); Fields v. McNamara, 189 Colo. 284, 540 P.2d 327 (1975); Weaver v. Mann, 90 F.R.D. 443 (D.N.D. 1981).

232. Trans-World Investments v. Drobny, 554 P.2d 1148 (Alaska 1976) (patient waived privilege by filing personal injury suit); Wright by Wright v. Group Health Hosp., 130 Wash. 2d 192, 691 P.2d 564 (1984) (plaintiff's attorney in malpractice action may interview employees of HMOs *ex parte*; improper for defendant to advise employees not to speak to attorneys representing adverse interests).

233. United States v. Kansas City Lutheran Home and Hosp. Ass'n, 297 F. Supp. 239 (W.D. Mo. 1969).

234. United States v. Providence Hosp., 507 F. Supp. 519 (E.D. Mich. 1981). *See also* United States v. Cherry Hill Women's Center, Inc., 512 F. Supp. 1303 (E.D. Pa. 1981) (IRS may compel abortion clinic owned by physician to produce records without patient's consent).

235. United States v. Westinghouse Electric Corp., 638 F.2d 570 (3d 1980); General Motors Corp. v. Director of NIOSH, 636 F.2d 163 (6th Cir. 1980).

236. United States v. University Hosp. of State Univ. of N.Y. at Stony Brook, 575 F. Supp. 607 (E.D.N.Y. 1983).

237. 729 F.2d 144 (2d Cir. 1984).

238. 575 F. Supp. At 611.

239. *Id*. at 615–16.

240. *In re* Michael Artery: A Witness Before Special April 1980 Grand Jury, No. 80 GJ 1435 (N.D. Ill., Aug. 13, 1981).

241. Hawaii Psychiatric Soc'y v. Ariyoshi, 481 F. Supp. 1028 (D.C. Haw. 1979).

242. *In re* Zuniga, 714 F.2d 632 (6th Cir. 1983).

243. Camperlengo v. Blum 56 N.Y.2d 251, 436 N.E.2d 1299, 451 N.Y.S.2d 697 (1982). *Accord, In re* Grand Jury Investigation, 441 A.2d 525 (R.I. 1982). *See also* State of Ill. v. Herbert, 438 N.E.2d 1255 (Ill. App. 1982) (grand jury may subpoena records of Medicaid patients; privileged communication does not apply because state had patient's consent; constitutional protection against self-incrimination does not apply because subpoena limited to records required by law); *In re* June 1979 Allegheny County Investigating Grand Jury, 415 A.2d 73 (Pa. 1980) (grand jury may subpoena patient's tissue reports).

244. People v. Doe, 116 Misc. 2d 626, 455 N.Y.S.2d 945 (1982).

245. Board of Medical Quality Assurance v. Hazel Hawkins Memorial Hosp., 135 Cal. App. 3d 561, 185 Cal. Rptr. 405 (1982) (patient's records of disciplinary proceedings, without names, may be subpoenaed); *cf.* Division of Medical Quality v. Gherardini, 93 Cal. App. 3d 669, 256 Cal. Rptr. 55 (1979) (records of five identified patients not subject to subpoena unless state interest overcomes state's constitutional right of privacy).

246. Several cases illustrate the impropriety of releasing medical information to the police. *E.g.,* Matter of Grand Jury Investigation of Onondaga County, 463 N.Y.S.2d 758 (1983) (names and addresses of patients treated for knife wounds during given period are not discoverable by district attorney investigating a murder; hospital may assert privilege on behalf of patient); State of N.J. v. Dyal, 97 N.J. 229, 478 A.2d 390 (1984) (without subpoena police may not obtain results of blood-alcohol test made for medical purposes when patient was not in custody or under arrest). See also discussion in Chapter 11, "Consent for Treatment and the Withholding of Consent," pp. 376–78.

MEDICAL STAFF APPOINTMENTS AND PRIVILEGES

T his chapter will discuss the rights of licensed physicians and other professional practitioners to acquire and retain appointments on a hospital's medical staff. The focus of the discussion will be the relationship between the independent fee-for-service private practitioner and the community general hospital, usually a private not-for-profit organization. The chapter will explore the differences between physicians' rights vis-à-vis publicly owned (governmental) hospitals and their rights when the hospital is a private corporation. This chapter will also explore the differences in the hospital-physician relationship occasioned by the growing trend of hiring physicians as employees.

Excluded from this analysis are situations in which hospitals limit their service to particular patients, such as the mentally ill or children, and situations involving appointment in the medical school as a prerequisite to staff privileges.

Hospital's Duty to Use Reasonable Care in Appointment of Staff

The hospital, as a legal entity, bears ultimate responsibility for the quality of the clinical practice rendered within the organization. The hospital's governing board (typically referred to as the board of trustees or directors) has a duty to the institution's patients to exercise reasonable care in the appointment and retention of the physicians on its medical staff. Failure to do so can result in liability, even though the physicians are technically independent contractors.[1] And obviously, liability under the doctrine of *respondeat superior* will apply when the physicians are employees, as is more and more frequently the case.

The hospital's duty to exercise reasonable care in the selection and retention of the independent medical staff practitioners has traditionally been separate and distinct from the hospital's vicarious liability for injuries to patients from malpractice or negligence committed in the institution.[2] Patients who sue for a breach of this duty need not allege and prove that an employment relationship exists between the hospital and the physician, nor is it necessary to prove that the doctor's negligence was within the scope of his or her employment.[3] All that is needed is to allege and establish that the hospital was negligent in granting or renewing staff privileges and that this negligence was the proximate cause of injury to the patient. If the hospital knew or should have known that the physician appointed to its staff was incompetent, liability will attach. Breach of this duty is sometimes referred to as "corporate" or "institutional" liability.

The institution's duty to use reasonable care in granting medical staff privileges cannot be delegated to the organized medical staff, to the local medical society, or to any other group or individual. The hospital's governing board may not abdicate its legal duties regarding management of the institution, whether in business or clinical affairs. Although it has been suggested that the governing body, which may be composed primarily or even entirely of lay persons, is incapable of judging professional competence, courts and legislatures have decided emphatically that responsibility must be vested in the governing board.[4] The board may authorize the medical staff to make recommendations about staff appointments and clinical privileges (which recommendations are generally approved, by the way) but the staff's role is limited to giving advice; the board retains ultimate responsibility for final decisions.[5]

For these reasons, the corporate institution itself must create a workable system for the hospital medical staff to review and evaluate the quality of care being rendered within the institution. The staff must be well organized to carry out the role delegated to it by the governing body. All powers of the medical staff flow from the board of trustees, and the staff must be held strictly accountable to the governing board for quality control.

The medical staff bylaws must clearly define the structure of the medical staff, the lines of communication among staff committees and between the staff and the board of trustees, and the areas of delegated authority. The hospital attorney should play a key role in making these matters clear. In a multihospital organization, furthermore, there must be a mechanism for the system governing board to communicate with each facility's medical staff and for each medical staff to interact with the corporate levels in matters relating to patient care services. This can be accomplished by an advisory board arrangement whereby each specific hospital can respond directly to the chief executive officer of the whole organization. More commonly today, however, healthcare systems have a physician employed full time as a corporate director of medical affairs. This position serves as liaison between the various medical staff and the corporate office.

Two issues emerge with respect to the hospital-physician relationship:

1. How can the physician be best integrated into the management of hospital affairs to encourage institutional responsibility and loyalty?
2. The second issue is a legal question: What are the rights of a licensed physician to attain and retain a hospital staff appointment?

Clearly if the institution has the responsibility to select and retain its medical staff, which in turn requires the governing board to see that medical staff conducts an effective and continuing process of peer review, it is advisable to have physicians on the board. In the past when business and medical administration of a hospital were separate, it was thought that conflicts of interest would exist if members of the medical staff were also members of the board. Although it is true that conflicts of interest can occur when physicians are placed on the governing body, the problem is no different than with the lay members and can be readily resolved by full disclosure and by making certain that the interested trustee, whether a physician or not, takes no part in decisions before the board in which he or she has a personal interest. The reasons in favor of integrating physicians into the management of hospitals far outweigh those in favor of a board of trustees consisting entirely of lay members.[6] The medical staff of a particular hospital, however, should not be granted the privilege of electing a "representative" to the board. All trustees are to be appointed or selected in accordance with corporate law and the corporate bylaws, and all must serve the institution, not represent a particular group of individuals or special interests.

Without staff privileges a physician or other professional practitioner is severely handicapped in practice and suffers an irreparable financial detriment. The legal issues concerning a licensed practitioner's right to attain and retain a hospital staff appointment with defined or delineated privileges are resolved in particular controversies by reference to constitutional law, statutory enactments, or simply the common law of judicial decision. The relevant law and the resolution of a particular case will of course depend on the allegations made in the plaintiff's complaint, the facts of the case, and the philosophy of the court rendering the opinion.

In a sense both case and statutory law surrounding the related problems of hospital liability and medical staff privileges are attempts to resolve a dilemma. How should American legal doctrines balance the sometimes conflicting interests and public policies? On one hand, as has been amply demonstrated in the preceding chapter, the hospital is responsible for adequately controlling the quality of care. On the other hand, it is generally in the public interest to allow licensed physicians the greatest possible individual freedom to practice their profession. Are these propositions irreconcilable? Control of quality implies, perhaps, maximum discretion on the part of the hospital in selecting staff physicians and regulating their professional practice. Individual freedom to practice implies the opposite—an absence of hospital control over medical staff appointments and the least possible discretionary control over individual doctors' privileges, once they have gained appointment.

This dilemma will be apparent throughout the ensuing discussion of some of the many recorded cases dealing with medical staff privileges. Because the courts have traditionally approached these controversies by first categorizing the hospital involved as either public of private—which in turn may determine the relevant rule or rules of law to apply—the discussion will follow a similar pattern.

Public Hospitals—Due Process and Equal Protection Requirements

More than 50 years ago the U.S. Supreme Court held that a licensed physician does not have a constitutional right to a medical staff appointment, even when the hospital involved is public.[7] However, if the hospital is a public or governmental hospital, the Fourteenth Amendment's provision that "*no state* [shall] deprive any person of life, liberty, or property, without *due process of law*; nor deny to any person . . . *the equal protection of the laws*" comes into play [emphasis supplied]. But the Fourteenth Amendment only applies to a *state*. Therefore, for private parties (including hospitals), the constitutional requirement applies only when they are engaged in "state action."[8]

What constitutes state action? It is something more than the mere receipt by a hospital of substantial federal funds. The U.S. Court of Appeals for the Second Circuit once affirmed a lower federal court ruling that a private hospital that revoked a physician's privileges who pleaded guilty to a charge of criminal assault was not engaged in state action in soing so.[9] According to the Second Circuit and the majority of courts, state action sufficient to entitle the doctor to constitutional protection is present only in the following extremely limited situation in which:

1. government involvement with the private hospital is significant;
2. state activity causes the alleged injury to the doctor (the "nexus" requirement); and
3. the state aids, encourages, or *connotes approval* of the activity.[10]

In applying this three-pronged standard, the Second Circuit held that government does not aid or approve the activity or cause the injury simply by providing funding to the hospital or by regulating the institution through licensure, certificate-of-need legislation, or other controls.[11] The court further stated that a private hospital is not performing a public function when it appoints physicians to its medical staff.[12] Today it is generally recognized that private hospitals, although highly regulated and funded in large part by government, are not instrumentalities of the state for constitutional purposes.

If state action can be established (as, for example, when the organization is city-, county-, or state-owned), hospitals must extend both substantive and procedural due process and equal protection to any physician who makes an initial application for a medical staff appointment and to any current staff member subject to disciplinary action.[13] Substantive due process creates and defines the rights and duties existing under the legal relationship between the hospital and the physician. The issue arises when property or other rights are directly affected by state action. Substantive due process and equal protection require the hospital to act reasonably, not capriciously or arbitrarily, and in accordance with permissible objectives. Procedural due process relates to the way substantive rules are made and administered. It requires a hospital to implement and enforce its rules and regulations fairly. More will be said about substantive reasonableness and procedural fairness throughout this chapter.

Because public or governmental hospitals are clearly involved in state action, they must grant due process and equal protection to physicians applying for an appointment to the medical staff and to current members of the staff being subjected to disciplinary proceedings. Most courts addressing this issue, however, have held that private not-for-profit hospitals and proprietary institutions need not accord physicians these rights. Thus, physicians' constitutional due process rights differ depending on whether the institution is public or private. Some commentators have suggested that this dichotomy is neither just nor equitable because both public and private hospitals serve the same community.[14] In fact, several sources of law are now imposing requirements of reasonableness on the private hospital that are essentially equivalent to the constitutional standards applicable to public hospitals. The clear trend of the law—statutory and case—thus reflects a narrowing of the distinction between the duties of public and private hospitals although a distinction between public and private ownership remains.

Qualifications of Staff Physicians

On the basis of various state and federal laws, no public hospital or private institution receiving federal financial assistance (including funds for Medicare) may discriminate in medical staff appointments on the basis of race, creed, color, sex, disability, national origin, or other prohibited category.[15] Such discrimination violates not only specific statutory prohibitions but also the equal protection clause of the Fourteenth Amendment.[16] The specific requirements were clarified in *Sosa v. Board of Managers of Val Verde Hospital.*[17]

In *Sosa* the court upheld the hospital that had denied Dr. Sosa admission to the medical staff. As a county institution, the defendant hospital was clearly subject to the Fourteenth Amendment. The factors considered by the medical staff credentials committee in recommending that the board deny the application—the applicant's character, qualifications, and standing in the community—were deemed by the court to be reasonable and not arbitrary.[18] A significant part of the ruling held that all standards and reasons for rejection need not be spelled out precisely in the medical staff bylaws.[19] The court discussed at length the application of the due process clause:

> [S]taff appointments may be constitutionally refused if the refusal is based upon "any reasonable basis such as the professional and ethical qualifications of the physicians or the common good of the public and the Hospital. Admittedly, standards such as "character, qualifications, and standing" are very general, but this court recognizes that in the area of personal fitness for medical staff privileges precise standards are difficult if not impossible to articulate. The subjectives of selection

simply cannot be minutely codified. The governing board of a hospital must therefore be given great latitude in prescribing the necessary qualifications for potential applicants. So long as the hearing process gives notice of the particular charges of incompetency and ethical fallibilities, we need not exact a précis of the standard in codified form.

On the other hand, it is clear that in exercising its broad discretion the board must refuse staff applicants only for those matters which are reasonably related to the operation of the hospital. Arbitrariness and false standards are to be eschewed. Moreover, procedural due process must be afforded the applicant so that he may explain or show to be untrue those matters which lead the board to reject his application.[20]

The court noted that there was considerable evidence regarding Dr. Sosa's lack of ethical and professional competency. It was reluctant to substitute its own evaluation of such matters for that of the board because the board, not the court, is charged with the responsibility of providing a competent staff of doctors.[21]

Procedural due process means *fundamental fairness* under all the facts and circumstances. The concept has no fixed, ironclad definition; it is related to the time, place, and circumstances of each case. More will be said later in this chapter about these procedural matters.

Charges of lacking surgical judgment, being without a surgical assistant, and assisting another who had no surgical privileges, all supported by medical records of specific instances, constituted "sufficient notice" for discipline in the case of *Woodbury v. McKinnon*.[22] The court also held that the hearing can be informal, the plaintiff's attorney need not be permitted to question the other doctors present, as long as the plaintiff could ask questions, and cross-examination need not be a part of every hearing to satisfy due process.[23]

A governmental hospital may thus exercise considerable discretion with respect to medical staff appointments and privileges when the motive is to enhance the quality of care. It has been held proper for a governmental hospital to have and enforce rules regarding the maintenance and completion of medical records.[24] Rules stating well-recognized professional qualifications as prerequisites for defined privileges will be upheld by the courts as long as the rules are reasonable, definite, certain, and capable of objective application.[25] The key to validating a particular rule is that it be related to an individual's specific qualifications rather than to class-based distinctions such as race or creed. In formulating the rules, which should be stated in the hospital or medical staff bylaws, the board may rely on professional standards recommended by the medical staff. Thus in *Selden v. City of Sterling* the court approved a rule that stated that an associate medical staff member could not perform major surgery without having a full staff member in attendance.[26] Similarly, in the interests of patient care a governmental hospital may have a closed staff in the radiology department as long as the reasons for such a decision can be adequately documented.[27]

Does a like philosophy prevail with respect to physicians who do not hold the M.D. degree? With osteopathic physicians, for example, local legislation is an important consideration. If the licensing statutes and other legislation equate doctors of medicine and osteopathy, it can be argued that the osteopathic physician must be accorded equal substantive rights and opportunities on the basis of individual training and qualifications.[28] Because the medical and osteopathic professions have essentially merged, and because the antitrust statutes apply to the hospital-physician relationship, it is contrary to public policy for hospitals to exclude osteopathic or other non-M.D. physicians as a group.

Access of Limited and Allied Health Care Practitioners to the Hospital

Statutes are also crucial in determining chiropractors' and other allied health professionals' rights to practice in governmental institutions. For example, North Carolina and North Dakota extend to chiropractors the right to practice in public hospitals within the scope of their licenses.[29] On the other hand, Oklahoma and Oregon make a clear distinction between physicians and chiropractors that permits the latter to be excluded from the staff of a county hospital.[30]

Bylaws that allow exclusion of an entire class of persons, such as podiatrists or physician's assistants—who are authorized by law to perform limited healthcare functions—may be rejected as unreasonable and contrary to constitutional law, state statutes, or common law.[31] When local law gives rights of limited practice to designated individuals, hospitals are required to act reasonably and not arbitrarily with respect to these persons' privileges.[32] It is not, however, necessary to grant full clinical privileges within the scope of license to these practitioners. Instead, hospitals are required to evaluate applications for privileges by allied health care professionals fairly and objectively and to base their decisions on reasonable criteria.[33] Such evaluation calls for an assessment of the individual's training, experience, and competence in relation to recognized standards of patient care and institutional objectives. Of course neither an evaluation of this kind nor a due process hearing necessarily requires actually granting privileges.[34]

A North Carolina case illustrates this concept. In *Cameron v. New Hanover Memorial Hospital, Inc.* the governing board of a governmental hospital granted limited privileges to two podiatrists but denied them the privilege to perform major surgery, which they sought.[35] The denial was based on the fact that the plaintiffs had not been declared eligible or certified by the American Board of Podiatric Surgery. Because the hospital required all persons appointed to the medical staff to meet the standards of eligibility or certification set by their specialty boards, the hospital board's decision was upheld as reasonably related to the operation, needs, and goals of the hospital. Further, a complete review of the podiatrists' experience and training had been conducted and procedural due process had been followed.

The Joint Commission approved a revised "Medical Staff Standard" recognizing that the "medical staff" may "include other licensed individuals permitted by law and the hospital to provide patient care services independently."[36] This standard was effective July 1, 1984, and noncompliance became a factor in accreditation decisions rendered in 1985. A careful interpretation of the standard reveals that a given hospital is not actually required to accept limited practitioners unconditionally as members of the medical staff. Such persons may be appointed to membership and then granted clinical privileges consistent with their scope of practice as articulated by local licensure law and the individual's training, experience, and demonstrated competence. The standard will be more fully discussed in the context of the private hospital's right to select medical staff.

Discipline of Professional Staff

A public hospital, again in the interest of its patients' care, may discipline, suspend, or refuse to reappoint a staff physician if there is sufficient evidence of incompetence or intolerable behavior.[37] In *Koelling v. Skiff Memorial Hospital* the Iowa court upheld an indefinite suspension of a staff physician charged with preparing deceptive and misleading medical records, giving fabricated, inconsistent explanations for his handling of a case, and rendering seriously inadequate medical care. In such circumstances physicians are entitled to a hearing, the right to present proof, and the right to cross-examine witnesses, and these were accorded in the *Koelling* case.[38]

The 1972 case of *Moore v. Carson-Tahoe Hospital* is most instructive with respect to the hospital's twofold duties: to exercise reasonable care in the selection and retention of medical staff, and to extend both substantive and procedural rights of due process to the physician when disciplinary action is undertaken.[39] *Moore* involved a contested termination of a medical staff appointment at a Nevada public hospital. Dr. Moore had been licensed to practice in Nevada, was certified by the board, and had specialized in obstetrics and gynecology. Acting in accordance with the medical staff bylaws, the governing body terminated his appointment on the ground of unprofessional conduct.

The specific acts precipitating the termination were not, however, expressly prohibited in the medical staff bylaws or the hospital's rules and regulations. The doctor had allegedly attempted to administer a spinal anesthetic to an obstetrics patient but had failed to employ a proper sterile technique in that he had prepared the medication, performed a minimal skin preparation, and handled the spinal needle, all without the use of sterile gloves. Further, he was not successful in several attempts at spinal puncture. Two days later the chief of the medical staff, with concurrence of another physician, canceled

Dr. Moore's scheduled surgery for that day, considering that he was "in no condition physically or mentally to perform surgery."

Dr. Moore brought suit to regain his hospital privileges. He did not allege any violation of his rights to procedural due process. Indeed, at the medical staff hearing he was permitted to have counsel present, to call friendly witnesses, and to cross-examine adverse witnesses. He did maintain, however, that he was denied *substantive* due process of law by reason of the uncertain meaning of "unprofessional conduct," the basis on which his privileges were revoked.[40] The Nevada Supreme Court disagreed, citing a Florida case that said: "Detailed description of prohibited conduct is concededly impossible, perhaps even undesirable in view of rapidly shifting standards of medical excellence and the fact that a human life may be and quite often is involved in the ultimate decision of the board."[41]

The *Moore* court held that the standard of "unprofessional conduct" was sufficiently objective, then went on to say,

> Today in response to demands of the public, the hospital is becoming a community health center. The purpose of the community hospital is to provide patient care of the highest possible quality. To implement this duty of providing competent medical care to the patients, it is the responsibility of the institution to create a workable system whereby the medical staff of the hospital continually reviews and evaluates the quality of care being rendered within the institution. The staff must be organized with a proper structure to carry out the role delegated to it by the governing body. All powers of the medical staff flow from the board of trustees, and the staff must be held accountable for its control of quality. The concept of corporate responsibility for the quality of medical care was forcibly advanced in *Darling v. Charleston Community Memorial Hospital,* wherein the Illinois Supreme Court held that hospitals and their governing bodies may be held liable for injuries resulting from imprudent or careless supervision of members of their medical staffs.
>
> The role of the hospital vis-à-vis the community is changing rapidly. The hospital's role is no longer limited to the furnishing of physical facilities and equipment where a physician treats his private patients and practices his profession in his own individualized manner.
>
> The right to enjoy medical staff privileges in a community hospital is not an absolute right, but rather is subject to the reasonable rules and regulations of the hospital. Licensing, *per se,* furnishes no continuing control with respect to a physician's professional competence and therefore does not assure the public of quality patient care. The protection of the public must come from some other authority, and that in this case is the Hospital Board of Trustees. The Board, of course, may not act arbitrarily or unreasonably in such

cases. The Board's actions must also be predicated upon a reasonable standard.[42]

In addition to the court's holding that the board had followed sufficiently objective standards and rules and regulations, involving no denial of substantive due process, the court further held that the documented evidence at the hearing justified the decision to terminate Dr. Moore's privileges.

The *Moore* case provides an excellent illustration of how the duly organized medical staff assumes its properly delegated function of recommending corrective action to the hospital's governing body to enforce reasonable rules and regulations *before* actual injury to a patient occurs.[43]

Appointments in Private Hospitals

Statutory Standards Regulating Appointments

The fundamental trends of the law in many jurisdictions point toward equating private hospitals with public (governmental) institutions in terms of the standards for medical staff appointments. Voluntary hospitals must therefore also act reasonably and not arbitrarily when considering medical staff appointments and must use fair procedures in applying their rules and regulations. Several legal or quasi-legal developments lead to this result, depending on the facts of the given case and the relevant statutory or judicial law:

- state statutory enactments that prohibit defined forms of discriminatory or arbitrary decisions by a hospital governing board;
- state judicial law that simply requires the hospital to act reasonably and with fairness as a matter of public policy;
- application of state and federal antitrust statutes prohibiting unlawful restraints of trade;
- rules prohibiting malicious interference with a licensed physician's right to practice medicine; and
- application of federal statutory civil rights legislation and occasionally of the Fourteenth Amendment to the private, voluntary hospital.

Furthermore, both the Medicare *Conditions of Participation: Hospitals* and the standards of the Joint Commission on Accreditation of Healthcare Organizations require the essence of due process. All these developments reduce the range of freedom and discretion previously enjoyed by the private hospital's board of trustees in appointing or reappointing staff physicians and improve considerably the doctor's ability to gain appointment.

As noted earlier in the context of the governmental hospital, if medical staff bylaws of a private hospital arbitrarily exclude certain named classes of practitioners or allied health care professionals from consideration for clinical privileges, they may be invalid either because a local state statute prohibits such discriminatory conduct or simply by virtue of common law. Statutes, for example, may prohibit a hospital from summarily dismissing an application solely because the applicant is an osteopathic physician, a podiatrist, or other specifically identified practitioner entitled to consideration.

One of the more comprehensive statutes of this type is the District of Columbia's, which grants procedural safeguards to clinical psychologists, podiatrists, nurse-midwives, nurse-anesthetists, and nurse-practitioners.[44] In short, applications for hospital access from these practitioners must be evaluated fairly in light of the individual's qualifications, current competence, and the needs of the hospital. A few statutes go further by providing that certain designated licensed practitioners must be allowed to use the hospital's facilities.[45] As a general rule, however, these statutes do not require that the limited or allied practitioner be granted medical staff membership or sole authority to admit patients to the hospital. Moreover, medical staff bylaws should always provide for a credentialing process and for well-defined physician supervision of practitioners who are entitled to render medical services only under such direction.

In Ohio, as a further example of legislative influence, the relevant anti-discriminatory statute reads:

> The governing body of any hospital, in considering and acting upon applications for staff membership or professional privileges within the scope of the applicants' respective licenses, shall not discriminate against a qualified person solely on the basis of whether such person is certified to practice medicine or osteopathic medicine, or podiatry, or dentistry.[46]

The purpose of the statute is to prevent *classwide* discrimination against the named applicants for access to the hospital while still observing the hospital's responsibility to establish reasonable standards for its staff and to determine the qualifications for each individual. Hence, hospital rules that required podiatrists to complete two years of postgraduate training in an approved residency program in addition to board certification or eligibility, as well as rules that prohibited podiatrists from conducting surgical procedures with anesthesia and denied them the right to vote or hold office within the staff organization, were all *prima facie* discriminatory.[47] Such provisions were unreasonable and lacked any rational purpose because less than 10 percent of all podiatric graduates in the United States had completed a two-year residency, no residency programs were available in Ohio, and similar restrictions did not apply to dentists or oral surgeons.

As noted earlier, in 1985 the Joint Commission implemented a revised "Medical Staff Standard" recognizing that a hospital's organized medical staff may "include other licensed individuals permitted by law and the hospital to provide patient care service independently."[48] In essence the standard and its interpretation authorize but do not require a hospital to grant medical staff membership and clinical privileges to limited practitioners consistent with their legally authorized scope of practice and each individual's training, experience, and demonstrated competence. Previously the standards had restricted membership to licensed medical practitioners and dentists, unless otherwise provided by local law. State statutes or rules and regulations of the medical licensure board may identify those persons who are entitled to medical staff membership. For example, a given statute or rule may restrict membership to physicians and dentists; others may extend the right of membership to osteopathic physicians, podiatrists, psychologists, and other named classes of practitioners. Unless local law prohibits the granting of staff membership to others than physicians, the standards of the Joint Commission thus permit a hospital to extend membership status to a limited practitioner.

When state law recognizes a given practitioner as having the right to practice independently—podiatrists and nurse-midwives, for example—and the hospital agrees to grant such a person access, then the hospital is required to delineate clinical privileges on an individual basis. An independent practitioner is one permitted to provide healthcare services without direction or supervision by a physician. The commission's standard does not make it mandatory for the hospital to extend staff membership to such a person, however, because the granting of clinical privileges is not necessarily conditional upon membership. According to the JCAHO standard:

- a dependent practitioner may render services only under medical direction and supervision;
- the right to admit patients may be limited to members of the medical staff;
- initial staff appointments may be provisional;
- a majority of the medical staff's executive committee must be physicians;
- heads of departments are responsible for monitoring the clinical performance of all persons in the department;
- quality assurance programs must be in place; and
- the hospital's governing body remains ultimately responsible for standards of clinical performance.

In promulgating the revised "Medical Staff Standard" the Joint Commission was simply responding to economic, social, and legal developments. Patients have increasingly demanded the services of limited and allied health care practitioners; economists and managed care organizations have suggested that these practitioners can provide quality care at less cost than physicians; and political lobbying and litigation have prompted hospitals and their medical staffs to accept the allied practitioner as a component of the healthcare team. It follows that the concept of due process and fundamental fairness should be extended to all recognized practitioners.

Statutes in Louisiana and New York further illustrate the equivalency of private and public institutions. Louisiana provides that a voluntary hospital may not deny medical staff membership solely because of a physician's participation in a group medical practice or lack of membership in a specialty body or professional society.[49] New York hospitals, both public and private, may not reject applicants on the basis of their participation in a group practice or a not-for-profit health insurance plan.[50] Hospital counsel and professional staff must be alert to such local statutory provisions.

The Common Law

Traditionally the courts have regarded voluntary hospitals as private institutions and hence their governing bodies could adopt and enforce whatever rules they wished to control medical staff appointments and staff discipline, so long as the action was not capricious and was without malice.[51] The range of discretion extended to the hospital's board of trustees by this judicial attitude is almost unlimited because the courts have hesitated to intrude into the internal management of hospitals and thus have not inquired into the arbitrariness or reasonableness of rules concerning eligibility for an initial staff appointment or reappointment. Procedurally, an applicant for a staff appointment, or a current member of the medical staff who is not to be reappointed or is subject to discipline, has not been entitled to a hearing or other procedural safeguards unless the bylaws of the hospital or medical staff positively provided such protection.[52]

Neither receipt of federal or state funds nor possession of tax-exempt status changes the private status of a voluntary hospital, and accordingly neither brings into play the rules of judicial review pertaining to a government hospital.[53] The cases of *Shulman v. Washington Hospital Center*[54] and *Foote v. Community Hospital of Beloit*[55] illustrate the traditional approach, granting to the voluntary hospital's governing board a nearly absolute discretion in denying staff privileges. In the *Foote* case the Kansas court indicated that it was not necessary for the hospital to grant a hearing to an applicant for a staff position upon denial of his application.[56] In other words, the decision of the hospital's governing board is final and not subject to judicial review.[57]

The traditional judicial attitude of allowing the private hospital an almost unlimited discretion in matters relating to medical staff appointments is tempered, however, by the common-law doctrine that interference with a physician's right to practice, committed maliciously, constitutes a cause of action.[58] There is never a privilege to act with malice. Accordingly, where it was established that certain doctors were motivated by their own financial interests in preventing the plaintiff from obtaining staff privileges in the only hospital in the county, an action could be brought against the hospital, the doctors, and the individuals on the governing body.[59]

Further, state common law pertaining to unlawful restraints of trade can be used as a legal theory to attack a voluntary hospital's arbitrary denial of medical staff privileges. The action can be brought against individual members of the board of trustees, the medical staff, and/or the hospital corporation, when the defendant intentionally and without good faith prevents admission to hospital practice on some other basis than the plaintiff's professional qualifications or standards of patient care.[60] In such an action the major problem consists of balancing the physician's interest in practicing medicine against the hospital's interest in regulating or preventing their practice. Certainly public policy must play a large role in the court's approach. For example, in *Blank v. Palo Alto-Stanford Hospital Center* the court held that a contract granting exclusive privileges to a group of radiologists for the operation of a hospital's radiology department did not violate California's restraint-of-trade concepts when it was established that the contract was entered into to ensure high-quality care—thus being in the best interests of both the public and the hospital's medical staff.[61]

In the 1980s, especially, physicians used antitrust laws with increasing frequency (but without much success) to challenge adverse decisions regarding medical staff appointments. Both the states and the federal government have antitrust statutes, and either can be the foundation for a lawsuit. As would be expected, however, the federal statutes are the more significant and are used more often than state legislation by plaintiffs alleging an illegal restraint of trade. For a variety of legal and practical reasons the plaintiff physicians have generally failed. Application of the antitrust laws to the hospital-physician relationship is discussed thoroughly in Chapter 7, "Antitrust Law."

More significant than the concepts discussed above, which only slightly limit the power of a private hospital to appoint and reappoint medical staff, is the distinct departure in 1963 from the historical and traditional judicial law under which the private hospital had nearly unlimited discretion. This was evident in New Jersey in the case of *Griesman v. Newcomb Hospital*. Without benefit of state statute or constitutional law doctrine the court held that a hospital could not arbitrarily refuse to consider the application of an osteopathic physician.[62] The basis of the decision was simply public policy: a private hospital is vested with a public interest and possesses a "fiduciary relationship" to both the patient and the medical community, especially when the hospital is the sole institution in the locality.[63]

The New Jersey court invalidated bylaws requirements that all staff physicians be graduates of a medical school approved by the American Medical Association and be members of the county medical society.[64] Specifically the court held that the voluntary hospital must at least *consider* the application of an osteopathic physician. This conclusion relied heavily on *Falcone v. Middlesex County Medical Society,* in which the defendant's denial of medical society membership to a licensed osteopathic physician was found to violate the state's public policy.[65] Accordingly the New Jersey court indicated its willingness to inquire into the reasonableness of a rule pertaining to staff privileges and to strike down the rule if it found it too arbitrary and not necessarily directly related to standards of patient care or other legitimate hospital concerns.

Following *Griesman,* another New Jersey court held that a voluntary hospital could not refuse applicants without giving them the opportunity to have a hearing and learn the reasons for the rejection.[66] The hearing need not be in the nature of a courtroom trial, but applicants have the right to appear in person if they wish and present evidence and witnesses in their behalf. An appeal procedure should be provided. This, of course, does not mean that all applicants must be given hospital privileges. It was proper to defer the application of an osteopathic physician whose academic record was shown to be only fair, who had no postgraduate training, and who had privileges elsewhere.[67] In other words, these New Jersey cases have established that all applications must be fully considered and evaluated and that all applicants are entitled to fair consideration in accordance with due process of law.[68]

Courts other than those of New Jersey are mindful of both substantive and procedural due process and of unreasonable and discriminatory action when they consider the discretion allowed a private hospital in appointment and reappointment of staff physicians.[69] The implication is that the court will intervene on behalf of the doctor if it finds the hospital's action to be unreasonable, arbitrary, or procedurally inconsistent with fairness and objectivity. Essentially the position of the voluntary hospital is equated in New Jersey and other jurisdictions with that of the governmental institution.

California followed New Jersey's lead by holding that private as well as public hospitals must provide the essence of due process to physicians who are denied staff appointments or who are disciplined, even if hospital bylaws do not require such procedures. In *Ascherman v. San Francisco Medical Society, et al.* the physician had privileges at Franklin Hospital, Hahneman Hospital, and St. Joseph's Hospital.[70] All three institutions denied him annual reappointment to their respective staffs without granting a hearing and without giving him the reasons for denial. The hospitals maintained that their bylaws required a hearing only if the doctor were disciplined during the term of annual appointment but not if annual reappointment was withheld.

Dr. Ascherman then applied for appointment at French Hospital, but his application was rejected, again without a hearing and without stated reasons for the action. The San Francisco Medical Society had also removed the physician's name from its referral service, apparently because of certain philosophical or political differences that arose between Dr. Ascherman and others in the early 1960s. As a consequence, Dr. Ascherman suddenly found himself excluded from the staffs of four hospitals and without professional referrals. He brought suit against the medical society, the hospitals, the mal-practice insurance carrier that insured members of the medical society (which had canceled his insurance), and various individuals who participated in these decisions. His suit asked not only for an injunction that would restore his privileges but also for compensatory and punitive damages. The trial court directed a verdict in favor of all defendants on all of plaintiff's claims.

The California Court of Appeals disagreed and in part reversed the judgment of the trial court. The opinion rejected the traditional rule that a court will not review the nearly unlimited discretion granted to a private hospital in excluding or disciplining staff physicians. In essence it held that a private institution affects the public interest, possesses a fiduciary duty, and must provide minimal due process to staff physicians with respect to both initial appointments and renewal of appointments. Minimal due process includes at least appropriate notice, an opportunity for a hearing, a written statement of charges or reasons for denial of appointment or reappointment, and the following rights:

- to call witnesses on the physician's behalf;
- to cross-examine the hospital's witnesses;
- to demand that the decision of the hearing body be supported by substantial evidence produced at the hearing; and
- to have the decision of the hearing body in writing, along with the basis of the decision.[71]

Under this ruling the physician is not necessarily entitled to have counsel present at the hearing, but if the hospital's counsel is present then the doctor may likewise be represented by an attorney. Most significant, as in the New Jersey cases, this judicial decision was based simply on public policy and was not grounded on rights guaranteed by the Fourteenth Amendment to the U.S. Constitution. Accordingly, the California Court of Appeals reversed the trial court's judgment in favor of the San Francisco Medical Society and the several hospitals, thus requiring them to afford due process to Dr. Ascherman.

Reasonable Rules and Regulations

After the decision in *Ascherman*, the same physician filed suit against St. Francis Memorial Hospital challenging a medical staff bylaw that required that applicants be supported by three letters of recommendation from active members of the medical staff. The bylaw was struck down as unreasonable because it would allow active members of the staff to exclude applicants arbitrarily or for discriminatory reasons.[72] This does not mean of course that a hospital cannot require applicants to submit letters of recommendation, but it does mean that the hospital must grant each applicant a fair hearing and evaluate letters of recommendation objectively without specifying that the letters be from a particular source.

As previously noted the private hospital is sometimes called on to act reasonably and fairly in medical staff appointments by the application of the Fourteenth Amendment and federal civil rights legislation regarding the physician-hospital relationship. Moreover, 42 U.S.C. § 1983 authorizes a civil action for deprivation of civil rights when the alleged deprivation is caused by a person "acting under color of state law." This means that physicians applying for staff privileges are entitled to constitutional equal protection and due process when the hospital is engaged in "state action" or when it acts under "color of law."[73]

A private hospital is not often found to be engaged in state action. Various sources of law, however, including constitutional and statutory authority as well as administrative regulations at both the state and federal levels of government, specifically prohibit private hospitals and certain other institutions serving the public from discriminating with respect to accommodations, services, or privileges on the basis of race, color, creed, national origin, and sex. It is also important to note that the application of the 1964 Civil Rights Act is not dependent on the concept of state action.[74] Title VII of the Civil Rights Act prohibits discriminatory practices when hiring employees (as distinct from granting or denying medical staff appointments), and Title VI protects individuals who are the intended beneficiaries of governmental financial assistance.[75]

In addition to the foregoing legal rules and local case law, which requires the private hospital to act reasonably and not arbitrarily and to afford procedural fairness, both the "Conditions of Participation for Hospitals" contained in the Medicare regulations[76] and the Standards of the Joint Commission on Accreditation of Healthcare Organizations dictate essentially the same conclusions.[77] The "Conditions" require the hospital's governing body to appoint physicians and establish privileges on the basis of written, defined criteria. Criteria for selection are individual character, competence, training, experience, and judgment. All qualified candidates are to be considered by the credentials committee of the medical staff, which then makes recommendations to the governing board. Similarly, the Standards of the Joint Commission require that the appointment and reappointment of physicians as well as the delineation of an individual's clinical privileges, whether or not that person is a member of the medical staff, be based on the periodic reappraisal of each practitioner's training, experience, current competence, and health.[78]

It should be noted that in other contexts as well the law has equated the duties of public and private healthcare institutions. For example, public and private hospitals that maintain an emergency room may not refuse to see a patient who comes seeking emergency care if the hospital represents itself as equipped and staffed to provide such care.[79] All hospitals that have received federal funds under the Hill-Burton Act must also provide a certain volume of free care to patients unable to pay.[80] Further, many states have overturned the doctrine of sovereign immunity, which holds that public hospitals are immune from tort liability, just as courts earlier reversed the doctrine of charitable immunity. The Michigan Supreme Court, for example, held in 1960 that it would impose tort liability on a charitable hospital,[81] and in 1978 it rejected governmental immunity for a public hospital even though such immunity was granted by statute to any governmental agency performing a "governmental function." Regarding tort liability to its patients, according to the Michigan court the ownership and operation of a hospital did not sufficiently represent a "governmental function" to support a difference between private and public hospitals.[82]

As a matter of the developing law as well as sound managerial practices, all hospitals, public or private, should implement policies that observe the essence of both substantive and procedural due process. All hospitals should serve their patients and physicians in accordance with uniform, reasonable, and nondiscriminatory standards. Fairness and logic suggest that all hospitals should be held to the same standards in appointing physicians to their medical staffs or delineating clinical privileges. Accordingly, it would seem that the sole general guideline for making medical staff appointments and defining privileges should be the quality of professional care rendered in light of the hospital's objectives and capabilities. Any rule or criterion for medical staff appointment that relates objectively to standards of patient care, the purposes of the hospital, and the clinical and ethical behavior of the individual physician will be upheld as reasonable and not arbitrary and thus consistent with substantive equal protection and due process.

Many cases support hospitals' efforts to improve the quality of care. To illustrate, a hospital may require physicians to sign and abide by reasonable medical staff bylaws,[83] to serve on a rotating basis in the emergency room,[84] and to be responsible for timely completion of medical records.[85] It may require applicants for a staff appointment to supply references[86] and to hold consultations in surgical or medical cases as defined by medical staff.[87] Physicians may have to carry malpractice insurance coverage because such a requirement protects the institution's fiscal integrity.[88] Surgical or specialty privileges can be restricted; for example, performance of major surgery in a given specialty may be limited to those who are board certified, board eligible, or Fellows in the American College of Physicians and Surgeons, or who have a minimum of ten years' experience in the specialty, as approved by the medical staff executive committee.[89] Such restrictions regarding major surgery may be adopted by the board of trustees on recommendation of the medical staff and may even be applied to physicians who had previously been performing major surgery. It is not unreasonable, arbitrary, or capricious to exclude from further practice of a specialty a physician who is unable to meet professionally approved criteria.

Both public and private hospitals act reasonably in suspending, disciplining, or refusing to appoint physicians who are professionally incompetent.[90] Even when a physician is legally entitled to due process, summary suspension for clinical incompetence will be upheld as long as a hearing is granted within a reasonable time after suspension.[91]

One of the more perplexing current issues is how far a hospital can go in denying a staff appointment or in disciplining a member of its staff for personal behavior considered contrary to generally accepted ethical, social, and moral behavior. In ethical and moral issues, hospital administrators must have a precise set of facts if a move to deny or withdraw staff privileges is to succeed. For example, a California court upheld a hospital's suspension of a physician's privileges following his conviction of conspiracy to murder his wife.[92] The court rejected the doctor's arguments that the event was unrelated to his competence as a practitioner and that the loss of hospital privileges prior to final resolution of the matter on appeal violated his rights to due process. A physician's past wrongful conduct may not be a proper basis, however, for denying a current application for appointment. On the other hand, the physician must give evidence of reformation and rehabilitation, and if references fail to provide this evidence, the hospital may deny the appointment.[93] Moreover, the "good character, qualifications, and standing" of the applicant are legitimate and justifiable areas of inquiry provided the criteria are applied fairly and there is evidence at the hearing that the physician was unsuited to the assigned tasks either physically or because of social behavior.[94] Substantial evidence indicating that an applicant for staff privileges has falsified information in the application has been a cause for denial of privileges.[95]

"Intolerable personal behavior" consisting of unacceptable language and rudeness in the presence of patients and visitors has also been held sufficient to dismiss a physician from the staff.[96] A physician's failure to document "adherence to the ethics of [the applicant's] profession, good reputation and ability to work with others," as required by the hospital's medical staff bylaws, was likewise found to be a proper basis for rejecting the doctor's application for appointment to the staff.[97]

A California case, however, held that a requirement that applicants for staff privileges be able to work with others must be reasonably related to standards of patient care. If an applicant is rejected, the hospital must be prepared to show that his or her inability to "work with others" presented a "real and substantial danger that patients . . . might receive other than high quality medical care."[98] If the hospital can meet this proof, then bylaw provisions relative to ability to work with others are valid. Vague and ambiguous provisions that are susceptible to arbitrary or discriminatory implementation, such as a provision requiring applicants to be "temperamentally and psychologically suited for cooperative staff-functions," have been rejected by the courts.[99]

Many states require hospitals to file a report with a designated state agency whenever disciplinary action is taken against a staff physician.[100] In addition, some local laws or regulations require that certain licensed healthcare practitioners—for example, physicians, nurses and pharmacists—are to report any impairment of the abilities or any professional misconduct of fellow practitioners. These statutory reporting requirements developed as a result of the "malpractice crisis" of the mid-1970s and were enacted as a component of the reform legislation designed to improve the quality of healthcare furnished to patients. A major difficulty, however, is that statutory requirements are either not well known or not properly understood by practitioners, and as a result appropriate and timely reports are frequently not filed. An impaired or incompetent physician, even when disciplined by a given hospital, can thus continue in practice simply by having patients move from one hospital to another or by practicing in a different locale. The difficulty is compounded when other hospitals do not adequately perform their duty to discover a physician's experiences elsewhere and to ascertain whether the doctor was ever subject to discipline by a hospital, licensure authority, or a court. The reporting statutes provide for certain administrative penalties and fines for failure to report instances of professional misconduct or incompetence. The penalties, however, are not severe and are frequently not imposed to their full extent because state agencies, along with hospitals and professional societies, would rather effect the rehabilitation of impaired physicians than adopt a punitive approach at an early stage of the problem.

It is readily apparent from this discussion that courts will uphold the decisions of hospital boards that follow documented recommendations of relevant committees that are meant to improve the quality of care, at least when the procedures are fundamentally fair. As stated by the Supreme Court of Ohio, "It is the board, not the court, which is charged with the responsibility of providing a staff of competent physicians. The board has chosen to rely upon the advice of medical staff, and the court may not surrogate for the staff in discharging their responsibility."[101]

Exclusive Contracts with Physicians

Along with the governing board's responsibility to select a competent medical staff, the board has the authority to enter into an exclusive contract with a given physician or group of physicians for specialty services. Hospitals frequently enter into exclusive contractual arrangements for staffing the radiology, emergency, or pathology departments, for example. Such contracts have been upheld, even for a governmental hospital, as long as the reasons relate to standards of patient care and efficient hospital operation, are adequate, and can be satisfactorily documented.[102]

In a leading case involving principles of constitutional law, *Adler v. Montefiore Hospital Association of Western Pennsylvania*, a private hospital employed Dr. Edward Curtiss as full-time salaried director of the cardiology laboratory and granted him the exclusive privilege of performing cardiac catheterizations, thereby excluding other qualified cardiologists from performing this specialized procedure. In the subsequent lawsuit by Dr. Adler challenging this arrangement it was stipulated by the parties that the hospital was "at least a quasi-public institution" and that the doctrine of state action would apply. Nevertheless, the exclusive arrangement was upheld as reasonable and related to the hospital's objectives, especially because it was a teaching institution.[103] Catheterization, the court held, was a laboratory procedure like radiology— as distinct from surgery, for example—and thus there had been no denial of plaintiff's right to admit his private patients to the hospital or treat them;

neither was there denial of a corresponding right in the patient to select his own physician. The exclusive contract was a part of the general advancement of medical specialization designed to protect both the patient's safety and the hospital's operation, as evidenced by the following factors established by expert testimony: the procedure of catheterization requires a team, and a single physician can best train and supervise the team; physicians can best maintain their competence if they perform more than just a few catheterizations over an extended period; failure of equipment can be minimized by having only one physician responsible for its use and maintenance; scheduling problems for patients can be reduced or minimized; a full-time physician is better able to teach students; it is in the patient's best interest that the physician performing procedure be on the hospital premises at all times in the event of complications; finally, the hospital board can better monitor the quality of care when one person is in charge of the laboratory. Accordingly, there was no violation of Dr. Adler's rights to substantive due process and equal protection because he must yield to reasonable rules intended to benefit the hospital's patients, their physicians, and the university, its students, and the public.

Courts in other jurisdictions have also refused to intervene in decisions of hospital authorities to confer exclusive privileges on designated physicians. All of the cases concerned arrangements for exclusive rights with respect to medical diagnosis and care and treatment of patients, as distinct from services such as that characterized in *Adler* as a "laboratory procedure." These cases therefore have the effect of restricting the medical staff privileges of other qualified and competent staff physicians.[104]

Exclusive service contracts have been frequently challenged as violating federal or state antitrust legislation. The underlying purpose of antitrust law is to foster competition in the marketplace, and the argument is that exclusive contracts reduce competition and may amount to a "group boycott." For the most part, however, the challenges have not been successful because an exclusive contract can be justified as a *reasonable* restraint of trade consistent with institutional goals of providing quality healthcare.[105] The leading cases are discussed in Chapter 7, "Antitrust Law."

Protecting the Institution's Fiscal Integrity

The financial integrity of the institution has become more central in recent years as the emphasis on cost containment intensified. Decisions of staff physicians in caring for patients directly affect the financial well-being of the institution where they practice. To an increasing extent hospitals are monitoring staff physicians to judge their efforts to contain costs without compromising recognized standards of practice. Cost effectiveness of a doctor's practice was made especially significant by the government's change in 1983 to reimbursement for Medicare patients on the basis of the diagnostic-related groups system. Two particular cases may provide some guidance regarding the extent that a hospital will be able to restrict or refuse to review privileges to support the fiscal objectives of the institution.

In Georgia a governmental hospital authority purchased a whole-body CAT scanner and then resolved that "if a treatment, procedure, diagnostic test or other service is ordered for a patient . . . and that procedure, test or service is routinely offered by the Hospital, then the [hospitalized] patient will receive that service within the confines of the Hospital complex."[106] Staff physicians who privately owned and operated a CAT scanner outside the hospital complex challenged this policy as arbitrary, unreasonable, and a restriction on their medical judgment. In upholding the hospital's policy as reasonable and as "strikingly similar" to exclusive service contracts, the Supreme Court of Georgia observed:

> This appeal represents a classic confrontation between two entities who play major roles in the health and welfare of the citizens of our state. The relationship which exists between hospital and physician is delicate, each one exercising exclusive as well as concentric areas of responsibility in the treatment and diagnosis of patients. In addition to the roles played by these two entities in providing this essential health service, the state has the duty of monitoring this function in order to protect the health and welfare of its citizens. . . .
>
> The Hospital Authority's resolution requiring use of in-house facilities and services for hospitalized patients rather than permitting them to be taken from the hospital to utilize like facilities or services elsewhere is reasonable and reflects a well intentioned effort by the Authority to deal with the intricate and complex task of providing comprehensive medical services to the citizens of our state. The preeminent consideration in the adoption of such a resolution by the Authority was the health, welfare and safety of the patient. . . . The Authority's resolution is a reasonable and rational administrative decision enacted in order for the Authority to carry out the legislative mandate that it provide adequate medical care in the public interest. The resolution does not invade the physician's province. Although he is required to use the facilities and equipment provided within the hospital complex for testing rather than similar facilities and equipment outside, he is nevertheless free to interpret the results of such tests and free to diagnose and prescribe treatment for all his patients.[107]

In 1983 a Pennsylvania court sustained a bylaw of a private hospital requiring that each of three physicians specializing in obstetrics and gynecology accept every third indigent patient admitted to the hospital for obstetrical treatment.[108] The rule was adopted at the insistence of the state's commissioner of health to implement its regulations established for community service in conformity with federal Hill-Burton legislation. When one of the physicians was suspended from the medical staff for failure to comply with the hospital bylaw he was entitled to the constitutional protection of due process because this private institution, according to these facts, was engaged in state action. Nevertheless, he was told by the court that the rule was reasonable, was not arbitrary, and was rationally related to a permissible governmental interest rather than an arbitrary interference with the doctor's right to practice medicine. The permissible governmental goal was to provide medical care to indigent patients, the hospital being the institutional conduit for achieving the goal. The court concluded: "The requirement that appellant accept indigent patients is onerous yet reasonable. It is both severe and not arbitrary. In short, it does not work a violation of substantive due process."[109]

It is generally advisable that medical staff bylaws state criteria for appointing staff members and granting clinical privileges that protect and preserve the fiscal integrity of the institution. The courts will uphold well-stated and regularly reviewed rules that balance the size and character of the medical staff with the facilities and supportive services provided by the hospital. Thus, as economic factors force hospitals to restrict the availability of their facilities or services, the courts are likely to uphold the denial of privileges to physicians who are not needed or who will not help the institution to reach its legitimate financial goals.

Procedural Due Process

According physicians procedural due process is often preferable to being unduly concerned about whether a given standard or criterion is "reasonable and nonarbitrary" as a matter of substance because denial of procedural fairness is more likely to generate hostility and litigation by an aggrieved physician. Physicians generally accept a substantive rule they do not agree with better than they accept procedures they consider arbitrary. A physician's attorney can also more easily attack the procedure by which the client was denied a medical staff appointment or subjected to discipline than challenge the merits of the rule or requirement. Hospitals accredited by the Joint Commission on Accreditation of Healthcare Organizations are required to have bylaws providing for procedural due process.[110] As a matter of "preventive law," it is therefore advisable for private hospitals to grant the essence of procedural due process to current members of the staff as well as to new applicants, whether or not the law of the particular jurisdiction actually mandates due process.

What is procedural due process? As a matter of constitutional law, it may be simply but accurately defined as fundamental fairness under all the facts and circumstances. The specific elements of a fair procedural evaluation of a physician's qualifications and competence may thus differ depending on time, place, and circumstance.

To meet the minimal requirements of procedural due process, the physician is entitled to:

1. written notice of reasons for denial of appointment or for the charges against him or her;
2. after such notice an opportunity for a timely hearing by a relatively impartial body;
3. an opportunity to produce evidence and witnesses on his or her behalf and to refute the hospital's proffered evidence;
4. a finding by the hearing body based on substantial and credible factual evidence;
5. written notice of the hearing body's recommended decision together with the reasons for the decision; and
6. an opportunity to appeal the decision.[111]

If the institution is attempting to suspend or diminish a physician's privileges, the notice of charges against the doctor must be sufficiently specific to allow an answer. To give the physician time to prepare an adequate response, the particulars of the evidence, including incident reports, references to specific cases or alleged deficiencies, and peer review records must be furnished to the doctor before the hearing.[112] Medical and administrative staff should collect and prepare this information carefully and treat it discreetly to avoid delays in the proceedings and to minimize the possibility of a lawsuit.

Hearing requirements The hearing panel can consist exclusively of physicians or include both physicians and lay persons. Members must, however, be impartial, though they need not be entirely divorced from the case or without prior knowledge of it. The test of constitutional impartiality is good faith. Persons asked to render a decision are thus not disqualified simply because they were already familiar with the situation or participated in the investigation that led to the charges.[113] Monitoring a physician's clinical performance and also serving as a member of the review committee does not preclude fairness.[114] The premise is that responsible and honest persons within the hospital can make fundamentally fair decisions.

On the other hand, in hospitals having a relatively small medical staff the risk of bias and partiality increases. A hearing panel composed of persons from outside the hospital may then be necessary. In *Applebaum v. Board of Directors of Barton Memorial Hospital,* for example, the medical staff of a private, not-for-profit community hospital consisted of Dr. Applebaum and 13 other persons.[115] After investigating complaints of clinical incompetence, an ad hoc committee recommended to the medical staff's executive committee that Dr. Applebaum's obstetrical privileges be suspended. The complaining physician was a member of the ad hoc investigative committee and also a practitioner in the same specialty; moreover, some of those serving on the ad hoc committee were also members of the executive committee. In these particular circumstances the court held that the doctor had been denied fundamental fairness. (It should also be noted that this case was tried in

California, where the courts impose these procedural standards on the staff of private hospitals simply as a matter of state common law and not of constitutional due process. Because the hospital was not engaged in state action, constitutional doctrine as such did not apply.)

These hearings need not be conducted with the formality and technicality of a courtroom proceeding. Hearing panels do not have the power of subpoena and they cannot compel the attendance of witnesses. Therefore there is no legal right to confront and to cross-examine witnesses unless they testify voluntarily. Cross-examination of those who supply adverse information is not an essential ingredient of due process.[116] As noted earlier, however, doctors seeking redress must be permitted to present their own witnesses and refute adverse evidence. The burden of proof at the hearing may be placed on the physician, but the decision must be based on and documented by substantial credible evidence in light of the record.[117] Most reviewing courts will not make a complete, independent review of the facts, and their decision must be based solely on evidence produced at the hearing, not on knowledge acquired elsewhere.[118]

Several cases have held that the physician is not entitled as a matter of law to representation by legal counsel at the hearing.[119] In New Jersey, however, it was held that, subject to reasonable rules specified by the hospital, the physician could choose whether to have counsel.[120] The attorney would be allowed to marshall evidence, explain adverse material, and present argument. In jurisdictions not following New Jersey's rule, the physician should be allowed counsel at the hearing if the hospital's lawyer is present.

Notices denying a physician's application for privileges and notices of disciplinary proceedings must be timely, and the opportunity for a hearing must be promptly granted. Undue deferral of an application also violates due process, because a refusal to render a decision or to provide reasons for it deprives the doctor of a fair hearing. Fundamental fairness under all circumstances is nevertheless the guiding rule. Thus, although in one case the bylaws provided that a hearing would be held within ten days of a request by a doctor who had been notified of his suspension from the staff, there was no violation of procedural due process when the hearing was convened 15 days after the request.[121] The delay of five days was insignificant because the doctor was not damaged or prejudiced by the minor technical violation of the bylaws.

Generally a doctor has a right to appeal the recommendation of a hearing committee to the hospital's board of trustees. The appeal can be and should be restricted to reviewing whether the bylaws were followed and whether there was substantial evidence to support the recommended decision. As mentioned earlier, the final decision is the responsibility of the board.

When is a hearing and review procedure required? Physicians are frequently entitled to due process when an initial application for appointment is denied or when an existing appointment is not renewed, is suspended, or is revoked. The Joint Commission requires fair procedures, including a hearing, when recommendations regarding clinical privileges are "adverse" to an applicant.[122] The meaning of adverse in this context, however, is not clear. With respect to appointment and reappraisal of clinical privileges, the following activities should not be considered as generating a right to a hearing and an appeal: medical staff programs for monitoring an individual's professional performance; a letter of reprimand or admonition directed to a physician; a requirement for consultation; a requirement that a physician seek additional training or education; or a requirement for limited supervision of the doctor's clinical practice. In short, peer review and quality assurance programs can be implemented without conducting hearings.[123] To argue otherwise would be to disregard the hospital's duty to protect the quality of professional practice. To avoid misunderstanding, the line dividing peer review of a physician's practice from curtailment, suspension, or revocation of privileges should be concisely explained in the medical staff bylaws or rules and regulations.

When a physician has a grievance, the hearing and appeal procedure provided by the hospital must be invoked before the case is taken to court. As a general principal of administrative law, administrative remedies must be exhausted before a solution to the controversy is sought in a judicial proceeding. Several cases regarding medical staff appointments are to this effect.[124]

By the same token in most jurisdictions and by prevailing doctrine both public and private hospitals must follow the provisions of their current bylaws.[125] Even if local law does not mandate that a private hospital grant due process to a physician whose application has been rejected or whose appointment as a staff member is terminated, the doctor may obtain an injunction requiring adherence to the procedural requirements set forth in the hospital's own bylaws. As noted earlier, however, insignificant deviations from bylaw provisions do not offend the physician's rights.

Peer Review of Professional Practice

In addition to the governing board's responsibility in monitoring the professional qualifications of the medical staff, the medical staff itself should continually assess the quality of care being provided in the facility. "Peer review" is the term used to describe formal, periodic review of care by the persons who provide that care (such as physicians or nurses). It is used to provide retrospective review of a single case or group of cases and to provide standards or goals for future care. Typically it is done by a committee or group of people with the same training as the subject matter being reviewed: for example, obstetricians reviewing obstetricians. Peer review includes such diverse activities as:

- utilization review (review of patients' lengths of stay);
- infection review (study of patterns of infections within the hospital);
- credentials review (review of the credentials of physicians applying for medical staff privileges); and

- review of such hospital functions as the emergency department, operating room radiology, and so on.

Other quality assurance activities such as process improvement and total quality management also relate to the peer review function.

Two major legal issues arise in the context of peer review and quality improvement: confidentiality and potential liability. The records of peer review committees are often sought by plaintiffs' attorneys to support their case, and physicians who are disciplined often allege that the peer review function has damaged their character or professional practice. This section will briefly outline the law relating to these two issues.

Obviously, to be most effective the peer review process must involve an honest and candid assessment of practitioners' activities. Confidentiality of the peer review committee's minutes and deliberations is essential to their success. As one court stated, "There is an overwhelming public interest in having those [peer review] meetings held on a confidential basis so that the flow of ideas can continue unimpeded."[126] The court also stated:

Confidentiality of peer review records

> Confidentiality is essential to effective functioning of these staff meetings; and these meetings are essential to the continued improvement in the care and treatment of patients. Candid and conscientious evaluation of clinical practices is a *sine qua non* of adequate hospital care. To subject these discussions and deliberations to the discovery process, without a showing of exceptional necessity, would result in terminating such deliberations. Constructive professional criticism cannot occur in an atmosphere of apprehension that one doctor's suggestion will be used as a denunciation of a colleague's conduct in a malpractice suit.[127]

Following this line of reasoning, beginning in the early 1970s various state legislatures began to address the confidentiality issue. Today nearly all jurisdictions have some form of legislation establishing a degree of privilege in certain described circumstances. For example, the Georgia statute, upheld in *Eubanks v. Ferrier*,[128] immunized medical review committee proceedings from both pretrial discovery and use in evidence in civil actions against a healthcare provider. It also stated that no person in attendance at a meeting of a review committee could be required to testify with respect to evidence presented during committee proceedings.

It must be noted that, as is usually the case, the statutes vary from state to state as to such matters as the type of legal proceeding to which they apply; whether the information is protected from discovery, admission into evidence, or both; the type of information and the nature of the committee whose records are confidential; and various express exceptions to the protection. The application of the privilege to particular sets of facts is, therefore, likely to vary from state to state and even court to court. Furthermore, almost universally the privilege does not apply to records (such as medical records and routine business records) created for purposes other than peer review.

Liability of quality assurance participants

Members of medical staff executive, peer review, credentials, and similar committees are often concerned that their activities while serving on such committees may subject them to legal liability for their words and actions. The major areas of potential liability involve defamation and interference with a person's professional practice or business relationships.

Under the law of defamation, there is a protection (known as a "privilege") provided either by judicial or statutory law for people who carry out important duties that are in the public interest. For the privilege to be recognized, the communication in question must have been made in good faith for the purpose of upholding a moral or legal duty, limited in scope to that purpose, made in a proper manner on a proper occasion, and transmitted only to proper and interested parties. It seems clear that physicians and other members of peer review–type committees will be protected by this privilege under most circumstances. Numerous cases have so held.[129] In addition, the majority of states have enacted statutes in an attempt to confirm and clarify the existence of the common-law privilege for medical review activities.

With regard to the second concern, the actions of a peer review committee may constitute an alleged intentional tort such as interference with one's profession or business relationships, interference with economic expectancy, wrongful suspension of staff privileges, and so on. The law in this area is similar to that concerning defamation. As noted earlier, all states have some form of protective statute for peer review functions, and most of these contain protection from personal liability of the participants. There are few if any cases in which members of a peer review committee have been held liable in the absence of malice or bad faith. Thus participants may proceed in good faith with confidence that their committee deliberations and actions will not subject them to legal exposure.

Contractual Rights of Employed Physicians

A final note is warranted. A physician-employee is in a different legal position than that of private fee-for-service physicians appointed to the medical staff of a hospital. Traditionally an employed person, whether a physician or other professional, is entitled to neither substantive nor procedural due process. An employee's rights to continued employment depend instead on the terms of the employment contract. Unless the contract provides otherwise, either expressly or by implication, the employee can be dismissed at will without a hearing, without prior notice, and without a statement of the reasons for the dismissal.[130] Similarly, nonrenewal of an exclusive service contract with radiology specialists does not require a hearing.[131] Thus a municipal hospital that had engaged in an oral contract at will making a doctor its director of pathology could discontinue the arrangement without following the due process procedures contained in the hospital bylaws.[132] In this latter case, moreover, and most significant, the doctor's staff privileges remained in effect.

Continued employment as such is not usually a property interest protected by constitutional guarantees.[133] On the other hand, rights conferred by contract or institutional policy may grant an employee a right to know the reasons for dismissal and the right to a hearing. In an instance in which a governmental hospital published an employees' handbook that purported to limit terminations to specified charges and also outlined a grievance procedure, a discharged employee was entitled to the essential elements of due process.[134] Similarly, at least one decision has elevated implied contractual rights contained in the personnel manual of a municipal hospital to a property interest protected by the Fourteenth Amendment, and accordingly it has held that the rights are constitutionally supported.[135]

In addition to distinguishing clearly between an employment contract at will and an agreement providing the essence of due process, one must be cautious in differentiating an employment relationship from a practice-privilege relationship. In a 1983 decision the U.S. Court of Appeals for the Fourth Circuit held that clinical privileges of physical therapists granted by a county hospital were sufficiently analogous to a physician's privileges to constitute a property or liberty interest within the context of constitutional law. Hence, allegations that these privileges were terminated without the safeguards of procedural due process presented a colorable constitutional claim, and the complaint should not have been dismissed.[136]

Conclusion

Judicial review of controversies concerning medical staff privileges is limited to determining whether the decision of the hospital's governing board was based on reasonable and not arbitrary criteria and was accompanied by the requisites of procedural due process. When there is sufficient credible evidence to show that the decision was reasonable in the circumstances, the court will not interfere and substitute its own judgment for that of the hospital's board. As stated by the U.S. Court of Appeals for the Fifth Circuit,

> No court should substitute its evaluation of such matters for that of the Hospital Board. It is the Board, not the court, which is charged with the responsibility of providing a competent staff of doctors. The Board has chosen to rely on the advice of its Medical Staff, and the court cannot surrogate for the Staff in executing this responsibility. Human lives are at stake, and the governing board must be given discretion in its selection so that it can have confidence in the competence and moral commitment of its staff. The evaluation of professional proficiency of

doctors is best left to the specialized expertise of their peers, subject only to limited judicial surveillance. The court is charged with the narrow responsibility of assuring that the qualifications imposed by the Board are reasonably related to the operation of the hospital and fairly administered. In short, so long as staff selections are administered with fairness, geared by a rationale compatible with hospital responsibility, and unencumbered with irrelevant considerations, a court should not interfere.[137]

Notes

Reprinted and revised with permission from MEDICOLEGAL NEWS, vol. 9, no. 1; © 1981, American Society of Law & Medicine.

1. Joiner v. Mitchell County Hosp. Auth., 125 Ga. App. 1, 186 S.E.2d 307 (1971), *aff'd*, 229 Ga. 140, 189 S.E.2d 412 (1972); Purcell v. Zimbelman, 18 Ariz. App. 75, 500 P.2d 335, 341 (1972); Gonzales v. Nork, No. 228566 (Sacramento County Super. Ct., Cal. 1973), *rev'd on other grounds*, 131 Cal. Rptr. 717, 60 Cal. App. 3d 728 (1976); Corleto v. Shore Memorial Hosp., 138 N.J. Super. 302, 350 A.2d 534 (1975); Johnson v. Misericordia Community Hosp., 99 Wis. 2d 708, 301 N.W.2d 156 (1981); Sophia Elam v. College Park Hosp., 132 Cal. App. 3d 332, 183 Cal. Rptr. 156, *modified*, 133 Cal. App. 3d 94 (1982); *compare* Schenck v. Government of Guam, 609 F.2d 387 (9th Cir. 1979) (district court did not err in declining to apply emerging theory of independent or corporate hospital liability).
2. *See generally*, Chapter 5, "Liability of the Healthcare Institution," pp. 131–57.
3. When there is no employment relationship, there is no vicarious liability; a hospital is not liable for the negligence of a physician who is an independent contractor. Cooper v. Curry, 92 N.M. 417, 589 P.2d 201 (1979).
4. *See supra* notes 1 and 2. *See also* Mich. Comp. Laws Ann. § 333.21513 (1980 & Supp. 1986); MICH. STAT. ANN. § 14.15(21513) (West Supp. 1986); IND. CODE ANN. § 16-10-1-6.5 (West 1984 & Supp. 1986); and ARIZ. REV. STAT. ANN. § 35-445 (1986) as examples of statutory expression of the corporate negligence doctrine as well as the statutes of Wisconsin and California discussed in Chapter 5.
5. Shields, *Guidelines for Reviewing Applications for Privileges*, 9 HOSP. MED. STAFF 11 (Sept. 1980); Leonard v. Board of Directors, Power County Hosp. Dist., 673 P.2d 1019 (Colo. App. 1983) (governing board has authority to reject a medical staff committee's recommendation and terminate a physician's privileges); Ad Hoc Executive Comm. of the Medical Staff of Memorial Hosp. v. Runyan, 716 P.2d 425 (Colo. 1986) (executive committee of medical staff has no standing to challenge decision of board restoring a physician's privileges).

6. Physicians or committees controlled by physicians should not, however, be the ultimate decision makers on medical staff appointments and the delineation of individual clinical privileges because such control raises antitrust legal issues. These issues are discussed in Chapter 7. In addition, tax-exempt organizations need to be aware that physicians and other "insiders" on the governing board are prohibited from taking part in decisions relating to their own compensation. This issue is discussed in more detail in Chapter 6.

7. Hayman v. Galveston, 273 U.S. 414, 416–17 (1927) (exclusion of osteopathic physician does not violate equal protection clause of Fourteenth Amendment).

8. See Shelley v. Kraemer, 334 U.S. 1 (1948); Burton v. Wilmington Parking Auth., 365 U.S. 715 (1961).

9. Barrett v. United Hosps., 376 F. Supp. 791 (S.D.N.Y. 1974), *aff'd mem.*, 506 F.2d 1395 (2d Cir. 1974). *See also* Waters v. St. Francis Hosp., 618 F.2d 1105 (5th Cir. 1980) (codification of common-law right authorizing revocation of staff privileges does not convert revocation to state action); Hodge v. Paoli Memorial Hosp., 576 F.2d 563, 564 (3d Cir. 1978) (mere receipt of Hill-Burton funds is insufficient to support state-action claim); *accord* Loh-Seng Yo v. Cibola Gen. Hosp., 706 F.2d 306 (10th Cir. 1983) (private hospital not engaged in state action); Modaber v. Culpeper Memorial Hosp., Inc., 674 F.2d 1023 (1982) (private not-for-profit hospital not engaged in state action).

10. *Barrett, supra* note 9, at 797.

11. *Id*. at 800–5.

12. *Id*. at 799; *accord* Lubin v. Critenden Hosp. Ass'n, 713 F.2d 414 (8th Cir. 1983), *cert. denied*, 465 U.S. 1025 (1984).

13. *E.g.,* Sosa v. Board of Managers of Val Verde Memorial Hosp., 437 F.2d 173 (5th Cir. 1971) (notice of charges "reasonably related to operation of hospital" is required for denial of admission to medical staff); Moore v. Board of Trustees of Carson-Tahoe Hosp., 88 Nev. 207, 495 P.2d 605 (1972), *cert. denied*, 409 U.S. 879 (1972).

14. Southwick, *The Physician's Right to Due Process in Public and Private Hospitals: Is There a Difference?* 9:1 MEDICOLEGAL NEWS 4 (1981).

15. Civil Rights Acts of 1964, 42 U.S.C.A. § 2000 (d) (1981); 42 U.S.C.A. §§ 1395-1395zz (1983 & Supp. 1987).

16. Foster v. Mobile Hosp. Bd., 398 F.2d 227 (5th Cir. 1968); Meredith v. Allen County War Memorial Hosp., 397 F.2d 33 (6th Cir. 1968); Eaton v. Grubbs, 329 F.2d 710 (4th Cir. 1964); Simkins v. Moses H. Cone Memorial Hosp., 323 F.2d 959 (4th Cir. 1963), *cert. denied*, 376 U.S. 938 (1964) (a private hospital receiving governmental financial support is subject to the Fourteenth Amendment); Birnbaum v. Trussell, 371 F.2d 672 (2d Cir. 1966).

17. 437 F.2d 173 (5th Cir. 1971).

18. There was evidence at the hearing that the doctor (a) abandoned obstetrical patients in active labor because they could not pay his bill; (b) possessed an unstable physical demeanor and showed nervousness, both

of which were likely to jeopardize surgical patients; (c) failed to retain and use basic surgical techniques; (d) manifested an unstable mental condition by numerous fits of anger and rage; (e) had unsatisfactory references; (f) engaged in an itinerant medical practice over the years; (g) pled guilty to two felony charges in criminal courts; (h) had his license to practice suspended in both Michigan and Texas (since restored in Texas). *Id.* at 175.

19. *Id.* at 176.

20. *Id.* at 176–77 (citations omitted).

21. *Id. See also* Shooler v. Navarro County Memorial Hosp., 375 F. Supp. 841 (N.D. Tex. 1973), *aff'd*, 515 F.2d 509 (5th Cir. 1975) (when procedural due process is followed, a hospital may deny staff appointment if there is evidence that the physician displayed an inability to work harmoniously with other doctors and hospital personnel and charged patients excessive fees).

22. 447 F.2d 839 (5th Cir. 1971).

23. *Id.* at 844. In the proper circumstances a summary suspension of privileges will not violate due process as long as the physician is afforded an opportunity for a hearing within a reasonable time. Citta v. Delaware Valley Hosp., 313 F.Supp. 301 (E.D. Pa. 1970)(Fourteenth Amendment applied to private hospital because it had received federal funds).

24. Board of Trustees of the Memorial Hosp. v. Pratt, 72 Wyo. 120, 262 P.2d 682 (1953); *accord* Peterson v. Tucson Gen. Hosp., Inc., 559 P.2d 186 (Ariz. Ct. App. 1976) (private hospital).

25. Green v. City of St. Petersburg, 154 Fla. 399, 17 So. 2d 517 (1944); Selden v. City of Sterling, 316 Ill. App. 455, 45 N.E.2d 329 (1942); Jacobs v. Martin, 20 N.J. Super. 531, 90 A.2d 151 (1952). *Cf.* Armstrong v. Board of Directors of Fayette County Gen. Hosp., 553 S.W.2d 77 (Tenn. 1977) (a public hospital could not require certification or eligibility for certification by the American Board of Surgery for the granting of specified surgical privileges when the physician was in fact competent).

26. 316 Ill. App. 455, 45 N.E.2d 329 (1942).

27. Rush v. City of St. Petersburg, 205 So. 2d 11 (Fla. App. 1967); Benell v. City of Virginia, 258 Minn. 559, 104 N.W.2d 633 (1960). *See also* Letsch v. County Hosp., 246 Cal. App. 2d 673, 55 Cal. Rptr. 118 (1966); Blank v. Palo Alto–Stanford Hosp. Center, 234 Cal. App. 2d 377, 44 Cal. Rptr. 572 (1965).

28. Stribling v. Jolley, 241 Mo. App. 1123, 253 S.W.2d 519 (Mo. 1952). A Wisconsin statute, WIS. STAT. ANN. § 50.36 (3) (Supp. 1985–86), prohibits denial of hospital staff privileges to any licensed physician solely on the basis that he is an osteopath. The crucial importance of statutory law with respect to the rights of osteopathic physicians is also illustrated by Taylor v. Horn, 189 So. 2d 198 (Fla. App. 1966).

29. N.C. GEN. STAT. § 90-153 (1985); N.D. Rev. Code § 43-06-17 (1978). These statutes also apply to almost all private hospitals. *See also* NEV.

REV. STAT. §§ 633.161, 450.430 (1986) (public institutions may not discriminate against dentistry, psychology, podiatry, Eastern medicine).

30. Boos v. Donnell, 421 P.2d 644 (Okla. 1966); Samuel v. Curry County and Curry Gen. Hosp. Bd., 55 Or. App. 653, 639 P.2d 687 (1982).

31. Shaw v. Hospital Auth. of Cobb County, 507 F.2d 625 (5th Cir. 1975) (podiatrist entitled to a hearing); Davidson v. Youngstown Hosp. Ass'n, 19 Ohio App. 2d 246, 250 N.E.2d 892 (1969) (private hospital must act reasonably in passing on applications for staff membership); Touchton v. River Dist. Community Hosp., 76 Mich. App. 251, 256 N.W.2d 455 (1977) (application of podiatrist cannot be summarily dismissed). *Cf.* Limmer v. Samaritan Health Serv., 710 P.2d 1077 (Ariz. App. 1985) (private hospital may deny privileges to osteopath; bylaws were not unreasonable or arbitrary). Some state statutes prohibit hospitals from arbitrarily discriminating against persons practicing in certain allied health professions. *E.g.* CAL. HEALTH & SAFETY CODE § 1316 (1974) and § 1316.5 (1978); NEV. REV. STAT. §§ 450.005, .430 (1975).

32. N.Y. PUB. HEALTH LAW § 2801-b (McKinney 1976) (podiatrists and others may not be denied staff privileges without stating reasons). In this connection see Fritz v. Huntington Hosp., 39 N.Y.2d 399, 348 N.E.2d 547 (1976); Fried v. Straussman, 393 N.Y.S.2d 334, 361 N.E.2d 984 (1977).

33. *See* Reynolds v. St. John's Riverside Hosp., 382 N.Y.S.2d 618 (Sup. Ct. 1976) (physician's assistants must be considered for privileges by a hospital).

34. Shaw v. Hospital Auth. of Cobb County, 614 F.2d 946 (5th Cir. 1980), *cert. denied,* 449 U.S. 955 (1980).

35. 293 S.E.2d 901 (N.C. App. 1982), *appeal dismissed,* 297 S.E.2d 399 (1982).

36. Joint Commission on Accreditation of Hospitals, ACCREDITATION MANUAL FOR HOSPITALS, 109 (1987); this statement is now contained in Standard MS. 1.1.1, JCAHO 1998 Hospital Accreditation Standards at 226.

37. *See, e.g.,* Mizell v. North Broward Hosp. Dist., 175 So. 2d 583 (Fla. App. 1965) (proof that a physician's mistakes in diagnosis were too frequent is an adequate basis for suspension of surgical privileges).

38. 259 Iowa 1185, 146 N.W.2d 284 (1966). *See also* Anderson v. Caro Community Hosp., 10 Mich. App. 348, 159 N.W.2d 347 (1968) (Michigan appellate court upheld the right of a public hospital to dismiss a staff physician who was extended the right of a hearing, when documented behavior clearly violated adequately defined standards of conduct).

39. 88 Nev. 207, 495 P.2d 605 (1972), *cert. denied,* 409 U.S. 879 (1972).

40. Nevada statutes authorize the board of trustees of a public hospital to adopt bylaws, rules, and regulations governing admission of physicians to the staff, and they grant the board power to organize the staff. The bylaws of the medical staff authorized alteration or revocation of privileges on

recommendation of medical staff for "unprofessional conduct." NEV. REV. STAT. §§ 450.160, .180, .440 (1986).

41. North Broward Hosp. Dist. v. Mizell, 148 So. 2d 1, 5 (Fla. 1962).

42. 88 Nev. At 211, 212, 495 P.2d at 608 (citations omitted). *See also* Southwick, *Hospital Medical Staff Privileges,* 18 DePaul L. Rev. 655 (1969).

43. A dissent by two justices was based on the following arguments: "Unprofessional conduct" is a vague and an ambiguous standard, not defined, even generally, in the medical staff bylaws. Hence, there is "substantial danger or arbitrary discrimination" and a grant to the board of "almost unlimited power, susceptible of abuse." Moreover, the dissent said that Dr. Moore's use of an anesthetic without sterile gloves was no more than an isolated instance of negligence that did not result in injury of damage to the patient, and thus was not a reasonable basis for revocation of privileges. Because the hospital could not have been liable to the patient as a result of this occurrence, arbitrariness was indicated. 88 Nev. At 214, 495 P.2d at 610.

44. D.C. Code Ann. § 32-1307 (Supp. 1986). *See also, e.g.,* Wis. Stat. Ann. § 50.36 (3) (Supp. 1985) (osteopathic physician); N.M. Stat. Ann. § 61-10-14 (1986) (osteopathic physician); Fla. Stat. § 395.011 (1986) (osteopathic physician, dentist, podiatrist); Va. Code § 32.1-134.2 (1985) (podiatrist); Okla. Stat. tit. 63, § 1-707A (1984) (osteopaths and podiatrists).

45. *E.g.,* Cal. Health & Safety Code §§ 1316, 1316.5 (West 1979 & Supp. 1986) (hospital must provide for use of facilities by podiatrists and allow them staff privileges; it may afford privileges to clinical psychologists).

46. Ohio Rev. Code Ann. § 3701.35.1(B) (Baldwin Supp. 1986).

47. Dooley v. Barberton Citizens Hosp., 11 Ohio St. 3d 216, 465 N.E.2d 58 (1984). *Cf.* Fort Hamilton-Hughes Memorial Hosp. Center v. Southard, 12 Ohio St. 3d 263, 466 N.E.2d 903 (1984) (Ohio Rev. Code Ann. § 3701.35.1(B) does not apply to chiropractors; private hospitals need not accept patients referred by a chiropractor for x-rays).

48. *See* note 36 and accompanying text.

49. La. Rev. Stat. Ann. § 37:1301 (1974 & Supp. 1986).

50. N.Y. Pub. Health Law § 206A (McKinney Supp. 1986). Moreover, the New York statutes provide that hospitals must *not* deny or withhold staff membership or diminish privileges of a physician, a dentist, or a podiatrist without stating the reasons. The law provides an appeal mechanism to the public health council of the state. N.Y. Pub. Health Law § 2801-b (McKinney 1985). Fritz v. Huntington Hosp., 39 N.Y.2d 339, 384 N.Y.S.2d 92, 348 N.E.2d 547 (1976) (a private hospital may not reject applications of two osteopathic physicians solely on the basis that they had not completed a training program, approved by the American Medical Association, because the statute requires that reasons for rejection must be related to standards of patient care or welfare, objectives of the hospital, or character and competency of physician); Fried v. Straussman, 393 N.Y.S.2d 334, 361 N.E.2d 984 (1977) (if reasons for rejection

meet statutory criteria, neither the public health council nor the courts may review the evidence on which the hospital acted). A New York trial court has ruled that a private hospital must at least consider fairly the application of a physician's assistant for privileges to practice, apply relevant criteria for determining the individual's credentials, training, and experience, and grant the applicant procedural due process. The decision was based on statutory language of the New York Hospital Code setting forth the rules of licensure of hospitals. Reynolds v. Medical and Dental Staff of Andrus Pavilion of St. John's Riverside Hosp., 382 N.Y.S.2d 618, 86 Misc. 2d 418 (Sup. Ct. 1976).

51. *See, e.g.,* Edson v. Griffin, 21 Conn. Supp. 55, 144 A.2d 341 (1958); West Coast Hosp. Ass'n v. Hoare, 64 So. 2d 293 (Fla. 1953); Levin v. Sinai Hosp., 186 Md. 174, 46 A.2d 298 (1946); Moore v. Andalusia Hosp., Inc., 284 Ala. 259, 244 So. 2d 617 (1969) (*Moore* held that the appointment of medical staff to a private hospital is solely in the discretion of the governing body, and a refusal to appoint is not subject to judicial review); Van Campen v. Olean Gen. Hosp., 210 A.D. 204, 205 N.Y.S. 554 (1924); Lakeside Community Hosp. v. Levenson, 710 P.2d 727 (Nev. 1985) (decision refusing appointment or declining to renew was not subject to judicial review); Hoffman and Rasansky v. Garden City Hosp., 115 Mich. App. 773, 321 N.W.2d 810 (1982).

52. Joseph v. Passaic Hosp. Ass'n, 26 N.J. 557, 141 A.2d 18 (1958); Berberian v. Lancaster Osteopathic Hosp. Ass'n, 395 Pa. 257, 149 A.2d 456 (1959). *Cf.* Natale v. Sisters of Mercy of Council Bluffs, 243 Iowa 582, 52 N.W.2d 701 (1952) (medical staff bylaws providing for a statement of charges against a physician subject to discipline and a hearing were not binding on the hospital board, and the board could dismiss the doctor without a statement of charges and hearing). *Cf.* St. John's Hosp. Medical Staff v. St. John Regional Medical Center, 245 N.W.2d 472 (S.D. 1976) (medical staff bylaws adopted and approved by the hospital's governing body reciting that they are equally binding on the governing body and medical staff are a "contract" and may not be amended without adherence to a provision requiring a two-thirds vote of medical staff, citing *Berberian* and *Joseph*). *See also* Gashgai v. Maine Medical Ass'n, 350 A.2d 571 (Me. 1976) (bylaws of a medical association were contractual and enforceable by court in a disciplinary matter); Jain v. Northwest Community Hosp., 67 Ill. App. 3d 420, 385 N.E.2d 108 (1978) (private hospital must follow its own bylaws in reducing doctor's staff privileges). See also cases cited in note 125, *infra.*

　　Moreover, the Joint Commission has provided that neither the hospital's governing body nor the medical staff may unilaterally amend the medical staff bylaws. Joint Commission on Accreditation of Hospitals, Accreditation Manual for Hospitals, 112 (1987).

53. Shulman v. Washington Hosp. Center, 222 F. Supp. 59 (D.D.C. 1963), *aff'd on rehearing,* 319 F. Supp. 252 (D.D.C. 1970); *West Coast Hosp. Ass'n, supra* note 51; Halberstadt v. Kissane, 51 Misc. 2d 634, 273 N.Y.S.2d 601 (Sup. Ct. 1966), *aff'd,* 31 A.D.2d 568, 294 N.Y.S.2d 841

(1968); Bricker v. Sceva Speare Memorial Hosp., 111 N.H. 276, 281 A.2d 589 (1971), *cert. denied*, 404 U.S. 995 (1971). See cases cited in note 9, *supra*.

54. *Shulman, supra* note 53.

55. Foote v. Community Hosp., 195 Kan. 385, 405 P.2d 423 (1965).

56. *Id*. A sequel to this case is Kansas State Bd. of Healing Arts. v. Foote, 200 Kan. 447, 436 P.2d 828 (1968), where the Supreme Court of Kansas upheld the Board of Healing Arts decision in revoking Dr. Foote's license to practice on the grounds of "extreme incompetency," even though the statute authorizing revocation for "unprofessional conduct" did not specifically include incompetency within unprofessional conduct. However, under a similar statute the attorney general of Michigan rendered an opinion contrary to the *Foote* case. Op. Mich. Att'y Gen. 4423 (1967). This opinion would appear to support the author's assertion earlier in this text that medical licensing laws often do not cope adequately with the problem of the quality of medical care rendered within hospitals. However, the Michigan Medical Practice Act has subsequently been revised to strengthen the authority of the licensing board.

57. *See also* Sams v. Ohio Valley Gen. Hosp. Ass'n, 149 W.Va. 229, 140 S.E.2d 457 (1965) (where the doctor was apparently denied staff privileges as a consequence of his participation in a closed panel group practice, although such was never formally stated as a reason for his exclusion; this state court decision upheld the hospital's denial of privileges to Dr. Sams). *See also* Mauer v. Highland Park Hosp. Found., 90 Ill. App. 2d 409, 232 N.E.2d 776 (1967) (medical staff privilege decisions by private hospital not subject to judicial review).

58. Raymond v. Cregar, 38 N.J. 472, 185 A.2d 856 (1962).

59. Cowan v. Gibson, 392 S.W.2d 307 (Mo. 1965). *See also* Burkhart v. Community Medical Center, 432 S.W.2d 433 (Ky. 1968); Nashville Memorial Hosp., Inc. v. Brinkley, 534 S.W.2d 318 (Tenn. 1976) (allegations of conspiracy without justification or excuse to injure another in the practice of a profession constitute a cause of action; moreover, express allegations of malice are not necessary, as malice is inferred from allegations that damage was done intentionally without legal justification). *Cf*. Campbell v. St. Mary's Hosp., 252 N.W.2d 581 (Minn. 1977) (unsubstantiated broad allegations of malice do not create a cause of action when staff privileges were revoked).

60. Willis v. Santa Ana Community Hosp. Ass'n, 58 Cal. App. 2d 806, 376 P.2d 568, 26 Cal. Rptr. 640 (1962).

61. 234 Cal. App. 2d 377, 44 Cal. Rptr. 572 (1965). *See also* Rush v. City of St. Petersburg, 205 So. 2d 11 (Fla. 1967) (court rejected plaintiff's argument that an exclusive privilege contract with a medical specialist constituted illegal corporate practice of medicine); Letsch v. Northern San Diego County Hosp. Dist., 246 Cal. App. 2d 673, 55 Cal. Rptr. 118 (1966).

62. 40 N.J. 389, 192 A.2d 817 (1963); *contra* Limmer v. Samaritan Health Serv., 710 P.2d 1077 (Ariz. App. 1985) (private hospital may deny privileges to osteopath; bylaws not arbitrary and capricious).

63. 40 N.J. at 403–4, 192 A.2d at 825.

64. *Id.* at 394, 192 A.2d at 819.

65. 34 N.J. 582, 170 A.2d 791 (1961). *See also* Blende v. Maricopa County Medical Soc'y, 96 Ariz. 240, 393 P.2d 926 (1964). The court ruled that a local medical society cannot arbitrarily deny membership if there is a relation between society membership and hospital staff privileges. But later litigation established that there was no definite, formal relation between society membership and hospital staff privileges, and therefore the society could not be required to admit the doctor as a member. Maricopa County Medical Soc'y v. Blende, 5 Ariz. App. 454, 427 P.2d 946 (1967).

66. Sussman v. Overlook Hosp. Ass'n, 95 N.J. Super. 418, 231 A.2d 389 (1967).

67. Schneir v. Englewood Hosp. Ass'n, 91 N.J. Super. 527, 221 A.2d 559 (1966).

68. *See also* Davis v. Morristown Memorial Hosp., 106 N.J. Super. 33, 254 A.2d 125 (1969) (documented evidence of lack of beds in the obstetrical department is sufficient reason to deny a physician's appointment to staff); Guerrero v. Burlington County Memorial Hosp., 70 N.J. 344, 360 A.2d 334 (1976) (a private hospital may deny applications for appointments to the staff of a satellite medical/surgical facility by two eminently qualified surgeons when denial was based on documented evidence of limited bed capacity, and the facts that current staff was providing adequate surgical coverage and the needs of the community would not be served by adding to the surgical staff). *Cf.* Walsky v. Pascack Valley Hosp., 145 N.J. Super. 393, 367 A.2d 1204 (1976), *aff'd per curiam,* 156 N.J. Super. 13, 383 A.2d 154 (1978) (a moratorium on additions to medical staff violated rights of physician applicants and the public policy of the state; adopted when hospital utilization was approximately 96 percent, and renewed annually without review, it sometimes resulted in arbitrary and capricious treatment of applicants without accomplishing its intended purpose of reducing utilization).

69. Woodard v. Porter Hosp., 125 Vt. 419, 217 A.2d 37 (1966); Hagan v. Osteopathic Gen. Hosp., 102 R.I. 717, 232 A.2d 596 (1967) (the court held for the hospital in a privilege controversy, stressing that due process of law had been observed and that there were adequate reasons for rejecting the applicant); Davidson v. Youngstown Hosp. Ass'n, 19 Ohio App. 2d 246, 250 N.E.2d 892 (1969); Bricker v. Sceva Speare Memorial Hosp., 111 N.H. 276, 281 A.2d 589 (1971), *cert. denied,* 404 U.S. 995 (1971); Hawkins v. Kinsie, 540 P.2d 345 (Colo. App. 1975) (osteopathic physician stated a claim for damages by alleging that the decision of a private hospital not to renew his privileges was arbitrary, capricious, and unreasonable); Park Hosp. Dist. v. District Court of the Eighth Judicial Dist. in the County of Larimer, 555 P.2d 984 (Colo. 1976); McElhinney v. William Booth Memorial Hosp., 544 S.W.2d 216 (Ky. 1977) (whether a hospital is public or private, the court will review its bylaws and require sufficiently definite standards prescribing physicians' conduct to justify revocation of staff privileges); Storrs v.

Lutheran Hosps. of Am., 609 P.2d 24 (Alaska 1980) (where private
hospital was only one in community, where construction was financed by
governmental grants, and where more than 25 percent of revenue was
derived from government, hospital was quasi-public and may not violate
due process); Barrows v. Northwestern Memorial Hosp., 505 N.E. 2d
1182 (Ill. App. 1st Dist. 1987) (private hospital's medical staff decisions
subject to judicial review). *Cf.* Moles v. White, 336 So. 2d 427 (Fla.
Dist. Ct. App. 1976) (allegations that the private hospital serves a public
purpose did not make it a public institution requiring the process).

70. 39 Cal. App. 3d 623, 114 Cal. Rptr. 681 (1974).

71. *Id.* at 648, 114 Cal. Rptr. at 697.

72. Ascherman v. St. Francis Memorial Hosp., 45 Cal. App. 3d 507, 119 Cal.
Rptr. 507 (1975).

73. Truly v. Madison Gen. Hosp., 673 (5th Cir. 1982), *cert. denied,* 459
U.S. 909 (1982) (governmental hospital is subject to jurisdiction of 42
U.S.C. § 1983; plaintiff's evidence, however, failed to show that staff
privileges were denied on basis of race). *Cf.* Loh-Seng Yo v. Cibola Gen.
Hosp., 706 F.2d 306 (10th Cir. 1983) (private hospital is not subject to
jurisdiction of 42 U.S.C. § 1983).

74. Civil Rights Act of 1964, 42 U.S.C.A. § 2000(c) (1981); 42 U.S.C.A.
§§ 1395-1395zz (1983 & Supp. 1987).

75. Gomez v. Alexander Brothers Hosp. of San Jose, 698 F.2d 1019 (9th Cir.
1982) (written agreement to operate a hospital emergency department
was on the facts an employment agreement as distinct from an agreement
with an independent contractor; Title VII of Civil Rights Act of 1964
applied); Vuciecevic v. MacNeal Memorial Hosp., 572 F. Supp. 1424
(D.C. Ill. 1983) (physician applying for privileges at a private hospital
is not an intended beneficiary of Medicare and Medicaid funds; Title
VI of Civil Rights Act does not apply); *see also* Chowdhury v. Reading
Hosp. and Medical Center 677 F.2d 317 (3d Cir. 1982), *cert denied,*
U.S. 1229 (1983); Amro v. St. Luke's Hosp., 39 Fair Empl. Prac. Cas.
(BNA) 1574 (E.D. Pa. 1986) (physician completing surgical residency
and making application for hospital privileges is entitled to protection of
Title VII; evidence, however, does not show that the denial constituted
discrimination).

76. 42 C.F.R. § 482.12

77. *See* Joint Commission on Accreditation of Healthcare Organizations,
1998 HOSPITAL ACCREDITATION STANDARDS 231–35; *see generally*
Darling v. Charleston Community Hosp., 33 Ill. 2d 326, 211 N.E.
2d 253 (196), *cert. denied,* 383 U.S. 946 (1966) (Joint Commission
standards are admissible in court and failure to adhere to them can
constitute evidence of negligence).

78. Joint Commission on Accreditation of Healthcare Organizations, *supra*
note 77, at 231-233.

79. Emergency Medical Treatment and Active Labor Act, 42 U.S.C. §
1395dd. Guerrero v. Copper Queen Hosp., 22 Ariz. App. 611, 529
P.2d 1205 (1974), *aff'd mem.,* 537 P.2d 1329 (1975) (private hospital);

Williams v. Hospital Auth. of Hall County, 119 Ga. App. 626, 168 S.E.2d 336 (1969) (public hospital).

80. 42 U.S.C. §§ 291–291o, §§ 300–300a-8; 44 Fed. Reg. 29372 (1979). See discussion in Chapter 9.

81. Parker v. Port Huron Hosp., 361 Mich. 1, 105 N.W.2d 1 (1960) (charitable immunity exception to general rule of tort liability, the reasons for which are no longer held compelling).

82. Parker v. Highland Park Hosp., 404 Mich. 183, 273 N.W.2d 413 (1978) (operation of a hospital is not "state action"; the fact that a public hospital operates for the "common good of all" does not distinguish it from a private hospital because modern hospitals, public or private, operate essentially as businesses).

83. Yeargin v. Hamilton Memorial Hosp., 226 Ga. 661, 171 S.E.2d 136 (1969), *cert. denied*, 397 U.S. 963 (1970).

84. Yeargin v. Hamilton Memorial Hosp., 229 Ga. 870, 195 S.E.2d 8 (1972).

85. Board of Trustees of the Memorial Hosp. of Sheridan County v. Pratt, 72 Wyo. 120, 262 P.2d 682 (1953); Peterson v. Tucson Gen. Hosp., Inc., 559 P.2d 186 (Ariz. Ct. App. 1976).

86. Rao v. Board of County Commiss'rs, 80 Wash. 2d 695, 497 P.2d 591 (1972).

87. Fahey v. Holy Family Hosp., 32 Ill. App. 3d 537, 336 N.E.2d 309 (1975) (a rule requiring that any physician not a member of the department of obstetrics and gynecology must obtain consultation before performing major surgery in this specialty is reasonable and may be enforced against a physician who had been performing such surgery without consultation).

88. Pollock v. Methodist Hosp., 392 F. Supp. 393 (E.D. La. 1975). *Accord* Homes v. Hoemako Hosp., 573 P.2d 477 (Ariz. 1977); *see also* Jones v. State Bd. of Medicine, 555 P.2d 399 (Idaho 1976) (statutory requirement that both physicians and hospitals obtain malpractice insurance as condition of licensure is constitutional); Wilkinson v. Madera Community Hosp., 144 Cal. App. 3d 436, 192 Cal. Rptr. 593 (1983) (hospital may deny privileges when doctor's insurance company is not approved by California Department of Insurance; rule is reasonable); Kling v. St. Paul Fire and Marine Ins. Co., 626 F. Supp. 1285 (C.D. Ill. 1986) (agreement between hospital and insurance company requiring staff to carry a minimum amount of malpractice insurance does not have a substantial effect on interstate commerce and thus is not subject to jurisdiction of Sherman Act).

89. Khan v. Suburban Community Hosp., 45 Ohio St. 2d 39, 340 N.E.2d 398 (1976). *Cf.* Armstrong v. Board of Directors of Fayette County Gen. Hosp., 553 S.W.2d 77 (Tenn. 1977) (a public hospital may not require board certification or eligibility for major surgical privileges).

90. *E.g.,* Koelling v. Skiff Memorial Hosp., 259 Iowa 1185, 146 N.W.2d 284 (1966); Mizell v. North Broward Hosp. Dist., 175 So. 2d 583 (Fla. App. 1965); *Sosa, supra* note 13; Moore v. Board of Trustees of Carson-Tahoe Hosp., 88 Nev. 207, 495 P.2d 605 (1972), *cert. denied*, 409 U.S. 879 (1972); Klinge v. Lutheran Charities Ass'n of St. Louis, 383 F. Supp. 287

(Mo. 1974), *modified,* 523 F.2d 56 (8th Cir. 1975); Storrs v. Lutheran Hosp. and Homes Soc'y of Am., Inc., 661 P.2d 632 (Alaska 1983).

91. Citta v. Delaware Valley Hosp., 313 F. Supp. 301 (E.D. Pa. 1970); Duby v. Baron, 369 Mass. 614, 341 N.E.2d 870 (1976) (rule allowing for summary suspension of physician was sustained when there was an immediate threat to patients' safety).

92. Miller v. National Medical Hosp. of Monterey Park, Inc., 124 Cal. App. 3d 81, 177 Cal. Rptr. 119 (1981).

93. Theissen v. Watonga Mun. Hosp. Bd., 550 P.2d 938 (Okla. 1976); Wyatt v. Tahoe Forest Hosp. Dist., 345 P.2d 93 (Cal. App. 1959). *Contra* Peterson v. Tucson Gen. Hosp., 114 Ariz. 66, 559 P.2d 186 (1976).

94. *Sosa, supra* note 13.

95. Unterthiner v. Desert Hosp. Dist. of Palm Springs, 33 Cal. 3d 285, 188 Cal. Rptr. 590, 656 P.2d 554 (1983), *cert. denied,* 464 U.S. 1068 (1984).

96. Anderson v. Caro Community Hosp., 10 Mich. App. 348, 159 N.W.2d 347 (1968). *See also* Greer v. Medders, 178 Ga. App. 408, 336 S.E.2d 328 (1985) (patient has cause of action for the tort of intentional infliction of emotional distress when physician used threatening, profane language in the presence of the patient's wife and a nurse).

97. Huffaker v. Bailey, 273 Or. 273, 276, 540 P.2d 1398, 1399 (1975) (bylaw was not unduly vague and was reasonably related to quality of patient care), quoted in Ladenheim v. Union County Hosp., 76 Ill. App. 3d 90, 394 N.E.2d 770 (1979).

98. *See, e.g.,* Miller v. Eisenhower Medical Center, 166 Cal. Rptr. 826, 835, 614 P.2d 258, 267 (1980); *see also* Staube v. Emanuel Lutheran Charity Bd., 287 Or. 375, 600 P.2d 381 (1979), *cert. denied,* 445 U.S. 966 (1980); Robbins v. Ong, 452 F. Supp. 110 (S.D. Ga. 1978); Pick v. Santa Ana-Tustin Community Hosp., 130 Cal. App. 3d 970, 182 Cal. Rptr. 85 (1982) (abrasive personality, difficulty in working with staff, applicant's behavior, and unfavorable reference letters were sufficient to deny privileges). *Cf.* Newcomb v. Patton, 608 S.W.2d 145 (Mo. App. 1980) (harassment of administrator justifies nonrenewal of physician's privileges).

99. Rosner v. Eden Township Hosp. Dist., 58 Cal. 2d 592, 375 P.2d 431, 25 Cal. Rptr. 551 (1962).

100. *E.g.,* CAL. BUS. & PROF. CODE § 805 (Deering 1986); TEX. REV. CIV. STAT. ANN. art. 4495b, § 4.14 (Vernon 1987); MICH. COMP. LAWS ANN. §§ 333.16233, 333.16243, 333.21513 (Supp. 1986). Further, the federal Health Care Quality Improvement Act of 1986 (Pub. L. No. 99-660) requires hospitals to report certain disciplinary actions and malpractice claims data to a national clearinghouse.

101. Khan v. Suburban Community Hosp., 45 Ohio St. 2d 39, 43–44, 340 N.E.2d 398, 402 (1976).

102. Rush v. City of St. Petersburg, 205 So. 2d 11 (Fla. App. 1967); Benell v. City of Virginia, 258 Minn. 559, 104 N.W.2d 633 (1960); Blank v. Palo

Alto–Stanford Hosp. Center, 234 Cal. App. 2d 377, 44 Cal. Rptr. 572 (1965) (radiology).

103. Adler v. Montefiore Hosp. Ass'n of W. Pa., 453 Pa. 60, 311 A.2d 634 (1973), *cert. denied,* 414 U.S. 1131 (1974); *see also* Lewin v. St. Joseph Hosp., 82 Cal. App. 3d 368, 146 Cal. Rptr. 892 (1978) (renal hemodialysis).

104. Dell v. St. Joseph Mercy Hosp. of Detroit, Inc., Civil No. 4070668 (E.D. Mich. 1974) (unreported opinion) (hospital may designate certain private cardiologists as having the exclusive right to make "official interpretations of electrocardiograms for the official hospital records"); Sokol v. University Hosp., Inc., 402 F. Supp. 1029 (Mass. 1975) (hospital's restriction of cardiac surgery to a single surgeon did not violate either antitrust or civil rights statutes); Moles v. White, 336 So. 2d 427 (Fla. Ct. App. 1976) (exclusive contract for open-heart surgery did not violate state antitrust statutes, constitutional principles, or common law); Dillard v. Rowland, 520 S.W.2d 81 (Mo. App. 1974) (private hospital having an affiliation agreement with a university's medical school may restrict staff appointments to those physicians who also hold a university faculty appointment).

105. *E.g.,* Dattilo v. Tucson Gen. Hosp., 23 Ariz. App. 392, 533 P.2d 700 (1975) (exclusive contract for nuclear medicine did not violate either state or federal antitrust laws); Harron v. United Hosp. Center, Inc., Clarksburg, W. Va., 522 F.2d 1133 (4th Cir. 1975), *cert. denied,* 424 U.S. 916 (1976) (exclusive radiology contract does not violate the federal Sherman Antitrust Act or the civil rights statutes); 42 U.S.C. §§ 1981, 1983, 1985.

106. Cobb County-Kennestone Hosp. Auth. v. Prince, 242 Ga. 139, 141–42, 249 S.E.2d 581, 583 (1978).

107. *Id.* at 143, 150, 249 S.E.2d at 584, 587–88.

108. Clair v. Centre Community Hosp., 317 Pa. Super. Ct. 25, 463 A.2d 1065 (1983).

109. *Id.,* 463 A.2d at 1072.

110. Joint Commission on Accreditation of Healthcare Organizations, 1998 HOSPITAL ACCREDITATION STANDARDS, Standards MS. 5.2 and MS. 5.3–MS. 5.3.2 at 231–32.

111. Silver v. Castle Memorial Hosp., 53 Haw. at 484–85, 497 P.2d at 571–72, *cert. denied,* 409 U.S. 1048 (1972).

112. Garrow v. Elizabeth Gen. Hosp., 155 N.J. Super. 78, 92, 382 A.2d 393, 400 (1977).

113. Klinge v. Lutheran Charities of St. Louis, 523 F.2d 56 (8th Cir. 1975); Hortonville Joint School Dist. No. 1 v. Hortonville Educ. Ass'n, 426 U.S. 482, 493 (1976).

114. Atassi v. Massillon Community Hosp., Ohio Slip Op. No. CA 6075 (1983).

115. 104 Cal. App. 3d 648, 163 Cal. Rptr. 831 (1980).

116. Woodbury v. McKinnon, 447 F.2d 839 (5th Cir. 1979); Ascherman v.

San Francisco Medical Soc'y, 39 Cal. App. 3d 623, 114 Cal. Rptr. 681 (1974).

117. *Silver, supra* note 111, 497 P.2d at 571; *Ascherman, supra* note 116, 114 Cal. Rptr. at 697.

118. *Id.*

119. Anton v. San Antonio Community Hosp., 140 Cal. Rptr. 442, 567 P.2d 1162 (1977). *Accord, Silver, supra* note 111.

120. Garrow v. Elizabeth Gen. Hosp. & Dispensary, 79 N.J. 549, 401 A.2d 533 (1979).

121. Brickman v. Board of Directors of W. Jefferson Gen. Hosp., 372 So. 2d 701, 705 (La. App. 1979).

122. Joint Commission on Accreditation of Healthcare Organizations, 1998 HOSPITAL ACCREDITATION STANDARDS, Standard MS. 5.2 at 231.

123. Johnson, *How Much Process Is Due?* 32:10 TRUSTEE 12 (Oct. 1979).

124. *E.g., Garrow, supra* note 128, 401. A.2d at 538; *Brickman, supra* note 121; Shulman v. Washington Hosp. Center, 121 App. D.C. 64, 348 F.2d 70 (1965).

125. Margolin v. Morton F. Plant Hosp. Ass'n, 348 So. 2d 57 (Fla. App. 1977); Yarnell v. Sisters of St. Francis Health Servs., Inc., 446 N.E.2d 359 (Ind. App. 1983); Knapp v. Palos Community Hosp., 125 Ill. App. 3d 244, 465 N.E.2d 554 (1984) (private hospital's denial of reappointment is not subject to judicial review as long as bylaw provisions are followed). *Cf.* Bello v. South Shore Hosp., 429 N.E.2d 1011 (Mass. 1981) (initial applicant to the staff of private hospital does not have standing to contest noncompliance with existing medical staff bylaws; current staff members are entitled to disciplinary procedures specified in bylaws). See also cases cited in note 52, *supra.*

Moreover, the Joint Commission has provided that neither the hospital's governing body nor the medical staff may unilaterally amend the medical staff bylaws. Joint Commission on Accreditation of Hospitals, ACCREDITATION MANUAL FOR HOSPITALS, 112 (1987).

126. Bredice v. Doctors Hospital, 50 F.R.D. 249, 251 (D.DC 1970), *aff'd,* 479 F.2d 920 (D.C. Cir. 1973).

127. 50 F.R.D. at 250.

128. 245 Ga. 763, 267 S.E.2d 230 (1980).

129. *See, e.g.,* Spencer v. Community Hosp. of Evanston, 87 Ill. App. 3d 214, 408 N.E.2d 981 (1980) *and* Raymond v. Cregar, 38 N.J. 472, 185 A.2d 856 (1962).

130. Burkette v. Lutheran Gen. Hosp., 595 F.2d 255 (5th Cir. 1979).

131. Kushner v. Southern Adventist Health and Hosp. Sys., 151 Ga. App. 425, 260 S.E.2d 381 (1979).

132. Engelstad v. Virginia Mun. Hosp. and Va. Hosp. Comm'n, 718 F.2d 262 (8th Cir. 1983).

133. Alonso v. Hospital Auth. of Henry County, 175 Ga. App. 198, 332 S.E.2d 884 (1985). *Cf.* Pollack v. Baxter Nursing Home, 716 F.2d 545 (8th Cir. 1983) (a constitutionally protected liberty interest was violated when an employee of a county-owned nursing home was fired for

allegedly falsifying her daughter's time cards, and the home subsequently disclosed that information to a prospective employer. Even though the allegations were true, the employee was entitled to a due process hearing upon termination and an opportunity to protect her reputation).

134. Conley v. Board of Trustees of Grenada County Hosp., 707 F.2d 175 (5th Cir. 1983).

135. Vinyard v. King, Adm'r of Clinton Regional Hosp., 728 F.2d 428 (10th Cir. 1984).

136. Yurko v. Carteret County Gen. Hosp. Corp., 718 F.2d 1094 (E.D. N.C. 1983).

137. Laje v. R.E. Thomason Gen. Hosp., 564 F.2d 1159, 1163 (5th Cir. 1977) (quoting *Sosa, supra* note 13).

LIST OF CASES

SUBJECT INDEX

ABOUT THE AUTHOR

J. Stuart Showalter, J.D., MFS, has more than 25 years' experience dealing with health law issues. He has a law degree from Washington University in St. Louis and a Masters in Forensic Science from George Washington University, Washington, D.C. He served in the U.S. Navy from 1972 to 1980 in various positions including in-house counsel to a 1,000-bed medical center, malpractice claims defense attorney, and counsel to the Navy Surgeon General.

From 1980 to 1996, Mr. Showalter was vice president and in-house counsel to the Catholic Health Association of the United States, headquartered in St. Louis, Missouri. Thereafter he was a partner in a St. Louis law firm, where he specialized in health law and corporate compliance until joining Orlando Regional Health System as Director of Compliance in March 1998.

While in St. Louis, Mr. Showalter taught health law and public policy in the health administration program, Washington University School of Medicine, where he was twice named teacher of the year. In addition to this book, he has authored a health law casebook.